Kritisch-exegetischer Kommentar über das Neue Testament

Begründet von
Heinrich August Wilhelm Meyer
herausgegeben von
Dietrich-Alex Koch

Band 15
Der Brief des Jakobus
13. Auflage

Vandenhoeck & Ruprecht

Der Brief des Jakobus

übersetzt und erklärt
von
Oda Wischmeyer

1. Auflage dieser Auslegung

Vandenhoeck & Ruprecht

Frühere Auflagen dieses Kommentars

Bearbeitung durch Johannes Eduard Huther
1. Auflage 1857
2. Auflage 1863
3. Auflage 1870

Bearbeitung durch Willibald Beyschlag
4. Auflage 1882
5. Auflage 1888
6. Auflage 1898

Bearbeitung durch Martin Dibelius
7. Auflage 1921
8. Auflage 1956
9. Auflage 1957
10. Auflage 1959
11. Auflage 1964
12. Auflage 1984

Bibliografische Information der Deutschen Bibliothek:
Die Deutsche Nationalbibliothek verzeichnet diese Publikation in
der Deutschen Nationalbibliografie; detaillierte bibliografische Daten sind
im Internet über https://dnb.de abrufbar.

© 2024 Vandenhoeck & Ruprecht, Robert-Bosch-Breite 10, D-37079 Göttingen,
ein Imprint der Brill-Gruppe (Koninklijke Brill BV, Leiden, Niederlande; Brill USA Inc., Boston MA,
USA; Brill Asia Pte Ltd, Singapore; Brill Deutschland GmbH, Paderborn, Deutschland;
Brill Österreich GmbH, Wien, Österreich)
Koninklijke Brill BV umfasst die Imprints Brill, Brill Nijhoff, Brill Schöningh,
Brill Fink, Brill mentis, Brill Wageningen Academic, Vandenhoeck & Ruprecht, Böhlau und V&R unipress.
Alle Rechte vorbehalten. Das Werk und seine Teile sind urheberrechtlich geschützt.
Jede Verwertung in anderen als den gesetzlich zugelassenen Fällen bedarf der vorherigen
schriftlichen Einwilligung des Verlages.

Satz: pagina, Tübingen
Druck und Bindung: Hubert & Co, Ergolding
Printed in the EU

Vandenhoeck & Ruprecht Verlage | www.vandenhoeck-ruprecht-verlage.com

ISBN 978-3-525-57362-4

Dem päpstlichen Bibelinstitut in Rom als einer herausragenden Stätte des internationalen Bibelstudiums gewidmet

Vorwort

1998 übertrug mir Ferdinand Hahn (1926–2015) die Neukommentierung des Jakobusbriefes. Der Kommentar sollte 2004 erscheinen. Zwanzig Jahre später als geplant und gut 100 Jahre nach Erscheinen von M. Dibelius, Der Brief des Jakobus, KEK 15, Göttingen 1921, tritt jetzt ein neuer Jakobuskommentar der KEK-Reihe neben den Dibeliuskommentar.

Dibelius' Kommentar war zu seiner Zeit einer der modernsten neutestamentlichen deutschsprachigen Kommentare und bleibt zudem einer jener ganz wenigen Kommentare, die weiterhin gelesen werden und an dessen Thesen sich die internationale Forschung abarbeitet. Dibelius erklärte den Brief auf der Grundlage der Formgeschichte und im Zusammenhang der paränetischen Literatur des antiken Judentums und des entstehenden Christentums des 1. und 2. Jahrhunderts n. Chr. Er verstand den Brief als pseudonymes Schreiben aus den letzten Jahrzehnten des 1. Jahrhunderts und überwand die bis dahin geführte Debatte um die Verfasserschaft durch den Herrenbruder Jakobus.

Nach rund hundert Jahren intensiver internationaler exegetischer Beschäftigung mit dem Jakobusbrief lassen sich gegenwärtig die interpretatorischen Schwerpunkte neu setzen. Dabei sind die zwanzig zusätzlichen Jahre seit dem ursprünglich anvisierten Erscheinungsdatum 2004 dem Ergebnis der Kommentierung zugute gekommen, denn in dieser Zeit sind sowohl mehrere bedeutende Kommentare als auch wegweisende monographische Untersuchungen und Aufsätze erschienen, die bei der jetzt vorgelegten Kommentierung berücksichtigt werden konnten. Zu den Untersuchungen zur Form-, Traditions- und Motivgeschichte sind die Fragen nach der Textproduktion und Textstrukturierung durch den literarischen Autor sowie nach seiner literarischen Intention getreten. Zugleich spielen das literarische Genre des Diasporabriefes und Stil und Semantik des Schreibens eine erhebliche Rolle bei der Neuinterpretation. Die genannten Fragestellungen führen dazu, dass sich das viel umstrittene individuelle historische, sozialgeschichtliche und religionsgeschichtliche Profil des Briefes anders und viel genauer beschreiben lässt, als es Dibelius im Rahmen der Form- und Motivgeschichte möglich war.

Die Kommentierung des Jakobusbriefes hat mich fünfundzwanzig Jahre begleitet, führte mich in die verschiedensten Bereiche der neutestamentlichen Wissenschaft und ermöglichte vielfältige wissenschaftliche Gespräche in Forschung und Lehre über einen langen Zeitraum hinweg. Dankbar blicke ich auf diese Zeit und alle Diskussionen und Anregungen aus Lehrveranstaltungen, Tagungen oder Workshops zurück. Einige Kolleginnen und Kollegen seien besonders erwähnt. Viel habe ich von den Teilnehmerinnen und Teilnehmern der Konferenzen *Imitation and Classicism in Hellenistic Textual Worlds* 2017 in Sandbjerg / Dänemark, veranstaltet von Sigurvin Lárus Jónsson, und *Who was »James?«* 2019 in Münster, veranstaltet von Eve-Marie Becker, Sigurvin Lárus Jónsson und Susanne Luther, gelernt. Ihnen danke ich vor allem. Meinem Mann, Wolfgang Wischmeyer, danke ich für viele Hinweise aus dem Bereich der frühen Kirchengeschichte und für vielfaches sorgfältiges Korrekturlesen.

Bei der Fertigstellung des Manuskripts halfen die studentischen Hilfskräfte des Lehrstuhls für Neues Testament von Professorin Dr. Eve-Marie Becker, Universität Münster, denen ich allen danke: Rebecca Meerheimb, Isabelle Kastner und Jan Hemling. Jan Hemling hat das Manuskript in die Druckvorlage eingetragen. Ohne seine großartige, monatelange akribische Arbeit wäre dieser Kommentar nicht publiziert worden. Frau Kollegin Becker gilt ein besonderer Dank für diese Unterstützung. Dem Herausgeber von KEK, Professor em. Dr. Dietrich-Alex Koch, danke ich für die Hilfe bei der Herstellung der endgültigen Druckvorlage und wichtige Korrekturvorschläge.

Der Kommentar ist dem Päpstlichen Bibelinstitut Rom als einer weltweit herausragenden Institution der Bibelstudien gewidmet. Im Wintersemester 2019 / 20 war ich als Gastprofessorin im *Pontificium Institutum Biblicum* eingeladen und konnte in der wunderbaren Bibliothek arbeiten. Die Erfahrung, täglich in Gemeinschaft mit vielen Studierenden aus allen Kontinenten an biblischen Texten zu arbeiten, war ein Geschenk. Die konzentrierte Arbeitsatmosphäre des *Instituto* hat meine Arbeit am Kommentar beflügelt und zu dessen Abschluss beigetragen. Mein abschließender Dank gilt dem damaligen Rektor des Instituts, Prof. Michael Francis Kolarcik S. J.

Erlangen am 6. Januar 2024 Oda Wischmeyer

Inhalt

Vorwort 7

Literatur 11
  1. Quellen: Textausgaben, Übersetzungen, Kommentare und Sammlungen 11
  2. Hilfsmittel 16
  3. Kommentare zum Jakobusbrief 17
  4. Monographien, Sammelbände und Aufsätze 17
  5. Abkürzungen und Zitierweise 34
    A) Abkürzungen 34
    B) Zitierweise 35

Einleitung 37
  A. Der Kommentar. Grundlinien der Interpretation 37
    1. Die Neukommentierung des Jakobusbriefes 38
    2. Burchard, Allison, Metzner 42
  B. Der Text. Historische, literarische und thematische Charakteristik 48
    1. Historische Charakteristik 48
    2. Literarische Charakteristik 64
    3. Thematische Charakteristik 97

Kommentar 141
  A. Inscriptio 141
  B. Präskript 141
  C. Briefcorpus 151
    1. Erster Hauptteil: Belehrungen über das richtige Ethos für die
      Christus-gläubigen Gemeinden (Kap. 1) 151
    2. Zweiter Hauptteil: Belehrungen über das Ansehen der Person
      und über das Verhältnis von Glauben und Tun (Kap. 2) 205
    3. Dritter Hauptteil: Warnungen vor Gefahren (Kap. 3) 254
    4. Vierter Hauptteil: Mahn- und Gerichtsreden gegen verschiede-
      ne Gruppierungen (Kap. 4,1–5,6) 284
    5. Schlussteil (Kap. 5,7–20) 329
  D. Subscriptio 369

LITERATUR

1. Quellen: Textausgaben, Übersetzungen, Kommentare und Sammlungen

Claudius Aelianus

VALDÉS, M. G. u. a. (Hg.), Claudius Aelianus, De natura animalium, BSGRT, Berlin / New York 2009.

Äthiopisches Henochbuch

KNIBB, M. A., The Ethiopic Book of Enoch. A New Edition in the Light of the Aramaic Dead Sea Fragments, 2 Bd. Oxford 1982.

NICKELSBURG, G. W. E., 1Enoch. A Commentary on the Book of 1 Enoch, Chapters 1–36; 81–108, Hermeneia, Minneapolis 2001.

– / VANDERKAM, J. C., 1 Enoch. The Hermeneia Translation, Minneapolis 2012.

– / –, 1 Enoch. A Commentary on the Book of 1 Enoch, Chapters 37–82, Hermeneia, Minneapolis 2012.

UHLIG, S., Das Äthiopische Henochbuch, JSHRZ V / 6, Gütersloh 1984.

Apostolische Väter

LINDEMANN, A./PAULSEN, H. (Hg.), Die Apostolischen Väter. Griechisch-deutsche Parallelausgabe, Tübingen 1992.

Cassius Dio

BOISSEVAIN, U. P. (Hg.), Cassii Dionis Cocceiani historiarum Romanarum quae supersunt, 3 Bd., Berlin 1895–1901, Bd. 4 comp. H. Smilda, Berlin 1995.

M. Tullius Cicero

WINTERBOTTOM, M. (Hg.), M. Tullius Cicero. De Officiis, OCT, Oxford 1994.

Diogenes Laertius

GÄRTNER, H. (Hg.), Diogenes Laertius, Vitae Philosophorum. Bd. 3, München / Leipzig 2002.

JÜRSS, F. (Hg.), Diogenes Laertius. Leben und Lehre der Philosophen, Stuttgart 2010.

MARCOVICH, M. (Hg.), Diogenes Laertius, Vitae Philosophorum. Bd. 1 und 2, Stuttgart / Leipzig 1999.

Dion Chrysostomos

VON ARNIM, H., Dionis Prusaensis quem uocant Chrysostomum quae exstant omnia, Berlin 1893–1896.

Epiktetos
SCHENKL, H. (Hg.), Epicteti dissertationes ab Arriano digestae. Accedunt fragmenta; enchiridion ex recensione Schweighaeuseri, gnomologiorum Epicteteorum reliquiae, Leipzig 1916.
SOUILHÉ, J./JAGU, A., Épictète, Entretiens, 4 Bd., CUFr, Paris 1963–1975.

Epiphanius
DEAN, J. E. (Hg.), Epiphanius' Treatise on Weights and Measures. The Syriac Version, SAOC 11, Chicago 1935.

Epistula Ieremiae
GUNNEWEG, A. H. J., Der Brief Jeremias, JSHRZ III / 2, Gütersloh 1975.

4 Esra
KLIJN, A. F. J. (Hg.), Die Esra-Apokalypse (4. Esra). Nach dem lateinischen Text unter Benutzung der anderen Versionen, GCS 18, Berlin 1992.
SCHREINER, J., Das 4. Buch Esra, JSHRZ V / 4, Gütersloh 1997.
STONE, M. E., Fourth Ezra. A Commentary of the Fourth Book of Ezra, Hermeneia, Minneapolis 1990.

Eusebius
MRAS, K., Eusebius Werke, Bd. 8.1.: Die Praeparatio evangelica. Einleitung, die Bücher I–X, Leipzig 1954.
–, Eusebius Werke, Band 8.2.: Die Praeparatio evangelica. Die Bücher XI–XV, Leipzig 1956.
SCHWARTZ, E. (Hg.), Eusebius, Kirchengeschichte, hg. v. E. Schwartz, Leipzig [5]1955.

Flavius Josephus
BARCLAY, J. M. G. u. a. (Hg.), Flavius Josephus. Translation and Commentary, Leiden 2000–2022.
NIESE, B. (Hg.), Flavii Iosephi opera, vols. 1–4, Berlin 1887 ff (repr. 1955).
SIEGERT, F. u. a. (Hg.) Josephus. Aus meinem Leben (Vita). Kritische Ausgabe, Übersetzung und Kommentar, Tübingen [2]2011.

Fragmente hellenistisch-jüdischer Historiker
HOLLADAY, C. R. (Hg.), Fragments from Hellenistic Jewish Authors. Vol. I: Historians, SBL.TT, Chico 1983.
WALTER, N., Fragmente hellenistisch-jüdischer Historiker, JSHRZ I / 2, Gütersloh 1976.

Hegesippus
PREUSCHEN, E., Antilegomena, Gießen [2]1905.
SCHLERITT, F. (Hg.), Hegesipp, Göttingen 2016.

Hieronymus
CERESA-GASTALDO, A. (Hg.), Gerolamo. Gli uomini illustri, Biblioteca patristica 12, Florenz 1988.

Iamblichos
DEUBNER, L. (Hg.), Iamblichi. De vita Pythagorica liber, Leipzig 1937.

1. Quellen: Textausgaben, Übersetzungen, Kommentare und Sammlungen

Irenäus
BROX, N. (Hg.), Adversus Haereses, 5 Bd., FC 8 / 1–5, Freiburg u. a. 1993–2001.

Joseph und Asenath
BURCHARD, CH., Joseph und Asenath, JSHRZ II / 4, Gütersloh 1983.
– u. a. (Hg.), Joseph und Aseneth, PVTG 5, Leiden / Boston 2003.

Jubiläenbuch
BERGER, K., Jubiläenbuch, JSHRZ II / 3, Gütersloh 1981.
VANDERKAM, J. C., The Book of Jubilees. A Critical Text, CSCO 510 f., Leuven 1989.

Jüdische Schriften aus hellenistisch-römischer Zeit
KÜMMEL, W. G. u. a. (Hg.), Jüdische Schriften aus hellenistisch-römischer Zeit, 5 Bd., Gütersloh 1973–2003.

Justinus der Märtyrer
MARCOVICH, M. (Hg.), Iustini Martyris Apologiae pro Chrstianis. Iustini Martyris Dialogus cum Tryphone, PTS 38 / 47, Berlin 2005.

Kleanthes
VON ARNIM, H. (Hg.), Stoicorum Veterum Fragmenta. 3 Bd., Berlin 1903–1905. Neuausgabe in 4 Bd., Berlin / Boston 1978 f.

Lukianus von Samosata
MACLEOD, M. D. (Hg.), Luciani Opera, 4 Bd., OCT, Oxford 1972–1987.

Menander
PERNIGOTTI, C., Menandri Sententiae, Florenz 2008.

Minucius Felix
KYTZLER, B. (Hg.), Octavius. Lateinisch-deutsch, München 1965.

Mischna
KRUPP, M. u. a. (Hg.), Die Mischna. Textkritische Ausgabe mit deutscher Übersetzung und Kommentar von M. Krupp u. a., Jerusalem 2002–2008.

Novum Testamentum
ALAND, B. u. a. (Hg.), Novum Testamentum Graece, Stuttgart [28]2012.
– u. a. Novum Testamentum. Editio Critica Maior, Bd. IV. Die Katholischen Briefe, Teil 1: Text; Teil 2: Begleitende Materialien, 1. Lieferung: Der Jakobusbrief, Stuttgart 1997.
ROBINSON, J. M. u. a. (Hg.), The Critical Edition of Q. Synopsis including the Gospels of Matthew and Luke, Mark and Thomas with English, German and French Translations of Q and Thomas, Leuven / Minneapolis, 2000.

Oracula Sibyllina
GAUGER, J.-D. (Hg.), Die Sibyllinischen Weissagungen. Griechisch-deutsch. Auf der Grundlage der Ausgabe von A. Kurfeß, Düsseldorf / Zürich 1998/[2]2002.

Origenes
GÖRGEMANNS, H./KARPP, H. (Hg.), Origenes. Vier Bücher von den Prinzipien, TzF 24, Darmstadt [3]1996.

Paralipomena Jeremiae

ALLISON, D. C., 4 Baruch. Paraleipomena Jeremiou, CEJL, Berlin 2019.
KRAFT, R./PURINTUN, A.-E. (Hg.), Paraleipomena Jeremiou, SBL.TT 1, 1972.
SCHALLER, B., Paralipomena Jeremiou, JSHRZ I/8, Gütersloh 1988.

Philon

COHN, L./ HEINEMANN, I. (Hg.), Philo von Alexandria. Die Werke in deutscher Übersetzung, 7 Bd., Breslau/Berlin 1909–1964.
– / WENDLAND, P. (Hg.), Philonis Alexandrini opera quae supersunt, 7 Bd., Berlin 1896–1930 (auch spätere Nachdrucke).

Platon

BURNET, J., (Hg.), Platonis opera. 5 Bd., Oxford 1900–1907.
EIGLER, G., (Hg.), Platon. Werke in 8 Bänden, Darmstadt 1970–1983, [6]2010.

Plutarchus

PLUTARQUE, Œuvres morales, 16 Bd., Paris 1972 ff.
WEISE, CH./VOGEL, M. (Hg.), Plutarch, Moralia. In zwei Bänden, Wiesbaden 2012.

Pseudo-Aristoteles

THOM, J. C. (Hg.), Cosmic Order and Divine Power. Pseudo-Aristotle: On the Cosmos, SAPERE XXIII, Tübingen 2014.

Pseudo-Libanius und Pseudo-Demetrius

MALOSSE, P.-L. (Hg.), Lettres pour toutes circonstances. Les Traités épistolaires du Pseudo-Libanios et du Pseudo-Démetrios de Phalère. Introduction, traduction et commentaire, Paris 2004.

Pseudo-Menander

ULLMANN, M. (HG.), Pseudo-Menander. Die arabische Überlieferung der sogenannten Menandersentenzen, Wiesbaden 1961.

Pseudo-Phokylides

VAN DER HORST, P. W., The Sentences of Pseudo-Phocylides. With Introduction and Commentary, SVTP 4, Leiden 1978.

Quintilianus

COUSIN, J. (Hg.), Quintilian, Institution Oratoire, 7 Bd., Paris 1975–1980.
RAHN, H. (Hg.), Marcus Fabius Quintilianus, Ausbildung des Redners. Zwölf Bücher, Lateinisch und Deutsch, Darmstadt [6]2015 (unveränderter Nachdruck der 3. Auflage 1995).

Sapientia Salomonis

NIEBUHR, K.-W. (Hg.), Sapientia Salomonis (Weisheit Salomos), SAPERE XXVII, Tübingen 2015.

L. Annaeus Seneca

HOSIUS, C. (Hg.), L. Annaei Senecae opera quae supersunt. 3 Bände in 4 Teilen, Leipzig 1898–1907. Band 1,2 (1900): De beneficiis libri VII. De clementia libri II, [2]1914.

Septuaginta

HARL, M. u. a. (Hg.), La Bible d'Alexandrie (LXX), Paris 1988 ff.

1. Quellen: Textausgaben, Übersetzungen, Kommentare und Sammlungen

KRAUS, W./KARRER, M. (Hg.), Septuaginta Deutsch. Das griechische Alte Testament in deutscher Übersetzung in Zusammenarbeit mit Eberhard Bons u. a., Stuttgart 2009.

RAHLFS, A. (Hg.), Septuaginta, id est Vetus Testamentum Graece iuxta LXX interpretes, Stuttgart 1935 u. a. Editio altera quam recognovit et emendavit Robert Hanhart, Stuttgart 2006.

Simplikios
HEIBERG, J. L. (Hg.), Simplicii in Aristotelis de caelo commentaria. Commentaria in Aristotelem Graeca Bd. 7, Berlin 1894.

Slavisches Henochbuch
BÖTTRICH, CH., Das Slavische Henochbuch, JSHRZ V/7, Gütersloh 1995.

VAILLANT, A., Le livre des secrets d'Hénoch. Texte slave et et traduction française, Paris ²1976.

Syrische Baruchapokalypse
BOGAERT, P.-M., L'Apocalypse Syriaque de Baruch. I und II, Paris 1969.

KLIJN, A. F. J., Die syrische Baruchapokalypse, JSHRZ V/2, Gütersloh 1976.

Syrische Didaskalia
ACHELIS, H./FLEMING, J., Die Syrische Didaskalia, Leipzig 1904.

VÖÖBUS, A., The Didaskalia Apostolorum in Syriac I/II, CSCO 401/407, Louvain 1979.

Testament Abrahams
JANSSEN, E., Das Testament Abrahams, JSHRZ III/2, Gütersloh 1975.

SCHMIDT, F., Le Testament grec d'Abraham. Édition critique des deux recensions, TSAJ 11, Tübingen 1986.

Testamente der XII Patriarchen
BECKER, J., Die Testamente der zwölf Patriarchen, JSHRZ III/1, Gütersloh 1974.

DE JONGE, M. u. a. (Hg.), The Testaments of the Twelve Patriarchs. A Critical Edition of the Greek Text, PVTG I/2, Leiden 1978 (Leiden/Boston 1997).

Thomasevangelium
PLISCH, U.-K., Das Thomasevangelium. Originaltext mit Kommentar, Stuttgart ²2016.

Testament Hiobs
BROCK, S. P./PICARD, J. C. (Hg.), Testamentum Iobi, PVGT 2, 1–59, Leiden 1967.

SCHALLER, B., Das Testament Hiobs, JSHRZ III/3, Gütersloh 1979.

Vitae Prophetarum
SCHWEMER, A. M., Vitae Prophetarum, JSHRZ I/7, Gütersloh 1997.

TORREY, CH.C. (Hg.), The Lives of the Prophets, JBL.MS 1, Philadelphia 1946.

Vulgata
WEBER, R./GRYSON, R. (Hg.), Biblia Sacra Iuxta Vulgatam Versionem, Stuttgart ⁵2007.

Xenophon
DINDORF, L. A., Xenophontis Scripta minora. 2: Respublica Lacedaemoniorium, Respublica Atheniensium, De vectigalibus liber, Hipparchicus, De re equestri liber, Cynegeticus, Leipzig ²1898.

MARCHANT, E. C. (Hg.), Xenophontis Opera Omnia, 5 Bd., 1900–1920.

2. Hilfsmittel

ALAND, K., Synopsis Quattuor Evangeliorum, Stuttgart ¹⁵1996.

BAUER, W., Griechisch-deutsches Wörterbuch zu den Schriften des Neuen Testaments und der frühchristlichen Literatur, 6. Aufl. v. K. und B. Aland, Berlin / New York 1988 (=BAUER / ALAND).

BALZ, H./SCHNEIDER, G. (Hg.), Exegetisches Wörterbuch zum Neuen Testament, 3 Bd., Stuttgart 1980–1983 (=EWNT).

BETZ, H. D. u. a. (Hg.), Religion in Geschichte und Gegenwart, 8 Bd., Tübingen ⁴2007 (=RGG).

BEYER, K., Semitische Syntax im Neuen Testament. Bd. I, Göttingen 1962.

BLASS, F./DEBRUNNER A., Grammatik des neutestamentlichen Griechisch, bearb. v. F. Rehkopf, Göttingen ¹⁵1979.¹⁷1990.¹⁸2001 (=BDR).

BONS, E. (Hg.), Historical and Theological Lexicon of the Septuagint. Bd. 1, Tübingen 2020 (=HTLS).

BOTTERWECK, G. J. u. a. (Hg.), Theologisches Wörterbuch zum Alten Testament, 10 Bd., Stuttgart u. a. 1970–2000 (=ThWAT).

CANCIK, H./SCHNEIDER, H. (Hg.), Der Neue Pauly. Enzyklopädie der Antike, 16 Bd., Stuttgart / Weimar 1996–2003 (=DNP).

COLLINS, J. J./HARLOW, D. C. (Hg.), The Eerdmans Dictionary of Early Judaism, Grand Rapids / Cambridge 2010 (=EDEJ).

CONCORDANCE TO THE NOVUM TESTAMENTUM GRAECE, hg. v. Institut für Neutestamentliche Textforschung, Berlin / New York ³1989.

DÖPP, S./GEERLINGS, W. (Hg.), Lexikon der Antiken Christlichen Literatur, Freiburg u. a. ³2002 (=LACL).

FREEDMAN, D. N. (Hg.), The Anchor Bible Dictionary, 6 Bd., New York u. a. 1992 (=ABD).

HATCH, E./REDPATH, H. A. (Hg.), A Concordance to the Septuagint and the Other Greek Versions of the Old Testament (including the Apocryphal Books). Bd. I und II, Graz 1954=Oxford 1897.

HENNECKE, E./SCHNEEMELCHER, W. (Hg.), Neutestamentliche Apokryphen in deutscher Übersetzung, 2 Bd., Tübingen ⁵1987/⁵1989.

KITTEL, G./FRIEDRICH, G. (Hg.), Theologisches Wörterbuch zum Neuen Testament, 11 Bd., Stuttgart 1933–1979. Neuausgabe 2019 (=ThWNT).

LIDDELL, H. G. u. a., A Greek-English Lexicon. With a Revised Supplement, Oxford ⁹1996 (=LSJ).

MARKSCHIES, CH./SCHRÖTER, J. (Hg.), Antike christliche Apokryphen in deutscher Übersetzung. 7. Auflage der von Edgar Hennecke begründeten und von Wilhelm Schneemelcher fortgeführten Sammlung der neutestamentlichen Apokryphen. I. Band in 2 Teilbänden. Evangelien und Verwandtes, Tübingen 2012 (=AcA).

SCHWERTNER, S. M., Internationales Abkürzungsverzeichnis für Theologie und Grenzgebiete, Berlin ³2014 (=³IATG).

SPICQ, C. O. P., Lexique Théologique du Nouveau Testament, Fribourg 1991.

STRACK, H. L./BILLERBECK, P., Kommentar zum Neuen Testament aus Talmud und Midrasch, 6 Bd., München ⁵1969 (=BILL).

3. Kommentare zum Jakobusbrief[1]

ALLISON JR., D. C., James. A Critical and Exegetical Commentary on the Epistle of James, ICC, London / New York 2013.

ASSAËL, J./CUVILLIER, É., L'Épître de Jacques, CNT 13A, Genf 2013.

BEDA VENERABILIS, In epistulam Iacobi expositio. Kommentar zum Jakobusbrief, FC 40, Freiburg 2000.

BEYSCHLAG, W., Der Brief des Jakobus, KEK 15, Göttingen ^{6}1897.

BLOMBERG, C./KAMELL KOVALISHYN, M., James, Zondervan Exegetical Commentary on the New Testament, Grand Rapids 2008.

BURCHARD, CH., Der Jakobusbrief, HNT 15 / 1, Tübingen 2000.

CHEUNG, L. L./SPURGEON, A. B., James. A Pastoral and Contextual Commentary, Asia Bible Commentary Series, Carlisle 2018.

DIBELIUS, M., Der Brief des Jakobus, KEK 15, Göttingen 1921.^{12}1984.

– / GREEVEN, H., James. A Commentary on the Epistle of James, Hermeneia, Philadelphia 1975.

FRANKEMÖLLE, H., Der Brief des Jakobus, 2 Bd., ÖTBK 17 / 1.2, Gütersloh / Würzburg 1994.

HECKEL, TH. K., Die Briefe des Jakobus, Johannes und Petrus, NTD 10, Göttingen 2019.

HERDER, J. G. VON, Briefe zweener Brüder Jesu in unserm Kanon. Sämmtliche Werke. Religion und Theologie. Achter Theil, Carlsruhe 1828.

HUTHER, J. E., Kritisch-exegetisches Handbuch über den Brief des Jakobus, KEK 15, Göttingen 1858.

JOHNSON, L. T., The Letter of James. A New Translation with Introduction and Commentary, AncB 37A, New Haven / London 1995.2005.

MAYOR, J. B., The Epistle of St. James, London / New York 1892.

MCCARTNEY, D. G., James, BECNT, Grand Rapids 2009.

METZNER, R., Der Brief des Jakobus, ThHK 14, Leipzig 2017.

MOO, D. J., The Letter of James, PiNTC, Grand Rapids / Cambridge 2000.

MUSSNER, F., Der Jakobusbrief, HThKNT XIII: Faszikel I, Freiburg ^{4}1981.

POPKES, W., Der Brief des Jakobus, ThHK, Leipzig 2001.

ROPES, J. H., A Critical and Exegetical Commentary of the Epistle of St. James, ICC, Edinburgh 1916.

SPITTA, F., Zur Geschichte und Litteratur des Urchristentums. Band II: Der Brief des Jakobus. Studien zum Hirten des Hermas, Göttingen 1896.

WINDISCH, H., Die Katholischen Briefe, HNT 15, Tübingen ^{3}1951.

4. Monographien, Sammelbände und Aufsätze[2]

AASGAARD, R., ›My Beloved Brothers and Sisters!‹ Christian Siblingship in Paul, Early Christianity in Context, JSNTS 265, London / New York 2004.

---

[1] Für eine umfassende Liste der Kommentare vgl. den Kommentar von R. Metzner. Ältere Kommentarliteratur seit den altkirchlichen Katenen vor allem im Kommentar von M. Dibelius (S. 81–84).

[2] Für eine umfassende bibliographische Dokumentation vgl. den Kommentar von D. C. Allison.

ADAMS, S. A., Greek Genres and Jewish Authors. Negotiating Literary Culture in the Greco-Roman Era, Waco 2020.

ADEWUYA, J. AYODEJI, An African Commentary on the Letter of James, Eugene 2023.

AHEARNE-KROLL, St.P. (Hg.), Oxford Handbook of the Synoptic Gospels, Oxford 2023.

ALETTI, J.-N., James 2,14–26. The Arrangement and Its Meaning, Bibl 95, 2014, 88–101.

ALLISON, D. C., Eldad and Modad, JSP 21, 2011, 99–131.

–, Job in the Testament of Abraham, JSP 12, 2001, 131–147.

AMSTUTZ, J., Haplotes, Theophaneia 19, Bonn 1968.

ARZT-GRABNER, P., ›Brothers‹ and ›Sisters‹ in Documentary Papyri and in Early Christianity, RivBib 50, 2002, 192–195.

ASCOUGH, R. S. (Hg.), Christ Groups and Associations. Foundational Essays, Waco 2022.

AUGOUSTAKIS, A., Literary Culture, in: A. ZISSOS (Hg.), A Companion to the Flavian Age of Imperial Rome, BCAW, Chichester 2016, 376–392.

AUNE, D. E. (Hg.), Greco-Roman Literature and the New Testament. Selected Forms and Genres, Sources for Biblical Studies 21, Atlanta 1988.

–, Reconceptualizing the Phenomenon of Ancient Pseudepigraphy, in: J. Frey u. a. (Hg.), Pseudepigraphie und Verfasserfiktion in frühchristlichen Briefen (Pseudepigraphy and Author Fiction in Early Christian Letters), WUNT 246, Tübingen 2009, 789–824.

BAASLAND, E., Literarische Form, Thematik und geschichtliche Einordnung des Jakobusbriefes, in: ANRW II 25/5, 1988, 3646–3684.

BAKER, W. R., Personal Speech-Ethics in the Epistle of James, WUNT II 68, Tübingen 1995.

BALTRUSCH, E., Art. Luxus II (Luxuskritik), RAC 23, 2010, 711–738.

BARCLAY, J. M. G., Paul and the Gift, Grand Rapids/Cambridge 2015.

BARTH, G., Glaube und Zweifel in den synoptischen Evangelien, ZThK 72, 1975, 269–292.

BATTEN, A. J., Friendship and Benefaction in James, Emory Studies in Early Christianity 15, Blandford Forum 2010.

–, James the Dramatist, in: E.-M. Becker u. a. (Hg.), Who was ›James‹? Essays on the Letter's Authorship and Provenance, WUNT 485, Tübingen 2022, 313–330.

–, The Urban and Agrarian in the Letter of James, JECH 3, 2013, 4–20.

–, The Urbanization of Jesus Traditions in James, in: A. J. Batten/J. S. Kloppenborg (Hg.), James, 1&2 Peter and the Early Jesus Tradition, LNTS 478, London/New York 2014, 78–96.

–, What Are They Saying About the Letter of James?, New York 2009.

– / OLSON, K. (Hg.), Dress in Mediterranean Antiquity. Greeks, Romans, Jews, Christians, London/New York 2021.

BAUCKHAM, R. J., James. Wisdom of James, Disciple of Jesus the Sage, London/New York 1999.

–, The Spirit of God in Us Loathes Envy. James 4:5, in: G. N. Stanton u. a. (Hg.), The Holy Spirit and Christian Origins (FS J. D. G. Dunn), Grand Rapids 2004, 270–281.

BAUER, Th. J., Der Jakobusbrief und das Bild des Jakobus im Kontext antiker und frühchristlicher Epistolographie, in: E.-M. Becker u. a. (Hg.), Who was ›James‹? Essays on the Letter's Authorship and Provenance, WUNT 485, Tübingen 2022, 77–98.

BAUERNFEIND, O., Art. στρατεύομαι κτλ., ThWNT 7, 1964, 701–713.

BAUS, K., Der Kranz in Antike und Christentum, Theophaneia 2, Bonn 1940.

BECKER, E.-M., Der Begriff der Demut bei Paulus, Tübingen 2015.

4. Monographien, Sammelbände und Aufsätze

–, EIS THEOS und 1Kor 8. Zur frühchristlichen Entwicklung und Funktion des Monotheismus, in: W. Popkes / R. Brucker (Hg.), Ein Herr und ein Gott. Zum Kontext des Monotheismus im Neuen Testament, BThSt 68, Neukirchen-Vluyn 2004, 65–99.

–, Paulus als *doulos* in Röm 1,1 und Phil 1,1. Die epistolare Selbstbezeichnung als Argument, in: Dies., Der Philipperbrief des Paulus. Vorarbeiten zu einem Kommentar, NET 29, Tübingen / Basel 2020, 205–222.

–, Σοφία ἄνωθεν *versus* ἄνω κλῆσις? Jas 3:15–17 and Phil 3:14 in Comparison, in: Dies. u. a. (Hg.), Who was ›James‹? Essays on the Letter's Authorship and Provenance, WUNT 485, Tübingen 2022, 219–236.

–, Was die »arme Witwe« lehrt. Sozial- und motivgeschichtliche Beobachtungen zu Mk 12,41–44par., NTS 65, 2019, 148–165.

–, Wer ist »Jakobus«? Ein typologischer Blick im Rahmen der frühchristlichen Briefkultur, in: Dies. u. a. (Hg.), Who was ›James‹? Essays on the Letter's Authorship and Provenance, WUNT 485, Tübingen 2022, 57–76.

– u. a. (Hg.), Who was ›James‹? Essays on the Letter's Authorship and Provenance, WUNT 485, Tübingen 2022.

–, u.a. (Hg.), Handbuch Brief – Antike, Berlin 2025.

– / BABUSIAUX, U., Paulus, der »Sklave Jesu Christi« (Gal 1,10; Röm 1,1; Phil 1,1) im Lichte des römischen Rechts, NTS 69, 2023, 365–385.

BELLANTUONO, A. u. a., Art. ἄνθρωπος, HTLS I, 2020, 743–768.

BEMMERL, CH., Der Jakobusbrief in der Alten Kirche. Eine Spurensuche vom Neuen Testament bis zu Origenes, WUNT II 558, Tübingen 2023.

–, Die frühe Rezeption des Jakobusbriefs und die Geschichte des neutestamentlichen Kanons, ASEs 34, 2017, 513–535.

– u.a. (Hg.), Handbuch Brief – Antike, Berlin 2025

BENDEMANN, R. VON, Die Heilungen Jesu und die antike Medizin, EaC 5, 2014, 273–312.

BENDLIN, A., Art. Personifikation I und II, DNP 9, 2001, 639–643.

BENSON, G., A Paraphrase and Notes on the Seven commonly called Catholic Epistles, London 1749 (repr. 2012).

BERGER, K., Art. Abraham II. Im Frühjudentum und Neuen Testament, TRE 1, 1977, 372–382.

–, Hellenistische Gattungen im NT, in: ANRW II 25 / 2, 1984, 1031–1432.

BERGES, U./HOPPE, R., Arm und Reich, NEB Themen 10, Würzburg 2009.

BEYER, H., Art. εὐλογέω κτλ., ThWNT 2, 1935, 751–763.

BIEBERSTEIN, S., Art. Rahab (Person), WiBiLex 2010 (https://bibelwissenschaft.de/stichwort/31780/).

BIGONI, L. u.a., Art. ἀλήθεια κτλ., HTLS I, 2020, 513–554.

BLANTON IV., TH.R., Wealth, Poverty, Economy, in: St.P. Ahearne-Kroll (Hg.), Oxford Handbook of the Synoptic Gospels, Oxford 2023, 296–319.

BLOMBERG, C. L., Neither Poverty Nor Riches. A Biblical Theology of Material Possessions, New Studies in Biblical Theology 7, Leicester 1999.

BOLKESTEIN, H./KALSBACH, A., Art. Armut I, RAC I, 1950, 698–705.

BORMANN, L. (HG.), Abraham's Family. A Network of Meaning in Judaism, Christianity, and Islam, WUNT 415, Tübingen 2018.

BOWLEY, J. E., Art. Abraham, EDEJ, 2010, 294f.

BRAND, M., Evil Within and Without. The Source of Sin and Its Nature as Portrayed in Second Temple Literature, JAJ Sup 9, Göttingen 2013.

BREMER, J., Art. Demut (AT), WiBiLex 2015 (https://www.bibelwissenschaft.de/stichwort/16317).

–, Die Armentheologie als eine Grundlinie einer Theologie des Psalters, Hebrew Bible and Ancient Israel 5, 2016, 350–390.

–, Wo Gott sich auf die Armen einlässt. Der sozio-ökonomische Hintergrund der achämenidischen Provinz Yəhūd und seine Implikationen für die Armentheologie des Psalters, BBB 174, Göttingen 2016.

BREU, C., Prosopopoiie im Jakobusbrief aus dekonstruktiver Perspektive, in: E.-M. Becker u. a. (Hg.), Who was ›James‹? Essays on the Letter's Authorship and Provenance, WUNT 485, Tübingen 2022, 99–120.

BROWN, M. J., Paul's Use of δοῦλος Ἰησοῦ Χριστοῦ in Romans 1:1, JBL 120, 2004, 725–728.

BROX, N., Art. Hermas, LACL, ³2003, 319 f.

BÜCHNER, D. u. a., Art. ἁμαρτάνω κτλ., HTLS I, 2020, 598–622.

BÜCHSEL, F., Art. θυμός κτλ., ThWNT 3, 1938, 167–173.

– / HERNTRICH, V., Art. κρίνω κτλ., ThWNT 3, 1938, 920–955.

BULTMANN, R., Art. ἔλεος κτλ., ThWNT 2, 1935, 474–483.

BURCHARD, CH., Gemeinde in der strohernen Epistel. Mutmaßungen über Jakobus, in: D. Lührmann / G. Strecker (Hg.), Kirche (FS G. Bornkamm), Tübingen 1980, 315–328.

–, Zu einigen christologischen Stellen des Jakobusbriefes, in: C. Breytenbach / H. Paulsen (Hg.), Anfänge der Christologie (FS F. Hahn), Göttingen 1991, 353–368.

CAPELLE, W./MARROU, H. I., Art. Diatribe, RAC 3, 1957, 990–1009.

CARLTON PAGET, J. N., Jewish Christianity, in: CHJud III, 2000, 731–775.

–, Jews, Christians and Jewish Christians in Antiquity, WUNT 251, Tübingen 2010.

–, Rezension zu Dale C. Allison, James. A Critical and Exegetical Commentary, EaC 5, 2014, 393–416.

CARMINATI, M. u. a., Art. ἀτιμάζω, HTLS I, 2020, 1262–1286.

CHEUNG, L. L., The Genre, Composition and Hermeneutics of the Epistle of James, PBTM, Carlisle 2003.

CHILTON, B./EVANS C. A. (Hg.), Authenticating the Words of Jesus, NTTS 28 / 1, Leiden u. a. 1999.

– / NEUSNER, J. (Hg.), The Brother of Jesus: James the Just and His Mission, Louisville 2001.

CHORRINI, E., Iterazioni sinonimiche nella Lettera di Giacomo. Studio lessicografico ed esegetico, Analacta 89, Mailand 2020.

CLAUSSEN, C., Versammlung, Gemeinde, Synagoge. Das hellenistisch-jüdische Umfeld der frühchristlichen Gemeinden, StUNT 27, Göttingen 2002.

COLLINS, J. H., Exhortation to Philosophy. The Protreptics of Plato, Isocrates, and Aristotle, New York 2015.

CONZELMANN, H./ZIMMERLI, W., Art. χαίρω κτλ., ThWNT 9, 1973, 349–404.

COTTON, H., Language Gaps in Roman Palestine and the Roman Near East, in: Dies./ Pogorelsky, O., Roman Rule an Jewish Life. Collected papers, Studia Judaica 89, Berlin / Boston 2022, 195–212.

– / POGORELSKY, O., Roman Rule an Jewish Life. Collected papers, Studia Judaica 89, Berlin / Boston 2022.

DALE, J. M., Demonic Faith and Demonic Wisdom in James. A Response to Kenneth M. Wilson, JBL 121, 2022, 177–195.

DALFERTH, I., Über Einheit und Vielfalt des christlichen Glaubens. Eine Problemskizze, in: W. Härle / R. Preul (Hg.), Glaube, MJTh 4, Marburg 1992, 99–137.

DASSMANN, E./Davies, P., Art. Hiob, RAC 15, 1991, 366–442.

DAVIDS, P. H., The Meaning of ἀπείραστος in James I.13, NTS 24, 1978, 386–392.

–, The Epistle of James in Modern Discussion, ANRW II 25 / 5, 1988, 3621–3645.

DE VOS, J. C., The Decalogue in Pseudo-Phocylides and Syriac Menander. ›Unwritten Laws‹ or Decalogue Reception? in: D. Markl (Hg.), The Decalogue and Its Cultural Influence, HBM 58, Sheffield 2013, 41–56.

DEINES, R., God or Mammon. The Danger of Wealth in the Jesus Tradition and in the Epistle of James, in: M. Konradt / E. Schläpfer (Hg.), Anthropologie und Ethik im Frühjudentum und im Neuen Testament. Wechselseitige Wahrnehmungen, WUNT 322, Tübingen 2014, 327–385.

–, Jakobus. Im Schatten des Größeren, Biblische Gestalten 30, Leipzig 2017.

DEISSMANN, A., Licht vom Osten, Tübingen ⁴1923.

–, Prolegomena zu den biblischen Briefen und Episteln, in: Ders., Bibelstudien, Marburg 1895, 187–254.

DELLING, G., Art. τέλος κτλ., ThWNT 8, 1969, 50–88.

DENIS, A.-M., Introduction à la littérature religieuse judéo-hellénistique, 2 Bd., Turnhout 2000.

DEPPE, D. B., The Sayings of Jesus in the Epistle of James, Chelsea 1989.

DINKLER, E./DINKLER-VON SCHUBERT, E., Art. Friede, RAC 8, 1972, 434–501.

DOCHHORN, J., Art. Zitat II. Neutestamentlich, LBH, 2009, 690.

–, Der Adammythos bei Paulus und im hellenistischen Judentum Jerusalems, WUNT 469, Tübingen 2021.

– u. a. (Hg.), Das Böse, der Teufel und Dämonen – Evil, the Devil, and Demons, WUNT II 412, Tübingen 2016.

DOERING, L., Ancient Jewish Letters and the Beginnings of Christian Epistolography (Antike jüdische Briefe und der Anfang der christlichen Epistolographie), WUNT 298, Tübingen 2012.

–, Art. ἀδελφός κτλ., HTLS I, 2020, 165–184.

DOGNIEZ, C./HARL, M., La Bible d'Alexandrie 5, Le Deutéronome, Paris 1992.

DOWNING, F. G., Ambiguity, Ancient Semantics, and Faith, NTS 56, 2010, 139–162.

DREXHAGE, H. J., Art. Handel I.II, RAC 13, 1986, 519–547.

DRIESBACH, J. K., Art. ἀπαρχή, HTLS I, 2020, 865–878.

EDGAR, D. H., Has God Not Chosen the Poor? The Social Setting of the Letter of James, JSNTS 206, Sheffield 2001.

EDSMAN, C. M., Schöpferwille und Geburt Jac 1,18. Eine Studie zur altchristlichen Kosmologie, ZNW 38, 1939, 11–44.

ELLIS, N. J., A Theology of Evil in the Epistle of James. Cosmic Trials and the *Dramatis Personae* of Evil, in: C. Keith / L. Stuckenbruck (Hg.), Evil in Second Temple Judaism and Early Christianity, WUNT II 417, Tübingen 2016, 262–281.

ELY WHEELERS, S., Wealth as Peril and Obligation. The New Testament on Possessions, Grand Rapids 1995.

ENGEMANN, J., Art. Kranz (Krone), RAC 21, 2006, 1006–1034.

ERNST, J., Art. Brüderliche Zurechtweisung I. Biblisch, LThK 2, ³1994, 715–716.

ESDERS, S., Art. Schwur, RAC 30, 2021, 29–79.

FALCETTA, A., Early Christian Teachers. The ›Didaskaloi‹ from Their Origins to the Middle of the Second Century, WUNT II 516, Tübingen 2020.

FERNGREN, G. B., Art. Krankheit, RAC 21, 2006, 966–1006.

FEWSTER, G. P., Ancient Book Culture and the Literacy of James. On the Production and Consumption of a Pseudepigraphical Letter, ZAC 20, 2016, 387–417.

FLURY, A., Art. Eid / Schwur (AT), WiBiLex 2014 (https://bibelwissenschaft.de/stichwort/16992/).

FÖRSTER, H., Der Versucher und die Juden als seine Vortruppen, ZThK 115, 2018, 229–259.

FÖRSTER, N., »Elia war ein Mensch uns gleichgeartet« (Jak 5,17). Jakobus, Elia und das Gebet des Gerechten in der Perspektive des Jakobusbriefes, in: E.-M. Becker u.a. (Hg.), Who was ›James‹? Essays on the Letter's Authorship and Provenance, WUNT 485, Tübingen 2022, 15–27.

FOSTER, R. J., The Significance of Exemplars for the Interpretation of the Letter of James, WUNT II 376, Tübingen 2014.

FRANCIS, F. O., Form and Function of the Opening and Closing Paragraphs of James and I John, ZNW 61, 1970, 110–126.

FRANKEMÖLLE, H., Art. πραΰτης, EWNT 3, 1983, 351–353.

FREY, J., Art. Ebionitenevangelium, WiBiLex 2013 (https://bibelwissenschaft.de/stichwort/47872/).

–, Der Brief des Judas und der zweite Brief des Petrus, ThHK 15 / II, Leipzig 2015.

–, The Letter of Jude and the Second Letter of Peter. A Theological Commentary, Waco 2018.

– u.a. (Hg.), Pseudepigraphie und Verfasserfiktion in frühchristlichen Briefen (Pseudepigraphy and Author Fiction in Early Christian Letters), WUNT 246, Tübingen 2009.

FRÖHLICH, I./KOSKENNIEMI, E. (Hg.), Evil and The Devil, LNTS 481, London 2013.

GANSELMAYER, CH., Der Autor des Jakobusbriefs aus linguistischer Perspektive, in: E.-M. Becker u.a. (Hg.), Who was ›James‹? Essays on the Letter's Authorship and Provenance, WUNT 485, Tübingen 2022, 121–157.

GARRISON, R., Redemptive Almsgiving in Early Christianity, JSNTS 77, Sheffield 1993.

GEMÜNDEN, P. VON, Vegetationsmetaphorik im Neuen Testament und seiner Umwelt, NTOA 18, Fribourg / Göttingen 1993.

GERSTENBERGER, E., Art. ʿānāh II, ThWAT 6, 1989, 247–270.

GILLMAN, F. M., Art. James, Brother of Jesus, ABD 3, 1992, 620–621.

GLÖCKNER, M., Bildhafte Sprache im Jakobusbrief. Form, Inhalt und Erschließungspotential der metaphorischen Rede einer frühchristlichen Schrift, ABIG 69, Leipzig 2021.

GOLDMANN, A., Art. Gelegenheit und Anlass, in: Handbuch Brief, Berlin 2025.

GRUEN, E. S., Diaspora. Jews Amidst Greeks and Romans, Cambridge 2002.

–, Ethnicity in the Ancient World – Did it Matter?, Berlin / Boston 2020.

GRUNDMANN, W., Art. δόκιμος, ThWNT 2, 1935, 258–264.

HAGNER, D.A., Art. James, ABD 3, 1992, 616–618.

HAHN, F., Theologie des Neuen Testaments. Bd. II, Tübingen 2002.

– / MÜLLER, P., Der Jakobusbrief, ThR 63, 1998, 1–73.

HARLAND, PH.A., Familial Dimensions of Group Identity. ›Brothers‹ (Ἀδελφοί) in Associations of the Greek East, JBL 124, 2005, 491–513.

HARTIN, P. J., The Letter of James. Its Visions, Ethics and Ethos, in: J. G. van der Watt (Hg.), Identity, Ethics, and Ethos in the NT, BZNW 141, Berlin / New York 2006, 445–471.

4. Monographien, Sammelbände und Aufsätze

–, James and the Jesus Traditions. Some Theological Reflections and Implications, in: K.-H. Niebuhr / R. W. Wall (Hg.), The Catholic Epistles and Apostolic Tradition, Waco 2009, 55–70.

–, James and the Q-Sayings of Jesus, Sheffield 1992.

HAUCK, F. Art μένω κτλ., ThWNT 4, 1942, 578–593.

– / BAMMEL, E., Art. πτωχός, ThWNT 6, 1959, 885–915.

– / BERTRAM, G., Art. μακάριος, ThWNT 4, 1942, 365–373.

– / KASCH, W., Art. πλοῦτος, ThWNT 6, 1959, 316–330.

HAYWARD, R. / EMBRY, B. (Hg.), Studies in Jewish Prayer, JSStSuppl 17, Oxford 2005.

HEATH, J., The Righteous Gentile Interjects (James 2:18–19 and Romans 2:14–15), NT 55, 2013, 272–295.

HEININGER, B., Die Parusie des Kyrios, in: F. W. Horn (Hg.), Paulus Handbuch, Tübingen 2013, 299–305.

HELLHOLM, D., Der Hirt des Hermas, in: W. Pratscher (Hg.), Die Apostolischen Väter. Eine Einleitung, Göttingen 2009, 226–253.

HENGEL, M., Der Jakobusbrief als antipaulinische Polemik, in: G. F. Hawthorne / O. Betz (Hg.)., Tradition and Interpretation in the New Testament (FS E. E. Ellis), Grand Rapids 1987, 248–265.

–, Der Jakobusbrief als antipaulinische Polemik, in: Ders., Paulus und Jakobus. Kleine Schriften III, WUNT 141, Tübingen 2002, 511–548 [erweiterte Fassung].

HENZE, M., Art. Baruch, Second Book of, EDEJ, 2010, 426–428.

HERRMANN-OTTO, E., Art. Sklave, RAC 30, 2021, 691–751.

HESZER, C., Jewish Slavery in Antiquity, Oxford 2005.

HINGE, G., The Hexameter in James 1:17. Metrical Forms in Graeco-Roman Prose Literature Between Emulation and Quotation, in: E.-M. Becker u. a. (Hg.), Who was ›James‹? Essays on the Letter's Authorship and Provenance, WUNT 485, Tübingen 2022, 239–277.

HINTZEN, B. u. a., Art. γι(γ)νώσκειν κτλ., HTLS I, 2020, 1863–1882.

HOEGEN-ROHLS, CH., Form und Funktion, Realia und Idee der Paulusbriefe, in: O. Wischmeyer / E.-M. Becker (Hg.), Paulus. Leben – Umwelt – Werk – Briefe, utb 2767, Tübingen ³2021, 247–278.

HÖLSCHER, M. u. a. (Hg.), Antike Fluchtafeln und das Neue Testament. Materialität – Ritualpraxis – Texte, WUNT 474, Tübingen 2021.

HORBURY, W. u. a. (Hg.), The Cambridge History of Judaism. Vol. 3: The Early Roman Period, Cambridge 2000.

–, Pedagogues and Primary Teachers, from Paul to Mishnah, in: G. J. Brooke / R. Smithuis (Hg.), Jewish Education from Antiquity to the Middle Ages (FS P. S. Alexander), Leiden 2017, 95–127.

HORN, F. W. (Hg.), Glaube, utb 5034 (Themen der Theologie 13), Tübingen 2018.

HORRELL, D. G., From adelphoi to oikos theou. Social transformations in Pauline Christianity, JBL 120, 2001, 293–311.

ILAN, T., Lexicon of Jewish Names in Late Antiquity. Part I: Palestine 330BCE – 200 CE, TSAJ 91, Tübingen 2002.

JACKSON-MCCABE, M., Logos and Law in the Letter of James. The Law of Nature, the Law of Moses, and the Law of Freedom, NT.S 100, Leiden 2001.

JEREMIAS, J., Art. Ἠλ(ε)ίας, ThWNT 2, 1935, 930–943.

–, The Prayers of Jesus, London 1967.

JEWETT, R., Romans. A Commentary, Hermeneia, Minneapolis 2007.

JOHNSON, L. T., Brother of Jesus and Friend of God. Studies in the Letter of James, Grand Rapids 2004.

JÓNSSON, S. L., James among the Classicists. Reading the Letter of James in Light of Ancient Literary Criticism, SANt 8, Göttingen 2021.

–, The Letter of James as Ethopoeia, in: E.-M. Becker u. a. (Hg.), Who was ›James‹? Essays on the Letter's Authorship and Provenance, WUNT 485, Tübingen 2022, 371–389.

KAISER, S., Krankenheilung. Untersuchungen zu Form, Sprache, traditionsgeschichtlichem Hintergrund und Aussage zu Jak 5,13–18, WMANT 112, Neukirchen-Vluyn 2006.

KAMELL KOVALISHYN, M., The Epistle of James, in: St. McKnight / N. K. Gupta (Hg.), The State of New Testament Studies. A Survey on Recent Research, Grand Rapids 2019, 407–424.

–, The Prayer of Elijah in James 5. An Example of Intertextuality, JBL 137, 2018, 1027–1045.

KARAMANOLIS, G./ZANELLA, F., Art. Seele, RAC 30, 2021, 107–177.

KATZ, ST. T., Introduction, in: Ders. (Hg.), The Cambridge History of Judaism. Vol. 4: The Late Roman-Rabbinic Period, Cambridge 1984, 11–22.

KEITH, C./STUCKENBRUCK, L. (Hg.)., Evil in Second Temple Judaism and Early Christianity, WUNT II 417, Tübingen 2016.

KEMEZIS, A., Flavian Greek Literature, in: A. Zissos (Hg.), A Companion to the Flavian Age of Imperial Rome, BCAW, Chichester / Malden 2016, 450–468.

KENSKY, M., Trying Man. Trying God. The Divine Courtroom in Early Jewish and Christian Literature, WUNT II 289, Tübingen 2010.

KESSLER, R., Art. Armut / Arme (AT), WiBiLex 2006 (http://www.bibelwissenschaft.de/stichwort/13829/).

KIM, S. K.-J., Stewardship and Almsgiving in Luke's Theology, JSNTS 155, Sheffield 1998.

KLEIN, TH., Bewährung in Anfechtung. Der Jakobusbrief und der Erste Petrusbrief als christliche Diasporabriefe, NET 18, Tübingen 2011.

KLEINKNECHT, H. u. a., Art. ὀργή, ThWNT 5, 1954, 382–448.

– / GUTBROD, W., Art. νόμος κτλ., ThWNT 4, 1942, 1016–1084.

KLOPPENBORG, J. S., Christ's Associations. Connecting and Belonging in the Ancient City, New Haven 2019.

–, Cursing in the Corinthian Christ Assembly, in: M. Hölscher u. a. (Hg.), Antike Fluchtafeln und das Neue Testament. Materialität – Ritualpraxis – Texte, WUNT 474, Tübingen 2021, 409–424.

–, James 1:2–15 and Hellenistic Psychagogy, NT 52, 2010, 37–71.

–, James, NTGu, London / New York 2022.

–, Judaeans or Judaean Christians in James? in: Z. A. Crook / P. A. Harland (Hg.), Identity and Interaction in the Ancient Mediterranean. Jews, Christians and Others (FS S. G. Wilson), London 2007, 113–135.

–, Poverty and Piety in Matthew, James, and the Didache, in: H. de Sandt / J. K. Zangenberg (Hg.), Matthew, James, and Didache. Three Related Documents in Their Jewish and Christian Settings, Atlanta 2008, 201–232.

–, Rezension von S. L. Jónsson, James among the Classicists. Reading the Letter of James in Light of Ancient Literary Criticism, SANt 8, Göttingen 2021, NT 64, 2022, 409–411.

–, The Author of James and His Lexical Profile, in: E.-M. Becker u. a. (Hg.), Who was ›James‹? Essays on the Letter's Authorship and Provenance, WUNT 485, Tübingen 2022, 197–211.

–, The Emulation of Jesus Tradition in the Letter of James, in: L. Webb / J. H. Kloppenborg (Hg.), Reading James with New Eyes. Methodological Reassessments of the Letter of James, LNTS 342, London / New York 2007, 121–150.

–, The Reception of the Jesus Tradition in James, in: J. Schlosser (Hg.), The Catholic Epistles and the Tradition, BETL 176, Leuven 2004, 93–141.

– / BAUCKHAM, R., James and Jesus, in: B. Chilton / J. Neusner (Hg.), The Brother of Jesus. James the Just and His Mission, Louisville 2001, 100–137.

KOCH, D.-A., Geschichte des Urchristentums, Göttingen ²2014.

KONRADT, M., Christliche Existenz nach dem Jakobusbrief, StUNT 22, Göttingen 1998.

–, Ethik im Neuen Testament, Göttingen 2022.

–, Theologie in der »strohernen Epistel«. Ein Literaturbericht zu neueren Ansätzen in der Exegese des Jakobusbriefes, VF 44, 1999, 54–78.

–, Werke als Handlungsdimension des Glaubens. Erwägungen zum Verhältnis von Theologie und Ethik im Jakobusbrief, in: F. W. Horn / R. Zimmermann (Hg.), Jenseits von Indikativ und Imperativ, WUNT 238, Tübingen 2009, 309–327.

–, / SCHLÄPFER, E. (Hg.), Anthropologie und Ethik im Frühjudentum und im Neuen Testament. Wechselseitige Wahrnehmungen, WUNT 322, Tübingen 2014.

KORN, H. J., ΠΕΙΡΑΣΜΟΣ. Die Versuchung des Gläubigen in der griechischen Bibel, BWANT 20, Stuttgart 1937.

KOSKENNIEMI, E., Greek Writers and Philosophers in Philo and Josephus. A Study of Their Secular Education and Educational Ideals, Studies in Philo of Alexandria 9, Leiden 2019.

KOTZÉ, A., Art. Protreptik, RAC 28, 2017, 372–393.

KRAMER, H., Lukas als Ordner des frühchristlichen Diskurses um »Armut und Reichtum« und den »Umgang mit materiellen Gütern«, NET 21, Tübingen 2015.

KRANEMANN, B., Art. Krankenöl, RAC 21, 2006, 915–965.

KRAPINGER, G., Art. Propositio, HWRh 7, 2005, 307–315.

KRAUSE, J.-U., Art. Klassen (Gesellschaftsschichten), RAC 20, 2004, 1169–1227.

KRAUTER, ST., Vater Abraham und *pater Aeneas*. Eine Auseinandersetzung mit einem neuen Interpretationsvorschlag zu Röm 4, in: J. Frey u. a. (Hg.), Paulusmemoria und Paulusexegese, Tübingen 2023, 63–96.

KRISPENZ, J. u. a., Art. Zitat, LBH, 2009, 689–695.

KRISTEVA, J., Bakhtine, le mot, le dialogue et le roman, Critique XXIII, 1967, 438–465.

–, Wort, Dialog und Roman bei Bachtin (1967), in: J. Ihwe (Hg.), Literaturwissenschaft und Linguistik. Ergebnisse und Perspektiven, Bd. 3: Zur linguistischen Basis der Literaturwissenschaft II, Frankfurt am Main 1972, 345–375.

KRÜGER, R., Arm und Reich im Jakobusbrief von Lateinamerika aus gelesen. Die Herausforderung eines prophetischen Christentums, Diss. Universität Amsterdam 2003 (=Der Jakobusbrief als prophetische Kritik der Reichen, Beiträge zum Verstehen der Bibel 12, Münster 2005).

LANG, B., Die Bibelkommentare der Kirchenväter (ca. 200–600). Kleines Kompendium mit Forschungsstand und Beispieltexten, in: D. Kästle / N. Jansen (Hg.), Kommentare in Recht und Religion, Tübingen 2014, 57–98.

LANG, F., Art. πῦρ κτλ., ThWNT 6, 1959, 927–953.

LAST, R., The Pauline Church and the Corinthian Ekklēsia. Greco-Roman Associations in Comparative Context, SNTS.MS 164, Cambridge 2015.

– / HARLAND, PH.A. (Hg.), Group Survival in the Ancient Mediterranean. Rethinking Material Conditions in the Landscape of Jews and Christians, London 2020.

LATTKE, M., Art. κενός, EWNT 2, 2011, 693–695.

LEINEWEBER, M., Lukas und die Witwen. Eine Botschaft an die Gemeinden in der hellenistisch-römischen Gesellschaft, Europäische Hochschulschriften, Reihe 23: Theologie 915, Frankfurt/M. 2011.

LEVINE, L. I., Art. Synagogues, EDEJ, 2010, 1260–1271.

LINCICUM, D., Art. ἀπάτη, HTLS I, 2020, 877–888.

LIST, N., Δίψυχος. Moving Beyond Intertextuality, NTS 67, 2021, 85–104.

LOHFINK, N., Von der ›Anawim-Partei‹ zur ›Kirche der Armen‹. Die bibelwissenschaftliche Ahnentafel eines Hauptbegriffs der ›Theologie der Befreiung‹, Bibl 67, 1986, 153–176.

LÖHR, H., Studien zum frühchristlichen und frühjüdischen Gebet. Untersuchungen zu 1Clem 59 bis 61 in seinem literarischen, historischen und theologischen Kontext, WUNT 16, Tübingen 2003.

LONGENECKER, B. W. (Hg.), Greco-Roman Associations, Deities, and Early Christianity, Waco 2022.

LÜHRMANN, D., Art. Glaube, RAC 11, 1981, 48–122.

–, Glaube im frühen Christentum, Gütersloh 1976.

–, Pistis im Judentum, ZNW 64, 1973, 19–38.

LUTHER, S., Der Jakobusbrief in der aktuellen Situation. Tendenzen und Perspektiven der neueren Forschung, ZNT 50, 2023, 5–25.

–, Die Ethik des Jakobusbriefes, in: R. Zimmermann (Hg.), Ethik des Neuen Testaments, [im Druck].

–, Profiling the Author of the Letter of James. Dealing With Traditions in the Light of Epistolary Authorship Conceptions, in: E.-M. Becker u. a. (Hg.), Who was ›James‹? Essays on the Letter's Authorship and Provenance, WUNT 485, Tübingen 2022, 29–56.

–, Protreptic Ethics in the Letter of James. The Potential of Figurative Language in Character Formation, in: R. Zimmermann u. a. (Hg.), Moral Language in the New Testament. Interrelatedness of Language and Ethics in Early Christian Writings, WUNT II 296, Tübingen 2010, 330–364.

–, Sprachethik im Neuen Testament. Eine Analyse des frühchristlichen Diskurses im Matthäusevangelium, im Jakobusbrief und im 1. Petrusbrief, WUNT II 394, Tübingen 2015.

–, The Christ of James' Story, in: P. Dragutinović u. a. (Hg.), Christ of the Sacred Stories, WUNT II 453, Tübingen 2015, 191–200.

–, Von Feigenbäumen und Oliven. Die Rezeption, Transformation und Kreation sprachethischer Traditionen im Jakobusbrief, ASEs 34, 2017, 381–401.

LUZ, U., Das Evangelium nach Matthäus (Mt 1–7), EKK I/1, Düsseldorf u. a. ⁵2002.

MAAS, W., Unveränderlichkeit Gottes. Zum Verhältnis von griechisch-philosophischer und christlicher Gotteslehre, PaThSt 1, München u. a. 1974.

MALHERBE, A. J., Godliness, Self-Sufficiency, Greed, and the Enjoyment of Wealth. 1Tim 6:3–19 Parts I and II, NT 52, 2010, 378–405; NT 53, 2011, 73–96.

–, The Letters to the Thessalonians, AncB 32, New Haven/London 2000.

MALINA, A., »I demoni credono e tremano« (Gc 2,19), ASEs 34, 2017, 457–468.

MASON, S., Jews, Judaeans, Judaizing, Judaism. Problems of Categorizing in Ancient History, JSJ 38, 2007, 457–512.

MAURER, CH., Art. φυλή, ThWNT 9, 1993, 240–245.

MAYNARD-REID, P. U., Poverty and Wealth in James, Maryknoll 1987.

METZNER, R., Der Lehrer Jakobus. Überlegungen zur Verfasserfrage des Jakobusbriefes, ZNW 104, 2013, 238–267.

MEYER, A., Das Rätsel des Jacobusbriefes, Gießen 1930.

MICHAELIS, W., Art. ὁδός, ThWNT 5, 1954, 42–118.

MIRGUET, F., The Study of Emotions in Early Jewish Texts. Review and Perspectives, JSJ 50, 2019, 1–47.

MITCHELL, M. M., The Letter of James as a Document of Paulinism, in: L. Webb / J. S. Kloppenborg (Hg.), Reading James with New Eyes. Methodological Reassessments of the Letter of James, LNTS 342, London / New York 2007, 75–98.

MITCHELL, S./VAN NUFFELEN, P. (Hg.), One God. Pagan Monotheism in the Roman Empire, Cambridge 2010.

MONGSTAD-KVAMMEN, I. A. K., Toward a Postcolonial Reading of the Epistle of James. James 2:1–13 in Its Roman Imperial Context, Biblical Interpretation Series 119, Leiden / Boston 2013.

MORALES, N. R., Poor and Rich in James. A Relevance Theory Approach to James's Use of the Old Testament, Bulletin for Biblical Research Supplement 20, Pennsylvania 2018.

MORGAN, TH., Roman Faith and Christian Faith. Pistis and Fides in the Early Roman Empire and Early Churches, Oxford 2015.

–, The New Testament and the Theology of Trust. ›This Rich Trust‹, Oxford 2022.

MUELLER, J. G., Art. Presbyter, RAC 28, 2017, 86–112.

MURPHY-O'CONNOR O. P., J., Paul the Letter-Writer, Good News Studies, Collegeville 1995.

NAYMAN, H., Past Renewals, Interpretative Authority, Renewed Revelation and the Quest for Perfection in Jewish Antiquity, JStJ.S 53, Leiden 2010.

NEILL, E. N., De cupiditate divitiarum (Moralia 523C–528B), in: H. D. Betz (Hg.), Plutarch's Ethical Writings an Early Christian Literature, SCHNT 4, Leiden 1978, 289–362.

NEUMANN, N., Armut und Reichtum im Lukasevangelium und in der kynischen Philosophie, SBS 220, Stuttgart 2010.

NIEBUHR, K.-W., »A New Perspective on James?« Neuere Forschungen zum Jakobusbrief, ThLZ 129, 2004, 1019–1044.

–, Der Jakobusbrief im Lichte frühjüdischer Diasporabriefe, NTS 44, 1998, 420–443.

–, Glaube im Stresstest. Πίστις im Jakobusbrief, in: B. Schliesser u. a. (Hg.), Glaube. Das Verständnis des Glaubens im frühen Christentum und seiner jüdischen und hellenistisch-römischen Umwelt, WUNT 373, Tübingen 2017, 473–501.

–, Jakobus und Paulus über das Innere des Menschen und den Ursprung seiner ethischen Entscheidungen, NTS 62, 1–30.

–, Luther und der Jakobusbrief. Zur Diskussion um die »stroherne« Epistel im frühen 16. Jahrhundert, ZNT 50, 2023, 27–49.

–, Rezension zu A. Peter, Akoluthiebewahrung und Jesusüberlieferung im Jakobusbrief, WUNT II 536, Tübingen 2020, RBL 24.2022, 437–439.

NIEHOFF, M. R., Auf den Spuren des hellenistischen Judentums in Caesarea. Ein jüdischer Psalmenforscher in Origenes' Glosse im Kontext Rabbinischer Literatur, ZAC 27, 2023, 31–76.

–, Rezension zu E. Koskenniemi, Greek Writers and Philosophers in Philo and Josephus. A Study of Their Secular Education and Educational Ideals, Studies in Philo of Alexandria 9, Leiden 2019, BMCR 19.05. 2022.

NÜRNBERGER, A., Zweifelskonzepte im Frühchristentum. Dipsychia und Oligopistia im Rahmen menschlicher Dissonanz- und Einheitsvorstellungen in der Antike, NTOA / StUNT 122, Göttingen 2019.

NUTTON, V., Rhodiapolis and Allianoi. Two Missing Links in the History of the Hospital? EaC 5, 2014, 371–389.

ÖHLER, M., Geschichte des frühen Christentums, utb 4737, Göttingen 2018.

OSTMEYER, K.-H., Jüdische Gebete aus der Umwelt des Neuen Testaments. Ein Studienbuch, BTSt 37, Leuven 2019.

–, Kommunikation mit Gott und Christus. Sprache und Theologie des Gebets im Neuen Testament, WUNT 197, Tübingen 2006.

PEACHIN, M., Attacken und Erniedrigung als alltägliche Elemente der kaiserzeitlichen Regierungspraxis, in: R. Haensch / J. Heinrichs (Hg.), Herrschen und Verwalten. Der Alltag der Aministration des Römischen Reiches in der Kaiserzeit, KHAb 46, Köln u. a. 2007, 117–125.

PENNER, T. C., The Epistle of James in Current Research, CR.BS 7, 1999, 257–308.

PETER, A., Akoluthiebewahrung und Jesusüberlieferung im Jakobusbrief, WUNT II 536, Tübingen 2020.

POGORZELSKI, R., Centers and Peripheries, in: A. Zissos (Hg.), A Companion to the Flavian Age of Imperial Rome, BCAW, Chichester 2016.

PETRACCA, V., Gott oder das Geld. Die Besitzethik des Lukas, TANZ 39, Tübingen / Basel 2003.

PROSINGER, F., Das eingepflanzte Wort der Wahrheit, SBS 243, Stuttgart 2019.

QUELL, G./FÖRSTER, W., Art. κύριος κτλ., ThWNT 3, 1938, 1038–1098.

REISER, M., Die Gerichtspredigt Jesu. Eine Untersuchung zur eschatologischen Verkündigung Jesu und ihrem frühjüdischen Hintergrund, NTA NF 23, Münster 1990.

RENGER, J. u. a., Art. Handel, DNP 5, 1998, 106–127.

RENGSTORF, K. H., Art. δοῦλος κτλ, ThWNT 2, 1935, 264–283.

RHEE, H. (Hg.), Wealth and Poverty in Early Christianity, Ad Fontes, Minneapolis 2017.

–, Loving the Poor, Saving the Rich. Wealth, Poverty, and Early Christian Formation, Grand Rapids 2012.

RÖHSER, G., Metaphorik und Personifikation der Sünde. Antike Sündenvorstellungen und paulinische Hamartia, WUNT II 25, Tübingen 1987.

ROHDE, J., Art. ἐπισκέπτομαι, EWNT 2, 1981, 83–85.

RUDNIG-ZELT, S., Der Teufel und der alttestamentliche Monotheismus, in: Dochhorn u. a. (Hg.), Das Böse, 1–20.

SÄNGER, D., Art. διασπορά, διασπείρω, EWNT 1, 1992/³2011, 553–555.

SASS, G., Zur Bedeutung von δοῦλος bei Paulus, ZNW 40, 1941, 24–31.

SAUR, M., Der Blick in den Abgrund. Bilder des Bösen, in der alttestamentlichen Weisheitsliteratur, in: Dochhorn u. a. (Hg.), Das Böse, 21–42.

SCHÄFER, K., Gemeinde als »Bruderschaft«. Ein Beitrag zum Kirchenverständnis des Paulus, EHS 333, Frankfurt / M., 1989.

SCHENK, W., Art. κριτής, EWNT 2, 1981, 795–797.

SCHENK-ZIEGLER, A., Correctio fraterna im Neuen Testament. Die »brüderliche Zurechtweisung« in biblischen, frühjüdischen und hellenistischen Schriften, fzb 84, Würzburg 1997.

SCHIMA, S., Art. Prozessrecht, RAC 28, 2017, 744–771.

SCHLIESSER, B. u. a. (Hg.), Glaube. Das Verständnis des Glaubens im frühen Christentum und seiner jüdischen und hellenistisch-römischen Umwelt, WUNT 373, Tübingen 2017.

–, Was ist Glaube? Paulinische Perspektiven, Theologische Studien N. F. 3, Zürich 2011.

–, Zweifel. Phänomene des Zweifels und der Zweiseeligkeit im frühen Christentum, WUNT 500, Tübingen 2022.

Schlosser, J. (Hg.), The Catholic Epistles and the Tradition, BETL 176, Leuven 2004.

Schmauder, M., Art. Ring, RAC 29, 2019, 123–130.

–, Art. Schmuck, RAC 29, 2019, 978–1006.

Schmidt, K. L., Art. διασπορά, ThWNT 2, 1935, 98–104.

Schneider, J., Art. ὀμνύω, ThWNT 5, 1954, 177–185.

Schnider, F./Stender, W., Studien zum neutestamentlichen Briefformular, NTTS 11, Leiden 1987.

Schöttner, M., Der vollkommene Mensch. Zur Genese eines frühchristlich-gnostischen Konzepts, Ntl. Abh. NF 61, Münster 2019.

Schröter, J., Jesus Tradition in Matthew, James, and the Didache. Searching for Characteristic Emphases, in: H. van de Sandt/J. K. Zangenberg (Hg.), Matthew, James, and Didache. Three Related Documents in Their Jewish and Christian Settings, Atlanta 2008, 233–255.

Schwartz, S., Political, Social, and Economic Life in the Land of Israel, 66–c.235, in: CHJud IV. The Late Roman-Rabbinic Period, Cambridge 1984, 23–52.

Schwemer, A. M., Studien zu den frühjüdischen Prophetenlegenden. Vitae Prophetarum. Bd. II: Die Viten der kleinen Propheten und der Propheten aus den Geschichtsbüchern, Tübingen 1996.

Scornaienchi, L., Polemik im Jakobusbrief und deren Bedeutung für die Konfiguration des Autors, in: E.-M. Becker u. a. (Hg.), Who was ›James‹? Essays on the Letter's Authorship and Provenance, WUNT 485, Tübingen 2022, 331–369.

–, Rezension zu E. Chorrini, Iterazioni sinonimiche nella Lettera di Giacomo: Studio lessicografico ed esegetico, Analacta 89, Mailand 2020, RBL 07.2022.

–, Sarx und Soma bei Paulus. Der Mensch zwischen Destruktivität und Konstruktivität, NTOA/StUNT 67, Göttingen 2008.

Seesemann, H., Art. πεῖρα κτλ., ThWNT 6, 1959, 23–37.

Seiler, S. u. a., Art. Intertextualität, LBH, 2009, 300–306.

Severus, E. von, Art. Gebet, RAC 8, 1972, 1134–1258.

Siegert, F., Einführung in die hellenistisch-jüdische Literatur. Apokrypha, Pseudepigrapha und Fragmente verlorener Autorenwerke, Berlin/Boston 2016.

Skehan, P. W./di Lella, A. A., The Wisdom of Ben Sira, AncB 39, New York 1987.

Soden, H. von, Art. ἀδελφός κτλ., ThWNT 1,1933, 144–146.

Sommer, A., Der Begriff der Versuchung im Alten Testament und Judentum, Diss. Breslau, Breslau 1935.

Spanneut, M., Art. Geduld, RAC 9, 1976, 243–294.

Spicq, C. O. P., Notes de Lexicographie Néo-Testamentaire I/II, OBO 22/1 und 2, Fribourg/Göttingen 1978.

Spitaler, P., Διακρίνεσθαι in Mt.21:21, Mk. 11:23, Acta 10:20, Rom. 4:20, 14:23, Jas. 1:6, and Jude 22 – the »Semantic Shift« That Went Unnoticed by Patristic Authors, NT 49, 2007, 1–39.

Stählin, G., Art. φίλος κτλ., ThWNT 9, 1973, 144–169.

–, Art. ἡδονή, ThWNT 2, 1935, 911–928.

Stanley, Ch.D., Paul and the Language of Scripture. Citation technique in the Pauline Epistles and the Contemporary Literature, SNTSMS 69, Cambridge 1992.

STARR, J. M./ENGBERG-PEDERSEN, T. (Hg.), Early Christian Paraenesis, BZNW 125, Berlin 2004.

STEIMER, B., Art. Didaskalia, LACL, ³2002, 196f.

STEINBERG, J., Art. Seligpreisung (AT), WiBiLex 2013 (https://bibelwissenschaft.de/stichwort/45569/).

STEMBERGER, G., Judenchristen, in: Ders., Judaica Minora. Bd. II: Geschichte und Literatur des rabbinischen Judentums, TSAJ 138, Tübingen 2010, 228–245.

STOWERS, S. K., Art. Diatribe, ABD 2, 1992, 190–193.

–, Letter Writing in Greco-Roman Antiquity, Philadelphia 1986.

STRECKER, G., Art. Ebioniten, RAC 4, 1959, 487–500.

–, Art. μακάριος, EWNT 2, 1992, 925–932.

STUIBER, A., Art. Diaspora, RAC 3, 1957, 972–982.

THIEL, CH., Art. Kettenschluss, EPhW 2, 1996, 390.

THÜR, G., Art. Gnome, DNP 4, 1998, 1108–1116.

– / PIELER, P. E., Art. Gerichtsbarkeit, RAC 10, 1978, 360–492.

THURÉN, L., Risky Rhetoric in James?, NT 37, 1995, 262–284.

TILLY, M., Besitzethik und Menschenbild bei Pseudo-Phokylides, in: M. Konradt / E. Schläpfer (Hg.), Anthropologie und Ethik im Frühjudentum und im Neuen Testament. Wechselseitige Wahrnehmungen, WUNT 322, Tübingen 2014, 309–325.

TREU, K., Art. Gottesfreund, RAC 11, 1981, 1043–1060.

TREU, N., Das Sprachverständnis des Paulus im Rahmen des antiken Sprachdiskurses, NET 26, Tübingen 2018.

TSUJI, M., Glaube zwischen Vollkommenheit und Verweltlichung. Eine Untersuchung zur literarischen Gestalt und inhaltlichen Kohärenz des Jakobusbriefes, WUNT II 93, Tübingen 1997.

UEDING, G./STEINBRINK, B., Grundriß der Rhetorik, Stuttgart ⁵2011.

URBANZ, W., Gebet im Sirachbuch. Zur Terminologie von Klage und Lob in der griechischen Textradition, Herders Biblische Studien 60, Freiburg 2009.

VAN DE SANDT, H./ZANGENBERG, J. K. (Hg.), Matthew, James, and Didache. Three Related Documents in Their Jewish and Christian Settings, Atlanta 2008.

VAN DER EIJK, PH., Galen and Early Christians on the Role of the Divine in the Causation and Treatment of Health, EaC 5, 2014, 337–370.

VAN DER HORST, P., Art. Father of the Lights, Dictionary of Deities and Demons in the Bible, Leiden u. a. ²1995, 628f.

VAN DER WATT, G. (Hg.), Identity, Ethics, and Ethos in the NT, BZNW 141, Berlin / New York 2006.

VAN VOORST, R. E., The Ascents of James. History and Theology of a Jewish-Christian Community, SBLDS 112, Atlanta 1989.

VOITILA, A., Art. ἁπλοῦς, ἁπλότης, HTLS I, 2020, 927–938.

VOLLENWEIDER, S., Freiheit als neue Schöpfung. Eleutheria bei Paulus und in seiner Umwelt, FRLANT 147, Göttingen 1989.

WACHOB, W. H./JOHNSON, L. T. (Hg.), The Sayings of Jesus in the Letter of James, in: B. Chilton / C. A. Evans (Hg.), Authenticating the Words of Jesus, NTTS 28 / 1, Leiden u. a. 1999, 413–450.

WACHT, M., Art. Reichtum, RAC 28, 2018, 830–856.

WAGNER, A. Emotionen in alttestamentlicher und verwandter Literatur – Grundüberlegungen am Beispiel des Zorns, in: R. Egger-Wenzel / J. Corley (Hg.), Emotions from Ben Sira to Paul, DCLY 2011, Berlin / Boston 2012, 27–68.

WAGNER-LUX, U., Art. Jerusalem I, RAC 17, 1996, 631–718.

WALL, R. W., The Intertextuality of Scripture. The Example of Rahab (James 2:25), in: P. W. Fint (Hg.), The Bible at Qumran. Text, Shape, and Interpretation, Grand Rapids 2001, 217–226.

WATSON, D. F., James 2 in Light of Greco-Roman Schemes of Argumentation, NTS 39, 1993, 94–121.

WATSON, F., Roman Faith and Christian Faith, NTS 64, 2018, 243–247.

WEBB, L./KLOPPENBORG, J. S. (Hg.), Reading James with New Eyes. Methodological Reassessments of the Letter of James, LNTS 342, London / New York 2007.

WEISER, A./BULTMANN, R., Art. πιστεύω κτλ., ThWNT 6, 1959, 174–230.

WEISS, A., Soziale Elite und Christentum. Studien zu ordo-Angehörigen unter den frühen Christen, Millenium-Studien 52, Berlin / Boston 2015.

WEISSENRIEDER, A., What Does »To be Saved by Childbearing« Mean (1 Timothy 2:15)? Insights from Ancient Medical and Philosophical Texts, EaC 5, 2014, 313–336.

WEKSLER-BDOLAH, SH., Aelia Capitolina – Jerusalem in the Roman Period. In Light of Archeological Research, MnS 432, Leiden / Boston 2019.

WENGER, S., Der wesenhaft gute Kyrios. Eine exegetische Studie über das Gottesbild im Jakobusbrief, AThANT 100, Zürich 2011.

WESSEL, K., Art. Elias, RAC 4, 1959, 1141–1163.

WETTLAUFER, R. D., No Longer Written. The Use of Conjectural Emendations in the Text of the New Testament. The Epistle of James as a Case Study, NTTSD 44, Leiden 2013.

WHITE, J., Die Erstlingsgabe im Neuen Testament, TANZ 45, Tübingen 2007.

WHITE, J. L., Introductory Formulae in the Body of the Pauline Letter, JBL 90, 1971, 91–97.

–, New Testament Epistolary Literature in the Framework of Ancient Epistolography, ANRW II 25 / 2, 1984, 1730–1756.

WIEGER, M./PERRY, K., Art. ἀγαπάω κτλ., HTLS I, 2020, 25–64.

WILK, F. (Hg.), Das Vaterunser in seinen antiken Kontexten, FRLANT 266, Göttingen 2016.

WILSON, K. M., Reading James 2:18–20 with Anti-Donatist Eyes. Untangling Augustine's Exegetical Legacy, JBL 139, 2020, 385–407.

WINDISCH, H., Zur Rahabgeschichte, ZNW 37, 1917 / 18, 188–198.

WISCHMEYER, O., Abraham unser Vater. Aspekte der Abrahamsgestalt im Neuen Testament, in: H. Lichtenberger / U. Mittmann (Hg.), Biblical Figures in Deuterocanonical and Cognate Literature, DCLY 2008, Berlin / New York 2009, 567–585.

–, Art. Epistel, in: Handbuch Brief, Berlin 2025.

–, Beobachtungen zu Kommunikation, Gliederung und Gattung des Jakobusbriefes, in: D. Sänger / M. Konradt (Hg.), Das Gesetz im frühen Judentum und im Neuen Testament (FS Ch. Burchard), NTOA 57, Göttingen / Fribourg 2006, 319–327.

–, Das Gebot der Nächstenliebe bei Paulus. Eine traditionsgeschichtliche Untersuchung, in: Dies., Von Ben Sira zu Paulus, 137–162.

–, Der Jakobusbrief, in: E.-M. Becker u. a. (Hg.), Der »Kritisch-exegetische Kommentar« in seiner Geschichte. H. A. W. Meyers KEK von seiner Gründung 1829 bis heute, KEK.S, Göttingen 2018, 436–453.

–, Emotionen als formative Elemente neutestamentlicher Ethik am Beispiel des Paulus, Journal of Ethics in Antiquity and Christianity 2, 2020, 25–39.

–, Glaube, der durch die Liebe tätig wird (Galater 5,6). Überlegungen zu den Grundlagen paulinischer Theologie, in: B. Bargel/A. Frank (Hg.), Christlicher Glaube in seinen Anfängen. Kulturelle Begegnungen und theologische Antworten (FS B. Heininger), Würzburg 2023, 101–130.

–, Jak 3,13–18 vor dem Hintergrund von 1Kor 1,17–2,16. Frühchristliche Weisheitstheologie und der Jakobusbrief, ASEs 34, 2017, 403–430.

–, Liebe als Agape. Das frühchristliche Konzept und der moderne Diskurs, Tübingen 2015 (engl.: Love as Agape. The Early Christian Concept and Modern Discourse, Waco/Tübingen 2021).

–, Luther's Prefaces to the New Testament in Their Hermeneutical and Theological Dimension. Read from an Exegetical Perspective, in: M. W. Elliott u. a. (Hg.), Studies in the History of Exegesis, HBE 2, Tübingen 2022, 109–122.

–, Paulus als Hermeneut der GRAPHE, in: M. Witte/J. C. Gertz (Hg.), Hermeneutik des Alten Testaments, VWGTh 47, Leipzig 2017, 71–94.

–, Polemik im Jakobusbrief. Formen, Gegenstände und Fronten, in: Dies./L. Scornaienchi (Hg.), Polemik in der frühchristlichen Literatur. Texte und Kontexte, BZNW 170, Berlin/Boston 2011, 357–379.

–, Reconstructing the Social and Religious Milieu of James. Methods, Sources, and Possible Results, in: H. van de Sandt/J. K. Zangenberg (Hg.), Matthew, James, and Didache. Three Related Documents in Their Jewish and Christian Settings, Atlanta 2008, 33–41.

–, Rezension zu J. Assaël, et É. Cuvillier, L'Épître de Jacques, CNT XIIIa, Genève 2013, ThLZ 141, 2016, 613–616.

–, Rezension zu F. Prosinger, Das eingepflanzte Wort der Wahrheit, SBS 243, Stuttgart 2019, RBL 12.2020.

–, Rezension zu R. Metzner, Der Brief des Jakobus, ThHK 14, Leipzig 2017, RBL 07.2018.

–, Rezension zu S. McKnight, The Letter of James, NICNT, Grand Rapids/Cambrige 2011, ThLZ 137, 2012, 677–680.

–, Rezension zu Th.K. Heckel, Die Briefe des Jakobus, Johannes und Petrus (NTD 10), Göttingen 2019, Biblica 101, 2020, 471–476.

–, Rezension zu W. Popkes, Der Brief des Jakobus, ThHK 14, Leipzig 2001, TRev 101, 2005, 212–215.

–, Scriptual Classicism?, in: E.-M. Becker u. a. (Hg.), Who was ›James‹? Essays on the Letter's Authorship and Provenance, WUNT 485, Tübingen 2022, 277–312.

–, The Book of Ben Sira From a Reception-Historical Perspective. Hubert Frankemölle's Commentary on the Letter of James, in: F. M. Macatangay/F.-J. Ruiz-Ortiz (Hg.), Ben Sira in Conversation with Traditions (FS N. Calduch-Benages), DCLS 47, Berlin/Boston 2022, 285–300.

–, The Prayer of Faith – the Prayer of the Righteous (Jas 5:13–18). Where the »Ways« Intersect, in: N. Calduch-Benages u. a. (Hg.), On Wings of Prayer. Sources of Jewish Worship (FS S. C. Reif); DCLS 44, Berlin/Boston 2019, 151–168.

–, THEON AGAPAN bei Paulus. Eine traditionsgeschichtliche Miszelle, in: Dies., Von Ben Sira zu Paulus, 162–166.

–, Von Ben Sira zu Paulus. Gesammelte Aufsätze zu Texten Theologie und Hermeneutik des Frühjudentums und des Neuen Testaments, hg. von E.-M. Becker, WUNT 173, Tübingen 2004.

4. Monographien, Sammelbände und Aufsätze

–, Who was »James«? Der Herrenbruder, ein »Namenloser aus den Vielen«, ein »role model« oder ein frühchristlicher Lehrer mit dem Namen Jakōbos? Die Neukommentierung des Jakobusbriefes für Meyers Kritisch-Exegetischen Kommentar, in: E.-M. Becker u. a. (Hg.), Who was ›James‹? Essays on the Letter's Authorship and Provenance, WUNT 485, Tübingen 2022, 179–195.

–, Wie kommt Abraham in den Galaterbrief? Überlegungen zu Gal 3,6–29, in: M. Bachmann / B. Kollmann (Hg.), Umstrittener Galaterbrief. Studien zur Situierung der Theologie des Paulus-Schreibens (FS I. Broer), BThSt 106, Neukirchen-Vluyn 2010, 119–163.

–, Wie spricht der Jakobusbrief von Gott? Theologie im Jakobusbrief, in: R. Egger-Wenzel u. a. (Hg.), Weisheit als Lebensgrundlage (FS F. V. Reiterer), DCLS 15, Berlin / Boston 2013, 385–409.

–, Zitat und Allusion als literarische Eröffnung des Markusevangeliums, in: J. Jakob / M. Mayer (Hg.), Im Namen des Anderen. Die Ethik des Zitierens, Ethik – Text – Kultur 3, München 2010, 175–186.

–, Zwischen Gut und Böse. Teufel, Dämonen, das Böse und der Kosmos im Jakobusbrief, in: Dochhorn u. a. (Hg.), Das Böse, 153–168.

Wissmann, E., Das Verhältnis von πίστις und Christusfrömmigkeit bei Paulus, FRLANT 40, Göttingen 1926.

Witte, M., Barmherzigkeit mit den Bedürftigen und Notleidenden und ihre anthropologische Grundlage, in: M. Konradt / E. Schläpfer (Hg.), Anthropologie und Ethik im Frühjudentum und im Neuen Testament. Wechselseitige Wahrnehmungen, WUNT 322, Tübingen 2014, 387–412.

Wold, B., Apotropaic Prayer and the Matthean Lord's Prayer, in: Dochhorn u. a. (Hg.), Das Böse, 101–112.

Wolmarus, J. L. P., The Tongue Guiding the Body. The Anthropological Presuppositions of James 3.1–12, Neot 26, 1992, 523–530.

Woolf, G., Writing Poverty in Rome, in: M. Atkins / R. Osborne (Hg.), Poverty in the Roman World, Cambridge 2006, 83–99.

Wuellner, W. H., Der Jakobusbrief im Licht der Rhetorik und Textpragmatik, LingBibl 43, 1978, 5–66.

Wypadlo, A., Viel vermag das inständige Gebet eines Gerechten (Jak 5,16). Die Weisung zum Gebet im Jakobusbrief, fzb 110, Würzburg 2006.

Yarbo Collins, A., Mark. A Commentary, Hermeneia, Minneapolis 2007.

Yoshiko Reed, A., Art. Job, Testament of, EDEJ 2010, 814–816.

Zager, W., Albert Schweitzers Anleitung zu selbständiger exegetischer Arbeit. Kleine Lesefrüchte aus den Kollegheften Albert Schweitzers, ZNW 85, 1994, 286–289.

Zeller, D., Der erste Brief an die Korinther, KEK 5, Göttingen 2010.

Zilliacus, H., Art. Anredeformen, RAC Suppl I, Stuttgart 2001, 465–497.

Zimmermann, Ch., Die Namen des Vaters. Studien zu ausgewählten neutestamentlichen Gottesbezeichnungen, AJEC 69, Leiden / Boston 2007.

Zissos, A. (Hg.), A Companion to the Flavian Age of Imperial Rome, BCAW, Chichester 2016.

5. Abkürzungen und Zitierweise

A) Abkürzungen

1. Die bibliographischen Abkürzungen sind aus dem [3]IATG übernommen.
2. Weitere verwendete Abkürzungen:

AcA	Antike christliche Apokryphen
Bibl	Biblica
BCAW	Blackwell Companions to the Ancient World
BMCR	Bryn Mawr Classical Review
c.I.	Conditio Iacobea
EaC	Early Christianity
ECM	Novum Testamentum. Editio critica maior
EDEJ	The Eerdmans Dictionary of Early Judaism
HTLS	Historical and Theological Lexicon of the Septuagint
LBH	Lexikon der Bibelhermeneutik
NTGu	New Testament Guides
SANt	Studia Aarhusiana Neotestamentica
SAPERE	Scripta Antiquitatis Posterioris ad Ethicam REligionemque pertinentia
WiBiLex	Das wissenschaftliche Bibellexikon im Internet

3. Die Abkürzungen der biblischen Bücher und der antiken jüdischen Literatur sind der [4]RGG entnommen.

4. Die Werke der antiken Autoren einschließlich Philo und Josephus sind nach DNP abgekürzt:

Aelianus, nat.: De natura animalium
Cicero, off.: De officiis
Dion Chrysostomos, or.: Orationes
Epiktet, Diss.: Dissertationes
Eusebius, HE.: Historia ecclesiastica
Eusebius, Pr. Ev.: Praeparatio Evangelica
Hieronymus, vir. ill.: De viris illustribus
Iamblichos, v. P.: De vita Pythagorica liber
Josephus, ant. Iud.: Antiquitates
Justin, apol.: Apologia Prima
Justin, dial.: Iustinus Martyr dialogus cum Tryphone
Kleanthes Frgm.: Fragmenta

Philo, Abr.: De Abrahamo
Philo, agr.: De agricultura
Philo, conf.: De confusione linguarum
Philo, congr.: De congressu eruditionis gratia
Philo, decal.: De decalogo
Philo, det.: Quod deterius potiori insidiari soleat
Philo, ebr.: De ebrietate
Philo, Flacc.: In Flaccum
Philo, fug.: De fuga et inventione
Philo, imm.: Quod Deus sit immutabilis
Philo, Jos.: De Josepho
Philo, leg.all.: Legum allegoriae
Philo, migr.: De migratione Abrahami
Philo, mut.: De mutatione nominum
Philo, opif.: De opificio mundi
Philo, plant.: De plantatione
Philo, post.: De posteritate Caini
Philo, praem.: De praemiis et poenis
Philo, prob.: Quod omnis probus liber sit
Philo, prov.: De providentia
Philo, sacr.: De sacrificiis Abeli et Caini
Philo, spec.leg.: De specialibus legibus
Philo, virt.: De virtutibus
Platon, leg.: Leges
Platon, Tht.: Platon, Theaitetos
Plutarch, mor.: Moralia
Ps.-Aristoteles, mund.: De mundo
Quintilian, inst.: Institutio oratoria
Seneca, benef.: De beneficiis
Simplikios, CAG.: Commentaria in Aristotelem Graeca
Xenophon, mem.: Memorabilia

B) Zitierweise

Die Kommentarliteratur zum Jakobusbrief wird mit dem Verfassernamen und der Abkürzung Jak zitiert. Dies gilt auch für die fremdsprachigen Kommentare. Die übrige Literatur wird in der Regel mit dem Verfassernamen und dem ersten Substantiv des Titels zitiert.

Einleitung

A. Der Kommentar. Grundlinien der Interpretation

Was ist die Aufgabe eines Kommentars (commentarii quid operis habent)? … Er soll die Meinungen vieler wiedergeben und sagen: Die einen erklären diesen Abschnitt so, andere interpretieren ihn so. … So kann der kritische Leser (prudens lector), wenn er verschiedene Erklärungen liest und Annehmbares und Unannehmbares erfährt, selbst urteilen, was eher zutrifft. Wie ein tüchtiger Geldwechsler soll er falsche Münzen ausscheiden.

Hieronymus, Apologia adversus libros Rufini I, 16

Nicht Commentar. Meine Ungerechtigkeit gegen Commentare … Im Grunde ein geistloses Erzeugnis der Litteratur. Kein Verdienst NT mit Handkommentar. Gesetzes Werk. Schwächung des Intellekts.

Albert Schweitzer[1]

Vor dem neuen Kommentar, der hier vorgelegt wird, stehen die bisherigen Kommentare. Jeder neue Kommentar knüpft in Konzeption, Innovation, Weiterführung, Widerspruch und Ablehnung – kurz in dauerndem Gespräch – an die vorliegenden Kommentare an und muss sich an ihnen messen lassen. Daher beginnt die Neuauslegung des Jakobusbriefes für den KEK mit einem Blick auf die bisherigen Kommentare.[2]

---

[1] Zitiert nach W. Zager, Albert Schweitzers Anleitung zu selbständiger exegetischer Arbeit. Kleine Lesefrüchte aus den Kollegheften Albert Schweitzers, ZNW 85, 1994, 286–289, 288. Ich danke James N. Carleton Paget, Cambridge, für den Hinweis.

[2] Zur Forschungsgeschichte zu Jak vgl. P. H. Davids, The Epistle of James in Modern Discussion, in: ANRW II, 25/5, 1988, 3621–3645; F. Hahn / P. Müller, Der Jakobusbrief, ThR 63, 1998, 1–73; M. Konradt, Theologie in der »strohernen Epistel. Ein Literaturbericht zu neueren Ansätzen in der Exegese des Jakobusbriefes«, VF 44, 1999, 54–78; T. C. Penner, The Epistle of James in Current Research, CR.BS 7, 1999, 257–308; A. J. Batten, What Are They Saying about the Letter of James?, New York 2009; O. Wischmeyer, Der Jakobusbrief, in: E.-M. Becker / F. W. Horn / D.-A. Koch (Hg.), Der »Kritisch-exegetische Kommentar« in seiner Geschichte. H. A. W. Meyers KEK von seiner Gründung 1829 bis heute, KEK.S, Göttingen 2018, 436–453; M. Kamell Kovalishyn, The Epistle of James, in: S. McKnight / N. K. Gupta (Hg.), The State of New Testament Studies. A Survey of Recent Research, Grand Rapids 2019, 407–424; O. Wischmeyer, Who was »James«? Der Herrenbruder, »ein Namenloser aus den Vielen«, ein »role model« oder ein frühchristlicher Lehrer mit Namen Iakōbos? Die Neukommentierung des Jakobusbriefes für Meyers Kritisch-Exegetischen Kommentar, in: E.-M. Becker / S. L. Jónsson / S. Luther (Hg.), Who was ›James‹? Essays on the Letter's Authorship and Provenance resulting from a Conference on the Occasion of Oda Wischmeyer's 75th Birthday, WUNT 485, Tübingen 2022, 179–195; Dies., Luther's Prefaces to the New Testament in Their Hermeneutical

38 Einleitung

1. Die Neukommentierung des Jakobusbriefes

Am Beginn dieses Kommentars soll der Hinweis darauf stehen, dass in der heutigen Welt ständiger Ausweitung der Produktion der internationalen Exegese und zunehmender Beschleunigung globaler digitaler Kommunikation Kommentare wie der KEK vornehmlich die Funktion der Ordnung des jeweils aktuellen exegetischen Diskurses haben. Ihr Einfluss, ihre Reichweite und ihre »Lebenszeit« sind kürzer als die ihrer Vorgänger. Auch der jetzt vorliegende Kommentar ist weniger für die Ewigkeit als vielmehr für die Gegenwart bestimmt und ist aus der Gegenwart heraus geschrieben. Als Teil des KEK ist er weiter der historisch-kritischen Exegese verpflichtet.[3] Das heißt für Jak: Der Brief wird als antiker Text im Zusammenhang sprachlicher, historischer und literarischer Bedingungen erklärt und interpretiert und besonders in die Zusammenhänge antiker jüdischer und entstehender frühchristlicher religiöser, ethischer und sozialer Literatur, Kultur und Weltinterpretation gestellt. Der Kommentar ist darum bemüht, den Platz des Jak in seiner Zeit und in seinem religiös-kulturellen Milieu zu bestimmen und seine ethischen und theologischen Aussagen in diesem Zusammenhang darzustellen.

Ein Blick auf die Forschungsgeschichte zeigt, wie schwierig diese Aufgabe schon immer war: Der Wechsel der Erklärungsparadigmen seit dem ersten KEK-Kommentar von J. E. Huther macht deutlich, wie sehr die jeweiligen Kommentierungen von den exegetischen Rahmenbedingungen ihrer Zeit abhängen und wie jede Neukommentierung um ihre Sicht auf Verfasser, Text und Aussage des Textes ringt. Martin Dibelius hat mit seinem Jakobuskommentar selbst diese Bedingungen – kurz gesagt die Prämissen der Formgeschichte und ihrer literaturgeschichtlichen und sozialgeschichtlichen Implikationen – mitgeformt und war insoweit ein Ausnahmekommentar.

---

and Theological Dimension. Read from an Exegetical Perspective, in: M. W. Elliott / R. C. Heth / A. Zautcke (Hg.), Studies in the History of Exegesis, History of Biblical Exegesis 2, Tübingen 2022, 109–122. Aktuell: S. Luther, Der Jakobusbrief in der aktuellen Diskussion. Tendenzen und Perspektiven der neueren Forschung, ZNT 50, 2023, 5–24; K.-W. Niebuhr, Luther und der Jakobusbrief. Zur Diskussion um die »strohene Epistel« im frühen 16. Jahrhundert, ZNT 50, 2023, 27–49. Eine größere theologiegeschichtliche Perspektive vertritt L. Scornaienchi in seinem Beitrag: Polemik im Jakobusbrief und deren Bedeutung für die Konfiguration des Autors, in: Who was ›James‹?, 331–369. Eine umfassende Übersicht über die Geschichte der Jakobusexegese gibt L. T. Johnson, The Letter of James. A New Translation with Introduction and Commentary, AncB 37A, New Haven / London 1995.2005, 124–161. – Zum Bibelkommentar in der christlichen Antike einführend: B. Lang, Die Bibelkommentare der Kirchenväter (ca. 200–600). Kleines Kompendium mit Forschungsstand und Beispieltexten, in: D. Kästle / N. Jansen (Hg.), Kommentare in Recht und Religion, Tübingen 2014, 57–98. Das Hieronymuszitat findet sich bei Lang auf S. 57.

[3] Zu anderen Fragestellungen und Paradigmen vgl. S. Luther, Der Jakobusbrief.

A. Der Kommentar. Grundlinien der Interpretation 39

Fünfzig Kommentare zum Jakobusbrief seit Beda Venerabils[4] verzeichnet Rainer Metzner 2017[5], ohne Anspruch auf Vollständigkeit zu erheben. Berücksichtigt man Metzners eigenen Kommentar und den von Theo K. Heckel von 2019[6] sowie die aktuellen in Arbeit befindlichen Kommentierungen für die Reihen Hermeneia, EKK und andere gerade vor der Fertigstellung stehende oder und bereits publizierte Kommentare[7], sind wir mindestens bei sechzig Kommentierungen. Im Fall von Meyers KEK wird der Vorgängerband von Martin Dibelius aus dem Jahr 1921[8], der bis heute höchstes Ansehen genießt und gleichermaßen Gegenstand andauernder Kritik ist, nicht ersetzt, sondern die hier gebotene Neukommentierung wird neben ihn gestellt. Dibelius' Kommentar erschien vor hundert Jahren und hat so viel Substanz, dass er in *pro* und *contra* im letzten Jahrhundert die interpretatorischen Maßstäbe für den Umgang mit dem Jakobusbrief gesetzt hat und ein bleibendes Dokument innovativer Kommentararbeit des 20. Jahrhunderts darstellt. Der Kommentar erlebte bis 1984 zwölf Auflagen, wurde ins Englische übersetzt[9] und ist immer wieder revidiert und ergänzt worden, zuletzt durch Ferdinand Hahn.[10]

Nun bedarf eine Neukommentierung innerhalb einer Reihe nach 100 Jahren keiner besonderen Rechtfertigung. Aber jeder neue Kommentar erfordert eine eigene Strategie, um sinnvoll im Konzert der Kommentare bestehen zu können. Ist es – wie üblich – ein Reihenkommentar, so ist er einerseits der *ratio* und dem Profil seiner Reihe und speziell seinem Vorgänger verpflichtet[11] und soll andererseits gerade

---

[4] Beda Venerabilis, In epistulam Iacobi expositio. Kommentar zum Jakobusbrief, FC 40, Freiburg 2000. Die Geschichte der Jakobus-Kommentierungen wird in den großen Kommentaren jeweils ausführlich dargestellt und wird hier nicht wiederholt. Kurzdarstellung bei Wischmeyer, Who was ›James‹?, 179–195.

[5] R. Metzner, Der Brief des Jakobus, ThHK 14, Leipzig 2017, XVf: Liste der Kommentare.

[6] Th.K. Heckel, Die Briefe des Jakobus, Johannes und Petrus, NTD 10, Göttingen 2019.

[7] D. J. Moo, The Letter of James, Grand Rapids / Cambridge 2000; C. Blomberg und M. Kamell Kovalishyn, James, Zondervan Exegetical Commentary on the New Testament, Grand Rapids 2008; D. G. McCartney, James, BECNT, Grand Rapids 2009; L. L. Cheung und A. B. Spurgeon, James: A Pastoral and Contextual Commentary, Asia Bible Commentary, Carlisle 2018; J. S. Kloppenborg, James, NTGu, London / New York / Dublin 2022 (kein Kommentar, sondern eine Einführung, also gleichsam der Einleitungsteil eines Kommentars); J. Ayodeji Adewuya, An African Commentary to the Letter of James, Eugene 2023.

[8] M. Dibelius, Der Brief des Jakobus, KEK 15, Göttingen 1921.¹²1984.

[9] M. Dibelius / H. Greeven, James: A Commentary on the Epistle of James, Hermeneia, Philadelphia 1975.

[10] Dazu Wischmeyer, Der Jakobusbrief, 436–453. Für den Umstand, dass in der jüngeren Jakobusforschung Dibelius oft als Negativfolie herhalten muss, gilt: Viel Feind', viel Ehr'!

[11] Dieser wichtige Punkt wird nur selten diskutiert. Vgl. für den Meyer-Kommentar insgesamt: E.-M. Becker u. a (Hg.), Geschichte. Dibelius sah die Verpflichtung gegenüber seinen Vorgängern Huther (J. E. Huther, Kritisch exegetisches Handbuch über den Jakobusbrief, KEK, Göttingen 1858) und Beyschlag (W. Beyschlag, Der Brief des Jakobus, KEK 15, Göttingen ⁶1897) *nicht*, als er im Vorwort zur 1. Auflage seines Kommentars schrieb: »Daß er mit diesem [Beyschlags Kommentar, Dibelius nennt nicht einmal den Namen] nur die Stellung im Rahmen des Meyerschen Sammelwerks gemeinsam hat, brauche ich nach allem schon Gesagten kaum mehr zu betonen« (Dibelius, Jak, 8). Auch D. C. Allison, A Critical and Exegetical Commentary on the Epistle of James, ICC, London / New York 2013, und R. Metzner, Jak, verweisen *nicht* auf ihre bedeutenden Vorgänger in ICC (Ropes) und ThHK (Popkes). Zum Verhältnis von Ropes und Allison

40 Einleitung

diesen hinter sich lassen, nicht ihn wiederholen. Letztlich wird er aber immer die Stimme seines eigenen Autors in dessen eigener Zeit darstellen: Der Kommentar legt die Stimme des Textes in der Zeit des Verfassers frei und ist zugleich selbst von der Gegenwart des Kommentators geleitet und dieser verpflichtet.[12] Eine Einleitung in einen Kommentar tut daher gut daran, den gewählten Ansatz und Zugriff bei der Kommentierung zu reflektieren und gegenüber der Leserschaft des Kommentars zu erläutern.

Die Arbeit am vorliegenden Kommentar bewegt sich zwischen Text, Übersetzung, eigener Texterfassung und -erklärung, dem Blick auf den Dibeliuskommentar und die Vorgängerkommentare. Dabei ist es notwendig, sich Rechenschaft über den eigenen Umgang mit den Erklärungen der bereits vorliegenden Kommentare zu geben und sich zu fragen, wo man den Vorgängern folgen kann und einfach referierend auf sie verweist, ohne sie zu wiederholen, wo man sich explizit zustimmend oder kritisch auf sie bezieht, wo man Neues findet und markiert und wie man den eigenen Erkenntnisbeitrag angesichts der bereits vorhandenen umfassenden interpretatorischen Leistungen der Vorgängerkommentare profilieren will. Die dreifache Schlüsselfrage lautet: 1. Was muss *stets* (wieder oder weiterhin) gesagt werden, 2. was muss *nicht* noch einmal gesagt werden, 3. was kann *neu* gesagt werden? Für den hier vorgelegten Kommentar soll gelten: (Ad 1.) *Stets* muss die grammatische und semantische Basis des Textes philologisch dargestellt werden, da der Kommentar sonst ohne Fundament bliebe. (Ad 2.) *Nicht* noch einmal müssen alle zu einzelnen Textstellen im Laufe der Kommentierungsgeschichte vorgeschlagenen Parallelen und Interpretationsvorschläge, die sich nicht bewährt haben, dokumentiert und diskutiert werden. Hier genügen – wenn überhaupt – Hinweise in den Anmerkungen. Ein Schneeballsystem ist zu vermeiden. Dem Verständnis des Jak ist nicht geholfen, wenn der Kommentar unter der wenig aussagekräftigen Überschrift der »Parallelen« zu einem Handbuch antiker Metaphern und Motive wird. Dasselbe gilt für die Literaturnachweise. (Ad 3.) Nach *neuen* Interpretationsvorschlägen wird jeder Kommentator streben. Ob dem hier vorgelegten Kommentar neue Erkenntnisse zu entnehmen sind und ob sie sich bewähren, muss die Kritik entscheiden. Der Spielraum ist nicht groß. Die philologisch-interpretatorische Arbeit, die die Exegeten an den fünf Kapiteln des Jakobusbriefes geleistet haben, ist – im Gegensatz zu dem, was man immer noch an Unzutreffendem über die Randstellung oder Vernachlässigung oder gar Verkennung des Jakobusbriefes, vor allem verursacht durch Martin Luther, lesen kann[13] – so immens und qualitativ hochstehend, dass

---

vgl. die wichtigen kritischen Überlegungen bei J. N. CARLETON PAGET, Dale C. Allison, James: A Critical and Exegetical Commentary, EaC 5, 2014, 393–416.

[12] Dies findet sich in klassischer Kürze bei ALLISON, Jak, ausgedrückt: »Commentators probably do best to write about what interests them, and as long as there are readers with similar interests ... their book will continue to see the light of day« (3).

[13] Nachklänge immer noch bei METZNER, Jak, 1–3, und HECKEL, Jak, 9. Dagegen realistischer schon im

A. Der Kommentar. Grundlinien der Interpretation 41

jede Neuinterpretation der bereits gesammelten Menge des Wissens wie der Hypothesen, die zu dem Text vorliegen, ihren Respekt erweisen muss.

Die gegenwärtig vorhandenen Kommentare – und das gilt für alle großen Kommentare seit Mayor[14], Ropes[15] und Dibelius und jetzt besonders für Allison – sind hervorragend. Dazu kommt die Flut der Literatur außerhalb der Kommentare, zu der jeder Kommentator auch noch selbst mit Spezialaufsätzen beiträgt. Bloße Wiederholungen oder weitere Anhäufungen von Argumenten und Bibliographien müssen daher *a limine* vermieden werden. Ist da überhaupt noch Platz für einen neuen Kommentar? Nun sind gerade die herausragenden Kommentare in ihren historischen Einschätzungen zu den Themen der Autorschaft, der Adressaten und der Entstehungszeit sowie der religiösen Zuordnung so unterschiedlich, dass die Suche nach neuen Lösungen für alte Fragen oder zumindest die begründete Positionierung zu bestimmten Thesen wie der apostolischen oder pseudepigraphen Verfasserschaft ein Desiderat bleibt. Dale Allison formuliert die kontroverse Forschungslage in der Einleitung zu seinem Kommentar in klassischer Kürze:

> Critical opinion regarding the letter is unusually diverse.[16]

Das hat sich aber auch mit Allisons Kommentar nicht geändert, wie James Carleton Paget urteilt. »Das Rätsel des Jacobusbriefes«[17] bleibt für Paget auch nach Allisons Kommentar ungelöst:

> Is it the case that we now know more about James than we did in 1916 when Ropes published the first ICC commentary on James? I would aver that after reading this commentary James remains as much of an enigma it was at the time of Ropes, that for all Allison's erudition, acuity of observation and even occasionally originality, there is little that he has said which clearly indicates an advance on Ropes, advance understood narrowly as movement towards certitude or greater certitude than it was the case before.[18]

Jahr 2000 CH. BURCHARD, Der Jakobusbrief, HNT 15/1, Tübingen 2000, 2: »Inzwischen ist Jak exegetisch so zersagt wie fast die ganze Bibel«. Positiv gewendet ist diese Wahrnehmung bei ALLISON, Jak, 109. Allison betont die umfangreiche exegetische Forschung zum Jakobusbrief (»the academic study of James is prospering at the moment«) und weist außerdem auf seine allgemeine Relevanz hin: »The most important and far-reaching business with James has taken place elsewhere, outside of both, church and academy«.

[14] J. B. MAYOR, The Epistle of St. James, London/New York 1892.

[15] J. H. ROPES, A Critical and Exegetical Commentary of the Epistle of St. James, ICC, Edinburgh 1916.

[16] ALLISON, Jak, 1. Vgl. die Einschätzung von JOHNSON, Jak, 151: »By the end of the nineteenth century, the battles within the historical-critical approach had reached a stalemate. Using the same methods and identical evidence, scholars came to diametrically opposed conclusions. No one convinced anyone else … Commentaries became more and more self-referential«.

[17] A. MEYER, Das Rätsel des Jacobusbriefes, Gießen 1930.

[18] PAGET, Dale C. Allison, James, 413. Paget bezieht sich auf den ersten Satz des Kommentars von Allison, der wiederum A. Deissmann zitiert. ALLISON, Jak, 1: »The book of James has been dubbed ›the enigma of the New Testament‹«.

Die Frage nach dem weiteren Erkenntnisfortschritt stellt sich also noch einmal neu seit dem Allison-Kommentar. Das ernüchternde Urteil Pagets verpflichtet jede weitere Kommentierung einerseits zu sorgfältigem Umgang mit dem bereits Erarbeiteten und andererseits zu methodischen und sachlichen Überlegungen zur Bedeutung des eigenen Beitrages.

Aus der Fülle der Kommentare[19] werden im vorliegenden Kommentar folgende Werke vor allem als Referenzwerke herangezogen: Mayor (1892.[3]1913), Ropes (1916), Dibelius (1921), Mußner (1963.[5]1987)[20], Frankemölle (1994)[21], Johnson (1995)[22], Burchard (2000), Popkes (2001)[23], Allison (2013), Metzner (2017). Die vorliegende Kommentierung befindet sich in einem andauernden *Gespräch* mit den genannten Kommentaren und dokumentiert damit die Bedeutung der forschungsgeschichtlichen Dimension jeder neuen Textauslegung. Neben Dibelius[24] sind an erster Stelle Burchard, dann Metzner, drittens Allison Dauergesprächspartner. Diese Werke führen selbstverständlich immer wieder zu den Lexika und Grammatiken sowie zu den anderen Kommentaren und zur Spezialliteratur.[25] Die drei genannten Kommentarwerke werden im Folgenden kurz hinsichtlich ihrer Textwahrnehmung und Schwerpunktsetzungen charakterisiert.

2. Burchard, Allison, Metzner

2.1 Burchard

Text und Kommentar stehen in einem engen Bezugsverhältnis zueinander: Der Kommentar erklärt den Text. Aus dieser klassischen Perspektive darf der Kommentar von Christoph Burchard nach wie vor für den gewissenhaftesten und zuverlässigsten Führer zum Text des Jakobusbriefes gehalten werden. Er zeichnet sich vor allem durch die große Bescheidenheit des Verfassers aus, der sich nie mit literatur-, sozial- oder religionsgeschichtlichen Hypothesen, mit kultur- und sozialwissen-

---

[19] Vgl. auch die Rezensionen von O. Wischmeyer zu: W. Popkes, Der Brief des Jakobus, ThHK 14, Leipzig 2001, ThRv 101, 2005, 212–215; Rez. zu: S. McKnight, The Letter of James, NICNT, Grand Rapids/Cambridge 2011, ThLZ 137, 2012, 677–680; Rez. zu J. Assaël et É. Cuvillier, L'Épître de Jacques, CNT(N) XIII a, Genève 2013, ThLZ 141, 2016, 613–616; Rez. zu R. Metzner, Der Brief des Jakobus, ThHK 14, Leipzig 2017, RBL 07/2018 (dazu auch s. unten in diesem Kommentar); Rez. zu Th.K. Heckel, Die Briefe des Jakobus, Johannes und Petrus, NTD 10, Göttingen 2019, Bibl 101, 2020, 471–476. Zum Kommentar von M. Dibelius vgl. die ausführliche Besprechung in: Wischmeyer, Der Jakobusbrief.

[20] F. Mussner, Der Jakobusbrief, HThKNT XIII: Faszikel I, Freiburg [4]1981.

[21] H. Frankemölle, Der Brief des Jakobus, 2 Bd., ÖTBK 17/1.2, Gütersloh/Würzburg 1994.

[22] Johnson, Jak.

[23] W. Popkes, Der Brief des Jakobus, ThHK 14, Leipzig 2001.

[24] Zu Dibelius und seinen Vorgängern im KEK vgl. Wischmeyer, Der Jakobusbrief.

[25] In den letzten Jahren ist eine Fülle wichtiger Aufsätze und Monographien zu Jak erschienen, die neues Licht auf den Text werfen. Der vorliegende Kommentar stellt besonders wichtige Beiträge ausführlicher vor.

A. Der Kommentar. Grundlinien der Interpretation   43

schaftlichen Theorien, mit kirchen- oder theologiegeschichtlichen Zuschreibungen, mit theologischen Haltungen[26] oder mit ermüdender Dokumentation der Forschungsliteratur *über* den Text stellt, sondern mit viel *common sense*, Geduld und enormem sprachlichem und literarischem Wissen nach Vokabular, Grammatik, Semantik, Rhetorik, Thematik und Aussage des Textes fragt und den Text zugleich umfassend in seine frühchristlichen, frühjüdischen und griechisch-römischen Kontexte stellt. Burchard weiß sich dem wissenschaftlichen Ethos des HNT als eines Glossenkommentars[27] verpflichtet. Die gelehrte Literatur findet umfassend Berücksichtigung, ohne dass ihre Dokumentation *vor* die Texterklärung tritt. Vielmehr wird sie so behandelt, wie Burchard seine eigene Rolle sieht, als dienender, nicht als beherrschender Teil der Kommentierung. Die Leserschaft kann darauf vertrauen, dass Burchard die Literatur umfassend berücksichtigt, ohne dass jede einzelne Aussage vor dem Hintergrund der gesamten Literatur gerechtfertigt werden muss.

Burchard gibt nicht vor, zu wissen, was er nicht weiß[28] oder was sich nicht wissen lässt, und ist bei aller Gelehrsamkeit zu gelegentlichen erfrischend unkonventionellen Bemerkungen wie: »Es hilft wohl nichts, Jak ist ein pseudepigrapher (nicht: pseudonymer) Brief«[29] fähig. Dem im Umfang begrenzten Schreiben von fünf Kapiteln und der randständigen Position im Kanon entspricht der Umfang des Kommentars von 200 – allerdings eng bedruckten und äußerst informationsreichen – Seiten. Den 30 Seiten der »Einleitung« stehen gute 150 Seiten der »Auslegung« gegenüber. Die »Literatur« beansprucht 16 Seiten. Die Proportionen zwischen Text und Auslegung sowie zwischen Einleitung, Auslegung und Literatur sind hier vorbildlich bewahrt. Allerdings hat seit Burchard die exegetische Literatur derartig zugenommen, dass der Einleitungsteil im hier neu vorgelegten Kommentar deutlich ausgeweitet werden musste. Die 27 teilweise kurzen Exkurse bei Burchard erschließen Hintergründe der Interpretation, ohne die Textkommentierung zu überlagern. Burchard gibt in seiner Einführung[30] eine ebenso kurze und klare wie präzise und hinreichende Erklärung seiner Vorgehensweise. Sein eigenes Verständnis des Textes fasst er in klassischer Kürze und Selbstbescheidung in vier »Grundannahmen«[31] zusammen:

- Der Brief ist ein pseudepigraphes Schreiben aus den letzten Jahrzehnten des 1. Jhs. n. Chr.[32]

---

[26] Jakobusexegese wird zu einem nicht ganz unerheblichen Teil von evangelikaler Seite betrieben. Katholische Kommentare setzen eigene Akzente. Anti-lutherische Grundeinstellungen scheinen bei mehreren Kommentaren durch.

[27] BURCHARD, Jak, 1.

[28] »Wie Jak als pseudepigraphischer Brief wirklich unter die Leute kam, weiß man nicht«: BURCHARD, Jak, 6.

[29] BURCHARD, Jak, 5.

[30] BURCHARD, Jak, 1f.

[31] BURCHARD, Jak, 1.

[32] Ebd.

44   Einleitung

- Der Brief ist stark traditionsgebunden, aber keine Sammlung von Traditions-
stoffen.[33]
- Jak vertritt eine stark jüdisch grundierte Form von Christentum.[34]
- Jak setzt sich nicht mit Paulus oder seiner Nachwirkung auseinander.[35]
Der letzten der vier Thesen schließt sich der vorliegende Kommentar ausdrücklich
nicht an.

2.2 Allison

Der Kommentar von Allison ist an sprachlicher Gründlichkeit, bibliographischer
dokumentarischer Vollständigkeit und durchgängiger Einbeziehung der gesamten Auslegungsgeschichte seit der Alten Kirche nicht zu überbieten und verdient
höchste Bewunderung. Die Vorstellung des Kommentars kann hier kurz ausfallen,
da die umfangreiche und äußerst kluge Rezension von James Carleton Paget vorliegt.[36] Der Kommentar umfasst knapp 800 Seiten, davon sind 110 Seiten der Einleitung gewidmet. Allisons Ausführungen zu den literarischen und vorliterarischen
Beziehungen zur Literatur des antiken Israel, der frühchristlichen und paganen
frühkaiserzeitlichen Literatur sind ebenso umfassend wie seine Texterschließung:
Vokabular, Wendungen, Stilzüge, Metaphern, intertextuelle Bezüge. Die Versexegese dokumentiert jeweils alle möglichen bzw. bisher vorgeschlagenen Auslegungs-
vorschläge. Allisons Kommentar ist daher zugleich maßgeblicher aktueller Stan-
dardkommentar und unentbehrliches Handbuch für alle Jak betreffenden Fragen.
Entscheidend bleibt Allisons Position zum Milieu des Briefes. Er stellt Jak in den
Zusammenhang des Judenchristentums am Anfang des 2. Jahrhunderts und ordnet
den Brief den Ebioniten zu. Damit erhält er ein präzises Bild von der Intention und
Kommunikation des Briefes:

> Our letter is not a systematic or comprehensive statement of its author's personal theo-
> logy or religious convictions. The content is rather dictated and circumscribed by the
> particular goals its author had in mind; and as this commentary discerns an attempt to
> promote irenic relations between Christian Jews and non-Christian Jews, the dearth of
> unambiguously Christian beliefs is readily explained. So too the traditional character
> of most of the letter: it is full of conventional material because James wanted his group
> to be perceived as conventional. That is, he wanted Christian Jews to be perceived as
> Jews. So the letter is in large measure a statement of beliefs shared by Jews and Chris-
> tians.[37]

---

[33] Ebd.
[34] Ebd.
[35] Ebd.
[36] Paget, Dale C. Allison, James. Paget geht neben Grundfragen zum Genus neutestamentlicher Kommentare einerseits und zum möglichen Erkenntnisfortschritt in Kommentaren andererseits auf die wichtigen
Positionen Allisons ausführlich ein: Neben den Einleitungsfragen sind dies der »Sitz im Leben« des Jak und
das Verhältnis von Jak und Paulus.
[37] Allison, Jak, 88.

A. Der Kommentar. Grundlinien der Interpretation

Dies Textprofil wird im Folgenden in unterschiedlichen thematischen Zusammenhängen einer kritischen Prüfung unterzogen. Der vorliegende Kommentar arbeitet die Zuordnung des Verfassers zum Judenchristentum in modifizierter Form neu aus, ohne sich der Ebionitenthese anzuschließen, und verortet den Brief lokal und kirchengeschichtlich anders als Allison. Auch der These, der Verfasser habe im Brief seine eigene Theologie nicht expliziert, schließt sich der hier vorgelegte Kommentar nicht an.

2.3 Metzner

In den 17 Jahren, die zwischen den Kommentaren von Burchard und Metzner liegen, hat die Produktion gelehrter Literatur zum Jakobusbrief stark zugenommen, und vor allem ist 2013 der Allison-Kommentar erschienen, der eine Herausforderung für jeden Folgekommentar darstellt. Auf diese Situation reagiert Rainer Metzner mit seinem Kommentar von 2017 auf gut 300 Seiten souverän und legt eine sehr sorgfältige philologische Neukommentierung des Briefes für den Theologischen Handkommentar (Nachfolge Popkes) vor. Umfangreiches Hintergrundwissen wird in elf teilweise ausführlichen Exkursen (in Petit) vermittelt. Seine fünfzig Seiten umfassende Einleitung ist ungemein materialreich und fast eine Aufsatzsammlung. Die sprachliche Kommentierung ist ähnlich zuverlässig wie bei Burchard. Zugleich setzt Metzner andere Akzente. Wesentlich deutlicher als Burchard zeichnet er die Argumentation des Verfassers nach. Die Texteinheiten werden stärker berücksichtigt. Gleichzeitig betont Metzner die Bedeutung von Sprache und Stil für den literarischen Anspruch des Verfassers. Anders als Burchard geht Metzner von einer eigenen Hypothese zum Verfasser aus, die seinem Kommentar eine Sonderstellung verschafft. Er hält den Jakobusbrief für »ein orthonymes Schreiben«[38] eines frühchristlichen Lehrers mit literarischen Ambitionen:

Autorfiktionale Elemente im Brief fehlen.[39]

Damit stellt sich Metzner gegen alle Exegeten, die »Jakobus den Gerechten« bzw. »Jakobus den Herrenbruder« entweder als Verfasser[40] annehmen und eine enge Beziehung zum ethischen Spruchgut der synoptischen Evangelien feststellen oder aber mit einem pseudepigraphen Schreiben rechnen, in dem Jakobus der Gerechte als *role model* in dem Sinne fungiert, dass ein unbekannter frühchristlicher Lehrer mit Hilfe von Ethopoiie einen moralischen Kompass für seine Gemeinden entworfen habe.[41] Metzner erklärt dagegen die ethische Thematik des Jakobusbriefes ohne

---

[38] METZNER, Jak, 10.

[39] Ebd.

[40] So Exegeten von Herder bis zu Mayor und R. DEINES, Jakobus. Im Schatten des Größeren, Biblische Gestalten 30, Leipzig 2017.

[41] So jetzt S. L. JÓNSSON, James among the Classicists: Reading the Letter of James in Light of Ancient Literary Criticism, SANt 8, Göttingen 2021. Dazu siehe unten.

Bezugnahme auf *James the Just* als *role model*. Er entwirft ein schlüssiges Bild eines frühchristlichen Lehrers Ἰάκωβος, der seine frühchristlichen Adressaten theologisch und ethisch mit Hilfe verschiedener frühjüdischer und frühchristlicher Traditionen unterweist, aber auch ein eigenes theologisches Profil hat. Diese Hypothese wird im Folgenden kritisch geprüft. Der vorliegende Kommentar hält Metzners These weiter für diskussionswürdig, übernimmt sie aber nicht, sondern kommt zu einem anderen Ergebnis.

2.4 Fazit

Angesichts der drei besprochenen Kommentare ist nicht ein »Noch mehr, noch genauer und noch vollständiger« gefragt, sondern ein »Noch einmal zurück zum Text« als Frage nach neuen Perspektiven des Textverstehens. Besonders Allisons Position in der religionsgeschichtlichen Zuordnung (Diasporajuden, Ebioniten[42]), die Burchard entgegengesetzt ist, und Metzners singuläre Orthonymitätshypothese stimulieren weitere Überlegungen. Dabei ist stets Dibelius' nachdenkliches Votum mitzuhören:

> Es ist überhaupt die Frage, ob wir einen eng umgrenzten religionsgeschichtlichen Bezirk angeben können, in den unsere Schrift gehört.[43]

Das Fazit für den vorliegenden Kommentar ist ein doppeltes: Die *erste* Aufgabe des vorliegenden Kommentars ist die *Texterklärung*, nicht die vollständige Dokumentation der gelehrten Literatur und ihrer Hypothesen zum Jakobusbrief und seinem Verfasser im Zusammenhang der jüdischen und frühchristlichen Religionsgeschichte des 1. Jahrhunderts n. Chr. und der exegetischen Kategorisierungsversuche (dafür steht bereits Allison), auch nicht die ausführliche Nachzeichnung der frühjüdischen und frühchristlichen Traditionen im Brief (dafür steht bereits Dibelius, gefolgt von Burchard, Johnson, Popkes und anderen). Auch allgemeinere literaturgeschichtliche, religionsgeschichtliche, sozialgeschichtliche und traditionsgeschichtliche Fragestellungen stehen nicht im Vordergrund des Kommentars, sondern werden nur zur Texterklärung herangezogen. Die umfassende Frage nach dem Verhältnis von Judentum und entstehendem Christentum im 1. und 2. Jh. – besonders das Phänomen des sog. Judenchristentums – lässt sich nicht in einem Kommentar zu Jak bearbeiten. Dasselbe gilt für das allgemeine Thema der synoptischen Tradition.[44] Schließlich dokumentiert der Kommentar nicht das jeweilige gesamte semantische Tableau jedes Begriffs, sondern gibt Hinweise auf spezielle Parallelen oder bestimmte Herkunftsbereiche einzelner Wörter, Syntagma, Metaphern oder

---

[42] ALLISON, Jak, 32–50. Dazu PAGET, Dale C. Allison, James.

[43] DIBELIUS, Jak, 40.

[44] Dazu im Zusammenhang mit Jak: J. SCHRÖTER, Jesus Tradition in Matthew, James, and the Didache: Searching for Characteristic Emphases, in: Van de Sandt / Zangenberg (Hg.), Matthew, James, and Didache, 233–255.

A. Der Kommentar. Grundlinien der Interpretation 47

Motive, soweit sie für den Text des Jak relevant sind. Die Texterklärung richtet ihr besonderes Interesse zunächst auf die Sprache: die Syntax, die Semantik, die Stilfiguren, die Metaphern und rhetorischen Züge, auf die Intertextualität, dann auf die Motivik und theologische Themen, weiter auf den Textaufbau und die kleinen literarischen Formen, schließlich auf die Entwicklung der Argumentation. Erstes Ziel des Kommentars ist also die genaue Nachzeichnung der *Textproduktion*.

Die *zweite* Aufgabe ist die *Textinterpretation*, die den Brief als Ganzen in seinen Charakteristika, seiner Intention und seiner Position in der Literatur seiner Zeit in den Blick nimmt. Im Mittelpunkt der vorliegenden Interpretation steht der Text eines frühchristlichen Lehrers[45], der mit Hilfe eines literarisch ambitionierten brieflichen Schreibens seine literarischen Adressaten auf Grundwerte ihres christlichen Glaubens anspricht (2,1), die er im »Gesetz« Israels formuliert findet. Damit rück-verpflichtet er seine Adressaten gleichsam auf die Grundlagen der Theologie und Ethik Israels. Zugleich spricht er sehr konkrete Defizite in ihrer Ethik an. Pointiert gesagt: der vorliegende Kommentar interpretiert den Jakobusbrief als *Produkt frühchristlicher theologisch-ethischer Briefliteratur* auf der Basis einer eigenen theozentrischen Tat-Ethik des frühchristlichen Lehrers mit dem Pseudonym Jakobus, der seine Adressaten auf das Gesetz Israels rück-verpflichtet und ohne christologische oder pneumatologische ethische Begründungen auskommt, wie sie Paulus in die entstehende Ethik der Christus-bekennenden Gemeinden eingeführt hatte. Damit steht Jak für einen *eigenen Typus* frühchristlicher Theologie und Ethik.

Die *dritte* Aufgabe dieses Kommentars wird es sein, den Brief in einen plausiblen *historischen Kontext* zu stellen. Die Rekonstruktion dieses Ortes und Milieus ist besonders umstritten. Der vorliegende Kommentar schlägt eine eigene Lösung vor und verortet den Brief um die Jahrhundertwende in der Christus-gläubigen Gemeinde in Jerusalem. Diese Zuordnung ergibt sich aus dem Zusammenspiel von literarischer Form – Diasporabrief – und theologisch-ethischem Profil. Beide Elemente weisen nach Jerusalem, aber nicht in das Jerusalem des Herrenbruders selbst, sondern in die Jerusalemer Christus-bekennende Gemeinde, die die Tradition des Herrenbruders hochhält und gegen einen progressiven Paulinismus verteidigt, von dem die beginnende Sammlung der Paulusbriefe und der Paulinismus der Jahrhundertwende zeugen.

---

[45] Es geht primär um den *Text* dieses Lehrers, nicht um *seinen* Glauben und *seine* »Religion«!

B. Der Text. Historische, literarische und thematische Charakteristik

1. Historische Charakteristik

Im Folgenden werden die klassischen Fragen nach Autor, Leserschaft, Zeit und Ort der Entstehung des Schreibens behandelt. Dabei gilt stets im Gefolge Christoph Burchards, dass Textbezug sowie philologische und historische Genauigkeit exegetische Tugenden sind, dass religions- und philosophiegeschichtliche Konstruktionen, Kategorisierungsversuche und weiträumige Kontextualisierungen eher knapp dargestellt werden und die Einleitungsfragen an keinem Punkt monographische Ausdehnung annehmen können. Sie sollen zum Text und zur Texterklärung hinführen. Sie sind notwendig und deshalb auch dem Textkommentar vorangestellt, diesem aber nicht aber sachlich vorgeordnet. Die Darstellung im vorliegenden Kommentar gibt jeweils den Stand der Diskussion in den leitenden Kommentaren an, führt zudem in wichtige aktuelle Beiträge der exegetischen Literatur ein und bezeichnet die Position des vorliegenden Kommentars.[46] Für umfangreiche Dokumentationen zum jeweiligen Thema wird vor allem auf die Kommentare von Dale C. Allison und Rainer Metzner verwiesen. Die dort gebotenen Darstellungen werden im vorliegenden Kommentar nicht ausführlich wiederholt.

1.1 Textüberlieferung

Die textliche Überlieferung des Jak ist in der Editio Critica Maior (ECM) des Novum Testamentum Graece dargestellt.[47] Die ECM bietet eine vollständige kritische Ausgabe von Jak. Ryan Wettlaufer hat außerdem eine kritische Untersuchung zu den Konjekturen zu Jak vorgelegt.[48]

Aus dem 3. Jahrhundert sind fünf Papyrusfragmente mit Texten aus Jak erhalten:

P^{20} = P. Oxy. IX 1171	Jak 2,19–3,2; 3,3–9	200–300 n. Chr.
P^{23} = P. Oxy. X 1229	Jak 1,10–12.15–18	250–300 n. Chr.

---

[46] Eine ältere Bestandsaufnahme findet sich in: R. L. WEBB / J. S. KLOPPENBORG (Hg.), Reading James with New Eyes: Methodological Reassessments of the Letter of James, LNTS 342, London / New York 2007. Zum aktuellen Stand vgl. den umfangreichen Band: E.-M. BECKER u. a. (Hg.), Who was ›James‹? Beide Bände spiegeln die Entwicklung der Fragestellungen und methodischen Zugänge der letzten Jahrzehnte im Bereich der Jakobusphilologie. Wichtige Beiträge zum religionsgeschichtlichen, traditionsgeschichtlichen und sozialgeschichtlichen *setting* von Jak auch in: VAN DE SANDT / ZANGENBERG (Hg.), Matthew, James, and Didache.

[47] B. ALAND, K. ALAND, G. MINK und K. WACHTEL, ECM, Bd. 4. Die Katholischen Briefe, Teil 1: Text; Teil 2: Begleitende Materialien, 1. Lieferung: Der Jakobusbrief, Stuttgart 1997.

[48] R. D. WETTLAUFER, No Longer Written: The Use of Conjectoral Emendations in the Restauration of the Text of the New Testament, the Epistle of James as a Case Study, NTTSD 44, Leiden 2013.

P[54] = P. Princ. 15	Jak 2,16–18.22–23; 2,4–26; 3,2–4	5./6. Jh. n. Chr.
P[74] = P. Bodmer XVII	Jak 1,1–5,20 (Lakunen)	7. Jh. n. Chr.
P[100] = P. Oxy. LXV 4449	Jak 3,13–4,4; 4,9–5,1	200–300 n. Chr.

Die beiden großen aus dem 4. Jahrhundert stammenden Pergamenthandschriften Codex Sinaiticus und Codex Vaticanus enthalten Jak vollständig.[49] Der vorliegende Kommentar folgt der ECM und dokumentiert wichtigere textkritische Varianten zum laufenden Text. Basis der Textkritik ist durchgehend die ECM, die auch digital zur Verfügung steht: https://www.uni-muenster.de/INTF/ECM.html. Im Einleitungsteil 1*–10* werden alle benutzten kritischen Zeichen erklärt.

Christian Bemmerl hat die Rezeptionsgeschichte des Jak in der Alten Kirche noch einmal umfassend monographisch untersucht.[50] Bemmerl ist äußerst zurückhaltend gegenüber den bekannten Kandidaten für eine frühe Bezeugung des Jak: 1Petr, Jud, 1Clem, Herm. Er hält keine der oft diskutierten Spuren einer Bezugnahme auf Jak bei den genannten Schriften für evident:

> Die ersten beiden Jahrhunderte sind, was den Jak anbelangt, von einem Schweigen gekennzeichnet. Die Suche nach verwertbaren Spuren verläuft weitgehend ergebnislos. Beginnend bei den neutestamentlichen Schriften, treten insbesondere 1 Petr und Jud in das Blickfeld, da beide Texte eine Vielzahl an Übereinstimmungen bieten. Aufgrund der Beschaffenheit dieser Verbindungen ist die beste Erklärung hierfür allerdings nicht in einer direkten literarischen Abhängigkeit zu sehen, sondern wohl eher in einem unabhängigen Rückgriff auf Teile der LXX oder, was noch wahrscheinlicher ist, auf eine Sammlung paränetischer Traditionen, was auch die ähnliche Abfolge der Übereinstimmungen erklären würde.[51]

Wie Bemmerl überzeugend nachweist, findet sich die erste direkte bzw. kanonische Bezeugung bei Origenes.[52] Sein Fazit zu Jak bei Origenes lautet:

> Nichtsdestotrotz spricht die große Zahl nachgewiesener Rezeptionen, Echos und Anklänge des Jak bei Origenes dafür, dass er den Jak benutzte wie niemand vor ihm und dass dieser ihm für seine Argumentationen auch durchaus hilfreich erschien, da auch theologische Spezifika des Jak, wie etwa dessen Rechtfertigungslehre (Jak 2,20–26),

---

[49] Zu allen Einzelheiten vgl. ECM, zur Textgeschichte außerdem vgl. die sehr gründliche Darstellung bei BURCHARD, Jak, 20–26, und einführend KLOPPENBORG, James, 17–19.

[50] CH. BEMMERL, Die frühe Rezeption des Jakobusbriefs und die Geschichte des neutestamentlichen Kanons, ASEs 34, 2017, 513–535 (527 zu Origenes als erstem Zeugen für den »kanonischen« Jak); monographisch DERS., Der Jakobusbrief in der Alten Kirche. Eine Spurensuche vom Neuen Testament bis zu Origenes, WUNT II/588, Tübingen 2023 (umfangreiche Forschungsgeschichte, Literaturdokumentation und kritische Diskussion der möglichen Zeugen vor Origenes).

[51] BEMMERL, Der Jakobusbrief in der Alten Kirche, 227. Besonders wichtig ist die Diskussion des Judasbriefes in Auseinandersetzung mit J. FREY, Der Brief des Judas und der zweite Brief des Petrus, ThHK 15/II, Leipzig 2015 (BEMMERL, 38–41).

[52] BEMMERL, Der Jakobusbrief in der Alten Kirche, 150–219.

aufgegriffen werden und nicht nur Elemente, bei denen es sich um Traditionsgut handelt. Dabei kennzeichnet Origenes Zitate aus dem Jak teils auch mit expliziten Hinweisen darauf in Einleitungen.[53]

Wichtig ist Bemmerls Hinweis darauf, dass Origenes Jak nicht in Alexandria, sondern erst in Caesarea genauer kennengelernt hat:

> Die beste Erklärung hierfür ist, dass Origenes den Jak in Alexandrien maximal bruchstückhaft gekannt und erst ab 231/232 in Cäsarea entscheidend kennengelernt hat, vielleicht in einer Gemeinde, die ihn intensiver benutzt hat. Damit ließe sich auch verstehen, weshalb sein Lehrer, Clemens von Alexandrien, den Jak nicht zu kennen schien.[54]

Der vorliegende Kommentar schließt sich Bemmerls vorsichtigem Urteil an. Aus neutestamentlicher Sicht ist seine Analyse des Verhältnisses von Jak und Judas besonders relevant.[55] Bemmerl plädiert gegen ein »literarisches Abhängigkeitsverhältnis«[56], ohne es allerdings auszuschließen.[57]

1.2 Autor

Die Verfasserfrage hat spätestens seit Johann Gottfried Herders[58] Votum für den Herrenbruder als Verfasser des Jakobusbriefes immer wieder zu kontroversen Antworten in der exegetischen Literatur geführt und wurde als ein Schlüssel zur Interpretation des Briefes verstanden. Die exegetischen Positionen zur Autoren- und Adressatenfrage hängen vor allem an der Interpretation von Jak 1,1. Die wichtigsten Positionen, die in den Kommentaren vertreten werden, sind: Orthonymie (der Herrenbruder Jakobus oder ein späterer frühchristlicher Lehrer mit Namen Jakobus als Autor) oder Pseudepigraphie, damit verbunden entweder frühe Entstehungszeit

---

[53] BEMMERL, Der Jakobusbrief in der Alten Kirche, 230.

[54] Ebd. – KLOPPENBORG, James, 14, hält die Bezeugung in Alexandria für entscheidend. Origenes, De principiis I 3,6, zitiert Jak 4,17 (»inquit« ohne Angabe der Herkunft von Jak). Kloppenborg bezieht sich bei seiner Lokalisierung des Jak nach Alexandria unter anderem auf diese Erstbezeugung (s. u. zur religionsgeschichtlichen Einordnung). Die Caesarea-Hypothese führt näher nach Jerusalem.

[55] BEMMERL, Der Jakobusbrief in der Alten Kirche, 38–41.

[56] BEMMERL, Der Jakobusbrief in der Alten Kirche, 41.

[57] »Damit steht Jud in Abhängigkeit zu Jakobus, aber nicht zwingend zum Jak, wie Frey vorschlägt, der mit der Selbstvorstellung als ›Bruder des Jakobus‹ eine bestimmte Traditionsbindung sieht, die sich primär sogar nicht auf die Person des Herrenbruders, sondern auf die ihm zugeschriebene Schrift bezieht«, BEMMERL, Der Jakobusbrief in der Alten Kirche, 39. Inhaltliche Hinweise auf eine Anknüpfung des Jud an Jak fehlen. Die Formulierung des Absenders lässt sich als parallele literarische Bezugnahme auf den Herrenbruder Jakobus verstehen, könnte allerdings das Wissen um einen bereits bestehenden Jakobusbrief voraussetzen: Der Verfasser würde dann auf Judas als autorisierende Gestalt »ausweichen«. Klarheit ist hier nicht zu erzielen.

[58] J. G. HERDER, »Briefe zweener Brüder Jesu in unserm Kanon« von 1775 (J. G. von Herders sämmtliche Werke. Religion und Theologie. Achter Theil. Carlsruhe 1828). Vgl. WISCHMEYER, Who was »James«, in: Who was ›James‹?, 179–195 (dort Hinweis darauf, dass die altkirchliche Tradition den Autorbegriff und die Autor-Zuschreibung nicht primär vom »Herrenbruder« ableitet, sondern von der *auctoritas* des Briefes in den Gemeinden) und: DIES., Scriptual Classicism?, in: Who was ›James‹?, 277–312 (dort ausführlichere Auseinandersetzung mit den Kommentarvorschlägen).

B. Der Text. Historische, literarische und thematische Charakteristik 51

zu Lebzeiten des Herrenbruders, Entstehung gegen Ende des 1. Jahrhunderts oder Entstehung in den ersten Jahrzehnten des 2. Jahrhunderts, außerdem eine jüdische oder frühchristliche intendierte Leserschaft, reale oder literarische Adressaten. Die Rekonstruktionen sind divergent, die unterschiedlichen Lösungen zu Autor und Adressaten miteinander verknüpft. Die Literatur ist zuletzt mit großer Sorgfalt bei Dale C. Allison (1) und Rainer Metzner (2) dokumentiert.[59] Sigurvin Jónsson hat einen literaturwissenschaftlich argumentierenden weiterführenden Vorschlag zur Pseudepigraphiehypothese vorgelegt (3), den der vorliegende Kommentar in modifizierter Form weiterführt (4).

(1) Allison rekapituliert noch einmal sehr ausführlich und systematisch die möglichen Antworten auf die Frage nach dem Verfasser.[60] Die These, der Verfasser sei der Bruder Jesu gewesen, lehnt er wie Burchard vor allem aus sprachlichen, kanongeschichtlichen (späte Bezeugung und Aufnahme in den Kanon[61]) und rezeptionsgeschichtlichen Gründen (die unklaren Notizen bei Euseb und Hieronymus) klar ab:

> This commentary adopts the thesis that James is a pseudepigraphon.[62]

Auf die Frage, weshalb der Autor gerade den Namen des Herrenbruders gewählt habe, gibt Allison vier mögliche Antworten[63]: (1) Der Verfasser sucht Autorität. (2) Der Verfasser war Judenchrist (anders z. B. Burchard) und repräsentierte die Art von Glauben, der mit Jakobus dem Gerechten assoziiert wurde. (3) »If a Christian wished to address a letter to Jews, James was an obvious candidate for authorship«.[64] Dies dritte Argument ist wichtig, wenn man die Adressaten für Juden im Literalsinn hält.[65] (4) Deutlicher als Dibelius, Burchard und Metzner findet Allison das Profil des Jakobus im Jakobusbrief:

> 1.1 implies that James is a Jew writing from Palestine, probably Jerusalem, which is consistent with the traditions about our purported author in Acts and Galatians.[66]

Die jüdischen wie die christlichen Leser konnten also ihnen bekannte Züge von »Jakobus dem Gerechten« im Ethos des Briefes finden. Allisons Rekonstruktion des primär jüdischen Adressatenprofils fügt seiner Verfasserrekonstruktion einen bedeutenden Aspekt bei.

---

[59] METZNER, Jak, 3–8. Vgl. auch KLOPPENBORG, James, 20–38.
[60] ALLISON, Jak, 3–28.
[61] ALLISON, Jak, 13–18 (ausführliche kritische Dokumentation).
[62] ALLISON, Jak, 28.
[63] Eine orthonyme Autorschaft eines frühchristlichen Lehrers erwägt Allison nicht.
[64] ALLISON, Jak, 30.
[65] Dazu Weiteres unter »Adressaten«.
[66] ALLISON, Jak, 127 f.

(2) Anders Rainer Metzner[67]: er führt keine der bisher genannten Verfassertheorien weiter, sondern setzt ganz neu ein. Er zieht den weitgehenden Konsens, in Jak 1,1 sei – ob orthonym oder pseudonym – auf jeden Fall Jakobus der Herrenbruder gemeint, in Zweifel und plädiert für einen unbekannten christlichen Gemeindelehrer Jakobus als orthonymen Verfasser. Metzner stellt alle Argumente, die gegen ein orthonymes Schreiben des Herrenbruders sprechen, nochmals zusammen – vor allem das gute Griechisch[68] und das Fehlen spezifisch jüdischer Themen sowie die späte Bezeugungsgeschichte. Ebenso kritisiert er aber die Pseudepigraphiehypothese[69] mit dem Argument, dass das in der außer- und nachneutestamentlichen Jakobusliteratur gezeichnete Bild des Herrenbruders, des Gerechten und Asketen, des Märtyrers und des ersten Bischofs von Jerusalem im Brief eben gerade nicht zu finden sei. Nach Metzner »ist der Jakobusbrief völlig unpersönlich gehalten«.[70] Metzner meint besonders im Hinblick auf Euseb und Hieronymus, der Brief sei »erst in späterer Zeit mit der Autorität des Herrenbruders verbunden« worden[71]:

> Die Sammlung der Katholischen Briefe mit Jak an der Spitze erfolgte zu einer Zeit, als der Brief bereits irrtümlich als Dokument des Herrenbruders gelesen wurde.[72]

Metzner entwirft zugleich ein eigenes Bild des Verfassers aufgrund von Jak 3,1 (Lehrer) und anhand der Semantik, des Stils und der pädagogischen Zielsetzung des Briefes.[73] Wichtig ist Metzners Hinweis auf den sozialen Status des Verfassers, den Metzner aus dessen Literarizität und seinem pädagogischen Leitungsanspruch ableitet: Er habe »der christlichen Oberschicht« angehört.[74] Der Begriff »Oberschicht« ist wohl weniger sozialgeschichtlich gemeint als vielmehr auf eine entstehende christliche Bildungselite bezogen.[75] Zeitlich denkt Metzner an das 2. Jahrhundert: Der Brief sei »im Laufe des 2. Jh.s verfasst« worden.[76]

---

[67] METZNER, Jak, 3–13; vgl. schon DERS., Der Lehrer Jakobus. Überlegungen zur Verfasserfrage des Jakobusbriefes, ZNW 104, 2013, 238–267.

[68] Vgl. auch JÓNSSON, James, 194 f. Jónsson stellt noch einmal Positionen aus der angelsächsischen exegetischen Literatur zusammen, die im Anschluss an Mayor für gute griechische Sprachkenntnisse bei Jakobus dem Herrenbruder plädieren.

[69] Breite Auseinandersetzung mit der exegetischen Literatur: METZNER, Jak, 5–8. Metzner unterscheidet die Traditions-, Milieu-, Leerstellen- und Fortschreibungshypothese.

[70] METZNER, Jak, 7.

[71] METZNER, Jak, 9.

[72] Ebd. Vgl. besonders Anm. 68 mit Literaturangaben zu Entstehungshypothesen zur Sammlung der Katholischen Briefe. Metzners Vorschlag könnte natürlich auch dann gelten, wenn der Brief einen pseudepigraphen Verfasser hätte.

[73] METZNER, Jak, 11–13.

[74] METZNER, Jak, 13.

[75] KLOPPENBORG, James, 92, spricht von den Adressaten als von »urban and middeling addressees«, was auch ein Licht auf den Verfasser selbst wirft.

[76] METZNER, Jak, 10. Dazu unten.

B. Der Text. Historische, literarische und thematische Charakteristik

(3) An dieser Stelle muss auf Sigurvin L. Jónssons Monographie »James among the Classicists«[77] hingewiesen werden, da Jónsson das Thema »Autor« in einer eigenen Weise bearbeitet, die noch in keinen Kommentar Eingang finden konnte.[78] Er analysiert an ausgewählten Textpartien Sprache und Stil des Briefes, statt primär nach dem historischen Verfasser zu fragen.

Dadurch gelingt es ihm, das Bild des literarischen Autors wesentlich genauer als Metzner zu schärfen und Metzners These, der Brief beziehe sich nicht auf das Ethos des Herrenbruders, in Frage zu stellen:

> The author presents a speech-in-character in the shape of a letter to establish his ethos (Chapter 2); he employs vocabulary and style to signal his education implicitly (Chapters 3&4); and includes himself in the category of sage, teacher and exegete explicitly (Chapter 5).[79]

Jónsson fügt außerdem den Aspekt des »socio-economic prophet« in das Bild des impliziten Autors ein.[80] Damit wird in der Monographie »James among the Classicists« für die Frage nach dem Autor des Jakobusbriefes in doppelter Hinsicht eine weitere neue Perspektive eröffnet. Erstens: nicht der historische Verfasser, sondern der literarische Autor und seine kulturelle Welt stehen im Zentrum des Interesses. Zweitens treibt Jónsson die Pseudepigraphie-These voran und entwickelt die seit Dibelius unterschiedlich bewertete Ethopoiiethese weiter. Dabei dienen ihm die Definitionen in der Progymnasmataliteratur als Wegweiser.[81] Von Jónssons Analyse aus muss besonders die Textwahrnehmung Metzners, der Brief sei nirgends auf die Person des Herrenbruders hin konzipiert, relativiert werden.

(4) Vor diesem forschungsgeschichtlichen Hintergrund ist die *Position des vorliegenden Kommentars* die folgende: Die Verfasserschaft durch Jakobus, den Herrenbruder, darf spätestens seit J. S. Kloppenborgs Aufsatz von 2022 als sprachlich *widerlegt* gelten.[82] Die Orthonymitäts-These Metzners sieht den historischen Verfasser als einen unabhängigen und selbständigen Autor des 2. Jahrhunderts, der seinen Status als frühchristlicher Lehrer mit seiner literarischen Ambition verbindet und

---

[77] Jónsson, James, 54–66. Vgl. die Rezension von J. S. Kloppenborg, NT 64, 2022, 409–411.

[78] Vgl. auch den dekonstruktivistischen Zugang von C. Breu, Prosopopoiie im Jakobusbrief aus dekonstruktiver Perspektive, in: Who was ›James‹?, 99–120. Im Ergebnis ähnlich aus linguistischer Sicht: Ch. Ganslmayer, Der Autor des Jakobusbriefs aus linguistischer Perspektive, in: Who was ›James‹?, 121–157.

[79] Jónsson, James, 7. Als Exeget erweist sich der Autor vor allem in 2,14–26.

[80] Jónsson, James, 193.

[81] Jónsson, James, 74–92. S. 78 gibt Jónsson Definitionen beider Begriffe nach Hermogenes, Progymnasmata 9: Ethopoiie bezieht sich auf die nachahmende Darstellung des Charakters einer Person, Prosopooiie dient der Personifikation. Aelius Theon, Progymnasmata 8, benutzt Prosopopoiie »for all kinds of speech-in-character, although his examples are exclusively ethopoietic« (79). Theon nennt den Protreptikos und die Epistel als literarische Formen, in denen Prosopooiie eingesetzt werden kann (dazu besonders S. 91). Zum Ausdruck P. vgl. S. 89.

[82] Kloppenborg, The Author of James and His Lexical Profile, in: Who was ›James‹?, 197–217. Dazu unten unter »literarische Charakteristik«.

54 Einleitung

eine ethische Epistel verfasst. Diese These hat wegen des schwachen Autorenprofils, wegen der guten sprachlich-literarischen Gestalt des Briefes und auch wegen ihrer Einfachheit eine gewisse Plausibilität und sollte weiter in der Diskussion bleiben.[83] Allerdings wird die Pseudepigraphiethese in der Form, wie sie von Kloppenborg und Jónsson vertreten wird, dem Profil des Briefes als ethischer Epistel in höherem Maße gerecht und dient dem vorliegenden Kommentar als Arbeitshypothese. Metzner ist zwar zuzustimmen, wenn er keine *direkte* Anspielung auf Jakobus den Herrenbruder als den Gerechten und Märtyrer und Bischof im Brief findet. Aber die ethische Unterweisung, die der Autor gibt, bezieht ihre Autorität nicht nur aus der sprachlichen Kompetenz und aus der jüdischen literarischen Bildung des Verfassers, sondern auch aus dem Ethos, das er vertritt: Vollkommenheit, Geduld, tätiger Glaube, Weisheit, Gerechtigkeit – ein Profil, das im Zusammenhang mit dem gewählten Verfassernamen durchaus auf Jakobus den Gerechten verweisen kann, wie schon Dibelius erkannte. Der Fortschritt liegt bei Jónsson vor allem darin, den Verfasser als *literarischen Autor* zu beschreiben[84], der ein ethisches Profil oder Programm für seine Leserschaft entwirft. Im vorliegenden Kommentar wird der Verfasser daher als ein frühchristlicher literarisch gebildeter Lehrer rekonstruiert, der unter dem Pseudonym des Herrenbruders Jakobus schreibt. Die historische Zuordnung dieses Autors kann erst am Ende der Darstellung der Einleitungsfragen vorgenommen werden. Zunächst gilt für den vorliegenden Kommentar: Der Name Jakobus ist *programmatisch* für einen Typus von Theologie und Ethik gewählt, wie er im entstehenden Christentum vor allem der *Jerusalemer* »Säule« Jakobus, dem Herrenbruder, zugeschrieben wurde.[85] Das literarische Profil des Autors weist in die judenchristliche Gemeinde in Jerusalem vor dem Zweiten Jüdischen Krieg. Die literarische Gestaltung als Diasporabrief deutet ebenso auf Jerusalem wie die Nähe zum 2Bar. Die theologie- und religionsgeschichtlichen Implikationen dieser Rekonstruktion werden im Zusammenhang der Rekonstruktion des historischen Profils des Jak dargestellt werden.[86]

---

[83] Vgl. WISCHMEYER, Who was »James«? und DIES., Scriptual Classicism: hier habe ich vorsichtig Metzners These übernommen (191 f und 379), aber auf das »low profile« des Briefes hingewiesen. Eine erneute Prüfung der Argumente im Lichte der Analyse von Jónsson hat mir gezeigt, dass Metzner wie schon Dibelius die ethopoietischen Elemente des Jak doch zu niedrig gewichtet (s. oben).

[84] GANSLMAYER, Autor, 132, formuliert zugespitzt: »Meines Erachtens ist die Frage nach der realen Person des Verfassers in diesem Fall also verfehlt, und es liegt näher, davon auszugehen, dass es dem Autor womöglich gar nicht wichtig war, eindeutig identifizierbar zu sein … Die Frage »Who was ›James‹?« sollte somit weniger auf Jakobus als historische Person, die Identität des Verfassers oder auch die Autorinszenierung, deren Bewertung ebenfalls viele offene Variablen beinhaltet, abzielen, sondern vielmehr auf die Individualität des Verfassers«. Außerdem will Ganslmayer die Untersuchung des Jak auf die »sprachliche Einordnung des Verfassers im Kontext des NT und der griechisch-hellenistischen Textkultur insgesamt fokussieren« sowie »auf die Rekonstruktion der Positionen des Verfassers« (133).

[85] Dazu siehe unten (Jakobus und Paulus).

[86] Siehe unten.

B. Der Text. Historische, literarische und thematische Charakteristik

1.3 Adresse und Adressaten

Die Adresse und die angeschriebenen Adressaten werfen einerseits zusätzliches Licht auf den Autor, andererseits stellen sie eigene Fragen, vor allem nach der religionsgeschichtlichen Zuordnung, nach der literarischen bzw. idealen Qualität der Adresse (1) – diese beiden Aspekte sind miteinander verbunden – und nach ihren möglichen sozialgeschichtlichen Implikationen (2).

(1) Die Anschrift: »An die zwölf Stämme in der Zerstreuung« weist im Wortsinn auf ein jüdisches Lesepublikum außerhalb des Landes Israel hin. In 2,1 werden die Adressaten dagegen klar als Mitglieder Christus-gläubiger Gemeinden angesprochen. Daher verbietet es sich, die Adressaten nur von 1,1 her zu rekonstruieren. Drei Aspekte sind zu unterscheiden: die *realen* Adressaten bzw. das reale Lesepublikum, die Adressaten der *literarischen* Formulierung der Briefadresse, die *intendierten* Adressaten. Über die realen Adressaten wissen wir fast nichts. Die literarischen Adressaten sind zumindest *idealiter* Diasporajuden: »die zwölf Stämme in der Diaspora«. Die intendierten Adressaten sind Mitglieder Christus-bekennender Gemeinden, ohne dass diese Gemeinden näher spezifiziert werden können.

Die Adressaten werden im Präskript genannt: ταῖς δώδεκα φυλαῖς ταῖς ἐν τῇ διασπορᾷ. Die Wendung ist ohne Parallele. Es ist zwischen Literalsinn und Metapher zu unterscheiden. Im *Literalsinn* handelt es sich um eine ökumenische Sammeladresse für die Gesamtheit der *jüdischen* Leserschaft im Imperium Romanum außerhalb »des Landes Israel«.[87] Hier liegt wie bei der Verfasserangabe jüdisch-frühchristlicher Soziolekt vor, der die Leserschaft in einer ganz bestimmten Weise anspricht und sie an die Geschichte Israels zurückbindet.[88] Für das 1. bzw. 2. Jahrhundert n. Chr. handelt es sich dabei unabhängig von der religiös-ethnisch-institutionellen Zuordnung *von vornherein* um eine historisch-ethnisch-religiöse *Metapher*: Das historische, längst nicht mehr bestehende Zwölf-Stämme-Volk wird auf das zeitgenössische ἔθνος Ἰουδαίων außerhalb des Landes Israel *oder* auf Christus-bekennende Gemeinden, die sich als *Israel* verstehen, bezogen. In diesem zweiten Fall liegt eine doppelte Metaphernbildung vor. Die Wendung als solche zielt auf ein jüdisch vorgestelltes Lesepublikum, im Zusammenhang mit dem christologischen Anfang, 2,1 und Kap. 5 ist an eine frühchristliche Leserschaft gedacht, die in den theologischen Zusammenhang Israels gestellt werden soll.

Der Zusatz »in der Zerstreuung« ist in besonderem Maße durch den jüdisch-frühchristlichen Soziolekt charakterisiert. Die literarisch-theologische Perspektive ist von Jerusalem her gewählt: Zentrum – Zerstreuung / Diaspora. Die Adressatenformulierung macht deutlich, dass das Schreiben literarisch als aus Jerusalem gesendet konzipiert ist und von dorther seine Autorisierung erfährt.[89] Von hieraus fällt

---

[87] Möglicherweise kann man auch an die Judenschaft in Babylon denken. Zur antiken jüdischen Diaspora vgl. E. S. GRUEN, Diaspora: Jews amidst Greeks and Romans, Cambridge MA 2002.

[88] Ex 24,4LXX; Ex 36,21; Num 1,44; Dtn 1,23; Jos 4,5; 3Kön 18,31LXX.

[89] Vgl. 1Petr 5,13: dort wird der theologisch-metaphorische Städtename Babylon als Absenderort angegeben.

56 Einleitung

weiteres Licht auf die Verfasserfrage. Es ist plausibel, dass dabei an Jakobus als den Gemeindeleiter gedacht wurde, dessen Autorität in Jerusalem begründet war, aber über Jerusalem hinausreichte, wie der sog. Antiochenische Zwischenfall zeigt (Gal 2,12). Allerdings ist historisch zu bedenken, dass der Herrenbruder Jakobus zwar Autorität innerhalb der Christus-bekennenden Diasporagemeinden hatte, aber weder Weisungsbefugnis noch Autorität über die Diasporajudenschaft besaß. Die Kombination des Pseudonyms Jakobus und der Zwölf-Stämme-Metapher hat hier einen Riss. Immerhin stützt die Adresse im vorliegenden Wortlaut doch noch einmal deutlich die Pseudepigraphiethese.[90] An Metzners Orthonymitätsthese muss die Frage gestellt werden, wieweit es plausibel ist, dass ein selbständiger frühchristlicher Autor des 2. Jahrhunderts an »die zwölf Stämme in der Zerstreuung« schrieb.[91]

Gegenwärtig werden von D. C. Allison, R. Metzner und J. S. Kloppenborg unterschiedliche Positionen zur Adressatenfrage vertreten. Rainer Metzner schließt sich deutlich an Christoph Burchard an, für den die Adressaten »gestandene Christen« sind.[92] Er zeichnet das Profil der Adressaten als Mitglieder von »Ortsgemeinden« mit typischen Problemen, die der Verfasser anspricht.[93] Metzner verschiebt die Akzente noch weiter als Burchard auf die Reichen und die Kaufleute, die Mitglieder prosperierender Gemeinden sind und die Gefahren von »Wohlstand und Prestige« in die Gemeinden tragen.[94]

Dale C. Allison geht hier in doppelter Hinsicht einen eigenen Weg.[95] Erstens liest er die Adresse als primär an ein jüdisches Lesepublikum gerichtet, wenn auch durch die generalisierende Formulierung Christusbekenner nicht ausgeschlossen sind:

> This commentary argues throughout that James envisages a mixed audience, one that includes Christian and non-Christian Jews.[96]

Das heißt, dass Allison ausschließlich mit ethnisch *jüdischen* Adressaten rechnet. Zweitens ordnet er die Christus-bekennenden Adressaten – wie den Verfasser – im Gegensatz zu Burchard religions- bzw. kirchengeschichtlich als Judenchristen in der Nähe der Ebioniten ein.[97] Dabei verweist Allison besonders auf die pseudoclemen-

---

[90] Vgl. auch Apg 15: dort dieselbe Perspektive; 15,25–29: Jakobus ist wesentlich an der Abfassung des Schreibens beteiligt (seit V. 13 wird nur Jakobus namentlich genannt). Allerdings bestehen wesentliche Unterschiede zwischen Apg 15 und Jak im Absender und bei den Adressaten sowie im Briefgenre.

[91] Vgl. allerdings Herm sim 9.17.1.

[92] METZNER, Jak, 15; CH. BURCHARD, Gemeinde in der strohernen Epistel: Mutmaßungen über Jakobus, in: D. Lührmann / G. Strecker (Hg.), Kirche, FS G. Bornkamm, Tübingen 1980, 315–328, 317.

[93] METZNER, Jak, 16.

[94] METZNER, Jak, 15.

[95] ALLISON, Jak, 127–133.

[96] ALLISON, Jak, 131.

[97] ALLISON, Jak, 32–50.

B. Der Text. Historische, literarische und thematische Charakteristik 57

tinischen Retractationes 1.27–71 (Ascents of James).[98] Hier rekonstruiert Allison allerdings – wenn überhaupt – eher das religiöse Milieu des Verfassers als das der Adressaten. Für die Adressatenfrage ist weniger Allisons Ebioniten-Hypothese als vielmehr seine Wahrnehmung wichtig, dass im literarischen Sinn Juden *und* Judenchristen angesprochen werden: Auch wenn die Adresse literarisch ist, bleibt doch die *kommunikative* Richtung des Verfassers auf das Judentum deutlich: Frühchristliche Gemeinden sollen mit dem ideellen Israel verbunden werden. Hier hat Allison schärfer als Burchard und Metzner gesehen. Andererseits betont Metzner mit Recht, dass jüdische Themen im engeren Sinn – Tempel, Beschneidung, Sabbat, Kalenderfragen – in Jak keine Rolle spielen und der für Paulus konstitutive Gegensatz von Juden und »Völkern« gar nicht thematisiert wird. Die Warnung Dibelius' vor einer Überzeichnung der Adressaten bleibt daher bestehen.

Kloppenborg wählt einen Mittelweg. Er folgt Allison zwar in seiner allgemeinen Einschätzung, ohne aber auf die Ebioniten-These einzugehen, und plädiert für einen »bi-focal discourse« der Briefkommunikation:

> ›James‹, who makes no pretense about his connection with the Jesus movement, nevertheless composed a letter that has in mind diaspora Jews as potential readers … The distinctives of the Jesus movement are suppressed … The explicit arguments of James are based on appeals to the Jewish Bible, in particular the Decalogue, Leviticus 19 … James is framed as a discourse to Jews and offers arguments designed to appeal to Jews based on common values. But at another level it speaks to Christ followers.[99]

Der vorliegende Kommentar versteht anders als Allison und Kloppenborg die Adresse wie schon die Verfasserangabe als durchgehend literarisch-theologisch stilisiert. Der Verfasser stellt sich eindeutig als Christusbekenner vor, der unter dem Pseudonym des Herrenbruders Jakobus das epistolographische Szenario eines Rundschreibens aus Jerusalem an eine griechischsprachige Christus-bekennende Leserschaft entwirft, die religiös-metaphorisch im jüdisch-frühchristlichen Soziolekt als die »Zwölf Stämme in der Diaspora« angesprochen und damit durch ihre Verbindung zu Israel definiert wird. Die Adressatenschaft ist nicht als reales, sondern als *ideelles* Israel verstanden. Die Adresse zielt damit im Literalsinn auf ein jüdisches, im metaphorischen Sinn auf ein frühchristliches Lesepublikum. Im Brief werden keine Fragen behandelt, die ausschließliche oder rein spezifisch jüdische und/oder spezifisch frühchristliche Themen berühren. Es fehlt Beides: eine deutliche Christologie, wie sie nicht nur die Paulusbriefe, sondern auch und gerade 1Petr zeigen, und eine Jerusalem-Israel-Thematik, die exemplarisch im 2Bar entwickelt wird. Ebenso

---

[98] ALLISON, Jak, 49 mit Anm. 276 zu Themen der PsClem, die auch im Jak eine Rolle spielen. Zu den Ascents of James als einer Quelle der pseudoclementinischen Retractationen vgl. R. E. VAN VOORST, The Ascents of James: History and Theology of a Jewish-Christian Community, SBLDS 112, Atlanta 1989 (Einführung, Übersetzung und Kommentar). Weiteres s. unten.

[99] KLOPPENBORG, James, 91. Allison prägt den Ausdruck »Janus-faced« für das, was Kloppenborg »bi-focal« nennt: ALLISON, Jak, 48.

58 Einleitung

wenig findet sich ein judenchristliches Sonder-Milieu im Sinne der pseudoclementinischen Recognitionen in Jak. Stattdessen entwirft der Brief eine Gesetzesethik, die sich am Dekalog und am Gebot der Nächstenliebe orientiert und einen eigenen frühchristlichen Ethiktypus vertritt[100], den der Verfasser Jakobus dem Gerechten zuordnet. Die Christus-gläubigen Adressaten werden auf ihr jüdisches Erbe verpflichtet.

Der Verfasser will *einerseits* ein möglichst *allgemeines* Schreiben vorlegen, bei dem er die Kommunikation mit seinem Lesepublikum sucht. Über die gedachte Art der brieflichen Verteilung oder über einen frühchristlichen Buchmarkt – und damit um reale Adressaten – lässt sich allerdings nichts sagen.[101] Das avisierte umfassende Publikum gibt dem Brief eine erhöhte Bedeutung und dem Verfasser eine besondere Position und Autorität als einem Beauftragten (δοῦλος) Gottes und Jesu Christi. *Andererseits* sucht sich der Autor ein Lesepublikum nicht nur im Bereich der *Christusbekenner* (2,1), sondern potentiell auch bei jüdischen Leserinnen und Lesern (1,1) – nicht aber in einem paganen gebildeten Publikum. Er selbst versteht sich als Christus-gläubiger Lehrer, der seine primär Christus-gläubige Leserschaft zu dem allgemeinen Ethos des Tuns (Kap. 1–4) wie zu bestimmten Verhaltensformen in den Gemeindeversammlungen (Kap. 5) ermahnt.

Einen indirekten Hinweis auf die intendierten Adressaten geben die literarische Gattung seines Schreibens, das Briefformat, das in Form und Thematik in den Bereich der frühchristlichen Briefliteratur gehört[102], sowie Sprache und Stil des Briefes, der ein gebildetes griechischsprachiges Publikum anspricht.[103] Dafür sind schließlich die *inscriptio* und der briefliche Gruß aufschlussreich. Jak ist die einzige neutestamentliche briefliche Schrift, die den Gattungsbegriff ἐπιστολή so betont, dass er Teil der *inscriptio* ist. Damit hat der Jak ein Alleinstellungsmerkmal unter den neutestamentlichen Schriften und befindet sich in der Nähe zu den genannten Apostolischen Vätern, genauer: zum Barnabasbrief. Zweites Alleinstellungsmerkmal in der neutestamentlichen Briefliteratur ist der briefliche Gruß χαίρειν. Hier benutzt der Verfasser nicht die paulinische Formulierung, wie sie sich auch in den anderen katholischen Briefen (1. und 2. Petrus, abgewandelt in Judas) findet, son-

---

[100] Dazu s. u.

[101] BURCHARD, Jak, 6, lapidar: »Wie Jak als pseudepigraphischer Brief wirklich unter die Leute kam, weiß man nicht«. D. E. AUNE, Reconceptualizing the Phenomenon of Ancient Pseudepigraphy, in: J. Frey u. a. (Hg.), Pseudepigraphie und Verfasserfiktion in frühchristlichen Briefen (Pseudepigraphy and Author Fiction in Early Christian Letters), WUNT 246, Tübingen 2009, 789–824, 805, weist ebenfalls darauf hin, dass die postalische Verteilung der pseudepigraphen Schreiben ungeklärt ist. Ausnahme: Paulusapokalypse 1–2. Auch G. P. FEWSTER, Ancient Book Culture and the Literacy of James: On the Production and Consumption of a Pseudepigraphal Letter, ZAC 20, 2016, 387–417, fragt nach dem Publikationsmodus des Jak. Er postuliert eine frühchristliche Lesegemeinschaft: »James' production and reception as a pseudepigraphal letter fits within a broader initiative within early Christianity to promote themselves and their early leaders as literate« (389). Das ist zutreffend, klärt allerdings auch nicht die Art der Verbreitung.

[102] Dazu Weiteres siehe unten.

[103] Darauf verweist GANSLMAYER, Autor.

B. Der Text. Historische, literarische und thematische Charakteristik 59

dern die gemeingriechische Grußformel.[104] An diesem Punkt beweist der Verfasser gleich am Anfang des Schreibens literarischen Anspruch im Sinne der hellenistischen Gräzität. Mit Beidem scheint sich der Verfasser – anders sowohl als der paulinische Briefkreis als auch die übrigen sog. katholischen Briefe – der griechischen Epistolographie zuzuordnen.[105]

Für die Frage, wo der Ursprung der singulären Konstellation »Jakobus – die zwölf Stämme in der Diaspora« zu suchen sei, wird stets die Adresse in 1Petr 1,1: Πέτρος ἀπόστολος Ἰησοῦ Χριστοῦ ἐκλεκτοῖς παρεπιδήμοις διασπορᾶς Πόντου, Γαλατίας, Καππαδοκίας, Ἀσίας καὶ Βιθυνίας, herangezogen.[106] Hier werden Petrus und die in der »Diaspora« lebenden Christusgemeinden literarisch verbunden. Darüber hinaus kann aber auch auf Apg 8,1.4; 11,19 hingewiesen werden. Lukas benutzt das Partizip διασπαρέντες – »die Zerstreuten« – für die Jerusalemer Gemeinde, die vor Verfolgung floh, vermerkt aber ausdrücklich, die *Apostel* hätten Jerusalem nicht verlassen. Lukas beschreibt diese Diaspora-Gemeindeglieder als Judenchristen (11,19). Damit will Lukas eine historische[107] Konstellation schildern: Die Apostel blieben in Jerusalem – Christus-gläubige Gemeindeglieder gingen in die Diaspora. Sie predigten nur Juden und waren Paulus gegenüber kritisch eingestellt. Der Verfasser des Jakobusbriefes, der wahrscheinlich später als Apg anzusetzen ist, kann bei der Wahl seiner Eingangs-Metaphern durchaus eine derartige historische Situation im Blick gehabt haben.[108] Diese Situation würde der Eingangsadresse eine gewisse historische Plausibilität verschaffen.

(2) Wissen wir etwas über die sozialgeschichtliche Position der Adressaten?[109] Sollen wir uns eine Christus-gläubige Gemeinde in Jerusalem vorstellen? Oder spiegelt der Jak lediglich ethische und soziale Beobachtungen, Erfahrungen und Überzeugungen seines Verfassers, ohne dass sich diese einer oder mehreren realen Gemeinden zuordnen lassen? Da der vorliegende Kommentar von einer literarischen Adresse des Jak ausgeht, lässt sich mit Sicherheit nur sagen, dass Jak weder ein sozialgeschichtlich differenziertes Bild von einer bestimmten Gemeinde, der der *Verfasser* angehörte, noch einen Hinweis auf bestimmte *Adressatengemeinden* gibt. Was sich erheben lässt, ist dagegen das soziale *Milieu*, das der Verfasser zeichnet

---

[104] Singulär unter den ntl. Briefen, vgl. aber Apg 15,23; 23,26 sowie die Ignatiusbriefe außer IgnPhld.

[105] Dazu s. u. (Form).

[106] Siehe den Kommentar zur Stelle.

[107] Zur kritischen Diskussion des Nachrichtenwertes dieses historischen Bildes, das Lk zeichnet, s. u. Für Jak ist wichtig, dass Lk eine Diasporasituation der Jerusalemer Gemeinde beschreibt, die der Verfasser des Jak im Rückblick für historisch halten konnte.

[108] Die hier angestellte Vermutung geht auf eine mündliche Anregung von Eve-Marie Becker zurück.

[109] Vgl. dazu den Exkurs bei Burchard, Jak, 102 f: »Zur sozialen Lage der Adressaten des Jakobusbriefs«. Burchard geht von Adressaten aus, die »zur städtischen Unterschicht oberhalb der Armutsgrenze … gehört haben« (103). Dabei berücksichtigt er die Implikationen des literarischen Niveaus des Briefes. Andererseits weist er darauf hin, dass Jak »Mittel und wahrscheinlich auch Organisation« in den Adressatengemeinden voraussetzt. Auch Frankemölle, Jak 1, 59, nimmt eine »bildungsmäßig und sozial geschichtete Adressatengruppe« an (ausführlich Exkurs 3: »Die soziale Situation der Adressaten«, 251–259).

und innerhalb dessen er sozial-kritisch argumentiert. John S. Kloppenborg spricht von den »urban and middeling addressees«.[110] Aus dem Umstand, dass in Jak 2,2 eine συναγωγή erwähnt wird, die Kloppenborg als synagogalen Bau deutet, schließt Kloppenborg:

> Thus, while James is critical of wealth and the improper attachment to wealth, he also plainly supposes that his addressees supported their respective groups, and were in a position to aid for the poor. This takes money and resources.[111]

Dies dürfte das Äußerste sein, was sich zu dem sozialen Milieu des Briefes sagen lässt. Allerdings scheint auch Kloppenborg noch zu sicher zu sein, dass sich aus Jak das reale Milieu der Adressaten erschließen lasse. Es geht aber strenggenommen um das Milieu, das der Verfasser *literarisch* entwirft und das er sich als relevant für die Adressaten *vorstellen* kann, nicht um das realistische Milieu der Adressaten, die sich nicht fassen lassen.[112]

1.4 Ort

Der *literarisch-theologische* Ort des Schreibens ist Jerusalem, auch wenn dies nicht ausgesprochen, sondern mit der Diasporametapher umschrieben wird: Die Diaspora definiert sich von Jerusalem aus. Würde man den Brief dem Herrenbruder zuschreiben, wäre der Jakobusbrief als einziger neutestamentlicher Text in Jerusalem entstanden, und zwar vor 62 n. Chr. Setzt man wie der vorliegende Kommentar den Brief in die dritte christliche Generation[113], stehen mehrere Städte als Entstehungsort zur Disposition.[114]

Die Adresse selbst gibt keine Auskunft über den realen Abfassungsort. Während einige Kommentatoren – prominent Dibelius – grundsätzlich auf eine lokale Zuordnung verzichten[115], bemühen sich die meisten Kommentare doch mittels literarischen Vergleichs und Milieuforschung um eine Lokalisierung. Die Kommentatoren haben verschiedene Vorschläge zur historischen Situierung gemacht, die von Metzner noch einmal sorgfältig dokumentiert worden sind[116]: »Palästina bzw.

---

[110] Kloppenborg, James, 92; Ders., Christ's Associations: Connecting and Belonging in the Ancient City, New Haven 2019; A. J. Batten, The Urbanization of Jesus Traditions in James, in: dies. / J. S. Kloppenborg (Hg.), James, 1&2 Peter and the Early Jesus Tradition, London / New York 2014, 78–96.

[111] Kloppenborg, James, 97.

[112] Die sozialgeschichtlich relevanten Einzelaussagen des Jak werden daher im Kommentarteil zu den entsprechenden Texten behandelt. – Zu neuen Beiträgen zu ethischen und speziell sozialethischen Kontexten des Jak vgl. S. Luther, Jakobusbrief, 14–17.

[113] S. unten.

[114] D.-A. Koch, Geschichte des Urchristentums, Göttingen ²2014, 375–385. Weiteres unten.

[115] So Dibelius, Jak, 69; Popkes, Jak, 69.

[116] Metzner, Jak, 23–25. Vgl. auch die Zusammenstellung bei Allison, Jak, 94, und sehr ausführlich Kloppenborg, James, 26–35. Kloppenborg votiert für Alexandria, weil Jak dort zuerst bezeugt ist (34 f). Vgl. dazu kritisch Bemmerl, Der Jakobusbrief in der Alten Kirche, 230 (siehe oben).

B. Der Text. Historische, literarische und thematische Charakteristik 61

Jerusalem«[117], Antiochia[118], Alexandria[119], Rom.[120] Die einzelnen Argumente sind schon oft beschrieben worden und müssen hier nicht noch einmal wiederholt werden. Für Palästina gibt es keine Evidenz.[121] Metzner schreibt zurecht: »Palästinisches Lokalkolorit lässt sich nicht nachweisen«.[122] Die Bildwelt ist die der großen Handelsstädte an der östlichen Mittelmeerküste. Damit erschöpfen sich aber bereits die Evidenzen. Für eine Lokalisierung in Antiochia fehlen triftige Gründe[123], ebenso für Alexandria.[124] Metzner stellt einige Argumente für Rom zusammen: neben Handel und Häfen vor allem die Nähe zum 1Petr, 1 und 2Clem und dem Hirten des Hermas.[125] Allerdings räumt er ein:

> Da es für direkte literarische Beziehungen zwischen diesen Schriften keine ausreichenden Anhaltspunkte gibt, genügt die Annahme, dass Jakobus auf in Rom zirkulierende Stoffe zurückgreift.[126]

Trotz dieser grundsätzlichen Einschränkung kann die frühchristliche Literaturproduktion in Rom als weiteres Argument für römische Entstehung gewertet werden. So entscheidet sich Allison mit einigen beachtlichen Überlegungen für Rom:

> While conceding that the evidence is circumstantial and fragile, … the best bet is Rome.[127]

---

[117] METZNER, Jak, 23 Anm. 195.

[118] METZNER, Jak, 24 Anm. 203.

[119] METZNER, Jak, 24 Anm. 204, Dazu kritisch-ironisch BURCHARD, Jak, 7: »Daß wir über alexandrinisches Christentum im 1. Jh. wenig wissen, macht die Lokalisierung dort ebenso schwierig wie reizvoll«.

[120] METZNER, Jak, 24, Anm. 205.

[121] JOHNSON, Jak, 121, plädiert aufgrund seiner Autor-Hypothese dafür, Jak als »a very early writing from a Palestinian Jewish Christian source« zu lesen. Zu einer möglichen Lokalisierung in Jerusalem siehe unten.

[122] METZNER, Jak, 23. Vgl. O. WISCHMEYER, The Social and Religious Milieu of James; Methods, Sources, and Possible Results, in: Matthew, James, and Didache, 33–41; A. J. BATTEN, The Urban and Agrarian in the Letter of James, Journal of Early Christian History 3, 2013, 4–20.

[123] Trotz BURCHARD, Jak, 7, der schreibt: »Wenn ich mich entscheiden muss: Antiochia, wegen des Apostelkonzils samt seinen Folgen und einiger Nähe zu Matthäus«. In diesen Zusammenhang gehören auch Zuschreibungen nach Syrien: ALLISON, Jak, 94. SCORNAIENCHI, Polemik im Jakobusbrief, votiert wieder für Syrien, »weil dort die judenchristlichen Gemeinden besonders stark waren« (365). Mit dem Hinweis auf die Bedeutung der jüdischen Einwohnerschaft Alexandrias kann man allerdings auch für Alexandria votieren.

[124] Der Hinweis auf die Papyri 20.23 und 100 sowie auf Philo-Parallelen und die Bezeugung bei Origenes ist nicht aussagekräftig genug. KLOPPENBORG, James, 29–31, votiert für Alexandria. Seine Gründe sind (1) die Ersterwähnung bei Origenes in seiner alexandrinischen Zeit (De Principiis I 3,6), (2) lexikalische und metaphernsprachliche Eigenarten von Jak, die sich auch in der alexandrinischen Literatur finden (Philo und Pseudo-Phokylides), (3) Hinweise auf andere Jakobus-Literatur in Ägypten. Es handelt sich aber bei den drei Gründen nur um literarische Hinweise. Eine plausible frühchristliche Gemeindesituation zeichnet Kloppenborg nicht.

[125] METZNER, Jak, 24.

[126] METZNER, Jak, 25.

[127] ALLISON, Jak, 95, zu den Gründen S. 96 f. Allison weist auch auf Markion hin: 97 f.

Allison versucht zusätzlich, ein randständiges judenchristliches Lokalmilieu in Rom zu rekonstruieren, dem der Brief entstammen könnte und das auch seine schwache Überlieferungsgeschichte erklären würde. Damit wäre Rom die wahrscheinlichste Hypothese. Allerdings erscheint die Annahme, in Rom habe sich ein frühchristlicher Lehrer als Jakobus vorgestellt, angesichts der starken Petrus- und Paulustradition in Rom um 100 n. Chr. (1Clem) sehr unwahrscheinlich. Allisons Überlegungen weisen eher auf Jerusalem als auf Rom. Die von Allison und anderen genannten Texte: 1Petr, 1 und 2Clem und Herm haben jeweils ihr eigenes literarisches und theologisches Profil. Gemeinsamkeiten mit Jak beziehen sich vor allem auf das Feld von Traditionen und Motiven. Eine Textgruppe, deren Ursprung in einem spezifischen theologischen, ethischen und institutionellen Milieu, etwa in Rom, zu verorten wäre, lässt sich nicht evident machen. Auch die Situierung in Alexandria, für die John S. Kloppenborg aufgrund der Erstbezeugung in Alexandria votiert[128], bleibt unbefriedigend. Hinweise auf Spuren hellenistisch-jüdischer allegorischer Schriftinterpretation fehlen ebenso wie eine Bezugnahme auf platonische und stoische philosophische Diskurse.[129] Der vorliegende Kommentar hält daher weder Antiochia noch Alexandria noch Rom für plausible Entstehungsorte, sondern schlägt *Jerusalem* vor. Diese Hypothese erhält ihre Plausibilität nicht nur durch literaturgeschichtliche Überlegungen zum Diasporabrief und zur Jakobustradition, sondern beruht vor allem auf der religionsgeschichtlichen, theologie- und kirchengeschichtlichen Verortung des Jak im Rahmen der Entstehung der frühchristlichen Literatur und ihrer Gemeinden und kann erst in den entsprechenden Zusammenhängen vorgestellt und diskutiert werden.[130]

1.5 Zeit

Der vorliegende Kommentar geht davon aus, dass Jak nicht ein Schreiben des Herrenbruders ist und damit nicht am Beginn der neutestamentlichen Literatur steht, wie Willibald Beyschlag annahm und auch Luke T. Johnson vorsichtig erwägt.[131] Welche Kriterien für eine Datierung lassen sich im Rahmen der Pseudepigraphiethese finden? Mit Allison ist davon auszugehen, dass der Verfasser Röm und Gal[132] – damit ist Jak in jedem Fall zeitlich post-paulinisch – und 1Petr kannte, außerdem ist die Nähe zu 2Bar 78–86 und zu Teilen des 1Clem evident. Möglicherweise kannten der Verfasser des Judasbriefes[133] und der Verfasser des Hirten des

---

[128] Siehe oben.
[129] Zur Psychagogie, die Kloppenborg, James, 97 ff, annimmt, s. u.
[130] S. u.
[131] Johnson, Jak, 121.
[132] Dazu siehe unten (Paulus und Jakobus).
[133] Die Adresse des Jud bezieht sich wahrscheinlich auf Jak (vgl. oben).

B. Der Text. Historische, literarische und thematische Charakteristik

Hermas[134] bereits den Jakobusbrief. Das schränkt die Entstehungszeit auf die ersten Jahrzehnte des 2. Jahrhunderts ein, wie Allison urteilt:

A date of 100–120 would fit the bill.[135]

Dieser Zeitrahmen fällt ungefähr mit dem zusammen, was exegetisch als dritte Christus-bekennende Generation bezeichnet wird. Auf einen entsprechenden Rahmen deuten auch allgemeinere theologiegeschichtliche Überlegungen zur Stellung des Briefes im Zusammenhang der Katholischen Briefe und im judenchristlichen und Paulus-kritischen Kontext der ersten Hälfte des 2. Jahrhunderts.[136] Eine genauere zeitliche Eingrenzung ist nicht möglich. Auch der Hinweis auf jüdische Aufstände zwischen 115 und 117 in Ägypten, der Cyrenaica und Zypern und auf sozio-ökonomische Bedrückung in Jerusalem durch die flavische Steuergesetzgebung können keine weiteren Hinweise geben.[137]

1.6 Gelegenheit und Anlass

Lassen sich Aussagen zu Gelegenheit und Anlass des Jak machen, die vor und mit der Adresse die Grundkomponenten eines Briefes darstellen?[138] Das briefliche Format, die diatribischen Partien, der teilweise protreptische Gestus[139] und die Thematik der πειρασμοί mögen zwar auf einen konkreten Anlass hindeuten. Der Verfasser sieht schwere ethische Missstände bei seinen Adressaten: Diese Wahrnehmung ließe sich unter Umständen als »Anlass« rubrifizieren. Die exegetische Analyse zeigt aber, dass es sich im Einzelnen jeweils um literarische Inszenierung, nicht um Darstellung realer Vorgänge handelt.[140] Der Jak wird von Typisierung bzw. Stereotypenbildung und dem Rückgriff auf Traditionen beherrscht. Situative Elemente fehlen. Der Ursprung der brieflichen Aussagen in der Realität – mögliche Verfolgungssituation, ethisches Fehlverhalten der Adressaten – lässt sich daher nicht genauer bestimmen. Der Verfasser ist offensichtlich daran interessiert, angesichts seiner negativen Wahrnehmungen allgemeine Belehrungen und Mahnungen zu formulieren und die Bedeutung seines Briefes vom Situativen ins Normative zu heben.[141]

---

[134] Datierung in der ersten Hälfte des 2. Jahrhunderts bei D. HELLHOLM, Der Hirt des Hermas, in: W. Pratscher (Hg.), Die Apostolischen Väter. Eine Einleitung, Göttingen 2009, 226–253.

[135] ALLISON, Jak, 29. Vgl. auch KLOPPENBORG, James, 35 f: »first half of the second century« (36).

[136] METZNER, Jak, 69, plädiert für »die Wende vom 1. zum 2. Jh.«. Diese zeitliche Ansetzung scheint zu früh zu sein, wenn Jak Röm und 1Petr gekannt hat.

[137] Zur Zeitgeschichte: ST.T. KATZ (Hg.), CHJud IV. The Late Roman-Rabbinic Period; darin: DERS., Introduction, 1–22; S. SCHWARTZ, Political, social, and economic life in the Land of Israel, 66 – c. 235, 23–52.

[138] Zur dieser epistolographischen Begrifflichkeit vgl. N. GOLDMANN, Art. Gelegenheit und Anlass, in: Handbuch Brief (im Druck): Goldmann bezeichnet Gelegenheit als übergeordnetes Prinzip, Anlass als jeweiligen Anstoß. Mit diesen Kategorien kann nach Realitätsbindung und Literarizität der Brieftexte gefragt werden.

[139] Zu diesen Apekten siehe unten.

[140] Dazu siehe unten zu Jak 5,1–6 und der Frage nach *ingroup violence.*

[141] Zur Gelegenheit im Sinne der *occasion* s. u.

64 Einleitung

2. Literarische Charakteristik

Umso wichtiger ist die literarische Analyse des Briefes. Im Rahmen der Diskussion der Einleitungsfragen ist der literarische Anspruch des Jakobusbriefes bereits deutlich geworden. Diese Thematik, der neuerdings viel Aufmerksamkeit entgegengebracht wird, wird jetzt in ihren Einzelaspekten dargestellt.

2.1 Autorisierung

Der Verfasser autorisiert sich selbst eingangs nicht als Apostel[142] oder als Jesu Bruder[143]. Er verzichtet auch auf einen expliziten Verweis auf seine mögliche Stellung in einer Institution wie dem Sanhedrin (Diasporabrief-Rahmung) oder in der Jerusalemer Gemeinde der Christusbekenner (Jakobus als »Säule« der Jerusalemer Gemeinde). Implizit sind allerdings beide Autorisierungen in der Adresse alludiert. Der Verfasser schreibt unter dem Namen Jakobus explizit als δοῦλος »Gottes und des Herrn Jesus Christus« und leitet seine Autorität damit einleitend bzw. grundsätzlich in doppelter Weise religiös her: von Gott und von Jesus Christus als seinem Herrn und dem Herrn der Adressaten. Mit dem δοῦλος-Titel verwendet der Verfasser den durch Paulus geprägten Soziolekt frühchristlicher Führer, der seinerseits auf die Tradition der Bibel Israels zurückgeht und für die großen Führer Israels verwendet wurde. Dibelius hat diese Selbstvorstellung richtig als »apostolischen Ehrentitel« interpretiert.[144] Paulus verwendet in Phil 1,1 dieselbe Formulierung für sich und Timotheus, so dass mit einer bereits erfolgten frühchristlichen Interpretation des sich auf Israel rückbeziehenden Titels zu rechnen ist.[145] Weitere Autorität liegt in der weitgespannten Adresse: Der Verfasser schreibt im Literalsinn mit dem Anspruch, die gesamte Judenschaft außerhalb des Landes Israel zu belehren.

Aus Jak 3,1 lässt sich zusätzlich entnehmen, dass der *historische* Verfasser selbst zu den frühchristlichen διδάσκαλοι gehört und damit eine besondere Verantwortung trägt. Anders als Paulus schreibt er also als Lehrer.[146] Zugleich legt er sich mit der pseudonymen Selbstvorstellung apostolische Autorität zu. Die Autorisierung erfolgt weiterhin durch die paränetische Rhetorik einerseits, durch die Schriftverweise andererseits, aber auch durch seine allgemeine Bildung. Gregory Fewster weist darauf hin, dass im Jakobusbrief wie in allen neutestamentlichen Briefen – unabhängig

---

[142] Vgl. die paulinischen und deutero- und tritopaulinischen Briefe mit Ausnahme von 1Thess (vgl. aber 2,6) und Phil (Παῦλος καὶ Τιμόθεος δοῦλοι Χριστοῦ Ἰησοῦ; »Freundschaftsbrief«). Jud schließt sich an Jak an und verweist auf Jakobus als autorisierende Größe.

[143] Anders Jud 1: der Verfasser bezeichnet sich als »*Bruder* des Jakobus«.

[144] Dibelius, Jak, 94.

[145] Röm 1,1: Παῦλος δοῦλος Χριστοῦ Ἰησοῦ, κλητὸς ἀπόστολος ἀφωρισμένος εἰς εὐαγγέλιον θεοῦ und Tit 1,1: Παῦλος δοῦλος θεοῦ, ἀπόστολος δὲ Ἰησοῦ Χριστοῦ fügen den Aposteltitel hinzu. Vgl. auch 2Petr 1,1. Allison, Jak, 122 Anm. 53, hält Tit 1,1 für die »closest parallel before Origen«. Zu Paulus vgl. E.-M. Becker und U. Babusiaux, Paulus, der »Sklave Christi Jesu« (Gal 1,10; Röm 1,1; Phil 1,1), im Lichte des römischen Rechts, NTS 69, 2023, 365–385.

[146] Siehe dazu den Kommentar zur Stelle.

B. Der Text. Historische, literarische und thematische Charakteristik 65

von ihrer Autorschaft – bereits das Faktum des Briefeschreibens (*literacy*)[147] selbst
Teil der Autorisierung ist, da die *literacy* als Ausdruck eines gehobenen Sozialstatus
verstanden werden muss. Sigurvin L. Jónsson hat dies Argument vertieft ausgearbeitet.[148] Der Titel διδάσκαλος enthält nach Jónsson drei wichtige autoritätsstiften-
de Faktoren: Die frühchristlichen Lehrer werden von den Gemeinden unterstützt,
ihre Stellung beruht auf Bildung (Schrift und Toraauslegung), die Lehrer haben
eine herausgehobene Position, an die besondere Anforderungen gestellt werden.
Diese drei Faktoren erzeugen Autorität.[149]

Rainer Metzner konstruiert auf der Basis seiner Autoren nicht nur das Profil,
sondern auch die Autorität des Schreibens noch eindeutiger von dem Lehrertitel
her, den der Verfasser verwendet:

> Jakobus schreibt nicht als Apostel oder Prophet, sondern als Lehrer, dem nicht an
> seiner Person, sondern an seiner Botschaft gelegen ist. Den ganzen Jakobusbrief durch-
> ziehen pädagogische Töne.[150]

Zusammengefasst: die Autorität des *historischen* Autors leitet sich aus seinem pä-
dagogisch-ethischen Anspruch und seiner Stellung als frühchristlicher Lehrer her.
Dieser Anspruch findet seine *literarische* Form im pseudepigraphen Rekurs auf den
frühchristlichen Jerusalemer Gemeindeleiter Jakobus sowie in der Rahmung seines
Schreibens als Diasporabrief.[151] Der Verfasser verwendet eine erweiterte frühchristliche religiöse Autorisierungsformel, die auf Gott und auf Jesus Christus als den
Herrn verweist und zugleich die implizite wie die tatsächliche Leserschaft unter
diese Doppelherrschaft stellt. Zusätzlich bezieht er sich mehrfach auf die »Schrift«
Israels. Diese besondere Form der Autorisierung wird im Folgenden vorgestellt.

2.2 Intertextualität. Zitate. Allusionen. Traditionen

Der Intertextualität des Jak ist sehr viel exegetische Aufmerksamkeit zuteil geworden. Dabei werden die verschiedensten Suchbegriffe: Zitat, Anspielung, Tradition
bzw. Motiv und sprachliches und literarisches Milieu, verwendet. Für den Jakobusbrief sind neben der allgemeinen Intertextualität (2.2.1) vor allem Zitate (2.2.2),
Allusionen (2.2.3) und Traditionen (2.2.4) vielverhandelte Themen.

2.2.1

Intertextualität ist ein Terminus der neueren Literaturwissenschaft (Julia Kristeva).[152] Das Phänomen wird in der neutestamentlichen Exegese seit langem unter

---

[147] Das häufig gebrauchte englische Substantiv ist mehrdeutig: Schreibfähigkeit, Schreib- und Lesefähig-
keit, eigene Textproduktion. Ausführliche Darstellung mit Lit.angaben bei FEWSTER, Ancient Book Culture.
[148] JÓNSSON, James, 193–218.
[149] JÓNSSON, James, 215.
[150] METZNER, Jak, 11.
[151] Dazu s. unten.
[152] J. KRISTEVA, Bakhtine, le mot, le dialogue et le roman, 1967; dt.: J. KRISTEVA, Wort, Dialog und Roman

verschiedenen Begriffen verhandelt. Dibelius hat in seinem Kapitel »Literarische Beziehungen«[153] einen souveränen Überblick über den Platz des Jakobusbriefes in der traditionell gehaltenen paränetischen Literatur seiner Zeit gegeben und damit das weite Gebiet ethischer Traditionen abgesteckt, in dem in der Folgezeit der Jakobusbrief immer wieder neu verortet wurde.[154] Die Kommentare sind der grundsätzlichen Option für »Traditionen« bei Dibelius weitgehend gefolgt, obwohl in der Jakobusexegese ein methodischer Paradigmenwechsel von der formgeschichtlichen Methode zur literaturwissenschaftlichen Perspektive erfolgt ist. So legt auch Burchard das Hauptgewicht auf den Umgang mit der Jesustradition.[155] Dale Allison gibt eine überaus gründliche Einführung in die fünf Bereiche, die als Quellen – er entschränkt den Begriff »Quelle« praktisch in Richtung auf Traditionen und literarische Milieus – für den Jak infrage kommen: LXX, frühjüdische Schriften außerhalb der LXX, hellenistische Popularphilosophie, Jesustradition, weitere frühchristliche Traditionen und Texte.[156] Die Zitate aus LXX führt er als Bestandteil einer langen Liste von Zitaten, Bezugnahmen und Anspielungen auf LXX-Texte als »citations« oder »quotations« auf.[157] Indem er die expliziten Zitate derart kontextualisiert, nimmt er ihnen allerdings gleichzeitig die besondere autoritative Bedeutung, die sie in der Argumentation des Verfassers haben. Allisons Darstellung darf abgesehen von ihren definitorischen Unschärfen als gegenwärtig umfangreichste und vollständigste Dokumentation der Thematik gelten.

Die Überordnung des Traditionen-Begriffs hat sich trotz unterschiedlicher Terminologien im Ganzen von Dibelius bis Metzner also nicht grundlegend geändert. Allerdings wird das Feld von Zitat – Allusion – Tradition gegenwärtig weniger aus der quellen- und traditionsgeschichtlichen Perspektive, sondern verstärkt unter literaturgeschichtlichen Fragestellungen erschlossen. Exemplarisch am Zitat dargestellt: Zitate sagen ebenso viel über Autorisierungsstrategien wie über die materiale oder virtuelle Bibliothek des Autors, über seine Bildungswelt und über den Bildungsstand der intendierten Leserschaft aus. Der vorliegende Kommentar trägt diesem Umstand Rechnung, indem zwischen Zitat (2.2.2), Allusion, (2.2.3) und

---

bei Bachtin, 1967, in: J. Ihwe (Hg.), Literaturwissenschaft und Linguistik. Ergebnisse und Perspektiven. Bd. 3: Zur linguistischen Basis der Literaturwissenschaft II, Frankfurt am Main 1972, 345–375. Vgl. S. Seiler u. a., Art. Intertextualität, LBH, 300–306; zu Intertextualität in Jak: Wischmeyer, Scriptual Classicism?; dies., The Book of Ben Sira from a Reception-Historical Perspective: Hubert Frankemölle's Commentary on the Letter of James, in: F. M. Macatangay / F.-J. Ruiz-Ortiz (Hg.), Ben Sira in Conversation with Traditions. A Festschrift for Prof. Núria Calduch-Benages on the Occasion of Her 65th Birthday, DCLS 47, Berlin / Boston 2022, 285–300.

[153] Dibelius, Jak, 43–53, unterscheidet zurecht zwischen den »wenigen wirklichen Zitaten« aus LXX (er nennt 2,23 und 4,6) und »Anklängen« (43).

[154] Vgl. aber schon Mayor, Jak, lxviii–ciii (»Relations«).

[155] Burchard, Jak, 17 f.

[156] Allison, Jak, 51–71.

[157] Allison, Jak, 51: Jak 2,23 (Gen 15,6); 2,11 (Ex 20,13 f); 2,8 (Lev 19,18); 4,6 (Spr 3,34); 4,5 (Eldad und Modad?).

B. Der Text. Historische, literarische und thematische Charakteristik   67

Traditionen (2.2.4) unterschieden wird. Gerade bei dem Jakobusbrief als einem Text, der mit vielen ethischen Traditionen arbeitet und mit vielen Texten aus der frühjüdischen und frühchristlichen Literatur verbunden ist, müssen die verschiedenen Grade der Intertextualität sichtbar gemacht werden.[158]

2.2.2

Jakobus *zitiert* mit einer Ausnahme nur »die Schrift«.[159] Die Liste der *Schriftzitate* ist die folgende:

(1) Εἰ μέντοι νόμον τελεῖτε βασιλικὸν **κατὰ τὴν γραφήν·** ἀγαπήσεις τὸν πλησίον σου ὡς σεαυτόν, καλῶς ποιεῖτε(2,8), Zitat aus Lev 19,18.

(2) ὁ γὰρ εἰπών· μὴ μοιχεύσῃς, εἶπεν καί· μὴ φονεύσῃς (2,11), Zitat aus Ex 20,13 f.

(3) **καὶ ἐπληρώθη ἡ γραφὴ ἡ λέγουσα·** ἐπίστευσεν δὲ Ἀβραὰμ τῷ θεῷ, καὶ ἐλογίσθη αὐτῷ εἰς δικαιοσύνην (2,23), Zitat aus Gen 15,6.

(4) ἢ δοκεῖτε ὅτι κενῶς **ἡ γραφὴ λέγει·** πρὸς φθόνον ἐπιποθεῖ τὸ πνεῦμα ὃ κατῴκισεν ἐν ἡμῖν (4,5), unbekanntes Zitat.[160]

(5) **διὸ λέγει·** ὁ θεὸς ὑπερηφάνοις ἀντιτάσσεται, ταπεινοῖς δὲ δίδωσιν χάριν (4,6), Zitat aus Spr 3,34 f.

Die zahlenmäßig seltenen expliziten Zitate im Jakobusbrief dienen nicht primär dem literarischen Schmuck. Sie sind auch nicht einfach Traditionsstücke oder Ausweis der Belesenheit des Verfassers oder Hinweise auf seine Bibliothek.[161] Sie dienen in erster Linie der Bestätigung und Autorisierung entscheidender Aussagen des Verfassers.[162] Zitate[163] im Sinne expliziter Referenz oder wörtlicher Wiedergabe im Jakobusbrief beziehen sich bis auf eine Ausnahme auf die Septuaginta.[164] Die Schrift (γραφή)[165] wird mehrfach explizit zitiert oder als νόμος argumentativ eingesetzt.[166]

Jakobus zitiert dreimal aus der Tora – Gen, Ex, Lev – und zwar Sätze, die mehrfach als Zitate und in wichtigen Zusammenhängen im frühen Christentum Ver-

---

[158] Auch KLOPPENBORG, James, 61–81, unterscheidet zwischen: allusions, paraphrase and aemulatio, quotations und Jesus tradition. Interessant ist die Kapitelüberschrift: »The Fabric of James: The Jewish Bible and the Jesus Tradition« (61). Hier nimmt Kloppenborg die Perspektive der Textproduktion ein.

[159] Ausnahme: Zitat Nr. 4, das von Jakobus aber als Schriftzitat eingeführt wird.

[160] Zu der komplizierten Diskussion über die mögliche Quelle siehe ALLISON, Jak, 51–71 und den vorliegenden Kommentar zur Stelle.

[161] Zu den Fragen der Bibliothek des Verfassers vgl. WISCHMEYER, Classicism.

[162] Gegnerische Zitate fehlen, vgl. aber den fiktiven Dialog in Jak 2,14–19. In V. 14 und 18 können mindestens positionell gegnerische Argumente gefunden werden.

[163] Vgl. J. KRISPENZ u.a., Art. Zitat, LBH 2013, 689–695. Zum Begriff vgl. O. WISCHMEYER, Zitat und Allusion als literarische Eröffnung des Markusevangeliums, in: J. Jacob / M. Mayer (Hg.), Im Namen des Anderen. Die Ethik des Zitierens, Ethik – Text – Kultur 3, München 2010, 175–186, Definitionen und Lit. S. 175–177.

[164] Vgl. dazu ausführlich WISCHMEYER, Classicism.

[165] 2,8.23; 4,5.

[166] 1,25; 2,8. 9. 10.11.12; 4,11.

68 Einleitung

wendung finden – gleichsam klassische Stellen.[167] Einmal ist das Zitat den Sprüchen entnommen. Das Proverbienzitat findet sich ebenso in 1Petr 5,5. Das unbekannte Zitat benutzt Jakobus in direktem Zusammenhang mit dem Zitat aus Proverbien.[168]

Mit den Zitaten stellt sich Jakobus in die doppelte autorisierende Tradition Israels und des frühen Christentums.[169] Die Zitation des Gebotes der Nächstenliebe und der Verweis auf den Dekalog zeigt den Autor im *mainstream* frühchristlicher LXX-Zitatpraxis, ebenso das Proverbienzitat. Ungewöhnlich, ja kühn, ist nicht seine Benutzung, sondern seine *Interpretation* von Gen 15,6.[170]

Wichtig sind neben den Schriftzitaten die ethischen *exempla*, alle aus dem Alten Testament genommen: Abraham (2,21–23), Rahab (2,25), die Propheten und Hiob (ὑπόδειγμα 5,10 f) sowie Elia (5,17 f).[171] Bis auf Rahab handelt es sich um sehr bekannte Beispiele. Explizite Verweise auf die ältere oder zeitgenössische stoische Moralphilosophie fehlen demgegenüber völlig, ebenso fehlt eine Auseinandersetzung mit verschiedenen philosophischen Schulmeinungen, wie sie ansatzweise in der Apostelgeschichte aufscheint.[172] Zitate aus den synoptischen Evangelien fehlen ebenfalls. Jesus wird nicht explizit als Autorität herangezogen. Anders als bei Paulus und später bei Papias werden Herrenworte nicht angeführt.

Festzuhalten ist: Im Vergleich mit frühchristlichen Briefen wie dem Römerbrief oder vor allem dem Hebräerbrief setzt Jakobus explizite Zitate aus der Schrift *selten*.[173] Mit einer Ausnahme verwendet er sehr bekannte Zitate.[174] Diese haben ein erhebliches Gewicht in argumentativer und paränetischer Hinsicht und dienen jeweils der Bestätigung des Autors. Eine eigenständige Interpretation legt der Verfas-

---

[167] Lev 19,18: vgl. Röm 12,19; 13,9; Gal 5,14 (zitiert ebenfalls in Mt, Mk, Lk, Joh); Ex 20,13–17 zitiert ebenfalls in Röm 13,9 (kritisch zitiert in Mt 5,21); Gen 15,6 zitiert auch in Röm 4,3.9; Gal 3,6 (alludiert in Hebr 11,8). Auffallend ist, dass Jakobus Zitate verwendet, die auch in den Paulusbriefen eine wichtige Rolle spielen. Die »Zettelkasten«-Hypothese von Popkes, Jak, 29, (mit Hinweis auf Plutarch) ist reizvoll, führt aber an dem Umstand vorbei, dass Jakobus nur wenige und sehr bekannte Zitate bringt, für die man keine Unterstützung brauchte – weder durch Zettelkästen noch durch Originalschriften (vgl. dazu die Überlegungen bei Metzner, Jak, 34).

[168] Das kann auf eine gemeinsame Überlieferung zurückgehen, die uns aber nicht bekannt ist (s. zur Stelle).

[169] Jónsson, James, 218–225, weist auf zwei Ergebnisse in Ch.D. Stanleys Studie: Paul and the Language of Scripture: Citation Technique in the Pauline Epistles and the Contemporary Literature, MSSNTS 69, Cambridge 1992, hin, die auch für Jak gelten: »Quotations were used as a marker of authority in Jewish and Greco-Roman circles and as a caution and against overestimating historically the literacy of ancient audiences« (222).

[170] Siehe unten (Paulus und Jakobus).

[171] Dazu monographisch R. J. Foster, The Significance of Exemplars for the Interpretation of the Letter of James, WUNT II / 376, Tübingen 2014; Jónsson, James, 243–256.

[172] Das unbekannte Zitat und das Rahab-Exempel weisen darauf hin, dass Jakobus auch aus uns unbekannten Quellen schöpft (dazu ausführlich Allison, Jak, jeweils zur Stelle).

[173] O. Wischmeyer, Paulus als Hermeneut der Graphe, in: M. Witte / J. C. Gertz (Hg.), Hermeneutik des Alten Testaments, VWGTh 47, Leipzig 2017, 71–94.

[174] Ob er auf eine Sammlung zurückgreift, lässt sich nicht klären: vgl. J. Dochhorn, Art. Zitat II. Neutestamentlich, LBH, 690: Testimonien sind »erst später bezeugt«.

B. Der Text. Historische, literarische und thematische Charakteristik 69

ser zu Gen 15,6 vor.[175] Jesus-*Zitate* bzw. als Zitat markierte Herrenworte begegnen *nicht*. Die LXX-Zitate stellen die unangefochtene gemeinsame Autoritätsgrundlage für mögliche jüdische und christliche Adressaten des Briefes dar.

2.2.3

Anspielungen auf bekannte Texte gehören zur Bildungsliteratur aller Kulturen. Hier zeigen sich einerseits die Belesenheit des Verfassers und andererseits die Literaturkenntnis der Hörer- bzw. Leserschaft. Beides bleibt so lange verborgen, wie der Autor seine Intention nicht zu erkennen gibt und die Rezipienten keine Stimme haben. Das bedeutet von vornherein, dass die Benennung von Allusionen stets weitgehend im Bereich der Mutmaßung bleibt. Unabhängig von dieser Beweisnot sind Allusionen aber ein wichtiges Instrument vor allem traditioneller Literaturen und stellen das Gewebe her, aus dem der Intertext besteht, dem der Jakobusbrief angehört.[176] Dem Lesepublikum eröffnen Allusionen eine besondere Art wissender Teilhabe und konstituieren eine Gemeinschaft literarisch gebildeter Lesender bzw. Hörender. Für Jak werden vor allem LXX-Allusionen[177] (1), besonders Anspielungen auf Jesus Sirach (2) nachgewiesen. Weiter werden Allusionen auf die Paulusbriefe (3) sowie auf 1Petr (4) und den Hirten des Hermas (5) diskutiert.

(1) Dale Allisons Kommentar bietet die beste Einführung in dies Thema. Auf die Liste von LXX-Texten, die er zusätzlich zu den Zitaten unter den Stichworten »borrowing«, »summary«, »allusion« zusammengestellt hat[178], kann hier verwiesen werden. Im Zusammenhang der Frage, wieweit das Erkennen von Anspielungen vom Verfasser intendiert war, ist Allisons Hinweis auf solche Stellen hilfreich, für die gilt:

> At least some of James' borrowing from the LXX is intended to be noticed; that is, certain lines are designed to function as allusions and so don divine authority.[179]

Hier werden nur diejenigen Anspielungen genannt, die Allison für unzweifelhaft hält: Gen 1,26 f; Lev 19,13; Lev 19,15.[180] Der vorliegende Kommentar schließt sich dieser Bewertung an. Dass die Liste von Anspielungen im weiteren Sinn diejenige der Zitate um ein mehrfaches übertrifft, weist darauf hin, dass es dem Verfasser nicht nur um die Autorität der wörtlich angeführten Schrift in wichtigen Fragen ging, sondern darüber hinaus um einen autoritativen Fundus gemeinsamer ethischer und religiöser Grundwerte – so etwa eben um das Verbot der Prosopolempsie,

---

[175] Dazu weiter s. unten.
[176] Zur Intertextualität in Jak vgl. WISCHMEYER, Classicism, 389–405.
[177] Anspielungen auf LXX-Texte setzen feste Texte voraus, seien diese dem Autor mündlich (im Synagogal- oder frühchristlichen Gemeindeversammlungsvortrag) oder aber schriftlich zugänglich.
[178] ALLISON, Jak, 51. Vgl. Anm. 284 und 285: Allison weist darauf hin, dass vor allem Johnson (Leviticus) und Frankemölle (Sirach) sowie Wachob (Psalmen) eine höhere Anzahl von Allusionen annehmen.
[179] ALLISON, Jak, 52.
[180] Vgl. den Verskommentar.

70 Einleitung

das für Jakobus so wichtig ist, dass er zweimal darauf anspielt (2,1.9). In 2,9 verkürzt er das Gebot mittels des verbalen Neologismus προσωπολημπτεῖν.

Gen 1,26 f καὶ εἶπεν ὁ θεός Ποιήσωμεν ἄνθρωπον κατ᾽ εἰκόνα ἡμετέραν καὶ καθ᾽ ὁμοίωσιν.
Jak 3,9 καὶ ἐν αὐτῇ καταρώμεθα τοὺς ἀνθρώπους τοὺς καθ᾽ ὁμοίωσιν θεοῦ γεγονότας.
Lev 19,13 οὐκ ἀδικήσεις τὸν πλησίον καὶ οὐχ ἁρπάσεις, καὶ οὐ μὴ κοιμηθήσεται ὁ μισθὸς τοῦ μισθωτοῦ παρὰ σοὶ ἕως πρωί.
Jak 5,4 ἰδοὺ ὁ μισθὸς τῶν ἐργατῶν τῶν ἀμησάντων τὰς χώρας ὑμῶν ὁ ἀπεστερημένος ἀφ᾽ ὑμῶν κράζει, καὶ αἱ βοαὶ τῶν θερισάντων εἰς τὰ ὦτα κυρίου σαβαὼθ εἰσεληλύθασιν.
Lev 19,15 Οὐ ποιήσετε ἄδικον ἐν κρίσει· οὐ λήμψῃ πρόσωπον πτωχοῦ οὐδὲ θαυμάσεις πρόσωπον δυνάστου, ἐν δικαιοσύνῃ κρινεῖς τὸν πλησίον σου.
Jak 2,1 Ἀδελφοί μου, μὴ ἐν προσωπολημψίαις ἔχετε τὴν πίστιν τοῦ κυρίου ἡμῶν Ἰησοῦ Χριστοῦ τῆς δόξης.
Jak 2,9 εἰ δὲ προσωπολημπτεῖτε, ἁμαρτίαν ἐργάζεσθε ἐλεγχόμενοι ὑπὸ τοῦ νόμου ὡς παραβάται.

An dieser Stelle wird deutlich, dass der Verfasser nicht nur auf einen LXX-Text anspielt, sondern ihn literarisch verbessert, d. h. das Prinzip der *aemulatio* bewusst im Sinne literarischer Modernisierung eingesetzt hat.[181] Sigurvin Jónsson hat besonders Lev 19 im Hinblick auf *imitatio* und *aemulatio* in Jak diskutiert[182], während John Kloppenborg die *aemulatio* vornehmlich für die Jesustradition in Jak thematisiert.[183]

Im Zusammenhang der literaturwissenschaftlichen Perspektive hat Jónsson den Umgang des Verfassers mit der Schrift in Zitat und Allusion unter der Überschrift »James as Exegete« noch einmal auf den Prüfstand gestellt.[184] Sein Resümee, dem sich der vorliegende Kommentar anschließt, lautet:

> (Jakobus) is both original and traditional: He is traditional in the sense that he primarily utilizes scriptual references that we know circulated in early Christian circles and in that he generally stays true to the spirit of the scripture(s) he cites. But he is also original in his interpretation and incorporation of scripture to fit his rhetorical purpose, corresponding to Longinus' last two categories of literary imitation – to ensure that a borrowing is made one's own, and that the source is improved upon and surpassed.[185]

---

[181] Vgl. den Verskommentar.
[182] Jónsson, James, 231–238.
[183] J. S. Kloppenborg, The Emulation of Jesus Tradition in the Letter of James, in: R. L. Webb / J. S. Kloppenborg (Hg.), Reading James with New Eyes: Methodological Reassessments of the Letter of James, LNTS 342, London 2007, 121–150. Dazu Wischmeyer, Classicism, 397–401.
[184] Jónsson, James, ausführliche Darstellung 218–257.
[185] Jónsson, James, 257.

B. Der Text. Historische, literarische und thematische Charakteristik

Ein Aspekt ist hinzuzufügen: Originell ist Jakobus vor allem in der schriftgelehrten Interpretation von Gen 15.[186] Das bringt John Kloppenborg für den Vergleich von Röm 4,5 mit Jak 2 im exegetischen Umgang mit Gen 15,6 auf den Punkt:

> It is hard to imagine a more direct confrontation with the view that is taken by James in Jas 2:14–26, where he declares that trust (in God) absent of deeds is dead.[187]

(2) Hubert Frankemölle hat Jak weitgehend auf der Grundlage von Jesus Sirach interpretiert.[188] Seine Belege müssen hier nicht wiederholt werden.[189] Eine Fallstudie zu Jak 3,1–12 im Vergleich mit Sir 28,8–26 zeigt deutlich Zweierlei: erstens die Bezugnahme des Jak auf den griechischen Sirachtext, zweitens die literarischen Veränderungen, die Jak am Sirachtext vornimmt:

> In terms of motifs, Jas 3 is obviously dependent on Sir 28: strife, fire, tongue, Hades (Jas 3:6 φλογιζομένη ὑπὸ τῆς γεέννης), death: these motifs form a cluster of their own to which James refers. Frankemölle is right in terms of »tradition history« when he writes that James »found this antithetical thinking with regard to the positive and negative powers of the tongue in Jesus Sirach [Frankemölle, Jak 2, 485].« He is also right when he interprets James against the background of Sirach. But even our brief comparison has shown that the two texts I have chosen as comparative examples follow different literary concepts while dealing with the same subject matter. James has emancipated himself from the wisdom saying, the basis of wisdom literature: he chooses instead the literary genre of the ethical epistle and works with the means of contemporary rhetoric.[190]

Jakobus bezieht sich auf Motivik und Kernaussagen Sirachs zur »Zunge«, gestaltet aber eine kleine Ekphrasis zum Thema, die den Sirachtext literarisch strafft, modernisiert und in den Kontext zeitgenössischer Literatur stellt.

(3) Zu Allusionen auf Paulustexte vertreten die Kommentare unterschiedliche bis gegensätzliche Positionen. Lorenzo Scornaienchi stellt die Forschungsgeschichte zu Jak seit Ferdinand Christian Baur unter dem Gesichtspunkt des Verhältnisses des Jakobusbriefes zu Paulus dar und weist zurecht auf die grundsätzliche theologiegeschichtliche Dimension der Fragestellung hin.[191] Bei dem Thema der möglichen Paulus-Allusionen geht es allerdings noch nicht um eine Rekonstruktion der Geschichte des entstehenden Christentums, sondern zunächst »nur« um die kritische Diskussion textlicher Übereinstimmungen zwischen Paulus- und Jakobustexten.

---

[186] Siehe unten.
[187] KLOPPENBORG, James, 71.
[188] Siehe oben. Vgl. weiter dazu: WISCHMEYER, The Book of Ben Sira From a Reception-Historical Perspective, 285–300, besonders 289 f.
[189] Vgl. auch die Zusammenstellung bei ALLISON, Jak, 53 Anm. 292.
[190] WISCHMEYER, The Book of Ben Sira, 298.
[191] SCORNAIENCHI, Polemik im Jakobusbrief, 331–370, 340–348.

72 Einleitung

Diese Untersuchung kann dann als Basis für weitere theologiegeschichtliche Zuordnungen dienen.[192]

Allison hält es für eher wahrscheinlich, dass Jakobus mindestens den Römerbrief, wohl auch 1Kor und Gal kannte. Der vorliegende Kommentar geht mit Allison davon aus, dass mindestens Jak 2,21–26 Anspielungen auf Paulus*texte*, nicht nur auf Paulus*parolen*, enthält.[193] Anspielungen, die über ein gemeinsames Traditionsvokabular hinausgehen und Textkenntnisse wahrscheinlich machen, finden sich noch an anderen Stellen in Jak.[194] Die deutlichsten Beziehungen bestehen zwischen folgenden Texten:

Jak 1,13–15	Röm 7,7–13	Begierde, Sünde und Tod[195]
Jak 2,14–17	Gal 2,16; 3,6–9	Das Verhältnis von Glaube und Werken und
Jak 2, 18–26	Röm 3,27–31	Abrahams Glaube
	Röm 4,1–5	
Jak 3,13–18	1 Kor 1,17–2,16	Weisheit von oben und irdische Weisheit[196]

Der vorliegende Kommentar knüpft daher an Allisons Urteil an:

James was – or perhaps some of his sources were – more likely than not familiar with Romans and perhaps also with 1Corinthians and / or Galatians,[197]

---

[192] Dazu s. unten.

[193] Weiteres siehe unten in der Einleitung und unter dem Verskommentar.

[194] ALLISON, Jak, 64–67 nennt Röm 3,28; Gal 2,16; Röm 3,30 (»ein Gott«); Röm 2,12 (»durch das Gesetz gerichtet werden«) und 1Kor 12,8–9 (»Glauben haben«). Er setzt sich kritisch mit M.M. MITCHELL, The Letter of James as a Document of Paulinism?, in: R.L. Webb / J.S. Kloppenborg (Hg.), Reading James with New Eyes: Methodological Reassessments of the Letter of James, LNTS 342, London 2007, 75–98 auseinander. MITCHELL, The Letter, plädiert dafür, dass Jakobus außer Röm sowohl Gal als auch 1Kor kannte, und führt Hinweise auf die Kenntnis von 1Kor an: 90–93. ALLISON, Jak, 65f, reduziert Mitchells Liste und lässt für 1Kor nur zwei Belege gelten: die Formel Εἴ τις δοκεῖ + εἶναι (1Kor 3,18 und Jak 1,26) sowie 1Kor 2,14–3,3 und Jak 3,15–16. Weitere Vergleichstexte Allisons aus Röm 2; 3 und 4: S. 66f. Wichtig ist Allisons Beobachtung zum Diatribestil in Jak 2,14–26 im Vergleich mit Röm 2. Allison vermutet eine polemische *imitatio* des paulinischen Stils bei Jak (67). O. WISCHMEYER, Jak 3,13–18 vor dem Hintergrund von 1Kor 1,17–2,16. Frühchristliche Weisheitstheologie und der Jakobusbrief, ASEs 34, 2017, 403–430, weist darauf hin, dass Jak 3,13–18 auf 1Kor Bezug nimmt. E.-M. BECKER, Σοφία ἄνωθεν versus ἄνω κλῆσις? Jas 3:15, 17 and Phil 3:14 in Comparison, in: Who was ›James‹?, 219–236, plädiert mit guten Gründen dafür, dass Jakobus sich auch auf den Philipperbrief bezieht. Daraus leitet sie eine wichtige Folgerung ab: ›If James – especially in 3:13ff. – interacts with Paul's letter to the Philippians, we might even reach a more elaborated understanding of what σοφία means: By implementing and defining σοφία as a concrete source of proper *moral* conduct James might want to shape a decisive contrast to Paul's notion of the ἄνω κλῆσις as an eschatological idea. This might also mean that James' theology finally refuses to be »Weisheitstheologie« as such‹ (234). SCORNAIENCHI, Polemik im Jakobusbrief, 340–344, besonders 343f, weist zusätzlich auf folgende Themen hin: ζῆλος, καυχᾶσθαι, διακρίνειν, ἀκατάστατος/ἀκαταστασία, προσωπολημψία, sowie auf weitere sprachliche Wendungen.

[195] Vgl. den Verskommentar.

[196] Vgl. den Verskommentar. Zum Vergleich der beiden Texte: MITCHELL, The Letter, 91.

[197] ALLISON, Jak, 67.

B. Der Text. Historische, literarische und thematische Charakteristik

und rechnet mit der Kenntnis von Röm, 1Kor und Gal, wohl auch von Phil. Für die Gesamtinterpretation des Jakobusbriefes sind die Anspielungen auf Paulusbriefe in mehrfacher Hinsicht wichtig. Erstens ist Jak eine *nachpaulinische* Schrift, die sich modifizierend und kritisch mit gewissen theologischen Gedanken des Paulus auseinandersetzt. Zweitens steht Jak damit im Zusammenhang der entstehenden frühchristlichen *Brieftheologie*. Allison schließt daher richtig:

> that James did not live in a Christian backwater appears from his knowledge of Pauline theology and his likely dependence upon one or more Pauline epistles.[198]

(4) Dale Allison dokumentiert ebenfalls sorgfältig die Allusionen des Jakobusbriefes auf den 1Petr.[199] Er zählt zwölf Parallelen auf, die von der *adscriptio* in Jak 1,1 bis zu dem Bruchstück eines Proverbienzitates in 5,20 reichen und damit den gesamten Brief betreffen.[200] Zudem ist die Reihenfolge der Parallelen in beiden Briefen fast gleich.[201] Allison urteilt daher, der Verfasser des Jakobusbriefes habe 1Petr gekannt.[202] Allison zieht zwei wichtige Schlüsse aus dem Verhältnis beider Briefe zueinander: Erstens bezieht sich Jak auf 1Petr, da dieser zwischen 80 und 100 n. Chr. datiert wird und damit älter als Jak ist.[203] Zweitens hat der Verfasser des Jak bewusst kein christologisches Argument oder auch nur christologische Sprache aus 1Petr übernommen. Die *Reduktion der Christologie* in Jak ist also gewollt. Allison weist auch darauf hin, dass 1Petr im 2. Jahrhundert bekannt und beliebt war. Jak reiht sich also unter die unterschiedlich profilierten Briefe, die von 1Petr inspiriert sind: 2Petr, Jud und eben Jak.[204] Rainer Metzner hat das Urteil Allisons zur Abfolge von 1Petr und Jak wieder infrage gestellt. Nach Metzner

> muss 1Petr dem Jakobus nicht literarisch vorgelegen haben. Es genügt die Annahme, dass Jakobus das gemeinsame Material in modulierter Form kennengelernt hat.[205]

Angesichts der Adresse, der langen Liste der Übereinstimmungen und ihrer Abfolge sowie der LXX-Zitate hält der vorliegende Kommentar Allisons Darstellung für wahrscheinlicher.

---

[198] ALLISON, Jak, 60. MITCHELL, The Letter, 83: »The Epistle of James breathes the same air as Pauline Christianity, and this ›air‹ constitutes a Pauline literary culture«, formuliert dagegen überpointiert. Die deutliche sachliche antipaulinische Polemik, die sich in Jak 2 findet, wird bei dieser Einordnung vernachlässigt. Dazu kritisch SCORNAIENCHI, Polemik im Jakobusbrief, 343 f.

[199] ALLISON, Jak, 67–70, dort auch die Auseinandersetzung mit der exegetischen Literatur.

[200] ALLISON, Jak, 67 f: Jak 1,1 / 1Petr 1,1; Jak 1,2 / 1Petr 1,6–9; Jak 1,3–4 / 1Petr 1,7–9; Jak 1,10 / 1Petr 1,24 [Jes 40,6–8]; Jak 1,18 / 1Petr 1,23; Jak 1,21 / 1Petr 2,1; Jak 3,13 / 1Petr 2,12; Jak 4,1 f / 1Petr 2,11; Jak 4,6 / 1Petr 5,5 [Spr 3,34]; Jak 4,7 / 1Petr 5,8 f; Jak 4,10 / 1Petr 5,6; Jak 5,20 / 1Petr 4,8 [Spr 10,12].

[201] ALLISON, Jak, 68.

[202] ALLISON, Jak, 68: »In this writer's judgement, a literary relationship is likely«.

[203] Siehe oben zur Datierung.

[204] ALLISON, Jak, 69.

[205] METZNER, Jak, 40.

(5) Die engen sprachlichen und thematischen Beziehungen zwischen Jak und dem Hirten des Hermas sind oft dokumentiert und bewertet worden.[206] Dabei verbietet es sich, von Allusionen an Hermas bei Jak zu sprechen, da nicht anzunehmen ist, dass Hermas in irgendeiner Gestalt dem Jakobus schriftlich vorlag. Stattdessen muss von Parallelen in der Motivik gesprochen werden. Allison und Metzner geben die wichtigsten Parallelen an.[207] Klarheit über eine genauere Verhältnisbestimmung und mögliche Benutzung des einen Textes durch den anderen oder über zugrunde liegende Quellen lässt sich von Jak her nicht erzielen. Die Entstehungsgeschichte des Hirten ist komplex und die zeitliche Einordnung unsicher.[208] Allison weist darauf hin, dass Hermas – nach allgemeiner Meinung vor 150 n. Chr. in Rom entstanden[209] – ein Zeuge für die Zirkulation des Jak in Rom im ersten Drittel des 2. Jahrhunderts wäre, wenn Hermas sich tatsächlich auf Jakobus bezöge.[210] Sicherheit lässt sich nach Allison aber auch hier nicht erzielen. Auch Metzner legt sich nicht auf eine literarische Abhängigkeit fest, sondern diagnostiziert »eine gemeinsame Atmosphäre«, die sich aus »Wendungen, Motive(n) und Gedanken« speist und »ein vergleichbares soziales Milieu, das durch das Auftreten selbsternannter Lehrer« und weitere vergleichbare Erscheinungen in den Gemeinden gekennzeichnet ist.[211] Für den vorliegenden Kommentar ist die Beziehung zwischen Jak und Hermas vor allem bei der Diskussion um Ort und Zeit der Entstehung des Jak – unter Umständen Rom in der ersten Hälfte des 2. Jahrhunderts – wichtig.[212] Metzner weist auch auf Beziehungen zu den übrigen Apostolischen Vätern hin und stellt im Rahmen seiner Verfasserhypothese Jak in die Nähe dieser Schriftengruppe.[213] Allerdings sind die literarischen Formate beider Schriften so unterschiedlich, dass jedenfalls vom Hirten des Hermas kein Licht auf Jakobus fällt. Die Motiv- und »Parallelen«- Forschung stößt hier an ihre interpretatorischen Grenzen. Bemmerl verneint zurecht literarische Abhängigkeit und geht davon aus,

> dass der *Hirt des Hermas* und Jak unabhängig voneinander auf verschiedene Traditionen zurückgriffen, die für Christen des zweiten Jahrhunderts besonders relevant waren und sich diese deshalb auch in verschiedenen Texten dieses Zeitraums wiederfinden … Deshalb stellt sich auch die Frage nach einer Rezeptionsrichtung hier nicht.[214]

---

[206] Ältere Lit. bei ALLISON, Jak, 20 Anm. 101. Weitere Lit. bei METZNER, Jak, 18 f, Anm. 128 und 129. Vergleichende Tabelle bei BEMMERL, Der Jakobusbrief in der Alten Kirche, 71–73.

[207] ALLISON, Jak, 20–22, METZNER, Jak, 19 f.

[208] HELLHOLM, Hirt: im Verlauf der ersten Hälfte des 2. Jahrhunderts.

[209] N. Brox datiert auf 140 n. Chr. (N. BROX, Art. Hermas, LACL ³2003, 319 f).

[210] ALLISON, Jak, 23. Allerdings lässt sich die Bezugnahme nicht belegen, wie die sorgfältige Analyse bei BEMMERL, Der Jakobusbrief in der Alten Kirche, 45–74, zeigt.

[211] METZNER, Jak, 19.

[212] Siehe oben kritisch dazu.

[213] METZNER, Jak, 21.

[214] BEMMERL, Der Jakobusbrief in der Alten Kirche, 74.

B. Der Text. Historische, literarische und thematische Charakteristik

2.2.4

Anders als die Frage nach Allusionen auf *Texte* betrifft die Suche nach *Traditionen* in Jak den Umgang des Jak mit dem weiten Feld alttestamentlicher und frühjüdischer wie frühchristlicher Traditionen, die primär nicht in schriftlicher *Text*gestalt Wirkung entfalten, sondern sprachliche, motivische und thematische *Milieus* bilden, an denen ein Autor partizipiert. Hier sollen nur die hauptsächlichen Schwerpunkte der exegetischen Debatte zur Jesustradition in Jak dargestellt werden, die für die Jakobusexegese bereits seit Herder eine wichtige Rolle spielen. Die vielfältigen Beziehungen zu den Traditionsmilieus von Septuaginta und nicht-kanonischen Schriften des antiken Judentums sind bereits in den Kommentaren von Dibelius bis zu Allison und Metzner (vgl. auch besonders Frankemölle und Popkes) dargestellt worden und können hier vorausgesetzt werden.

In den letzten Jahrzehnten werden vor allem die Geschichte und der Umfang der Jesustradition im Jakobusbrief diskutiert. Besonders in der angelsächsischen Exegese ist hier umfangreich gearbeitet worden.[215] Antworten auf die Frage nach Jesustradition bei Jak hängen in erheblichem Maß von der Position zur Autorenfrage ab. Wird der Herrenbruder Jakobus als Verfasser angenommen, gewinnt die Identifizierung von Jesuslogien notwendig an Bedeutung. Folgt man dem bewusst unspezifischen Paränese-Ansatz des formgeschichtlichen Paradigmas von Dibelius[216], tritt die Frage zurück. Ähnliches gilt für die Pseudepigraphiethese. Für die Zuweisung einzelner Jakobussätze zur Jesustradition fehlt auf jeden Fall die Evidenz, weil Jakobus kein Jesuslogion zitiert oder auf Herrenworte verweist. Alle Zuweisungen haben den Status der Hypothese.

Allisons Kommentar widmet dem Thema der Jesustradition besondere Sorgfalt, indem er vor allem die detaillierte angelsächsische Diskussion ausführlich doku-

---

[215] Dazu D. B. Deppe, The Sayings of Jesus in the Epistle of James, Chelsea 1989; P. J. Hartin, James and the Q-Sayings of Jesus, Sheffield 1992; ders., James and the Jesus Traditions. Some Theological Reflections and Implications, in: K.-W. Niebuhr / R. W. Wall (Hg.), The Catholic Epistles and Apostolic Tradition, Waco 2009, 55–70; W. H. Wachob / L. T. Johnson, The Sayings of Jesus in the Letter of James, in: B. Chilton / C. A. Evans (Hg.), Authenticating the Words of Jesus, NTTS 28 / 1, Leiden / Boston / Köln 1999, 413–450; R. J. Bauckham, James. Wisdom of James, Disciple of Jesus the Sage, London / New York 1999; J. S. Kloppenborg, The Reception of the Jesus Tradition in James, in: J. Schlosser (Hg.), The Catholic Epistles and the Tradition, BETL 176, Leuven 2004, 93–141; ders., The Emulation of the Jesus Tradition in the Letter of James, in: R. L. Webb / J. S. Kloppenborg (Hg.), Reading James, LNTS 342, London / New York 2007, 121–150; J. Schröter, Jesus Tradition, in: van de Sandt / Zangenberg (Hg.), Matthew, James, and Didache, 233–255; A. Peter, Akolothiebewahrung und Jesusüberlieferung im Jakobusbrief, WUNT II / 536, Tübingen 2020, hier ausführliche und klare Darstellung der Forschungsgeschichte und der gegenwärtigen Lösungsvorschläge: 5–61 und 63–105 (vgl. die Rezension von K.-W. Niebuhr, RBL 04 / 2022). Kloppenborg spricht jetzt sehr allgemein von »The Fabric of James: The Jewish Bible and the Jesus Tradition«: Kloppenborg, James, 61–81. Dabei fasst er die Bibel Israels »and related documents« zu den »cultural resources« von Jak zusammen (62).

[216] Dazu Dibelius, Jak, 43–45: LXX, Sir, TestXII, Philo.

76 Einleitung

mentiert und kommentiert.[217] Er geht davon aus, dass Jak mindestens folgende synoptischen Logien aus Q (1.–6.), Mk / Mt (7.), Mt (8.) und Lk (9. und 10.) kannte[218]:

1. Mt 5,3=Lk 6,20 — Jak 2,5 — Seligpreisung der Armen
2. Mt 5,11–12=Lk 6,22–23 — Jak 1,2 (1,12) — Seligpreisung der Verfolgten
3. Mt 7,1–5=Lk 6,37,41–42 — Jak 4,11–12 — Verbot des Richtens
4. Mt 7,24–27=Lk6,47–49 — Jak 1,22–23 — Hörer und Täter
5. Mt 7,7–11=Lk 11,9–13 — Jak 1,5.17; 4,3 — Gott der Geber
6. Mt 6,19–21=Lk 12,33–34 — Jak 5,1–3 — Vergängliche Schätze
7. Mk 11,23=Mt 21,21 — Jak 1,6 — Glaube und Zweifel
8. Mt 5,34 — Jak 5,12 — Verbot des Schwörens
9. Lk 6,24 — Jak 5,1–3 — Wehe über die Reichen
10. Lk 6,25 — Jak 4.9; 5,1 — Wehe über die jetzt Lachenden[219]

Dabei schließt er an Dibelius' Urteil zu der Sonderstellung von Jak 5,12 an[220]:

> Indeed, with the exception of 5.12=Mt 5.33–37, emulating logia without reproducing them is characteristic of him.

Allison verwendet hier den Schlüsselbegriff der *aemulatio* und weist zugleich darauf hin, dass dieser Begriff das Thema so kompliziert macht:

> If an author is deliberately not reproducing his sources but rather creatively rewriting them for his own ends, it may not be so easy to decide when to attribute parallels to design and when to give coincidence its due.[221]

Es ist nochmals wichtig, zu betonen, dass die Art der Verbindungen zwischen Jesustradition und Sätzen aus Jak hypothetisch bleiben muss. Plausibilisierungen können nur gelingen, wenn längere Texte und Themen einbezogen werden. Sonst reduziert sich die Analyse von Traditionen auf Motivforschung. Allison fragt daher auch nach thematischen Parallelen wie Burchard und nach »language that mirrors the Jesus tradition«[222], so dass er in gewisser Weise zu Dibelius' Traditionsbegriff zurückkehrt, aber unter neuen methodischen Vorzeichen. Die Möglichkeit, dass die Jesustradition und die entsprechenden Jakobustexte jeweils unabhängig voneinander auf gemeinsame alttestamentliche und frühjüdische Traditionen zurückgreifen, erörtert er allerdings nicht. In Bezug auf die Kenntnis von Evangelien bleibt er sehr

---

[217] ALLISON, Jak, 56–62.
[218] ALLISON, Jak, 56 f.
[219] KLOPPENBORG, James, 72, zählt mit Deppe und Hartin 21 Parallelen auf.
[220] DIBELIUS, Jak, 46.
[221] ALLISON, Jak, 57. Allison verweist auf KLOPPENBORG, Emulation (ALLISON, Jak, 57, Anm. 306).
[222] ALLISON, Jak, 58.

B. Der Text. Historische, literarische und thematische Charakteristik

vorsichtig.[223] Insgesamt geht Allison von der Prägung des Jakobus durch das frühchristliche Milieu und hier besonders durch die Jesustradition aus. Das Fehlen von *Zitaten* aus der Jesustradition erklärt Allison mit dem nach seinem Urteil jüdischen und judenchristlichen Adressatenprofil:

> Our text does not appeal to Jesus as an authority because Jesus was not an authority for all of the envisaged audience.[224]

Metzner behandelt das Thema trotz seiner Orthonymie-These, die ihn in gewisser Weise am ehesten von der Pflicht oder mindestens der Aufgabe entlastet, Jesustradition in Jak zu finden, noch einmal sehr ausführlich unter Einbeziehung der Forschung der letzten Generation und des Allisonkommentars.[225] Er macht deutlich, wie weit Hypothesen zu Jak von Hypothesen zur Entstehung und zum Text von Q und Mt abhängen und letztlich mit der Einschätzung der Geschichte der Jesusüberlieferung im Ganzen verbunden sind – einer Einschätzung, die allerdings nicht vom Jakobusbrief aus geleistet werden kann. Für erfolgreich hält Metzner mit Allison das Konzept der *aemulatio* (Quintilian, inst. 10,5.5[226]), das John S. Kloppenborg in die Jakobusexegese eingeführt hat[227] und auf das Metzner sich noch konsequenter als Allison stützt. Metzner geht wie Allison davon aus, dass »Jakobus die in den Gemeinden verbreitete Jesustradition nicht einfach zitiert, sondern *moduliert und paraphrasiert*.« Dabei benutzt Jakobus anders als Q und als die Evangelien die Tradition eben nicht als »Quellen, die sie leicht edieren«, sondern »als Ressource[228], die er nicht wortwörtlich übernimmt, sondern kreativ neu formuliert«.[229] Metzner weist mit Recht besonders auf die Nähe zu »Stoffe(n) der Bergpredigt« und auf eine besondere Nähe zu Mt[230] hin – die sich allerdings eben auf die Bergpredigt beschränkt:

Jak 1,17<Mt 7,11   Gott gibt denen, die bitten
Jak 2,5<Mt 5,3.5   Gott hat die Armen erwählt
Jak 2,13<Mt 5,7   Selig sind die Barmherzigen

---

[223] So bleibt auch die Möglichkeit, Jakobus habe Mt gekannt, für ihn eine Hypothese (ALLISON, Jak, 61).
[224] ALLISON, Jak, 59. Dies Urteil ist wenig wahrscheinlich.
[225] METZNER, Jak, 34–37, besonders die Liste »der häufigsten Parallelen, die in der Forschung benannt werden« (35). S. 35, Anm. 291, stellt Metzner die Hypothesen zur Benutzung von Q und Mt durch Jak zusammen.
[226] QUINTILIAN, inst. X 5,5: neque ego paraphrasin esse interpretationem tantum volo, sed circa eosdem sensus certamen atque aemulationem. Auch möchte ich nicht, daß die Paraphrase (der Dichtung) nur eine Übersetzung liefert, sondern es soll um die gleichen Gedanken ein Wettkampf und Wetteifern stattfinden. Übersetzung: Marcus Fabius Quintilianus, Ausbildung des Redners Zwölf Bücher. Lateinisch und Deutsch. Herausgegeben und übersetzt von Helmut Rahn, Darmstadt 2011, unveränderter Nachdruck der 3. Auflage 1995, Teil II, S. 517.
[227] KLOPPENBORG, Emulation.
[228] Vgl. die Formulierung von BURCHARD, Jak, 17.
[229] METZNER, Jak, 36.
[230] Ebd.

Jak 3,18<Mt 5,9	Selig sind die Friedenstifter
Jak 5,2 f<Mt 6,19 f	Gegen das Schätzesammeln
Jak 5,9a<Mt 7,1	Gegen das Richten
Jak 5,12<Mt 5,33–37	Gegen das Schwören

2.2.5

Zusammengefasst bleiben drei Punkte bedenkenswert, die nicht isoliert voneinander bedacht werden können. *Erstens* gibt es auffallende Übereinstimmungen zwischen der synoptischen ethischen Jesustradition und dem Jakobusbrief. Gleichzeitig begegnen die vielfältigen christologischen Traditionen der Synoptiker bei Jak *nicht*. *Zweitens* sind nur sehr wenige Logien aus der synoptischen Jesustradition betroffen. Das gilt auch für Q und die Bergpredigt, auf die Kloppenborg als Bezugstexte hinweist. Eine umfangreichere Bezugnahme des Jakobus auf die synoptischen Evangelien lässt sich nicht nachweisen.[231] *Drittens* zitiert Jakobus anders als Paulus keine Herrenworte trotz seiner Nähe zur ethischen Jesustradition.[232]

Drei miteinander verwandte Erklärungen bieten sich hier an: (1) *aemulatio*, (2) Paränese, (3) das Briefformat. (1) Nach der *aemulatio*-Hypothese hat Jakobus die Herrenworttradition literarisch intentional im Sinne der *aemulatio* verwandelt und zitiert deshalb nicht.[233] Das impliziert, dass Jesuslogien für Jakobus nicht autoritative »Herrenworte« waren, deren Wortlaut feststand, sondern paränetische Tradition bzw. ethisches Material, das er literarisch variierte und überbot. *Aemulatio* lässt sich häufig nicht zweifelsfrei nachweisen, passt aber zu dem anspruchsvollen Stil des Jak und stellt ein wichtiges methodisches Instrument im Zusammenhang der Frage nach Jesustradition bei Jak dar. (2) Allison weist auf Untersuchungen zur Paränese hin:

> Since paraenesis …, is not argument but exhortation, sources are not usually cited.[234]

Die Benutzung von LXX-Zitaten im paränetischen Zusammenhang des Jak macht diese Annahme aber eher unwahrscheinlich. (3) Am ehesten lässt sich vor dem Hintergrund der dargestellten Forschungen eine dritte Erklärung plausibel machen, die die *aemulatio*-Hypothese weiterdenkt und mit der literarischen Gattung des *Briefes* verbindet: Die Jesustradition wird in den Erzählungen der *Evangelien* gesammelt, die frühchristlichen *Briefe* transportieren demgegenüber nicht primär Jesustraditi-

---

[231] Vgl. dazu Allison, Jak, 57 mit Anm. 306: Hinweis auf J. S. Kloppenborg / R. J. Bauckham, James and Jesus, in: B. Chilton / J. Neusner (Hg.), The Brother of Jesus: James the Just and His Mission, Louisville 2001, 100–137.

[232] O. Wischmeyer, Paulus als Hermeneut, 71–94.

[233] Vgl. dazu auch Metzner, Jak, 37 mit Anm. 303: »Jakobus kennzeichnet seine Stoffe nicht als Herrenworte, weil Paraphrasen in antiken Texten nicht auf die Herkunft von Vorgängertexten verweisen und voraussetzen, dass die Hörer und Leser die Quellen kennen«.

[234] Allison, Jak, 58 f.

B. Der Text. Historische, literarische und thematische Charakteristik

on[235], sondern sind die literarische Form für die Entwicklung der Ethik, Theologie und Institutionenleitung der frühchristlichen Gemeindeleiter und Lehrer unter Zuhilfenahme verschiedener Traditionen, zu denen auch Jesustraditionen gehören, die aber anders als in den Evangelien weder quantitativ noch normativ anderen Traditionen übergeordnet sind. Diese Erklärung verzichtet auf kausale Hypothesen und geht rein deskriptiv vor. Welche Gründe diese Zweiteilung der Geschichte der Jesustradition hat, ist damit nicht gesagt. Im Ergebnis haben wir es jedenfalls in Jak im Hinblick auf die Jesustradition mit einer literarischen Strategie des Autors zu tun, der seine Paränese nicht durch Herrenworte autorisiert, sondern ein *eigenes* ethisch-literarisches Schreiben ausarbeitet. Der Autor wählt für seine Gemeindeermahnung das Briefformat, das es ihm erlaubt, selbständig zu argumentieren, wobei er zugleich auf seine Kenntnis der Jesustradition und mindestens einiger Paulusbriefe zurückgreift.[236]

Eine vierte kurze Beobachtung sei hier angeschlossen: Die literarische Bildung des Verfassers bezieht sich ausschließlich auf die Literatur Israels, wie die Analyse der Zitate und Allusionen zeigt. Vergleicht man die literarische Bildung des Jakobus mit Philo und Josephus[237], wird der eingeschränkte Radius des Jakobus sehr deutlich.

2.3 Sprache. Stil. Metaphern. Kleine Formen

Besondere Aufmerksamkeit verdienen die literarischen Milieus, an denen der Brief in Sprache und Stil sowie in seinen Formen und seiner Argumentation partizipiert. Sprache und Stil des Jak sind häufig ausführlich untersucht und von den Kommentatoren dargestellt worden (2.3.1). Jüngst sind wichtige Spezialuntersuchungen zu Lexikon[238], Ethopoiie, Rhythmus, sowie zur Metaphorik hinzugekommen (2.3.2). Weiter tragen Untersuchungen zu den kleinen literarischen Formen und zur Diatribe zur Konturierung des literarischen Profils des Jak bei (2.3.3).

2.3.1

Bereits die Kommentare von Mayor und Ropes haben die Standards für die Behandlung nicht nur von Sprache, Stil und Metaphorik, sondern auch von Fragen des Prosarhythmus des Jak gesetzt und müssen immer noch für diese Themen her-

---

[235] Schon Paulus setzt nur sehr *selten* Herrenworte ein und versteht sich offensichtlich nicht als Tradent der Jesusüberlieferung. Zur Entstehungszeit des Jak existieren bereits Evangelien, die diese Aufgabe erfüllen.

[236] Vgl. dazu oben zu Paulusallusionen und zu ALLISON, Jak, 60.

[237] Vgl. zu Philo und Josephus: E. KOSKENNIEMI, Greek writers and philosophers in Philo and Josephus: a study of their secular education and educational ideals, Studies in Philo of Alexandria 9, Leiden 2019 (vgl. die kritische Rez. von M. R. Niehoff, BMClR 2022.05.19).

[238] J. S. KLOPPENBORG, The Author of James and His Lexical Profile, in: Who was ›James‹?, 197–217, 198 Anm. 4 gibt eine ausführliche Bibliographie. Vgl. auch KLOPPENBORG, James, 30 f., zu »alexandrinischem« Vokabular, 31–34, zu römischem Vokabular. KLOPPENBORG, James, 35, relativiert selbst diese Lokalzuschreibungen, indem er auf den Verkehr zwischen den Metropolen hinweist. Die lokale Zuordnung bestimmter Vokabeln in der frühkaiserzeitlichen Welt überdehnt die Aussagekraft der Lexikographie.

80 Einleitung

angezogen werden. Besonders Joseph B. Mayor hat in Kapitel 8 und 9 seines Kommentars Grammatik[239] und Wortschatz[240] sowie Stilzüge (rhetorische Figuren und Rhythmus)[241] umfassend dargestellt. In seiner Wortschatzanalyse stellt er die *hapax legomena*[242] des Jak im neutestamentlichen Zusammenhang sowie 13 Neologismen[243] zusammen. Die Stilzüge resümiert er wie folgt:

> These would be best summed up in the terms, energy, vivacity, and, as conducive to both, vividness of representation.[244]

Vividness steht vor allem für die Metaphorik[245] und für die literarischen Szenen z. B. in Kap. 2, außerdem für die Kürze und Wucht der Paränese in Kap. 4 und 5. Sigurvin Jónsson hat die Stilkriterien von Dionysius Halikarnassus zusammengestellt und die Bedeutung, die *vividness* bei Dionysius hat, unterstrichen.[246]

Dass auch eine gründliche Sprachanalyse nicht zu eindeutigen Ergebnissen bei der Bestimmung des Autorenprofils führt, zeigt ein Vergleich der Kommentare von Mayor und Allison. Dale Allison, der die Tradition der englischsprachigen Kommentare mit ihrem großen Interesse an Philologie fortsetzt, beschreibt das Griechisch des Autors ähnlich wie Mayor, setzt dann aber den Verfasser in die griechischsprachige Diaspora um die Jahrhundertwende statt wie Mayor in das Jerusalem zur Zeit des Herrenbruders. Diese Divergenz in der Einschätzung zeigt die Grenzen nicht nur der lokalen, sondern auch der historischen Kompetenz semantischer Analysen. Allison hat die gesamte Thematik nochmals detailliert dokumentiert und kritische Listen der Stichwortanschlüsse, Wortspiele, Alliterationen, Parallelismen, aphoristischen Stilzüge[247], antithetischen Formulierungen, Semitismen und diatribischen Elemente[248] erstellt.[249] Wichtig ist sein Hinweis, dass sich

---

[239] MAYOR, Jak, clxx–clxxxiv.

[240] MAYOR, Jak, cxc–cxciii.

[241] MAYOR, Jak, cxciii–ccii. Mayor listet die Beispiele von Paronomasie, Alliteration und Homoioteleuta sowie Asyndeton auf. Ausführlich bespricht er Syntax und Prosarhythmus (dazu s. unten). ALLISON, Jak, reduziert die Neologismen auf: ἀνεμιζόμενος (1,6), θρησκός (1,26), χρυσοδακτύλιος (2,2) und ἀνέλεος (2,13). Weitere Wörter, die Allison nicht als Neologismen wertet s. S. 85, Anm. 443.

[242] Dazu jetzt aus textlinguistischer Sicht vertieft GANSLMAYER, Autor, 144–150, besonders S. 147 zu der autorenspezifischen Bedeutung der Hapaxe.

[243] MAYOR, Jak, cxci.

[244] MAYOR, Jak, ccii. Ganz ähnlich ROPES, Jak, 24–27: »The vivacity, simple directness, and general attractiveness and effectiveness of his style are conspicuous even to the reader of the English version« (24). Ropes weist besonders auf die Nähe zur LXX hin und spricht von »a distinct Biblical flavour to the style in general«. Dabei denkt er besonders an die Genitivverbindungen in 1,25; 2,4; 1,25 / 2,12; 3,6; 1,23 (26).

[245] Liste der Metaphern bei MAYOR, Jak, cxciv. Bezugsfelder: ländliches Leben, Meer, Sterne, häusliches Leben, öffentliches Leben. Weiteres s. unten.

[246] JÓNSSON, James, 156–164.

[247] ALLISON, Jak, 85: 1,17.19; 2,13b.17.26; 3,16; 4,47. 8. 10.17; 5,16b.

[248] ALLISON, Jak, 88, kritisch gegenüber ROPES, Jak, 10–18. Allison reduziert Ropes' Beispiele, möchte aber doch die Gattungsbezeichnung der Diatribe beibehalten. Dazu s. unten.

[249] ALLISON, Jak, 81–88.

B. Der Text. Historische, literarische und thematische Charakteristik 81

die genannten Stilzüge im gesamten Brief finden. Daher urteilt er in Bezug auf die Sprache (implizit gegen Dibelius) zutreffend:

> James was not just a collector but also an author.[250]

2.3.2

Gegenwärtig liegen neue *Spezialstudien* zu (1) Lexikon, (2) Ethopoiie, (3) Rhythmus, (4) Metapher und (5) Stil vor, die hier kurz vorgestellt werden.

(1) John S. Kloppenberg bestätigt und vertieft Allisons Sprach- und Stilanalyse noch einmal in seiner computerbasierten Spezialuntersuchung des *Lexikons* des Jak.[251] Er wertet die Einzelanalysen zunächst in Bezug auf die *historische* Verfasserfrage aus. Dabei wiederholt er Allison: Aus sprachlichen Gründen verbietet sich eine Verfasserschaft durch den Herrenbruder. Stattdessen plädiert Kloppenborg für eine Entstehung des Jak im frühen 2. Jahrhundert außerhalb Jerusalems, vielleicht in Rom.[252] Er verortet den Verfasser präzise in dem Sprachmilieu des literarisch ambitionierten Diasporajudentums und frühen Christentums:

> The point is that whether James employs such common terms as ἀκατάστατος, πηδάλιον, κυβερνήτης and δαμάζω, or rare terms like δίψυχος or χαλιναγωγέω, he uses these terms in the registers of philosophical discourse that concern the therapy of the self, and the control of both the passions and the product of the passions, especially speech … It should be obvious by now that owing to James' use of the rhetorical practice of *aemulatio*, his high-register vocabulary, evocations of Homer, and the interest in philosophical psychagogy, it is virtually inconceivable that the author is James of Jerusalem.[253]

(2) Ebenso wichtig sind Kloppenborgs Überlegungen zu dem Zusammenhang zwischen der anspruchsvollen Sprache und der Verfasser*fiktion*: Ist es plausibel, den Herrenbruder wie einen gebildeten Diasporajuden schreiben zu lassen? Die Lösung findet er hier im Anschluss an die Dissertation von Sigurvin Jónsson in der *Ethopoiie*.[254] Kloppenborg gibt eine knappe Definition von Ethopoiie:

> At its most general ἠθοποιία refers to the construction of ἦθος in any writing. Rhetorical training involved constructing speeches that might have been spoken on either well known occasions by notable figures.[255]

---

[250] ALLISON, Jak, 85.

[251] KLOPPENBORG, The Author of James.

[252] KLOPPENBORG, The Author of James, 198.

[253] KLOPPENBORG, The Author of James, 206. In Bezug auf das psychagogische Vokabular knüpft Kloppenborg auch an einen seiner Aufsätze an: J. S. KLOPPENBORG, James 1:2–15 and Hellenistic Psychagogy, NT 52, 2010, 37–71. Zur Kritik an Kloppenborg s. o.

[254] Dazu zuletzt: JÓNSSON, The Letter of James as Ethopoeia, in: Who was ›James‹?, 371–389. Jónsson weist in seinem Fazit darauf hin, dass die Verbindung von Sprache und Ethos literarische und sachliche Autorität aufbaut (386).

[255] KLOPPENBORG, The Author of James, 207.

82 Einleitung

Kloppenborg fragt, welch Ethos für Jakobus den Herrenbruder in den Augen des Verfassers angemessen sein könnte und antwortet:

> Ethos of James had to be established by two means: recollection of what was commonly known about James of Jerusalem, and the construction of ethos appropriate to the type of discourse represented by James.[256]

Kloppenborg bezieht sich auf die zweite Möglichkeit und findet anders als Metzner wichtige Charakteristika des Herrenbruders von Jak 1,1 über die Schriftzitate des Jak bis zu der antipaulinischen Sach-Polemik in Kap. 2. Aus der Perspektive seiner eingehenden Sprachanalyse kommt er zu folgendem Schluss, mit dem der gegenwärtige Stand der Sprachanalyse des Jak überzeugend markiert ist:

> While we might find ›James‹ use of high register vocabulary unrealistic and incongruous, the pseudepigraphical writer's construction of James as a teacher, and indeed as the head of a Jesus-school, required him to have ›James‹ speak in a register appropriate to a teacher and to express an ἦθος appropriate to such a figure.[257]

(3) Besondere exegetische Beachtung hat der Hexameter in 1,17 gefunden[258], eine Versart, die in der antiken jüdischen Literatur nicht unbekannt ist.[259] Dass Jakobus in seinem Brief einen Hexameter verwendet, zeigt seine literarische Ambition. George Hinge analysiert Jak 1,17 und stellt den Vers in den größeren Zusammenhang der Klauseln des Briefes im Vergleich mit griechischer Prosa. Er kommt zu dem Resultat:

> There can be no doubt that the author of the Epistle of James was extremely conscious about his style. The many rhetorical and stylistic figures and the preference for short rhythmical clauses have not escaped the notice of the commentators, and even though we find syntactical constructions that are alien to the rules of good Classical (and Atticist) prose, the language of the text is more idiomatic and polished than most New Testament Greek.[260]

Abschließend bringt er den wichtigen Aspekt des mündlichen Vortrags ins Spiel:

> Yet, it is evident that these texts were not written for the eye but for the ear. A person who had learned how to write in Greek would automatically try to give his text what he believed was an agreeable form. So, with the highly polished rhythmical prose and with

---

[256] KLOPPENBORG, The Author of James, 211.

[257] KLOPPENBORG, The Author of James, 215.

[258] Zum Hexameter und zur rhythmischen Prosa bei Jak vgl. G. HINGE, The Hexameter in James 1:17: Metrical Forms in Graeco-Roman Prose Literature Between Emulation and Quotation in: Who was ›James‹?, 239–277.

[259] Buch 3 der Sib: Sibyllinische Weissagungen. Griechisch-deutsch. Auf der Grundlage der Ausgabe von A. Kurfeß, hg. und neu übersetzt von J.-D. GAUGER, Düsseldorf/Zürich 1998, 66–111.

[260] HINGE, Hexameter, 272. Ausführlich JÓNSSON, James, 120–132.

B. Der Text. Historische, literarische und thematische Charakteristik

the many explicit and implicit quotations, the author James meets the expectations of his Hellenized audience.[261]

(4) Großes Interesse haben immer die sprachlichen Bilder, Metaphern, Vergleiche und Beispiele erweckt. Den entsprechenden Darstellungen in den Kommentaren hat Michael Glöckner eine detaillierte monographische Studie hinzugefügt[262], in der das gesamte metaphorische Inventar des Jak unter den theologischen Stichworten Theologie, Anthropologie und Ethik sowie Soteriologie und Eschatologie analysiert wird. Jakobus benutzt ein außergewöhnlich reiches Spektrum von Metaphern aus den Bereichen Kultur, Natur, Technik, Militär und Wirtschaft.[263] Glöckner betont diese Breite der Bildspenderbereiche und verweist auf zahlreiche Parallelen zur frühjüdischen und frühkaiserzeitlichen ethischen Literatur.

(5) Elisa Chiorrini hat die Synonyme des Jak untersucht.[264] Ihre Analyse zeigt, dass die zahlreichen Synonyme vor allem aus rhetorischen Gründen gesetzt werden.

2.3.3

Auf weitere Qualitäten des Briefes, die sich stilistisch der literarischen Diatribe zuordnen lassen, haben jetzt Alicia Batten und Lorenzo Scornaienchi[265] vertieft hingewiesen. Alicia Batten lenkt den Blick auf Typendarstellungen – der Reiche, der Arme, der Kaufmann – und Szenarien wie den Vorfall der Bevorzugung des Reichen in der Versammlung (Jak 2). Sie verortet diese Darstellungsformen in der antiken Satire:

> This is not to say that James constitutes satire, but simply that there are important satirical aspects to the letter. I will borrow the notion of »masks« or *personae* that one finds in studies of satirical authors.[266]

Lorenzo Scornaienchi rückt das Thema der literarischen Polemik in den Vordergrund: Jakobus arbeitet mit den polemischen Mitteln von Invektiven, ungenannten Gegnern (τίς,), Interlokutoren, Antithesen, gegenständigen Typen, rhetorischen Fragen und Drohszenarien.[267] Batten und Scornaienchi tragen mit ihren Untersuchungen zur Konturierung von Stil und kleinen literarischen Formen im Jak bei. Sie schaffen neue Parameter für das Thema der kleinen literarischen Formen in Jak,

---

[261] HINGE, Hexameter, 273.

[262] M. GLÖCKNER, Bildhafte Sprache im Jakobusbrief. Form, Inhalt und Erschließungspotential der metaphorischen Rede einer frühchristlichen Schrift, ABIG 69, Leipzig 2021. Einführung in die Forschungsgeschichte: 21–38.

[263] GLÖCKNER, Sprache, 63.

[264] E. CHIORRINI, Iterazioni sinonimiche nella Lettera di Giacomo: Studio lessicografico ed esegetico, ASBF 89, Mailand 2020 (vgl. die Rezension von L. Scornaienchi, RBL 07 / 2022).

[265] A. J. BATTEN, James the Dramatist, in: Who was ›James‹?, 313–330; SCORNAIENCHI, Polemik im Jakobusbrief.

[266] A. J. BATTEN, Dramatist, 314.

[267] SCORNAIENCHI, Polemik, 339 f. Zu Scornaienchis These, der Jak sei gegen »Person und Theologie des Paulus« gerichtet (365), siehe unten.

das seit Dibelius kontrovers verhandelt wird. Jak muss in dem Spannungsbogen zwischen diatribischen Stilzügen und Formen einerseits (1) und Einzelspruch und Spruchreihe (2) andererseits diskutiert werden.

(1) Wie weit Jak als *Diatribe* zu verstehen ist, wird seit Ropes und Dibelius diskutiert. Dibelius differenziert zwischen der literarischen Gattung und dem literarischen Stil. Beide sind für Dibelius entscheidende Hilfen bei dem Verstehen des Jakobusbriefes »als Ganze(n)«.[268] Er verwendet den Begriff der Diatribe für Stilzüge und für einzelne Textabschnitte: Für ihn besteht das »Kernstück des Jak, 2,1–3,12« aus »drei abhandlungsartigen Ausführungen«[269]: vom Ansehen der Person (2,1–13), von Glauben und Taten (2,14–26) und von der Zunge (3,1–12). Hier findet er »die Art der Diatribe, wie wir sie vor allem aus Epiktet und in anderer Gestaltung beispielsweise aus Philos Schriften kennen«.[270] »Diatribe« als literarische Bestimmung des gesamten Jak zu verwenden, lehnt Dibelius aber ab, weil er den Brief als Ganzes eher als »Spruchsammlung« denn als »Abhandlung« sieht.[271] Allison geht auf diese Differenzierung nicht ein. Er nimmt mit Bezug auf Ropes »Diatribe« als stilistischen Rahmenbegriff für Jak deutlicher in Anspruch. Die neuen Spezialuntersuchungen zu den satirischen Zügen und der scharfen Polemik des Briefes unterstützen das Urteil von Ropes und Allison[272] sowie von Stanley Stowers. Stowers hat bereits 1992 den größeren literaturgeschichtlichen und gattungsgeschichtlichen Rahmen für diatribische Elemente in Jak gezeichnet:

> In the diatribe, then, early Christian speakers and writers adapted a style of teaching and exhortation which had developed in circles of philosophical teachers and their students. By the 1st century A. D. this style had been widely influential in moral literature and philosophical rhetoric. In the NT the style of the diatribe is most important in Paul's letters, especially in Romans, and the epistle of James. An understanding of its features and functions is invaluable for the exegesis of these texts.[273]

Sein Urteil, das auch Licht auf das Verhältnis des Jak zu den Paulusbriefen wirft, wird durch die neuen Untersuchungen von Batten und Scornaienchi noch plausibler.

(2) Mit dem Verweis auf die stilistische Bedeutung der Diatribe für Jak ist aber Dibelius' Verweis auf die basale *Spruchstruktur* des Jak und damit auch die Frage nach den kleinen Formen im Brief noch nicht ausdiskutiert. Dibelius versteht den *Spruch* als das Rückgrat der unterschiedlichen kleinen Formen, die für ihn großen-

---

[268] DIBELIUS, Jak, 1.

[269] DIBELIUS, Jak, 14.

[270] Ebd.

[271] DIBELIUS, Jak, 57. Damit wendete sich Dibelius gegen die Verwendung von »Diatribe« als Gattungsbezeichnung.

[272] ALLISON, Jak, 88: »An early Christian could borrow rhetorical features from diatribe«.

[273] S. K. STOWERS, Art. Diatribe, ABD 2, New York 1992, 190–193, 193 (Lit.). Vgl. auch W. CAPELLE / H. I. MARROU, Art. Diatribe, RAC 3, 1957, 990–1009.

B. Der Text. Historische, literarische und thematische Charakteristik

teils Spruchreihen sind. Er findet in Jak neben den kleinen Diatriben vor allem Spruchreihen (1,2–18; 1,19–27; 5,7–20) und Spruchgruppen (3,13–4,12; 4,13–5,6), die nach den stilistischen Vorgaben der frühjüdischen und frühchristlichen Traditionen formuliert sind, denen sie entstammen.[274] Dibelius' Beobachtungen zur Bedeutung des Spruches in Jak bleiben wichtig, besonders im Zusammenhang mit den Beobachtungen zur synoptischen Tradition in Jak. Die Bezeichnungen, die Dibelius wählt, sind aber – gerade für Kap. 4 und 5 – unbefriedigend. Hier muss neu nach den *kleinen Formen* gefragt werden, die die Lebhaftigkeit der Textur des Briefes bewirken. Der Text geht nirgendwo in die Breite wie beispielsweise 1Clem oder spielt mit Wiederholungen wie Sirach. *Brevitas* ist nicht nur im Stil, sondern auch in den Darstellungsformen vorherrschend.[275] 4,1–6; 4,7–12; 4,13–17 und 5,1–6 sind thematisch konzise Gerichtsreden an die »Weltfreunde« (4,4), die Sünder (4,8), an die planungssüchtigen Kaufleute (5,13) und an die Reichen (5,1). Jakobus nimmt Motive und Themen aus der spruchbasierten Weisheit auf, bearbeitet sie aber stilistisch und thematisch im Rahmen zeitgenössischer argumentativer Prosa-Briefliteratur, darin vor allem Paulus ähnlich, wie ein Vergleich von Röm 2 und Jak 2 zeigt. Eine vergleichende Studie zu Sir 28,2–26 und der kleinen Ekphrasis über die Zunge in Jak 3,1–12 kommt zu folgendem Ergebnis:

> The text of Sirach is much more extensive than Jas 3. The sentence structure inhibits argumentative progress in favor of self-contained and literarily ambitious text units (stichs), based on individual sentences. Ben Sira emphasizes repetition, doubling, enumeration of examples, and the accumulation of linguistic images even in a single verse. In short, Sirach cultivates a style that seeks to convince through vividness, breadth, repetition and the accumulation of examples. James, on the other hand, develops an argumentative style. Examples are clearly distinguished from argumentative and paraenetic sentences (v. 5). The text culminates in rhetorical questions. Through brevity and thematic concentration, James creates a text that is immediately convincing. The rapid and pointed argumentation of James contrasts with the rather broad and leisurely accumulation of sayings in Sirach, who loves to go into details and does not omit any possible related motif.[276]

Der Jakobusbrief ist also ein Beispiel für argumentativ-paränetische *Literarisierung* der Spruchdichtung. Das Urteil von Dibelius, es handele sich um eine Art Sammlung paränetischen Materials, wird im vorliegenden Kommentar daher nicht geteilt, wenn auch Dibelius' Beobachtungen zur unterliegenden Spruchtextur, die sich aus der weisheitlichen Literatur Israels und der Jesustradition herleitet, weiterhin Gewicht haben.

---

[274] DIBELIUS, Jak, 14: Spruchgruppen: »kleinere Abschnitte, die in sich geschlossen sind«, Spruchreihen: lose Kombination thematisch verwandter Sprüche.

[275] Zu *brevitas* siehe oben.

[276] WISCHMEYER, The Book of Ben Sira From a Reception-Historical Perspective, 298.

2.3.4

Zusammengefasst: der Brief weist in Lexikon, Syntax und Stilzügen in den Bereich des gehobenen Griechisch der frühen Kaiserzeit. Der Verfasser schöpft vor allem aus Septuagintawortschatz, -wendungen und -stilzügen, aber auch aus philosophischem und poetischem Vokabular. Was entsteht, ist eine sorgfältige Mischung zwischen gut verständlicher, häufig topischer, zugleich aber literarisch nicht unanspruchsvoller paränetischer argumentativer Prosa und ständigem Rückgriff auf Vokabular und Metaphorik der Septuaginta. Wortschatz – gekennzeichnet durch gewählte Begriffe, *hapax legomena* und Neologismen – und Stil, vor allem die durchgehende Metaphorik und Synonymik, sind bemerkenswert und auf jeden Fall im Vergleich mit ähnlichen frühchristlichen Texten ambitioniert. Diatribische Stilelemente und kleine diatribische Formen durchziehen den gesamten Brief. Der Text basiert auf unterschiedlichen Form- und Motivtraditionen aus den Bereichen der Septuaginta, vor allem antiker jüdischer Weisheitsschriften, und frühchristlicher Jesustradition und verarbeitet diese zu einem einheitlichen literarischen Brief vor allem ethischen Inhalts auf einem guten literarischen Niveau. Der Brief gehört literaturgeschichtlich in den Zusammenhang der sich rasch entwickelnden nachpaulinischen frühchristlichen Briefliteratur, behauptet in diesem literarischen Zusammenhang aber einen eigenen Platz, der ebenso durch eine gewisse stilistische Qualität wie durch die formale Nähe sowohl zum frühchristlichen Gemeindebrief wie zum jüdischen Diasporabrief ausgezeichnet ist. Es handelt sich mit Allison um Autorenliteratur, nicht um eine Sammlung von Traditionen, wie Dibelius annahm.

2.4 Gliederung

Die Diskussion um Sprache, Stil und kleine Formen führt weiter zur Analyse der Binnenstruktur des Textes und damit zur Gliederung. Die Einheitlichkeit des Briefes wird bei den Kommentatoren vorausgesetzt, die Gliederung ist dagegen kontrovers. Seit Luther wird bekanntlich immer wieder eine stringente Gliederung des Briefes bestritten.[277] Rainer Metzner schließt sich dem bereits dargestellten Vorschlag von Dibelius an, in Kap. 2–4 »kleinere, oft assoziativ miteinander verbundene Essays (Abhandlungen)« zu finden, wobei besonders für 3,1–4,12 »ein engerer Zusammenhang« besteht.[278] Allison bleibt noch allgemeiner:

> This commentator largely agrees with Bauckham. 1.1 is the prescript, 1,2–27 serves as an introduction of sorts, and 2,1–5,20 is the main body, or at least the rest of the letter[279] –

---

[277] Die Gliederungsvorschläge sind bei ALLISON, Jak, 76–81 (besonders 77, Anm. 415), und bei METZNER, Jak, 30–32, zusammengestellt. Vgl. auch J.S. KLOPPENBORG, James, 51–58. Vgl. auch F. PROSINGER, Das eingepflanzte Wort der Wahrheit, SBS 243, Stuttgart 2019 (Rez. O. Wischmeyer, RBL 12/2020).

[278] METZNER, Jak, 31.

[279] ALLISON, Jak, 78. Allison verweist auf R.J. BAUCKHAM, Wisdom, 61–67. Bauckhams Detailanalyse (BAUCKHAM, Wisdom, 63f) folgt Allison nicht (ALLISON, Jak, 78, Anm. 418).

B. Der Text. Historische, literarische und thematische Charakteristik

eine reduktionistische bzw. pessimistische Einschätzung, der der vorliegende Kommentar nicht folgt.

2.4.1

Gliederungsvorschlag: Ein Überblick zeigt, dass die Exegeten über die grobe Textaufteilung relativ einig sind. 1,2–27; 2,1–13; 2,1–26; 3,1–12; 3,13–18; 4,1–12; 4,13–5,6; (5,12); 5,13–20 werden als »main sections« des Briefes verstanden.[280] Auf der doppelten Grundlage dieser *main sections* und der kleinen Formen und ihrer kommunikativen Pragmatik arbeitet der vorliegende Kommentar mit folgender *sachlicher* Gliederung des Briefes:

Erster Hauptteil: Belehrungen über das richtige Ethos (Geduld in Anfechtungen und Vollkommenheit) für die Christus-gläubigen Gemeinden (Kap. 1)
Adresse: 1,1
A. 1,2–18 Belehrung über die πειρασμοί
1. Texteinheit: 1,2–4 πειρασμοί als Grund zur Freude (*propositio generalis*)
2. Texteinheit: 1,5–8 Warnung vor Zweifel bei der Bitte um Weisheit
3. Texteinheit: 1,9–11 Der Niedrige und der Reiche
4. Texteinheit: 1,12 Seligpreisung
5. Texteinheit: 1,13–15 Diskussion über die Ursache der Versuchungen
6. Texteinheit: 1,16–18 Abschließende Belehrung über Gott als Geber des Guten

B. 1,19–27 Belehrung über das Wort
1. Texteinheit: 1,19–21 Belehrung über das richtige Sprechen
2. Texteinheit: 1,22–25 *Erstes* Fallbeispiel: Hörer des Wortes
3. Texteinheit: 1,26–27 *Zweites* Fallbeispiel: der »Religiöse«, und Resümee

Zweiter Hauptteil: Belehrungen über Ansehen der Person und über das Verhältnis von Glauben und Tun (Kap. 2)
A. 2,1–13 Belehrung über das Ansehen der Person
1. Texteinheit: 2,1–4 *Drittes* Fallbeispiel: Der Arme in der Gemeindeversammlung
2. Texteinheit: 2,5–7 Belehrung über die Behandlung der Armen
3. Texteinheit: 2,8–11 Belehrung über das richtige Halten des Gesetzes
4. Texteinheit: 2,12–13 Abschließende Belehrung über Reden und Tun nach dem Gesetz der Freiheit

B. 2,14–26 Belehrung über Glaube und Taten
1. Texteinheit: 2,14–17 *Viertes* Fallbeispiel
2. Texteinheit: 2,18–19 *Fünftes* Fallbeispiel
3. Texteinheit: 2,20–26 Abschließende Belehrung über das Verhältnis von Glauben und Taten

---

[280] ALLISON, Jak, 80. KLOPPENBORG, James, 55–58, spricht von »local structures«.

Dritter Hauptteil: Warnungen vor Gefahren (Kap. 3)
A. 3,1–12 Warnung vor der Macht der Zunge

B. 3,13–18 Warnung vor irdischer Weisheit

Vierter Hauptteil: Mahn- und Gerichtsreden gegen verschiedene Gruppierungen (4,1–5,6)
A. 4,1–12 Reden gegen Sünder
1. Texteinheit: 4,1–6 Mahnrede gegen »Ehebrecher« und Weltfreunde
2. Texteinheit: 4,7–10 Mahnrede gegen Sünder und Zweiseeler
3. Texteinheit: 4,11–12 Mahnrede gegen das Richten

B. 4,13–17 Rede gegen Kaufleute

C. 5,1–6 Rede gegen Reiche

Schluss: Ratschläge und Schlussbelehrung an die Adressaten und ihre Gemeinden (5,7–20)
1. Texteinheit: 5,7–11 Mahnung zur Geduld
2. Texteinheit: 5,12 Verbot des Schwörens
3. Texteinheit: 5,13–18 Ratschläge zum Gebet
4. Texteinheit: 5,19.20 Schlussbelehrung zur Umkehr

2.4.2
Auswertung: Diese Gliederung verbindet thematische und formale Merkmale und kann dadurch die Binnenstruktur des Briefes nachzeichnen. Der Brief zeigt eine klare Thematik und einen deutlichen Spannungsbogen (1). Gleichzeitig ist er kleinteilig gegliedert – besonders in Kap. 1 (2). Die umfangreicheren Teile, aber auch die kleinen Texteinheiten sind sorgfältig komponiert und werden jeweils deutlich abgeschlossen (3).

(1) Die vier Hauptteile und die Schlussermahnung folgen einem deutlichen *Spannungsbogen*: Situationsanalyse und Themenvorgabe in Teil 1, Belehrung über theologisch-ethische Grundfragen in Teil 2, Warnungen vor Gefahren in Teil 3, spezielle Mahn- und Gerichtsreden in Teil 4, praktische Ratschläge im Schlussteil. Dabei wird sowohl in Teil 4 als auch im Schlussteil zunehmend eine eschatologische Perspektive aufgemacht. Auf die Eschatologie folgt die praktische Perspektive. Den Abschluss bildet eine Septuaginta-nahe Gnome über die Errettung von Sünden. Die *Themen*, über die Jakobus in den Kapiteln 1–3 seine Leserschaft belehrt, sind: richtiges Verhalten in πειρασμοί, richtiger Glaube und Gefahren des Streites. Im Folgenden – Kap. 4 und 5,1–6 – wird der Modus der *Warnung* weitergeführt. Jakobus warnt vor den Gefahren bestimmter Sünden (Freundschaft mit der Welt, »Zweiseeligkeit«, gegenseitiges Verurteilen bzw. »Richten«) und vor dem Verhalten

B. Der Text. Historische, literarische und thematische Charakteristik

bestimmter Gruppen. Schließlich klagt er die Reichen wegen Gewaltausübung und Mord an. In 5,7–20 wendet er sich dem gemeindlichen Leben der Adressaten zu und gibt *Mahnungen und Ratschläge* zu Geduld und Gebet.

(2) Besonderes Interesse gilt Kap. 1. Hier werden Ton und Themen des Briefes gesetzt. 1,2–4 kann als *propositio generalis* gelesen werden.[281] Der Autor verbindet seine Diagnose des Zustandes der Adressaten (Leben in πειρασμοί) mit einer grundsätzlichen Belehrung darüber, wie sie diese Situation deuten und in ihr leben sollen. Er formuliert sein Ziel für die Adressaten: Vollkommenheit. 1,5–18 führt dies zentrale Thema eines Ethos der Geduld und des einfachen Glaubens nach verschiedenen Seiten hinaus. 1,19–27 knüpft an 1,11–18 an, erläutert, was »Geburt durch das Wort der Wahrheit« für die Adressaten bedeutet, verweist nochmals auf die Vollkommenheit (V. 25 und 27a und b) und legt zugleich den Grund für Teil 2 und 3.

Jak weist eine kohärente syntaktische, kommunikative und literarische *Feinstruktur* auf. Verschiedene Elemente stehen nebeneinander: Eine starke Adhäsion wird durch Stichwortanschlüsse, Wiederholungen bzw. Wiederaufnahmen von Lexemen und Themen sowie Parallelismen hergestellt.[282] Denselben Effekt hat das dichte Netz direkter Anreden (»Brüder«), Imperative und diatribischer Gesprächselemente mit Opponenten oder imaginierten Personen, die der Verfasser zur Belehrung und Überzeugung seiner Adressaten benutzt. Argumente, Lehrsätze, Erläuterungen, Begründungen durch Beispiele, imperativische Aufforderungen wechseln einander ab.[283] Zugleich sind die einzelnen Textteile sorgfältig gestaltet und meist klar voneinander abgehoben. Was entsteht, ist ein sehr lebhafter Text, der starke rhetorische Elemente enthält, die im Kommentarteil eigens untersucht werden müssen.

(3) Auffallend sind bei aller epistolaren Homogenität des Jak die klaren Konturen der Einzeltexte (siehe oben). Besonders deutlich sind die *thematischen* Texteinheiten der Kapitel 2–5, die zum Teil als bestimmte literarische Kleinformen gestaltet sind, konturiert: 2,1–7 (Prosopolempsie); 2,8–13 (Gesetz); 2, 14–26 (Glaube und Taten); 3,1–12 (die Zunge, literarische Kleinform: Ekphrasis), 3,13–18 (himmlische und irdische Weisheit, literarische Kleinform: Synkrisis), 4,13–17 (Kaufleute, literarische Kleinform: Mahnrede), 5,1–6 (Reiche, literarische Kleinform: Gerichtsrede), 5,7–11 (Geduld), 5,13–18 (Gebet). Mehrfach werden diese Texte mit Gnomen abgeschlossen: 2,13b; 2,26; 3,12b; 3,18; 4,17; Schluss von 5,11.

---

[281] *Propositio generalis* ist term. techn. der Rhetoriklehre: vgl. ausführlich G. Krapinger, Art. Proposition, HWRh 7, Stuttgart 2005, 307–315. G. Ueding / B. Steinbrink, Grundriß der Rhetorik, Stuttgart ⁵2011, 263, definieren *p.* als Teil der *narratio* wie folgt: »Mit *propositio* bezeichnet man den zusammenfassenden Überblick über das Thema«. Kloppenborg, James, 55 weist darauf hin, dass in Jak 1, 2–5 logisch ein *sorites*, ein Kettenschluss, vorliegt (Ch. Thiel, Art. Kettenschluss, EPhW 2, Stuttgart 1996, 390).

[282] Dazu die Aufstellungen bei Allison, Jak, 80. 82–84.

[283] O. Wischmeyer, Beobachtungen zu Kommunikation, Gliederung und Gattung des Jakobusbriefes, in: D. Sänger / M. Konradt (Hg.), Das Gesetz im frühen Judentum und im Neuen Testament. FS Christoph Burchard zum 75. Geburtstag, NTOA 57, Göttingen / Fribourg 2006, 319–327.

2.5 Rhetorik. Argumentation

Nach der Frage nach der sachlich-thematischen Textgliederung stellt sich die Frage nach der Textkomposition und nach einem möglicherweise rhetorisch durchstrukturierten Aufbau von Jak. Die methodisch erschließende Frage in diesem Zusammenhang gilt nicht primär der *Rekonstruktion der Vorgeschichte des Textes*, die bei Dibelius eine wichtige Rolle spielt, sondern der *Rekonstruktion der Textproduktion* im Sinne des gedanklichen Aufbaus und der rhetorisch-epistolographisch konzipierten Durchführung des Schreibens. *Dass* eine Disposition vorliegt, wurde bereits in der diesem Kommentar zugrunde liegenden Gliederung dokumentiert (gegen Dibelius). *Wie* ist nun der Aufbau zu beschreiben, und wie kam der Verfasser zu dieser Disposition? Hier sind zwei Fragen unter Aufnahme zweier Kategorien aus der Rhetoriklehre auseinanderzuhalten, *inventio* (1) und *dispositio* (2).

(1) Erstens zur *inventio*[284]: Jakobus bezieht sich – wie bereits gezeigt – auf die Septuaginta und auf bekannte Themen aus der frühjüdischen Theologie, aus der Jesustradition und aus der Theologie des Paulus. Ein Beispiel steht für zahlreiche: das Thema der Güte Gottes, die zugleich unmöglich macht, Gott mit dem Bösen in Verbindung zu bringen. Das Thema findet sich bei Philo wie bei Jak. Philo verwendet den Topos öfter ebenso kurz wie Jak gleichsam als philosophisch-theologischen Glaubenssatz in unterschiedlichen Zusammenhängen[285] oder aber in einer längeren, stilistisch gefälligen Argumentation mit Beispielen.[286] Hier bietet sich viel Vergleichsmaterial.[287] Außerdem lässt sich der Verfasser Themen aus den zeitgenössischen frühchristlichen Gemeinden, wie er sie wahrnimmt, vorgeben: Zweifel, mangelnde Demut, mangelnde Fürsorge für die Armen und Schwachen, Prosopolempsie, Streit, Weltlichkeit und Gewalttätigkeit. Diese Wahrnehmungen bearbeitet er literarisch mit Bezugnahmen auf die Septuaginta und mit den Mitteln der epistolaren Protreptik.[288]

(2) Zweitens geht es um die *dispositio*[289], die sich aus der Gliederung ergibt: Ermahnung und Aufbau von Ethos (Kap. 1), theologisch-ethische grundsätzliche Belehrung (Kap. 2), Warnungen (Kap. 3 und 4), Gerichtsandrohung und Ausblick auf das »Kommen des Herrn« (Kap. 5), praktische Ratschläge und Schluss (Kap. 5). Ist hier eine *rhetorische* Disposition zu erkennen? Zunächst ist festzuhalten, dass es

---

[284] Vgl. UEDING / STEINBRINK, Grundriß der Rhetorik, 214: »*Inventio* ist die Bezeichnung für das Auffinden der Gedanken und stofflichen Möglichkeiten, die sich aus einem Thema bzw. aus einer Fragestellung entwickeln lassen.«

[285] Siehe Kommentar zu 1,13.

[286] So in prov. II.

[287] Dazu durchgehend der Kommentar.

[288] Siehe unten zur Ethik.

[289] Vgl. UEDING / STEINBRINK, Grundriß der Rhetorik, 215: »Die gefundenen und nach ihrer Bedeutung und Stichhaltigkeit in Anbetracht der Sachlage abgewogenen Beweisgründe gilt es nunmehr zu ordnen. Diese Anordnung des Stoffs, »eine Form der Zusammenstellung, die in der rechten Weise das Folgende mit dem Vorausgehenden verknüpft« (Quint. VII,1,1), ist Gegenstand der *dispositio*«.

B. Der Text. Historische, literarische und thematische Charakteristik

sich bei Jak nicht um eine religiöse oder ethische Rede, sondern um einen Brief handelt.[290] Eine Anwendung rhetorischer Kategorien kann daher nicht die Frage betreffen, ob es sich im Jak um eine Rede in einer der drei *genera dicendi, genus iudiciale, genus deliberativum* oder *genus demonstrativum* handele – offensichtlich trifft keines der *genera* auf Jak zu. Diskutiert wird aber die Frage, ob die Gliederung des Jak mit rhetorischen Mustern zu erklären sei.

Rainer Metzner gibt anders als die anderen Kommentare eine detaillierte Darstellung der Forschungsvorschläge zu einer rhetorischen Disposition von Jak seit Wilhelm Wuellner.[291] Er selbst sieht aber keinen »Bauplan«[292] in Jak. Er betont stattdessen »das Geflecht der Argumentationsstruktur«, das »mit dem der Traditionsverarbeitung« zusammengeht.[293] Allerdings müssen rhetorische Disposition und Verflechtung traditioneller Motive und Themen einander nicht ausschließen. Unterschiedliche Vorschläge zu einer rhetorischen Gliederung des Jak oder seiner Teiltexte wurden außer von Wuellner vor allem von Ernst Baasland[294], Duane F. Watson[295] und Lauri Thurén[296] gemacht.[297] Dabei werden die Einzelschritte von *exordium, propositio, argumentatio* und *peroratio* entweder auf den ganzen Brief oder auf einzelne Kapitel angewendet.[298] Die Entwürfe enthalten aber keine texterklärenden Einsichten, die über die inhaltlichen und formalen Strukturanalysen hinausführen. Das gilt für die einzelnen rhetorischen Analysen, die in der Tat wenig mehr aussagen, als bereits die Sachgliederung ergibt. John Kloppenborg weist allerdings auf einen wichtigen Punkt hin: auf die »local structures« des Briefes:

> There is a general acknowledgement that 2:1–13, 2:14–26, and 3:1–12 are identifiable argumentative units. The existence of these longer units distinguishes James from the sententious approach to paraenesis that is seen in Ankhsheshonq and Ps-Phocylides, which lack extended argumentative structures extending over several lines.[299]

---

[290] Dazu siehe unten.

[291] Metzner, Jak, 47–58. W. H. Wuellner, Der Jakobusbrief im Licht der Rhetorik und Textpragmatik, LingBibl 43, 1978, 5–66.

[292] Metzner, Jak, 57.

[293] Metzner, Jak, 58.

[294] E. Baasland, Literarische Form, Thematik und geschichtliche Einordnung des Jakobusbriefes, in: ANRW II, 25/2, Berlin 1988, 3646–3684.

[295] D. F. Watson, James 2 in Light of Greco-Roman Schemes of Argumentation, NTS 39, 1993, 94–121; ders., James 3:1–12 and a Classical Pattern of Argumentation, NT 35, 1993, 48–64.

[296] L. Thurén, Risky Rhetoric in James?, NT 37, 1995, 262–284.

[297] Metzner, Jak, 48; Kloppenborg, James, 51–58.

[298] Zu den Einzelheiten Thuréns siehe Kloppenborg, James, 51–54. Kloppenborg scheint vor allem Watsons Vorschlag zu einer rhetorischen Gliederung von 2,1–13; 2,14–26 und 3,1–12 etwas abzugewinnen, resümiert aber zu den verschiedenen Vorschlägen: »Several others have attempted to see James as a coherent rhetorical argument, each proposing different divisions of the text … none of them manages convincingly to compass the entire contents of the letter within the standard five divisions of a rhetorical speech« (54).

[299] Kloppenborg, James, 55.

92   Einleitung

Damit kommt Kloppenborg zu einem differenzierten Fazit, das im vorliegenden Kommentar geteilt wird:

> When James is placed in a more appropriate context, that of moral and paraenetic letters, it is clear that James is among the *better* organized specimens of these ancient moral letters ... James has moved far beyond the sententious nature of Ps-Isocrates' *To Demonicus* and has formulated units of a dozen or so sentences in length, offering four rhetorically structures[300] arguments and several smaller units.[301]

Fazit: eine genaue rhetorische Disposition liegt Jak nicht zugrunde, aber der Umstand, dass rhetorische Dispositionen im Brief im ganzen oder in einzelnen Teilen gefunden werden *können*, weist noch einmal darauf hin, dass sich in Jak sich deutliche Verbindungen zur zeitgenössischen paganen epistolaren, an Rhetorik geschulten Literatur finden lassen. Das heißt: Die Adressaten konnten Jak im Kontext ihrer rhetorischen Bildung lesen.

2.6 Genre

Die Thematik von kleinen Formen, Gliederung, Aufbau und rhetorischer Struktur führt zu der Frage nach dem literarischen Genre von Jak. Von Dibelius bis zu Metzner und Kloppenborg haben sich die Überlegungen zur Gattung des Jak ständig weiterentwickelt und verändert. Gegenwärtig wird mehrheitlich Jak *gegen* Dibelius als *Brief* gelesen (1). Ein besonderer Fokus liegt auf der Diskussion um den Diasporabrief (2). Der vorliegende Kommentar betont gegenüber Metzner und Allison besonders die *literarische* Dimension der Briefadresse (3).

(1) Allison und Metzner lesen Jak als *Brief*, kommen dabei aber zu unterschiedlichen religionsgeschichtlichen und literaturgeschichtlichen Zuordnungen. Rainer Metzner präzisiert die Bestimmung »Brief« gattungsgeschichtlich, indem er Jak mit Verweis auf die spätantiken Briefsteller Pseudo-Demetrius und Pseudo-Libanius den paränetischen Briefen zuordnet und damit die Wende von der inhaltlichen Bestimmung bei Dibelius zur Gattungsbestimmung durchführt.[302] Damit ist nicht gesagt, dass der Verfasser des Jak die Gattung des paränetischen Briefes bewusst gewählt habe, wohl aber, dass sein Schreiben in diesem Zusammenhang gelesen werden konnte und damit auch anschlussfähig an die zeitgenössische Brieflitera-

---

[300] »Structured«?

[301] Kloppenborg, James, 58.

[302] Metzner, Jak, 29 f mit Anm. 247. Metzner bezieht sich auf Pseudo-Demetrius »Briefliche Typen« und Pseudo-Libanius »Briefliche Charaktere«. Textausgabe und Einführung: Lettres pour toutes circonstances. Les traités épistolaires du Pseudo-Libanios et du Pseudo-Démétrios de Phalère. Introduction, traduction et commentaire par Pierre-Louis Malosse, Paris 2004. Während Pseudo-Demetrius den symbouleutischen Brief kennt (Kategorie II bei Pseudo-Demetrius), nennt Pseudo-Libanius die Kategorie des paränetischen Briefes. Vgl. dazu S. K. Stowers, Letter Writing in Greco-Roman Antiquity, Philadelphia 1986, 94–96. Für die antike jüdische Literatur vgl. S. A. Adams, Greek Genres and Jewish Authors: Negotiating Literary Culture in the Greco-Roman Era, Waco 2020, 152–163 (Lit.).

B. Der Text. Historische, literarische und thematische Charakteristik 93

tur war. Metzner hat mit dieser Zuordnung eine wichtige gattungsgeschichtliche Bestimmung gewonnen, die formale und inhaltliche Kriterien berücksichtigt und grundsätzlich über Dibelius hinausführt.

(2) Auch Allison liest Jak als Brief[303], schließt sich aber der seit Tsuji, Niebuhr, Bauckham und anderen Exegeten[304] vertretenen spezielleren Gattungsbestimmung als Diasporabrief an.[305] Er kommt mit Joel White zu dem Urteil:

> In any event, James combines the didactic letter with the diaspora letter; it is a ›paranetically oriented early-Jewish diaspora-letter‹.[306]

Damit stellen sich die Fragen, was eine solche Bezeichnung bedeute[307] und ob und in welcher Hinsicht Jak als Diasporabrief[308] zu bezeichnen sei. Beide Fragen werden von Allison nicht im Einzelnen erörtert. Er stellt zehn formale und inhaltliche Kriterien zusammen[309], die Jak mit den Diasporabriefen teilt. Was sein Vergleich aber nicht enthält, ist der Hinweis auf das *Fehlen* entscheidender Themen wie Jerusalem, Israel, Tempel, Exodus und Rückführung u. a. und generell der Beziehung zwischen Jerusalem und der Diaspora, weshalb Metzner die Bezeichnung Diasporabrief für Jak ablehnt.[310]

Beide gegenwärtig vertretenen Positionen: Diasporabrief oder Gemeindebrief, übersehen bestimmte Aspekte. Metzner muss sich fragen lassen, ob der Verfasser nicht doch mit der Verbindung der Stämme- und der Diasporametapher eine *in-*

---

[303] Er weist darauf hin, dass die meisten griechischen Manuskripte in *inscriptio* oder *superscriptio* ἐπιστολή haben (siehe den Kommentar).

[304] M. Tsuji, Glaube zwischen Vollkommenheit und Verweltlichung. Eine Untersuchung zur literarischen Gestalt und zur inhaltlichen Kohärenz des Jakobusbriefes, WUNT II / 93, Tübingen 1997; K.-W. Niebuhr, Der Jakobusbrief im Lichte frühjüdischer Diasporabriefe, NTS 44, 1998, 420–443; R. J. Bauckham, Wisdom.

[305] Vergleichsbeispiele, die Allison, Jak, 73 nennt: Jer 29 (36LXX); EpJer; 2Makk 1,1–9; 1,10–2,18; 2Bar 78–87; ParJer 6,16–25; San 2,6; Targum des Jeremia 10,11.

[306] Übersetztes Zitat von J. White, Die Erstlingsgabe im Neuen Testament, TANZ 45, Tübingen 2007, 242.

[307] Zum Diasporabrief grundlegend L. Doering, Ancient Jewish Letters and the Beginnings of Christian Epistolography [Antike jüdische Briefe und der Anfang der christlichen Epistolographie], WUNT 298, Tübingen 2012 (Lit.). Einführend: Th. Klein, Art. Diasporabrief, in: Handbuch Brief (im Druck). Zum Verhältnis von Jak und 1Petr vgl. Ders., Bewährung in Anfechtung. Der Jakobusbrief und der Erste Petrusbrief als christliche Diasporabriefe, NET 18, Tübingen 2011. Wieweit der Diasporabrief eine Subgattung des antiken jüdischen Briefes darstellt und wieweit überhaupt derartige religiös basierte gattungsgeschichtliche Kategorien nützlich sind, kann im Rahmen dieses Kommentars nicht erörtert werden. Vgl. dazu die einführenden Überlegungen bei Klein, Art. Diasporabrief.

[308] Vgl. Allison, Jak, 73 f (Lit.). Für Jak als Diasporabrief votiert auch Adams, Genres, 159 f. Vgl. auch L. L. Cheung, The Genre, Composition and Hermeneutics of the Epistle of James, PBTM, Carlisle 2003.

[309] Allison, Jak, 74: Adresse an die zwölf Stämme in der Zerstreuung, »authorship by recognized authority«, griechische Sprache [gilt nur für vier Beispiele], paränetische Element, prophetische Elemente, Trost, Bedeutung des Gesetzes, »appeal to God's generous / merciful nature«, Hoffnung auf göttliche Rettung, Gericht über die Ungerechten. Kriterium 1–3 sind formale Kriterien, bei 4–10 handelt es sich um theologisch-ethische Motive, die Jak mit den genannten Diasporabriefen teilt.

[310] Metzner, Jak, 28.

94 Einleitung

tendierte Verbindung zu dem Instrument der antiken jüdischen Diasporakorrespondenz seit Jer 29 herstellt und die Adresse zur literarischen Autorisierung nutzt.[311] Allison übersieht, dass diese Jakobusadresse keinen realen religionsgeschichtlichen Bezug auf das zeitgenössische Judentum außerhalb Palästinas hat, sondern metaphorischen, d. h. verfremdenden Charakter trägt. Kloppenborg[312] spricht das Defizit an Bezug auf das außerpalästinische Judentum an und modifiziert damit Allisons Position:

> Even though James does not exhibit many of the features of other diaspora letters, it shares with those letters the fiction of authorities in Jerusalem writing to Jews elsewhere.[313]

Er interpretiert Jak 1,1 als literarisches Mittel, die dominierende Position, die Jakobus laut Paulus in Jerusalem hatte, in Analogie der jüdischen Diasporabriefe seit Jeremia für die Autorenschaft des Jak fruchtbar zu machen:

> Hence, James of Jerusalem was the optimal figure, analogous to Jeremiah or Baruch, to whom to attribute a paraenetic letter addressed to the diaspora. The exemplary way of life that he was reputed to have exhibited made him an ideal figure to promote conceptions of Torah-centered piety in Hellenistic Judaism.[314]

Im Vergleich mit 1Petr zeigt sich allerdings, dass hier für Jak noch weiter gedacht werden muss. Der enzyklische Anspruch, der sich in den Paulusbriefen schon abzeichnet[315], wird in 1Petr 1,1 ausgeweitet und literarisiert: 1Petr 1,1 richtet sich an kleinasiatische Christen in der »Diaspora«: Πέτρος ἀπόστολος Ἰησοῦ Χριστοῦ ἐκλεκτοῖς παρεπιδήμοις διασπορᾶς Πόντου, Γαλατίας, Καππαδοκίας, Ἀσίας καὶ Βιθυνίας.[316] Diese Adresse geht davon aus, dass die Christus-gläubigen Gemeinden in der »Zerstreuung« und damit in einer gewissen Analogie zu den Juden in der »Diaspora« leben und dass der Brief an die verschiedenen Gemeinden weitergegeben wird. Wie das praktisch aussah, bleibt offen. Die Ausweitung der Adresse findet ihren Abschluss im 2Petr, der ganz ohne eine konkrete Adressatenschaft auskommt auf: Συμεὼν Πέτρος δοῦλος καὶ ἀπόστολος Ἰησοῦ Χριστοῦ τοῖς ἰσότιμον ἡμῖν λαχοῦσιν πίστιν ἐν

---

[311] METZNER, Jak, 54f, betont, es fehle die Bezeichnung »Israels« für die zwölf Stämme und die »Diaspora« sei nicht geographisch gemeint, sondern auf die christliche Existenz bezogen. Beides ist richtig, ändert aber nichts an der deutlichen Bezugnahme auf den jüdischen Diasporabrief.

[312] KLOPPENBORG, James, 47–49.

[313] KLOPPENBORG, James, 48.

[314] KLOPPENBORG, James, 49.

[315] Der enzyklische Anspruch der Adresse weist einerseits auf die paulinischen Gemeindebriefe zurück, die neben ihrem situativen Charakter bereits eine explizite enzyklische Dimension haben, wie 1Kor 1,2 zeigt: τῇ ἐκκλησίᾳ τοῦ θεοῦ τῇ οὔσῃ ἐν Κορίνθῳ, ἡγιασμένοις ἐν Χριστῷ Ἰησοῦ, κλητοῖς ἁγίοις, σὺν πᾶσιν τοῖς ἐπικαλουμένοις τὸ ὄνομα τοῦ κυρίου ἡμῶν Ἰησοῦ Χριστοῦ ἐν παντὶ τόπῳ, αὐτῶν καὶ ἡμῶν (vgl. 2Kor 1,1; Gal 1,2; auch Kol 4,15f), andererseits auf 1Petr 1,1. Zu 1Petr vgl. KLEIN, Bewährung, 225–272.

[316] Dazu speziell KLEIN, Bewährung, 260–272.

B. Der Text. Historische, literarische und thematische Charakteristik 95

δικαιοσύνη τοῦ θεοῦ ἡμῶν καὶ σωτῆρος Ἰησοῦ Χριστοῦ (2Petr 1,1). Hier ersetzt die neue religiöse Zugehörigkeit die lokale oder regionale Bindung und Konkretisierung.[317]

Bereits die Adresse des 1Petr bezieht sich semantisch und in der Provinzliste deutlich auf das jüdische Genus der Diasporabriefe und gewinnt damit gegenüber den Paulusbriefen sowie den Pastoralbriefen eine eigene epistolare Kontur. Zugleich macht 1Petr aber deutlich, dass Christus-bekennende Autoren das Genus des Diasporabriefes für ihre eigenen kommunikativen Zwecke benutzen konnten. Ein Diasporabrief hat (1) *autoritativen* Charakter (*top down* von Jerusalem in die Diasporajudenschaft bzw. an die Christus-bekennenden Gemeinden) und (2) eine besondere *kommunikative* Funktion: Von vornherein ist eine bestimmte – theoretisch umfassende – Öffentlichkeit des ἔθνος Ἰουδαίων in der Diaspora im Blick. (3) Die Gattungsbezeichnung enthält außerdem eine *religiös-theologische* Konnotation: Es geht um Themen der religiösen Praxis des ἔθνος Ἰουδαίων.

Was heißt das für Jak? Jak 1,1 nimmt Elemente aus 1Petr 1,1 auf und formt sie um. So ist bereits in 1Petr 1,1 der Diasporagedanke formuliert, dort auf Christus-bekennende Gemeinden in einigen Provinzen Kleinasiens bezogen. Jak 1,1 generalisiert und theologisiert den Diasporagedanken: Das Präskript knüpft damit an die theologische Komponente des 1Petr an[318], vermeidet aber *geographische* Zuordnungen ebenso wie die klare *religiöse* Festlegung (1Petr 1,2) und öffnet stattdessen durch die idealisierende Formulierung von den »Zwölf Stämmen« die Adressatenschaft ebenso ins Allgemeine wie ins jüdische religiöse Milieu hinein. Die Verbindung von Jakobus und der Zwölfstämme-Metapher schafft damit eine *hybride transhistorische Verfassersituation*: Jerusalem als Mittelpunkt der jüdischen Diaspora und Jakobus als Leiter der Jerusalemer Gemeinde der Christusgläubigen werden in Jak 1,1 miteinander zu einer singulären Autoritätskonstellation verbunden, die ein literarisch und theologisch produktiver frühchristlicher Lehrer nutzt, um seine eigene theologische Ethik zu kommunizieren.

(3) Das Fazit ist nicht unkomplex und muss Einsichten von Metzner, Allison und Kloppenborg integrieren und neu gewichten. Jak ist ein briefliches Schreiben. Der Brief ist *literarisch* an »die zwölf Stämme in der Zerstreuung«, *faktisch* primär an Christus-bekennende »Brüder«[319] und Gemeinden, gerichtet, schließt aber durch die Adresse *ideell* eine jüdische Diasporaleserschaft ein. Der Verfasser steht in der literarischen Tradition des Paulus und in der Gattungstradition der frühchristlichen

---

[317] Ebenso Jud 1.

[318] Παρεπίδημος noch 1Petr 2,11 und Hebr 11,13 nach Gen 23,4. Abraham sagt: Πάροικος καὶ παρεπίδημος ἐγώ εἰμι μεθ᾽ ὑμῶν.

[319] »Schwestern« werden nicht in der Kommunikation erwähnt (aber 2,15 als Gemeindeglieder). Vgl. KLOPPENBORG, James, vii (»James's rather androcentric language«).

Gemeindebriefe[320] und nutzt *zugleich* den literarischen Zusammenhang der Subgattung des jüdischen *Diasporabriefes*.[321]

Wer im ersten oder frühen zweiten Jahrhundert einen Brief an *Christus-Bekenner* schreibt, schreibt in irgendeiner Weise – in Anknüpfung, Veränderung oder Widerspruch – in der literarischen Tradition des Paulus.[322] 2Petr macht das besonders deutlich, da der Verfasser theologische Schwierigkeiten mit Paulus hat, aber doch meint, ihn nennen zu müssen.[323] Jak steht des Näheren im Zusammenhang der (pseudepigraphen) Schreiben der dritten Generation, d. h. einerseits der Pastoralbriefe, die explizit an die paulinische literarische Tradition anknüpfen, und andererseits der Katholischen Briefe, vor allem in der Nähe des 1Petr (Absender und Adressaten) und des Jud (Absender), die in Konkurrenz zur paulinisch-nachpaulinischen Briefproduktion unterschiedliche *alternative* Autorisierungsstrategien – Bezugnahme auf Jakobus, Petrus und Judas – verfolgen. Für Jak sind die Beziehungen zu den beiden letztgenannten Briefen besonders wichtig, was Datierungs-, Situierungs-, Autorisierungs- und Theologie- bzw. Paränesethematik angeht. All diesen brieflichen Schreiben gemeinsam ist die Literarisierung des paulinischen Gemeindebriefes und seiner Kommunikationsfunktion. D. h. diese Schreiben übertragen die ursprüngliche Kommunikationsfunktion der paulinischen Briefe, die einzelnen Gemeinden und einzelnen Personen galten und zur öffentlichen Verlesung in den Gemeindeversammlungen bestimmt waren, auf ein allgemeines frühchristliches Hör- und Lesepublikum. Ein begrenztes reales Publikum wird durch ein virtuelles literarisches Publikum ersetzt. Diese Briefe stehen daher dem näher, was Adolf Deissmann als Epistel bezeichnet[324], als den Paulusbriefen, die aus biographischen Situationen heraus geschrieben wurden und auf Situationen in den Gemeinden reagierten. Was Jak über 1 und 2Petr hinaus kennzeichnet, ist sein literarisch-theologisches Spiel mit der Zwölf-Stämme-Diaspora-Metaphorik, das nach zwei Richtungen bedeutsam ist: Auf der einen Seite wird explizit eine griechischsprachige

---

320 Dazu einführend CH. HOEGEN-ROHLS, Form und Funktion, Realia und Idee der Paulusbriefe, in: O. Wischmeyer / E.-M. Becker (Hg.), Paulus. Leben – Umwelt – Werk – Briefe, Tübingen ³2021, 247–278; O. WISCHMEYER, Art. Paulusbriefe, in: Handbuch Brief (im Druck). Die Anknüpfung von Jak an den paulinischen Brief wird besonders betont bei E.-M. BECKER, Wer ist »Jakobus«? Ein typologischer Blick im Rahmen der frühchristlichen Briefkultur, in: Who was ›James‹?, 57–76.

321 KLEIN, Bewährung, schlägt die Brücke zwischen beiden Richtungen mit dem Terminus »christliche Diasporabriefe« (438–443), den er inhaltlich füllt: »Hier wie dort [sc. im Frühjudentum und im Frühchristentum] bediente man sich angesichts der in der Fremdlingsexistenz begründeten Herausforderungen des Mediums ›Rundbrief‹, um die Glaubensgeschwister in der Zerstreuung zu trösten und zu ermahnen« (438).

322 Dazu BECKER, Wer ist »Jakobus«?; TH.J. BAUER, Der Jakobusbrief und das Bild des Jakobus im Kontext antiker und frühchristlicher Epistolographie, in: Who was ›James‹?, 77–98. Das Gesagte gilt auch für den johanneischen Literaturkreis: Auch hier sind Briefe notwendig.

323 Die Apostelgeschichte ist das wichtigste Zeugnis für die Bedeutung des Paulus in der zweiten und dritten Generation. Allerdings erwähnt Lukas anders als 2Petr die Briefe des Paulus nicht.

324 A. DEISSMANN, Prolegomena zu den biblischen Briefen und Episteln, in: Ders., Bibelstudien, Marburg 1895, 187–254. Dazu WISCHMEYER, Art. Epistel, in: Handbuch Brief (im Druck).

B. Der Text. Historische, literarische und thematische Charakteristik

Leserschaft aus den Städten der jüdischen Diaspora angesprochen[325] – die Grenzen zwischen synagogaler und ekklesialer Leserschaft waren permeabel –, andererseits wurden die Christus-bekennenden Adressaten auf ihre Herkunft aus dem Zwölf-Stämme-Volk Israel verpflichtet. Über eine mögliche Reaktion von Leserschaften jüdischer Synagogalgemeinden wissen wir nichts.

3. Thematische Charakteristik

Der Jakobusbrief ist ein *ethisches Lehr- und Mahnschreiben* auf der *theologischen Basis* von Belehrung über Gott, autorisiert mit Schriftzitaten und Schriftauslegung sowie Beispielen aus der Schrift. Theologie und Ethik bilden die thematische Doppelstruktur des Jak. Die seit den Paulusbriefen eröffneten *neuen* frühchristlichen Themenfelder von – kurz genannt – Christologie, Pneumatologie und Ekklesiologie behandelt Jakobus nicht.[326] Sein Engagement gilt der Formierung von innerer Haltung (Ethos) und ethischem Verhalten bzw. praktischem Tun anhand des Gesetzes für seine als »zwölf Stämme in der Diaspora« angeredeten Adressaten. Ethische und theologische Belehrung hängen bei Jak zusammen, müssen aber thematisch eigenständig erschlossen werden. Das kommunitäre und soziale Handeln und die innere Haltung der Adressaten werden durch das Gesetz – auch als »Schrift« konkretisiert – bestimmt und damit direkt auf Gott zurückgeführt. Gott ist der Gesetzgeber und der Richter (4,12). Die Adressaten stehen unter dem Gesetz. Dieser grundlegende Sachverhalt verbindet die theologische und ethische Thematik in Jak.

3.1 Situationen. Konfrontationen

Der Verfasser des Jak reagiert durchaus auf die Realität in den Gemeinden, die sein literarisches Gegenüber bilden. Dabei geht er aber anders vor als Paulus. Jakobus reagiert nicht *explizit* auf aktuelle Gemeindesituationen und ihre realen Rahmenbedingungen.[327] Er gestaltet vielmehr ethisch relevante *Mustersituationen* nach stereotypen Vorgaben. Was entsteht, sind – wie schon gezeigt – eindrucksvoll kleine literarische Szenen und Bilder mit einer eigenen Plausibilität: der Arme und der Reiche in der Gemeindeversammlung, der Mann, der mit seinem Glauben prahlt, die Kaufleute mit ihren großsprecherischen Reden, die Lohnarbeiter auf den Feldern. Auch *Konfrontationen* inszeniert Jakobus literarisch, einerseits mit imaginierten Gemeindegliedern, die sagen: »Ich habe Glauben«, ohne diesen Glauben ethisch umzusetzen (2,14–26), andererseits mit Reichen (2,1–7; 5,1–6), Streitsüchtigen bzw.

---

[325] Man könnte an Personen wie den Vater des Paulus denken: ein griechisch sprechender Jude aus Tarsus, der zum Stamm Benjamin gehörte.

[326] Hamartologische (1,13–15), soteriologische (1,21; 5,20) und eschatologische Argumente (5,7–11) setzt der Verfasser (nur) *ad hoc* ein.

[327] Metzner, Jak, 27 betont zurecht die situativen Kontexte des Jak, weist aber nicht darauf hin, dass diese anders als in den Paulusbriefen nicht explizit gemacht werden.

98 Einleitung

Hochmütigen (4,1–10) oder Kaufleuten (4,13–17). In Kap. 2 entwickelt Jakobus mit Mitteln der Diatribe (Interlokutoren, Diskussionen) eine primär *theologische* Konfrontation mit ethischen Konsequenzen, während die Beispiele in Kap. 3–5 größenteils in den Bereich der *Ethik* gehören. Auch hier liegt literarische Gestaltung mit Mitteln der Diatribe (Stereotypik, Ekphrasis, Polemik und Satire) vor. Wieweit die theologischen und ethischen Auseinandersetzungen und Belehrungen trotz ihrer Topik auch auf reale religiöse, soziale und juristische Situationen und Zustände in den Gemeinden der Adressaten Bezug nehmen, muss im Einzelnen in der Exegese geklärt werden. Das sog. *mirror reading* kann für Jak jedenfalls nur mit großer Vorsicht angewendet werden[328], da es sich bei Jak um ein literarisch durchstilisiertes briefliches Schreiben mit einer zweifach verschlüsselten Adresse handelt: Jakobus spricht mit der Metapher von den zwölf Stämmen eine *generelle* und *ideelle* Adressatenschaft an. Was die literarisch situativ gestalteten Texte spiegeln, ist nicht die ethische und soziale Realität, sondern das, was die Wahrnehmung und Wertung des Verfassers als Realität stilisiert. So hören und lesen die Adressaten nicht direkt ihre soziale Wirklichkeit, sondern die Diagnose der Fehlentwicklungen und Gefahren in ihren Gemeinden, die der Verfasser stellt.

3.2 Theologische Themen

Der Jakobusbrief entwickelt keine eigenen theologischen Entwürfe wie Paulus.[329] Er basiert auf Grundüberzeugungen Israels zum *Wesen und Wirken Gottes als Schöpfer, Gesetzgeber, Erhalter und Richter der Menschen.*[330] Im Folgenden werden zunächst die Positionen der leitenden Kommentare dargestellt (3.2.1). Es folgt ein Blick auf die theologische Sprache des Jak (3.2.2) sowie auf die theologischen Themen (3.2.3). Besonderes Interesse gilt dem Thema »Paulus und Jakobus« (3.2.4).

---

[328] O. WISCHMEYER, Milieu, 34–36. Grundlegend bleibt DIBELIUS, Jak, 7: »Im Jakobus-Brief handelt es sich eben nicht um die Wirklichkeit einer bestimmten Gemeinde, sondern um die Möglichkeiten der gesamten Urchristenheit«.

[329] Die Kommentare fragen immer wieder den Text nach Theologie, Christologie, Anthropologie und Eschatologie ab. Auch Metzners leicht geänderte Terminologie: Gottesbild, Christusbild, Menschenbild (METZNER, Jak, 42–46) ändert daran wenig. Burchard präsentiert einen detaillierten Katalog theologischer Themen oder besser Motive (BURCHARD, Jak, 18–20). O. WISCHMEYER, Wie spricht der Jakobusbrief von Gott? Theologie im Jakobusbrief, in: R. Egger-Wenzel / K. Schöpflin / J. F. Diehl (Hg.), Weisheit als Lebensgrundlage. FS F. V. Reiterer, DCLS 15, Berlin / Boston 2013, 385–409, weist darauf hin, dass in Kap. 2,14–26 durchaus »Theologie« im qualifizierten Sinn stattfindet. Zur Christologie vgl. den Kommentar von ASSAËL / CUVILLIER, Jak, 68–94; S. LUTHER, The Christ of James' Story, in: P. Dragutinovic u. a. (Hg.), Christ of the Sacred Stories, WUNT II / 453, Tübingen 2017, 191–200. Eine besondere Position vertritt Allison im Zusammenhang seiner religionsgeschichtlichen Zuordnung des Verfassers. Er bezweifelt die Ursprünglichkeit der christologischen Sätze in 1,1 und 2,1 und kommt zu dem Schluss: »The Ebionites, according to the church fathers, did not believe in Jesus' divinity. What did James believe? We do not know« (ALLISON, Jak, 91). Als »leading ideas« identifiziert er Theologie, Gesetz und Ethik. Die Eschatologie ist (nur) eine Funktion der Ethik (James, 88–94).

[330] Vgl. monographisch: S. WENGER, Der wesenhaft gute Kyrios. Eine exegetische Studie über das Gottesbild im Jakobusbrief, AthANT 100, Zürich 2011.

3.2.1

Die *Kommentare* beschäftigen sich alle mit dem Profil der Theologie des Jak. Dabei entwickelt sich von Dibelius zu Metzner durchaus eine gewisse Dynamik: Der »Theologie«, neuerdings auch der »Christologie« wird sukzessiv mehr Interesse entgegengebracht. Am Anfang steht das Diktum von Dibelius:

> Zunächst hat der Jak keine »Theologie«[331],

das ebenso bekannt wie bestritten und missverstanden ist. Meist wird übersehen, dass Dibelius unter »Theologie« nicht »Theologie« im Sinne Bultmanns versteht, sondern die »Entfaltung und Durchführung religiöser Ideen«[332] und seine entsprechenden Ausführungen großzügig und wenig spezifisch unter »Religionsgeschichtliche Beziehungen« einordnet.[333] Einen deutlichen Akzent auf die Christologie des Jak hat Christoph Burchard gelegt und in diesem Zusammenhang Dibelius' Jak-Interpretation ironisch als »freischwebende ethische Hausapotheke« bezeichnet – eine Charakteristik, die nicht nur auf die Grenzen von Dibelius' theologischer Gewichtung des Jak hinweist, sondern vor allem auf die Grenzen einer primär traditionsgeschichtlich-motivgeschichtlich-intertextuellen Analyse auf der Basis der Formgeschichte aufmerksam macht.[334] Luke Timothy Johnson gibt eine sorgfältige Analyse der Rede von Gott bei Jak und vertritt eine differenzierte eigene, im Ergebnis Dibelius entgegengesetzte Position zur Theologie des Jakobus:

> In our discussion of James' Christian character, we saw how little explicit Christology James has to offer. And the letter clearly does not present an innovative or complex set of reflections on ultimate reality. Nevertheless, it is not far wrong to consider James one of the most »theological« writings in the NT.[335]

Allison legt Wert darauf, das jüdische Profil der Theologie des Jak zu betonen[336], und zieht das entsprechende Fazit zu den Gottesaussagen:

> None of these is distinctively Christian. On the contrary ... everything that James teaches about God has multiple parallels in the Bible and in Jewish texts.[337]

Dabei geht er allerdings nicht auf die Paulus-Jakobus-Texte in Kap. 2 ein. Hier liegt ein deutliches Defizit seiner Darstellung. Seine Einschätzung zum Thema Christologie ist lakonisch:

---

[331] DIBELIUS, Jak, 36 (gesperrt).
[332] Ebd.
[333] DIBELIUS, Jak, 35–43.
[334] CH. BURCHARD, Zu einigen christologischen Stellen des Jakobusbriefes, in: C. Breytenbach / H. Paulsen (Hg.), Anfänge der Christologie, Göttingen 1991, 353–368.
[335] JOHNSON, Jak, 85–88, Zitat 85.
[336] Ebd.
[337] Ebd.

James is theocentric, not Christocentric … [338] The upshot is that we know next to nothing about the Christology of our author.[339]

Dies Urteil trifft den Text, auch wenn man nicht die Schlüsse zum Ebionitismus des Verfassers zieht, die Allison daran anschließt, und wenn die Frage, weshalb Christologie fehlt, eigens beantwortet werden muss.

Metzner urteilt anders. Er findet in Jak ein ausgearbeitetes Gottesbild, dazu auch ein qualifiziertes Menschenbild, das Anthropologie und Ethik verbindet.[340] Bei der Frage nach der Christologie schließt er sich neueren Untersuchungen an, nach denen Jak jedenfalls eine implizite Christologie hat und auch große Teile der Lehre Jesu teilt.[341] Metzner kommt zu dem Urteil:

> Im ursprünglichen Sinn des Wortes betreibt er [Jakobus] »Theologie«, freilich nicht als Explikation christlicher Lehrtopoi, … sondern als *qualifizierte Rede von Gott, Christus, Wort, Glaube usw.*[342]

Das Fehlen wichtiger frühchristlicher theologischer Themen erklärt Metzner damit, dass Jak ein »Gelegenheitsschreiben« sei und unstrittige Themen nicht erwähnen müsse.[343] Er spricht daher von dem »Fehlen einiger christlicher Lehren«.[344] Dieser Einschätzung schließt sich der vorliegende Kommentar nicht an, da Metzner an diesem Punkt das klare Profil des Jak verwischt. In Jak fehlen nicht *einige* Themen, sondern insgesamt eine ausgearbeitete umfassende frühchristliche Theologie[345] im Sinne der neuen von Paulus gesetzten Themen von Christus, Geist, ἐκκλησία u. a. und ihren deuteropaulinischen Weiterungen, der jeweils eigenen Christologie der Petrusbriefe und der Johannesbriefe oder der christologischen Schrifttheologie im Hebräerbrief. Dies Fehlen ist besonders im Vergleich mit 1Petr auffallend und lässt sich nicht mit dem Briefformat erklären.[346]

3.2.2

Für Jakobus, den literarisch ambitionierten Verfasser, ist die theologische *Sprache* besonders wichtig. Jak benutzt die theologische bzw. religiöse Sprache programmatisch im *lobenden* und damit zugleich im stilistisch elaborierten Sinn (3,9 f), nicht

---

[338] ALLISON, Jak, 89.

[339] ALLISON, Jak, 90.

[340] K.-W. NIEBUHR, Jakobus und Paulus über das Innere des Menschen und den Ursprung seiner ethischen Entscheidungen, NTS 62, 2016, 1–30.

[341] METZNER, Jak, 44 f, mit Anm. 366 (Lit.). Metzner nimmt damit die Tendenz der Jakobusexegese der letzten Jahrzehnte auf, die den Text generell aufwertet (SCORNAIENCHI, Polemik).

[342] METZNER, Jak, 42. Auch hier sind wie bei Burchard Fragezeichen angebracht: Wo findet sich eine qualifizierte Rede von Christus?

[343] METZNER, Jak, 43.

[344] Ebd.

[345] WENGER, Der wesenhaft gute Kyrios; WISCHMEYER, Wie spricht der Jakobusbrief von Gott?

[346] So auch KLOPPENBORG, James, 85.

B. Der Text. Historische, literarische und thematische Charakteristik

als Mittel wohl als spaltend empfundener Definitionen.[347] Er sucht nach hochwertigen verallgemeinernden Umschreibungen im Zusammenhang mit Gottes Gaben und seinem Gesetz und setzt hochsprachliche Redewendungen und Begriffe für diese Themen ein, ohne diese in *spezifischer* Weise religiös zu konturieren. Keines der Gottesepitheta und der religiös konnotierten Begriffe in Jak lässt sich dem frühen Christentum oder dem antiken Judentum *eindeutig* oder gar ausschließlich zuordnen. Das gilt besonders für die Begriffe Wort und Gesetz, die religiös, philosophisch oder politisch konnotiert sein können. Jakobus scheint nach einer literarisch elaborierten *lingua franca* von Religion zu suchen.[348] Typisches Beispiel ist ein metaphorisches Syntagma wie »Vater der Lichter« für »Gott«. Eine Liste der entsprechenden Wendungen – vorwiegend Genitivverbindungen in Anlehnung an Septuagintadiktion – umfasst:[349]

1. Die gute und vollkommene Gabe von **oben** 1,17
2. Der **Vater** der Lichter 1,17
3. Das **Wort** der Wahrheit 1,18
4. Erstlinge seiner **Geschöpfe** 1,18
5. Das eingepflanzte **Wort**, das Seelen rettet 1,21
6. Das vollkommene **Gesetz** der Freiheit 1,25
7. Der reine und unbefleckte **Gottesdienst** 1,27
8. Der gute **Name** 2,7
9. Das königliche **Gesetz** 2,8
10. Das **Gesetz** der Freiheit 2,12
11. Die Weisheit von **oben** 3,15.17
12. Die Frucht der **Gerechtigkeit** 3,18.

Zentrale Begriffe sind Gesetz, Wort und der spatial-umschreibende Ausdruck »von oben«[350], dem die Bezeichnung »der Lichter« korrespondiert. Das »Gesetz« wird mit den lobenden Epitheta von Freiheit – ein Paradoxon –, königlich und vollkommen bezeichnet, das »Wort« mit Wahrheit und Rettung. Die genannten Grundbegriffe werden nicht erklärt, eher geradezu literarisch verklärt. Der Verfasser sucht nach einer hohen Sprache für die theo-logische Rede.

---

[347] Das gilt trotz seiner Vorbehalte gegenüber der »Zunge«. Definitorische Sprache benutzt vor allem der Verfasser von 1 und 2Joh.

[348] Die lobende theologisch-religiöse Diktion bedeutet aber nicht die Zugehörigkeit des Jak zum *genus epideiktikon* der Rhetorik (siehe oben).

[349] Vgl. dazu jeweils die Exegese.

[350] Alle drei Begriffe begegnen bereits prominent bei Paulus.

3.2.3

Sachlich lassen sich folgende theo-logische[351] *Aussagen*, nach Kapiteln geordnet, beschreiben.[352] In Kap. 1 dominiert das Theologumenon »Gott als guter Geber«. Gott gibt gern und freigebig, das gilt auch für die Weisheit. Gott gibt ἁπλῶς gemäß seiner Einheit und Einfachheit. Einem Zweifler aber gibt Gott nicht: Glaube und Gabe gehören zusammen. Die »Krone des Lebens« gibt Gott dem Mann, der die Anfechtung erduldet. Gott als gut und als Geber des Guten – das impliziert, dass Gott niemanden versucht und mit dem Zusammenhang von Versuchung – das Böse – Begierden – Sünde – Tod nicht in Verbindung gebracht werden kann (1,13–15). Zugleich ist Gott Vater (1,27[353]) und Schöpfer (1,17 f[354]): Er gibt, erhält und vollendet Leben. Falls 1,18 (»Er hat uns geboren, ... damit wir Erstlinge seiner Geschöpfe seien«) auf die Wiedergeburt der Christus-gläubigen Adressaten in der Taufe anspielt, hat der Verfasser diese Anspielung bewusst verdeckt.

In Kap. 2 ist zunächst das Theologumenon von der βασιλεία τοῦ θεοῦ zentral. Gott erwählt die Armen und macht sie zu Erben seines Reiches. Zugleich ist Gott Gesetzgeber und Richter (so auch 4,12 und 5,9) und setzt damit die Norm für die Gerechtigkeit des Menschen (V. 24).[355] In 2,19 bezieht sich Jakobus auf das Bekenntnis zu Gott als dem Einen (Dtn 6,4), um dann aber mit einer sarkastischen Bemerkung die Begrenztheit des Bekenntnisses zu demonstrieren: Es ist korrekt, und auch die Dämonen glauben es. Hier wird »glauben« auf ein »monotheistisches« Bekenntnis bezogen *(fides quae creditur)*. Die Begrenztheit des bloßen Bekenntnisses liegt in der mangelnden Umsetzung in Werke – die Tragik der Dämonen, die nicht ethisch agieren können. Das bedeutet: Gott erwartet nicht nur das Sch'ma, sondern ein respondierendes *Verhalten* im Sinne der βασιλεία τοῦ θεοῦ. Gott wird also grundsätzlich im Zusammenhang mit den Menschen gesehen. Theologie ohne Ethik ist nicht sinnvoll. In der Relativierung der Bedeutung des Sch'ma liegt ein wichtiger theologischer Gedanke vor, der in anderem Zusammenhang auch von Paulus[356] und in Mk 12,28–34par ausgeführt wird.[357]

In Kap. 3 beschwört Jakobus die »Weisheit von oben«, die die ethischen Standards für die Adressaten setzt, vor allem Frieden, Güte, Barmherzigkeit (so auch nachdrücklich 5,11: πολύσπλαγχνός ἐστιν ὁ κύριος καὶ οἰκτίρμων) und Gerechtigkeit – einerseits Eigenschaften Gottes, andererseits ethische Standards für seine Geschöpfe.[358]

---

351 Eine klare Trennung zwischen Theologie und Ethik ist häufig nicht möglich.

352 Auch hier ist jeweils die Versexegese zu vergleichen.

353 Auch 3,9.

354 Auch 3,9. Allusion auf Gen 1,26 f.

355 Vgl. unten zur Eschatologie.

356 1Kor 8,4–7: das Wissen um den einen Gott reicht nicht, die Rücksichtnahme auf den schwachen Bruder muss hinzutreten.

357 Jesus beantwortet die Frage nach dem »höchsten Gebot« mit dem Doppelgebot von Sch'ma und Gebot der Nächstenliebe.

358 Vgl. Mt 5,48. Hier liegt dieselbe reziproke Struktur vor.

B. Der Text. Historische, literarische und thematische Charakteristik   103

Kap. 4 beschreibt den Dualismus zwischen Gott und Welt bzw. Teufel aus der Perspektive der Adressaten: Sie sollen Freunde Gottes, nicht der Welt sein und seine Nähe suchen, dem Teufel aber widerstehen und ihn fliehen. Hier bedient sich Jakobus klassischer jüdischer Vorstellungen[359], die sich auch bei den Synoptikern und in den späteren Briefen finden (1Petr 5,8; 1Joh 3,10). Jakobus geht von der Realität des Teufels aus, der an die Menschen herantritt und dem sie widerstehen sollen und können.[360] Gott »gibt den Demütigen Gnade«, die Adressaten sollen sich ihm unterordnen, er wird sie erhöhen. Der κύριος regiert das Leben der Menschen (4,15). In Kap. 4 und 5 spannt Jakobus den Bogen von den Gefahren der »Welt« zu Gott dem Richter, der »kommt« und die Geduldigen recht richtet. 5,15 und 5,20 vermitteln dabei eine Hoffnungsperspektive: Gott wird heilen und vergeben, und Sünder können bekehrt werden.

Alle hier genannten Theologumena sind, wie Allison feststellt, aus dem antiken jüdischen Kontext zu erklären: Jak vertritt einen bestimmten Typus einer streng theozentrischen jüdischen Theologie. Auffallend ist einerseits die vollständige Reduktion der alttestamentlichen und frühjüdischen Geist-Theologie. Hier liegt auch ein entscheidender Unterschied zu Paulus.[361] Außerdem fehlen wesentliche Elemente einer expliziten Israel-Theologie: Israel, Bund, Beschneidung, Mose, Tempel, Sabbat, Reinheits- und Speisegebote.[362] Auf Jerusalem wird nur indirekt durch die Adresse angespielt. Explizit erwähnt werden Gesetz[363] und Schrift[364] sowie das Beispiel Abrahams. Das Gesetz ist der leitende theologisch-ethische Begriff. In Jak 4,12 wird das Gesetz *theologisch* an den Gesetzgeber zurückgebunden: εἷς ἐστιν ὁ νομοθέτης καὶ κριτής. *Ethisch* wird das Gesetz durch Nächstenliebe, Unparteilichkeit und Barmherzigkeit (ἔλεος[365]) in Kap. 2 sowie das Verbot der Verleumdung in Kap. 4 charakterisiert: also durch zwei normative ethische Begriffe und durch zwei Beispiele des praktischen Ethos in den Gemeinden. Das Gesetz ist im Jak *die* normative ethische Größe, die nicht weiter erklärt, sondern angewendet werden muss. Differenzierende *Diskussionen* um *Gesetzesauslegung* oder *Gesetzesverschärfung* wie in Lk 10,29 (Wer ist mein Nächster?) oder den Antithesen der Bergpredigt oder

---

359 Vgl. auch 5,4: während im übrigen Brief stets von Gott dem Vater oder Schöpfer oder dem κύριος gesprochen wird, nennt Jakobus in 5,4 im Zitat τὰ ὦτα κυρίου σαβαώθ und damit das einzige explizit jüdische Gottesepitheton des Briefes.

360 Vgl. die narrative Gestaltung des Theologumenons in Mt 4,1–11. In der Versuchungsgeschichte begegnen »Versucher« und »Teufel«: Der Versucher tritt an Jesus heran und will ihn verführen. Er scheitert und »verlässt« Jesus. Es handelt sich um eine Bewährungserzählung, nicht um eine theologische Auseinandersetzung über die Frage nach der Herkunft und der Macht des Teufels und über das Verhältnis von Gott und Teufel. Dasselbe gilt für Jak 4.

361 Jak 2,26 und 4,5 beziehen sich nicht auf den Geist Gottes.

362 Bei Paulus finden sich die genannten Elemente: vgl. nur die Aufzählung in Röm 9,4f. Dazu auch KLOPPENBORG, James, 85f.

363 Jak 1,25; 2,8.9.10.11.12; 4,11 (viermal).

364 Jak 2,8.23; 4,5.

365 Jak 2,13 und 3,17.

104   Einleitung

heilsgeschichtlich-christologisch begründete *Gesetzeskritik* im Sinn paulinischer Theologie fehlen bei Jak. Jakobus weist lediglich darauf hin, dass nicht *ein*, sondern *alle* Gebote des Dekalogs zu halten seien. Allison liest Jak 2,10 f.

> 10 ὅστις γὰρ ὅλον τὸν νόμον τηρήσῃ, πταίσῃ δὲ ἐν ἑνί, γέγονεν πάντων ἔνοχος. 11 ὁ γὰρ εἰπών· *μὴ μοιχεύσῃς*, εἶπεν καί· *μὴ φονεύσῃς* · εἰ δὲ οὐ μοιχεύεις, φονεύεις δέ, γέγονας παραβάτης νόμου,

daher von Mt 5,20 her:

> Λέγω γὰρ ὑμῖν ὅτι ἐὰν μὴ περισσεύσῃ ὑμῶν ἡ δικαιοσύνη πλεῖον τῶν γραμματέων καὶ Φαρισαίων, οὐ μὴ εἰσέλθητε εἰς τὴν βασιλείαν τῶν οὐρανῶν

und resümmiert: »The whole law is still valid«.[366] Bei Jak findet sich aber kein Hinweis auf ein Gesetzesverständnis, das über ethische Grundnormen hinausgeht, die Jak mit synoptischen und paulinischen Texten zu Dekalog und Leviticusgeboten teilt. Ob man mit Allison Jakobus und die Gemeinden, die er repräsentiert, als Tora-observant verstehen soll oder ob die Tora im frühchristlichen Kontext bereits ethisiert worden ist, lässt sich Jak *nicht* entnehmen.[367]

3.2.4

Diese Frage führt direkt zu dem Thema »Paulus und Jakobus«, das – anders als bei Dibelius, Johnson, Allison und Metzner – im vorliegenden Kommentar als zentraler Bestandteil der Denk- und Traditionswelt[368] des Jak und seiner *eigenen Theo-logie* verstanden wird. »Paulus und Jakobus« ist eins der »klassischen Themen« der Jakobusexegese.[369] Hier ist eine sorgfältige Analyse erforderlich. Die intertextuelle Analyse ergab bereits, dass Jakobus 1Kor, Gal und Röm – unter Umständen auch Phil – kannte und sich auf *Texte* aus diesen Briefen bezieht. Daher gilt allgemein: Im vorliegenden Kommentar werden die Texte in Kap. 1; 2 und 3 als konstitutiver Teil der Auseinandersetzung des Jakobus mit Texten und Themen des Paulus verstanden. Dabei geht es um folgende *Themen*: um Sünde und Herkunft des Bösen (Kap. 1), um Glauben und Werke (Kap. 2), um Abraham als Gottesfreund (Kap. 2) und um die irdische und himmlische Weisheit (Kap. 3). Im Zusammenhang der *Theo-logie* des Jak führen diese Texte zu drei sachlichen Fragen. *Erstens*: wie verhält sich Jak zu den entsprechenden Paulustexten über Sünde und Herkunft des Bösen (1)? *Zweitens* wie ist das Verhältnis zu den Paulustexten über die irdische und himm-

---

[366] ALLISON, Jak, 91. Vgl. die Argumentation S. 27: »One can plausibly construe 2.10 as forwarding a rigorous nomism«.

[367] Dazu siehe unten.

[368] KLOPPENBORG, James, 107 f, geht zwar davon aus, dass Jak an mehreren Stellen direkt gegen Paulustexte polemisiert, sieht aber Paulus nicht als Teil der »fabric of James« (61–81), zu der er nur die jüdische Bibel und die Jesustradition rechnet und damit sowohl die gattungsbedingte (Gemeindebrief) als auch theologische (Glaube und Taten) Bezugnahme auf Paulus zu gering veranschlagt.

[369] POPKES, Jak, 36.

B. Der Text. Historische, literarische und thematische Charakteristik 105

lische Weisheit und über Glauben und Werke und über Abraham (2)? Die *dritte* und wichtigste Frage lautet: Wie lässt sich im Gegenüber zu Paulus die eigene Jakobus-Theologie beschreiben (3)? Dabei gilt allgemein: Im vorliegenden Kommentar werden die Texte in Kap. 1; 2 und 3 als konstitutiver Teil der Auseinandersetzung des Jakobus mit Texten und Themen des Paulus verstanden.

(1) Zur Sünde: Jak 1 schließt das Thema »Versuchung« theologisch ab, indem klargestellt wird, dass die Versuchung nicht von Gott ausgeht.[370] Jak 1,13–15 ist vor dem Hintergrund von Röm 7 zu lesen. Metzner widmet dem Abschnitt einen kleinen Exkurs[371] und geht genauer auf das Verhältnis von Röm 7 und Jak 1 ein.[372] Er findet in Jak 1 »paulinisches Gedankengut in veränderter, von Paulus losgelöster Form«.[373] Allerdings besteht nicht nur eine enge Sachbeziehung zwischen der paulinischen Kausalreihe: Sünde – Begierde – Tod und der Reihe in Jak 1: Begierde – Sünde – Tod, sondern auch eine analoge mythologisierend-personifizierende Diktion. Im vorliegenden Kommentar wird daher für wahrscheinlich gehalten, dass Jak sich *korrigierend* auf Röm 7 *bezieht*: Jakobus betont die Bedeutung der »eigenen Begierde« und damit die ethische Verantwortung des Einzelnen. Eine von außen kommende Erlösung – ein Grundelement der paulinischen Christologie – wie in Röm 7 ist hier nicht vorgesehen.

(2) Zur Weisheit: bei der Beurteilung der Beziehung zwischen 1Kor 2,14 und Jak 3,13–18 findet Metzner höchstens sprachliche Ähnlichkeiten:

> Die Sprechweise des Jakobus könnte von der paulinischen Tradition beeinflusst sein … Doch anders als Paulus (und Jud 19) kennt Jakobus die urchristlich fest verankerte Opposition ψυχικός – πνευματικός nicht … Sofern also (noch) vorhanden, ist paulinische Sprechweise nur abgeschwächt und moduliert da.[374]

Ähnlich vorsichtig urteilt Allison:

> One might even detect Pauline influence here … But James' use of ψυχική could equally derive from a hellenistic Jewish anthropology …[375]

Er übersieht dabei aber den Zusammenhang mit der Weisheitsthematik, die Paulus zuerst in 1Kor 2 in die entstehende frühchristliche Theologie aufgenommen hat. Jak 3,13–18 lässt sich plausibel auf dem Hintergrund von 1Kor 1,17–2,16 lesen, wie Verfasserin des vorliegenden Kommentars in einer Studie vorschlägt:

> Die Vorstellung von der geistlichen bzw. oberen und »psychischen«, d. h. physischen oder irdischen Weisheit und das irenische Weisheitskonzept bei »Jakobus« lassen sich

---

[370] So auch Paulus: 1Kor 7,5 (Satan); 1Thess 3,5 (Versucher).
[371] METZNER, Jak, 81f.
[372] ALLISON, Jak, 254, erwähnt eine mögliche Beziehung zu Röm nur in Anm. 253.
[373] METZNER, Jak, 82.
[374] METZNER, Jak, 203.
[375] ALLISON, Jak, 577.

am ehesten als Echo des 1. Korintherbriefes verstehen. Aber der Verfasser des Jakobusbriefes hat durch die radikal ethische Reduktion des paulinischen Weisheitskonzeptes zugleich Paulus implizit kritisiert oder zumindest den komplexen theologischen Einfluss paulinischer Texte und Theologeme zurückzudrängen versucht.[376]

Den beiden genannten Jakobustexten ist eine Tendenz zur Vereinfachung und zur Applikation paulinischer theologischer Texte gemeinsam. Dabei geht es in erster Linie um eine praktische Indienstnahme paulinischer Begriffe und Themen im Rahmen der Theo-logie des Jakobus.

(3) Die Frage nach »Paulus und Jakobus« entscheidet sich an der Beurteilung der Texte in Jak 2 und den Aussagen des Jak zu Glauben und Taten und zu Abraham. Hier ist eine genaue Analyse notwendig. Drei Positionen lassen sich unterscheiden: die antipaulinische Interpretation (3.1), die *new perspective on James* (3.2) sowie die sog. mittlere Position (3.3). Der vorliegende Kommentar entwickelt in drei Schritten eine eigene Position (3.4). Metzners sehr materialreicher und zugleich die Fragestellung klar strukturierender Exkurs »Jakobus und Paulus«[377] beschreibt und ordnet die exegetischen Positionen und ihre theologische Bedeutung und verbindet dabei zwei Aspekte: Metzner zeichnet die Wende von einer theologischen (Luther) zu einer theologie*geschichtlichen* Perspektive auf die Konstellation Paulus – Jakobus nach und stellt gleichzeitig die gegenwärtig drei möglichen Optionen in der Verhältnisbestimmung Paulus – Jakobus detailliert anhand der Literatur dar.[378] Metzner unterscheidet zwischen *erstens* der »antipaulinische(n) Stoßrichtung«[379], *zweitens* der »new perspective on James«, d. h. »keine Frontstellung gegenüber Paulus oder Paulinisten«[380], *schließlich* »eine(r) mittlere(n) Position«, bei der Jakobus zwar Paulus voraussetzt, »ohne jedoch Paulus oder seine Nachfolger attackieren zu wollen«, also eine Spielart einer post-paulinischen Position.[381]

(3.1) *Die antipaulinische Stoßrichtung*: diese *erste* Option, die gegenwärtig zugunsten der zweiten Position zurückgetreten ist, wird aktuell von Lorenzo Scornaienchi aufgenommen und weiterentwickelt.[382] Scornaienchi knüpft an Martin Hengel an[383], der im gesamten Jakobusbrief verdeckte aktuelle Polemik gegen Paulus,

---

[376] Wischmeyer, Jak 3,13–18 vor dem Hintergrund von 1Kor 1,17–2,16, 429 f.

[377] Metzner, Jak, 163–166.

[378] Besonders wichtig die umfangreiche Literaturdokumentation zu den einzelnen Positionen.

[379] Vertreten von wichtigen Lehrbüchern zur ntl. Ethik und Theologie der zweiten Hälfte des letzten Jahrhunderts (Metzner, Jak, 164 Anm. 253).

[380] Metzner, Jak, 164. In der deutschsprachigen Exegese besonders vertreten von K.-W. Niebuhr, »A New Perspective on James?«. Neuere Forschungen zum Jakobusbrief, ThLZ 129, 2004, 1019–1044 (vgl. Metzner, Jak, 164 Anm. 255).

[381] Metzner, Jak, 165.

[382] Scornaienchi, Polemik im Jakobusbrief.

[383] M. Hengel, Der Jakobusbrief als antipaulinische Polemik, in: G. F. Hawthorne / O. Betz (Hg.), Tradition und Interpretation in the New Testament. Essays in Honor of E. Earle Ellis for his 60th Birthday, Grand Rapids 1987, 248–265 (erweiterte Fassung: Der Jakobusbrief als antipaulinische Polemik, in: M. Hengel, Paulus und Jakobus. Kleine Schriften III, WUNT 141, Tübingen 2002, 511–548).

B. Der Text. Historische, literarische und thematische Charakteristik 107

seine Theologie und seine Beziehung zu den Reichen fand und dementsprechend Jakobus den Herrenbruder für den Autor des Jak hielt. Scornaienchi nimmt die Polemik in Jak ähnlich ernst wie Hengel, kommt aber zu einer anderen Lösung der Autor-Frage und damit auch zu anderen theologiegeschichtlichen Ergebnissen, da er die Herrenbruder-Hypothese nicht teilt. Scornaienchi ist von der Frage geleitet:

> Ist der Jakobusbrief dann insgesamt eine *ethische Schrift*, die sich der Polemik bedient, oder ist er eine *polemische Schrift*, die moralische Korrektheit für sich beansprucht?[384]

Er votiert für die zweite Möglichkeit. Seine methodische Überlegung:

> Der springende Punkt in der Diskussion, ob hier wirklich Paulus im Spiel ist, ist gerade die offensichtliche *Intertextualität dieses Teils des Briefes mit dem corpus paulinum*[385],

ist richtig und wird von dem vorliegenden Kommentar geteilt. Gegenüber Scornaienchis genereller Einordnung des Jak als einer polemischen Schrift ist aber Zurückhaltung angebracht. Weder Hengels noch Scornaienchis durchgehende polemische Analyse trifft den ethisch-belehrenden Ton des Jak. Nun bleibt Scornaienchi anders als Hengel aber nicht bei dem Urteil des Anti-Paulinismus stehen, sondern denkt auch in Richtung auf die dritte bzw. mittlere Lösung weiter. Er geht von einem judenchristlichen Verfasser aus, der Vertreter einer spezifisch judenchristlichen post-paulinischen Richtung ist. Damit nähert sich Scornaienchi der religionsgeschichtlichen Position Allisons, der seinerseits allerdings weniger interessiert an einer antipaulinischen Theologie des Jak ist.[386] Scornaienchi resümmiert zu Jak:

> Dieser befürwortet eine zentrale Funktion des νόμος und die Überwindung der paulinischen Rechtfertigungslehre, die Gesetz und Werke geringschätzt. Als möglicher Abfassungsort des Briefes kommt Syrien in Frage, weil dort die judenchristlichen Gemeinden besonders stark waren. … Die Untersuchung über die Polemik im Brief hat gezeigt, dass es sich nicht um eine individuelle Abrechnung eines Autors gegen Paulus' Person und Lehre handelt. Der Jakobusbrief vertritt eine Richtung im Frühchristentum, die literarisch einen neuen judenchristlichen Kanon bildet, und ist daher *in primis* ein Projekt, die Auffassung der Säulen, der Jerusalemer Apostel, sprechen zu lassen.[387]

Letztere Standortbestimmung des Jak wird auch im vorliegenden Kommentar vertreten.

---

[384] SCORNAIENCHI, Polemik, 336.
[385] SCORNAIENCHI, Polemik, 343.
[386] ALLISON, Jak, 49, geht von einer Nähe des Jak zu den Ebioniten aus und charakterisiert Jak in diesem Zusammenhang auch als antipaulinisch: »The text bears witness to a Greek speaking Christian Judaism that opposed Paul, upheld the law, and regarded James as its hero.« Allison thematisiert diesen Aspekt aber nicht ausführlicher.
[387] SCORNAIENCHI, Polemik, 365.

(3.2) *Die new perspective on James*: für die zweite Möglichkeit, das Verhältnis von Paulus und Jak zu bestimmen, tritt besonders wirksam Luke Timothy Johnson ein. Unter der Überschrift »Loosening the Pauline Connection« schreibt er:

> No real progress can be made in the historical reconstruction of earliest Christianity or in the theological appreciation of its diverse canonical witnesses until the Pauline connection is loosened.[388]

Johnson kämpft für eine neue Sicht auf die theologiegeschichtliche Entwicklung des frühen Christentums, weg von ›paulinisch-orthodox contra häretisch‹ hin zu einer größeren Bandbreite theologischer Positionen:

> It is in principle important to assert that James could have held a different theology than Paul, without necessarily also asserting that James was against Paul's mission.[389]

Die deutlichen Beziehungen zwischen Jak 2 und paulinischen Positionen erklärt Johnson mit dem Hinweis auf gemeinsame frühjüdische Sprache (»forensic language«[390]) sowie auf Thematik und Rolle als ethische Lehrer, geht aber über die gegensätzlichen Positionen und die argumentative Protreptik von Jak 2 hinweg. Hier liegen deutliche Mängel der Analyse Johnsons. Johnson votiert außerdem für eine frühe Datierung des Jak, die im vorliegenden Kommentar abgelehnt wird.[391]

(3.3) *Die mittlere Position*: Metzner selbst votiert daher für die *dritte* Option[392] und plädiert dafür,

> dass Jak 2,14–26 lediglich die sprachliche Vorarbeit und bestimmte Koordinaten von Paulus voraussetzt, ohne jedoch Paulus oder seine Nachfolger attackieren zu wollen[393]. … Beurteilt man Jak im Licht dieser späteren theologiegeschichtlichen Entwicklung im 2. Jh., legt sich die Vermutung nahe, dass Jakobus die durch die paulinischen Briefe bekannte Zusammenschau »Glaube – Werke – Rechtfertigung« in einer bereits verselbständigten Form kannte, mit bekannten jüdischen Abraham- und (bei Paulus nicht belegten) Rahabtraditionen verband und in Reaktion auf untätige Christen zu einer eigenständigen Argumentation in der vorliegenden Gestalt ausbildete, ohne dabei Paulus im Blick zu haben, gegen ihn oder seine Anhänger vorgehen zu wollen. … Die Übereinstimmungen lassen sich auch durch sprachliche Konventionen in den paulinischen Missionsgebieten erklären, die Jakobus in einer bereits von Paulus losgelösten, durch gemeindliche Lehre und Predigt assimilierten Form kennengelernt hat. Paulus … liegt so weit zurück, dass er für Jakobus kein Thema mehr ist.[394]

---

[388] JOHNSON, Jak, 111.

[389] JOHNSON, Jak, 114.

[390] JOHNSON, Jak, 59.

[391] Siehe oben.

[392] METZNER, Jak, 165 mit Anm. 265.

[393] Ebd.

[394] METZNER, Jak, 166.

B. Der Text. Historische, literarische und thematische Charakteristik

Metzners Schwäche liegt in seiner Ablehnung einer produktiven theologischen Bezugnahme des Jak auf paulinische *Texte*. In dieser Richtung geht die Diskussion weiter. Eve-Marie Becker ordnet in ihrem Beitrag: Wer ist »Jakobus«? das Forschungsfeld ähnlich wie Metzner: einerseits Anti-Paulinismus[395], andererseits Unabhängigkeit von Paulus (K.-W. Niebuhr), benennt dann allerdings zwei weitere neuere modifizierende Positionen, Margaret Mitchell und Oda Wischmeyer. Nach Mitchell ist der Jakobusbrief ein Dokument »from within Paulinism«.[396] Diese Position könnte vereinfacht eine weitere Position, nämlich als Pro-Paulinismus bezeichnet werden. Mit Allison wurde diese Position bereits als zu einseitig kritisiert.[397] Die Verfasserin dieses Kommentars verfolgt nach Becker dagegen die post-paulinische Interpretation weiter:

> Der Brief ist so im weiteren Umfeld eines post-paulinischen ethischen Diskurses zu sehen, in dem weder primär ein Anschluss an Paulus (so Mitchell) noch eine Frontstellung gegen Paulus (so Hengel) versucht wird.[398]

Eve-Marie Becker denkt selbst ebenfalls auf dieser literarisch-theologischen Spur weiter und stellt den post-paulinischen ethischen Diskurs des Jak – so auch der vorliegende Kommentar – in den Zusammenhang des epistolaren Typus des Briefes als Gemeindebrief in der Tradition des Paulus:

> Der Jakobusbrief lässt sich gewiss nicht unabhängig von der ihn umgebenden frühchristlichen Briefliteratur und deren prototypischer Prägung durch Paulus verstehen … Jak greift wie die pseudopaulinischen Briefe, 1Clem und PolPhil den »Glaube-Taten«-Diskurs auf – mehr als alle anderen post-paulinischen Briefe beschäftigt ihn dieser Diskurs … Der Verfasser des Jak gestaltet ein vormals für Gal und Röm charakteristisches paulinisches Thema – unter Aufnahme von, wie es scheint, lange vergessenen Motiven, die neu in die Mode kommen (Rahab-Motivik) – offensichtlich bewusst neu.[399]

Auch John S. Kloppenborg geht von einer Kenntnis paulinischer Texte bei Jak aus:

> The only way to make sense of the argument in 2:14–26 is to see that James is invoking the distinction made by *Paul* in Galatians and Romans between *pistis* (›faith‹) and deeds (*erga*). Paul used these terms in a very particular way: the deed in question was the circumcision of males, and the faith in question was a faith in the redemptive power of Christ's death and resurrection. The distinction that James invokes only makes

---

[395] BECKER, Wer ist »Jakobus«?, 57–76, 58, verweist auf J. E. HUTHER, Kritisch-exegetisches Handbuch über den Brief des Jakobus, KEK 15, Göttingen 1858, 20; neuerdings wieder HENGEL, Der Jakobusbrief als antipaulinische Polemik, in: Ders. Paulus und Jakobus. Kleine Schriften III, 526.
[396] BECKER, Wer ist »Jakobus«?, 59. MITCHELL, The Letter, 75–98.
[397] Siehe oben.
[398] BECKER, Wer ist »Jakobus«?, 59.
[399] BECKER, Wer ist »Jakobus«?, 73.

> sense if we assume that he is referring to *Paul's* language of Galatians and Romans; no
> other Jew would make such a distinction.[400]

Kloppenborg schließt daraus:

> James is confronting Paul directly.[401]

Dabei findet Kloppenborg wie auch Scornaienchi nicht einen personal, sondern
einen sachlich verstandenen Anti-Paulinismus und ordnet seine Beobachtungen
seinerseits in ein eigenes theologiegeschichtliches Szenario ein:

> James was framed as the letter of a principal representative of the Jesus movement, but
> one reputed to be faithful to the Torah. The letter is almost certainly written in the
> diaspora and to an urban audience. It fictively addresses all diaspora Jews, but its actual
> readers were probably Jews in Alexandria or perhaps Rome.[402]

Er liest den Brief als paränetisches Schreiben, das an Psychagogie interessiert ist
und die Tora als Gesetz der Freiheit und als eingepflanzten Logos versteht. Was er
nicht erklärt, ist die Frage, weshalb ein christlicher Lehrer an die Juden Alexandrias
schreiben sollte, wenn sich seine theologisch-ethische Botschaft nicht von der des
Judentums unterscheidet und speziell anti-paulinisch ist. Der vorliegende Kommentar folgt Kloppenborgs Rekonstruktion an diesem Punkt nicht und geht von
Christus-gläubigen Adressaten aus.

(3.4) Wie positioniert sich der vorliegende Kommentar insgesamt in dem unübersichtlichen Feld von Ante-Paulinismus, Iuxta-Paulinismus, Anti-Paulinismus,
Post-Paulinismus und Pro-Paulinismus (M. M. Mitchell), in dem es oft um Nuancen geht und die Unterschiede sehr fein sind? Grundsätzlich empfiehlt sich eine
Unterscheidung zwischen persönlich-biographischer, sachlich-theologischer und
historischer Verhältnisbestimmung zwischen Paulus und Jakobus. Der vorliegende
Kommentar liest Jak als Dokument des sachlichen und historischen *Post-Paulinismus*. Das ist im Rückblick auf die Forschungsgeschichte in *vier* Schritten zu präzisieren. Erstens werden die Defizite der nicht post-paulinischen Positionen benannt.
Zweitens werden die theologischen Tendenzen des Post-Paulinismus bei Jak skizziert. Drittens werden die Charakteristika der post-paulinischen Position in den
Zusammenhang der verschiedenen exegetischen Lösungsvorschläge eingeordnet.
Viertens wird das Ergebnis der Paulus – Jakobus – Diskussion in eine Gesamtdarstellung der Jakobus-Theologie integriert.

Erstens ist deutlich, dass sich – obgleich Paulus nicht genannt wird – die theologischen Themen: »Glaube und Werke« und der »Glaube Abrahams« auf *paulinische*
Positionen und auf Paulus*texte* beziehen und dass der Verfasser auf dieser Grundlage

---

[400] KLOPPENBORG, James, 107.
[401] KLOPPENBORG, James, 108.
[402] KLOPPENBORG, James, 109. Der vorliegende Kommentar stimmt dieser Hypothese nicht zu. Siehe unten.

B. Der Text. Historische, literarische und thematische Charakteristik

seine eigene Position entwirft. Weder das *loosening the Pauline connection* (Johnson) noch die Hypothese einer bloßen Aufnahme paulinischer Themen oder Schlagworte (Dibelius, Metzner) erklärt die präzise Übernahme paulinischer Begrifflichkeiten in Jak 2. Die *ante*-paulinische Position, die prominent von Herder über Beyschlag bis Mayor vertreten wurde, lässt sich schon angesichts der lexikalischen Studie von Kloppenborg nicht mehr vertreten. Eine Variation dieser Position, nämlich eine Interpretation der Theo-logie des Jak *abseits* (iuxta) eines sachlichen Bezuges auf Paulus oder neben diesem, wie Johnson und Niebuhr vorschlagen, greift zu kurz und unterschätzt die Bedeutung der Theologie des Paulus und ihrer Begrifflichkeit in der post-paulinischen Entwicklung ebenso wie die Bedeutung der eigenen theologischen Argumentation des Jakobus in Kap. 2. Ähnliches gilt für Metzners »mittlere« Position, die die die Sach-Polemik gegen das paulinische Glaubenskonzept nicht scharf genug abbildet. Hier sind Becker und Kloppenborg textnäher. Die *durchgängig anti*paulinische Interpretation des Jakobusbriefes bei Lorenzo Scornaienchi dagegen kann ihrerseits nicht erklären, dass Jakobus weder Paulus selbst noch den wesentlichen Rahmen der paulinischen Glaube-Werke-Diskussion: die Rechtfertigung aus Glauben an Christus, nennt. Hier gilt es, weiterzudenken. Die einleuchtendste Erklärung für dies Fehlen eines expliziten Bezuges auf Paulus ist: Jak war nicht mehr mit dem Thema der möglichen Beschneidung und des möglichen Einhaltens der Reinheits- und Speisegebote für Christus-gläubige Heiden befasst – Themen, die Paulus in Gal und Röm beschäftigen mussten (Kloppenborg). Jak schreibt *nach* den Kämpfen um die Frage der Geltung des Gesetzes für Heidenchristen und der Botschaft des Paulus vom rettenden Glauben, deren problematische Auswirkungen in den Gemeinden er aber zu erkennen glaubt und heftig kritisiert. Allerdings ergibt sich dann keine realistische Situation mehr, in der ein christlicher Lehrer an Juden schreibt, wie Kloppenborg vorschlägt.

Zweitens: der Blick auf die Forschungsdebatte zeigt, dass Dibelius bereits grundsätzlich Paulus und Jakobus in die angemessene historische und theologische Balance gebracht hat: Es geht bei Jak um *Post*-Paulinismus (Wischmeyer, Becker). Allerdings unterschätzt Dibelius die gedankliche Auseinandersetzung des Jakobus mit Paulus und seine direkte Bezugnahme auf Paulustexte. Damit unterschätzt Dibelius zugleich auch die selbständige theologische Argumentation des Jakobus. Jak sieht die ethischen Schwächen und Fehler in den Christus-bekennenden Gemeinden nachpaulinischer Zeit, die seiner Wahrnehmung nach wieder das Gesetz – nun als Richtschnur des Tuns – brauchten und gleichzeitig gewisse Einseitigkeiten des paulinischen Ansatzes aufdeckten. Glaube allein reichte nicht, um das Ethos der Gemeinden zu stabilisieren. Allerdings bearbeitet Jakobus nicht die Frage, welche Teile der Tora Ethos-stabilisierend sein könnten. Er scheint an Dekalog, Gebot der Nächstenliebe und soziale Richtlinien aus Leviticus zu denken. Im Zusammenhang mit dem Gesetz ist ihm enkomiastische Sprache wichtiger als Analyse und fallbedingte Anwendung des Gesetzes.

Zwei Tendenzen des Post-Paulinismus bei Jak lassen sich beschreiben. *Einerseits* betreibt Jak theologische *Komplexitätsreduktion* zugunsten paränetischer Kontextualisierung bzw. Applikation. So werden die Thematik der Herkunft des Bösen und der »oberen« und der »psychischen« Weisheit kürzer und eher im Stil des elementarisierenden Rückgriffs auf vorhandenes Grundwissen und im Hinblick auf richtiges Verhalten und Handeln behandelt. Theologisch-spekulative Elemente der paulinischen Bearbeitung der Themen werden rigoros zurückgedrängt. *Andererseits* entwickelt Jak aber bei dem Thema »Glaube und Werke« sowie bei Abraham eine ausführliche eigene theologische Argumentation. Hier agiert Jakobus als *polemisch-korrektiver Rezipient* des Paulus.[403] Er benutzt Polemik – hier muss mit Scornaienchi nicht nur Johnson, sondern auch Dibelius widersprochen werden – und konfrontative Korrektur, wie die Argumentationsanalyse und die Protreptikdiskussion[404] zeigen (Kloppenborg, Scornaienchi). Dabei erweist sich Jakobus auch als Schriftinterpret[405], der Gen 15,6 *selbständig* auslegt.

Drittens: vor einer abschließende Charakteristik der *Jakobus-Theologie* ist zu bedenken, dass diese Charakteristik immer eine Gratwanderung bleiben wird und mit vielen anderen Fragestellungen verbunden ist, die in eine plausible Konstellation zueinander gebracht werden müssen: die zeitliche Ansetzung des Jak (ante-paulinisch, iuxta-paulinisch, post-paulinisch?), das Verhältnis zu den paulinischen Briefen (Kenntnis von Schlagworten oder Textkenntnis?), die Bestimmung und Bedeutung der Briefgattung (Gemeindebrief oder Diasporabrief?), die Gewichtung der Polemik (sachlich: Wischmeyer, oder dezidiert antipaulinisch: Scornaienchi), die Rekonstruktion des religiösen Milieus (jüdische Diaspora: Kloppenborg, judenchristliche Gemeinden: Scornaienchi, ebionitische Gemeinden: Allison, oder christliche Gemeinden der dritten Generation: Dibelius, Burchard, Metzner).

Viertens kann nun das Ergebnis der Paulus-Jakobus-Diskussion in die Darstellung der eigenen *Jakobus-Theologie* integriert werden. Die Jakobus-Theologie setzt sich aus drei Elementen zusammen:

(1.) alttestamentlich-frühjüdische Grundüberzeugungen über Gott den Schöpfer, Gesetzgeber, Richter und Retter,

(2.) Paulus verkürzende Theologumena zu Sünde und Weisheit,

(3.) bestimmte Themen paulinischer Theologie, die Jakobus korrigiert.

Der dritte Punkt verdient besonderes exegetisches Interesse. Jakobus interpretiert »Glaube und Werke« und »Glaube Abrahams« mit den argumentativen Mitteln der Protreptik *anders* als Paulus und zum Teil sachlich deutlich *gegen* ihn. Die paulini-

---

[403] Über die genannten Themen hinaus, die Jakobus als einen Kritiker des Paulus zeigen, lassen sich viele Gemeinsamkeiten zwischen den Paulusbriefen und Jak namhaft machen. Hier ist besonders Johnson zu nennen, der eine umfangreiche Dokumentation von sprachlichen und sachlichen Gemeinsamkeiten registriert: 58–64.

[404] Dazu s. u.

[405] Vgl. JÓNSSON, James, 218–257 (»James as Exeget«); WISCHMEYER, Scriptual Classicism?

B. Der Text. Historische, literarische und thematische Charakteristik

sche Vorordnung des Glaubens vor die »Werke des Gesetzes« versteht Jakobus nicht mehr, da er nicht mehr mit dem Gesetzesdiskurs befasst ist. Er betont stattdessen die Notwendigkeit, den Glauben in praktisches soziales Handeln umzusetzen, und führt Abraham und die Akedah dafür als Beispiel an. Dazu weist er auf die Unfruchtbarkeit eines bloßen Bekenntnisglaubens hin. Hier liegt die *eigene* theologische Leistung des Jakobus, der eben nicht nur – wie dargestellt – bewahrender Tradent der Theo-logie Israels – so Allison –, sondern auch kritischer frühchristlicher Theologe in Auseinandersetzung mit bestimmten Themen paulinischer Theologie ist. Allerdings hat Jakobus die Verschiebung der Koordinaten von Gesetz – Werke des Gesetzes – Glaube Abrahams von der Zeit des Paulus zu seiner eigenen Gegenwart nicht reflektiert. Bleibendes Alleinstellungsmerkmal und damit zugleich theologiegeschichtliches Problem der Jakobus-Theologie ist das Fehlen von Christologie, Pneumatologie und Ekklesiologie bei Jak. Der vorliegende Kommentar interpretiert dies Fehlen als bewusste Rückbildung paulinischer Theologie.

3.3 Soteriologischer und eschatologischer Horizont

Soteriologische und eschatologische Aussagen sind in Jak streng an die Theo-logie gebunden. Ein christologisches Rettungs- bzw. Endzeitmotiv fehlt in Jak.[406] Auch die messianische Motivik fehlt gänzlich. Die βασιλεία-Vorstellung ist ausschließlich auf Gott bezogen (2,5). Das *theo-logische Rettungsmotiv* begegnet in Jak in verbaler Form.[407] Grundsätzlich gilt 4,12: Gott ist der *Retter* (εἷς ἐστιν ὁ νομοθέτης καὶ κριτὴς ὁ δυνάμενος σῶσαι καὶ ἀπολέσαι). Wie geschieht das? Jak verwendet unterschiedliche Motive. Rettung geschieht durch »das eingepflanzte Wort, das eure Seelen *retten* kann« (1,21). Der Täter des Gesetzes wird *selig* sein in seiner Tat (1,25). Glaube ohne Taten kann nicht *retten* (2,14), wohl aber *rettet* das Gebet des Glaubens einen Kranken (5,15), und man kann einen Sünder von seinem sündigen Tun bekehren und so seine Seele aus dem Tod *retten* (5,20). Alle diese Motive sind alttestamentlich.

Dasselbe gilt für die ebenfalls ausschließlich theo-logisch basierten *Endzeitvorstellungen*.[408] Hier gilt grundsätzlich: Gott ist der endzeitliche *Richter*: 2,13, der Gerechtigkeit und Barmherzigkeit verbindet. Gottes Barmherzigkeit wird aber nur denen zuteil, die selbst Barmherzigkeit getan haben.[409] Nur Barmherzigkeit wird das Gericht besiegen. Das Gericht wird besonders den christlichen Lehrern gelten (3,1), da diese besondere Verantwortung für den Frieden in den Gemeinden

---

[406] Substantivisch besonders betont in Joh 4,42; Phil 3,20 und öfter (besonders in Past). Niebuhr, Wer war »Jakobus«, 166 f, weist zurecht auf die Bedeutung des christologischen Bekenntnisses in Jak 1,1 hin, ohne aber weiter darauf einzugehen, dass die Inhalte des Bekenntnisses, die er hinzufügt, gerade nicht in Jak erscheinen (167). Hier scheinen – wie bei Metzner – die Gewichte verschoben zu sein.

[407] Der atl. Titel σωτήρ begegnet nicht in Jak.

[408] Allison, Jak, 92–94. Allison urteilt: »Eschatological expectation is important for James, and it is present in every section. It is nonetheless not a topic in and on itself, and it remains undeveloped« (92 f).

[409] Vgl. Mt 23,23; Lk 10,37.

haben. In Kap. 4 und 5 wird der eschatologische Horizont drängender. Wieder gilt: εἷς ἐστιν ὁ νομοθέτης καὶ κριτὴς ὁ δυνάμενος σῶσαι καὶ ἀπολέσαι (4,12). Jakobus sagt in 5,3 den Reichen »die letzten Tage« an.[410] Darauf folgt die dreimalige Ansage des »Kommens des Herrn« (5,7.8.9) mit einer klimaktischen temporal-spatialen Steigerung: Μακροθυμήσατε ... ἕως τῆς παρουσίας τοῦ κυρίου, ἡ παρουσία τοῦ κυρίου ἤγγικεν, ἰδοὺ ὁ κριτὴς πρὸ τῶν θυρῶν ἔστηκεν. Dabei ist die Perspektive von Kap. 5,7–11 eine soteriologische. Hier verdient die Sprache besondere Aufmerksamkeit. Die Wendung »nahe vor der Tür« begegnet in Mt 24,33 in eschatologischem Zusammenhang, ebenso in Apk 3,20. Die Wendung παρουσία τοῦ κυρίου ist in Mt 24,3.27.37.39 (das »Kommen des Menschensohnes«) sowie in den Briefen[411] an Jesus Christus gebunden. Für Jak 5,7 lässt sich diese Zuschreibung nicht wahrscheinlich machen.[412] Jakobus versteht Gott als endzeitlichen Richter, dessen Gericht bald anbrechen wird: daher der Gerichtsernst besonders in 5,1–6. Jakobus vertritt deutlich eine rein theozentrische Naherwartung, ohne apokalyptische Motive einzusetzen oder eine christologische Interpretation des Motivs vorzunehmen. Eher umgekehrt: die frühchristliche christologische Überschreibung des theozentrischen Naherwartungsmotives wird rückgängig gemacht. Der Jakobusbrief verwendet Motive wie die *Parusie*, die auch spezifisch apokalyptisch eingesetzt werden können, in einem ethischen Weltdeutungsrahmen. Bei aller Angstbesetztheit seiner Gerichts-Eschatologie fehlen die positiven Motive keineswegs: 1,12.18; 2,5 und 4,10 weist Jakobus auf Leben[413], Erbschaft des Reiches und Erhöhung[414] hin. Es bleibt bei der allgemeinen theozentrischen eschatologischen Perspektive von 4,12.

Angesichts dieser Perspektive ist das Ziel des Briefes, die Adressaten zur Vollkommenheit zu führen, beschrieben mit der metaphorischen Wendung des »reinen Gottesdienstes«, konkretisiert als soziale Fürsorge und Distanz zur »Welt«. Den Rahmen bilden einerseits die Geschöpflichkeit des Menschen und Gottes gute Gaben, das »Gesetz der Freiheit«, die Taufe (implizit), Gottes Barmherzigkeit und sein Wort, andererseits das baldige »Kommen des Herrn« und das Gericht. Die Adressaten stehen zwischen Gott und Teufel (4,7), zwischen der Freundschaft mit der Welt und der Freundschaft mit Gott (4,4). Sie in Anfechtungen zu stärken und zur Wahrheit zu bekehren, ist ein gutes Werk und hilft zur »Rettung«, auf die alles ankommt (5,20). Eschatologie und Ethik sind eng aufeinander bezogen.

3.4 Ethos, Ethik, ethische Themen
Die Frage nach der Ethik des Jak führt ins Zentrum des Briefes. Die »Ethik des Jak« zeigt ein bestimmtes Sachprofil (3.4.1). Zugleich nimmt diese Ethik einen bestimm-

---

[410] Apg 2,17; 2Tim 3,1; Hebr 1,2; 1Petr 1,20; 2Petr 3,3.
[411] 1Kor 15,23; 1Thess 2,19; 3,13 u. ö.
[412] Vgl. 5,10 f.: κύριος auf Gott selbst bezogen.
[413] Wie dies vorzustellen sei, bleibt in 1,12.18 unklar.
[414] Auch diese Wendungen sind topisch und lassen sich inhaltlich nicht füllen.

B. Der Text. Historische, literarische und thematische Charakteristik   115

ten Platz im Diskursfeld frühchristlicher Ethik ein (3.4.2). Im Feld frühchristlicher ethischer Entwürfe stellt die Jakobus-Ethik einen eigenen Typus dar (3.4.3). Seit den Kommentaren von Mayor, Ropes und Dibelius ist die Ethik des Jak immer wieder sachlich und traditionsgeschichtlich neu vermessen worden. Susanne Luther führt jetzt auf dem neuesten Stand in die Themen und die Literatur der Jakobus-Ethik ein und schafft eine Plattform für weitere Untersuchungen.[415]

3.4.1

Der vorliegende Kommentar unterscheidet in Abwandlung einer Definition von Friedrich Wilhelm Horn[416] zwischen dem *Ethos* des Jak, wie es vor allem in Kap. 1 entworfen wird (1), der unterliegenden theologisch basierten *Ethik*, die besonders in Kap. 2 formuliert ist (2), und *ethischen Themen*, die besonders in Kap. 3 und 4,1–5,6 behandelt werden (3). Daraus ergibt sich zunächst ein Sachprofil der Ethik des Jak (4). Vorangestellt finden sich die leitenden positiven und negativen Normen in der Anordnung von Susanne Luther (nach der Reihenfolge im Text):[417]

Positive Normen neben dem Gesetz (bzw. aus dem Gesetz abgeleitet)
Standhaftigkeit und Bewährung in Anfechtung (Jak 1,2–12)
Geduld / Erdulden (Jak 1,3 f; 1,12; 5,7–11)
Vollkommenheit (Jak 1,4; 1,17; 2,22; 3,2)
Weisheit (Jak 1,5; 3,13–18)
Demut (Jak 1,10; 4,6–10; 4,13–17)
Armut (Jak 1,10 f; 2,5–13; 5,1–6)
Sanftmut (Jak 1,21; 3,13)
Barmherzigkeit (Jak 2,13)
(gute) Werke (Jak 2,14–26; 4,16)
Gerechtigkeit (Jak 2,23–25; 3,18; 5,16)
Integrität / keine innere Gespaltenheit (Jak 3,1–12; 5,12)
Wahrheit (Jak 3,14; 5,19 f)
Reinheit / Heiligkeit / Sündlosigkeit (Jak 3,17; 4,8)
Negative Normen
Reichtum (Jak 2,1–13)

---

[415] S. Luther, Die Ethik des Jakobusbriefes, in: R. Zimmermann (Hg.), Ethik des Neuen Testaments, Tübingen 2023, (im Druck) (umfangreiche Bibliographie). Vgl. weiter M. Konradt, Ethik im Neuen Testament, Göttingen 2022.

[416] »Ethik ist eine theoretische Reflexion über ein gefordertes menschliches Verhalten, und sie legt dessen Begründung, Inhalt und Zielsetzung dar … Die Darlegung einer Ethik des Neuen Testaments ist in jedem Fall eine konstruktive Aufgabe der Exegese. Demgegenüber beschreibt Ethos das faktische, oft unreflektierte, übliche Verhalten in den neutestamentlichen Schriften«: F. W. Horn, »Ethik (NT)«, WiBiLex, https://www.bibelwissenschaft.de/stichwort/47913/.

[417] S. Luther, Ethik, siehe oben. Die Frage, ob die Exegese hier von Normen oder Tugenden bzw. Lastern / Sünden sprechen solle, kann offen bleiben, da Jak keinen dieser Begriffe benutzt. Der Terminus Norm macht deutlich, dass es sich bei den entsprechenden Verhaltens- und Handlungsweisen nicht um bloße Vorschläge, sondern um Gebote oder Verbote handelt.

116 Einleitung

Ungerechtigkeit (Jak 3,6)

Sich Rühmen (Jak 4,13–17).[418]

(1) Ethos: für das *Ethos* des *Niedrigen* sind Geduld, Niedrigkeit bzw. Demut, Sanftmut, Glaube, Einseeligkeit (ἁπλῶς[419]), Nächstenliebe, kontrollierte Rede, Weisheit
und Frieden entscheidende Verhaltensformen. Der Niedrige erwartet alles von Gott
und lebt in der Haltung des einfachen und vertrauensvollen Bittens und Empfangens. In Jak 1,2–4 entwirft der Verfasser den Rahmen dieses Ethos, 1,5–27 dient
einer ersten Ausführung, die auch die wichtigsten Aspekte der folgenden Ausführungen bereits im Vorgriff anspricht: Geduld, Niedrigkeit, Ablehnung der Sünde,
Stellen unter Gottes Gaben und Wort, Tun des Gehörten, *caritas* und Distanz zur
Welt. In den folgenden Kapiteln folgen weitere Aspekte dieses Ethos: Verzicht auf
Bevorzugung sozial Höherstehender und Reicher (Prosopolempsie), Friedfertigkeit,
Güte, Barmherzigkeit[420], Verzicht auf Streit, Neid, Verleumdung, auf »Zweiseeligkeit« (δίψυχος[421]) bzw. Zweifel (διακρινόμενος[422]), auf wirtschaftliche Unterdrü-
ckung, Gewaltanwendung und Schwören – zusammengefasst als »Sünde« und Ver-
halten der »Welt« charakterisiert. Hier ist der Einzelne als ethisch verantwortliches
Subjekt im Blick.

John Kloppenborg bemerkt zurecht, dass Jak 1 mehr ist als bloße Tatethik, und
bringt dies Ethos in Zusammenhang mit antiker Psychagogie:

> A distinctive feature of James … is that James is not simply a list of do's and don'ts
> akin to what is found, for example, in Ps-Isocrates' *To Demonicus*, Ps-Phocylides, or the
> *Sentences of Sextus*. James is keenly interested in the conditions of the soul from which
> moral actions flow.[423]

Im vorliegenden Kommentar wird die Charakteristik als »Ethos« bevorzugt. Jak 1,21
und 5,20 belegen allerdings, dass Jak den Begriff der ψυχή im Sinne philosophischer
Seelenführung verwenden kann. Wichtig ist, dass in Kap. 1 die innere Haltung des
Individuums thematisiert wird. Zu dieser inneren Haltung (Ethos) gehört entscheidend die πίστις als festes Vertrauen auf Gottes Gabe (1.3.6; 2,5; 5,14). Gegenbegriff
ist Zweifel bzw. Zweiseeligkeit. Der Glaubensbegriff, der in Kap. 2 vorherrscht, ist
davon *unterschieden*. Jakobus stellt keine Verbindung zwischen den unterschiedlichen Bedeutungsinhalten von πίστις her. Es ist deutlich, dass sein eigener Glaubens-

---

[418] Hinzu kommen: Prosopolempsie (2,1); Vorenthalten des Lohnes (5,4); Schlemmen (5,5); ungerechtes
Richten (5,6); Schwören (5,12).

[419] Das Substantiv fehlt.

[420] »Gute Früchte« 3,17; vgl. die Liste der »Früchte des Geistes bei Paulus.

[421] Das Substantiv fehlt.

[422] Das Substantiv fehlt.

[423] KLOPPENBORG, James, 97–106, Zitat 97. Kloppenborg räumt ein, dass Jak keine theoretischen Refle-
xionen zur Seele anstellt und daher eine philosophiegeschichtliche Verbindung zur Stoa oder zu Philo nicht
hergestellt werden kann. Er weist aber auf Elemente eines Vollkommenheitsethos bei Jak hin, die Analogien
zu kaiserzeitlichen Überlegungen zu Ausdauer, Geduld, Training der Seele bzw. des Selbst aufweisen.

B. Der Text. Historische, literarische und thematische Charakteristik 117

begriff mit dem Ethos des festen und einfachen Gottvertrauens von Kap. 1 beschrieben werden kann. In Kap. 2 lässt er sich polemisch auf einen Glaubensbegriff ein, der aus einem anderen theologischen Zusammenhang stammt.

(2) Ethik: die Ethik des Jak ist auf den *post-paulinischen Diskurs um Glauben und Taten* konzentriert. Die theologisch-ethische Abhandlung in Kap. 2 ist reich binnengegliedert, behandelt aber *ein* Thema: das Verhältnis von Glauben und Taten, und ist insofern eminent ethisch:

2,1–4	Beispielerzählung für die Ungleichbehandlung in der Gemeindeversammlung
2,5–7	Mahnrede an die Adressaten: Grundsatz-Belehrung über das Gesetz
2,8–11 / 12 f	Ausblick auf das Gericht gemäß dem Gesetz und Grundsatzermahnung
2,14–17	Schulbeispiel zum synergetischen Verhältnis von Glauben und Werken
2,18 f	Schuldiskussion zum nutzlosen Glauben der Dämonen ohne Taten
2,20–26	Schulbeweis für die These: »Der Mensch wird durch Taten gerecht« anhand des Beispiels Abrahams.

Der Ausgangspunkt liegt in 2,1–7 und 2,14.17: Jakobus diagnostiziert einen Hiat zwischen Glauben (πίστις) und Taten (ἔργα) bei seinen Adressaten.[424] Mit dem Oppositionsbegriff »Werke« bzw. »Taten« wird πίστις aus dem Ethos-Diskurs in Jak 1 herausgenommen und in einen anderen ethischen Diskurs gestellt, der auf paulinische Begriffssprache rückverweist, diese aber eigenständig füllt und bewertet. Die Opposition Glaube – Taten ist das ethische Herzstück des bereits dargestellten theo-logischen Post-Paulinismus des Jakobus.

Der *ethische Post-Paulinismus* muss an dieser Stelle in Korrespondenz zur post-paulinischen *Theologie* ausführlicher dargestellt werden, da er die wichtigste sachliche Botschaft des Jak bildet. Jakobus entwickelt eine eigene Argumentation um die Begriffe *Glaube, Gerechtigkeit, Taten*, in der der Glaube allein (2,24) nicht zur Gerechtigkeit gemäß dem Gesetz – auch als Vollkommenheit bezeichnet (2,22) – führt, sondern mit Taten nach der Norm des Gesetzes zusammenwirken muss (2,22). Dafür führt Jakobus Abrahams Glauben als Beispiel an.[425] Dabei benutzt Jakobus einen gegenüber Kap. 1 veränderten Glaubensbegriff. πίστις bezeichnet nicht mehr das individuelle Ethos des Vertrauens, sondern ist Bestandteil von Bekenntnisformeln – hier zunächst als Bekenntnis zu dem Herrn Jesus Christus verwendet (μὴ ἐν προσωπολημψίαις ἔχετε τὴν πίστιν τοῦ κυρίου ἡμῶν Ἰησοῦ Χριστοῦ

---

[424] Zum Thema vgl. M. KONRADT, Werke als Handlungsdimension des Glaubens. Erwägungen zum Verhältnis von Theologie und Ethik im Jakobusbrief, in: F. W. Horn / R. Zimmermann (Hg.), Jenseits von Indikativ und Imperativ, WUNT 238, Tübingen 2009, 309–327.

[425] Die kursiv gesetzten Begriffe stellen das argumentative Netz dar, das Jakobus aus paulinischen Vorgaben neu knüpft.

τῆς δόξης), in V. 19 dann auf »den einen Gott« angewendet (σὺ πιστεύεις ὅτι εἷς ἐστιν ὁ θεός, καλῶς ποιεῖς· καὶ τὰ δαιμόνια πιστεύουσιν καὶ φρίσσουσιν). Damit formalisiert und depraviert Jakobus seinen eigenen Glaubensbegriff (einfaches kindliches Vertrauen auf Gottes Gabe) von Kap. 1. Offensichtlich reagiert er damit auf Gemeindeglieder, die ihren Christus-Glauben nicht in ethischer Verantwortung leben und formelhaft auf die Korrektheit ihrer πίστις verweisen. Jakobus findet die Wurzel dieses Fehlverhaltens in paulinischen Texten über »Gerechtigkeit aus Glauben« (λογιζόμεθα γὰρ δικαιοῦσθαι πίστει ἄνθρωπον χωρὶς ἔργων νόμου Röm 3,28[426]) und setzt sich mit diesem von ihm diagnostizierten Hintergrund des Fehlverhaltens in den Gemeinden auseinander. Wie ist sein Argument?

Für Jakobus sind beide Bekenntnisformeln korrekt, aber in ihrer Bedeutung begrenzt. Sie bleiben hinter dem Gesetz zurück. Denn Dämonen sprechen das Sch'ma – ohne ethisch handeln zu können. Und Christus-bekennende Gemeindeglieder begehen προσωπολημψία und verstoßen damit nicht nur gegen *ein* Gesetz, sondern gegen alle Gesetze (2,1–13). Korrektes Bekenntnis – Glaube an Jesus Christus und an den einen Gott – schützt also nach Jak nicht vor Versündigung am ganzen Gesetz, das als eschatologische Richtinstanz Gültigkeit behält (2,12 f) und allein retten wird (4,11). Der Glaube impliziert Verpflichtungen und muss praktisch umgesetzt werden. Jakobus nennt: gerechte bzw. gleiche Behandlung verschiedener sozialer Klassen (kein »Ansehen der Person« 2,1, »Ehre«[427] für die Armen 2,6), praktische Unterstützung Armer, Niedriger, Notleidender, Gerechtigkeit bzw. Gewaltverzicht gegenüber Abhängigen (arme Gemeindemitglieder, gegen die prozessiert wird 2,6 f; Lohnarbeiter, denen ihr Lohn verweigert wird 5,1–6). Auf den Punkt gebracht ist es die Gesetzeserfüllung (2,8) bzw. sind es die Taten, die retten, nicht der (Bekenntnis-) Glaube. Der Bekenntnis-Glaube wird als ethisch defizitär abgewertet, die Taten gemäß dem Gesetz werden als ethisch notwendig prämiert.

In Kap. 2 verbindet Jakobus die beiden großen Begriffspaare, die Paulus in Gal und Röm theologisch-*christologisch* und heilsgeschichtlich ausgearbeitet hat: *Gesetz und Gerechtigkeit* und *Glaube und Werke*, in einer sachlich anti-paulinischen, historisch aber post-paulinischen Verhältnisbestimmung. Dabei entsteht eine *eigene* theo-logisch-ethische Verknüpfung der Begriffe ohne die christologische Interpretation, die Paulus dem gesamten Zusammenhang von Glauben, Gerechtigkeit und Freiheit gegeben hatte. Für Jak gilt: Gerechtigkeit, verstanden als ethische Vollkommenheit (1,4), wird durch Gesetzeserfüllung, auch als »Werke« bezeichnet (2,24), erzielt. Bekenntnisglaube allein ist »tot« (2,17). Beide wirken zusammen: ἡ πίστις συνήργει τοῖς ἔργοις αὐτοῦ, und: ἐκ τῶν ἔργων ἡ πίστις ἐτελειώθη (2,22).

Damit stößt Jakobus in Kap. 2 zu der theologischen Begründung seiner eigenen Ethik vor: Die *erste und einzige Grundlage* ist das *Gesetz* (2,8–11 »das königliche

---

[426] Beachte das Sch'ma Israel in Röm 3,30.
[427] Das Substantiv fehlt bei Jak, das Verb begegnet in Jak 2,6 in verneinter Form: ἀτιμάζειν.

Gesetz« und V. 12 »das Gesetz der Freiheit«). Jakobus findet im sachlichen Gegensatz zu Paulus die Freiheit *im* Gesetz, das bis zum Endgericht in Geltung bleibt und dessen Befolgung soteriologische Funktion hat. Eine soteriologische Funktion Jesu Christi und die offenbarungsgeschichtliche Differenz zwischen der Zeit vor dem Kommen Jesu Christi und dem neuen Sein in Christus aus der paulinischen Theologie und Ethik fehlen. Wichtig ist hier, dass es Jakobus trotz der generalisierenden Diktion dabei konkret um Lev 19,15 geht: Οὐ ποιήσετε ἄδικον ἐν κρίσει· οὐ λήμψῃ πρόσωπον πτωχοῦ οὐδὲ θαυμάσεις πρόσωπον δυνάστου, ἐν δικαιοσύνῃ κρινεῖς τὸν πλησίον σου (Ihr sollt im Gericht kein Unrecht verüben. Du sollst das Angesicht eines Armen nicht in Augenschein nehmen und das Angesicht eines Machthabers nicht bewundern. In Gerechtigkeit sollst du über deinen Nächsten urteilen). Er verweist im Zitat aber auf die bekannten und überall in den frühchristlichen Schriften zitierten Gebote von Dekalog und Nächstenliebe. Dekalog und Liebesgebot stehen für *alle* Gebote des Gesetzes.[428] Wie diese Repräsentation aber zu verstehen sei – als »Erfüllung« im Sinne von Substitution oder im Sinne einer buchstäblichen Befolgung, sagt Jakobus nicht. Auch das Abraham-Beispiel bleibt der praktischen Einzeltat verbunden: Jakobus gründet die Gerechtigkeit Abrahams auf seinen Glaubensgehorsam, der sich im »Werk« des Isaakopfers realisiert. Paulus hatte in Röm 4,5 umgekehrt argumentiert: τῷ δὲ μὴ ἐργαζομένῳ πιστεύοντι δὲ ἐπὶ τὸν δικαιοῦντα τὸν ἀσεβῆ λογίζεται ἡ πίστις αὐτοῦ εἰς δικαιοσύνην (Dem aber, der nicht mit Werken umgeht [der keine Werke tut], aber an den glaubt, der den Gottlosen gerecht macht, dem wird sein Glaube zur Gerechtigkeit angerechnet). Es geht also in Jak 2 ausschließlich um gesetzeskonforme *Ethik*, nicht um die Themen von Gesetzeserfüllung oder um eine eigene Gesetzestheologie. Auch bei diesem Thema konzentriert sich Jak auf die praktische Dimension und übergeht die paulinischen theologischen Neuinterpretationen.

Zusammengefasst: Jakobus entwickelt seine theologische Ethik aus der Tora und aus einer unterstützenden Interpretation des Abraham-Glaubens, der im Gegensatz zu der Interpretation in Röm 4 durch Abrahams »Werke«, durch sein Tun bestimmt ist. Sowohl das Gesetz als auch der Glaube Abrahams werden in Jak 2 *ethisch* interpretiert und auf ihre ethische Dimension konzentriert und gegenüber Paulus auch reduziert. Dass diese Interpretation sich sachlich gegen paulinische theologische Vorstellungen richtet und Teil des Post-Paulinismus des Jakobus ist, wurde bereits dargelegt.

(3) Ethische Themen: von Kap. 3 an behandelt Jak verschiedene ethische Einzelthemen. Sprachethik (a), Ethik des friedlichen Zusammenlebens (b), Verzicht auf Gewalt und Selbstdurchsetzung (c) sind die übergeordneten Verhaltensformen, zu denen Jak teilweise in scharfer prophetisch gefärbter Gerichtssprache aufruft.

---

[428] Hier liegt ein entscheidender Unterschied zu Paulus. Gal 5,13 ist das ganze Gesetz im Gebot der Nächstenliebe erfüllt, und Paulus führt für diese Art der Gesetzeserfüllung den Begriff der Freiheit ein.

(a) *Sprachethik*: besondere Aufmerksamkeit – sachlich und formal[429] – schenkt er der Sprachethik. Der Brief ist ein Versuch, Sprachethik theologisch zu basieren und in den Gemeinden zu etablieren.[430] Sorgfältiger Umgang mit der Sprache – es geht um die Vermeidung von »Verfehlung im Wort« (3,2) –, die Entwicklung einer geeigneten ethischen Sprache für die frühchristlichen Gemeinden und für die praktische ethische Unterweisung für Haltung und Handeln greifen ineinander, zusammengehalten durch das literarische Format des an die frühchristlichen Gemeinden insgesamt gerichteten theologisch-paränetischen Briefes, der Maßstäbe setzt und autoritativ wirken will. Der Verfasser entwirft eine Sprache des theo-logischen Lobes[431], die dadurch vorbildlich ist, dass sie spaltende Definitionen vermeidet. Eine theoretische Erörterung von Sprache im Sinne einer Sprach- oder Sprechtheorie findet sich in Jak nicht.[432] Ebenso fehlen metaethische Überlegungen zum Thema. Was wir finden, sind einerseits Aussagen über das Wort (λόγος), die Rede bzw. das Reden (λέγειν, λαλεῖν), ein topisch geprägter ekphrastischer Text über die Zunge (γλῶσσα) bzw. das Hören und den Hörer (ἀκούειν, ἀκροατής) und andererseits über richtiges und falsches Handeln oder Tun (ποιεῖν, ποίησις, ποιητής) und die daraus folgenden Taten oder Werke (ἔργον, ἐργάζεσθαι). Das Interesse des Jakobus liegt auf dem Nachweis, dass Sprechen gegenüber Tun *a priori* defizitär ist. Das bedeutet auch, dass Sprechen gegenüber ethischem Tun moralisch abgewertet oder mindestens dem Tun nachgeordnet wird.

---

[429] Die *ekphrasis* über die Zunge ist der sprachlich-stilistisch am sorgfältigsten gestaltete Teiltext des Jak.

[430] Vgl. dazu S. Luther, Sprachethik im Neuen Testament. Eine Analyse des frühchristlichen Diskurses im Matthäusevangelium, im Jakobusbrief und im 1. Petrusbrief, WUNT II / 394, Tübingen 2015, 9–11. Luther bezieht sich auf die Definition von W. R. Baker, Personal Speech-Ethics in the Epistle of James, WUNT II / 68, Tübingen 1995, 2: »The term ›personal speech-ethics‹ is my own attempt to capture the idea of ethics or morality as applied to interpersonal communication. Simply put, it is the rights and wrongs of utterance. It involves when to speak, how to speak, and to whom to speak, as well as when, how, and to whom not to speak. It includes to a certain extent the process of human speech and its relationship to thoughts and actions. Only to a very limited extent does formal speech relate to it.« S. Luther, Sprachethik, 414–422; vgl. auch die kurze Aufzählung der sprachethisch relevanten Topoi in Jak bei S. Luther, Profiling the Author of the Letter of James: Dealing with Traditions in the Light of Epistolary Authorship Conceptions, in: Who was ›James‹?, 29–56, 33: »Various *topoi* of ancient speech-ethics discourse, including: wrathful speaking (Jas 1:19–27); the lack of human integrity, often reflected in verbal action (Jas 1:26–27; 3:9–12); the control of the tongue (Jas 1:26–27; 3:1–18); forms of inappropriate speech (Jas 4:1–4, etc.); interpersonal judgmental speech (Jas 4:11–12); the problem of oathtaking (Jas 5:12); and the necessity of interpersonal admonition (Jas 5:19–20)«. Kritisch zur Übernahme des Baker-Begriffs »Sprachethik« durch S. Luther äußert sich Scornaienchi, Polemik, 353–357: »Zweitens verzichtet die Philosophie im ersten und zweiten Jahrhundert darauf, eine eigene Ethik auszuarbeiten« (355).

[431] Siehe oben.

[432] Vgl. allerdings die Ansätze in 1Kor 12–14: N. Treu, Das Sprachverständnis des Paulus im Rahmen des antiken Sprachdiskurses, NET 26, Tübingen 2018. Interessant ist ein Vergleich zwischen 1Kor 12–14 und Jak 3: Paulus bemüht sich um eine theoretische Erfassung von »Sprache«, während Jakobus seine grundsätzliche Warnung vor Streit in eine literarisch ambitionierte Ekphrasis der »Zunge« kleidet, die auf der Motivik von Sirachpassagen beruht.

B. Der Text. Historische, literarische und thematische Charakteristik 121

Jak steht damit in der Tradition tiefen Misstrauens gegenüber der Rede als einem menschlichen Instrument, wie sie in der Weisheitsliteratur Israels formuliert wurde und in der Warnung vor »der Zunge« bei Jesus Sirach eine klassische Darstellung fand.[433] Nur der göttliche λόγος, in 1,18 (λόγῳ ἀληθείας) und 1,21 (τὸν ἔμφυτον λόγον) thematisiert, ist davon ausgenommen. Gerade der göttliche λόγος ist aber auf das Tun hin angelegt: Γίνεσθε δὲ ποιηταὶ λόγου (1,22 f). Nicht gesagt wird, ob sich 1,18 auf das göttliche Schöpfungswort oder auf die Taufformel bezieht[434] und ob 1,21 das Gesetz meint oder »a philosophical notion of law«.[435] Verkürzt lässt sich daher formulieren: Die Adressaten sollen tun, was das göttliche Wort impliziert – obgleich dieser Inhalt nirgendwo ausgesprochen wird. Hier wie so oft findet sich die jakobäische Komplexitätsreduktion. Diese Tradition schließt das Misstrauen gegenüber jeder Form religiöser Intellektualität ein (Lehrer) und betrifft damit interessanterweise auch den Glauben als Grundmodus des personal verantworteten Verhaltens gegenüber Gott, wie Paulus ihn beschreibt. Demgegenüber gilt nur das Tun der Gebote als ethisch gut und Gott entsprechend (Vollkommenheit). Der Gegensatz zwischen Theorie und Praxis, im Jak als Gegensatz zwischen πίστις und ἔργα oder ἀκούειν und ποιεῖν formuliert, lässt eine ethische Dimension von Sprache und damit auch von der Entwicklung theologischer Gedanken und Positionen, wie sie seit Paulus in den Gemeinden entstehen, nur ganz begrenzt zu. Grundsätzlich wird die Rede aus einer angstbesetzten Perspektive heraus beurteilt – paradoxerweise, da der Verfasser des Jakobusbriefes selbst literarische Fähigkeiten hat und mit Sprache umgehen kann.

(b) *Distanz zur Welt und zur Sünde*: schon in 3,13–18 weitet Jakobus das Thema des kontrollierten Sprechens zu einem Ethos des Friedens und der Güte aus. Er ordnet der »Weisheit von oben« einen Tugendkatalog zu und entwirft einen konträren Lasterkatalog für die irdische Weisheit. Damit führt er das bekannte dualistische Tugend-Laster-Konzept in seine Ethik ein und ordnet die ethische Welt nach Gott und Teufel, nach Freundschaft mit Gott und Freundschaft mit der Welt, nach Sünde und Gesetzesbefolgung. Es geht dabei um *Weltdistanz*, nicht um *Weltgestaltung*. Außer der klassischen jüdischen Witwen- und Waisenfürsorge, caritativem Verhalten in der Gemeinde und der gerechten Bezahlung der Lohnarbeiter wird nicht gestaltendes Handeln gefordert, sondern »keine Befleckung mit der Welt« (1,27). Der Brief hat das praktische Ziel der Stärkung der *passiven* Tugend der Geduld der Adressaten in ihren hauptsächlichen Versuchungen: Reichtum, Weltlichkeit, Selbstdurchsetzung, Luxus, Ungerechtigkeit.

(c) *Gewalt*: Jakobus diagnostiziert und verurteilt verschiedene Spielarten von Gewalt »von oben« in der Diskussion und in der Verurteilung anderer Menschen sowie

---

[433] WISCHMEYER, The Book of Ben Sira From a Reception-Historical Perspective.
[434] Vgl. den Kommentar zur Stelle.
[435] Vgl. dazu KLOPPENBORG, James, 106 mit Hinweis auf M. JACKSON-MCCABE, Logos and Law in the Letter of James: The Law of Nature, the Law of Moses, and the Law of Freedom, NT.S 100, Leiden 2001, 238.

in der Gestalt juristisch und sozial ungerechter Unterdrückung und schrankenloser Selbstdurchsetzung. Im Verlauf von Jak 4,1–5,6 lässt sich eine Steigerung der Kritik und Verurteilung beobachten, die in der rhetorischen Mordanklage von 5,6 gipfelt. Die Exegese zeigt, dass Jakobus besonders in 5,1–6 mit Elementen sozialkritischer Gesetzgebung der Tora und prophetischer Anklage gegen die Reichen arbeitet. Die archaisierende Topik trifft nicht die aktuelle Situation der Adressaten und wirkt eher verstörend als mahnend und erziehend. Jónsson argumentiert, hier liege Kritik an realen Vergehen der Reichen vor: Jakobus verurteile *in-group violence*.[436] Diese Analyse berücksichtigt zwei Aspekte nicht ausreichend: *erstens* die archaisierende Topik, die LXX-Wendungen benutzt, die nicht zu den sozialen und institutionellen Lebensbedingungen der Adressaten passen, *zweitens* die literarische Ambition und damit gepaarte emotionale Rhetorik des Verfassers, die sich in Kap. 3 und 4,1–5,6 zeigt. Jakobus arbeitet mit der sich steigernden Rhetorik der Gerichtsrede, um eine nachhaltige Wirkung bei den Adressaten zu erzielen: Betroffenheit, Angst, Umkehr – das Motiv, das in 5,19 f abschließend aufgerufen wird. Jakobus wird von der Angst getrieben, die Adressaten könnten im Zuge des Wachstums ihrer Gemeinden Reichen und Mächtigen Raum gewähren und damit die Armen und Ohnmächtigen unterdrücken und damit ihre eigene Existenz vor Gott zerstören.

(4) Profil: die Analyse des Netzes von Ethos, Grundlagenethik und ethischen Themen macht einen eigenen Typus frühchristlicher gesetzesbasierter *Vollkommenheitsethik* sichtbar.[437] Grundlage und ethische Norm ist das *Gesetz* Israels. Theologisch-ethisches Vorbild ist Abraham als paradigmatischer Vertreter gelebten Glaubensgehorsams (sog. mimetische Ethik).[438] Der Brief entwickelt auf dieser doppelten Basis eine eigene *Jakobus-Ethik* unter dem theologischen Signet des Pseudonyms Jakobus. Diese Jakobus-Ethik bezieht sich auf Christus-bekennende Gemeinden, kann aber nach der Vorstellung des Verfassers auch für Diasporajuden gelten. Andersherum formuliert gilt ebenfalls: Die Jakobus-Ethik bindet die frühchristlichen Gemeinden an das Gesetz als ethische Richtschnur und an Abrahams Glauben, der als Gesetzesgehorsam und Tatglaube definiert wird. Der Verfasser knüpft bereits in der Adresse an die Gesetzesethik Israels an, indem er sich als Jakobus vorstellt und seine Adressaten als Israel in der Zerstreuung anschreibt. Hinter dieser doppelten Zuschreibung verbirgt sich sein realer Status als frühchristlicher Lehrer (1,1; 3,1) und der reale Status seiner Adressaten als Mitglieder frühchristlicher Gemeinden (2,1). Der Verfasser entwirft aber unter der Autorität des Jakobus und eines enzyklischen Schreibens an die jüdische Diaspora eine eigene Jakobus-Ethik für Christus-bekennende Gemeinden. Er verzichtet dabei auf christologische, ekklesiologische oder pneumatologische Begründungen ethischen Verhaltens und Handelns seiner

---

[436] JÓNSSON, James, 274–282.
[437] 1,4.16 f.25; 2,8.22; 3,2; 5,11.
[438] 1,25; 2,8–13.

B. Der Text. Historische, literarische und thematische Charakteristik   123

Adressaten. Damit verzichtet er auf die neuen frühchristlichen Begründungsansätze, die Paulus entwickelt hat, die in der deuteropaulinischen Briefliteratur und in der großen Erzählung der Apostelgeschichte weiterentwickelt werden und die sich auf die institutionellen Bedingungen der ἐκκλησίαι und die Lebenswirklichkeit der Christus-gläubigen Gemeindeglieder beziehen.[439] Lediglich in Jak 5,13–20 scheint zum Ende des Briefes etwas von der realen zeitgenössischen »Gemeindeethik« auf, in der Verfasser und Adressaten leben. Insgesamt aber beschränkt Jakobus sein Ethikkonzept auf das Gesetz sowie auf Elemente der Sozialkritik der Propheten, auf weisheitliche Mahnungen und paradigmatische Gestalten aus der Geschichte Israels, ohne zu berücksichtigen, dass die Christus-gläubigen Gemeinden seiner Generation in ἐκκλησίαι, nicht in Synagogalverbänden leben. Jakobus konzipiert und lehrt *Toraethik*. Das wird besonders deutlich in 2,8–13 und in 2,20–26, wo der Verfasser Abraham als Urbild der »Gerechtigkeit durch Werke«, d. h. einer Tora-Ethik vorstellt. Diese ethische Interpretation von Gen 15,6 ist sachlich gegen die »Glaubensethik« des Paulus gerichtet, der Abraham als Urbild der Gerechtigkeit, die aus Glauben kommt, versteht (Röm 4,16).

3.4.2

Jak ist ein ethisches Schreiben. Das Sachprofil dieser Ethik wurde erhoben. Jetzt geht es um die Anschlussfrage: Wo ist der *Platz des Jak im Diskursfeld frühchristlicher Ethik*? Was trägt er *additiv*, was *konzeptionell* bei? Sucht er in anderer Weise Verbindungen zur frühkaiserzeitlichen ethischen Literatur als die Paulus-Briefe? Der Verfasser zitiert wie Paulus »Schrift« bzw. »Gesetz«, nicht aber griechische Philosophen oder zeitgenössische Ethiker. Gerade die Einsicht, dass es sich bei Jak nicht um *ad-hoc*-Korrespondenz, sondern um sorgfältig konzipierte *Briefliteratur* handelt, macht die Frage nach der Funktion des Schreibens und nach dem Platz dieser Art ethischer Epistel in der frühkaiserzeitlichen Literatur griechisch-römischer, jüdischer und frühchristlicher Provenienz umso wichtiger. Drei Merkmale sind in diesem Fragezusammenhang besonders wichtig: erstens die literarische Form der ethischen Texte des Jak(1), zweitens die Stellung des Briefes im Gesamtfeld frühkaiserzeitlichen Ethik (2), drittens das innovative oder traditionelle Potential der Jak-Ethik (3).

---

[439] Darauf weist besonders E.-M. Becker, Der Begriff der Demut bei Paulus, Tübingen 2015, 190, hin: »Paulus schreibt an konkrete Gemeinden (ἐκκλησία), deren Glieder κλητοί sind, so wie er als Apostel ›berufen‹ ist. Die Haltung des ταπειν- nimmt also nicht nur Maß an Christus (Phil 2,6 ff.), sondern stiftet Gemeinschaft und Einheit unter den in einer Ortsgemeinde versammelten ›Berufenen‹. Der Verfasser des Jak schreibt hingegen nicht an eine konkrete Gemeinde, sondern an die ›zwölf Stämme in der Diaspora‹ (1,1). Die Übung der Demut als ekklesiales Prinzip der Gemeinschaftsstiftung wird in der hier vorausgesetzten Situation der Adressaten kaum für die inter-personale Kommunikation in der Ortsgemeinde von Nutzen sein können. Gerade im Vergleich mit Paulus wird die sozialkritische und weisheitliche Prägung der Lexik im Jak evident werden«. Vgl. dies., Σοφία ἄνωθεν, in: Who was ›James‹?, 219–236.

124 Einleitung

(1) *Erstens* muss geklärt werden, um welche Form ethischer Rede es sich in Jak handelt. Dabei werden in der exegetischen Literatur vor allem die Begriffe Paränese und Protreptik benutzt. Dibelius hat – wie schon gezeigt – Jak weniger als Brief, sondern eher als »Paränese« charakterisiert:

> Wir dürfen also den »Jakobus-Brief« nach Prüfung seiner literarischen Art in allen seinen Teilen als Paränese bezeichnen.[440]

Er stellt den Brief »mit dieser Einordnung in eine große und bedeutsame Geschichte«[441]: in die Spruchdichtung der jüdischen Weisheitsliteratur, die Dibelius ebenso in den Paulusbriefen[442] wie in Hebr 13, in Barn und der Didache, aber auch in den Reden Jesu in Mt und Lk findet.[443] Besonders weist er auf die Mandata des Hermas hin[444], weiter auf die antike jüdische paränetische Literatur wie Tobit, Pseudo-Phokylides, Pseudo-Menander[445], Testamente der zwölf Patriarchen, Pirke Aboth. Allen diesen Texten ist nach Dibelius Folgendes gemeinsam: der »Eklektizismus«[446], das »Fehlen des Zusammenhangs«[447], die »Stichwort-Verbindung«[448], Wiederholungen.[449] Dabei handelt es sich um formale Kriterien, die ihre Bedeutung im Rahmen seiner formgeschichtlichen Konzeption haben und, wie gezeigt wurde, forschungsgeschichtlich überholt sind. Dibelius' Einordnung hat eine starke Wirkung in der Jak-Forschung gehabt, kann jedoch nicht zufriedenstellen. Allison weist auf die drei deutlichen Defizite bei Dibelius hin:

> Dibelius was far from being wholly wrong: James is indeed full of *paraenesis*, that is, moral exhortation. He erred, however, in setting aside James' character as a letter, in denying that it could have a concrete situation in view, and in falling to see that *paraenesis* can serve coherent argumentation.[450]

John Kloppenborg nimmt Allisons Einwände gegen Dibelius auf und will Jak statt in der Perspektive der Paränese eher im Zusammenhang der *Protreptik* lesen. Kloppenborg definiert Paränese allerdimgs anders als Dibelius weniger formal-traditionsgeschichtlich als inhaltlich-intentional:

---

[440] Dibelius, Jak, 16.
[441] Dibelius, Jak, 17.
[442] Dibelius, Jak, 15.
[443] Dibelius, Jak, 16.
[444] Ebd.
[445] Dazu J.C. de Vos, The Decalogue in Pseudo-Phocylides and Syriac Menander: ›Unwritten Laws‹ or Decalogue Reception? in: D. Markl (Hg.), The Decalogue and Its Cultural Influence, HBM 58, Sheffield 2013, 41–56.
[446] Dibelius, Jak, 19.
[447] Dibelius, Jak, 20.
[448] Dibelius, Jak, 21.
[449] Dibelius, Jak, 22.
[450] Allison, Jak, 75. Allison weist auch auf die Nähe zur ethischen Predigt (»sermon«) hin.

B. Der Text. Historische, literarische und thematische Charakteristik

The main characteristic of *paraenesis* is moral exhortation addressed to an individual or group, exhortations about behaviour – what is to be done and to be avoided.[451]

Nun ist deutlich, dass Jak nicht nur Verhaltensregeln und -empfehlungen gibt. Daher bevorzugt Kloppenborg für Jak das Protreptik-Konzept, das er mit James Collins als dialogisch, agonistisch, situativ und rhetorisch, d.h. weniger traditionsbezogen und argumentativ anspruchsvoller und damit für Jak geeigneter beschreibt.[452] Kloppenborg urteilt für Jak:

> James is not simply sententious wisdom but, ... [contains] structured arguments on the topics of favouritism and the Law, deeds *versus* mere expressions of belief, control of speech, and the characteristics of the perfect life.[453]

Der vorliegende Kommentar nimmt Kloppenborgs Beobachtungen in modifizierter Form auf und stellt sie in den größeren Zusammenhang, den Annemaré Kotzé entwirft. Die von Kloppenborg im Anschluss an Collins herausgestellten Unterschiede zwischen Paränese und Protreptik lassen sich nach Kotzé nicht ohne weiteres statuieren, sondern müssen differenziert werden. Kotzé weist darauf hin, dass Philo beide Begriffe kennt und verwendet und sie für gleichbedeutend zu halten scheint.[454] Dabei gilt: Protreptik wurde in der antiken Literatur eher »als Oberbegriff für exhortative Werke gebraucht«.[455] Kotzé rät daher dazu, Protreptik und Paränetik »am besten als heuristische Konzepte auf[zufassen], um unterschiedliche, aber eng verwandte kommunikative Ziele zu bezeichnen«[456], wobei Protreptik der umfassende Terminus ist.[457] Nun wurde Protreptik statt Paränese schon seit Längerem als Terminus für Jak vorgeschlagen. So hat vor allem Klaus Berger protreptische Texte aus dem NT zusammengestellt[458], und P.J. Hartin rechnet Jakobus zur protreptischen Literatur.[459] Für die Zuordnung des Jak zur protreptischen Literatur sprechen vor allem die *Merkmale* der Ethik des Jak, die Allison und Kloppenborg benennen: besonders das dialogische und das argumentative Moment sowie die

---

[451] Kloppenborg, James, 43.

[452] Kloppenborg, James, 44 f (nach J. H. Collins, Exhortations to Philosophy: The Protreptics of Plato, Isocrates, and Aristotle, New York 2015, 17 f).

[453] Kloppenborg, James, 45.

[454] A. Kotzé, Art. Protreptik, RAC 24, 2017, 373–394, 374 (ausführliche Lit. 392 f).

[455] Kotzé, Art. Protreptik, 375.

[456] Kotzé, Art. Protreptik, 380.

[457] Kotzé weist aber darauf hin, dass zur Beschreibung ethischer Texte im Neuen Testament nebeneinander Paränese, Paraklese und Protreptik verwendet werden können, allerdings unterschiedliche Akzentuierungen beinhalten und dass für Paulus gern der Begriff »Paraklese« verwendet wird, vgl. die Beiträge in: J. M. Starr / T. Engberg-Pedersen (Hg.), Early Christian Paraenesis, BZNW 125, Berlin 2004.

[458] K. Berger, Hellenistische Gattungen im NT, in: ANRW II, 25 / 2, Berlin 1984, 1031–1432.

[459] P. J. Hartin, The Letter of James. Its vision, ethics, and ethos, in: J. G. van der Watt (Hg.), Identity, ethics, and ethos in the New Testament, BZNW 141, Berlin / New York 2006, 445–471; vgl. auch S. Luther, Protreptic Ethics in the Letter of James: The Potential of Figurative Language in Character Formation, in: R. Zimmermann / J. G. van der Watt / S. Luther (Hg.), Moral Language in the New Testament. Interrelatedness of Language and Ethics in Early Christian Writings, WUNT II / 296, Tübingen 2010, 330–364.

126 Einleitung

Tendenz zu kleinen präzise komponierten thematischen Texteinheiten. Beides wurde von Dibelius unterschätzt.

(2) Eine Zuordnung zur Protreptik, wie sie gegenwärtig vor allem Kloppenborg vornimmt, stellt auch eine Weiche für die allgemeine Einordnung der Ethik des Jak. Während die Paränese deutlich mit der Spruchdichtung verbunden ist und die Paraklese als Kennzeichen paulinischer Ethik und ihrer gemeindeleitenden Intention gelten kann[460], macht die Zuordnung zum Oberbegriff der Protreptik Jak formal und auch thematisch anschlussfähig für literarisch-philosophische Zuordnungen. So verortet John Kloppenborg einige ethische Motive bei Jak in der Nähe der kaiserzeitlichen *Stoa*: die Frage nach dem »Selbst«, die Psychagogie und die Vorstellung des ἔμφυτος λόγος[461] – Motive eines Ethos des Individuums, die sich sehr ähnlich in 1Petr finden. Kloppenborg weist allerdings selbst darauf hin, dass es sich bei den genannten Motiven nicht um eine Übernahme aus der Stoa oder um Einflüsse oder Parallelen handelt, sondern eher um mögliche Konvergenzen bzw. Anknüpfungspunkte. Er nennt sie:

> points where James' perspective on testing, endurance, desire, and training and his notion of ›receiving‹ and implanted word make sense if seen in the broader context of Stoic philosophy.[462]

Es geht also nicht um eine mögliche philosophiegeschichtliche Verortung, sondern eher um eine gewisse Permeabilität einiger Motive und Intentionen. Damit zeigt sich, dass der traditionelle ethische Ansatz des Jak bei dem Gesetz Israels auch Anknüpfungspunkte für andere zeitgenössische ethische Konzepte bietet. Allerdings bleibt bei Jak doch der Rahmen der Gemeindeethik, wie oben gezeigt, leitend. Die Betonung eines Individual-Ethos, das Kloppenborg ins Zentrum seiner Gesamtinterpretation rückt:

> A paraenetic letter, James is especially interested in the guidance of the soul, or psychagogy,[463]

bezieht sich vor allem auf Kap. 1 und 5,19 f und gibt der grundsätzlichen Zuordnung des Jak zum frühchristlichen Gemeindebrief (Kap. 2 und 5) zu wenig Gewicht.

(3) Fragt man nach *additiven* ethischen Impulsen in Jak im zeitgeschichtlichen Kontext, wird man nichts finden, was über das bekannte Inventar frühjüdischer und frühchristlicher Ethik hinausgeht. Es handelt sich im Gegenteil eher um eine *selektive* oder *reduktive* Ethik, deren Sitz im Leben die Korrektur von Fehlentwick-

---

[460] Die paulinische Ethik trägt aber ihrerseits stark protreptische Züge, wie besonders Röm 2 zeigt. Röm 2 darf geradezu als formales Vorbild für Jak 2 gelten.

[461] KLOPPENBORG, James, 97–106; vgl. ausführlich KLOPPENBORG, Hellenistic Psychagogy, 37–71. Zu den genannten Stellen siehe den Kommentar.

[462] KLOPPENBORG, James, 106.

[463] KLOPPENBORG, James, 109.

B. Der Text. Historische, literarische und thematische Charakteristik 127

lungen in den Christus-gläubigen Gemeinden ist. Bestimmte ethische Themen: die Prosopolempsie, »die Zunge«, Streit, Selbstbestimmtheit der Kaufleute, Missachtung der Niedrigen und Ruchlosigkeit der Reichen werden besonders akzentuiert und literarisch sorgfältig präsentiert. Sie sind aber nicht neu. Jakobus arbeitet stets auf der Grundlage von Septuagintatexten. Er erarbeitet nicht ein neues Konzept, sondern reagiert auf Fehlentwicklungen.

Konzeptionelle Qualität haben allerdings zwei Aspekte der Ethik des Jak, die schon dargestellt wurden: erstens das *ethisch definierte Glaubensverständnis* (Tat-Ethik) mit seinem schriftinterpretierenden Hintergrund in Kap. 2, zweitens der Verzicht auf *Christologie und Pneumatologie zur Fundierung der Ethik.* Damit separiert sich der Verfasser des Jak von der Ethik der Katholischen Briefe – besonders deutlich im Vergleich mit 1Petr, mit dem Jak viele Gemeinsamkeiten teilt –, die auf der Basis der paulinischen Ethik in unterschiedliche Richtungen weiterentwickelt wurde. Die ethischen *Hauptelemente* des Jak: erstens das *Ethos* der demütigen und geduligen einfachen Seelenhaltung des Einzelnen, zweitens die normative *Tat-Ethik* von Kap. 2 (das Tun des Gesetzes / der Gebote in den Gemeinden) und drittens der allgemeine *Gerichtshorizont* weisen dagegen auf die Ethik Israels und kommen ohne die christologische Fundierung der Ethik des Paulus aus. Die Jakobusethik lässt sich ohne Abzüge innerhalb der Ethik des antiken Judentums verorten.[464]

3.4.3

Im Rückblick lassen sich vier Strukturelemente der *Jakobus-Ethik* benennen.[465] Die Jakobus-Ethik ist:

praktisch intendiert (Tat-Ethik),

normativ basiert (»Schrift«/Gesetz als alleinige normgebende Größe),

anachronistisch bzw. ideell-historisch konzipiert (Rückgriff auf Jakobus als Autorisierungsgestalt und die zwölf Stämme als Adressaten),

traditionell ausgearbeitet (Verzicht auf aktuelle ethische Institutionen und Themen).

Es handelt sich um einen literarisch ambitionierten Versuch eines frühchristlichen Lehrers, Fehlentwicklungen, die das Wachstum der Gemeinden mit sich brachte, durch einen Rekurs auf Jakobus und einen Rundbrief aus seiner Feder zu korrigieren. Im Zusammenhang der Geschichte des entstehenden Christentums stellt die *Jakobus-Ethik* einen *eigenen* Typus neben der paulinischen, pseudo-petrinischen (1 und 2Petr)[466], pseudo-paulinischen (Deutero- und Tritopaulinen) und pseudo-johanneischen (1–3Joh) epistolaren Gemeindeethik dar. Sie baut auf der

---

[464] Dibelius kommt aufgrund seiner formgeschichtlichen Perspektive zu einer sachlich ähnlichen Einschätzung, ohne allerdings die Problematik einer frühchristlichen Ethik »ohne Christus« bzw. »Nach / gegen / ohne Paulus« zu berücksichtigen. Hier zeigt sich die Grenze einer rein motivisch-traditionsgeschichtlichen Analyse.

[465] Vgl. die anders akzentuierte Darstellung bei Johnson, Jak, 80–88.

[466] Diese Ethik ist ähnlich christologisch geprägt wie die paulinische – ein Umstand, der bei Klein, Bewährung, im Schlussvergleich nicht genügend Beachtung findet (438–443).

128 Einleitung

Tora auf, kommt ohne christologische oder pneumatologische Argumente aus und schlägt sachlich – ohne dies eigens zu thematisieren – eine Brücke zwischen der Ethik Israels und der zeitgenössischen Synagoge einerseits und den frühchristlichen ἐκκλησίαι andererseits. Dabei setzt sie nicht auf Innovation, sondern auf *Kontinuität*. Ethisch relevante frühchristliche Stoffe werden durch Rekurs auf Jesustradition in die Jakobus-Ethik integriert. Damit ist eine gewisse Nähe vor allem zur Bergpredigt gegeben.[467]

3.5 Profil der Jakobus-Theologie und Jakobus-Ethik

Das Profil der Jakobus-Theologie und Jakobus-Ethik lässt sich am besten im Vergleich mit Paulus zeichnen. Der Christus-bekennende (1,1) Lehrer *Jakobus*, über dessen persönliche Biographie wir nichts wissen, entwickelt auf der Basis der Gottesvorstellung der Tora, der Propheten und der Weisheitsschriften Israels einen traditionellen Ansatz für die Institutionen und das Verhalten seiner Christus-bekennenden (2,1) Adressaten. Eine soteriologische oder paradigmatische Funktion des Glaubens an den κύριος Ἰησοῦς Χριστός, der in den Christus-gläubigen Gemeinden seit Paulus theologisch ausgearbeitet wurde, entwickelt Jakobus aber nicht. Auch das Bekenntnis des Sch'ma Israel entfaltet nur im Zusammenspiel mit dem Tun des Gesetzes seine Wirkung. Begrifflich formuliert: weder der Monotheismus Israels allein noch die Christologie des Paulus und der nachpaulinischen Lehrer schaffen gemäß dem Jak »Leben« und »Rettung«, sondern das *Tun* des Gesetzes. Welche Bedeutung der κύριος Ἰησοῦς Χριστός für den Verfasser und die Adressaten hat, bleibt ungesagt.

Der frühere Pharisäer *Paulus* aus Tarsus entwickelte bereits ein bis zwei Generationen *vor* Jakobus eine innovative Interpretation der theologischen und religiösen Basis und des Ethos Israels, wie er sie in »der Schrift« fand. Er überschrieb bzw. re-interpretierte die gesamte Theo-logie Israels christologisch und leitete daraus sein Konzept von ἐκκλησία und Ethik der Christus-gläubigen Gemeinden her. Zentrum seiner Interpretation war die »moderne«, d. h. in seinem Verständnis zeitgemäße (Gal 4,3–7), Vorstellung von »Gott, der *in Christus* den Kosmos mit sich versöhnte« (2Kor 5,19). Dieser theologische Neuansatz und seine ethischen Implikationen werden von allen frühchristlichen Autoren – Briefautoren wie Evangelisten – in unterschiedlichen Genera und Typen von Theologie und Ethik weiterentwickelt. Einzig Jakobus trägt diesen interpretatorischen Neuansatz nicht mit. Insofern ist Jak ein *Solitär* unter den neutestamentlichen Schriften. Anders als die anderen frühchristlichen Autoren der zweiten und dritten Generation verzichtet er gänzlich auf die inhaltliche Überschreibung der Theologie und Ethik Israels durch Christologie und

---

[467] Allerdings fehlt anders als in der Bergpredigt jede kritische Auseinandersetzung mit dem Gesetz. – Der umfangreiche Komplex der Jesus-Ethik in den synoptischen Evangelien stellt einen weiteren eigenen Typus frühchristlicher Ethik dar, ebenso die Ethik des Johannesevangeliums.

korrigiert die entsprechenden theologischen Ansätze des Paulus hin zu einer Rück-
kehr in eine idealisierte Vergangenheit – mit chiffriertem Verfasser und chiffrierten
Adressaten. Er entwirft auf der Basis der Schrift und frühjüdischer sprachlicher
und theo-logischer Topoi eine streng theo-logisch zentrierte *Jakobus-Theologie*, die
analog zur *Jakobus-Ethik* jede qualifizierte christologische Neuinterpretation der
Theologie Israels vermeidet und die Christus-bekennenden Gemeinden auf den in
der Tat bewährten, durch Abraham exemplarisch vorgelebten Glauben an Gott den
Vater verpflichtet. Damit unterscheidet sich Jakobus auch von der Bergpredigt –
dem einzigen Text im Kanon der neutestamentlichen Schriften neben dem Jakobusbrief, der eine Art von ethischem Manifest darstellt. Aber Mt 5–7 enthält auch
christologische Begründungen und zugleich grundsätzliche Diskussionen über das
richtige Verständnis und die Applikation der Tora. Beides fehlt im Jakobusbrief.

Ein Blick auf Jak aus der Perspektive *frühchristlicher Theologiegeschichte* wird sich
mit dem Phänomen auseinandersetzen müssen, dass ein Christus-gläubiger Lehrer
der dritten Generation seine Adressaten ohne Christologie und ohne Pneumatologie über Grundlagen ihrer Lebensführung und ihrer Zukunftshoffnung belehrte
und dass dies ethische Lehrschreiben Teil des kanonischen Neuen Testament wurde.

3.6 Religionsgeschichtliches Profil

Jede Kommentierung des Jak wird vor die Frage nach der Zuordnung des Briefes
zu einem religionsgeschichtlichen Milieu gestellt (3.6.1). Dale Allisons Kommentar
sucht wieder nach einem Platz für den Jak und seinen Verfasser im sog. Judenchristentum (3.6.2), speziell im Milieu der Ebioniten (3.6.3). Der vorliegende Kommentar schlägt eine andere Lösung vor (3.6.4): Er erprobt die Hypothese eines jüdischen griechischsprachigen Lehrers der Christus-gläubigen Gemeinde in *Jerusalem*
zwischen 100 und 120 n. Chr., der in der Autorität des Jakobus das traditionell
geprägte theologisch-ethische Erbe der Jerusalemer Christus-gläubigen Gemeinde
formuliert und in der literarischen Hybridform eines »apostolischen Diasporabriefes« an die Christus-gläubigen Gemeinden außerhalb des Landes Israel weitergibt.

3.6.1

Die Ausgangssituation in der Forschung: die *singuläre Stellung* des Jak in der frühchristlichen Literatur der dritten Generation, die sowohl die Aspekte der Gattung
und der sprachlichen und stilistischen Qualität als auch die zuletzt dargestellten
inhaltlichen Eigenarten der Jakobustheologie und Jakobusethik betrifft, hat seit
dem 19. Jahrhundert immer wieder zu neuen religions- und theologiegeschichtlichen Positionsbestimmungen des Autoren- *und* Textprofils geführt.[468] Eine iso-

---

468 Im Folgenden werden »religionsgeschichtlich« und »theologiegeschichtlich« nebeneinander gebraucht,
erstere Bezeichnung für die Zuordnung des Jak innerhalb des Spannungsfeldes von Judentum und entstehen-

130 Einleitung

lierte zeitliche und lokale Verortung der Person des Autors[469] bleibt dabei ebenso unbefriedigend wie eine bloße formale und inhaltliche Textanalyse.[470] Beides ist vielmehr untrennbar verbunden und muss als Einheit verstanden und zueinander in Beziehung gesetzt werden, da einerseits der Text das Produkt des Autors in Verarbeitung von und Auseinandersetzung mit seinem religiösen, kulturellen und sozialen Milieu ist, wir aber andererseits den Autor und sein Milieu ausschließlich aus seinem Text rekonstruieren können.[471] Sicher ist, dass sich das Schreiben am Schnittpunkt zwischen griechischsprachigem *Judentum* und griechischsprachigen *frühchristlichen Gruppierungen* bewegt. Die Welt der paganen Religionen und ihre Institutionen und Praktiken kommen anders als in den Paulusbriefen nicht in den Blick, ebenso wenig eine explizite Beziehung des Verfassers zu einer bestimmten Philosophenschule. Dasselbe gilt andererseits auch für eine einfache Zuordnung des Jak zum Judentums des 1. Jahrhunderts n. Chr.[472], wie sie in der älteren Literatur vorgeschlagen wurde (Massebieau)[473], angesichts der Überlieferungs- und Rezeptionsgeschichte aber nicht plausibel ist.

3.6.2

Dale Allison hat mit einer profilierten religions- und theologiegeschichtlichen Hypothese auf diese besondere Stellung des Jak zwischen jüdischer und frühchristlicher Literatur reagiert. Allison sucht folgerichtig das religiös-soziale und kulturelle Milieu des Jak und seinen »Sitz im Leben« in der verbindenden Zone zwischen antikem Judentum und frühem Christentum, d. h. im Bereich des sog. *Judenchristentums.*[474]

---

dem Christentum im 1. und 2. Jahrhundert n. Chr., letztere Bezeichnung für die »innerchristliche« Position des Jak. Beides hängt eng zusammen und lässt sich mit unseren Begriffen nur unzureichend beschreiben.

[469] Siehe oben.

[470] Siehe oben und Teil II: Kommentar.

[471] Die Adressatenperspektive ist dabei nur insoweit ein Aspekt der Fragestellung, wie der Autor seine Adressaten modelliert.

[472] Vgl. zu der Welt jüdischer Gruppierungen im 1. Jahrhundert n. Chr. die übersichtliche Darstellung in: W. Horbury / W. D. Davies / J. Sturdy (Hg.), CHJud III. The Early Roman Period, Cambridge 1999. Zur Christus-gläubigen Gemeinde in Jerusalem vgl. D.-A. Koch, Geschichte des Urchristentums, Göttingen ²2014, 375–385.

[473] Methodisch unbefriedigend ist auch die nicht weiter diskutierte oder begründete Zuordnung des Jak von S. A. Adams, Genres, 159 f, zu »Other New Testament Letters« als »Jewish Philosophical Treatises« (119) bzw. »Literary Letters« (155).

[474] Vgl. zur Frage die sehr vorsichtige grundsätzliche Beschreibung bei Niebuhr, Wer war »Jakobus«?, 166: »Begriffe wie »Judentum« *versus* »Christentum« oder »Judenchristen« *versus* »Heidenchristen« sind freilich missverständlich und anachronistisch und sollten bei der Charakteristik von Autor und Adressaten vermieden werden.« Das sympathische *Caveat* lässt sich angesichts der wissenschaftlichen Lit. zu Jak aber nicht einfach durchhalten. Spätestens seit F.Ch. Baur wird die Frage eines »Judenchristentums« kontrovers erörtert, vgl. die profunde Einführung bei J. N. Carleton Paget, Jewish Christianity, in: CHJud III, 731–775; ausführlich: ders., Jews, Christians and Jewish Christians in Antiquity, WUNT 251, Tübingen 2010, 289–324. Immerhin schlägt auch Paget, Jews, 320, vor, den Begriff »Judenchristen« durch »Torah observant« zu ersetzen und für Ebioniten, Elkasaiten usw. zu verwenden, d. h. implizit, polemische Ketzerbenennungen für obsolet zu halten. Dieser Vorschlag hat sich aber (noch) nicht durchgesetzt. In eine ähnliche Richtung argumentiert M. Jackson-McCabe, Jewish Christianity. The Making of the Christianity-Judaism Divide, AYBRL, New

B. Der Text. Historische, literarische und thematische Charakteristik   131

Diese Kategorie wurde schon oft für Jak in Anspruch genommen[475], ihre Definition und ihr Umfang sind aber im Fluss. Günter Stemberger weist auf die *generell* judenchristlichen Anfänge des Christentums hin, die eine spezifische Verwendung des Begriffs erschweren: »Der Herkunft nach ist die gesamte Kirche judenchristlich« und hat sich erst in der zweiten und dritten Generation ausdifferenziert.[476] Er definiert daher sehr allgemein:

> Wesentlich für das J.tum sind jüdische Herkunft u. bleibende Bindung an das Judentum; diese äußert sich in der religiösen Praxis u. in der Ausprägung des Glaubensbekenntnisses … Was die Praxis betrifft, ist das Festhalten am Gesetz der Tora oder zumindest wesentlicher Teile davon ein klares Kriterium.[477]

Letzteres trifft zumindest theoretisch auf Jak zu, wenn der Brief auch bezüglich der Tora im Allgemeinen bleibt.[478] James Carleton Paget bietet eine deutlicher konturierte »praxis-based definition« an:

> A Jewish Christian [is] … someone who accepts the messianic status of Jesus (the bare minimum required by someone wishing to be a Christian) but feels it necessary to keep, or perhaps adopt, practices associated with Judaism such as circumcision, in the case of males, the sabbath, the food laws and other related practices … A Jewish Christian is only to be differentiated from a non-Christian Jew by the fact of his acceptance of Jesus' messianic status (see Epiphanius, Pan. 29.7.2 and Rec. 1.43.2).[479]

Allerdings wird genau bei dieser praktischen Definition deutlich, wo das Problem einer Zuordnung des Jak liegt: Jak rekurriert weder auf Beschneidung noch Sabbat oder Speisegesetze bzw. das Problem ritueller Reinheit – lauter Fragen, die in der Jesustradition und in den Paulusbriefen thematisiert werden. Stemberger und – sehr ausführlich – Paget zeichnen weiterhin die komplexe und im Detail nur schwer zu rekonstruierende Entwicklung hin zu eigenen Gruppierungen in Abgrenzung von den jüdischen Synagogen und den frühchristlichen mehrheitlich heidenchrist-

---

Haven/London 2020 (neue Darstellung der komplizierten Begriffs- und Forschungsgeschichte). Die Problematik ist offen und muss weiter diskutiert werden. Sie kann nicht im Rahmen eines Jak-Kommentars bearbeitet werden. Der vorliegende Kommentar beschränkt sich darauf, Allisons Hypothese zu diskutieren.

[475] Vorgänger dieser Hypothese bei ALLISON, Jak, 49 Anm. 271. Wichtig bleibt das ablehnende Urteil bei BURCHARD, Jak, 5 (Jakobus »war … kein Judenchrist«).

[476] STEMBERGER, Art. Judenchristen, 228. Aktuell wird die Ausdifferenzierung teilweise deutlich später angesetzt.

[477] STEMBERGER, Art. Judenchristen, 229. Vgl. PAGET, Jewish Christianity, 742: »In the beginning all Christianity was Jewish Christianity«.

[478] Dazu allerdings kritisch PAGET, Jewish Christianity, 755: Paget geht eher davon aus, dass die Aussagen des Jak zum Gesetz die bleibende Bedeutung jener jüdischen Gesetze bestätigen, die Paulus für überwunden hält. Allerdings ist auch diese Sicht auf Paulus nicht unumstritten.

[479] PAGET, Jewish Christianity, 734.

132 Einleitung

lichen Gemeinden sowie die Tendenz der Kirchenschriftsteller, die Judenchristen als Häretiker zu bezeichnen, nach.[480]

3.6.3

Hier bringt nun Allison die *Ebioniten* ins Spiel.[481] Er regiert auf die Unschärfe des Begriffs »Judenchristentum«, indem er Jak nicht nur allgemein in einem judenchristlichen religiösen Milieu verortet:

> This commentary ... suggests that James represents Christian Jews who did not define themselves over against Judaism. That is, our book emerged from a Christ-oriented Judaism, from a group that still attended synagogue and wished to maintain irenic relations with those who did not share their belief that Jesus was the Messiah,[482]

sondern dabei im Besonderen an die Ebioniten denkt[483]:

> So the Pseudo-Clementines preserve religious traditions that are in important aspects akin to James. It is a reasonable hypothesis that our epistle and Rec 1.27–71 witness to related, and perhaps closely relate forms of the Christian Judaism known as Ebionitism. The chief difference is that James represents a group that still holds out hope for irenic relations with the synagogue. In the source behind the Recognitions, the separation from Judaism is a fait accompli.[484]

Bei den Ebioniten findet Allison mehrere spezifische Eigenarten, die ihm auch für Jak wichtig zu sein scheinen: Ablehnung des Paulus, das Matthäusevangelium als einziges Evangelium und die Parteinahme für die Armen.[485] Diese prononcierte Zuordnung muss sowohl in ihrer allgemeinen Ausrichtung (Judenchristen) als auch in der speziellen Zuordnung des Verfassers des Jak zu den Ebioniten diskutiert werden. Die Ebioniten als sog. häretische Gruppierung im Rahmen des Judenchristentums sind zum ersten Mal bei Irenäus bezeugt[486], (unter Umständen) als Bewegung allerdings doch älter. Zugeschriebene Kennzeichen sind – wie auch Allison betont – eine besondere Christologie, der Gegensatz zu Paulus und die Beschränkung auf das Matthäusevangelium. Die Bezeichnung der Kirchenschriftsteller geht unter

---

[480] PAGET, Jewish Christianity, 742–775.

[481] ALLISON, Jak, 49 f. Vgl. einführend G. STRECKER, Art. Ebioniten, RAC 4, 1959, 487–509; STEMBERGER, Art. Judenchristen, 228–245; J. N. CARLETON PAGET, Art. The Ebionites, in: EBR 7, 2013, 246–248. Ausführliche kritische Darstellung bei PAGET, Jews, 289–324 (umfangreiche Lit.).

[482] ALLISON, Jak, 43.

[483] Ähnlich argumentiert SCORNAIENCHI, Polemik im Jakobusbrief.

[484] ALLISON, Jak, 50. Dazu: The Ascents of James 1.43.2 f (Trennung von Juden und Christusbekennern wegen des Glaubens an Christus). Hinzuzufügen ist der wichtige Unterschied, dass die Recognitionen Jakobus stets als Bischof von Jerusalem bezeichnen und ihn nicht mit der jüdischen Diaspora in Verbindung bringen. – Vgl. oben das zum Autor Gesagte.

[485] Weitere Parallelen und Diskussion von Pseudoclementinen, besonders Recognitionen 1,27–71, ebd. mit Anm. 273–278.

[486] Haer. 1,26,2 (vgl. STEMBERGER, Art. Judenchristen, 233). Vgl. auch PAGET, Jews, ch. 11: The Ebionites in recent research, 325–379.

B. Der Text. Historische, literarische und thematische Charakteristik

Umständen auf eine »Selbstbezeichnung« bzw. einen »Ehrentitel der Jerusalemer Gemeinde« (»die Armen«) nach Gal 2,10 und Röm 15,26 zurück.[487] Diese Aspekte lassen sich nur teilweise zu Jak in Beziehung setzen. Die Tora-Zentrierung des Jak ist aber kein eindeutiges Zeichen für Ebionitismus – sie findet sich beispielsweise ebenso in 2Bar. Eine explizite Beschränkung auf das Matthäus*evangelium* lässt sich Jak nicht entnehmen, sie würde höchstens für die Bergpredigt gelten.

Andererseits ist von der »separation from Judaism«, die Allison selbst als Kennzeichen der Ebioniten nennt, gerade in Jak *nichts* zu spüren. Wenn man diesen letzten Punkt in Allisons eigenem Votum ernstnimmt, ergeben sich schwerlich jene genaueren religionsgeschichtlichen Zuordnungen für Jak, wie sie Allison vornimmt. Hinzu kommt: Der von Allison herangezogene Text der sog. *Ascents of James* zeigt an keinem Punkt – weder in der Gattung noch bei den ethischen Vorstellungen – eine *sachliche* Nähe zu Jak. Die *Ascents of James* lassen sich eher als eine Schrift verstehen, die – später als Jak entstanden – eine neue Phase der Trennung Christus-gläubiger Gemeinden und ihrer Autoren vom zeitgenössischen Judentum und von der entstehenden altkatholischen Kirche dokumentiert.[488]

Fazit: wieweit Jak ein Dokument einer *besonderen* Gruppierung aus dem Spektrum möglicher judenchristlicher Vereinigungen – von denen wir nur aus der späteren Perspektive der Kirchenschriftsteller erfahren – gewesen sein könnte, geht aus dem Brief *nicht* hervor. *Jak lässt sich weder einem ethnicity-Konzept noch einer speziellen judenchristlichen Gruppierung zuordnen.* Der Brief entwickelt keine Institutions- und Leitungsdirektiven und dient nicht der Konstruktion einer bestimmten religiösen Gruppenidentität, wie es für ein ebionitisches Dokument oder ein Dokument einer anderen Sondergruppierung anzunehmen wäre[489], sondern gibt im Gegenteil im selbstgewissen Gestus des Lehrers auf der als *selbstverständlich* vorausgesetzten Basis der Tora ethische Weisung für eine Leserschaft[490], deren Christus-Bekenntnis ebenfalls als *selbstverständlich* vorausgesetzt wird (2,1). Der Jakobusbrief lässt sich daher – gegen Allison – nicht als ebionitisches oder dem ebionitischen Milieu nahestehendes Schreiben verstehen, das durch die Verbindung zu den Ebioniten plausibler würde, sondern bleibt das gewichtigste Dokument eines frühchristlichen Welt- und Handlungsverständnisses, das sich in der Sache nicht signifikant von seiner jüdischen Grundlage entfernt hat und im weitesten Sinn als »judenchristlich« (Stemberger, Paget) bezeichnet werden kann, solange kein adäquaterer Begriff gefunden ist.[491]

---

[487] STEMBERGER, Art. Judenchristen, 233; kritisch PAGET, Jews, 344–349.

[488] VAN VOORST, The Ascents, datiert die Schrift »somewhere in the second half of the second century« (80). Die *Ascents* sind durchgängig von Vorstellungen geprägt, die Jak (noch?) nicht kennt bzw. die ihm nicht wichtig sind: Jakobus als Bischof, die Bedeutung Jesu und die Apostel, Auferstehung. Vgl. die kritische Analyse bei PAGET, Jews, 325–379.

[489] Dazu E. S. GRUEN, Ethnicity in the Ancient World: Did It Matter? Berlin 2020.

[490] ALLISON, Jak, 33: »The Jewish ethos is ubiquitous«.

[491] Hier ist Burchards zu enger Begriff des Judenchristentums zu korrigieren. – Allerdings bleibt unklar, ob

3.6.4

Der vorliegende Kommentar schlägt vor diesem Hintergrund eine eigene Lösung der Frage nach dem religiös-literarisch-kulturellen Milieu des Briefes und seiner *occasion*[492] vor, die oben bereits vorformuliert wurde. Als Autor des Jak lässt sich ein jüdischer griechischsprachiger Lehrer der Christus-gläubigen Gemeinde in *Jerusalem* zwischen 100 und 120 n. Chr. annehmen, der in der Autorität des Jakobus das theologisch-ethische Erbe der Jerusalemer Christus-gläubigen Gemeinde formuliert und in der hybriden Form eines »apostolischen Diasporabriefes« an die Christus-gläubigen Gemeinden in der Diaspora weitergibt. Diese Hypothese muss in *pro* (1) und *contra* (2) diskutiert werden und wird abschließend nochmals konturiert (3).

(1) Sechs Argumente und Überlegungen lassen sich *für* diese Hypothese anführen.

Erstens: die literarische Form des *Diasporabriefes* und die literarische Selbstvorstellung als *Jakobus* (Ethopoiie, Jakobus der Gerechte) sowie die literarische Adresse weisen auf *Jerusalem*.

Zweitens: die theologiegeschichtliche Ausrichtung ist sachlich deutlich *antipaulinisch*, was zumindest in Antiochia und Rom nicht sehr plausibel wäre, aber nach Apg für die Christus-gläubige Gemeinde in *Jerusalem* zutrifft. Außerdem gibt es weder in Antiochia noch in Rom oder Alexandria eine eigene Jakobustradition (anders die Petrustradition!). Das macht die Lokalisierung des Jak in einer dieser Großstädte problematisch.[493]

Drittens: das theo-logisch-ethische Profil des Jak lässt sich am ehesten aus einem gewissen traditionellen Milieu erklären, das nicht Teil der relativ schnellen Entwicklung der Christus-gläubigen Gemeinden in Kleinasien, Griechenland und Rom ist. Dafür kommt am ehesten *Jerusalem* in Frage, wo die Christus-gläubige Gemeinde nach allem, was wir wissen, nach dem Ersten Jüdischen Krieg nicht mehr wuchs. Dazu passt das schwache institutionelle Profil einerseits und die späte Kanonisierung andererseits. Verfasser und Gemeinde bzw. ideeller Adressatenkreis des Jak befinden sich nicht im *mainstream* der Entwicklung der sog. heidenchristlichen Gemeinden und ihrer Leiter, wie sie sich in den Deutero- und Tritopaulinen und den Petrusbriefen manifestiert.[494]

Viertens: das religionsgeschichtliche Milieu ist dezidiert *nicht heidenchristlich* und bezieht die Welt der »Völker« nicht ein. Diese Sicht trifft besonders für *Jeru-*

---

der zentrale Begriff des »Gesetzes« vollständig ethisiert war oder weiterhin die Observanz der Reinheits- und Feiertagsgebote einschloss. Hier gibt der Jakobusbrief keine weitere Auskunft.

[492] So der glückliche Terminus bei VAN VOORST, Ascents, 80.

[493] Siehe oben zum Ort des Jak.

[494] Das bedeutet aber nicht, dass der Verfasser sich nicht im Kontakt mit diesen Entwicklungen befand: Er kannte sie und kritisiert sie.

B. Der Text. Historische, literarische und thematische Charakteristik 135

salem zu, wäre dagegen besonders in Rom, Alexandria oder Antiochia nur schwer zu erklären.

Fünftens: das literarische, kulturelle, religiöse und theologische Milieu zeigt eine gewisse *Verwandtschaft zu 2Bar*, der gegen 100 n. Chr. in *Jerusalem* angesetzt wird. Deutlich sind die gemeinsamen Themen: Gott, Gesetz und Gericht[495], das schriftstellerische Können, der Bezug auf die Tora sowie die Gattung des Diasporabriefes (2Bar 78–87) und die kommunikative Richtung von Jak und 2Bar, die von Jerusalem in die Diaspora weist, speziell das Motiv des Trostes in Trübsalen in dem Diasporabrief 2Bar 78,5; 91,1; 92,1.

Sechstens: der Verfasser hat kein Interesse an eigenen Organisationsstrukturen, wie sie in der paulinisch-deuteropaulinischen Briefliteratur entwickelt werden. Die Nähe zu Synagogalgemeinden und zu der archaisierenden Darstellung der frühen *Jerusalemer* Christus-gläubigen Gemeinde in Apg ist deutlich.[496]

Der Gewinn der Hypothese liegt in der plausiblen Zusammenführung folgender Aspekte: der literarischen Adresse und der Gattung des »Diasporabriefes«, der theologiegeschichtlichen Richtung sowie bestimmter theologischer Themen in einer historisch aussagekräftigen Personen-, Milieu- und Lokalzuschreibung. Insbesondere die historische Tradition, die Lukas in Apg 8,1–3 weitergibt, bietet sich als literarisches Szenario für den Jakobusbrief an: Die Jerusalemer Gemeinde wird zerstreut, während die Apostel in Jerusalem bleiben.[497] Apg 15,22 entwirft das Szenario eines Sendschreibens des Jerusalemer Apostelgremiums an die Gemeinden außerhalb des Landes Israel: Οἱ ἀπόστολοι καὶ οἱ πρεσβύτεροι ἀδελφοὶ τοῖς κατὰ τὴν Ἀντιόχειαν καὶ Συρίαν καὶ Κιλικίαν ἀδελφοῖς τοῖς ἐξ ἐθνῶν χαίρειν (Wir, die Apostel und die Ältesten, eure Brüder, grüßen die Brüder aus den Heiden in Antiochia und Syria und Kilikien). Das Schreiben ist gänzlich auf moderate Toraeinhaltung konzentriert. Auf derartige Traditionen und ihre literarische Verarbeitung konnte ein Christus-gläubiger Lehrer im Jerusalem der Jahrhundertwende zurückgreifen, um das, was er für die ethische Botschaft des Jakobus hielt, in die Christus-gläubigen Gemeinden in der Oikumene / Diaspora zu vermitteln, die er in der Gefahr sah, die Grundsätze der Jerusalemer Tradition der Apostel zu vergessen.[498]

---

[495] Vor allem 2Bar 85,3: »Nichts haben wir jetzt mehr, nur den (All)mächtigen noch und sein Gesetz« (Übersetzung: A. F. J. KLIJN, Die Syrische Baruchapokalypse, JSHRZ V / 2, Gütersloh 1976, 103–191, 182).

[496] KOCH, Geschichte des Urchristentums, 504 f, weist auf die Bedeutung der Eigenorganisation für die entstehenden Christengemeinden des 2. Jahrhunderts hin. Jak hat hier ein deutliches Defizit. Die Apg betont für die frühe Gemeinde neben der apostolische Leitung die Gleichheit und den Ausgleich der Armut.

[497] Siehe oben.

[498] Dabei ist aber zu beachten, dass solche lokalen und geographischen Zuschreibungen durchaus symbolische Bedeutung haben können und nicht einfach Quellenwert haben. Ob die Gemeinde als ganze (ohne die Apostel) wirklich Jerusalem verlassen hat, wissen wir nicht. Hier kann nur auf die Bedeutung des lukanischen Konzepts für die Lokalisierung des Jak hingewiesen werden: Lukas bietet ein plausibles Szenario für den Jakobusbrief als Schreiben aus Jerusalem. Ich danke Sylvie Honigman, Münster, für entsprechende Hinweise.

136 Einleitung

(2) Bei dieser Hypothese ergeben sich vor allem zwei *Probleme*, die hier angesprochen werden müssen:

Erstens: die *Sprache*. Wir haben keine anderen griechischsprachigen Schriften in Jerusalem aus dem Zeitraum um 100 n. Chr. überliefert.[499] Möglicherweise wurde allerdings 2Bar ursprünglich auf Griechisch, nicht – wie gegenwärtig die Mehrheitsmeinung annimmt[500] – auf Hebräisch verfasst.[501] Damit wäre eine signifikante Parallele zu einem relativ zeitgleich in Jerusalem verfassten Jakobusbrief vorhanden. Die griechische Sprache des Jak würde aber auch unabhängig von 2Bar nicht gegen eine Herkunft in Jerusalem sprechen, da jüdische Autoren dort zwar im Allgemeinen nicht mehr Griechisch schrieben, aber selbstverständlich Griechisch beherrschten und Griechisch als Verkehrssprache im Osten des Imperium Romanum gängig war. Der Verfasser des Jak hätte dann *anders* als die Verfasser des 2Bar[502] und des 4Esra die griechische Sprache gewählt, um sich seinen griechischsprachigen Christus-gläubigen Adressaten im Imperium mitzuteilen. Das Sprachargument spricht jedenfalls nicht gegen die Jerusalem-Hypothese. Wichtig ist das Fazit, das Shlomit Weksler-Bdolah zur sprachlichen Situation in Jerusalem nach 70 n. Chr. aufgrund der epigraphischen Denkmäler zieht: »Most of the inscriptions belonging to the period between 70 CE and the early fourth century are written in Latin, which was the language of the military and the Roman administration, and a small number are in Greek – the language spoken by the local population. Hebrew and Aramaic are almost completely absent from the finds«.[503]

---

[499] Die griechische Erziehung von Josephus fällt in die Zeit vor dem Ersten Jüdischen Krieg.

[500] So Klijn, Die Syrische Baruchapokalypse, 110. Anna Maria Schwemer hält auch die Vitae prophetarum für eine griechische jüdische Schrift aus dem 1. Jahrhundert n. Chr. aus Jerusalem (A. M. Schwemer, Vitae Prophetarum, JSHRZ I / 7, Gütersloh 1997, 545.547.548). Vgl. die Eliatradition in VitProph.

[501] P.-M. Bogaert, L'Apocalypse Syriaque de Baruch, Sources Chrétiennes tom. I und II, Paris 1969, nimmt eine griechische Originalfassung an. So jetzt auch – vorsichtig – mündlich L. Stuckenbruck. M. Henze, Art. Baruch, Second Book of, EDEJ, Grand Rapids 2010, 426–428, plädiert für eine ursprüngliche hebräische Fassung, die verloren ging und auch in der rabbinischen Literatur keine Spuren hinterlassen hat (427), hält allerdings ein griechisches Original nicht für ausgeschlossen (mündliche Auskunft). Henze weist auf die Nähe von Partien des 2Bar zu ntl. Schriften hin, er nennt besonders Paulusbriefe (428). Sein Urteil: »2 *Baruch* has much to contribute to the study of the formation of first-century Christianities«, ist aber besonders für Jak wichtig. – Die Überlegungen zu einem griechischen 2Bar bleiben naturgemäß *hypothetisch*. Die Möglichkeit eines griechischen Originals des 2Bar macht aber die Hypothese einer Entstehung des Jak in Jerusalem weniger unwahrscheinlich.

[502] Vgl. aber die Möglichkeit eines griechischsprachigen Originals des 2Bar.

[503] Sh. Weksler-Bdolah, Aelia Capitolina – Jerusalem in the Roman Period. In Light of Archaeological Research, MnS 432, Leiden / Boston 2020, 205 mit Anm. 15. Vgl. auch H. M. Cotton / O. Pogorelsky, Roman Rule and Jewish Life: Collected Papers, Studia Judaica 89, Berlin / Boston 2022. Cotton weist nach, dass nach der Zerstörung Jerusalems und nach der Auflösung des Sanhedrin die Einwohner auf die römischen Gerichte angewiesen waren und eine griechische Sprache verwenden mussten. Wichtige Überlegungen zur Verwendung der griechischen Sprache im Raum Palästinas auch bei M. R. Niehoff, Auf den Spuren des hellenistischen Judentums in Caesarea. Ein jüdischer Psalmenforscher in Origenes' Glosse im Kontext Rabbinischer Literatur, ZAC 27, 2023, 31–76. Niehoff resümiert: »Das rabbinische Judentum war in der Tat mit der

B. Der Text. Historische, literarische und thematische Charakteristik   137

Zweitens: über *Christen* und eine christliche Gemeinde zu dieser Zeit in Jerusalem ist nichts Sicheres bekannt. Bekannt sind die allgemein als fiktiv beurteilten Bischofslisten[504] und die hypothetische Notiz bei Epiphanius, de mensuris et ponderibus 14 über die Versammlung von Christen auf dem Zionsberg.[505] Ute Wagner-Lux schreibt zu einer möglichen sog. judenchristlichen Gemeinde in Jerusalem: »Von ihr läßt sich nichts Näheres sagen, als daß es nach 70 in J. wiederum eine Gemeinde gegeben hat, die ihre Bedeutung für die Gesamtkirche aber verloren hatte.«[506] Und: »Die Geschichte der Jerusalemer judenchristl. Gemeinde (ging) mit dem Zweiten Jüd. Krieg zu Ende«.[507] Nach Euseb, HE. 3,10.11 wurde »nach dem Ende des Krieges [Erster Jüdischer Krieg] Symeon, ein Vetter Jesu, als Nachfolger für den 62 n. Chr. hingerichteten Herrenbruder eingesetzt. Symeon wurde nach Euseb, HE. 3,32,1/6 106/107 unter Trajan gekreuzigt«.[508] Das ließe sich als Hinweis auf die Anwesenheit und auf die bleibende Autorität der Familie Jesu in Jerusalem verstehen. Ob der Verfasser in dieser Gruppe zu vermuten ist, muss offen bleiben. Es geht hier nur um den Nachweis einer christlichen Gemeinde in Jerusalem vor Bar Kochba.[509] Dass es um die Jahrhundertwende keine Christus-gläubige Gemeinde in Jerusalem gegeben habe, ist historisch unwahrscheinlich. Die *Person* eines frühchristlichen Lehrers mit der griechischen Sprachkompetenz und der literarischen Fähigkeit des Verfassers des Jak bleibt auch in diesem hypothetischen Szenario ungewöhnlich. Andererseits lassen sich die thematische Verengung des Jak auf Toraethik, die Nähe zu synoptischer Tradition, die Polemik gegen paulinische Theologumena und die Bedeutung der Gestalt des Jakobus am besten aus einem Milieu in Jerusalem zwischen den beiden jüdischen Kriegen erklären.

(3) Welche *Konsequenzen* ergeben sich aus dieser Hypothese für die Interpretation des Jak? Ein Christus-gläubiger Lehrer schreibt in der Rolle des Jakobus, des berühmten (Josephus!) Leiters der frühchristlichen Gemeinde Jerusalems, an ein allgemeines Publikum von Christus-Bekennern außerhalb Jerusalem-Israels und

---

griechischen Sprache vertraut und nahm an der zeitgenössischen jüdisch-griechischen Kultur teil, besonders in Großstädten wie Caesarea« (43).

[504] U. Wagner-Lux, Art. Jerusalem I, RAC 17, 1996, 631–718, 690: »Eus. h.e. 3,11; 4,5,3 f: Jakobus bis Judas (ca. 44/134) = 15 judenchristliche Bischöfe«. Kritisch dazu: Koch, Geschichte des Urchristentums, 389.

[505] PG 43, 261.

[506] Wagner-Lux, Art. Jerusalem I, 669. Paget, Jewish Christianity, 747 f: »There is no reason to doubt the basic purpot of these traditions, namely that there was an organized presence of Jewish Christians in or near the city until the Bar Cochba revolt« (748).

[507] Ebd.

[508] Vgl. Koch, Geschichte des Urchristentums, 388.

[509] Siehe Paget, Jewish Christianity, 748. Koch, Geschichte des Urchristentums, 387–401 und 500–502 zur Entwicklung des Judenchristentums außerhalb von Jerusalem/Palästina (Did/Mt). Jak wird bei Koch nicht erwähnt. M. Öhler, Geschichte des frühen Christentums, Göttingen 2018, 271–273 ist sehr skeptisch gegenüber der Überlieferung bei Euseb. Öhlers Urteil (273) lautet: »Die späteren Jakobustraditionen präsentieren Jakobus vor allem als Repräsentanten einer toraobservanten Linie des Christentums … Im Jakobusbrief präsentiert sich dieses als großkirchlich«. Letzteres trifft allerdings sicher nicht zu. Der Begriff »großkirchlich« ist historisch unangemessen.

verpflichtet sie auf die theo-logischen Grundsätze des Gottes Israels und auf die individual- und sozialethischen Grundsätze der Tora sowie auf die soziale (1,27) und persönliche (1,1.2–4) Pflege ihrer Frömmigkeit (θρησκεία καθαρὰ καὶ ἀμίαντος 1,27) bzw. ihres Ethos als Gemeindeglieder und als Einzelpersonen. Offensichtlich ist der Verfasser dabei nicht an der Modellierung *religiöser Identität* interessiert, sondern an der Korrektur *ethischer Fehlentwicklungen in den Christus-bekennenden Gemeinden*. Dabei wird die Autorität des Jakobus als der zentralen Gestalt der frühen Christus-gläubigen Gemeinde in Jerusalem in Anspruch genommen.

Das Interesse der Schrift richtet sich nicht auf eine Verständigung zwischen Juden und Judenchristen (Allison) – dies Thema wird im Gegenteil sorgfältig ausgeklammert – oder darauf, in einer bi-fokalen Kommunikation von Juden und von Christus-gläubigen Gemeinden anerkannt zu werden (Kloppenborg) – weshalb sollte ein frühchristlicher Lehrer Synagogenmitglieder über den Dekalog belehren sollen? –, sondern auf die Bewahrung der Christus-bekennenden Adressaten außerhalb Jerusalems vor der »Welt« und ihren Sünden, auf die Belehrung über einen Glauben, der sich in Taten erweist, und auf die ethische Vervollkommnung ihrer Leserschaft im Sinn des »Gesetzes der Freiheit«. Dabei wird *Jakobus* als Garant dieser Tora-fundierten Ethik gesehen – sachlich im Gegensatz zu *Paulus* und zur Weiterentwicklung der paulinischen Theologie, Christologie, Ethik und Ekklesiologie und zugleich in sachlicher Übereinstimmung mit Teilen der *Jesus*tradition und Traditionen der *Jerusalemer* Gemeinde, zu der die fundierende Jakobustradition gehört, die von der Apostelgeschichte und von Josephus weitergegeben wird. Der Verfasser argumentiert literarisch (Diasporabrief) und theologisch von Jerusalem aus. Die Christus-bekennenden Gemeinden und ihre Mitglieder werden in Jak 1,1 auf ihre ideelle Zugehörigkeit zur jüdischen *Zwölfstämme-Diaspora* und ihrem Ethos verpflichtet, dem sich der Christus-bekennende Verfasser – wie schon der historische Jakobus – selbstverständlich und undiskutiert zugehörig weiß.

So gelesen erhält der Jakobusbrief einen Platz in der Geschichte des entstehenden Christentums, indem er ein Zeugnis der ethisch formierten Theologie und der literarisch ambitionierten Kultur der Christus-gläubigen Gemeinde in Jerusalem um die oder nach der Jahrhundertwende darstellt. Der literarisch versierte Autor[510] steht neben dem ebenfalls literarisch qualitätvollen jüdischen Autor des 2Bar und vertritt in diesem Spannungsfeld durchaus die Eigenarten frühchristlicher Literatur seit Paulus: griechische Sprache, gehobener Stil[511], argumentative Kraft, dabei eine gewisse Kürze und Abkehr von traditionellen Formen (Apokalypse) und Stilzügen (Breite, Wiederholung, Sprucheinheiten)[512] sowie die erfolgreiche und originelle Adaption des paulinischen Gemeindebriefes[513] in die jüdische Form des Diasporab-

---

[510] Ganz anders die extrem einfache literarische Qualität der *Ascents*.

[511] Vgl. die Analyse von JÓNSSON, James.

[512] Das wird bei ADAMS, Genres, übersehen. Dazu WISCHMEYER, The Book of Ben Sira.

[513] Jak lehnt sich nicht an die jüdische literarische Gattung der Apokalypse, sondern an den paulinischen

B. Der Text. Historische, literarische und thematische Charakteristik 139

riefs. Mit dieser Hypothese wird einerseits die allgemeine religiös-kulturelle Bedeutung Jerusalems um die Jahrhundertwende gestärkt, andererseits fällt neues Licht auf die Bedeutung Jerusalems im lukanischen Doppelwerk. Abschließend stellt sich daher die Frage, wieweit Jak im Zusammenhang mit dem lukanischen Doppelwerk als dem wichtigsten frühchristlichen literarischen Werk aus der flavischen Literaturepoche[514] gelesen werden muss und uns – als einzige erhaltene *literarische* Quelle – in das kulturelle Milieu der Christus-gläubigen Gemeinschaft in Jerusalem im Übergang zum 2. Jahrhundert führt.

Gemeindebrief in der Form des Diasporabriefes an.

[514] Im weiteren Sinn der Zeit Domitians und der frühen nachflavischen Zeit. Genauere zeitliche Einordnungen sind nicht möglich. Zur flavischen Literatur vgl. einführend: A. Zissos (Hg.), A Companion to the Flavian Age of Imperial Rome, BCAW, Chichester 2016, darin besonders: R. Pogorzelski, Centers and Peripheries (376–392); A. Augoustakis, Literary Culture (376–392); A. Kemezis, Flavian Greek Literature (450–468). – Diese letzte Überlegung verdanke ich Sigurvin L. Jónsson, Münster.

KOMMENTAR

A. Inscriptio

Brief des Jakobus

P74V. 01. 02 und einige Minuskeln haben keine inscriptio. P20. P23. P54. 04. 048 und andere Zeugen fallen hier aus. 03. 018 sowie einige Minuskeln schreiben ΙΑΚΩΒΟΥ ΕΠΙΣΤΟΛΗ. Nestle-Aland[28] vermerkt bei 03, es handele sich um den 2. Korrektor. ECM übernimmt diese Angabe nicht. 044 und andere schreiben ΕΠΙΣΤΟΛΗ ΙΑΚΩΒΟΥ. Verschiedene Minuskeln erweitern mit καθολικη, einige Minuskeln stellen καθολικη vor επιστολη. 467 u. a. fügen πρωτη hinzu. 400V u. a. fügen του αγιου ιακωβου επιστολη καθολικη hinzu. 025 stellt dem Namen noch den Titel »Apostel« nach.

Verschiedene Minuskeln fügen erklärende Zusätze zum Verfasser hinzu: αδελφοθεοιο (1739), αδελφοθεου (1501), αγιου (400V u. a.) oder geben Erklärungen zu den Adressaten: γραμμα προς εβραιους (1739), προς τους εν τη διασπορα πιστευσαντες ιουδαιους (94) sowie zum Abfassungsort: γραφεισα απο ιερουσαλημ (330) oder zum Text: το αναγνωσμα (1838 u. a.) ab.

επιστολη findet sich auch in der *inscriptio* von 1Petr: P72. 01 (1. Korrektor), 02 (lectio verisimilis), von 2Petr: P72. 04 und von Jud: P72. 02. επιστολη fehlt in den *inscriptiones* der Paulusbriefe, begegnet aber in der *subscriptio* von Röm (Mehrheitstext), 1Kor (1175 al), Gal (0278), Eph (0278), Kol (0278), Hebr (0285[vid]). επιστολη im Text begegnet in Röm, 1.2Kor, Kol, 2Thess, 2Petr. Weiterhin begegnet επιστολη in der *subscriptio* des Barnabasbriefes, im Text des Polykarpbriefes, im Text mehrerer Ignatiusbriefe, im Text des 1Clem und in der *subscriptio* des 1 und 2Clem sowie in der *inscriptio* des Diognetbriefes.

B. Präskript

(1,1) Jakobus, Gottes und des Herrn Jesus Christus Sklave[515], den zwölf Stämmen in der Zerstreuung[516] Gruß.

---

[515] SPICQ, NLNT I, 211–215 zu δοῦλος.

[516] Wörtlich: denen in der Zerstreuung.

Textkritik: Die Variante θεου πατρος statt θεου (429.614.630 pc) beseitigt die Unklarheit bezüglich der Selbständigkeit von θεου oder der Zugehörigkeit des Genitivs zu κυριου ιησου χριστου.

Der Jakobusbrief ist ein enzyklisches Schreiben, das sich in seinem kurzen Präskript als allgemeines Rundschreiben eines namentlich genannten Absenders Jakobus an eine ganz allgemein als die »zwölf Stämme in der Diaspora« bezeichnete Adressatenschaft einführt. Damit liegt – anders als in der paulinischen Korrespondenz – wie auch im 1.[517] und 2. Petrusbrief[518], im Judasbrief[519] und im Barnabasbrief[520] eine ideale Korrespondenzsituation vor. Der Verfasser unterlässt es, eine mögliche reale Situation, die eine Zustellung des Schreibens an »die zwölf Stämme« vorstellbar oder plausibel machen könnte, herzustellen. Der Jakobusbrief präsentiert sich damit im Präskript als ein nichtsituativer Text, der das Briefgenus mit seiner kommunikativ-situativen Struktur als literarischen Träger seiner Ausführungen benutzt. Das bedeutet auch, dass weder die reale Leserschaft mit den im Präskript genannten Empfängern bzw. Adressaten, »den zwölf Stämmen in der Zerstreuung«, noch der reale Verfasser mit dem literarischen Absender »Jakobus« identisch sein muss. Was aus 1,1 zu erschließen ist, ist die literarische Modellierung eines Absenders und einer Adressatenschaft in einem ebenfalls literarisch modellierten brieflichen Rahmen. Über den historischen Verfasser des Präskripts und über das reale Lesepublikum gibt das Präskript keine direkte Auskunft. Ob der Verfasser selbst schreibt oder (nur) diktiert, bleibt ebenfalls offen. Auf jeden Fall tritt er im Text von Anfang an als autoritative Person in Erscheinung: Eine *einzelne* Führungsperson verfasst ein autoritatives Schreiben an eine *umfassende* Adresse.

V. 1 Die Brieferöffnung folgt dem üblichen Schema von *superscriptio* (Sender), *adscriptio* (Empfänger) und *salutatio* (Gruß). Alle drei Elemente der Brieferöffnung fallen aber aus dem Rahmen der frühchristlichen Briefliteratur, der durch die Paulusbriefe geprägt ist.[521] Das ist umso auffallender, als Briefanfang und Briefschluss – im Jak fehlt dies Element – stets besonders stereotyp geprägt sind. Abweichungen von dem üblichen Formular verdienen daher besondere Aufmerksamkeit.

Am einfachsten lässt sich die Eigenart der im Jak gewählten Brieferöffnung bei der *salutatio* beschreiben, die hier daher zuerst betrachtet wird. Der Verfasser verwendet den gewöhnlichen Eingangsgruß der »Privatbriefe ptolemäischer u. frührö-

---

[517] 1Petr 1,1 werden immerhin Provinzen genannt: »Petrus, Apostel Jesu Christi, an die auserwählten Fremdlinge, die in der Zerstreuung leben (ἐκλεκτοῖς παρεπιδήμοις διασπορᾶς), in Pontus, Galatien, Kappadozien, der Provinz Asia und Bithynien.«

[518] 1,1 τοῖς ἰσότιμον ἡμῖν λαχοῦσιν πίστιν (an die, die mit uns denselben teuren Glauben empfangen haben).

[519] τοῖς ἐν θεῷ πατρὶ ἠγαπημένοις καὶ Ἰησοῦ Χριστῷ τετηρημένοις κλητοῖς (den Berufenen, die geliebt sind in Gott, dem Vater, und bewahrt für Jesus Christus).

[520] 1,1 »Seid gegrüßt (χαίρετε), Söhne und Töchter, im Namen des Herrn, der uns geliebt hat, in Frieden«.

[521] Dazu Ch. Hoegen-Rohls, Form und Funktion, Realia und Idee des Paulusbriefes, in: O. Wischmeyer / E.-M. Becker (Hg.), Paulus – Leben – Umwelt – Werk – Briefe, Tübingen ³2021, 247–278.

B. Präskript

mischer Zeit aus Ägypten«: χαίρειν.[522] Mit dieser Wendung ist der Jakobusbrief das einzige Schreiben aus der Gattung »Brief« im Neuen Testament, dessen *salutatio* nicht auf der religiös grundierten, substantivierten paulinischen Variante von χαίρειν basiert: χάρις ὑμῖν καὶ εἰρήνη.[523] Was wie ein Paradox erscheinen könnte, dass nämlich der nicht in eine originäre oder fingierte personale Kommunikationsbeziehung eingebundene Jakobusbrief gerade die *salutatio*-Formel des situativen griechischen Privatbriefs benutzt, erweist sich so als Teil der sorgfältigen literarischen Strategie des Verfassers.[524] Der Verfasser benutzt die allgemeine Grußformel der damaligen griechischsprachigen Welt und verzichtet auf die spezifische frühchristliche Formulierung, die paulinisch geprägt ist.

Anders verfährt der Absender bei der *superscriptio*: Ἰάκωβος θεοῦ καὶ κυρίου Ἰησοῦ Χριστοῦ δοῦλος. Er stellt sich in der deutlich ausgeweiteten *superscriptio* zuerst mit seinem *Namen* Ἰάκωβος vor, dem dann eine *religiöse* Selbstvorstellung angeschlossen ist, wie seit den Paulusbriefen im frühen Christentum üblich. Allerdings weicht die hier gewählte Selbstvorstellung von den paulinischen Formeln ab. Zunächst zum Namen: Ἰάκωβος ist die gräzisierte Form des hebräischen Namens, der auf den Patriarchen Jakob (Ἰακώβ[525]) zurückweist. Zugleich handelt es sich um die gräzisierte Form eines der beliebtesten jüdischen Namen[526], der den Verfasser als Juden ausweist und den – wie viele andere Juden aus frommen Familien – auch ein Bruder Jesu trug. Denselben Namen trugen nach Mk 3,13–19 par zwei Mitglieder des Zwölferkreises, den Jesus berief. Diese beiden Jakobi werden zur Unterscheidung in den Evangelien zusätzlich gekennzeichnet: »Sohn des Zebedäus« und »Sohn des Alphäus«[527]. In 1Kor 15,7 und in Apg 12,17; 15,13; 21,18 fehlt eine Kennzeichnung

---

[522] Vgl. H. ZILLIACUS, Art. Anredeformen, RAC.S I, Stuttgart 2001, 465–497, 475. Vgl. die Briefe Epikurs, weiter 1Makk 10,18.25; 11,30 u. ö., 2Makk 1,1–10 (erweitert) u. ö.; Apg 15,23; 23,26. χαίρειν auch in der *salutatio* der Mehrzahl der Ignatiusbriefe: IgnEph; IgnMagn; IgnRöm; IgnSmyr; IgnPolyk (in IgnPhld fehlt die salutatio). Sonst nicht bei den Apostolischen Vätern: Barn benutzt das flektierte Verb.

[523] Vgl. zu dem paulinischen Formular J. L. WHITE, Introductory Formulae in the Body of the Pauline Letter, JBL 90, 1971, 91–97; DERS., New Testament Epistolary Literature in the Framework of Ancient Epistolography, ANRW II 25.2, Berlin / New York 1984, 1730–1756; F. SCHNIDER / W. STENDER, Studien zum neutestamentlichen Briefformular, NTTS 11, Leiden 1987; D. E. AUNE (Hg.), Greco-Roman Literature and the New Testament. Selected Forms and Genres, Atlanta 1988; J. MURPHY-O'CONNOR O. P., Paul the Letter-Writer, Collegeville Min. 1995; H.-J. KLAUCK, Die antike Briefliteratur und das Neue Testament, UTB 2022, Paderborn u. a. 1998; CH. HOEGEN-ROHLS, Form, in: Wischmeyer / Becker (Hg.), Paulus, 247–278 (Lit.).

[524] Vgl. dasselbe Vorgehen in Apg 15,23.

[525] Wenn man die Namensdifferenz berücksichtigt, kann in Jak 1,1 kaum der Patriarch Jakob gemeint sein. Die ntl. Schriften verwenden für den Patriarchen ausnahmslos Ἰακώβ, auch für den Vater des Joseph in Mt 1,15 f.

[526] Zum Namen vgl. T. ILAN, Lexicon of Jewish Names in Late Antiquity. Part I: Palestine 330 BCE – 200 CE, TSAJ 91, Tübingen 2002. Zum neutestamentlichen Vorkommen vgl. D. A. HAGNER, Art. James, ABD 3, New York 1992, 616–618; zum Herrenbruder vgl. F. M. GILLMAN, Art. James, Brother of Jesus, ABD 3, New York 1992, 620–621. Ausführlich R. DEINES, Jakobus. Im Schatten des Größeren, Biblische Gestalten 30, Leipzig 2017.

[527] Sohn des Zebedäus: Mt 4,21 u. ö.; Sohn des Alphäus: Mt 10,3 u. ö. Das Lukasevangelium kennt ein

des Herrenbruders Jakobus durch Vater- oder Bruderangabe[528]: Offenbar ist sie nicht notwendig, da Paulus die Bedeutung und Identität des Jakobus als bekannt voraussetzen kann. Auch in Jak 1,1 fehlt eine unterscheidende Zusatzbezeichnung. Der Verfasser des Judasbriefes dagegen nennt aus Unterscheidungs- oder Autorisierungsgründen seinen eigenen (oder pseudepigraphen) Namen »Judas, Bruder des Jakobus«. Auch hier fehlt eine Zusatzbezeichnung wie »Bruder Jesu« oder »Bruder des Herrn«.[529] Alle drei genannten Jakobi kommen grundsätzlich als Verfasser in Frage. Die stilisierte Adressatenanrede weist allerdings eher auf den Herrenbruder als auf die in der Tradition blass bleibenden Jesusjünger. Möglich ist außerdem die Verfasserschaft durch einen Jakobus, der nicht aus der Verwandtschaft oder Umgebung Jesu stammt.[530]

Dieser zweite Teil der *superscriptio* fasst die religiöse Selbstvorstellung des Absenders in Analogie und Differenz zu den Selbstvorstellungen der Präskripte der Paulusbriefe in der sprachlich sperrigen Wendung θεοῦ καὶ κυρίου Ἰησοῦ Χριστοῦ δοῦλος[531] zusammen. Zunächst ist wie schon bei der – zeitlich späteren – *inscriptio* auffallend, dass der Absender nicht als ἀπόστολος, sondern als δοῦλος eingeführt wird.[532] Paulus selbst verwendet diese Selbstbezeichnung ohne den Apostel-Zusatz (nur) in dem als Freundschaftsbrief konzipierten Philipperbrief, in dem er Timotheus denselben Titel wie sich selbst gibt und offensichtlich auf die Selbstautorisierung als Apostel verzichtet.[533] Anders verfährt 1Petr, der den – zu erwartenden – Aposteltitel benutzt, während 2Petr beide Bezeichnungen verbindet: δοῦλος καὶ ἀπόστολος Ἰησοῦ Χριστοῦ. Hier dürfte eine Kenntnis des 1Petr und des Jak vorauszusetzen sein. Der Judasbrief verwendet ebenfalls den δοῦλος-Begriff, präzisiert den Namen aber durch die Verwandtschaftsbezeichnung: ἀδελφὸς δὲ Ἰακώβου, allerdings ohne die Verwandtschaft zu Jesus anzudeuten – darin dem Jakobusbrief gleich.[534] Demgegenüber stellt sich im Jakobusbrief der Absender als bekannt und

---

weiteres Mitglied der Zwölf mit Namen Judas, dessen Vater Jakobus heißt (6,16; Apg 1,13). Vgl. auch die Todesnotiz in Apg 12,2: hier wird Jakobus als »Bruder des Johannes« bezeichnet. Jakobus, der Sohn des Alphäus, spielt in der Geschichte der frühen Gemeinden keine erkennbare Rolle.

528 Ausnahme: Gal 1,19, wo Paulus anscheinend den klärenden Zusatz »Bruder des Herrn« nicht vermeiden kann (2,9.12 dann ohne diesen Zusatz). In Mk 6,3 / Mt 13,55 findet sich eine Liste mit Namen der Brüder Jesu: Jakobus, Joses, Judas, Simon.

529 Vgl. Mk 6,3par.

530 Dazu R. METZNER, Der Lehrer Jakobus. Überlegungen zur Verfasserfrage des Jakobusbriefes, ZNW 104, 2013, 238–267. Siehe oben die Einleitung zum Autor.

531 Ausnahme: 1Thess (auch 2Thess), dort nur namentliche Selbstvorstellung.

532 Spätere Handschriften haben das nachgeholt s. o.

533 Phil 1,1 (Παῦλος καὶ Τιμόθεος δοῦλοι Χριστοῦ Ἰησοῦ). Röm 1,1 (Παῦλος δοῦλος Χριστοῦ Ἰησοῦ, κλητὸς ἀπόστολος) und Tit 1,1 (Παῦλος δοῦλος θεοῦ, ἀπόστολος δὲ Ἰησοῦ Χριστοῦ) verbinden δοῦλος und ἀπόστολος (vgl. 2Petr 1,1). Phlm verwendet Παῦλος δέσμιος Χριστοῦ Ἰησοῦ. Vgl. dazu E.-M. BECKER, Der Begriff der Demut bei Paulus, Tübingen 2015, 130–137.

534 Ἰούδας Ἰησοῦ Χριστοῦ δοῦλος, ἀδελφὸς δὲ Ἰακώβου. Beide Präskripte beziehen ihre Autorisierung also nicht aus dem Verwandtschaftsverhältnis zu Jesus, sondern aus ihrer Dienstverpflichtung durch den erhöhten Jesus Christus. Vgl. zum Judasbrief J. FREY, The Letter of Jude and the Second Letter of Peter: A Theological

unabhängig und ausschließlich »Gott und dem Kyrios Jesus Christus« verpflichtet vor. Die *superscriptio* des Judasbriefes legt nahe, dass der Verfasser des Judasbriefes den Jakobusbrief bereits kannte, den Verfasser für den Herrenbruder hielt und dementsprechend eine eigene Verfasserschaft im Umkreis der Familie Jesu suchte.[535] Dieser rezeptionsgeschichtliche Hintergrund spricht zugleich gegen die These Rainer Metzners von einem späteren frühchristlichen Lehrer mit dem Namen Jakobus.

Die Wendung θεοῦ καὶ κυρίου Ἰησοῦ Χριστοῦ δοῦλος, bei der der Nominativ nachgestellt ist, erlaubt eine doppelte Auflösung: »Diener Gottes und des Kyrios Jesus Christus« oder »des *Gottes und Kyrios* Jesus Christus Diener«.[536] Eine grammatische Entscheidung lässt sich nicht treffen. Berücksichtigt man die Dominanz des Gottesbegriffs im Jakobusbrief und die (einmalige) analoge Wendung »unseres Kyrios Jesus Christus« in 2,1[537], wird man sich für die Übersetzung »Jakobus, Gottes und des Kyrios Jesus Christus Sklave« entscheiden, die die emphatische Voranstellung Gottes abbildet.[538] Der Absender erhält mit dieser Prädikation eine spezifische religiöse Identität, die auf einer doppelten verpflichtenden Zugehörigkeit, Abhängigkeit und damit verbundenen Autorisierung beruht: Er steht in einem Besitz- und Dienstverhältnis zu Gott selbst und zum Herrn Jesus Christus. Wie dies ausgesehen haben könnte, lässt sich dem Brief ebenso wenig entnehmen wie ein Amts- oder Leitungsverständnis. δοῦλος ist hap. leg. im Jakobusbrief, das paulinische Thema der δουλεία und das vor allem paulinische Motiv des δουλεύειν begegnen nicht im Jakobusbrief.

Der Verfasser stellt sich in doppelter Weise vor: zuerst mit einer traditionellen theologischen Autorisierungsfigur, dem Syntagma δοῦλος θεοῦ, das Septuagintasprache[539] und Teil des jüdischen religiösen Soziolekts ist. »Sklave Gottes« ist eine Ehrenbezeichnung für die Erzväter, Mose, Josua, David und die Propheten[540]. Die emphatische Rückbindung der Bezeichnung an Gott findet sich weder im Präskript

---

Commentary. Translated by K. Ess, Waco 2018, 21–32 (Judasbrief zwischen 100 und 120 n. Chr. als pseudonymes Schreiben verfasst, das an die Bedeutung des Jakobus, des Herrenbruders, im frühen Christentum anknüpft). Frey geht für Jak 1,1 von einem unbekannten Verfasser aus, der unter dem Pseudonym des Herrenbruders schreibt.

[535] So FREY, The Letter of Jude. Die Schwierigkeit, dass weder Jak noch Jud auf den »Herrenbruder« hinweisen, kann Frey für den pseudonymen Verfasser des Jakobusbriefes nicht auflösen (59 f.). – Vgl. oben die Einleitung zum Autor.

[536] Zur Textkritik s. o. Diese Auflösung wird prominent vertreten von J. ASSAËL / É. CUVEILLIER, Jak, 153 f.

[537] S. dort zu der Wendung τῆς δόξης. 3,9 dagegen bezieht sich auf Gott selbst. Zur Verwendung von κύριος in Kap. 5 s. dort.

[538] Dieselbe Reihenfolge 1Thess 1,1; 2Thess 1,1. Die Pastoralbriefe wandeln dies Schema ab. Gal 1,1 ist emphatisch »nicht von Menschen und nicht durch einen Menschen« vorangestellt, gefolgt von der inversen Verbindung »durch Jesus Christus und Gott den Vater« (ähnlich Eph 1,1 und Kol 1,1).

[539] K. H. RENGSTORF, Art. δοῦλος κτλ., ThWNT 2, 1935, 264–283.

[540] Vgl. RENGSTORF, ThWNT 2, 271.

146   Kommentar

des Judasbriefes[541] noch des Philipperbriefes[542], sondern nur in Tit 1,1 zusammen mit ἀπόστολος δὲ Ἰησοῦ Χριστοῦ und in Jak 1,1.[543] Es handelt sich also bei θεοῦ δοῦλος zunächst um einen jüdischen Ehrentitel[544], den der Autor sich selbst oder dem imaginierten Verfasser beilegt.

Durch die *zweite* Genitivverbindung wird diese Ehrenbezeichnung dann erweitert, aber auch religiös präzisiert: καὶ κυρίου Ἰησοῦ Χριστοῦ (δοῦλος). Mit diesem Zusatz stellt sich das Präskript zugleich in den Zusammenhang der paulinischen Briefschule und des 1. und 2. Petrusbriefes und des Judasbriefes[545], d. h. in den literarischen und theologischen Kontext der entstehenden frühchristlichen Briefliteratur nach Paulus. Die Wendung setzt Jak noch einmal in 2,1. Die in der paulinischen und nachpaulinischen Briefliteratur vielfach bezeugte Prädikation κύριος Ἰησοῦς Χριστός bleibt unerläutert, erweist sich aber in der Zusammenstellung mit »Sklave Gottes« als religiös konnotiert. κύριος ist in diesem Kontext nicht Gottestitel wie in Septuaginta, sondern ein eigener Hoheitstitel Jesu Christi.[546] Das Verhältnis zwischen Gott und dem κύριος Ἰησοῦς Χριστός wird nur soweit deutlich, als keine weiteren Götter oder göttlichen Kräfte genannt werden.[547] Das »und« zwischen θεοῦ und κύριος sagt auch nichts über eine Gleichberechtigung oder Nebenordnung aus. »Christologische« Reflexion fehlt ganz. Allerdings wird weder in den orthonymen und pseudonymen Paulusbriefen mit Ausnahme von Gal und Röm[548] noch in den Jakobus, Petrus und Judas zugeschriebenen Briefen das Christusverständnis der Absender in den Adressen näher erläutert. Im Rahmen der *superscriptio* geht es lediglich um die Zugehörigkeit des Absenders und um seine Autorisierung. So

---

[541] Ἰούδας Ἰησοῦ Χριστοῦ δοῦλος, ἀδελφὸς δὲ Ἰακώβου, τοῖς ἐν θεῷ πατρὶ ἠγαπημένοις καὶ Ἰησοῦ Χριστῷ τετηρημένοις κλητοῖς. Das Judaspräskript vereindeutigt sowohl die christologischen als auch die biographischen Uneindeutigkeiten des Jakobuspräskriptes. Die in Jak vorliegende Doppelbindung an Gott und Christus wird bei Judas auf die Adressaten verschoben.

[542] In den Apostolischen Vätern findet sich die Bezeichnung nur im Hirten des Hermas (sehr häufig) als allgemeine religiöse Bezeichnung der Gerechten. IgnRöm 4,3 verwendet den Begriff im speziellen Zusammenhang seiner Martyriumstheologie. In den Präskripten der Briefe begegnet die Bezeichnung nicht.

[543] Vgl. 1Petr 2,16.

[544] R. Jewett, Romans. A Commentary. Hermeneia, Minneapolis 2007, 100, macht für Röm 1,1 die politische Valenz von δοῦλος im Zusammenhang der Familia Caesaris sehr wahrscheinlich, mindestens für das Verständnis der Adressaten. In anderen neutestamentlichen Briefpräskripten lässt sich dies Verständnis nicht nachweisen. Lit: G. Sasse, Zur Bedeutung von δοῦλος bei Paulus, ZNW 40, 1941, 81–82; M. J. Brown, Paul's use of δοῦλος Ἰησοῦ Χριστοῦ in Romans 1:1, JBL 120, 2004, 725–728; E.-M. Becker, Paulus als *doulos* in Röm 1,1 und Phil 1,1: Die epistolare Selbstbezeichnung als Argument, in: dies., Der Philipperbrief des Paulus. Vorarbeiten zu einem Kommentar, NET 29, Tübingen-Basel 2020, 205–222; E. Herrmann-Otto, Art. Sklave, RAC 30, 2021, 691–751 (umfangreiche Lit.), 712 f zum Status der Sklaven im hellenistischen Judentum (Verweis auf C. Heszer, Jewish Slavery in Antiquity, Oxford 2005). Herrmann-Otto geht nicht auf die metaphorische Verwendung in den Titulaturen des Alten Orients und des Alten Testaments ein.

[545] Anders: Hebr und 1–3Joh.

[546] Dazu orientierend F. Hahn, Theologie des Neuen Testaments. Band II, Tübingen 2002, 207–209.

[547] Anders D. Zeller, Der erste Brief an die Korinther, KEK 5, Göttingen 2010, 283–293 zu 1Kor 8,1–6.

[548] In den beiden Briefen geht es um Apologetik des Paulus (in Gal gegenüber Gegnern, in Röm im Zusammenhang der Selbstvorstellung vor einer fremden Gemeinde).

B. Präskript

bleibt offen, ob die Adressaten mit der Wendung κύριος Ἰησοῦς Χριστός eine Prä-existenzchristologie verbinden sollen wie in Röm 1,1–7[549], ob im Hintergrund der potentielle politische oder religiöse (vgl. 1Kor 8,5[550]) Anspruch der Wendung steht, ob hier entweder Septuagintasprache gleichsam verdoppelt und auf Jesus Christus übertragen worden ist oder ob – noch einfacher – lediglich Gemeindeterminolo-gie Verwendung findet, die brieftechnisch in einer *superscriptio* erwartet wird. Der Absender weist sich jedenfalls als eine Person aus, die in einer direkten Abhängig-keits- und Beauftragungsverhältnis nicht nur zum Gott Israels steht, sondern zu jenen Gemeinden gehört, die Ἰησοῦς als κύριος bekennen (Röm 10,9; 1Kor 12,3). Der Verfasser empfängt selbst seine Autorisierung von dem erhöhten κύριος Ἰησοῦς Χριστός. In der *superscriptio* des Jakobusbriefes fungiert die Doppelwendung »Got-tes und des Herrn Jesus Christus Sklave« zugleich als schlichtes Erkennungssignal frühchristlicher Gemeindeliteratur.[551]

Die *adscriptio* des Jakobusbriefes erfolgt mittels der Wendung ταῖς δώδεκα φυλαῖς[552] ταῖς ἐν τῇ διασπορᾷ.[553] Die Wendung als ganze ist ohne Parallele. Sie ist von vorn-herein als literarisch stilisiert zu lesen. Die zweiteilige *adscriptio* ist eine in lokaler, temporaler, personaler und situativer Hinsicht unbestimmte Sammeladresse, die gleichzeitig ein sehr spezifisches Vokabular aufweist. Die »zwölf Stämme«[554] stehen metaphorisch für Israel, das selbst weder hier noch sonst im Jakobusbrief genannt wird.[555] Allison kommentiert den Ausdruck zutreffend: »[it] was a common way of referring to all Israel«.[556] ἐν τῇ διασπορᾷ ist ein Semitismus.[557] διασπορά begegnet in der Profangräzität sehr selten, zuerst bei Plutarch[558]. Im jüdischen Sprachgebrauch dagegen ist διασπορά seit der Septuagintaübersetzung *terminus technicus* für »die

---

[549] Vgl. JEWETT, Romans, 103–108.

[550] Vgl. allg. G. QUELL / W. FÖRSTER, Art. κύριος κτλ., ThWNT 3, 1938, 1038–1098.

[551] In welchem Nah- oder Fernverhältnis diese Gemeinden zu den jüdischen Synagogalgemeinden stehen, lässt sich dem Präskript nicht entnehmen.

[552] φυλή hap. leg. in Jak. Zwölf Stämme: Mt 19,28par [Q 22,30]; Lk 2,36 (Hanna aus dem Stamm Asser); Apg 13,21 (Saul aus dem Stamm Benjamin – wie Saulus-Paulus!); Röm 11,1; Phil 3,5; Hebr 7,13.14 (Stamm Juda); Apk 5,5 (Stamm Juda); 7,4–8 (jeweils 12 000 sind versiegelt aus den 12 Stämmen Israels, die aufgezählt werden); 21,12 (auf den Toren des himmlischen Jerusalems befinden sich die Namen der zwölf Stämme der Söhne Israels).

[553] Hap. leg. in Jak, im NT noch Joh 7,35 und 1Petr 1,1 (Verbindung zu Jak 1,1).

[554] CH. MAURER, Art. φυλή, ThWNT 9, 1973, 240–245.

[555] In den Katholischen Briefen begegnet »Israel« ebenso wenig wie »Jerusalem« und Ἰουδαῖος (alle drei Begriffe aber in Apk). Anders ist die Situation in den Paulusbriefen: zehnmal Jerusalem, häufig Ἰουδαῖος und Israel.

[556] ALLISON, Jak, 128.

[557] ALLISON, Jak, 129. Allison weist darauf hin, dass διασπορά im Sinne einer Sammelbezeichnung für die Juden außerhalb des Landes Israel weder in den griechischsprachigen Pseudepigraphen noch bei Philo und Josephus begegnet, in christlichen Schriften erst seit Justin.

[558] Plutarch, Non Posse Suaviter Vivi Secundum Epicurum 27; vgl. Philo, praem. 115.

148 Kommentar

Zerstreuung der Juden unter die Heidenvölker«[559]: Dtn 28,25; 30,4[560]; Neh 1,9; Jud 5,19; Ps 138 tit. (Hs. A[561]); Ps 146,2; Jes 49,6[562]; Jer 13,14 (Hs. S); 15,7 (Hs. A al.); 41,17; DanLXX 12,2; 2Makk 1,27; PsSal 8,3; 9,2 (vgl. auch Joh 7,35). »*In* Zerstreuung« begegnet in Dtn 28,24 f und in TestXII 10,7.[563] In der Adresse des 1Petr ist der Terminus bereits deutlich metaphorisch für frühchristliche Gemeinden in Kleinasien eingesetzt:

Πέτρος ἀπόστολος Ἰησοῦ Χριστοῦ ἐκλεκτοῖς παρεπιδήμοις διασπορᾶς Πόντου, Γαλατίας, Καππαδοκίας, Ἀσίας καὶ Βιθυνίας.

Petrus, Apostel Jesu Christi, den erwählten Fremdlingen der Diaspora in Pontus, Galatien, Kappadokien, der Asia und Bithynien.

Dass die frühen Christen diesen Begriff für ihre eigene Situation verwendeten, geht auch aus Apg 8,1.4 und 11,19 hervor: Lukas spricht von den »Zerstreuten«, die nach der Stephanushinrichtung Jerusalem verlassen mussten.[564] Jak 1,1 knüpft an diesen metaphorischen Gebrauch an, betont aber die jüdische Komponente durch die Adresse »an die zwölf Stämme«.

Die *adscriptio* macht deutlich, dass der Brief in *literarischer* Hinsicht an eine wie immer vorzustellende – reale oder ideale – *jüdische* Adresse gerichtet ist. Dadurch fällt auch weiteres Licht auf den Absender: Ein Träger des gräzisierten jüdischen Namens Jakobus, der sich zugleich als der Christus-bekennenden Gruppierung zugehörig ausweist, schreibt ideell an die Diasporajuden *in toto*. Zwei Schlüsse sind hieraus zu ziehen, erstens zur intendierten Leserschaft und zweitens zum Verfasser.

Erstens: die Wendung »die zwölf Stämme in der Zerstreuung« ist – wie gesagt – singulär.[565] Sie ist vor allem Ausdruck der *stilistischen* Ambition des Verfassers, die den ganzen Brief charakterisiert. Er vermeidet mit seiner Wortwahl eine terminologisch explizite und eindeutige ethnisch-religiöse Zuordnung der Leserschaft und bevorzugt eine metaphorisch-andeutende, umschreibende Diktion. Zugleich stellt sich die Frage, wieweit die literarisch intendierte jüdische Leserschaft als eine *reale*, religiös-ethnisch definierte zu verstehen sei, zumal im Verlauf des Jak kein Lexem

---

[559] K. L. Schmidt, Art. διασπορά, ThWNT 2, 1935, 98–104, 99; vgl. auch A. Stuiber, Art. Diaspora, RAC 3, 1957, 972–982. Stuiber weist darauf hin, dass διασπορά ein Septuaginta-Neologismus ist: RAC 3, 973: »Bezeichnenderweise ist der Ausdruck d. eine Schöpfung des D.-judentums u. seiner Bibelübersetzung«; D. Sänger, Art. διασπορά, διασπείρω, EWNT 1, ³2011, 553–555.

[560] Zitiert bei Philo, conf. 197.

[561] Die Stellung im Titulus: »Psalm des Zacharias ἐν τῇ διασπορᾷ« ist besonders interessant.

[562] Μέγα σοί ἐστιν τοῦ κληθῆναί σε παῖδά μου τοῦ στῆσαι τὰς φυλὰς Ιακωβ καὶ τὴν διασπορὰν τοῦ Ισραηλ ἐπιστρέψαι (Es ist etwas Großes für dich, dass du mein Knecht genannt wirst, um die Stämme Jakobs aufzurichten und die Zerstreuung Israels zurückzubringen).

[563] Jeweils ohne Artikel. J. Becker, Die Testamente der zwölf Patriarchen, JSHRZ III,1, Gütersloh 1974, 117 Anm. zu VII2a): zu »Diaspora« in TestXII.

[564] Vgl. die Einleitung.

[565] Belege nur bei den Kirchenvätern im Zusammenhang der Jakobusexegese (vgl. Jónsson, James Among the Classisists, 74 Anm. 424).

aus der spezifischen Lexik des Judentums begegnet.[566] Anders gesagt: schreibt der Autor wirklich an eine intendierte jüdische Leserschaft? Zunächst gilt: Seit dem Exil war die Vorstellung von den »zwölf Stämmen Israels« und die Zugehörigkeit zu einem dieser Stämme Bestandteil der ethnischen Identität und des sozialen Ranges eines Juden.[567] Dafür ist auch Paulus ein Beispiel. In Apg 26,7 spricht der *lukanische* Paulus in seiner Rede vor Agrippa von dem historischen Israel als von dem δωδεκάφυλον ἡμῶν. Lukas lässt Paulus bewusst jüdischen Soziolekt benutzen. Dass auch für den *historischen* Paulus die Phylen Israels eine besondere Bedeutung hatten, zeigen Röm 11,1 und Phil 3,5 (»aus dem Stamm Benjamin«). Die Wendung »Zwölf Stämme« wird auch im Protev 1,3[568] und in 1Clem 55,6[569] für das historische Israel benutzt. Christus-gläubige Schriftsteller konnten also die Wendung »zwölf Stämme« für das historische wie für das zeitgenössische Israel benutzen. Zugleich waren aber »die zwölf Stämme« auch mit der »Hoffnung auf die zukünftige Sammlung Gesamtisraels« verbunden.[570] Diese Hoffnung nun findet sich gleichermaßen in frühjüdischen[571] wie in frühchristlichen[572] Schriften. Mt 19,28par und Apk 7,4–8; 21,12 sind besonders aufschlussreich. In Mt 19 sagt Jesus den Zwölf zu, dass sie »die zwölf Stämme Israels« richten werden. In Apk 7,4–8 werden jeweils zwölftausend aus jedem der zwölf Stämme versiegelt. Die Versiegelten werden in 7,3 mit dem alttestamentlichen Ehrentitel als δοῦλοι τοῦ θεοῦ ἡμῶν bezeichnet. In beiden Texten wird nicht deutlich, ob speziell an Christus-gläubige Juden, generell an ethnisch-religiöse Juden oder auch an Christus-gläubige Nichtjuden gedacht ist. Wie in Jak 1 scheinen diese Differenzierungen in den genannten Texten keine Rolle zu spielen.[573]

Die Beispiele machen deutlich, dass Christus-gläubige Autoren die Zwölfstämme-Vorstellung nicht ausschließlich im historischen und / oder ethnisch-religiös definierenden Zusammenhang verwendeten.[574] Die Bezeichnung konnte auch andere Konnotationen haben. Das heißt: In der *adscriptio* des Jak ist im wörtlichen Sinn die jüdische Diaspora angesprochen. Das Profil dieser Adressatenschaft wird von dem Verfasser des Briefes im politisch-religiösen Deutungshorizont des Judentums konstruiert. Es können aber auch Christus-bekennende Juden oder Heiden-

---

566 Weder Lexeme mit Ἰουδ- noch Israel und Jerusalem sind belegt. Vgl. aber 5,4 *(τὰ ὦτα κυρίου σαβαώθ)*.

567 Bedeutung der Stammeszugehörigkeit für Paulus: Röm 11,1; Phil 3,5. Für Jesus: Apk 5,5 (nicht in den Stammbäumen bei Mt und Lk). Bei Josephus, vita. 1,1 fehlt ein Verweis auf seine φυλή.

568 Joachim sieht das »Zwölfstämmeregister« Israels ein.

569 δωδεκάφυλον τοῦ Ἰσραήλ.

570 MAURER, ThWNT 9, 243.

571 Arist 46–50; TestXII: eine Schrift, die nach Gen 49,1 konzipiert ist.

572 ›Frühchristlich‹ bezieht sich auf Schriften, in denen sich ein Christusbekenntnis findet (z. B. Ἰησοῦς Χριστός oder Ἰησοῦς Χριστός Κύριος etc.) oder die eine ausschließlich christliche Überlieferungsgeschichte haben. Damit ist noch kein historisches Urteil über die Religions- und Gruppenzugehörigkeit der Autoren und der Lesegemeinschaften dieser Schriften gefällt.

573 ALLISON, Jak, 128 Anm. 102, verweist nicht auf Apk 7. Er listet Mt 19 auf, ohne aber den Text zu interpretieren.

574 Das muss gegen ALLISON, Jak, 129–132 festgehalten werden.

150 Kommentar

christen, die sich dem Judentum verbunden fühlen, gemeint sein.[575] Worin etwa eine Differenz zwischen »Juden« allgemein und jenen »Juden, die dem Kyrios Jesus Christus zugehören«, bestehen könnte und ob der Verfasser eine solche Differenzierung überhaupt im Blick hatte, geht aus dem Präskript nicht hervor. *Nichtjuden* aber werden weder auf der Briefebene noch auf der Ebene der Metapher angesprochen. Jedenfalls wählt der Verfasser für seine intendierte Adressatenschaft eine sorgfältig ausgesuchte Metapher, die auf das historisch geprägte ›nationale‹ Selbstverständnis des antiken Judentums hinweist, ohne dass sie in exkludierender Weise ethnisch-religiös verstanden werden müsste.[576]

Zweitens: die Konstellation von Jakobus und den zwölf Stämmen in der Diaspora weist für eine jüdische wie für eine Christus-bekennende Leserschaft auf den weithin bekannten Herrenbruder Jakobus hin. Allerdings fehlt die Bezugnahme auf seine Leitungsfunktion in Jerusalem, auf das Epitheton der Gerechtigkeit oder ein gezielter Hinweis auf seine Stellung zu Jesus. Auf jeden Fall modelliert der Verfasser den Herrenbruder nicht (mehr?) als eine klar umrissene historische Gestalt. Vielmehr fungiert Jakobus als eine Art Passepartout für einen literarisch ambitionierten Verfasser, der seine Nähe zum Judentum betonen will und sich unter die Autorität eines religiösen Führers stellt.

Welches Signal sendet das Präskript damit insgesamt? Ein *literarisch ambitionierter Briefautor* schreibt unter dem gräzisierten jüdischen Namen Jakobus, der zugleich der Name verschiedener bekannter Leitungsgestalten aus der Jesusbewegung ist, einen Brief an eine *literarisch konstruierte Lesergemeinde*, die er mit einer *Metapher aus dem jüdischen Soziolekt* als Diasporajuden anspricht. Damit ist zugleich ein religiöser Rahmen gegeben. Seine eigene Autorität begründet der Verfasser mit der Doppelmetapher »Gottes und des Herrn Jesus Christus Sklave«, in der sich alttestamentlich-jüdischer Soziolekt mit frühchristlicher Bekenntnissprache verbindet. *Eindeutige* geographische, biographische oder religionsgeschichtliche Zuordnungen liegen nicht im Interesse des Verfassers und lassen sich dem Präskript nicht entnehmen. *Deutlich* ist dagegen die literarische Gestaltung des Schreibens als eines Briefes, der in der paulinischen Brieftradition steht, seine Leserschaft aber suchen muss und

---

[575] Vgl. R. METZNER, Jak, 13–16. Metzner formuliert die beiden religionsgeschichtlich basierten Zuordnungsmöglichkeiten: »Versteht man die Wendung *eigentlich*, sind Juden oder Judenchristen außerhalb Israels gemeint. Ist sie *übertragen* zu lesen, sind alle Christen und überall angesprochen« (13). Und: »Fehlen auf der einen Seite Hinweise auf eine jüdische Identität der Adressaten, so auf der anderen Seite auch auf eine heidnische Identität« (14).

[576] Vgl. auch den eschatologischen Aspekt der Zahl »Zwölf« in 4Esr 14,11: »Denn in zwölf Teile ist die Weltzeit geteilt« (Übersetzung: J. SCHREINER, Das 4. Buch Esra, JSHRZ V/4, Gütersloh 1981, 401). Zum ethnischen Verständnis des antiken Judentums vgl. besonders S. MASON, Jews, Judaeans, Judaizing, Judaism. Problems of Categorizing in Ancient History, JSJ 38, 2007, 457–512; vgl. zustimmend J. M. G. BARCLAY, Flavius Josephus. Translation and Commentary, Bd. 10: Against Apion. Translation and Commentary, Leiden 2007, XVII-LXXI, bes. LV-LXI; differenzierend E. GRUEN, Ethnicity in the Ancient World – Did it Matter? Berlin / Boston 2020.

seinen Verfasser nicht offenbart. Ob es sich bei dem *Verfasser* um den Herrenbruder handelt oder ob ein unbekannter Verfasser in der Autorität des Herrenbruders schreibt, wird durch das Präskript nicht eindeutig geklärt.[577] Die Konstellation von Namen, autoritativer religiös bestimmter Selbstvorstellung und griechisch-sprachiger jüdischer Leserschaft deutet auf den Herrenbruder Jakobus hin. Die *superscriptio* aber gibt gerade keinen deutlichen Hinweis. Weder »Bruder des Herrn« noch der Titel »der Gerechte« begegnen, so dass eine historische Zuschreibung ebenso wie auch eine pseudepigraphe Zuschreibung zu Jakobus, dem Bruder Jesu, offenbleibt. Die Leserschaft, soweit sie judenchristlich war, wird an Jakobus, den Herrenbruder, gedacht haben. Das Verhältnis der *Leserschaft* zum Judentum bleibt ebenfalls *offen*. Im Verlauf des Briefes wird dies Verhältnis nicht explizit thematisiert. Auf der Ebene des wörtlichen Verstehens richtet sich das Schreiben an die Diasporajudenschaft griechischer Sprache. Judenchristen, wie es Paulus und die anderen Apostel waren (Gal 2,15), sind durchaus einbegriffen. Ob sich auch Christus-gläubige Gemeinden und Gemeindeglieder, die nicht zum ἔθνος τῶν Ἰουδαίων gehörten, von der Adresse angesprochen fühlten oder fühlen sollten, ist weder zu beweisen noch auszuschließen. Seit Paulus wird der ethnisch-religiöse Begriff von Ἰουδαῖος bzw. von Ἰσραήλ neuen Definitionen jenseits des ἔθνος-Begriffs zugeführt, wie Röm 2,28 f; 9,6; 1Kor 9,20; 10,28; Gal 3,28; 6,16 zeigen. Die Jakobusadresse lässt sich auch im Sinne von 1Petr 1,1, d. h. der »wahren Diaspora«, d. h. der Christus-gläubigen Gemeinden lesen. Fazit: die Adresse ist gerade nicht an religiös-institutioneller Eindeutigkeit, sondern an Offenheit und stilistischer Gestaltung interessiert.

C. Briefcorpus

1. Erster Hauptteil: Belehrungen über das richtige Ethos für die Christus-gläubigen Gemeinden (Kap. 1)

Hauptteil 1 und 2 (Kapitel 1 und 2) gehören zusammen.[578] Sie sind der Belehrung über den richtigen *Glauben* in den Christus-gläubigen Gemeinden gewidmet, deren Mitglieder der Verfasser brieflich anspricht. Dabei geht es ab 1,3 um das δοκίμιον τῆς πίστεως, um die »Prüfung des *Glaubens*«, ab 2,1 um den »*Glauben*, der frei ist von sozialer Status-Bevorzugung«, ab 2,14 dann um das Verhältnis von *Glauben* und Taten. 2,14–26 ist einer der zentralen theologischen Glaubenstexte der neutestamentlichen Schriften. Den Schluss bildet eine Gnome über den *Glauben* (2,26). Ziel des Verfassers ist, die Adressaten zu dem in 2,26 formulierten *richtigen Glaubensverständnis* und dem damit verbundenen Ethos des *vollkommenen Lebenswandels* zu führen (1,4).

---

[577] Interessanterweise haben die Kirchenväter diese Unschärfe nicht als Problem empfunden, vgl. Wischmeyer, Who was »James«?, in: E.-M. Becker u. a. (Hg.), Who was ›James‹?, 179–195.
[578] Zur Gliederung des Briefes vgl. die Einleitung.

In Hauptteil 1 (Kapitel 1) entwirft Jakobus das richtige Ethos für seine Adressaten. Kap. 1 ist reich gegliedert. Jakobus beginnt mit der Belehrung über die πειρασμοί in 1,2–18 (Hauptteil 1 A mit sechs Texteinheiten). Es folgt in 1,19–27 die Belehrung über das Wort (Hauptteil 1 B mit drei Texteinheiten). *Thema* sind die πειρασμοί, die die Gemeindeglieder treffen können. Teil A gliedert sich zudem thematisch in *zwei* Teile: In A1 (1,2–12) sind die πειρασμοί Gegenstand einer einführenden Belehrung, in A2 (1,13–18) wird das Thema theologisch vertieft. Teil B ist thematisch nicht weiter untergliedert. Der gesamte erste Hauptteil ist im Modus der kommunikativen Belehrung gehalten. Die Adressaten werden auf ihre Einsicht, ihr Wissen und ihr Urteilsvermögen angesprochen.[579]

A. 1,2–18: Belehrung über die πειρασμοί

A1 (1,2–12) ist als Eröffnungstext besonders sorgfältig gestaltet. Es handelt sich um eine Ringkomposition. Der Autor eröffnet seine Argumentation in 1,2 mit einer These und einem Ratschlag: Versuchungen sind etwas Positives und sollen mit Zustimmung aufgenommen werden. V. 12 verstärkt und bekräftigt die Eingangsthese in der literarischen Gestalt einer Seligpreisung für diejenigen, die Versuchung erdulden und sich bewähren. In diesem Rahmen stellt 1,3 die vertiefende Begründung von 1,2 dar: Der Verfasser denkt an Glaubensprüfungen. Diese führen zu Geduld. 1,4 rundet die These mit der Aussicht auf Vollkommenheit in der Geduld ab. In diesem Vers formuliert der Verfasser zugleich die gemeindeleitende *Intention seines Schreibens*: Es geht um die *Vollkommenheit* der Adressaten. V. 2–4 können als die *propositio generalis* oder als das Programm des Briefes bezeichnet werden: in Versuchungssituationen den rechten Glauben und die Geduld zu bewahren, um vollkommen zu sein. In 1,25 führt Jakobus dann das »vollkommene Gesetz der Freiheit« als Maßstab dieser Vollkommenheit ein. In 1,5–8 und 9–11 konkretisiert er seinen Ratschlag von V. 2 durch drei praktische Zusatz-Mahnungen zu Weisheit, Glauben und Demut: *Erstens* soll man auf Vollkommenheit in der Weisheit achten und um sie bitten. *Zweitens* soll dies Gebet im einfachen Glauben erfolgen. *Drittens* soll die »Niedrigkeit« bzw. Demut der Gemeindemitglieder positiv bewertet werden, nicht ihr Reichtum. Die Mahnungen werden plausibilisiert, indem der Verfasser zwei negative Typen von Menschen zeichnet: den Zweifelnden und den Reichen. Beide Typen, die häufiger im Jak begegnen, werden nichts vom Herrn empfangen, d. h. sie sind von der guten Botschaft von 1,2 ausgeschlossen. Dem stehen der Glaubensstarke und der »Niedrige« gegenüber.

A2 (1,13–18) ist der vertiefenden theologischen Frage der Herkunft der Versuchung und der Gottesgaben gewidmet. Versuchung und Gottesgaben stehen in einem antithetischen Verhältnis zueinander. Der Verfasser stellt klar, dass Gott ausschließlich der Geber der guten Gaben ist. Die Versuchungen dagegen stammen

---

[579] ἡγήσασθε, γινώσκοντες, μὴ πλανᾶσθε, ἴστε, εἴ τις δοκεῖ.

aus dem Inneren des Menschen. 1,18 schließt mit der stärkenden Aussage, die Adressaten seien »die Erstlingsfrucht der Geschöpfe« Gottes. Mit dieser Botschaft ist der erste Argumentationszusammenhang des Briefes abgeschlossen. Zugleich sind damit die Grundlagen der *Theologie* des Verfassers gelegt: *Gott* ist der Geber der guten Gaben. Er ist der Schöpfer und der Garant der Unveränderlichkeit. Er hat die Christus-bekennende (1,1) Gemeinde ins Leben gerufen. Dieser Theologie soll das Verhalten der Adressaten korrespondieren: Sie sollen entsprechend der vollkommenen Gabe Gottes (V. 17) selbst vollkommen sein (V. 4). Ziel der Ausführungen ist die Stärkung in Glaubensprüfungen im Hinblick auf eine Vollkommenheitsethik.[580]

1. Texteinheit[581]: 1,2–4 πειρασμοί als Grund zur Freude (V.4 propositio generalis)

(2) Haltet es ganz für Freude[582], meine Brüder, wenn ihr in vielfältige Versuchungen geratet[583], (3) indem ihr wisst[584], dass die Echtheit eures Glaubens Geduld bewirkt. (4) Die Geduld aber möge ein vollkommenes Werk haben, damit ihr vollkommen und untadelig seid und in nichts zurückbleibt.

Textkritik: V. 3 δοκίμιον wird von 110.1241 pc zu δόκιμον vereinfacht (ebenso 1Petr 1,7). Statt ὑμῶν τῆς πίστεως lesen mehrere Minuskeln ἡμῶν τῆς πίστεως.

V. 2 Die Eingangsmahnung in V. 2.3 setzt das *Thema*: die Prüfung des Glaubens. Diese Prüfung muss bestanden werden und wird die Adressaten zur Vollkommenheit führen. Der Verfasser eröffnet das Briefcorpus mit einem Ratschlag zu den πειρασμοί, die die Brüder treffen können, und appelliert in V. 3 an ihr Erfahrungswissen. Es geht um das innere Verhalten bzw. das Verständnis gegenüber möglichen πειρασμοί: um ἡγεῖσθαι und γινώσκειν. V. 4 schließt den belehrenden Ratschlag mit einem Zusatz zu V. 3 ab. Der Rat wird im Imp.2.Pers.Pl. gegeben und richtet sich an »meine Brüder«.[585] Die Briefsituation des Präskripts wirkt in ihrer kommunikativen Grundstruktur weiter, der Verfasser wechselt aber unauffällig von der umfassenden und gleichsam offiziellen Adresse »an die zwölf Stämme in der Diaspora« zu einer Belehrung der »Brüder«. Die Kommunikationssituation ist jetzt die der Gleichwertigkeit zwischen Sender und Empfängern: »*meine* Brüder«. Damit nimmt die Kommunikation eine Wendung von einer allgemeinen, ›hoch‹ oder ideal, d. h.

---

580 Zum Text 1,2–15: J. S. Kloppenborg, James 1:2–15 and Hellenistic Psychagogy, NT 52, 2010, 37–71.

581 Die Textgliederung erfolgt nach dem subordinierenden Schema: Hauptteil, Teiltext, Texteinheit. Im vorliegenden Kommentar wird der Begriff »Texteinheit« jeweils für die kleinste formal und argumentativ zusammenhängende Verbindung von Sätzen gewählt. Dibelius arbeitete mit dem der Formgeschichte zugeordneten Begriff der »Spruchreihe«. Die unterschiedliche Anzahl von Texteinheiten in den fünf Hauptteilen und ihren Teiltexten (im Kommentar durch A, B, C gekennzeichnet) weist sowohl auf eine bleibende Verbindung der Prosa des Briefes zur Spruchdichtung der LXX hin wie auf die ebenso nachhaltige Bindung einzelner Motive und Argumentationen an LXX-Vorgaben. Weiteres siehe Einleitung.

582 Wörtlich: haltet es für ganze (deutsch besser: »reine«) Freude. – Aor. Imp.

583 Aor. Konj.

584 Modale Auflösung des Partizips.

585 L. Doering, Art. ἀδελφός κτλ., HTLS I, 165–184.

154 Kommentar

religiös-ethnisch, konzipierten literarischen Adressatenschaft (die zwölf Stämme in der Diaspora) zu der faktisch intendierten realen Leser- bzw. Hörerschaft, die grundsätzlich in dem kleinen, sich zu Jesus Christus als dem Kyrios bekennenden frühchristlichen Feld angesiedelt sein kann, ohne dass das große jüdische Feld ausgeschlossen wäre, da πειρασμός hier wie dort thematisiert wird. Ein eigener Akzent, der die Zugehörigkeit der »Brüder« näher definieren könnte, fehlt.[586] πειρασμός ist das prägnant gesetzte Eröffnungsthema des Briefes, das aber ausschließlich die erste thematische Einheit 1,1–18 bestimmt.[587]

Die Bezeichnung ἀδελφοί/ἀδελφός »Bruder« ist gleichermaßen Bestandteil des jüdischen wie des frühchristlichen Soziolekts.[588] Hans von Soden hat darauf hingewiesen, dass der frühchristliche Sprachgebrauch »deutlich aus jüdisch-religiöser Sitte übernommen« ist.[589] Lutz Doering spricht von »fellow compatriots«.[590] Seit Paulus ist die »Bruder«-Anrede auch breit als metaphorische Bezeichnung für die Mitglieder der frühchristlichen Gemeinden und als briefliche Anrede der Gemeindemitglieder[591] bezeugt. Nach der Selbstvorstellung des Verfassers in Jak 1,1 lässt sich die Bruder-Anrede sowohl im jüdischen als auch im paulinisch geprägten Kontext verorten. Der Verfasser des Jakobusbriefes verwendet die »Bruder«-Anrede durchgehend zur Herstellung der literarischen Briefkommunikation mit seinem Lesepublikum[592]. Dabei schwingt die jüdische ethnisch-religiöse Bedeutungskomponente ebenso mit wie die paulinische Gemeindekonzeption mit der Vermeidung neuer Hierarchien. Untersuchungen von D. G. Horrell[593], Ph.A. Harland[594], P. Arzt-Grabner[595] und R. Aasgard haben die soziologische und emotionale

---

[586] Auch bei Paulus sehr häufig am Beginn von Ermahnungen die einfache Anrede »Brüder« (z. B. 1Kor 1,10).

[587] Jak 1,2.12. Verb: 1,13 (zweimal).14.

[588] H. v. Soden, Art. ἀδελφός κτλ., ThWNT I, 1933, 144–146.

[589] ThWNT I, 145. So wird »Bruder« auch in der synoptischen Tradition gebraucht (Mt 5,22 und öfter).

[590] Doering, HTLS I, 175 für den frühjüdischen Sprachgebrauch, 176 für die frühchristliche Verwendung (besonders bei Paulus sehr häufige Verwendung für »fellow believers in Christ«); 177 weist Doering darauf hin: »The address ἀδελφοί (μου) is particularly frequent in James«, 182 f (Bibliographie).

[591] In den orthonymen Paulusbriefen begegnet die »Bruder«-Anrede überaus häufig. Paulus benutzt sie als entscheidendes Instrument für den brieflichen (Halb)-Dialog. Dieser Gebrauch fehlt in Eph und Kol sowie fast ganz in den Pastoralbriefen und 1.2Petr. Aber in Hebr 3,1.12; 10,19; 13,22 und häufig in 1Joh. Jak zeigt hier einen deutlichen Einfluss der paulinischen Korrespondenz. Zum paulinischen Gebrauch vgl. K. Schäfer, Gemeinde als »Bruderschaft«. Ein Beitrag zum Kirchenverständnis des Paulus, EHS.T 333, Frankfurt / M., 1989; R. Aasgaard, ›My Beloved Brothers and Sisters!‹ Christian Siblingship in Paul, Early Christianity in Context. JSNTS 265, London / New York 2004. Wichtig auch die häufige Bruderanrede bzw. -bezeichnung in Apg.

[592] 1,2.16.19; 2,1.5.14; 3,1.10.12; 4,11; 5,7.9.10.12.19.

[593] D. G. Horrell, From Adelphoi to Oikos Theou: Social Transformation in Pauline Christianity, JBL 120, 2001, 293–311.

[594] Ph.A. Harland, Familial Dimensions of Group Identity: ›Brothers‹ (ἀδελφοί) in Associations of the Greek East, JBL 124, 2005, 500.

[595] P. Arzt-Grabner, ›Brothers‹ and ›Sisters‹ in Documentary Papyri and in Early Christianity, RivBib 50, 2002, 192–195.

C. Briefcorpus

Bedeutung des Terminus im Vergleich mit Inschriften, Papyri und kaiserzeitlicher Literatur[596] akzentuiert. Alicia J. Batten hat die Bedeutung der Bruder-Anrede für die Freundschaftskonstruktion des Briefes als besondere Stärkung der Gruppenverbindung beschrieben.[597]

Der erste freundschaftlich-autoritative Rat[598], den der Verfasser seinen Lesern und Hörern gibt, stellt eine kräftig modellierte Einführung in die Thematik des πειρασμός dar, die den Text von 1,2–18 bestimmt. Bevor aber das Thema überhaupt gesetzt wird, akzentuiert der Verfasser die spezifische Haltung, die die Brüder dem Thema gegenüber einnehmen sollen: Freude. Diese Haltung ist ihm besonders wichtig. Die Semantik ist sorgfältig gewählt. ἡγεῖσθαι, halten für, begegnet im Jak nur hier.[599] χαρά – hier benutzt Jakobus die Anadiplose: χαίρειν-χαρά – wird in 1,2 nicht theologisch aufgewertet[600], sondern stilistisch und sachlich kontrastiv zum Thema der πειρασμοί im Sinne »freudiger Zustimmung« gesetzt.[601] πειρασμός darf als Bestandteil des Septuaginta-Soziolekts gelten[602] und weist von vornherein auf eine Autoren- und Leserschaft hin, der diese Thematik vertraut ist und die sich selbst davon betroffen fühlt. Eine Einführung oder nähere Konkretisierung des Begriffs ist offensichtlich überflüssig. Für die hier eingangs gesetzte Konstellation von Glaube, Freude und Anfechtung ist 1Petr 1,6–9 zu vergleichen[603]:

(6) ἐν ᾧ ἀγαλλιᾶσθε ὀλίγον ἄρτι, εἰ δέον ἐστίν, λυπηθέντας ἐν ποικίλοις πειρασμοῖς, (7) ἵνα τὸ δοκίμιον ὑμῶν τῆς πίστεως πολυτιμότερον χρυσίου τοῦ ἀπολλυμένου, διὰ πυρὸς δὲ δοκιμαζομένου εὑρεθῇ εἰς ἔπαινον καὶ δόξαν καὶ τιμὴν ἐν ἀποκαλύψει Ἰησοῦ Χριστοῦ (8) ὃν οὐκ ἰδόντες ἀγαπᾶτε, εἰς ὃν ἄρτι μὴ ὁρῶντες, πιστεύοντες δὲ ἀγαλλιᾶσθε χαρᾷ ἀνεκλαλήτῳ καὶ δεδοξασμένῃ (9) κομιζόμενοι τὸ τέλος τῆς πίστεως ὑμῶν σωτηρίαν ψυχῶν.

(6) Dann werdet ihr euch freuen, die ihr jetzt eine kleine Zeit, wenn es sein soll, traurig seid in mancherlei Anfechtungen, (7) damit euer Glaube bewährt und viel kostbarer

---

[596] Bes. Plutarch, De fraterno amore. Vgl. die Interpretation bei AASGAARD, ›My Beloved Brothers…‹, 92–106.

[597] A. J. BATTEN, Friendship and Benefaction in James, ESEC 15, Blandford Forum 2010, 46–48.

[598] Der kommunikative Ton verbindet Belehrung und Ratschlag.

[599] Vgl. Phil 2,3; 3,7 f; 2Petr 2,13; 3,15.

[600] In Jak noch 4,9: konventionell antithetisch zu Trauer.

[601] Paulinisches Vorzugswort, in Jak noch 4,9; auch Mt 5,11: Freude bei Verfolgung. Vgl. H. CONZELMANN / W. ZIMMERLI, Art. χαίρω κτλ., ThWNT 9, 1973, 349–404.

[602] Grundlegend: H. J. KORN, PEIRASMOS. Die Versuchung des Gläubigen in der griechischen Bibel, BWANT 20, Stuttgart 1937. Vgl. auch A. SOMMER, Der Begriff der Versuchung im Alten Testament und Judentum, Diss. Breslau, Breslau 1935; H. SEESEMANN, Art. πεῖρα κτλ., ThWNT 6, 1959, 23–37; ergänzend: C. SPICQ, Lexique Théologique du Nouveau Testament, Fribourg 1991, 1218–1224. Als Neologismus im Pentateuch wertet M. Harl das Substantiv: C. DOGNIEZ / M. HARL, La Bible d' Alexandrie, 5, Le Deutéronome, Paris 1992, 65. Anders περίστασις (nur Ez 26,8 und 2Makk 4,16). – Ich übersetze mit »Versuchungen«. »Anfechtungen« oder »Prüfungen« sind ebenso möglich, aber »Anfechtung« hat einen leicht moralisierenden Klang, »Prüfungen« ist im Deutschen nicht eindeutig, außer wenn es im Zusammenhang mit »Glaube« als »Glaubensprüfungen« gesetzt wird. Zum Thema auch: H. FÖRSTER, Der Versucher und die Juden als seine Vortruppen, ZThK 115, 2018, 229–259.

[603] Darüber hinaus sind 1Petr 1,3–25 und Jak 1,2–18 in mehrfacher Hinsicht verwandt. Vgl. DIBELIUS, Jak, 105. Ausführlich mit Tabelle FRANKEMÖLLE, Jak I, 185–188.

befunden werde als Gold, das vergänglich ist, obgleich es durchs Feuer geläutert wird, zu Lob, Preis und Ehre bei der Offenbarung Jesu Christi, (8) den ihr liebt, obgleich ihr ihn nicht gesehen habt, an den ihr glaubt, obwohl ihr ihn jetzt nicht seht; ihr werdet euch aber freuen mit unaussprechlicher und herrlicher Freude, (9) wenn ihr das Ziel eures Glaubens erlangt, nämlich die Rettung eurer Seelen.

Die Motivkombination von ποικίλοι πειρασμοί, »vielfältige Anfechtungen«[604], δοκίμιον τῆς πίστεως, »Bewährung des Glaubens« und χαρά, »Freude« verbindet Jak und 1Petr. Für die Erklärung von Jak 1,2–4 sind folgende Züge wichtig: (1) die thematische Stellung der πειρασμοί am Briefanfang, (2) die Verbindung von Trauer und Freude, (3) die zentrale Stellung des Glaubens in diesem Zusammenhang, (4) das Ziel der Vollkommenheit (Jak 1,4).[605] Im Unterschied zu Jak 1 wird in 1Petr dieser Zusammenhang allerdings in doppelter Weise theologisch gedeutet: (1) Die Ausführungen zu den πειρασμοί stehen nicht einfach in einem zeitlichen, sondern in einem eschatologischen Rahmen: Im ἄρτι (V. 6) herrschen während einer kurzen Zeitspanne (ὀλίγον) Anfechtung und Trauer, (V. 5) ἐν καιρῷ ἐσχάτῳ folgt die Freude[606]. (2) Dieser eschatologische Rahmen ist außerdem explizit christologisch, nämlich durch die Auferstehung Jesu Christi bestimmt (1Petr 1,3.7). (3) Auch die Freude ist theologisch, genauer: eschatologisch und soteriologisch, qualifiziert. Die Gläubigen freuen sich darüber, dass sie »das Ziel ihres Glaubens«, die σωτηρία ψυχῶν erlangen (1Petr 1,9). 1Petr 1 liest sich wie eine christologisch-soteriologisch-eschatologische Variante von Jak 1.[607] In Jak 1 fehlt die dreifache Qualifizierung: Es gibt kaum ein zeitliches Gefälle[608], der Glaube ist nicht auf Christus gerichtet und die πίστις nicht soteriologisch bestimmt. Ein weiterer thematisch verwandter Text mit einer anderen Pointe liegt in Hebr 10,33–36 vor. Der Verfasser weist auf eine Verfolgungssituation hin, die die Adressaten erlitten haben – ein Hinweis, der im Jak fehlt. Sie haben »den Raub ihrer Güter mit Freude hingenommen« (10,34) – hier findet sich dieselbe paradoxe Werteumwandlung wie im Jak. Die eschatologische Perspektive wird in Hebr 10,35–39 angedeutet. Geduld (10,36) und Glaube (10,38 f; Kap. 11) sollen die Verhaltensformen der Adressaten sein. Wie im Jak fehlt auch in Hebr 10 die christologische Perspektive.[609]

Welche semantischen Nuancen in Jak 1,2–4 bei πίστις, πειρασμός, χαρά und ὑπομονή im Spiel sind, wird im weiteren Verlauf der Belehrung in den Versen 5–8 deutlicher. Eingangs werden die Begriffe einfach als bekannt und selbsterklärend

---

[604] πειρασμοῖς περιπέσητε ποικίλοις: Alliteration und Assonanz (ALLISON, Jak, 146).

[605] »Vollkommenheit« begegnet nicht in 1Petr, stattdessen »heilig im ganzen Wandel« V. 15. Zu dem Motiv des verwelkten Grases s. zu V. 11.

[606] Vgl. Joh 16,22 (νῦν und λύπη). Im Johannesevangelium wird die Zukunft umschrieben: an jenem Tag, wenn Jesus die Jünger wiedersehen wird (Joh 16, 22 f).

[607] Ähnliches lässt sich im Verhältnis der beiden Präskripte beobachten.

[608] Luthers Übersetzung: »Die Geduld aber soll ihr Werk tun bis ans Ende« statt »ihr vollständiges Werk« führt eine zeitliche Dimension ein, die im Griechischen nicht eindeutig vorhanden ist.

[609] 10,37 deutet Jesu endzeitliches Wiederkommen an.

vorausgesetzt. Der Verfasser verwendet bei der Einführung des Themas die Stilmittel des Paradoxon – *Versuchungen* sollen als reine *Freude* verstanden werden – und der Anastrophe, indem er das Akkusativobjekt ›Freude‹ voranstellt. Er rät den Brüdern zu einer Umwertung der üblichen Werteordnung, in der πειρασμός negativ konnotiert ist, und erzeugt damit zu Beginn seines Schreibens sogleich Aufmerksamkeit.[610] Der Plural und das Attribut ποικίλοι[611] machen deutlich, dass hier nicht an eine spezifische Form der Versuchung gedacht ist, sondern an die allgemeine *condition croyante* der Adressaten. Eine Differenzierung zugunsten einer der Bedeutungsnuancen von Prüfung, Versuchung, Anfechtung[612] ist hier gerade noch *nicht* im Blick.[613] Offen muss auch bleiben, ob der Verfasser auf Mt 4,1–11 anspielen und die Adressaten mit dem Schicksal Jesu verbinden will, wie es in Hebr 2,18; 4,15 der Fall ist, oder ob er implizit bereits auf Abraham verweist (Hebr 11,17). Die Argumentation von 1,2–18 deutet allerdings in eine andere Richtung, wie die V. 13–15 zeigen werden. περιπίπτειν πειρασμοῖς ist eine eigene alliterierende Wendung des Verfassers.[614]

Wie weit die »Versuchungen« oder »Prüfungen« real sind und den Anlass des Schreibens darstellen, lässt sich angesichts der topischen Sprache nicht sagen. Anders als 1Petr bleibt Jak so allgemein, dass eher von einem pädagogisch-psychagogischen Interesse des Verfassers auszugehen ist als von einer konkreten Situation bei den Adressaten.

V. 3 Der imperativische Ratschlag wird mit einem Partizip + Objektsatz fortgeführt. Wirft Jak 1,2–4 auch anders als Hebr 10,34 kaum direkt Licht auf die Art der πειρασμοί, so wird doch in V. 3 f eine Kette von Gegenbegriffen genannt, die die πειρασμοί indirekt näher bestimmen: πίστις, ὑπομονή, ἔργον τέλειον. Dabei behaftet der Verfasser die Adressaten bei ihrem religiös-ethischen Erfahrungswissen: γινώσκοντες.[615] Es werden also nicht konkrete Verfolgungssituationen genannt, sondern ethische Haltungen, Aspekte des Ethos der Vollkommenheit. Dabei ist die πίστις der tragende Begriff.[616] Denn der Glaube ist es, der die so auffällig thematisierten πειρασμοί meistert, indem er Geduld bewirkt. Damit wird deutlich, dass der Verfasser bei den πειρασμοί an Glaubensprüfungen denkt. Das Thema Glaube beherrscht damit die gesamten Ausführungen der Kapitel 1 und 2 des Briefes. V. 3 und 4 stellen schon die Weiche in Richtung auf den Zusammenhang von Glauben und Taten, wenn die notwendige Geduld dem Glauben als Tat, d. h. als Ergebnis

---

[610] Vgl. nur Mt 6,13par!

[611] Selten im NT, hap. leg. in Jak. Vgl. die Parallele in 1Petr 1.

[612] Nach BAUER / ALAND, 1291.

[613] Die ausführliche Analyse von TH. KLEIN, Bewährung in Anfechtung. Der Jakobusbrief und der 1. Petrusbrief als christliche Diaspora-Briefe, NET 18, Tübingen / Basel 2011, 288–299, setzt Kap. 4 voraus.

[614] Vgl. 1Tim 6,9: ἐμπίπτουσιν εἰς πειρασμὸν

[615] γινώσκειν: vgl. B. HINTZEN / E. BELENKAJA / CH. LUSTIG, Art. γι(γ)νώσκειν κτλ., HTLS I, 1863–1882. Das Verb wird in Jak in rhetorisch-didaktischem Zusammenhang gesetzt: 1,3; 2,20; 5,20.

[616] Siehe Röm 5,1.

des Glaubens, beigesellt wird. Der Glaube selbst wird bei den Adressaten vorausgesetzt. Dem Verfasser geht es genauer gesagt um die Erprobung, Prüfung und Bestätigung des Glaubens, das δοκίμιον.[617] Dabei steht zunächst die Geduld im Vordergrund: Sie bestimmt die Thematik bis V. 12. Die Zusammenstellung von πίστις[618] und ὑπομονή[619] ist traditionell und den jüdischen Synagogalgemeinden ebenso vertraut wie den frühen christlichen Gemeinden.[620] Eine Konturierung der Semantik nimmt der Verfasser hier noch nicht vor.[621] Er konstruiert vielmehr eine kurze, lockere Kette von Begriffen, deren Bedeutung, Wichtigkeit und Zusammenhang er voraussetzt: Glaube, Geduld, Vollkommenheit – letztere in V. 4 adjektivisch ausgedrückt. Glaube und Geduld sind durch κατεργάζεσθαι verbunden, die Geduld soll bis zum Stand der Vollkommenheit *wirken*. κατεργάζεσθαι ist im neutestamentlichen Umfeld ein paulinisches Vorzugswort und ist außer in der paulinischen Briefliteratur nur in Jak 1,3.20 und 1Petr 4,3 bezeugt. Die Zusammenstellung von Glaube, Geduld und Vollkommenheit bzw. Vervollkommnung im Sinne eines Kettenschlusses ist im frühjüdischen und frühchristlichen Denken verbreitet.[622] Paulus stellt in Röm 5,3 f[623] eine etwas längere Kette von Begriffen zusammen, die ebenfalls durch κατεργάζεσθαι[624] zueinander in Beziehung gesetzt sind und in der δοκιμή einen eigenen Stellenwert hat[625]: Geduld – Bewährung – Hoffnung. Basis ist auch hier der Glaube (Röm 5,1). Bei Paulus in Röm 5,3 f ist die θλῖψις die Situation, die die Erprobung nötig macht und die Kette der Verhaltensweisen in Gang setzt:

---

[617] Zu δοκίμιον vgl. W. Grundmann, Art. δόκιμος, ThWNT 2, 1935, 258–264: »Prüfungsmittel« (259); Bauer / Aland, 408: »Echtheit«. δοκίμιον im NT nur in Jak 1,3 (hap. leg. in Jak) und 1Petr 1,7. LXX: Ps 11,7 und Spr 27,21.

[618] Vgl. zum »Glauben«: E. Wissmann, Das Verhältnis von πίστις und Christusfrömmigkeit bei Paulus, FRLANT 40, Göttingen 1926; R. Bultmann / A. Weiser, Art. πιστεύω κτλ., ThWNT 5, 1959, 193–230; D. Lührmann, Pistis im Judentum, ZNW 64, 1973, 19–38; ders., Glaube im frühen Christentum, Gütersloh 1976; ders., Art. Glaube, RAC 11, 1981, 48–122; B. Schliesser, Was ist Glaube? Paulinische Perspektiven, Theologische Studien NF 3, Zürich 2011; Th. Morgan, Roman Faith and Christian Faith: Pistis and Fides in the Early Roman Empire and Early Churches, Oxford 2015; B. Schliesser / J. Frey / N. Ueberschaer (Hg.), Glaube. Das Verständnis des Glaubens im frühen Christentum und in seiner jüdischen und hellenistisch-römischen Umwelt, WUNT 373, Tübingen 2017 (darin: K.-W. Niebuhr, Glaube im Stresstest. πίστις im Jakobusbrief, 473–501); F. Watson, Roman Faith and Christian Faith, NTS 64, 2018, 243–247; F. W. Horn (Hg.), Glaube, UTB 5034.Themen der Theologie 13, Tübingen 2018.

[619] F. Hauck, Art. μένω κτλ., ThWNT 4, 1942, 578–593.

[620] Röm 2,7; 5,3 und 8,25, aber auch 1Kor 13,7.

[621] Dieter Lührmann hat gezeigt, dass im antiken Judentum der Glaube in vier Themenkreisen eine besondere Rolle spielt: im Zusammenhang mit dem Gesetz, als Glaube an Gott den Schöpfer und Richter, als Glaube Abrahams und als »Kennzeichen des Frommen«: »G. ist die Haltung des Frommen, der lebt in Ausrichtung auf die inhaltlich bestimmten G.sätze u. das Gesetz«: Lührmann, RAC 9, 61. Diese Charakteristik trifft vollständig auf Jak zu. Eine semantische und argumentative Näherbestimmung nimmt der Verfasser des Jak erst in Kap. 2 vor.

[622] Ausführliche Dokumentation bei Burchard, Jak, 52 f. Rhetorisch: *sorites* (s. o. in der Einleitung).

[623] Dazu Frankemölle, Jak I, 185.

[624] Von Paulus häufig gebrauchtes Verb, besonders im Römerbrief. Jak 1,3.20; 1Petr 4,3.

[625] Dibelius, Jak, 104, hält »die Steigerung im dritten Glied [für] nicht so überzeugend«.

(3) οὐ μόνον δέ, ἀλλὰ καὶ καυχώμεθα ἐν ταῖς θλίψεσιν, εἰδότες ὅτι ἡ θλῖψις ὑπομονὴν κατεργάζεται, (4) ἡ δὲ ὑπομονὴ δοκιμήν, ἡ δὲ δοκιμὴ ἐλπίδα.

(3) Nicht allein das aber, sondern wir rühmen uns auch in den Trübsalen, wissend, dass die Trübsal Geduld bewirkt, (4) die Geduld aber Erprobung, die Erprobung aber Hoffnung.

Im Jak sind es die πειρασμοί, die Versuchungen oder Prüfungen. Hier muss noch einmal auf 1Petr 1,6 f hingewiesen werden:

(6) ἐν ᾧ ἀγαλλιᾶσθε ὀλίγον ἄρτι, εἰ δέον ἐστίν, λυπηθέντας ἐν ποικίλοις πειρασμοῖς, (7) ἵνα τὸ δοκίμιον ὑμῶν τῆς πίστεως πολυτιμότερον χρυσίου τοῦ ἀπολλυμένου, διὰ πυρὸς δὲ δοκιμαζομένου εὑρεθῇ εἰς ἔπαινον καὶ δόξαν καὶ τιμὴν ἐν ἀποκαλύψει Ἰησοῦ Χριστοῦ ...

(6) Dann werdet ihr euch freuen, die ihr jetzt eine kleine Zeit, wenn es sein soll, traurig seid in mancherlei Anfechtungen, (7) auf dass euer Glaube bewährt und viel kostbarer befunden werde als vergängliches Gold, das durchs Feuer geläutert wird, zu Lob, Preis und Ehre, wenn offenbart wird Jesus Christus.[626]

Das δοκίμιον wird in 1Petr in seiner LXX-Verwendung als Metallprüfung bzw. -läuterung eingesetzt. Dasselbe Bild steht in verkürzter Form hinter Jak 1,3. Die ὑπομονή begegnet in der längeren Kette von 2Petr 1,5–8 neben Glauben, ἐγκράτεια und anderen Verhaltensweisen. Zunächst ist deutlich, dass frühjüdische Verhaltensweisen gleichermaßen in die ethische Mahnung des Paulus, der Deuteropaulinen und der verschiedenen katholischen Briefe aufgenommen werden. Jak steht hier also im Zusammenhang mit frühjüdischen und frühchristlichen Ermahnungen zu rechter Lebensführung in Nöten oder »Versuchungen«.[627] Ob die evidente Nähe zu 1Petr 1,6 f mehr als ein Ausdruck des gemeinsamen frühchristlichen πειρασμός-Soziolekts und des damit verbundenen Ethos ist[628], kann an dieser Stelle nicht geklärt werden.

V. 4 Der Verfasser rundet den Gedanken von V. 3 ab und verleiht ihm Nachdruck. Das Dreieck von Versuchungen, Glaube und Geduld soll eine Art von erzieherischem Werk tun, das die Adressaten zur Vollkommenheit führt. Die Anadiplose erhöht die Bedeutung der ὑπομονή. Das Verb κατεργάζεσθαι wird ἔργον aufgenommen. Eine entsprechende Paronomasie findet sich in 2,20 (ἀργός/ἔργον). Damit schärft der Verfasser das Thema der beiden ersten Kapitel: Es geht nicht allgemein um den Glauben, sondern um die Bewährung des Glaubens im Tun, d. h. um das *Verhältnis von Glaube und Tun*. Die Brüder sollen τέλειοι καὶ ὁλόκληροι, ohne Mangel werden, und ihnen soll (ethisch) nichts fehlen (λείπειν[629]). Die drei adjektivisch-partizipialen Bestimmungen zusammen stehen für höchste Perfektion. τέλειος wird besonders in Jak 1 gesetzt.[630] Es geht um eine religiös-ethische

---

[626] Zum Vergleich s. DIBELIUS, Jak, 105.

[627] In 3.4Makk ist die Verfolgungs- und Martyriumssituation überdeutlich.

[628] Vgl. die Analyse bei DIBELIUS, Jak, 105. Dibelius betont die Unterschiede.

[629] Das Verb begegnet dreimal in Jak: 1,4.5; 2,15. Ebenso im Zusammenhang ethischer Vollkommenheit: Lk 18,22.

[630] τέλειος fünfmal in Jak: 1,4 (zweimal).17.25; 3,2. Im ethischen Zusammenhang ebenfalls Mt 5,48; 19,21; Röm 12,2; 1Kor 2,6; 14,20; Phil 3,15 u. ö. Vgl. G. DELLING, Art. τέλος κτλ., ThWNT 8, 1969, 50–88. ὁλόκληρος hap. leg. in Jak. Nur noch 1Thess 5,23 im NT, Substantiv in Apg 3,16. Vgl. SPICQ, NLNT II, 616 f (zahlreiche

160 Kommentar

Dauer-Haltung[631], einen Standard, der durch geduldigen und beharrlichen Glauben gekennzeichnet ist und zur Vollkommenheit führt. Dementsprechend müssen die Versuchungen ebenfalls als dauernd auftretend, gleichsam als stetiges Umfeld der Adressaten verstanden werden. V. 5–11 konkretisieren die Prüfungen. Die gemeindepädagogische Pragmatik wird bereits in diesen ersten Sätzen des Briefes ganz deutlich. Der Verfasser möchte »die Brüder« zu einer ethischen Elite erziehen. Diese Grundpragmatik bestimmt das gesamte Schreiben. Vollkommenheit ist das Ziel. Zusammengefasst: in V. 4 formuliert der Verfasser sein ethisches Grundsatzprogramm für die Adressaten.

2. Texteinheit: 1,5–8 Warnung vor Zweifel bei der Bitte um Weisheit

(5) Wenn aber jemand von euch an Weisheit zurückbleibt, so erbitte er (sie) von Gott, der jedem einfach gibt und keine Vorwürfe macht[632], und sie wird ihm gegeben werden. (6) Er bitte aber im Glauben, ohne zu zweifeln; denn der Zweifelnde gleicht einer Welle[633] des Meeres, die vom Wind bewegt wird[634] und hin und her treibt[635]. (7) Nicht meine nämlich jener Mensch, dass er etwas von dem Herrn empfangen werde – (8) ein Mann mit zwei Seelen[636], unbeständig auf (in) allen seinen Wegen.[637]

Textkritik: V. 5 ουκ statt μη schreiben einige Minuskeln und Byz. V. 7 τι fehlt in 01 und wohl in der ursprünglichen Lesart von 04 sowie in einzelnen Vulgatahandschriften.

Im Folgenden benennt der Verfasser Mängel in Bezug auf die erstrebte Vollkommenheit und gibt Ratschläge zur Behebung dieser Mängel. Der Verfasser nimmt eine *erste* Konkretisierung bzw. Weiterung seiner Eingangsmahnung vor, indem er die Bedeutung der *Weisheit* akzentuiert. Die dichte Argumentation der Passage wird

---

Papyrusbelege; in Votivgaben für Gesundheit gesetzt). – Ethische Verwendung 4Makk 14,17. Doppelte Bildung mit -ολο 1Thess 5,23. Zum Konzept ethischer Vollkommenheit: O. WISCHMEYER, Liebe als Agape. Das frühchristliche Konzept und der moderne Diskurs, Tübingen 2015, 201–204. Zur antiken Begriffsgeschichte vgl. die Studie von M. SCHÖTTNER, Der vollkommene Mensch. Zur Genese eines frühchristlich-gnostischen Konzepts, NTA NF 61, Münster 2019, 127–197.

[631] In Mt 5,48 und besonders in 19,21 geht es primär um spezielle Formen der Überbietung. Jak 1,4 ist näher bei Röm 12,2.

[632] BAUER / ALAND, 1155, spricht von einer »bes. Art des Scheltens«, die »Äußerungen des Mißvergnügens [darstellen], mit denen mancher seine Gabe begleitet« (mit verschiedenen Beispielen).

[633] DIBELIUS, Jak, 111, plädiert dafür, κλύδων mit »Brandung« statt mit Welle zu übersetzen. BAUER / ALAND, 888: »Wellenschlag«, »Seegang«. Das Bild wird mit dem Sing. »Welle« aber plausibler.

[634] ἀνεμίζω: hap. leg. im NT, BAUER / ALAND, 127: »vom Wind bewegt werden«.

[635] ῥιπίζω: hap. leg. im NT, BAUER / ALAND, 1474: »hin- und hertreiben, schaukeln«.

[636] ἀνὴρ δίψυχος statt ἄνθρωπος ist Septuagintasprache (DIBELIUS, Jak, 111). Burchard übersetzt »zweiseeliger Mann« (BURCHARD, Jak, 51) und bringt damit die Geringschätzigkeit des Verfassers gegenüber dem δίψυχος zum Ausdruck. Weiteres zur Herkunft des Adjektivs s. u.

[637] BAUER / ALAND, 58, übersetzt: »wankelmütig in allen seinen Handlungen«. Das Adjektiv im NT nur bei Jak: 1,8; 3,8. Zum Terminus vgl. Herm mand V 2,7; sim VI 4,5. Das Substantiv ἀκαταστασία öfter im NT (Aufruhr), auch Jak 3,16.

in folgenden Schritten entwickelt[638]: Der Verfasser konstruiert in V. 5 (a) hypothetisch einen Fall, gibt (b) den Rat zu einer Bitte und sagt (c) unter Hinweis auf das Wesen des Gebers (d) Erfüllung zu. In V. 6 fügt er (e) eine Bedingung an, die er in einem Bild begründet. In V. 7.8 weist er (f) auf die Möglichkeit des Scheiterns der Bitte hin, wenn die Bedingung nicht erfüllt wird. Das Thema der ethischen Vollkommenheit von V. 4 wird *ex negativo* mit dem Stichwortanschluss »fehlen, ermangeln« fortgesetzt, dabei wechselt der Verfasser den Modus der Kommunikation. Statt des Imperativs Plur. konstruiert er ein Fallbeispiel: Möglicherweise fehlt es einem Bruder an Weisheit. Die V. 5–8 sind also als *exemplum* im Zusammenhang mit der Vorstellung von der ethischen Vollkommenheit der Brüder zu lesen. Es wird zunächst nach der positiven, dann nach der negativen Seite hin entfaltet. Das *exemplum* wird im Modus der Mahnung in der 3.Pers.Sing. weitergeführt. Es steht für *fehlende* Vollkommenheit und rückt hypothetisch einen entscheidenden Mangel in den Mittelpunkt: die Weisheit. Die Nennung der Weisheit erfolgt nur scheinbar ebenso unvermittelt wie das Thema der Versuchungen in 1,2. Die traditions- und motivgeschichtliche Analyse zeigt aber, dass der Verfasser sich mit seinen Ermahnungen in traditionellen frühjüdischen und frühchristlichen Bahnen bewegt. σοφία gehört – anders als bei Paulus – in den deuteropaulinischen Briefen, besonders im Kolosserbrief, zum *set* geistlicher Gaben und ethischer Verhaltensformen.[639] Die stilistische Gestaltung ist sorgfältig. Jakobus benutzt Parallelausdrücke bzw. Synonyme[640] und einen ausgeführten Vergleich in V. 6. In V. 8 schließt Jakobus die Textpassage mit einer Gnome.

V. 5 Jakobus fährt mit dem Stichwortanschluss λείπεται fort und beginnt mit den Erläuterungen seines ethischen Programms von 1,2–4 im Sinne der Belehrung über den richtigen Glauben. Dazu ist Weisheit als eine besonders wichtige ethische Verhaltensform angesichts der Versuchungen notwendig. Dass gerade die Weisheit als erster Aspekt der Vollkommenheit erscheint, erklärt sich aus der traditionellen Verbindung von Prüfungen bzw. Versuchungen, Vollkommenheit und Weisheit in der Literatur des frühen Judentums.[641] Hier genügt der exemplarische Hinweis auf SapSal 9,6, wo ebenfalls mit einem τις-Beispiel argumentiert wird[642]:

κἂν γάρ τις ᾖ τέλειος ἐν υἱοῖς ἀνθρώπων, τῆς ἀπὸ σοῦ σοφίας ἀπούσης εἰς οὐδὲν λογισθήσεται.
Denn wenn (auch) einer vollkommen wäre unter den Menschenkindern – falls ihm die von dir (stammende) Weisheit fehlt, wird er für nichts gehalten werden.[643]

---

[638] Vgl. ähnlich Allison, Jak, 166.

[639] Vgl. besonders Eph 5,15: »Wandelt nicht als Unweise, sondern als Weise«.

[640] Allison, Jak, 166.

[641] Reiches Material bei Frankemölle, Jak I, 212–214.

[642] Zum Motiv der Prüfung durch die Weisheit vgl. Sir 4,17 ([Die Weisheit] wird ihn in ihren Rechtssätzen erproben). – Dibelius, Jak, 106, bestreitet, dass eine Konstellation wie die von SapSal 9 in Jak 1 zugrunde liege. Die Analyse von 1,2–19 wird aber zeigen, dass hier nicht nur mit Stichwortanschlüssen gearbeitet wird, sondern dass dem Text ein gedankliches Konzept zugrunde liegt.

[643] Zum Aufbau und zur Aussage des Satzes vgl. die Parallele in 1Kor 13,1–3: Vollkommenheit – Mangel –

Burchard kommentiert das τις in V. 5 richtig: Das Subjekt »ist generisch«.[644] Im Zusammenhang von 1,5–8 geht es thematisch noch nicht um die Weisheit selbst, sondern stattdessen um das *Woher* und um das *Wie der Bitte* um Weisheit. V. 5 entfaltet sich zwischen Bitten (αἰτεῖσθαι[645]) und Empfangen (διδόναι[646]). Jakobus beschreibt den Glauben (1,3) als Modus der zuversichtlichen Bitte und bestimmt ihn *ex negativo* näher, indem er zuversichtlichen Glauben und Zweifel einander gegenüberstellt. Das bedeutet: Ethische Perfektion, hier Weisheit, wird nicht einfach selbst gemacht, d. h. durch Unterricht oder ethisch korrektes Verhalten erworben, und ist damit nicht einfach so etwas wie ein *Werk* (ἔργον 1,4), sondern es ist Gegenstand des Bittgebets und zuerst *Gabe* (δόσις 1,17). An diesem Punkt kommt ebenso unversehens wie selbstverständlich Gott[647] ins Spiel: *Er* ist der Geber der Weisheit. Das Thema der guten Gabe Gottes wird bis 1,18 verfolgt. Die theologische Vertiefung und Basierung der Ethik, die der Verfasser anstrebt, erfolgt in 1,16–18, wird aber hier schon vorbereitet. Der Ratschlag, den der Verfasser im Rahmen des *exemplum* gibt, lautet: Wem es an Weisheit mangelt, der soll Gott um sie bitten. Könnten die Ratschläge in 1,2–4 im Sinne einer selbständigen ethischen Leistung (miss-)verstanden werden, wird hier schon unmissverständlich deutlich, dass der Verfasser auch in seiner ethischen Weisung letztlich stets *theo*logisch argumentiert, denn Gott setzt die Standards für das ethische Tun der Menschen und ermöglicht zugleich ethisches Tun.

Zunächst wird *Gott* mit zwei Wesensbestimmungen charakterisiert. *Erstens* gibt Gott allen (Menschen) ἁπλῶς, »ohne Nebenabsichten« und »gütig, freigebig«[648], d. h. er verhält sich wie jeder gute Geber. Dibelius bevorzugt zurecht mit Hin-

---

Wertlosigkeit. Bei Paulus nimmt die ἀγάπη die Rolle der Weisheit ein.

[644] BURCHARD, Jak, 61.

[645] Jak 1,5.6; 4,2.3 (zweimal); auffallend die jeweilige Wiederholung oder Häufung des Verbs, die Nachdruck bedeutet. Gebräuchliches Verb für das Bittgebet bei Synoptikern, Johannes und in 1Joh. Nicht in LXX. – Schon hier begegnet das Thema des Gebetes, das in Kap. 5 breiter thematisiert wird.

[646] δίδωμι noch Jak 2,16. Im Sinne des Geschenkes oder der Gabe von Gott vor allem sehr häufig im Joh, aber auch bei den Synoptikern (Mt 28,18). Vgl. auch 1Kor 3,5.

[647] »Gott« ist in 1,1 bereits eingeführt worden. Vgl. dazu S. WENGER, Der wesenhaft gute Kyrios. Eine exegetische Studie über das Gottesbild im Jakobusbrief, AThANT 100, Zürich 2011; WISCHMEYER, Wie spricht der Jakobusbrief von Gott?, 385–409. Weiteres in der Einleitung.

[648] Monographisch: J. AMSTUTZ, Haplotes, Theoph. 19, Bonn 1968. In LXX: Spr 10,9 ethisch (SapSal 16,27 und 2Makk 6,6: »einfach« im Sinne von »nur«). ἁπλότης in LXX nicht als Gottesattribut verwendet; ἁπλότης als Tugend in 1Chr 29,17; SapSal 1,1; DanLXX Su 63; 1Makk 2,37.60 (für Daniel); 3Makk 3,21; Röm 12,8; 2Kor 8,2; 9,11.13 im Zusammenhang der Kollekte. ἁπλῶς hap. leg. NT. Vgl. zu ἁπλῶς DIBELIUS, Jak, 106 f (auch ältere Lit.). Dibelius plädiert für die Übersetzung »ohne Bedenken«, zeigt aber auch die semantische Breite des Begriffs auf und urteilt: »Die Mahnung scheint zum Gemeingut griechischer wie jüdischer Moralweisheit zu gehören« (108). Reiches Belegmaterial auch bei SPICQ, NLNT I, 125–129. Spicq erklärt den ntl. Sprachgebrauch von LXX her: Das klassische Griechisch verwende die Wurzel im Sinn von »einfach«, LXX füge eine spirituelle Komponente im Sinn von *simplicitas* hinzu. Spicq versteht Jak 1,5 dementsprechend als »purement et simplement« (129). A. VOITILA, Art. ἁπλοῦς, ἁπλότης, HTLS I, 927–938, definiert: »liberally«, »the meaning of the adverb confers both sincerity and openness upon the giver« (933). In Jak 1 ist ἁπλῶς ein Vollkommenheitsprädikat. Es dient dem Anschluss an V. 4 und ist zugleich Auslöser für die Zweifelsthematik in V. 6–8.

blick auf die zweite Wesensbestimmung die Bedeutungsnuance »ohne Bedenken«.[649] *Zweitens* macht Gott dabei keine Vorwürfe: μὴ ὀνειδίζοντος.[650] Nicht zu fluchen oder Vorwürfe zu machen gehört ebenfalls in den Zusammenhang des guten Gebens:

> (αἰσχύνεσθε) ἀπὸ φίλων περὶ λόγων ὀνειδισμοῦ καὶ μετὰ τὸ δοῦναι μὴ ὀνείδιζε.
> (Schämt euch) vor Freunden wegen der Fluchworte, und fluche nicht, nachdem du gegeben hast (Sir 41,25).

Beide Bestimmungen hängen also topisch mit dem Thema der Gabe zusammen und stellen Gott als den guten Geber in der Tradition des frühen Judentums[651] und des frühen Christentums[652] dar.

V. 5 schließt mit der Versicherung: Wer Gott um *Weisheit* bittet, »dem wird sie gegeben werden«.[653] Auch die Erfüllung von Bitten durch Gott ist »ein geläufiger τόπος jüdisch-christlicher Spruchweisheit«.[654] Hier treffen wir zum ersten Mal auf einen Spruch, der nicht nur zum frühjüdischen und frühchristlichen Gemeingut gehört, sondern sich auch in deutlicher Nähe zu dem Spruch über das Gebet befindet, der in unterschiedlichen Versionen als *Jesuslogion* überliefert ist:

> Mk 11,22 f: καὶ ἀποκριθεὶς ὁ Ἰησοῦς λέγει αὐτοῖς· ἔχετε πίστιν θεοῦ. (23) ἀμὴν λέγω ὑμῖν ὅτι ὃς ἂν εἴπῃ τῷ ὄρει τούτῳ· ἄρθητι καὶ βλήθητι εἰς τὴν θάλασσαν, καὶ μὴ διακριθῇ ἐν τῇ καρδίᾳ αὐτοῦ ἀλλὰ πιστεύῃ ὅτι ὃ λαλεῖ γίνεται, ἔσται αὐτῷ.
> (22) Und Jesus antwortete und sprach zu ihnen: Habt Glauben an Gott. (23) Amen, ich sage euch, wer zu diesem Berg sagt: Heb dich empor und wirf dich ins Meer, und zweifelt in seinem Herzen nicht, sondern glaubt (vertraut), dass das, was er sagt, geschieht – dem wird es geschehen.
>
> Mt 21,21 f: [Der verdorrte Feigenbaum] ἀμὴν λέγω ὑμῖν, ἐὰν ἔχητε πίστιν καὶ μὴ διακριθῆτε, οὐ μόνον τὸ τῆς συκῆς ποιήσετε, ἀλλὰ κἂν τῷ ὄρει τούτῳ εἴπητε· ἄρθητι καὶ βλήθητι εἰς τὴν θάλασσαν, γενήσεται (22) καὶ πάντα ὅσα ἂν αἰτήσητε ἐν τῇ προσευχῇ πιστεύοντες λήμψεσθε.
> (21) Amen, ich sage euch, wenn ihr Glauben habt und nicht zweifelt, so werdet ihr nicht nur das (Zeichen mit) dem Feigenbaum tun, sondern wenn ihr zu diesem Berg sagt: heb dich empor und wirf dich ins Meer, wird es geschehen. (22) Und alles, was ihr bittet im Gebet – wenn ihr glaubt, werdet ihr empfangen.

---

[649] DIBELIUS, Jak, 107.

[650] Vgl. SPICQ, NLNT II, 623–625 Art. ὀνειδίζω, ὀνειδισμός, ὄνειδος, 624 Anm. 2 zu Lit. und weiteren Parallelen.

[651] Dazu J. M. G. BARCLAY, Paul and the Gift, Grand Rapids / Cambridge 2015, 194–328. Barclay interpretiert SapSal, Philo, 1QH[a], PsPhilo LibAntBibl, 4Esr und verortet Paulus im frühjüdischen Diskurs. Jak 1,18 erwähnt Barclay nur im Zusammenhang der rhetorischen Sprache zusammen mit Gabe / Gnade (68). Es wäre hier weiterführend gewesen, Paulus und den Jakobusbrief in einen thematischen Zusammenhang zu bringen. Das Thema der Gabe ist wie das Weisheitsthema eines der Nebenthemen, die Paulus und Jak neben dem Hauptthema ›Glaube und Werke‹ gemeinsam haben.

[652] Did 47; Barn 19,6.

[653] διδόναι: im Sinne der Gabe Gottes noch Jak 4,6 im Zusammenhang mit Spr 3,34 (s. u.).

[654] DIBELIUS, Jak, 108. Vgl. Herm mand IX 6.

164   Kommentar

Lk 17,5 f [Q]: [Glaubensstärkung] Stärke uns den Glauben (πίστιν) …
»Wenn ihr Glauben (πίστιν) hättet wie ein Senfkorn, würdet ihr zu diesem Feigenbaum
sprechen: Entwurzle dich und verpflanze dich ins Meer, und er würde euch gehorchen.«
Mt 17,20 [Q]: [Mangelnder Glaube der Jünger bei der Dämonenaustreibung] … wegen
eures Kleinglaubens (διὰ τὴν ὀλιγοπιστίαν ὑμῶν). Wahrlich, ich sage euch nämlich: Wenn
ihr Glauben (πίστιν) hättet wie ein Senfkorn, würdet ihr zu diesem Berg sagen: Rücke
von hier nach dorthin, und er würde wegrücken. Und nichts wird euch unmöglich sein.
Mt 7,7 f: [Letzter Teil der Bergpredigt: Vom Vertrauen beim Beten] Αἰτεῖτε καὶ δοθήσεται
ὑμῖν[655], ζητεῖτε καὶ εὑρήσετε, κρούετε καὶ ἀνοιγήσεται ὑμῖν· (8) πᾶς γὰρ ὁ αἰτῶν λαμβάνει καὶ
ὁ ζητῶν εὑρίσκει καὶ τῷ κρούοντι ἀνοιγήσεται.
(7) Bittet, und es wird euch gegeben werden, sucht, und ihr werdet finden, klopft an,
und es wird euch geöffnet werden. (8) Jeder nämlich, der bittet, empfängt, und wer
sucht, findet, und dem Anklopfenden wird geöffnet.
Lk 11,9 f: [Vaterunser und Gleichnis vom bittenden Freund] Κἀγὼ ὑμῖν λέγω, αἰτεῖτε καὶ
δοθήσεται ὑμῖν, ζητεῖτε καὶ εὑρήσετε, κρούετε καὶ ἀνοιγήσεται ὑμῖν·(10) πᾶς γὰρ ὁ αἰτῶν
λαμβάνει καὶ ὁ ζητῶν εὑρίσκει καὶ τῷ κρούοντι ἀνοιγ[ήσ]εται.
(9) Und ich sage euch auch, bittet, und es wird euch gegeben werden, sucht, und ihr werdet finden, klopft an, und es wird euch geöffnet werden. (10) Jeder nämlich, der bittet,
empfängt, und wer sucht, findet, und dem Anklopfenden wird geöffnet werden.

Die Tabelle zeigt, dass der Spruch in der synoptischen Tradition (Mk 11,23 und Q
17,6) in zwei unterschiedlichen Zusammenhängen begegnet: einmal kombiniert
mit der Glaubensthematik, zum andern mit dem Gebet selbst. In Jak 1,5 f sind
beide Themen verbunden, hinzu kommt eine speziell theologische Aussage: *Gott
ist der Geber*. V. 5 präzisiert wie schon dargestellt Gottes Geberschaft doppelt: Gott
gibt »ohne Hintergedanken« und »nicht vorwurfsvoll«. Hier werden gleichsam im
Vorübergehen Gottes Grundcharakteristik als des Gebers alles Guten zwei weitere
Gotteseigenschaften hinzugefügt, die gleichzeitig Tugenden sind: Einfachheit bzw.
Aufrichtigkeit und rückhaltloses Geben ohne innere Vorbehalte oder – gedachte
oder ausgesprochene – Vorhaltungen.[656] Der Verfasser vertieft diese Aspekte der
Gotteslehre an dieser Stelle nicht weiter, sondern kehrt zur Ermahnung, genauer
zur Aufforderung zu einer richtigen Haltung bei der Bitte (um Weisheit) zurück.
    V. 6 Die *zweite* Weiterung des Rates zur Ausdauer in Prüfungen dient der Prä-
zisierung und betrifft den *Modus* des Bittens: Der Bittende wird mit einem weiteren Ratschlag in der 3.Pers.Sing. aufgefordert, »im *Glauben* zu bitten und nicht zu
zweifeln«. Zweifel wird hier verbal als διακρίνομαι gefasst.[657] Damit wird der Glau-

---

[655] Dieselbe Beziehung zwischen Bitten und Empfangen in Jak 1,5.
[656] Sir 20,15; 41,19.
[657] διακρίνειν im Medium als »zweifeln« bei Jak: 1,6; 2,4; NT: Mt 21,21; Mk 11,23; Röm 4,20; 14,23; Apg
10,20; Jud 22; vgl. F. BÜCHSEL / V. HERNTRICH, Art. κρίνω κτλ., ThWNT 3, 1938, 920–955; G. BARTH, Glaube und Zweifel in den synoptischen Evangelien, ZThK 72, 269–929. Weiter: P. SPITALER, Διακρίνεσθαι in
Mt. 21:21, Mk. 11:23, Acts 10:20, Rom. 4:20, 14:23, Jas. 1:6, and Jude 22 – the »Semantic Shift« That Went
Unnoticed by Patristic Authors, NT 49, 2007, 1–39. Monographisch: B. SCHLIESSER, Zweifel. Phänomene

be[658] detaillierter durch einen Gegenbegriff bestimmt: den *Zweifel*. Frankemölle weist richtig darauf hin, dass der Verfasser den Zweifel für »eine weitere exemplarische, konkrete Versuchung seiner Adressaten« neben einem möglichen Mangel an Weisheit hält.[659] Die Relation von Glaube und Zweifel beim Gebet begegnet, wie schon gezeigt, in der Jesusüberlieferung in Mk 11,22 fpar in Jesu Logion vom Feigenbaum.[660]

Dieselbe Aussage findet sich bei Paulus. Paulus wendet die Verbindung von Glaube und »Nicht zweifeln« in Röm 4,20 f auf Abraham an:

(20) εἰς δὲ τὴν ἐπαγγελίαν τοῦ θεοῦ οὐ διεκρίθη τῇ ἀπιστίᾳ ἀλλ᾽ ἐνεδυναμώθη τῇ πίστει, δοὺς δόξαν τῷ θεῷ (21) καὶ πληροφορηθεὶς ὅτι ὃ ἐπήγγελται δυνατός ἐστιν καὶ ποιῆσαι.

(20) Er zweifelte aber nicht an der Verheißung Gottes im Unglauben, sondern wurde stark im Glauben und gab Gott die Ehre (21) und war voller Gewissheit, dass der, der etwas verheißt, auch die Macht hat, es zu tun.

Allerdings sind das synoptische Logion und das Paulus-*exemplum* auf den Wunderglauben bzw. auf das Vertrauen auf das Eintreten eines Wunders bezogen, während der Jakobusbrief von der Bitte um Weisheit spricht und damit schon hier die Weisheit religiös bestimmt, indem er sie mit glaubensstarkem Gebet verbindet und als himmlische Gabe darstellt. Es geht dem Verfasser also nicht um den Wunderglauben, sondern um die Glaubens*haltung*: hier die Haltung der ἁπλότης.[661] Der Glaubende soll sich wie Gott verhalten. Der Brief konstruiert die einfache Gleichung: wie der Geber (Gott), so der Beter. Das Gesagte wird in dem topischen Bild von der Welle, die für die Wankelmütigkeit des Zweifelnden steht, figurativ verdeutlicht. ἐοικέναι[662] ist hap. leg. im Neuen Testament. Das Verb wird zweimal in Jak im Zusammenhang mit einem Bild gesetzt (1,6.23). Der Vergleichspunkt ist die Unstetigkeit der Welle. Dibelius spricht zurecht von der »Beliebtheit dieses Bilderkreises« von Welle, Meer und Brandung.[663] Das Bild ist selbsterklärend. Eine genauere traditions- oder motivgeschichtliche Anbindung an die Septuaginta oder frühjüdische Texte ist für dies sprechende Bild nicht notwendig. Auffallend ist die sorgfältige sprachliche Gestaltung mit ausgefallenen Lexemen.[664]

---

des Zweifels und der Zweiseeligkeit im frühen Christentum, WUNT 500, Tübingen 2022. Schliesser bietet auf S. 33–40 eine detaillierte Darstellung der Übersetzungsproblematik des Verbs (Lit.). Zu Jak 1,6: 273–283. Vgl. auch Philo, mut. 177–186 (Abraham glaubte und zweifelte nicht).

[658] S. o. zu 1,3.

[659] FRANKEMÖLLE, Jak I, 232. Er versteht schon den Mangel an Weisheit als erste Prüfung. Das ist nach dem Text nicht erforderlich.

[660] SCHLIESSER, Zweifel, 283, spricht von einer »dezidierte(n) Aufnahme und Adaption«.

[661] AMSTUTZ, Haplotes.

[662] »Altes Pf. zu εἴκω gleichen«, BAUER / ALAND, 566.

[663] DIBELIUS, Jak, 111. Die Kommentare geben reiche Beispiele zum genannten Bildkreis: DIBELIUS, Jak, 110 f; FRANKEMÖLLE, Jak I, 234 f, verweist besonders auf Jes 57,20.

[664] κλύδων hap. leg. in Jak, im NT nur noch Lk 8,24 (»Sturm«). Die Hypothese von MAYOR, Jak, 41, ἀνεμίζειν, »vom Wind bewegt sein«, sei nicht nur ein hap. leg. im NT, sondern ein Neologismus des Jakobusbriefes, wird von DIBELIUS, Jak, 110 Anm. 2, begründet zurückgewiesen; vgl. auch BURCHARD, Jak, 60 f. ῥιπίζεσθαι, »hin- und hergeworfen werden«, ebenfalls hap. leg. im NT.

166 Kommentar

V. 7.8 Beide Verse bilden eine syntaktische Einheit. V. 8 ist eine ausführliche Apposition zum Subjekt ὁ ἄνθρωπος ἐκεῖνος von V. 7. Der Text kehrt zum Thema von Gabe und Empfangen (λαμβάνειν[665]) zurück und macht die Auswirkung des Zweifels im Gebet auf den Empfang der Weisheit deutlich: Der Mensch[666], der zweifelt, wird die erbetene Gabe der Weisheit *nicht* empfangen. κύριος ist hier Gottesprädikat (auf V. 5 bezogen).[667] οἴεσθαι, meinen, denken[668], ist ein sehr selten im Neuen Testament gebrauchtes Verb des Meinens und hap. leg. bei Jak.[669] Das Thema der Gabe wird in V. 8 vorläufig mit einem zweigliedrigen erläuternden Zusatz zu dem Zweifler abgeschlossen: ἀνὴρ δίψυχος, ἀκατάστατος ἐν πάσαις ταῖς ὁδοῖς αὐτοῦ.[670] Für die negative Charakterisierung des Zweifelnden verwendet Jakobus zwei neutestamentliche hapax legomena, zunächst das auffallende Adjektiv δίψυχος, das zuerst im Jakobusbrief begegnet[671], sowie ἀκατάστατος. »Der Mann[672] der zwei Seelen« ist ein Typus, den der Verfasser für gefährlich hält und vor dessen Haltung

---

[665] Jak 1,7.12; 3,1; 4,3 (ebenfalls »Erbetenes empfangen«); 5,7.10.

[666] ἄνθρωπος bei Jak: 1,7.19; 2,20.24; 3,8.9; 5,17. ἄ. meint stets den Menschen allgemein, auch wenn einzelne Menschentypen vorgestellt werden wie hier der Zweifler. A. BELLANTUONO et al., Art. ἄνθρωπος, HTLS I, 743–768 (Lit.).

[667] κύριος auch 2,1 (wie in 1,1 explizit auf Christus bezogen); 3,9; 4,10.15; 5,7.8.10.11.14.15.

[668] BAUER / ALAND, 1140. Hier im verneinten Imp. Präs. Sing. gesetzt. BURCHARD, Jak, 61, diskutiert, ob das Verbot generell oder speziell sei.

[669] Joh 21,25; Phil 1,17 (»in negativer Absicht«); Jak 1,7. Öfter in Hiob, mehrfach in Makkabäerbüchern.

[670] Auf die syntaktische Unklarheit der Apposition (eine A. mit einer weiteren Untererklärung oder zwei A.?) macht BURCHARD, Jak, 61, aufmerksam und fügt hinzu: »Semantisch sind die Unterschiede gering«.

[671] Neologismus. Im NT nur Jak 1,8 und 4,8; später in Did, Barn, 1.2Clem und häufig im Herm. Ebenso das Verb und διψυχία. Ältere Studie: S. E. PORTER, Is dipsuchos (James 1,8; 4,8) a »Christian« Word? Bibl 71, 1990, 469–498 (ausführliche Lit.benutzung). Porter plädiert für Neologismus und für eine Einschätzung als ›christliches Wort‹. Dieser Anspruch ist nicht entscheidend und kann hier offenbleiben. Für das Textverständnis ist wichtiger, dass sich der *Verfasser* einen eigenen Begriff schafft, den er in 4,8 nochmals verwendet und der auch von den Apostolischen Vätern verwendet wird. Burchard ordnet den Begriff ausführlich in die »Zweierbegriffe« der griechischen und frühjüdischen Lexik ein (BURCHARD, Jak, 62 f). FRANKEMÖLLE, Jak I, 238 f, erörtert das Verhältnis von Jak 1,8 und den Belegen im Hirten des Hermas (vgl. schon DIBELIUS, 111 f). Zwei neue Monographien präsentieren nochmals ausführlich das Material: A. NÜRNBERGER, Zweifelskonzepte im Frühchristentum. Dipsychia und Oligopistia im Rahmen menschlicher Dissonanz- und Einheitsvorstellungen in der Antike, NTOA / StUNT 122, Göttingen 2019, und B. SCHLIESSER, Zweifel, 40–50. Schliesser diskutiert im Anschluss an R. Bauckham und D. Allison erneut gründlich eine Herkunft des Ausdrucks aus einer Kombination von Zwei-Wege-Lehre (so die Belege in Did und Barn) und der Eldad-Modad-Quelle (so die Belege in Herm, zu Eldad und Modad s. o., Einleitung). Auf S. 50 formuliert er die vorsichtige Hypothese: »Zusammenfassend ist also damit zu rechnen, dass die Rede von der Zweiseeligkeit auf (mindestens) zwei voneinander getrennten, jüdischen Traditionslinien in das Gesichtsfeld frühchristlicher Autoren trat: das Apokryphon Eldad und Modad und Rezensionen eines Zwei-Wege-Traktats. Diese Hypothese bleibt aber mit etlichen Unsicherheiten behaftet.« Für Jak ergibt die Hypothese nichts Entscheidendes, denn eine Verbindung zur Zwei-Wege-Literatur findet sich nicht im Brief, und die Eldad-Modad-Beziehung bleibt unklar (s. o.). An dem Neologismusbefund für Jak ändert sich nichts. Schliesser (51 Anm. 178) verweist daher selbst zurecht abschließend auf die Position von LIST, Δίψυχος, 95, der den Ausdruck statt im Zusammenhang hypothetischer Quellenschriften lieber im »linguistic milieu of the Koine period« verortet und damit der sprachlichen Kompetenz des Jak-Verfassers Rechnung trägt (N. LIST, Δίψυχος. Moving beyond Intertextuality, NTS 67, 2021, 85–104).

[672] ἀνήρ bei Jak noch 1,12.20.23; 2,2; 3,2. Synonym mit ἄνθρωπος: generisch (vgl. METZNER, Jak, 66).

er warnt. Der Zusatz macht deutlich, dass der Verfasser hier nicht nur moralisch, sondern auch anthropologisch sprechen will. Hubert Frankemölle hat sowohl den allgemeinen frühjüdischen anthropologischen Horizont von V. 8 wie den speziellen Rückbezug auf das Sirachbuch herausgearbeitet. Unter Rückgriff auf die Studien von Joseph Amstutz verweist er auf »die hier sichtbar werdende frühjüdische Anthropologie«[673], wie sie sich besonders deutlich bei Philo von Alexandria findet. Für Philo sind Einheit und Einfachheit positive Werte und tugendhafte Verhaltensformen der Seele[674], Vielfalt, Zersplitterung, Schwanken und Wankelmut dagegen negativ konnotiert.[675] Dieser Wankelmut wird in Jak 1,8 mit dem zweiten Adjektiv ἀκατάστατος[676] ausgedrückt. Anders als Philo entfaltet der Jak diesen anthropologischen Gedanken aber nicht, sondern belässt es bei der knappen Anspielung auf anthropologisch-ethisches Wissen, das selbstevident ist. Die Schlusswendung ἐν πάσαις ταῖς ὁδοῖς αὐτοῦ verwendet die alttestamentliche Wegmetapher, die im Sinne von »Lebenswandel, Lebensführung« im antiken Judentum ebenso verbreitet ist wie im frühen Christentum.[677]

3. Texteinheit: 1,9–11 Der Niedrige und der Reiche

(9) Es rühme sich aber der Bruder, der niedrig ist, (in) seiner Höhe (10) und der Reiche (in) seiner Niedrigkeit, weil er wie die Blume des Grases vergehen wird. (11) Es geht nämlich die Sonne mit der Hitze auf[678] und verbrennt[679] das Gras, und seine Blume fällt ab, und seine Wohlgestalt[680] geht zugrunde. So wird auch der Reiche in seinen Unternehmungen[681] dahinschwinden[682].

Textkritik: V. 11 Minuskel 43.330.1563 lesen μωραινω (töricht machen) statt μαραινω (dahinschwinden).

Auch bei der *dritten* Weiterung des Eingangsrates benutzt der Verfasser ein *exemplum*: nun den demütigen Bruder im Gegensatz zum reichen (Bruder). Es geht dem Verfasser nicht nur (1) um die Einfachheit bei der Bitte um *Weisheit* und (2) um den nicht zweifelnden *Glauben*, sondern gleichermaßen (3) um die ethische

---

[673] FRANKEMÖLLE, Jak I, 233.

[674] ψυχή bei Jak: 1,21 und 5,20. ψυχή meint hier »das Verlangen, die Gesinnung« (METZNER, Jak, 67).

[675] Migr. 152f; Plant. 101. Vgl. auch die Belege bei FRANKEMÖLLE, Jak I, 233, die die Thematik der Einfachheit mit dem Gebet zusammenbringen.

[676] LXX: Jes 54,11 (Jerusalem). Nicht bei Philo. NT: Jak 1,8; 3,8. Substantiv 1Kor 14,33: »Nicht nämlich ist Gott [ein Gott] der Unruhe bzw. Unordnung, sondern des Friedens«. Weiter 2Kor 6,5; 12,20; Jak 3,16; Lk 21,9 (Aufruhr).

[677] ὁδός häufig im NT, in Jak: 1,8; 2,25; 5,20 (ebenfalls bildlich für Lebenswandel); vgl. W. MICHAELIS, Art. ὁδός, ThWNT 5, 1954, 42–118.

[678] Aor.

[679] Aor.

[680] Verkürzung von »die Wohlgestalt ihres Angesichtes«. »Ihres Angesichtes« muss im Deutschen nicht übersetzt werden.

[681] Oder konkreter: »Reisen« (vgl. BAUER / ALAND, 1387). Das würde zu Jak 4,13 passen.

[682] μαραίνω: SPICQ, NLNT II, 531f.

Haltung, nämlich um die *richtige Selbsteinschätzung* der Bittenden: Ohne die richtige Selbsteinschätzung können die Glaubensprüfungen nicht erfolgreich bestanden werden. Für den Verfasser ist die ταπείνωσις die richtige Form der Selbsteinschätzung. V. 9–11 führen diesen Gedanken aus, und zwar als Ratschlag mit Begründung. V. 9 und 10 bilden eine Einheit. Der Verfasser benutzt »einen antithetischen Satzparallelismus mit Ellipse in 10a«.[683] V. 10b liefert eine begründende Erläuterung in Form eines Vergleichs. V. 11a–d führen die Bildhälfte des Vergleichs weiter aus. V. 10b–11 tragen nicht zur Ermahnung von 1,2–12 bei, sondern dienen der rhetorischen Verstärkung von V. 10a. V. 11e enthält die abschließende Anwendung des Vergleichs. In den Versen 9–11 wird zudem der soziale Rahmen der Mahnung von 1,2–12 deutlicher: Es geht um *Brüder*, d. h. um Gemeindeglieder, wie der Folgetext (2,1–7) noch deutlicher zeigen wird. Die Deutung der Sprucheinheit ist in verschiedener Hinsicht kontrovers, und zwar sowohl was die Beurteilung des gedanklichen Zusammenhanges innerhalb 1,2–18 angeht als auch in Bezug auf die inhaltliche Interpretation von 1,9–11.

Martin Dibelius hat mit einer gewissen Schärfe einen *Zusammenhang* zwischen den Texten 1,6–8 und 1,9–11 bestritten.[684] Er spricht nicht nur von der »Fraglichkeit eines äußeren Anschlusses«, sondern auch von der »Aussichtslosigkeit einer gedanklichen Verbindung«[685] zwischen den Themen der Weisheit und des einfachen Glaubens mit der ταπείνωσις des Reichen und dem ὕψος des »Niedrigen«. Wir treffen hier auf die Bedeutung des formgeschichtlichen Ansatzes für die Exegese längerer Texteinheiten und Teiltexte. Dibelius versteht V. 9–11 als einen thematisch ganz selbständigen Spruch mit dem einen Thema: »Untergang des Reichen«.[686] Im Zusammenhang von 1,1–27 möchte Dibelius überhaupt nicht von »Gruppenbildungen«, sondern nur von lockeren »Spruchreihen« sprechen.[687] Der »gedankliche Zusammenhang« fehle hier wie anderswo.[688] Nun weist aber die besonders von Frankemölle durchgehend betonte Beziehung zu Sirach auf durchaus bestehende Zusammenhänge zwischen Einfachheit, Beständigkeit und festem Glauben einerseits sowie Reichtum und Niedrigkeit andererseits hin. Hinter den Sprüchen in Jak 1,2–12 steht die frühjüdische weisheitliche Thematik einer *guten Lebensführung*, die ἁπλότης, ταπείνωσις, vorsichtigen und sozial-caritativen Umgang mit Besitz sowie Geduld, Weisheit und Glauben verbindet. 1,9–11 muss vor dem Hintergrund dieses Ensembles einer untadeligen Lebensführung (1,4) gelesen werden. Insofern teilt der vorliegende Kommentar Dibelius' Urteil nicht. Im Sinne des Verfassers *ist* die Fort-

---

[683] Burchard, Jak, 63.

[684] Dibelius, Jak, 97: »Die Richtigkeit dieser Voraussetzung [der Form einer kleinen Diatribe hinter 1,2–12] ist mit aller Entschiedenheit zu bestreiten«.

[685] Dibelius, Jak, 113, mit Verweis auf S. 98 (»Gedankensprung vor 1,9«).

[686] Dibelius, Jak, 113. Dementsprechend fügt Frankemölle, Jak I, 251–259, schon an dieser Stelle den Exkurs 3: »Die soziale Situation der Adressaten« ein.

[687] Dibelius, Jak, 14.

[688] Ebd.

setzung von 1,2–8 in 1,9–11 plausibel. Aber Dibelius' Spruchanalyse hat auch Richtiges gesehen: Der Übergang von V. 8 zu V. 9 ist thematisch abrupt. Die Mikroeinheit schließt mit dem Ausblick auf das Ende des Reichen statt auf die Bewährung der Geduld. Dibelius betont zu Recht, dass der kommende Untergang des Reichen »nicht ohne Genugtuung« beschrieben wird.[689] Das führt doch von der Thematik der Glaubensprüfungen ab. Was Dibelius sieht, ist die relative Sperrigkeit und Eigenthematik des Spruchgutes mit dem Thema Reichtum, das der Verfasser benutzt. Er arbeitet mit einer negativen Konnotation des Themas Reichtum, wie die folgenden Kapitel noch deutlicher zeigen werden, und verzichtet nicht auf die destruktive Schlusspointe in V. 11 – analog zu V. 8. Auch dort schießt die Schlusspointe über die intendierte Thematik hinaus. Der Verfasser behält – ähnlich wie Jesus Sirach und anders als Paulus – die Spruchstruktur also so weit bei, dass Argumentation und Textpragmatik häufig unklar bleiben. Andererseits weist Burchard aber richtig auf die Parallelstruktur zwischen 1,5–8 und 1,9–11 hin, die beide Untereinheiten auch formal verbindet: Es geht nach dem Typus des »Zweiseelers« und des »Einfachen« wieder um die »Opposition zweier Menschen(typen oder -gruppen)«[690], den ταπεινός und den πλούσιος. Dabei fällt von vornherein eine gewisse sachliche Inkongruenz des chiastisch konstruierten antithetischen Parallelismus ins Auge[691]: Die erwartete Opposition zu »der Niedrige« wäre »der Hohe oder Hochmütige«, zu »der Reiche« wäre »der Arme« zu erwarten. V. 9.10a verschränken beide Motive, indem zwar in V. 9 der Niedrige erhöht, in V. 10 der Reiche aber nicht arm, sondern eben niedrig wird. Erst die V. 10b.11 fügen wenigstens implizit den Ausblick hinzu, dass der Reiche in Zukunft arm werde. Explizit erscheint das Thema der Armut nicht. Der Ton liegt auf der finalen Erfolglosigkeit der Existenz des Reichen, nicht auf seiner späteren Armut.

V. 9 Wer ist der »niedrige« oder »demütige« Bruder in V. 9? 1,9 f ist einer der beiden Texte zur Demut im Jakobusbrief. Der Verfasser setzt die Wurzel ταπειν- viermal ein: 1,9 und 4,6 als Adjektiv[692], 4,10 als Verb und 1,10 als Substantiv.[693] In beiden Textzusammenhängen, in Kap. 1 wie in Kap. 4, arbeitet der Verfasser mit dem Gegensatz hoch – niedrig.[694] Eve-Marie Becker hat das frühchristliche Konzept von Demut untersucht.[695] Sie verortet den Beitrag des Jak zum Thema der Demut in der nachpaulinischen frühchristlichen Literatur:

---

[689] Dibelius, Jak, 114.

[690] Burchard, Jak, 63.

[691] Die Spruchstruktur ist hier besonders deutlich.

[692] Bedeutungsaspekte nach Bauer / Aland, 1603 f: niedrig, kriechend (negativ), demütig (positiv). Bauer / Aland wählt für Jak 1,9 die erste Bedeutung.

[693] Bauer / Aland, 1605, schlägt für Jak 1,10 »Erniedrigung« vor (Aufnahme von Dibelius' ironischer Deutung von V. 10, dazu s. u.).

[694] 1,9: ὕψος (in sozialer Bedeutung nur hier im NT); 4,6: ὑπερήφανος (Spr 3,4LXX); 4,10: ὑψόω.

[695] E.-M. Becker, Der Begriff der Demut bei Paulus, Tübingen 2015, 188–195.

Die Gestaltung des Begriffsfeldes im Jak spiegelt … insgesamt wider, dass der durch Paulus geprägte frühchristliche Diskurs über Niedrigkeit bekannt war, dass aber zugleich die paulinische ›Erfindung‹ der Niedrig-Gesinnung als ekklesiales Prinzip der Christus-Orientierung in den Hintergrund tritt.[696]

Stattdessen weist Becker auf den »weisheitlichen Charakter der Demut als anthropologisches Wissen« bei Jak hin.[697] Für 1,9 f gilt aus dieser Perspektive: Die Sentenz, dass der Reiche sich seiner Niedrigkeit rühmen solle,

> gehört in den aus der LXX bereits bekannten weisheitlichen Diskurs über Niedrigkeit und Demut (z. B. Ps 89LXX), in dem besonders auf das Wissen um die Vergänglichkeit der menschlichen Existenz rekurriert wird.[698]

Während die Belege in Jak 4 eher von dieser demütigen Haltung sprechen, betont Burchard richtig zu 1,9 f, dass hier bei ταπεινός und ταπείνωσις zuerst an den finanziellen und sozialen Status zu denken sei: Denn der Gegencharakter, der πλούσιος, ist zunächst von seinem sozialen Status her entworfen.[699] Allerdings spreche Kap. 1 eben nicht von »dem Armen« (πτωχός) wie in Kap. 2, sondern von dem »Niedrigen«.[700] Die korrekte Antithese von arm *versus* reich begegnet erst in Kap. 2. Burchard interpretiert daher:

> Er [der Vf.] stellt dem Reichen mit dem Niedrigen den idealen Christen gegenüber, der nicht aus höheren Schichten stammt oder sich aus ihnen gelöst hat, bescheiden lebt und ist …, nicht den ärmsten [Christen].[701]

Burchards Formulierung »der ideale Christ« greift 1,4 auf. Wieder geht es um ethische Elitebildung in den Gemeinden, die der Verfasser anmahnt. Damit wird zugleich deutlich, dass durchaus auch die Haltung, nicht nur der soziale und wirtschaftliche Status im Blick sind. Eine einseitig soziale Akzentuierung ist nicht im Sinne des Textes.[702] Was in V. 9 deutlich werden soll, ist: Die ταπείνωσις ist ein Teil der Glaubensprüfungen von 1,2. Das impliziert, dass das vorangestellte Verbum καυχᾶσθαι mit Freude und Dank[703] zu verbinden ist. Bultmann paraphrasiert die

---

[696] Becker, Der Begriff der Demut, 189.

[697] Becker, Der Begriff der Demut, 191.

[698] Becker, Der Begriff der Demut, 193. B. verweist besonders auf Sir 2,17; 3,18. Weiteres zur Demut s. bei Kap. 4.

[699] Burchard, Jak, 64.

[700] Becker, Der Begriff der Demut, weist aber darauf hin, dass bei Jak »niedrig« und »arm« (als Gegensatz zu reich mitzudenken) zu *einem* semantischen Feld gehören (191).

[701] Ebd.

[702] Auch in der hebräischen Bibel stehen ʿānī (eher den Zustand beschreibend) und ʿānāw (eher die Haltung beschreibend) nahe beieinander. LXX übersetzt ʿānāw eher mit πραΰς oder ταπεινός. Vgl. E. Gerstenberger, Art. ʿānāh II, ThWAT 6, 1989, 247–270; H. Frankemölle, Art. πραΰτης, EWNT ³2011, III, 351–353.

[703] Vgl. R. Bultmann, Art. καυχάομαι κτλ., ThWNT 3, 1938, 646–654, 647 zur Bedeutung in AT, LXX und Judentum. Das Verb wird im NT ausschließlich und häufig von Paulus gebraucht. Ausnahme: Jak 1,9; 4,16. Ebenso καύχησις (außer bei Paulus nur Jak 4,16).

Haltung des Demütigen dahingehend, »daß er von Gott begnadet ist bzw. werden wird«.[704] Die semantische Nähe zu der Wendung »es für Freude halten« bzw. »sich freuen über« in 1,2 ist deutlich. Dieser Gnadenstand ist wirkliches ὕψος[705], hoher Standort bzw. »Stellung«[706] oder einfach Höhe oder Position. Im Zusammenhang ist damit deutlich: Dem ταπεινός fehlt nicht etwa etwas, sondern er ist gerade in seinem niedrigen Status reich bzw. hoch. Diese Wertschätzung des Status des Niedrigen ist nicht nur LXX-Erbe des Jak, sondern findet sich auch bei Paulus und bei den Synoptikern.[707]

V. 10 Anders steht es mit dem πλούσιος, der als Antitypos zu dem Demütigen eingeführt wird.[708] Dabei fehlt die zusätzliche Bezeichnung »Bruder«. Hier geht es noch nicht um das Thema des Reichen in der Gemeinde (2,1–8) und der Reichen als einer Gruppe, der das Gericht gepredigt wird (5,1–6), sondern »der Reiche« tritt (nur) als Negativfolie des Demütigen auf. Im Gegensatz zum Demütigen hat er einen Mangel (1,5) und ist insoweit Gegenstand der Mahnung, denn er ist grundlegend gefährdet. Der Topos »der Reiche« ist in der synoptischen Tradition verankert und grundsätzlich negativ besetzt.

Mt 19,23par	Lk 6,24	Lk 12,16
πλούσιος δυσκόλως εἰσελεύσεται εἰς τὴν βασιλείαν τῶν οὐρανῶν. Ein Reicher wird schwer ins Reich der Himmel kommen.	Πλὴν οὐαὶ ὑμῖν τοῖς πλουσίοις, ὅτι ἀπέχετε τὴν παράκλησιν ὑμῶν. Aber wehe euch Reichen, denn ihr habt euren Trost schon gehabt.	ἀνθρώπου τινὸς πλουσίου εὐφόρησεν ἡ χώρα. Eines reichen Menschen Feld hatte gut getragen.
Lk 16,1	Lk 16,19	Jak 1,10 f
ἄνθρωπός τις ἦν πλούσιος ὃς εἶχεν οἰκονόμον. Es war ein reicher Mensch, der hatte einen Verwalter.	Ἄνθρωπος δέ τις ἦν πλούσιος. Es war ein reicher Mensch.	ὁ δὲ πλούσιος ἐν τῇ ταπεινώσει αὐτοῦ, ὅτι ὡς ἄνθος χόρτου παρελεύσεται.

Die Beispiele zeigen, dass es in diesem Eingangsbereich des Jakobusbriefes nicht sinnvoll ist zu fragen, wer »der Reiche« sei und wie er sozialgeschichtlich verortet werden könne. Denkt der Verfasser auch hier an Brüder, d. h. an wohlhabende Neuchristen, ohne es auszusprechen? Oder bezieht er sich einfach auf den *Typos* des »Reichen« aus der Septuagintathematik, die Reichtum als Gegensatz zu Demut

---

[704] BULTMANN, ThWNT 3, 653.
[705] G. BERTRAM, Art. ὑψόω κτλ., ThWNT 8, 1969, 604–611.
[706] So BAUER / ALAND, 1695.
[707] BECKER, Der Begriff der Demut, 171–203.
[708] Jak 1,10.11; 2,5.6; 5,1. πλοῦτος: 5,2. Häufig in Lk. Vgl. F. HAUCK / W. KASCH, Art. πλοῦτος, ThWNT 6, 1959, 316–330.

172   Kommentar

bzw. Niedrigkeit versteht?[709] Dibelius plädiert zurecht dafür, die Frage offenzulassen. Allerdings wird man angesichts des gespaltenen Subjekts der V. 9.10a und der in den folgenden Kapiteln wieder aufgenommenen Thematik durchaus mit Frankemölle und Burchard bei »dem Reichen« auch an christliche Gemeindeglieder denken dürfen, wenn Jakobus sie hier auch noch nicht näher charakterisiert. Burchard prägt den glücklichen ironischen Begriff vom »Halbchristen«.[710] Damit ist bereits hier implizit gesagt, dass der Verfasser des Briefes sich keinen wirklich »vollkommenen« (1,4) reichen Christen vorstellen kann oder will.[711] Seine Abneigung dem Reichtum gegenüber ist bereits hier deutlich. Allerdings leiden die Verse 10 und 11 unter einer gewissen Unklarheit, die auch dann bestehen bleibt, wenn die Texteinheit nicht wie bei Dibelius als selbständig und kontextlos gedeutet wird. Zwar rät der Verfasser dem Reichen, sich seiner Niedrigkeit zu rühmen, (um die Glaubensprüfungen zu bestehen), und bewertet damit den Reichtum als ethischen Mangel (1,5) – aber wie soll das gehen? Man erwartet hier ethische Weisung: Besitzverzicht[712] oder Almosengeben bzw. Armenfürsorge.[713] Solche Konkretionen fehlen aber und scheinen dem Verfasser nicht am Herzen zu liegen. Dibelius schreibt zu Recht: »Untergang ist die letzte Aussicht, die Jak dem Reichen zeigt«.[714] Der Verfasser will den Reichen letztlich nicht ermahnen, sondern verurteilen und verlässt an diesem Punkt den Argumentationszusammenhang der V. 2–12. Nicht plausibel ist dagegen Dibelius' Vorschlag, V. 10a »ironisch« zu lesen.[715] Burchard trifft dagegen den Text, wenn er ταπείνωσις in V. 10 so deutet, »daß der Reiche sich selbst innerlich und wohl durch soziales Verhalten auch äußerlich … auf den Stand des ταπεινός herunterbringen oder bringen lassen und dann sich dessen rühmen soll«[716] oder sich über seinen niedrigen Stand freuen soll, da dieser ihn retten kann. Noch einmal: dem Verfasser ist dieser Aspekt nicht sehr wichtig. Stattdessen beleuchtet er das Schicksal

---

[709] Bei Philo, Jos. 150, sind der goldene Ring und die goldene Halskette statthafte Ehrenzeichen, dagegen soll sich der Reiche bei Jak seiner Niedrigkeit rühmen. Vgl. unten zu Jak 2,2.

[710] Burchard, Jak, 64.

[711] 2,1–7 zeigt, dass der Vf. sich solche Personen in den Gemeinden vorstellen kann, ihnen gegenüber aber negativ eingestellt ist.

[712] Vgl. Mk 10,17–22par.

[713] Armenfürsorge: vgl. die Kollekte des Paulus für die »Armen in Jerusalem« (2Kor 8.9). Vgl. besonders 2Kor 8,9: »Denn obwohl er [Christus] reich ist, wurde er um euretwillen arm, damit ihr durch seine Armut reich würdet«. Anders als in Jak 1 ist bei Paulus die chiastische Antithese stimmig. Zugleich bezieht sich die figurative Rede auf beide Pole der Antithese, während der Jakobustext zwischen materiellem Reichtum einerseits und eher ethischer Niedrigkeit andererseits schwankt. – Zum Thema insgesamt ausführlich: H. Kramer, Lukas als Ordner des frühchristlichen Diskurses um »Armut und Reichtum« und den »Umgang mit materiellen Gütern«, NET 21, Tübingen 2015. Zu Jakobus: R. Deines, God or Mammon. The Danger of Wealth in the Jesus Tradition and in the Epistle of James, in: M. Konradt / E. Schläpfer (Hg.), Anthropologie und Ethik im Frühjudentum und im Neuen Testament, WUNT 322, Tübingen 2014, 327–385. Weitere Lit. siehe zu Jak 2,14–17.

[714] Dibelius, Jak, 114. So auch teilweise in der synoptischen Tradition.

[715] Dibelius, Jak, 115 (im Anschluss an Beda).

[716] Burchard, Jak, 65.

des Reichen zunächst mit einem knappen Vergleich (ὡς) aus der Pflanzenwelt: Der Reiche wird »wie die Blüte[717] des Wildkrauts[718] (ἄνθος χόρτου) zugrunde gehen«.[719] Das Bild der »Blüte des Wildkrautes« ist Jes 40,6LXX entnommen und begegnet ebenfalls 1Petr 1,24. Während aber 1Petr 1,24f das Jesajazitat im ganzen Satz und im sachlich adäquaten Kontext des Gotteswortes verwendet, überträgt Jak 1,10 das Bild auf einen anderen Zusammenhang: das zukünftige Verderben des Reichen.[720] Dass dieser Aspekt dem Verfasser wichtiger ist, als es der Zusammenhang erfordert und gestattet, wurde schon gesagt.

V. 11 Der mehrgliedrige Satz widmet sich der Polemik gegen den Reichen in einem ausgeführten zweiteiligen Vergleich. Die Bildseite besteht aus einer kleinen viergliedrigen – vier Aussagesätze – Erzählung über das Schicksal der Blüte des Wildkrauts: Die Sonne geht auf (ἀνατέλλω)[721], das Gras wird versengt (ξηραίνω)[722], seine Blüten fallen ab, d.h. verwelken (ἐκπίπτω). Das vierte Glied der Erzählung bringt das Ergebnis: Die Schönheit der Blüte des Wildkrautes (εὐπρέπεια)[723] wird zerstört (ἀπόλλυμι)[724]. Die Sachseite oder Anwendung bezieht sich auf den Reichen und wiederholt in einem knappen Vergleichssatz das Urteil von V. 10. Das Bild vom aufblühenden und verwelkenden Gras als Topos der *Vergänglichkeit* ist verbreitet (Mt 6,30) und vielseitig einsetzbar.[725] Wieder steht Jes 40,6fLXX deutlich im Hintergrund. Ein Vergleich mit 1Petr 1,24 und Mk 4,6 zeigt die Allusionstechnik des Jak:

Jes 40,6f: Πᾶσα σὰρξ χόρτος, καὶ πᾶσα δόξα ἀνθρώπου ὡς ἄνθος χόρτου· ἐξηράνθη ὁ χόρτος, καὶ τὸ ἄνθος ἐξέπεσεν.
Alles Fleisch ist Gras und alle Herrlichkeit des Menschen wie die Blüte des Grases. Versengt ist das Gras und die Blüte abgefallen.

---

[717] Zu ἄνθος vgl. Bauer / Aland, 133. Hap. leg. in Jak (1,10f), im NT noch 1Petr 1,24a.b.

[718] Burchard, Jak, 65, übersetzt χόρτος mit »Wildgrün«. χόρτος nur in 1,10.11 in Jak, einige Male im NT.

[719] Zu παρέρχομαι vgl. Bauer / Aland, 1165. Hap. leg. in Jak. Das Verb hat ein breites Bedeutungsspektrum: vorübergehen, vorbeifahren, verlassen, aufhören, ein Ende finden (2Kor 5,17), vergehen im kosmologischen und apokalyptischen Zusammenhang (Mt 5,18par u.ö.). In Jak 1,10 ist es um »das Ende finden«, wobei ein apokalyptischer Aspekt anklingen mag (siehe die Perspektive in 5,7–11).

[720] Eine motivgeschichtlich genauere Zuordnung von Jak 1,10 zu Jes 40 und 1Petr 1 ist nicht nötig. Für 1,10f gilt insgesamt das Urteil von Burchard, Jak, 65: »Jak 1,10b–11 sind weder Zitat noch freie Anwendung von Jes 40, sondern ein neuer Text aus atl. Spolien«. Man kann auch von einem Allusionszusammenhang sprechen.

[721] Selten im NT, hap. leg. in Jak. Topisch im Zusammenhang mit dem Sonnenaufgang: Mt 5,45; 13,6 (dort im Zusammenhang mit der Hitze, die die Vegetation zerstört).

[722] Die Sonne trocknet das Gras aus (Aktiv). Das Verb nur hier in Jak.

[723] εὐπρέπεια hap. leg. im NT. Vgl. Spicq, NLNT I, 330, Belege.

[724] Im NT sehr häufig im Sinne von »vergehen«, »zerstören« (Jak 1,1; 4,12). Synoptisches Vorzugsverb, in Jak noch 4,12, dort endzeitlicher Kontext.

[725] Zur Metapher vgl. P. von Gemünden, Vegetationsmetaphorik im Neuen Testament und seiner Umwelt, NTOA 18, Freiburg / Göttingen, 1993, 305–309. Zum Text vgl. besonders Frankemölle, Jak I, 246–249.

174 Kommentar

1 Petr 1,24: διότι πᾶσα σὰρξ ὡς χόρτος καὶ πᾶσα δόξα αὐτῆς ὡς ἄνθος χόρτου· ἐξηράνθη ὁ χόρτος καὶ τὸ ἄνθος ἐξέπεσεν.
Denn alles Fleisch ist wie Gras und alle seine Herrlichkeit wie die Blüte des Grases. Versengt ist das Gras und die Blüte abgefallen.
Jak 1,11: καὶ ἐξήρανεν τὸν χόρτον καὶ τὸ ἄνθος αὐτοῦ ἐξέπεσεν.
Und sie (die Sonne) hat das Gras versengt, und seine Blüte ist abgefallen.
Mk 4,6par: καὶ ὅτε ἀνέτειλεν ὁ ἥλιος ἐκαυματίσθη καὶ διὰ τὸ μὴ ἔχειν ῥίζαν ἐξηράνθη.
Und als die Sonne aufging, verdorrte es (das Saatgut), und weil es keine Wurzel hatte, wurde es versengt.

Beide Verben aus Jes 40, ξηραίνω und ἐκπίπτω, begegnen ebenso in Jak 1,11, desgleichen die Substantive χόρτος und ἄνθος. Aber während 1 Petr den Jesajatext sowohl wörtlich als auch sinngemäß zitiert und mit dem Lob des Gotteswortes schließt, stellt Jakobus den Jesajatext in einen anderen Sachzusammenhang und benutzt dafür die *Bildqualität* und das damit verbundene Vergänglichkeitsvokabular Jesajas. Ähnlich verfährt das Markusevangelium. Der Markus- und der Jakobustext sind durch das narrative Element der Gleichnisrede bzw. des ausgeführten Vergleichs verbunden. Zur Vergänglichkeitssprache gehört auch das abschließende Verb in V. 11: μαραίνω heißt »auslöschen, vernichten«[726], wird aber gern für Pflanzen im Sinne von »welken« verwendet, so auch bildlich von verstorbenen Menschen.[727] V. 10 f enthalten ein kleines Lexikon von Verben, die das Ende, besonders das gewaltsame Ende im Sinne von »zugrunde gehen« apostrophieren: παρέρχομαι, ξηραίνω, ἐκπίπτω, ἀπόλλυμι, μαραίνω. Diese variationsreiche Kette von Verben zeigt einerseits die literarische Ambition des Verfassers, andererseits wird noch einmal deutlich, wie Recht Dibelius damit hat, dass dem Verfasser der Hinweis auf das negative Schicksal des Reichen besonders wichtig ist. πορεία[728] ist parallel zu 1,8 (ὁδός) gesetzt. Mindestens theoretisch ist für den Reichen, außer er erniedrige sich – wie immer dies auch praktisch zu realisieren wäre –, kein Platz in den Gemeinden, wie sie Jakobus sich vorstellt. Damit befindet sich Jakobus in der Nähe von Mk 10,25–27 (Vergleich eines Reichen mit einem Kamel). Hier geht es um dasselbe Urteil: In der Gottesherrschaft ist kein Platz für die Reichen, aber Gott kann sie retten. Jakobus argumentiert: Die Reichen werden vergehen, aber dennoch spricht er sie an und rät ihnen, sich ihrer Niedrigkeit zu rühmen.

Im *Rückblick* wird deutlich: Die Weiterungen von 1,5–11 rufen grundlegende ethische Wertvorstellungen auf: Weisheit, Glauben bzw. Einfachheit im Glauben und Niedrigkeit bzw. Demut. Diese ethischen Verhaltensformen führen materialethisch zur Tugend der Geduld, formalethisch zu der Vollkommenheit, die der

---

[726] BAUER / ALAND, 996.

[727] Ebd. Belege. Vgl. auch SPICQ, NLNT II, 531 f (reiche lexikographische Belege, besonders aus Philo).

[728] DIBELIUS, Jak, 116, deutet das Substantiv zu Recht nicht im Sinn von »Geschäftsreise« (4,13), sondern als Synonym von ὁδός im ethischen Sinn. Hap. leg. in Jak, im NT nur noch Lk 13,22 (Weg).

Verfasser für seine Adressaten erstrebt (1,2–4). Die Anfechtungen ermöglichen diese Perfektionierung der Adressaten. Dass dem Verfasser das Thema des Reichtums von Anfang an wichtig ist, wurde bereits deutlich. Beides fließt ineinander: grundsätzliche Kritik am Reichen und Misstrauen gegenüber der inneren Haltung eines reichen Christen. Trotzdem handelt es sich hier weder um Armentheologie noch um ein eschatologisches Szenario, wie Dibelius will[729], sondern um die *ethische* Haltung, das Ethos der ὑπομονή in den Anfechtungen, wie V. 12 resümiert.

4. Texteinheit: 1,12 Seligpreisung

(12) **Selig der Mann, der die Versuchung aushält[730], weil er, da er, ein Bewährter geworden[731], den Kranz des Lebens empfangen wird, den er (Gott) denen verheißen hat, die ihn lieben.**

Textkritik: 02 u.a. lesen ανθρωπος statt ανηρ (par zu V. 8). 018. 020 und einige Minuskeln haben Futur bei υπομενει. P20. 54 u.a. haben νικης statt ζωης (klareres Bild: sekundär). Verschiedene nachträgliche Ergänzungen des fehlenden Subjekts im abschließenden Relativsatz: κυριος (04), ο κυριος (025 u.a.), ο θεος (Minuskeln).

V. 12 verbindet eine klassisch formulierte Seligpreisung (prädikatloser Hauptsatz mit Relativsatz) mit einem Begründungssatz.[732] Diesem folgt ein Relativsatz, der sich auf das Akkusativobjekt des ὅτι-Satzes bezieht. Die Seligpreisung stellt den rhetorisch herausgehobenen Schluss des ersten Teils von 1,2–18 dar und fungiert als Variation und Bestätigung der Ermahnung in 1,2 und der damit verbundenen Perspektive in 1,3 f: πειρασμός wirkt Geduld und führt zur Vollkommenheit. Das ist Freude (1,2) und Glück (1,12). In 1,25 wird der Makarismus nochmals in variierter Form wiederholt. μακάριος lässt sich mit »glücklich« oder mit »selig« übersetzen.[733] Auf jeden Fall nimmt μακάριος den Gedanken von χαρά auf. Daher greift Dibelius' Urteil, es handele sich um einen nach vorn und nach hinten unverbundenen Einzelspruch, wieder zu kurz.[734] Allerdings weist Dibelius zu Recht darauf hin, dass in V. 12 eine semantische Veränderung eintritt, die den nächsten Teiltext 1,13–18 vorbereitet. πειρασμός wird jetzt im Sing. gesetzt, d. h. es geht nicht mehr um verschiedene *Situationen* der Glaubensprüfungen, sondern bereits um eine theologische Größe – weniger um Prüfungen als vielmehr um die »Versuchung«, über deren

---

[729] DIBELIUS, Jak, 113 f: »Jak spricht V. 9–11 die Erwartung einer bevorstehenden Umkehr der Verhältnisse aus, die dem Armen Erlösung, dem Reichen Erniedrigung bringt. Denn daß ὕψος und ταπείνωσις eschatologische Bedeutung haben, nicht etwa ethische, das ergibt sich mit Notwendigkeit aus der Geschichte des frommen Armen-Bewußtseins«.

[730] Vertont von Mendelssohn im Oratorium »Paulus« (Nr. 11 Chor); vgl. die Übersetzung von Julius Schubring: »Wir preisen selig, die erduldet haben«.

[731] Kausale Auflösung des Partizips.

[732] Der ὅτι-Anschluss ist eher ungewöhnlich. Vgl. ALLISON, Jak, 227: dort die LXX-Makarismen und der Hinweis darauf, dass der ὅτι-Anschluss auf die Jesustradition verweist.

[733] μακάριος bei BAUER / ALAND, 987; F. HAUCK / G. BERTRAM, Art. μακάριος, ThWNT 4, 1942, 365–373; G. STRECKER, Art. μακάριος, EWNT 2, 1992, 925–932.

[734] DIBELIUS, Jak, 118.

176 Kommentar

Herkunft der Verfasser seine Leser im Folgenden belehrt. Jakobus nimmt die *propositio generalis* von 1,2–4 wieder auf und bekräftigt sie. Dabei benutzt er hier deutlich die Formensprache der Bibel Israels, um seinem Urteil: »Anfechtung ist Freude« autoritatives Gewicht zu verleihen.

Die Einleitungswendung Μακάριος ἀνὴρ ὅς findet sich im NT nur noch in Röm 4,8 im Zitat aus Ps 32,2. Die vor allem bei den Synoptikern zahlreichen Makarismen sind überwiegend im Plural formuliert und beziehen sich auf bestimmte Personengruppen. Formulierungen im Singular (ohne ἀνήρ) finden sich in Mt 11,6; Lk 7,23; Röm 14,22; Apk 1,3; 16,15; 22,7. Der Makarismus schließt an entsprechende Seligpreisungen der Psalmen und der Weisheitsliteratur an.[735] V. 12b sind Dan 12,12LXX[736]; Jes 30,18LXX[737] und Sach 6,14LXX (ὁ δὲ στέφανος ἔσται τοῖς ὑπομένουσιν καὶ τοῖς χρησίμοις αὐτῆς. Der Kranz aber soll für die sein, die geduldig warten, und für seine tüchtigen Männer) besonders nahe. Der Sacharjatext könnte der Referenztext für Jak 1,12 sein, da hier vom Kranz die Rede ist. Der Zusammenhang bei Sacharja ist allerdings ein anderer: Es geht um die Krönung des Hohenpriesters und um seine Gefolgsleute.[738] Nachdem der Makarismus in 1,12 den Rat von 1,2 f bestätigend wiederholt, richtet der Begründungssatz den Blick in die Zukunft: Der Bewährte wird den Kranz des Lebens empfangen. Das Motiv des Empfangens weist auf Gott als den Geber zurück (1,5) und zugleich auf 1,16 f voraus, ebenso nimmt δόκιμος die Wendung τὸ δοκίμιον ὑμῶν τῆς πίστεως von 1,3 auf. Der Zukunftsaspekt, der schon in 1,10.11 eröffnet wurde, wird nun deutlicher akzentuiert: Der Reiche wird mit seinen Unternehmungen vergehen, während der in Anfechtungen Bewährte »das Leben« empfangen wird. Die metaphorische Wendung: »den Kranz des Lebens empfangen« lässt eine genauere zeitliche Zuordnung offen. Handelt es sich um eine eschatologische Aussage? Welche Verheißung ist gemeint? Der Kranz des Lebens[739] begegnet in Apk 2,10, dort im Zusammenhang mit Verfolgung (θλῖψις) und Leben nach dem Tod. Aus Apk 2,10 lässt sich die Bedeutung »ewiges Leben« für die Metapher erschließen. Der Jakobusbrief bleibt hier aber im Metaphorisch-Ungewissen. Die futurische Gerichtsperspektive begegnet erst in 2,13; 4,12; 5,7.

Der abschließende Relativsatz nimmt mit dem Verb ἐπηγγείλατο noch einmal die allgemeine Zukunftsperspektive auf. Die Wendung: »[Gott] hat etwas verheißen« begegnet öfter besonders in den späteren neutestamentlichen Schriften.[740] Die Vorstellung von Gottes Verheißung ist aber eher an das Substantiv geknüpft und

---

[735] Vgl. J. STEINBERG, Art. Seligpreisung (AT), WiBiLex, https://bibelwissenschaft.de/stichwort/45569/.

[736] Theodotion: μακάριος ὁ ὑπομένων (eschatologische Perspektive).

[737] »Selig, die in ihm bleiben«, ἐμμένοντες (in Gott).

[738] Vgl. ALLISON, Jak, 228: »James may ... rather express a theological commonplace«.

[739] Vgl. K. BAUS, Der Kranz in Antike und Christentum, Theoph. 2, Bonn 1940; J. ENGEMANN, Art. Kranz (Krone), RAC 21, 2006, 1006–1034. Weitere Lit: ALLISON, Jak, 230 Anm. 104.

[740] Tit 1,2; Hebr 6,13; 10,23; 11,11; 12,26; 1Joh 2,25 (fig. etym.); in Jak nur noch 2,5.

C. Briefcorpus

bezieht sich überwiegend auf das Schema von Verheißung und Erfüllung im Zusammenhang von Gottes Heilsansagen und -zusagen im Alten Testament.[741] »Die Verheißung des Lebens« wird in 1Tim 4,8 und 2Tim 1,1 angesprochen, in 2Tim 1,1 mit Christus Jesus verbunden. Dieser Aspekt fehlt – wie so oft – in Jak. 1Tim 4,8 führt zugleich eine interessante Differenzierung ein:

ἡ δὲ εὐσέβεια πρὸς πάντα ὠφέλιμός ἐστιν ἐπαγγελίαν ἔχουσα ζωῆς τῆς νῦν καὶ τῆς μελλούσης.

Die Frömmigkeit aber ist zu allem nützlich und hat die Verheißung des Lebens, des jetzigen und des kommenden.

Dieser doppelte Aspekt von Verheißung des Lebens kann unausgesprochen auch für Jak 1,12 zutreffen. Die Verheißung gilt denen, »die [Gott] lieben«. Die Wendung ist topisch und findet sich in der frühjüdischen und frühchristlichen Literatur.[742] Im Jak wird die Wendung auch in 2,5 benutzt. »Die Gott lieben« ist einer der verschiedenen Charakterzüge, mit denen der Verfasser die Adressaten, die ἀδελφοί, bezeichnet: vollkommen, untadelig, bewehrt, gottliebend.

Rückblickend erschließt sich V. 12 am ehesten vom Testament Hiobs her.[743] Die Motive von Geduld, Anfechtung, Bewährung und dem Kranz des Lebens sowie die Wendung »denen, die Gott lieben« finden sich in TestHiob 1,5; 4,6–10[744]; 5,1; 21,4; 26,5 und 27,4.7.

5. Texteinheit: 1,13–15 Diskussion über die Ursache der Versuchungen

(13) **Niemand sage, wenn er versucht wird**[745]: ›**Ich werde von Gott versucht‹**[746]. **Gott nämlich kann nicht vom Bösen versucht werden**[747], **aber (auch) er selbst versucht niemanden**[748]. (14) **Jeder aber wird von seiner eigenen Begierde versucht, fortgerissen und geködert.** (15) **Danach, wenn die Begierde empfangen hat**[749], **gebiert sie die Sünde, die Sünde aber, wenn sie vollendet ist**[750], **gebiert den Tod.**[751]

Textkritik: **V. 13** Minuskel 918 fügt zur Erläuterung εις αμαρτιαν zu πειραζομενος hinzu. Hier ist der semantische Wechsel von πειρασμος vom Schreiber bemerkt worden. Statt »ich

---

[741] Besonders in Apg, Röm, Gal und vor allem in Hebr.

[742] Vgl. O. WISCHMEYER, THEON AGAPAN bei Paulus. Eine traditionsgeschichtliche Miszelle, in: DIES., Von Ben Sira zu Paulus, WUNT 173, Tübingen 2004, 162–166. M. WIEGER / K. PERRY, Art. ἀγαπάω κτλ., HTLS I, 25–64.

[743] Vgl. auch unten zu Jak 5,11.

[744] 4,10: »Denn du wirst sein wie ein Wettkämpfer, der Schläge austeilt und Schmerzen erträgt und (am Ende) den (Sieges)Kranz empfängt« (Übersetzung: B. SCHALLER, Das Testament Hiobs, JSHRZ III 3, Gütersloh 1979, 331).

[745] Konditionale Auflösung des Partizips.

[746] ὅτι nicht übersetzt.

[747] Wörtlich: »ist unversuchbar vom Bösen (Plur.)«.

[748] Wörtlich: »Er versucht aber selbst niemanden«.

[749] Temporale Auflösung des Partizips.

[750] Temporale Auflösung des Partizips.

[751] K.-W. NIEBUHR, Jakobus und Paulus über das Innere des Menschen und den Ursprung seiner ethischen Entscheidungen, NTS 62, 2016, 1–30.

178 Kommentar

werde versucht« haben einige Minuskeln das blassere πειραζεται. Statt απο θεου liest οι υπο: »Unsicherheit in der Überlieferung« (DIBELIUS, Jak, 121). V. 15 haben einzelne Minuskeln Abweichungen bei den Verben: αποτικτει statt τικτει (1678), τελεσθεισα statt αποτελεσθεισα (1799), κυει statt αποκυει (mehrere Minuskeln, außerdem Fut. bei einigen), τικτει statt αποκυει (1848T. Wiederholung).

Der Verfasser hebt nun das ethische Thema der πειρασμοί auf die theologisch-anthropologische Ebene, wie der bereits erwähnte semantische Wandel von πειρασμός zeigt. Wieder sieht Dibelius eine scharfe Zäsur und bestreitet jede Verbindung zwischen 1,2–12 und 1,13–15.[752] Es handelt sich allerdings eher um einen Gedanken- und Argumentations*fortschritt* im thematischen Zusammenhang von Prüfungen / Versuchungen als um einen Neuanfang.[753] Was entstanden ist, ist aber ein thematisch und formal deutlich selbständiger Text. V. 13 verbindet einen theologischen Satz, der als ein warnendes Verbot fungiert, in Bezug auf den πειρασμός *theologisch* falsch zu argumentieren, mit einem zweiteiligen, antithetisch und asyndetisch gestalteten Begründungssatz zum Wesen Gottes. Diese theologische Belehrung wird dann in 1,16–18 vertieft. Zuvor erfolgt in V. 14.15 die *anthropologische* Klarstellung in Form eines Aussagesatzes. Der Verfasser klärt, woher der πειρασμός kommt, wenn denn nicht Gott sein Urheber ist. V. 15 präsentiert in äußerster Kürze und stilistischer Präzision eine anthropologische Erzählung in zwei formal parallel gestalteten Stadien: die Todesgeschichte der Begierde (ἐπιθυμία). Es macht die Eigenart der Texteinheit aus, dass hier Theologie und Anthropologie engstens verknüpft sind. Formal handelt es sich um eine Art von kleinem Schulgespräch im Diatribenstil.[754] Der fingierte Satz: »Ich werde *von Gott* versucht« (und nicht von meiner eigenen Schwäche), wird widerlegt, indem der verbotene Satz formuliert und vorab bereits zurückgewiesen wird: »Niemand sage …«.[755] Es folgt eine weitergehende Belehrung.

---

[752] DIBELIUS, Jak, 121.

[753] BURCHARD, Jak, 71, spricht richtig von einem »Perspektivwechsel«. Zur anthropologischen Dimension von »Versuchung« vgl. M. KENSKY, Trying Man, Trying God: The Divine Courtroom in Early Jewish and Christian Literature, WUNT II / 289, Tübingen 2010; KLEIN, Bewährung in Anfechtung, 274–367.

[754] So auch ALLISON, Jak, 240.

[755] DIBELIUS, Jak, 122, zieht bei Philo »exegetische Schul-Kontroversen« zum Thema in Erwägung. Texte: Philo, fug. 79 f: »Es gebührt sich also, daß wir die heimlich, auf hinterlistige Weise und mit Vorbedacht begangenen Übeltaten nie auf Gottes, sondern stets auf unseren eigenen Willen zurückführen. Denn in uns selbst liegen, wie ich schon sagte, die Schatzkammern des Schlechten, in Gott die des Guten allein«; 80: »Eine schwer oder aber überhaupt nicht wieder gut zu machende Schmähung ist die Behauptung, die Gottheit sei auch Urheberin der Übel«. Abr. 142 f: »einer der ›drei Männer‹ ist ›der wahrhaft Seiende‹, die beiden anderen sind ›Kräfte‹, die ›das Gegenteil‹ des Guten in Sodom bewirken, damit er [Gott] ›ausschliesslich für den Urheber des Guten, nicht aber für den Urheber irgend eines Übels gehalten würde‹«; conf. 161: Es gibt Menschen, die »die eigene Blutschuld Gott zu Last legen, der Urheber ist aller Güter, dagegen keines einzigen Übels«. Prov. 2,82: »Selbstverständlich wird durch die Vorsehung, wie wir behaupten, die Welt regiert, aber nicht in dem Sinn, als ob Gott die Ursache von allem wäre; denn ir ist nicht die Ursache des Schlechten noch dessen, was außerhalb der Natur geschieht … In gleicher Weise wird behauptet, daß die Welt durch die Vorsehung regiert wird, nicht weil Gott für alles sorgt, sondern weil es die Würde seiner Natur ist, auf jeden Fall gut und nützlich zu sein; das Gegenteil jedoch sind die Früchte des Irrtums entweder der Materie oder der Schlechtig-

V. 13 Die Wendung »Niemand sage« (Imp.3.Pers.Sing.) leitet die theoretische Aussage »Von Gott werde ich versucht« ein.[756] Sie ist formal und inhaltlich nahe bei Sir 15,11 f.[757] Dort heißt es:

(11) μὴ εἴπῃς ὅτι Διὰ κύριον ἀπέστην· ἃ γὰρ ἐμίσησεν, οὐ ποιήσει. (12) μὴ εἴπῃς ὅτι Αὐτός με ἐπλάνησεν· οὐ γὰρ χρείαν ἔχει ἀνδρὸς ἁμαρτωλοῦ.

(11) Sag nicht: ›Durch den Herrn bin ich abgefallen‹, denn was er hasst, wird er nicht tun. (12) Sag nicht: ›Er selbst hat mich getäuscht‹, denn er benötigt keinen sündigen Mann.

Der Verfasser des Jak rückt das Thema der πειρασμοί und des πειρασμός damit in den Zusammenhang des antiken jüdischen Diskurses über die Frage nach der Herkunft des Übels / des Bösen und nimmt mit seinem Text zugleich selbst an diesem Diskurs teil. Die wichtigsten entsprechenden Texte stammen, wie gezeigt, einerseits von Jesus Sirach, andererseits von Philo. Den größeren Rahmen bildet die »antike Gotteslehre«.[758] Der Verfasser schließt sich der antiken Grundüberzeugung an, die vom Judentum geteilt wird, Gott sei der »Vater alles Guten«, nicht aber die Ursache des Bösen.[759]

Damit ist zugleich deutlich, dass πειρασμός und πειράζειν[760] nun nicht mehr nur schwierige äußere Bedingungen wie Krankheit, Armut oder Verfolgung – also »Übel« – bezeichnen, sondern grundsätzlich negativ konnotiert sind und dem Bereich des Bösen (κακόν) zugeordnet werden:[761] Jak 1,13 ist mit verschiedenen

---

keit einer maßlosen Natur; Gott jedoch ist daran nicht schuld«. Det. 122: »Mose bezeichnet nicht wie einige gottlose Menschen die Gottheit als Ursache des Schlechten, sondern unsere eigenen Hände, worunter er sinnbildlich unsere eigenen Taten und die freiwilligen Neigungen unserer Seele zum Schlechteren versteht« (vgl. dazu Philo von Alexandria. Die Werke in deutscher Übersetzung, Hg. L. Cohn u. a. III, Berlin ²1962, 315 Anm. 2). Vgl. auch Arist 231: »Täter guter Werke und nicht des Gegenteils zu sein ist aber eine Gabe Gottes«. Bei Jak findet Dibelius dagegen keine theoretische Polemik, sondern »praktische ... Bekämpfung von Ausflüchten derer, die in der Versuchung gefallen sind«. Diese rein praktische Deutung greift angesichts von 1,16–18 zu kurz. Jak steht deutlich im Zusammenhang der Thematik, die besonders Philo mehrfach anspricht. Richtig ist aber auch, dass Jak anders als Philo argumentiert: nicht im Stil einer ethischen Untersuchung, sondern im Stil ethisch-religiöser Bilderrede.

[756] BURCHARD, Jak, 71: »Klage« (mit ὅτι). »Offenbar hat Jak dergleichen gehört«. Das ist nicht nötig: Es kann sich auch um einen fingierten Satz handeln.

[757] Vgl. besonders FRANKEMÖLLE, Jak I, 278–282.

[758] BURCHARD, Jak, 72: Diogenes Laertius, Plutarch, Marc Aurel u. a. Schon Homer, Od. I 32 ff; Platon, Tht. 176c; Kleanthes Frgm. 573,11 ff. Ausführlicher: O. WISCHMEYER, Wie spricht der Jakobusbrief von Gott?, 385–409 (398 f Diskussion der historischen Wahrscheinlichkeit, dass Positionen wie die bei Philo und Jak genannten von Juden vertreten wurden).

[759] Plutarch, mor. 1102d.

[760] S. o. zu 1,2.

[761] M. BRAND, Evil Within and Without. The Source of Sin and Its Nature as Portrayed in Second Temple Literature, JAJSup 9, Göttingen 2013; I. FRÖHLICH / E. KOSKENNIEMI (Hg.), Evil and the Devil, LNTS 481, London 2013; M. SAUR, Der Blick in den Abgrund. Bilder des Bösen in der alttestamentlichen Weisheitsliteratur, in: J. Dochhorn / S. Rudnig-Zelt / B. Wold (Hg.), Das Böse, der Teufel und Dämonen – Evil, the Devil, and Demons, WUNT II / 412, Tübingen 2016, 21–42; O. WISCHMEYER, Zwischen Gut und Böse. Teufel, Dämonen, das Böse und der Kosmos im Jakobusbrief, ebd., 153–168; N. J. ELLIS, A Theology of Evil in the Epistle of James: Cosmic Trials and the *Dramatis Personae* of Evil, in: C. Keith / L. T. Stuckenbruck

LXX-Texten und mit ntl. Texten zum Thema »Versuchung als Übel / Böses« verbunden. Dieser spezielle Diskurs des antiken Judentums ist vielfältig und hält unterschiedliche Stellungnahmen zum Thema bereit. Spätestens seit dem Hiobbuch ist der Teufel Bestandteil des Diskurses.[762] Er tritt als Versucher auf: bei Hiob, der die vom διάβολος verursachten Prüfungen / Versuchungen besteht[763], oder in der synoptischen Versuchungserzählung (Mk 1,12 f; Mt 4,1–11; Lk 4,1–13). In dieser äußerst komplexen Erzählung versucht der Teufel Jesus mit einem Schriftwort (Ps 91,11 f). Jesus entlarvt die Taktik des Teufels mit einem anderen Schriftwort zur Versuchung, indem er mit Dtn 6,16 antwortet:

Οὐκ ἐκπειράσεις κύριον τὸν θεόν σου, ὃν τρόπον ἐξεπειράσασθε ἐν τῷ πειρασμῷ.

Du sollst den Herrn, deinen Gott, nicht versuchen, wie ihr ihn (willentlich) versucht habt in der Versuchung.[764]

Im Ergebnis geht es nicht darum, ob Gott den Menschen versucht, sondern dass Gott nicht versucht werden darf, indem seine Hilfe mutwillig und ohne Not in Anspruch genommen wird. An diesem Punkt ist Jak 1 aufgrund seiner Gotteslehre radikaler als die Jesustradition: Gott ist grundsätzlich unversuchbar.[765] Das Verbaladjektiv ἀπείραστος[766] ist aus der Thematik heraus gewähltes ntl. hap. leg. Der korrespondierende Aussagesatz: »Gott versucht niemanden« geht aus dem Vordersatz hervor und beruht auf der Einheit des Wesens Gottes.[767] Damit ist Jak 1,13 auch von der Vaterunserbitte Mt 6,13a par entfernt[768]: καὶ μὴ εἰσενέγκῃς ἡμᾶς εἰς πειρασμόν. In dieser Bitte ist die Möglichkeit, dass Gott die Menschen selbst prüft bzw. versucht,

---

(Hg.), Evil in Second Temple Judaism and Early Christianity, WUNT II / 417, Tübingen 2016, 262–281. – Die eigentliche Theodizeefrage: *Weshalb lässt Gott das Böse zu?* wird hier aber nicht gestellt. Anders Paulus in Röm 5–7: Paulus fragt nach der Herkunft und der Funktion des Bösen / der Sünde im theologischen Kontext. Seine heilsgeschichtlich-spekulative These, die Sünde sei durch Adam in die Welt gekommen und durch das Gesetz den Menschen offenkundig gemacht, spielt in der Argumentation des Jak keine Rolle. Damit fallen einerseits die theologische Bedeutung bzw. Qualität der Sünde und andererseits auch die Grundlage der Bedeutung der heilsgeschichtlichen Rolle Jesu fort. Zum Thema J. DOCHHORN, Der Adammythos bei Paulus und im hellenistischen Judentum Jerusalems, WUNT 469, Tübingen 2021, zur Rolle und zum Begriff des Bösen in der Konstellation von Sünde-Teufel-Bösem, besonders 438–464.

762 S. RUDNIG-ZELT, Der Teufel und der alttestamentliche Monotheismus, in: Dochhorn / Rudnig-Zelt / Wold (Hg.), Das Böse, 1–20 (Lit.).

763 Auffallenderweise wird Hiob nicht in Jak 1,13, sondern erst in 5,11 als Beispiel für Geduld erwähnt. Zum Motiv der Versuchung durch den Teufel vgl. auch 1Thess 3,5; 1Kor 7,5.

764 Vgl. 1Kor 10,9.

765 Die allgemeine Gotteslehre des Jak ist theoretischer und damit »moderner« als Dtn 6. – Anders Jesus in Lk 4,12: hier *soll* Gott nicht versucht werden.

766 Nicht in LXX. BAUER / ALAND, 166: »Gott kann nicht zu bösen Dingen versucht werden«. Vgl. auch das Agraphon 21: ἀνὴρ ἀδόκιμος ἀπείραστος. Vgl. P. DAVIES, The Meaning of APEIRASTOS in James 1.13, NTS 24, 1978, 391–410.

767 Allgemein dazu: W. MAAS, Unveränderlichkeit Gottes. Zum Verhältnis von griechisch-philosophischer und christlicher Gotteslehre, Paderborn u. a. 1974.

768 Vgl. dazu F. WILK (Hg.), Das Vaterunser in seinen antiken Kontexten, FRLANT 266, Göttingen 2016.

gerade nicht ausgeschlossen – so aber in Jak 1.[769] Jak 1,13–15 zeigt in dem Diskurs um die Versuchung und das Böse ein eigenes Profil.

V. 14 Jakobus beantwortet die Frage, woher denn die Versuchung (und das Böse) komme, mit dem Verweis auf das Innere des Menschen: Die Versuchung ist innen, sie kommt nicht von außen. Die Antwort liegt also nicht im Bereich der Theologie oder Dämonologie, sondern der Anthropologie. Jakobus formuliert hier ebenso kurz wie merkwürdig unscharf.[770] Anders als in der Hiobtradition ist nicht der Satan der Versucher[771], sondern die Versuchung ist ausschließlich mit der versuchten Person verbunden, und zwar in Gestalt der eigenen ἐπιθυμία. Der Verfasser schreibt aber nicht, wie man erwarten könnte: ›Die Versuchung liegt in der Begierde des Menschen‹, sondern lässt den Zusammenhang zwischen Versuchung und Begierde offen. Ist die Begierde Ursprung der Versuchung, oder bleibt die Herkunft der Versuchung unbestimmt, und beschränkt sich der Verfasser darauf, die *Empfänglichkeit* des Menschen für die Versuchung darzustellen? Letzteres liegt deutlich im Interesse des Verfassers, wie die beiden Part. pass. zeigen: Die Begierde »reizt und lockt« (ἐξελκόμενος[772] καὶ δελεαζόμενος[773]). Die Wahl der sehr seltenen Verben[774] und die nachgestellte Position der Partizipien verrät schriftstellerische Raffinesse.[775] Dass die ἐπιθυμία ein bekannter Topos im thematischen Zusammenhang mit dem Bösen, mit Versuchung, Sünde und Tod sei, wird hier vorausgesetzt.[776] Das Objekt der Begierde bleibt ungenannt. V. 14 bleibt anthropologisch eher blass.[777] Das argu-

---

[769] So auch FRANKEMÖLLE, Jak I, 281. F. weist auch auf 1Kor 10,13 hin. ALLISON, Jak, 240, weist auf J. Jeremias hin, der einen Zusammenhang zwischen Jak 1,13 und Mt 6,13 annahm (J. JEREMIAS, The Prayers of Jesus, London 1967, 104), bemerkt aber kritisch: »One need not call upon the Lord's Prayer to explain it«. Zu Mt 6,13: auch U. LUZ, Das Evangelium nach Matthäus (Mt 1–7), EKK I / 1, Düsseldorf u. a. ⁵2002, 454 Anm. 130, bemerkt den Unterschied zwischen Jak und dem synoptischen Text. Zur Vaterunserbitte auch B. WOLD, Apotropaic Prayer and the Matthean Lord's Prayer, in: Dochhorn / Rudnig-Zelt / Wold (Hg.), Das Böse, 101–112. Wold denkt bei der Vaterunserbitte an Befreiung von »demonic evil« (112), ohne die Frage, ob es sich um eine apotropäische Gebetsformulierung handele, zu entscheiden. Zum Thema auch: N. J. ELLIS, A Theology of Evil in the Epistle of James: Cosmic Trials and the *Dramatis Personae* of Evil, in: Keith / Stuckenbruck, (Hg.), Evil in Second Temple Judaism, 262–281, 267 Anm. 16.

[770] FRANKEMÖLLE, Jak I, 285, weist zu Recht darauf hin, dass »die Verse [formkritisch] antithetisch zu 3 f.« stehen.

[771] Vgl. die synoptischen Texte! Besonders interessant Mk 8,33. Petrus wird metaphorisch als Satan angesprochen und seine Einlassung offensichtlich von Jesus als Versuchung (vgl. Mk 1,13) verstanden. – Im Jak wird der Satan nur in 4,7 erwähnt (s. dort).

[772] ἐξέλκω: »fortreißen«, ntl. hap. leg., »von der Begierde fortgerissen werden«: Platon, 7. Brief p. 325B (vgl. BAUER / ALAND, 554: weitere Belege).

[773] δελεάζω: verlocken, ködern, vgl. noch 2Petr 2,14.18 (dort zusammen mit: »geködert von den Begierden des Fleisches«). BAUER / ALAND, 348.

[774] BAUER / ALAND, 348, erwägt für beide Partizipien »Fischersprache«: »von der eigenen Lust herausgezogen u. geködert«.

[775] DIBELIUS, Jak, 124, weist zurecht darauf hin, dass schon hier die Begierde »fast wie eine Person erscheint«.

[776] Das Substantiv begegnet sonst nicht im Jak (Verb: Jak 4,2). Auffallend häufig in der ntl. Briefliteratur, besonders im Röm.

[777] Zum Begriff BURCHARD, Jak, 72 f. S. 73: »Die ἐπιθυμία ist keine überindividuelle Macht, sondern je

182   Kommentar

mentative Gewicht liegt auf der Beschreibung der Gewalt, mit der die Begierden den Menschen »in Versuchung führen« und in eine tödliche Richtung ziehen.

V. 15 Jakobus führt diese negative dynamische Tendenz fort: In einer lapidaren Erzählung (εἶτα: »danach«) verknüpft der Verfasser die Begierde mit zwei weiteren anthropologischen Grundbegriffen: mit Sünde und Tod. Begierde, Sünde und Tod werden personifiziert. Damit entsteht nun ein gewichtiges anthropologisches Narrativ, das im Zusammenhang mit Röm 7 gelesen werden muss.[778]

Der Satz ist äußerst sorgfältig aus zwei exakt parallel gestalteten kurzen Aussagesätzen zusammengesetzt: Subjekt mit Part. Aor., Präd., Akk.obj. Die Kombination von vorangestellten Partizipien und darauffolgenden Verben macht die Dynamik des Prozesses deutlich, der unausweichlich zum Tod führt. Die Diktion ist nicht so gewählt wie in V. 14[779], aber prägnant und bildhaft. Das Bild stammt aus dem Bereich weiblicher Geschlechtlichkeit und Sexualität und des Gebärens und wird durch drei Verben aufgebaut: συλλαμβάνειν[780] und die bedeutungsgleichen Verben τίκτειν[781] und ἀποκύειν »gebären« (*variatio*).[782] Die Substantive bilden die klimaktische[783] Kette: Begierde, Sünde, Sünde (*repetitio*), Tod.[784] Die Sünde ist hier der zentrale anthropologische Begriff, der durch Wiederholung besonders hervorgehoben wird. Die Substantive fungieren als Subjekte des Empfängnis- und Geburtsgeschehens.[785] Das Bild gehört in den Bereich naturhaft-mythologischer Szenarien[786], in dem die anthropologischen Größen Begierde, Sünde und Tod[787] personifiziert werden und als eigene Akteure im Zusammenhang des Versuchung und des Bösen auftreten.[788] Das Bild hat zwei Implikationen: *Erstens* wird die Person, die versucht wird, indirekt als in einen tödlich endenden Empfängnis- und Geburtsvorgang – dieser ist gedoppelt – verstrickt vorgestellt.[789] Dadurch schwingt

---

eigen«.

[778] Zum größeren thematisch-motivischen Umfeld von Röm 7 vgl. monographisch Dochhorn, Der Adammythos.

[779] ἀποτελέω allerdings im NT äußerst selten: als »vollenden« nur in Jak 1,15, als »vollbringen« Lk 13,32.

[780] συλλαμβάνω hap. leg. in Jak, als »empfangen«, »schwanger werden« im geschlechtlichen Sinn im NT (Bauer / Aland, 1550): Lk 1,24. 31. 36; 2,21; Jak 1,16 (metaphorisch).

[781] τίκτω, »gebären« (Bauer / Aland, 1628): hap. leg. in Jak, vgl. den metaphorischen Gebrauch auch in Hebr 6,7.

[782] ἀποκυέω, »gebären« (Bauer / Aland, 188), hap. leg. im NT, nur Jak 1,15.18 (metaphorisch).

[783] Die Klimax bedeutet zusätzliche Dynamik des Versuchungsprozesses.

[784] Zu den sog. Kettenschlüssen ausführlich mit Beispielen Dibelius, Jak, 125–129.

[785] Zur Sünde vgl. G. Röhser, Metaphorik und Personifikation der Sünde. Antike Sündenvorstellungen und paulinische Hamartia, WUNT II/25, Tübingen 1987. D. Büchner et al., Art. ἁμαρτάνω κτλ., HTLS I, 598–622. Jak 1 befindet sich in der Tendenz des Paulus, »Sünde« im absoluten Sinn zu verwenden (vgl. HTLS I, 619).

[786] Von Gemünden, Vegetationsmetaphorik, 336, zum Bildfeld.

[787] Der Tod wird durch die kausal-genealogische Verknüpfung mit Begierde und Sünde gleichfalls zur anthropologischen Größe.

[788] Auch Dibelius, Jak, 125, spricht von der »Personifikation« der Sünde.

[789] Parallelen zum Geburtsbild: Burchard, Jak, 73f. Am nächsten kommt Philo, post. 74. Post. 71–74 handeln von dem Kampf gegen die Lust. 74: »Wenn jedoch diese Leidenschaft (πάθος) schwanger ging

das Bild der verführenden und verführten Frau mit, ohne dass es explizit aufgerufen wird. Das Bild des Empfängnis- und Geburtsgeschehens konstruiert *zweitens* eine als unausweichlich beschriebene genealogische[790] Verbindung zwischen den drei anthropologischen Größen, die, theoretisch zu Ende gedacht, dem Menschen keinen Spielraum lässt.

Allerdings zieht der Verfasser diesen Schluss, der in der Konsequenz zur These vom grundsätzlich unfreien Willen führen würde, *nicht*, wie die folgende Texteinheit zeigen wird. Es geht ihm weder um eine Theorie des unfreien Willens noch um eine tiefere theologisch-anthropologische Diskussion des Bösen und der Sünde. Vielmehr liegt die textpragmatische Funktion dieses dichten und bedrückenden Bildes gerade in der *Warnung*, die ja Spielraum zum richtigen Verhalten lässt.[791] Der Mensch kann sich durchaus von dieser Geschichte der Versuchung zum Bösen freihalten. Genau dazu aufzurufen, ist die Absicht des Verfassers. Die Warnung hat hier wie öfter im Jakobusbrief die literarisch-rhetorische Gestalt der Drohung: Hier wird mit dem Tod gedroht.[792] Die *Emotion*, die der Verfasser hier und öfter erzeugen will, ist Angst. Ziel ist es, die Leserschaft zur Standhaftigkeit im πειρασμός zu bringen (1,2–4).

Hinter der Warnung stehen die Traditionen von der Herkunft des Bösen und der Sünde im antiken Judentum. Sie machen die Warnung des Verfassers plausibel. Die Literatur der Zeit des Zweiten Tempels entwirft verschiedene Szenarien, die sich als »interne« und »externe« Modelle beschreiben lassen.[793] Der Jakobusbrief kennt die kosmologisch-dämonologischen[794] Vorstellungen von der Ursache bzw. Verursachung von Sünde, betont aber ihre ethisch-anthropologische – d. h. interne – Seite.[795] ἁμαρτία ist kein zentraler, wohl aber ein wichtiger Begriff im Jak, der in verschiedenen Zusammenhängen begegnet.[796] Christoph Burchard kommentiert:

(κυοφορήσῃ), gebar (ἔτεκεν) sie unter schlimmen Wehen Krankheiten und Schwächen«. Philo schildert den ethischen Kampf zwischen brennender Begierde (φλεγούσης τῆς ἐπιθυμίας), die im Innern (ἐν ἡμῖν, ἔχοντες αὐτὰ ἐν ψυχῇ) »Krankheiten und Schwächen« zurücklässt, und deren vollständiger Vertreibung. Wird sie nicht vertrieben, folgt der Tod der Seele (θάνατος ὁ ψυχῆς).

[790] DIBELIUS, Jak, 124, bestreitet nachdrücklich, dass hier auf einen Mythos angespielt werde, und weist auch die Idee einer mythischen Genealogie in Jak 1,14 f zurück. Das ist richtig. Es geht nicht um den Mythos, wohl aber liegt mythologische Bildersprache vor.

[791] Richtig DIBELIUS, Jak, 129: »Unsere Stelle hat wie das ganze Schriftstück praktische Absicht; ein theoretisches Interesse spielt insofern mit, als falsche Aussagen über die Versuchung, mit denen sich der Sünder entschuldigen könnte, durch richtige ersetzt werden sollen.« Vgl. auch BURCHARD, Jak, 72, der darauf hinweist, dass der Verfasser weder über den freien Willen noch über »Sündenfall« bzw. »die Entstehung von Einzelsünden« schreibe. Auch der Schicksalsbegriff fehlt ganz.

[792] θάνατος bei Jak: nur 1,15; 5,20 (auch im Zusammenhang mit Sünde).

[793] Zu dieser Struktur vgl. besonders BRAND, Evil Within and Without, und ELLIS, A Theology of Evil in the Epistle of James.

[794] Dazu s. u.

[795] Vgl. WISCHMEYER, Zwischen Gut und Böse.

[796] 1,15; 2,9; 4,17; 5,15. 16. 20 (s. dort).

184 Kommentar

Die Personifizierung ist auch hier nur rhetorisch; Sünde ist für Jak weder überindividuelle Macht noch individuelle Sucht (so Röm 7,7–25), sondern Handeln wider Gottes Gesetz (s. 1,25).[797]

Die thematische Nähe zu Röm 7,7–25 ist deutlich.[798] Auch Röm 7 stellt eine Verbindung zwischen Begierde (7,7), Sünde (7,8), Tod (7,10) und dem Bösen (7,19) her. Die theologisch-anthropologische Konstellation ist aber grundlegend anders: Während Jak von der Wahrnehmung des πειρασμός ausgeht und vor dessen Gefahren warnt, denkt Paulus existenzialanthropologisch über sein Ich zwischen Gesetz / Geist und Sünde / Fleisch nach. Bei Jak sind weder das Ich noch das Gesetz[799] im Blick. Die selbständige Macht der Sünde ist bei Paulus unvergleichlich größer: Die Sünde ist ein eigener Akteur, der der Mensch verfallen ist. Rettung (Röm 7,24 f) kann nur von außen kommen: von Jesus Christus. Vor diesem Hintergrund der absolut pessimistischen Anthropologie des Paulus tritt die *positive, ja optimistische* Sicht des Jak hervor, die gegenüber der finsteren Metaphorik von 1,13–15 leicht übersehen wird. Jak ist überzeugt, dass seine Adressaten der Versuchung widerstehen und die Vollkommenheit erlangen können, zu der er sie erzieht (1,2–4). Einer Rettung von außen scheinen sie nicht zu bedürfen.

6. Texteinheit: 1,16–18 Abschließende Belehrung über Gott als Geber des Guten
(16) **Irrt nicht, meine geliebten Brüder.** (17) **Jede gute Gabe und jedes vollkommene Geschenk ist von oben, herabsteigend von dem Vater der Lichter[800], bei dem nicht ist Veränderung oder auch nur ein[801] Schatten des Wandels.** (18) **Willentlich[802] hat er uns geboren durch das Wort der Wahrheit, damit wir gleichsam die Erstlingsgabe[803] seiner Geschöpfe seien.**

Textkritik: V. **16** liest Minuskel 33 μηδε statt μη. V. **17** einige Minuskeln lesen κατερχομενον statt καταβαινον (stilistische Vereinfachung, vgl. Jak 3,15). Statt ενι (P23. 02. 03. 04. 044. Min. 33) lesen ἐστι(ν) 01. 025 sowie Minuskeln. παραλλαγη η τροπης αποσκιασμα lesen 01C2. 02. 04. 025, viele Minuskeln, byzantin. Codices. 044 hat ουδε statt η. Umstellung der Kasus: παραλλαγη η τροπη αποσκιασματος bei 614 und anderen Minuskeln. Unverständlich ist die Lesart von 01*. 03: παραλλαγη η τροπης αποσκιασματος. P23 liest παραλλαγης η τροπης αποσκιασματος. Weitere Varianten, teils mit anderen Lexemen, teils mit Erweiterungen, in

---

[797] BURCHARD, Jak, 74.

[798] Mit Burchard gilt daher: »Nächstverwandt ist wohl Röm 7,7–12« sowie: »Wenn Paulus nachklingt, dann ungenau; eher gemeinsame Tradition« (BURCHARD, Jak, 73). B. verweist auf Philo, post. 73 f (s. o.). DOCHHORN, Der Adammythos, 160, spricht von der Begierde als »Wurzelsünde« und erläutert: »Die Zusammenfassung des Gesetzes in dem einen Begierdeverbot [sc. in Röm 7,7] gewinnt ihre Logik aufgrund einer jüdischen Tradition, derzufolge von der Begierde die Tatsünden ausgehen«. Belege: 1Kor 10,6; 1Thess 4,15; Jak 1,15; Philo, decal. 173; Philo, spec.leg. IV,84; ApkMos 19,3.

[799] Vgl. unten zu Jak 1,25.

[800] Dazu C. SPICQ, NLNT Supplément, OBO 22 / 3, Fribourg / Göttingen 1982, 674–691.

[801] »Auch nur ein« ist im Deutschen hinzugefügt.

[802] Eine deutlichere Übersetzung wäre: »mit Absicht, intentional«.

[803] Philo, spec.leg. IV 179–181: Erstlingsgabe.

einzelnen Minuskeln. **V. 18** mehrere Minuskeln lesen εποιησεν statt απεκυησεν (stilistische Vereinfachung).

Auf die Warnung folgt die ex negativo umschreibende Belehrung (»Irrt nicht«) über die Gaben Gottes. Auffallend ist der Stil der *Umschreibung*: »Gott« wird nicht genannt. Ebenso fehlt jeder explizite Hinweis auf jüdische oder frühchristliche Vorstellungen. Damit entsteht ein kurzer theologischer Text in philosophierend-ethisierender Sprache und hohem Stil. Das literarische Bemühen ist deutlich.

V. 16 Die Neuanrede leitet einen eigenständigen Gedanken ein, nicht aber schon ein neues Thema.[804] Der Verfasser schließt das Thema der πειρασμοί positiv ab, indem er von den Gefahren, die aus dem Menschen selbst hervorgehen, fortlenkt und stattdessen *erstens* auf die gute Gabe, die von Gott kommt, hinweist. *Zweitens* versichert er den Adressaten, sie seien »die Erstlinge von Gottes Geschöpfen«. Die gebräuchliche Wendung[805] »Irrt nicht«[806] aus der literarischen und epistolographischen Kommunikation dient gleichermaßen der Textgliederung wie der Belehrung und Ermahnung. ἀγαπητοί als Zusatz zur Anrede »Brüder« intensiviert die kommunikative Beziehung zu den Adressaten.[807] Paulus benutzt zweimal diese Anrede: 1Kor 15,58 und Phil 4,1. »Geliebte« und »geliebte Brüder« sind Teil des frühchristlichen Soziolekts.

V. 17 Hier formuliert Jakobus den positiven theologischen Gedanken: Von Gott kommt alles Gute. Auf die sprachliche Formulierung dieser ebenso einfachen wie generalisierenden These verwendet der Verfasser besondere Sorgfalt.[808] Sie wird in einem Aussagesatz mit doppeltem, durch καί verbundenem Subjekt (Substantiv + Adjektiv, stilistische Variation) vorgetragen. Für das Prädikat greift der Verfasser zur sog. umschreibenden Konjugation[809]: Part. καταβαῖνον (die Abwärtsbewegung anzeigend) + ἐστιν. Dieser Verbkonstruktion sind in nicht eindeutiger Konstella-

---

[804] DIBELIUS, Jak, 129, weist richtig darauf hin, dass V. 17 f eine gewisse Selbständigkeit bewahren, was auf eine eigenständige Vergangenheit als Spruch hinweist. ALLISON, Jak, 264, möchte in 1,16 weniger eine »conclusion« als vielmehr eine »introduction« sehen. Allerdings bemerkt er die Uneindeutigkeit der Gliederungssignale und schlägt deshalb vor, V. 16 als »formula of transition« zu lesen. Von dem beherrschenden Thema der Rede von Gott her legt sich aber näher, V. 16–18 als Abschluss der ersten Texteinheit zu verstehen. – Zur Textgliederung von Jak vgl. die Einleitung.

[805] So bei Paulus 1Kor 6,9; 15,33; Gal 6,7. Auch 2Tim 3,13. πλανᾶσθαι, irren, noch Jak 5,19. BURCHARD, Jak, 75, spricht metaphorisch von »Kirchensprache« mit Hinweis auf Lk 21,8; 1Joh 3,7 und die Ignatiusbriefe.

[806] DIBELIUS, Jak, 129: Damit wird der (fehlende) Gedanke ergänzt: »Gott schickt nur Gutes und nichts Böses«.

[807] So auch 1,19; 2,5. Zu »Brüder« s. o. zu 1,2.

[808] POPKES, Jak, 120: »Die Wortwahl ist geradezu exquisit«.

[809] Vgl. auch 3,15 in einem thematisch verwandten Zusammenhang. Bei Paulus mehrfach (2Kor 9,12; Gal 4,24; auch Kol 2,23). Zur coniugatio periphrastica vgl. DBR, § 353: εἶναι mit Part. Präs. als Umschreibung des Ind. Präs. (§ 353.2a: »eine gewisse Emphase ... ist auch im NT bei der Umschreibung oft unverkennbar«, vgl. auch dort Anm. 7 zu Jak 1,17). Anders POPKES, Jak, 121 Anm. 108: Popkes löst das Partizip als nachgestellte Apposition auf.

tion[810] zwei Umstandsbestimmungen zugeordnet: ἄνωθέν (spatial)[811] und ἀπὸ τοῦ πατρὸς τῶν φώτων (auktorial). Die metaphorische Bestimmung »Vater der Lichter« wird durch einen mit einer Präposition eingeleiteten Relativsatz ergänzt. Auch der Relativsatz hat ein doppeltes Subjekt (stilistische Variation), dessen zweites Glied erweitert ist und aus dem Syntagma τροπῆς ἀποσκίασμα besteht (vorangestelltes Genitivobjekt). Die Sequenz: πᾶσα δόσις ἀγαθὴ καὶ πᾶν δώρημα τέλειον wird seit Benson und Baumgarten[812] als Hexameter gelesen.[813] Ob ein Zitat vorliegt, muss offenbleiben. Fest steht, dass der Satz mit großer sprachlicher Sorgfalt gestaltet ist. Dazu passt, dass Burchard die Verse 16–18 für »die theologisch grundlegende Stelle des Briefs« hält.[814] Wenn dies Urteil auch zu einseitig scheinen mag, verdienen doch V. 16–18 mit ihren verschiedenen Motiven auf jeden Fall besondere exegetische Aufmerksamkeit.

Das Thema der *Gabe* Gottes wurde bereits in 1,5 angesprochen: »Gott, der jedem gern (ἁπλῶς) gibt«. In V. 17 ist die Gabe-Thematik mit dem in V. 13–16 verhandelten Thema: »Woher kommt der πειρασμός?« verbunden. Es geht jetzt um die *guten* Gaben und ihre Herkunft von Gott. Das Motiv der guten Gabe wird doppelt ausgedrückt, wobei zwischen δόσις[815] und δώρημα[816] (Alliteration) – beide Substantive begegnen nur zweimal im NT – kein sachlicher Unterschied besteht, während τέλειον eine Steigerung von ἀγαθή ist.[817] Auch das Motiv des Vollkommenen ist bereits in 1,4 angesprochen. Die umschreibende Herkunftsbezeichnung »von oben«

---

[810] Die Verbindung »von oben herabkommend, vom Vater der Lichter« ist die plausibelste. Entscheidet man sich gegen die coniugatio periphrastica, erhält man: »jede Gabe … ist von oben, herabkommend vom Vater der Lichter«. Einen sachlichen Unterschied zwischen beiden Auflösungen gibt es nicht.

[811] Vgl. noch 3,15 für σοφία.

[812] G. Benson, A Paraphrase and Notes on the Seven commonly called Catholic Epistles, London 1749 (repr. 2012), 42 Anm. 17: »And this seems to have been an hexameter verse, quoted, by the apostle *James*, from some of the *Greek* poets.« B. hält es für möglich, dass der Apostel Jakobus griechische Dichter gelesen habe. S. J. Baumgarten, Auslegung des Briefes Jakobi, Halle 1750, 54: »Diese Worte machen einen völligen Hexameter der Scansion nach aus, woraus aber nicht geschlossen werden kan, daß dieselben aus einem alten griechischen Dichter genommen seyn«.

[813] Zu hellenistisch-jüdischer Hexameterdichtung vgl. Allison, Jak, 270 Anm. 105 (auch: Sib, Bücher 3 sowie z. T. 4 und 5). Ausführlich: F. Siegert, Einführung in die hellenistisch-jüdische Literatur, Berlin / Boston 2016, 483–512. Möglich ist eine Skandierung, die den 2. Versfuß: σις–α–γα als Tribrachys liest (drei kurze Betonungen). Vgl. Jónsson, James among the Classicists, 124–132, und die gründliche Untersuchung von George Hinge: G. Hinge, The Hexameter in James 1:17: Metrical Forms in Graeco-Roman Prose Literature Between Emulation and Quotation, in: »Who Was James«? 239–276 (»There can also be no doubt that an ancient reader would in fact recognize these words as a dactylic hexameter immediately. This is the metrical form most familiar to any speaker of ancient Greek«, 240).

[814] Es fehlen Einleitungsformel sowie bekannter Bezugstext. Daher muss es bei dem bewusst weitgefassten Urteil Dibelius' bleiben: »Daß Jakobus oder einer seiner Vorgänger hier zitiert oder einen geläufigen Vers ohne Kenntnis seiner Herkunft verwendet habe, darf als möglich gelten und entspricht auch dem Stil solcher Paränesen« (Dibelius, Jak, 130). Siehe auch schon Baumgarten (s. o.).

[815] Phil 4,15 und Jak 1,17 (hap. leg. in Jak).

[816] Röm 5,16 und Jak 1,17 (hap. leg. in Jak).

[817] Noch Jak 3,17 (»gute Früchte« der Weisheit).

begegnet später noch einmal für die Weisheit in 3,15.17.[818] καταβαίνειν[819] wird sehr häufig im Zusammenhang in kosmologisch-apokalyptisch-epiphaniehaft-pneumatischen Zusammenhängen verwendet.[820] Erstere sind hier nicht im Spiel. Die kosmologisch-theologische Metapher »Vater der Lichter«[821] ist dagegen stilistisch exquisit und ohne Parallele.[822] Sachlich verbindet sie bekannte Elemente gemeinantiker und alttestamentlicher Gottesvorstellungen: den Schöpfer als Vater der Menschen und die Schöpfung als Gabe, mit der Lichtmetapher, die ihrerseits sowohl auf die Schöpfung[823] als auch auf den Himmel verweist und mit den Bestimmungen »von oben« und »herabsteigen« zusammen gelesen werden muss.

Der präpositional angeschlossene Relativsatz benutzt noch einmal die *variatio* des zweiteiligen Subjekts und dient der zusätzlichen steigernden Bestimmung der Metapher »Vater der Lichter«. Sachlich betont der Relativsatz die Unwandelbarkeit Gottes. Die sprachliche Auflösung ist umstritten. Schon die Abschreiber hatten Schwierigkeiten mit dem Wortlaut.[824] Folgt man dem textkritischen Vorschlag der ECM und übersetzt »bei dem nicht ist Veränderung oder ein Schatten des Wandels«, so erhält man einen stilistisch ambitionierten Text – die drei neutestamentlichen hapax legomena παραλλαγή[825], τροπή[826] und ἀποσκίασμα[827] sind hier verbunden –, der das Gottesprädikat »unwandelbar« durch die Verneinung der fast bedeutungsgleichen Substantive von τροπή und παραλλαγή ausdrückt (*variatio*) – letzteres Substantiv durch vorangestelltes ἀποσκίασμα verstärkt. Umstritten bleibt, ob das doppelte Subjekt insgesamt im Kontext der Lichtmetaphorik der Bezugsmetapher »Vater der Lichter« als astronomische Metapher zu verstehen ist *oder* ob lediglich ἀποσκίασμα metaphorisch zur Beschreibung einer geringen Größe verwendet wird und letztlich eine weitere Spielart der Verneinung (οὐκ) darstellt. Im ersten Fall würde der Verfasser bei τροπή und παραλλαγή an den Wandel der Gestirne denken, und ἀποσκίασμα wäre der Schatten, den die Gestirne bei ihrem Wandel werfen.[828] Das logische Verhältnis zwischen »Vater der Lichter« und der Wandel-Metapher

---

[818] Die Umschreibung steht für Gott und ist literarischer Stilzug.

[819] Hap. leg. in Jak. Vgl. aber 3,15: ἡ σοφία ἄνωθεν κατερχομένη.

[820] Joh, Apk.

[821] »Vater« statt »Schöpfer«, »Lichter« statt »Licht« für Gestirne (Plural äußerst selten: BURCHARD, Jak, 75). Zum Thema P. VAN DER HORST, Art. Father of the Lights, DDD, Leiden 1995, 620f; C. ZIMMERMANN, Die Namen des Vaters. Studien zu ausgewählten neutestamentlichen Gottesbezeichnungen, Leiden / Boston 2011 [= Die Namen des Vaters. Studien zu ausgewählten neutestamentlichen Gottesbezeichnungen in ihrem frühjüdischen und paganen Sprachhorizont, AGJU 69, Leiden 2007], 149–151. Zimmermann sieht in Jak 1 die Nähe zur »griechischen kosmologischen Vatervorstellung« (149).

[822] BURCHARD, Jak, 76: »hoher Stil«.

[823] Sonne und Mond als »Lichter« (φωστῆρες). Gen 1,14–19: vierter Schöpfungstag; Ps 135,7LXX.

[824] S. Textkritik.

[825] LSJ, 1316: »transmission, change«. Auch im astronomischen Zusammenhang gebraucht.

[826] LSJ, 1826: »turn, change«. Im Plural meist im Zusammenhang mit den Gestirnen gebraucht.

[827] Sehr selten. LSJ, 217: »shadow«.

[828] So LSJ, 217: »A shadow cast by turning«. LSJ denkt an den Wandel der Gestirne, durch den Schatten erzeugt wird. Im astronomischen Sinn interpretiert ALLISON, Jak, 274–278.

188 Kommentar

wäre konträr: Gott als Herr der Gestirne wäre gerade dem Wandel der Gestirne in keiner Weise unterworfen. Im zweiten Fall hätte nur das zweite Subjekt ἀποσκίασμα metaphorische Qualität im Sinne des Diminuierenden[829], während die Substantive für Wandel / Wechsel keine metaphorische Bedeutung hätten und der Relativsatz im Ganzen nicht der Lichtmetaphorik zugehören würde. Das doppelte Subjekt »Wandel und Veränderung« wäre nicht metaphorisch auf die Gestirne hin zu lesen, sondern theologisch auf Gott selbst bezogen. Das Verhältnis zum Bezugsbegriff »Vater der Lichter« wäre komplementär: Gott ist Schöpfer und unwandelbar. Beide Auflösungen von V. 17 sind sprachlich möglich. Die zweite Variante ist vorzuziehen, weil offenbar der Akzent auf dem Gedanken des Unwandelbaren liegt – durch doppeltes Substantiv hervorgehoben –, was der Gestirnmetaphorik widerspricht.

Dass Gott unwandelbar sei, gehört zu den theologischen Grundüberzeugungen des antiken Judentums. Es genügt hier, auf die Schrift Philos zum Thema »Quod deus sit immutabilis« hinzuweisen[830], in der Philo anhand von Gen 6,5–7[831] ausführlich die falsche Meinung einiger Menschen widerlegt, Gott habe seine Meinung über die Menschen geändert: »Denn was könnte es für einen größeren Frevel geben als zu glauben, der Unveränderliche könne sich ändern?«[832]

V. 18 Dieser Satz richtet wieder den Blick auf Gottes Gabe (ἀπαρχή) und verbindet abschließend Gott und die Adressaten. Nicht genanntes Subjekt des Satzes ist *Gott*: »Willentlich hat *er* uns geboren«. Das Prädikat nimmt die Vatermetapher von V. 17 auf, indem sie in der Geburtsmetapher auf die Adressaten angewendet wird: »Wir« sind Kinder Gottes. Die Wendung zu den Adressaten wird in dem erweiterten Infinitiv vertieft: »damit wir eine Art Erstlingsgabe seiner Geschöpfe seien«. Der Satz ist stilistisch ebenso anspruchsvoll wie V. 17. Der Verfasser verwendet eine Metaphernüberlagerung: Kollektive Schöpfungs-[833] und Kultelemente (Erstlingsgabe seiner Geschöpfe) werden mit der individuellen Geburtsmetapher verbunden. Dabei ist die Wendung »er hat uns geboren« in sich *doppelt* metaphorisch: (1) der Vater gebiert statt der Mutter, (2) der Geburtsvorgang steht metaphorisch für die Aufnahme in die Christus-bekennende Gemeinde.

---

[829] So mit Burchard, Jak, 76 f, mit Hinweis auf Kyrill Alex., ep. 39 (PG 77, 1859, col. 180) und andere antike Parallelen zur Wendung »ein Schatten von etwas«. »Schatten« steht hier für eine starke Minderung, die zum Verschwinden einer Größe tendiert.

[830] Philo, imm. 20–32. Vgl. auch leg.all. II 89: Man vertraut Gott, »wenn man erfährt, dass alles andere sich wandelt und Gott allein unwandelbar ist« (μόνος δὲ αὐτὸς ἄτρεπτός ἐστι). Weitere Belege aus Philo bei Allison, Jak, 278 Anm. 159.

[831] Ἀπαλείψω τὸν ἄνθρωπον, ὃν ἐποίησα, ἀπὸ προσώπου τῆς γῆς (Ich werde den Menschen, den ich geschaffen habe, vom Angesicht der Erde hinwegnehmen).

[832] Quod deus sit immutabilis (τὸν ἄτρεπτον τρέπεσθαι). Zum Thema bei Philo: W. Maas, Unveränderlichkeit Gottes. Zum Verhältnis von griechisch-philosophischer und christlicher Gotteslehre, PaThSt 1, München u. a. 1974, 87–124. Zu Jak 1,17 ebd. 28–30. Maas übersetzt: »bei dem es keine Veränderung gibt und keinen Schatten *durch* Wendung«. Maas löst also die Metapher im astronomischen Sinn auf. An der Bedeutung: »Gott ist ohne Veränderung« ändert sich nichts. – Vgl. auch Röm 11,2: für Paulus ist es undenkbar, dass Gott sein Volk, das er erwählt hat, verstoßen könnte.

[833] Vgl. Jak 3,9: dort deutliche Anspielung auf Gen 1,27.

ἀποκύω ist ein sehr seltenes Verb aus dem »gewählte(n)« Wortschatz.[834] »Geburt«
ist hier positiv konnotiert im Gegensatz zu der negativen Konnotation in 1,15. Ob
hier metaphorisch die Taufe umschrieben ist, bleibt offen. Metzner bemerkt richtig:

> Vermutlich hat Jakobus das im NT nur bei ihm belegte Verb in Opposition zu ἀποκύειν
> θάνατον (1,15) selbständig auf Gott übertragen, um deutlich zu machen, dass Gott
> nicht Tod, sondern Leben erschafft.[835]

Eine explizite Bezugnahme auf die Motive von Wiedergeburt oder Taufe hat Jakobus hier vermieden. Der frühchristliche Taufsoziolekt scheint aber durch die
Geburtsmetapher[836] und die Wendung »Wort der Wahrheit« hindurch. Zudem bezieht sich das »wir« auf die Adressaten und den Autor, also auf die Christus-gläubige
Gemeinde. Zwei Ergänzungen treten zu der Geburtsmetapher hinzu: »willentlich«[837]
und »durch das Wort der Wahrheit«, d. h. durch die christliche Predigt.[838] Diese
Motive sind Bestandteil der antiken jüdischen und der frühchristlichen Gottesvorstellung: Gott handelt willentlich[839], Gott schafft durch das Wort, bei Gott ist
die Wahrheit. Jak 1,18 stellt diese Elemente der Gotteslehre mit einer anthropologischen Bestimmung – die Menschen sind Geschöpfe – zusammen. Die Infini-
tivkonstruktion (Präposition mit Acc.c.Inf.[840]) enthält die weitere Metapher der
Erstlingsgabe, bezogen auf »die Geschöpfe« und durch τινα leicht relativiert. Die
ἀπαρχή als Erstlingsgabe, die der Gottheit geweiht war, ist eine »Kultmetapher«[841],
die die besondere Wertschätzung ausdrückt und sowohl in der paganen wie frühjüdischen und frühchristlichen Literatur jeweils auf die eigene Gruppierung bezogen
werden kann.[842] Das beste Beispiel findet sich bei Philo in De Specialibus Legibus IV 180, bezogen auf das Volk Israel:

> Dennoch (ist das Volk nicht verlassen, denn) mit seiner Verweisung und Verarmung
> hat, wie Moses sagt, Erbarmen und Mitleid der Herrscher der Welt, dem es ange-
> hört, weil es wie eine Art Erstlingsgabe des ganzen Menschengeschlechts dem Schöpfer
> und Vater zugewiesen wurde (διότι τοῦ σύμπαντος ἀνθρώπων γένους ἀπενεμήθη οἷά τις
> ἀπαρχὴ τῷ ποιητῇ καὶ πατρί).

---

834 Im NT nur noch Jak 1,15. C. M. Edsman, Schöpferwille und Geburt Jac 1,18, ZNW 38, 1939, 11–44;
Burchard, Jak, 77. Vgl. Spicq, NLNT I, 134–136.

835 Metzner, Jak, 87.

836 Deutlicher Joh 3,3–7 (»Neue Geburt«).

837 Part. Aor. von βούλομαι: geläufig für »wollen« (auch Jak 3,4; 4,4).

838 Frühchristlicher Soziolekt aus der paulinischen Briefliteratur: ἡ ἀλήθεια τοῦ θεοῦ Röm 3,7; 15,8; ἐν λόγῳ
ἀληθείας 2Kor 6,7; Eph 1,13; Kol 1,5 ἐν τῷ λόγῳ τῆς ἀληθείας τοῦ εὐαγγελίου; 2Tim 2,15. Bei Jak noch 3,14 und
5,19. Vgl. L. Bigoni u. a., Art. ἀλήθεια κτλ., HTLS I, 513–554.

839 Gottes Wille: Philo, opif. 16. Weitere Belege bei Metzner, Jak, 86.

840 DBR, § 402f.

841 Burchard, Jak, 79. Vgl. J. K. Driesbach, Art. ἀπαρχή, HTLS I, 865–878 (876 zu Philo-Belegen zu
der Metapher der Erstlingsfrüchte).

842 Hap. leg. in Jak. Öfter bei Paulus. In Röm 16,5; 1Kor 16,15 als Ehrentitel für Erstbekehrte verwendet. In
2Thess 2,13 und Apk 14,4 für Christen gebraucht.

190   Kommentar

Der Zusatz »seiner Geschöpfe«[843] bindet die Metapher an die Gabe-Thematik zurück. Gott der Schöpfer hat die »Brüder« gleichsam als Erstlinge geboren, so dass sie nun die Erstlingsgabe der Geschöpfe sind und ihm in besonderer Weise angehören. Der Satz legt durchgehend den Schleier der Metaphorik über das Gemeinte. Weder Gott noch Menschen noch die Mitglieder der christlichen Gemeinden noch die christliche Verkündigung werden explizit genannt. Die Metaphorik dient nicht nur der stilistischen Überhöhung. Zugleich schafft sie so etwas wie eine theologische Tiefendimension, die die Adressaten mit einem religiösen Nimbus umgibt.

B. 1,19–27: Belehrung über den richtigen Umgang mit dem Wort

1,19–27 bilden den zweiten thematischen Teiltext von Teil 1, der deutlich kürzer als die erste Einheit ausfällt und in dem verhältnismäßig kleinteiliger argumentiert wird. *Thema ist »das Wort«.* Jakobus wechselt nun explizit in den Modus der Belehrung. Drei verschiedene Aspekte des Themas λόγος sind hier gebündelt: die christliche Verkündigung, die Art und Weise des Redens in der Gemeinde und das Handeln nach dem Wort. Es geht um die richtige Disposition *für* das Wort (V. 19–21) und den richtigen (V. 22–25) sowie den falschen Umgang *mit* dem Wort (V. 26–27). Wie in der ersten thematischen Einheit greifen theologische Aussagen und ethische Belehrung ineinander. Der Text setzt belehrend ein: »Wisst, meine lieben Brüder« (V. 19) und schließt mit einer theologisch-ethischen Definition (V. 27 θρησκεία … αὕτη ἐστίν). Das Thema des λόγος, in V. 18 bereits vorgegeben, wird gleichzeitig ethisch (V. 19) und theologisch (V. 21) entfaltet und anschließend in zwei Ansätzen konkretisiert (V. 22–25 und 26–27), indem zwei Fallbeispiele aufgerufen werden: jemand, der nur »Hörer des Wortes ist« (V. 23), und jemand, »der seine Zunge nicht im Zaum hält« (V. 26). Die Fallbeispiele verbinden jeweils ein negatives und ein positives *exemplum* (V. 25 und V. 27). Verbindender Hintergrund zwischen 1,1–18 (»Wort der Wahrheit«) und 1,19 ff (»Täter des Wortes«) ist letztlich die Intention, die Christus-gläubigen Lehrer zu erziehen (3,1). Die abschließende Definition in V. 27 leitet schon zum nächsten Thema, dem Verhalten im Gottesdienst, über.

1. Texteinheit: 1,19–21 Belehrung über das richtige Sprechen

(19) **Wisst, meine geliebten Brüder: es sei aber jeder Mensch schnell zum Hören, langsam zum Sprechen, langsam zum Zorn; (20) denn der Zorn des Mannes bewirkt nicht die Gerechtigkeit, die bei Gott gilt[844]. (21) Deshalb legt alle Unsauber-**

---

[843] κτίσμα hap. leg. in Jak. Für »Geschöpf« sehr selten im NT: 1Tim 4,4 (»Jedes Geschöpf Gottes ist gut«); Apk 5,13; 8,9.
[844] Gen. als obj. aufgelöst.

C. Briefcorpus

keit[845] **und den Überfluss der Bosheit ab und in Sanftmut das euch**[846] **eingepflanzte Wort an, das eure Seelen retten kann.**

Textkritik: **V. 19a** Der Anfang des Satzes ist unterschiedlich überliefert. P74. 02 und einige Minuskeln schreiben ιστε δε (Glättung mit besserem Anschluss zum vorangehenden Abschnitt). 025. 044 und zahlreiche Minuskeln lesen ὥστε ἀδελφοί μου, das ebenfalls als Verstärkung des Anschlusses gelten darf. **V. 19b** Das im Anschluss schwierige εστω δε (δε hier logisch überflüssig) wird von den qualitativ besten Zeugen 01. 03. 04. 025* und von Minuskeln bezeugt. Das passendere εστω ist durch 025C. 044 und sehr viele Minuskeln bezeugt. Der Lakonismus ταχυς εις το ακουσαι, βραδυς εις το λαλησαι wird von P74V und wenigen Minuskeln vertreten. Wenige Minuskeln fügen δε bzw. και hinzu. L422 liest ποιησαι statt λαλησαι. **V. 20** 01. 02. 03. 04C3. 018. 044 und sehr viele Minuskeln lesen ουκ εργαζεται (bessere Bezeugung), während 04*. 025. 0246 und sehr viel Minuskeln ου κατεργαζεται haben (»Neigung zum Kompositum«, Dibelius, Jak, 141; vgl. Jak 1,3). **V. 21** υμων lesen P74. 01. 02. 03. 04. 025. 044 und zahlreiche Minuskeln (bessere Bezeugung). ημων (lectio difficilior) lesen 020. 049. 056 und zahlreiche Minuskeln. 025 fügt zu πραυτητι noch σοφιας hinzu.

Die erste Texteinheit warnt vor dem Zorn und ruft zur Sanftmut auf, mit der das »eingepflanzte Wort« aufgenommen werden soll. Es geht dem Verfasser zunächst darum, die Emotion des Zornes zu kontrollieren und eine psychologische Kultur der Demut, πραΰτης, unter den angesprochenen Adressaten herzustellen.

V. 19 Das Ἴστε, ἀδελφοί setzt einen Neuanfang[847] und bestätigt zugleich die briefliche Kommunikation.[848] Ἴστε kann indikativisch oder imperativisch gemeint sein. Im Zusammenhang mit V. 16 und 22 legt sich die Imperativform nahe.[849] Den Inhalt dessen, was die Adressaten wissen sollen, bildet eine dreigliedrige, formal gleich gebaute Verhaltensregel: Adjektiv mit präpositional eingeleitetem substantiviertem finalem Infinitiv[850], zum Thema: Hören, Reden, Zorn. Die Einleitung mit δέ ist textkritisch gut bezeugt, scheint logisch aber sperrig. Dibelius schlägt vor, das δέ sei aus einem »älteren Zusammenhang« des Spruches zu erklären. Damit wäre ein solcher älterer Spruch aber gerade unselbständig gewesen, was unwahrscheinlich ist. Burchard liest dagegen das δέ als Unterstützung des Imperativs ἔστω.[851]

Die Mahnung zu aufmerksamem Zuhören, verbunden mit der Warnung vor (zu) schneller sprachlicher und emotionaler Reaktion ›im Zorn‹, ist konventionell-gemeinantik. Beispiele finden sich seit der Weisheitsliteratur des Alten Ägypten über-

---

[845] Spicq, NLNT II, 784f.

[846] »Euch« im Deutschen hinzugefügt.

[847] Vgl. Dibelius, Jak, 143.

[848] Ἴστε noch Hebr 12,17 (dort indikativisch). An das Wissen der Adressaten appelliert der Verfasser auch 3,1; 4,4.17.

[849] Vgl. DBR, § 99,2.

[850] Vgl. DBR, § 402,2. Die dritte Einheit ist substantivisch verknappt formuliert (ὀργή).

[851] Burchard, Jak, 81. Allerdings schlägt er auch vor, das δέ als gegen die Negation in V. 16 gesetzt zu verstehen (DBR, § 447,1), der Abstand zwischen beiden Sätzen scheint aber zu groß zu sein. Allison, Jak, 296, weist darauf hin, dass δέ nicht »adversative« sein muss, sondern im Jak öfter »continuative or transitional character« habe.

all: »Die ganze alte Welt … mahnt, zuzuhören … und wenig oder überlegt zu reden«.[852] Die Mahnung richtet sich an »jeden Menschen«[853] und ist zunächst nicht auf den Umgang mit bestimmten »Worten« wie der Tora oder der frühchristlichen Verkündigung (V. 18) bezogen[854], sondern dient als allgemein akzeptierte Basis der spezifischeren Mahnung in V. 21. Die letzte der drei Mahnungen, langsam zum Zorn zu sein, wird in V. 20 fortgesetzt, so dass die Verse 19 und 20 als zusammenhängende Aussage des Verfassers zum Thema ὀργή kommentiert werden müssen. Die Adressaten von V. 19 sind entsprechend der allgemeinen Mahnung ebenfalls bewusst allgemein gehalten: Die Regeln gelten für »jeden Menschen«.[855] Das trifft auch für V. 20 zu. Erst in V. 21 zieht der Verfasser die Konsequenzen für seine Adressaten und kehrt zur 2. Pers. Plur. zurück.

V. 19 fällt also nicht durch thematische Originalität, wohl aber durch geschliffenen Stil auf. Derartige gleichgebaute Triaden sind in der antiken jüdischen Literatur beliebt.[856] Sie finden sich ebenso auch bei Lukian und Dion Chrysostomos.[857] Gnomische Sätze halb definitorischen, halb pädagogischen Charakters, die auf Fragen antworten, begegnen in pädagogisch-paränetischen Zusammenhängen, wie sie prominent in den ›Protokollen‹ des Gelehrtengastmahls im Aristeasbrief vorliegen. König Ptolemaios stellt den jüdischen Übersetzern Fragen aus den Bereichen der Regierungskunst und der Ethik. Die Weisen antworten jeweils mit einem geschliffenen Satz.[858] Folker Siegert weist darauf hin, dass die Antworten inhaltlich durch »pure Ethik mit sehr wenig Politik dabei und noch weniger Theologie« gekennzeichnet sind.[859] Eben dies Profil findet sich in Jak 1,19. Jak spielt auch mit dem Gegensatz ταχύς[860] und βραδύς (zweimalige Setzung: Anapher).[861]

V. 20 Dieser Satz, durch Stichwortanschluss mit V. 19 verbunden, enthält eine theologisch vertiefte Begründung zu V. 19. Ob damit auch ein Indiz dafür vorliegt, dass V. 19 Zitatcharakter hat oder mindestens – wie Dibelius will – ein überlieferter Weisheitsspruch ist, kann offenbleiben.[862] Die Warnung vor dem Zorn als einem

---

[852] BURCHARD, Jak, 81. So auch ALLISON, Jak, 295: »Transparently good advice, presumably not news to the readers«. Reiches Parallelenmaterial bei BURCHARD, Jak, 81, und ALLISON, Jak, 296–300. DIBELIUS, Jak, 141, weist besonders auf die frühjüdisch-weisheitlichen Appelle zum Hören hin: Sir 5,11 u. ö. und Av 5,12. Eine schlagende Parallele aus dem paganen Bereich: Lukian, Demonax 51: »Einem, der fragte, wie er am besten herrsche, sagte er: Ohne Zorn und wenig redend, aber viel zuhörend«.

[853] ἄνθρωπος bei Jak: 1,7 (siehe dort).19; 2,20.24; 3,8.9; 5,17. Die Wendung »jeder Mensch« auch in Röm 3,4.

[854] Vgl. DIBELIUS, Jak, 141; ALLISON, Jak, 301f. Deutlich ist aber der formale Stichwortanschluss von V. 18 zu V. 19 (λόγῳ ἀληθείας und λαλῆσαι).

[855] DBR, § 275,3 (= »jeder beliebige« Mensch, d. h. »alle« Menschen).

[856] DIBELIUS, Jak, 142f.

[857] Zu Lukian s. oben. Außerdem Dion Chrysostomos, or. XXXII 2. Bei Dion findet sich auch die Zusammenstellung von Hören, Reden und Zorn (s. BURCHARD, Jak, 81).

[858] Dazu einführend F. SIEGERT, Einführung, 473f (Lit.).

[859] SIEGERT, Einführung, 473.

[860] Das Adjektiv ist hap. leg. im NT.

[861] Hap. leg. in Jak. Noch Lk 24,25.

[862] Diese Annahme ist nicht nötig, wie die Belege aus Lukian und Dion Chrysostomos zeigen.

ungerechten Verhalten steht nicht im Zentrum neutestamentlicher Paränese. Sie findet sich aber Eph 4,31; Kol 3,8; 1Tim 2,8, verbal mit ὀργίζομαι ausgedrückt auch Mt 5,22[863]; Eph 4,26 (Ps 4,5LXX). Ihren ursprünglichen Sitz hat die Warnung vor dem Zorn in der Weisheitsliteratur: Sir 1,22; Spr 15,1[864], die insgesamt ein Ethos der Zurückhaltung, Vorsicht und Selbstbeherrschung vertritt. ὀργὴ ἀνδρὸς: ἀνήρ wird wie ἄνθρωπος (Jak 1,19: variatio) in weisheitlicher Diktion gern in allgemeinen Sentenzen benutzt.[865]

Die auffallende Wendung δικαιοσύνην θεοῦ οὐ κατεργάζεται ist im Zusammenhang der V. 19.20 als stilistisch anspruchsvolle Umschreibung für die Aussage: »Zorn macht niemanden bei Gott gerecht« zu verstehen.[866] ἐργάζεσθαι bewirken, tun[867], mit δικαιοσύνη findet sich auch in Apg 10,35[868] und Hebr 11,33.[869] Dort wie hier in Jak 1,20 wird δικαιοσύνη als bekannt und selbsterklärend vorausgesetzt. In 3,18 wählt der Verfasser die Metapher »Frucht der δικαιοσύνη« in einem ethischen Kontext.[870] In diesem Kontext steht auch 1,20.[871] Dibelius schließt daher zurecht aus, dass in Kap. 1 paulinische Theologie im Sinne seiner Interpretation der δικαιοσύνη θεοῦ von Röm 4,1–8 vorliege, räumt aber ein, es sei denkbar, »daß die Formulierung des Paulus, völlig im Sinn verkehrt und verflacht, als gemeinchristliches Losungswort für ein im eigentlichen Sinn ›gerechtes‹ Leben hier wieder auftaucht«.[872] Zwei Aspekte müssen auf jeden Fall festgehalten werden: *Erstens* machen die genannten Beispiele deutlich, dass die Wendung »Gerechtigkeit tun bzw. bewirken« im antiken Judentum[873] und im frühen Christentum bekannt ist und den Status des richtigen Lebens vor Gott benennt. *Zweitens* wird in Kap. 2 das Gerechtigkeitsthema im Zusammenhang der Glaube-Werke-Thematik und der Abrahamstheologie theo-

---

[863] Besonders radikal: »Jeder, der seinem Bruder zürnt, ist des Gerichtes schuldig«. Zur Gesamtthematik der Emotionen und zu ὀργή als destruktiver Emotion: F. Mirguet, The Study of Emotions in Early Jewish Texts: Review and Perspectives, JSJ 50, 2019, 1–47, und O. Wischmeyer, Emotionen als formative Elemente neutestamentlicher Ethik am Beispiel des Paulus, Journal of Ethics in Antiquity and Christianity 2, 2020, 25–39.

[864] Vgl. H. Kleinknecht u. a., Art ὀργή, ThWNT 5, 1954, 382–448, 395.414; A. Wagner, Emotionen in alttestamentlicher und verwandter Literatur – Grundüberlegungen am Beispiel des Zorns, in: R. Egger-Wenzel / J. Corley (Hg.), Emotions from Ben Sira to Paul, DCLY 2011, Berlin / Boston 2012, 27–68.

[865] Jak 1,8.12.20.23; 2,2; 3,2.

[866] Die Unterscheidung zwischen forensischer und ethischer Interpretation von δικαιοσύνη θεοῦ ist hier künstlich (dazu Metzner, Jak, 92 f).

[867] Das Verb nur hier in Jak, das Substantiv ἔργον dagegen häufig.

[868] ἐν παντὶ ἔθνει ὁ φοβούμενος αὐτὸν καὶ ἐργαζόμενος δικαιοσύνην δεκτὸς αὐτῷ ἐστιν (In jedem Volk – wer ihn fürchtet und Gerechtigkeit tut, ist ihm willkommen): aus der Rede des Petrus in Cäsarea.

[869] οἳ διὰ πίστεως κατηγωνίσαντο βασιλείας, εἰργάσαντο δικαιοσύνην (Diese haben durch den Glauben Königreiche bezwungen, Gerechtigkeit getan), Subjekt: die Propheten.

[870] S. u. zur Stelle.

[871] Ähnlich Joh 6,28 fragen die Leute: τί ποιῶμεν ἵνα ἐργαζώμεθα τὰ ἔργα τοῦ θεοῦ (Was sollen wir tun, damit wir die Werke Gottes tun?); 1Kor 16,10: Timotheus τὸ γὰρ ἔργον κυρίου ἐργάζεται (Er tut nämlich das Werk des Herrn). Vgl. Apk 22,11 ὁ δίκαιος δικαιοσύνην ποιησάτω (Der Gerechte wird Gerechtigkeit tun).

[872] Dibelius, Jak, 142.

[873] Ps 14,2LXX: πορευόμενος ἄμωμος καὶ ἐργαζόμενος δικαιοσύνην (der ohne Tadel wandelt und Gerechtigkeit tut).

194 Kommentar

logisch diskutiert: 2,21 (Verb).23 (Substantiv: Gen 15,6[874]).24.25 (Verb). Jak 1,19.20 warnt lediglich vor dem Zorn.

V. 21 Jakobus zieht hier den Schluss aus dem in V. 19 Gesagten und gibt eine allgemeine Anwendung auf das Leben der Adressaten, wieder theologisch vertieft. Der Appell an die Adressaten, mit dem Imp.2.Pers.Pl. von δέχεσθαι[875], annehmen, formuliert, betrifft ihre innere Haltung, nicht ihre Handlungen. Die vorangestellte Partizipialkonstruktion arbeitet mit dem konträren Verb: ἀποτίθεσθαι, ablegen.[876] Auch hier geht es um innere Haltungen, nicht um Handlungen. Gezielt wird auf die Seelen (ψυχαί[877]) der Adressaten. Zu einer spezifischen Konzeption von ψυχή finden sich bei Jak keine Hinweise. Im Kontext geht es um das jetzige Leben der Adressaten und um ihre Haltung sowie ihr Verhalten.

Welche Haltung will der Verfasser bewirken? *Negativ*: den Verzicht auf ῥυπαρία[878] (Unsauberkeit) und κακία (Bosheit)[879]. ῥυπαρία ist im übertragenen, ethischen Sinn gebraucht. Wieder fällt die anspruchsvolle Diktion auf: Der Verfasser arbeitet hier mit ausgefallenen Begriffen. περισσεία verwendet Paulus einige Male in gehobenen sprachlichen Zusammenhängen. In der Parallele in 1Petr 2,1 heißt es einfach πᾶσα κακία, bei Jakobus sollen die Adressaten dagegen περισσείαν κακίας ablegen.[880] *Positiv*: der Verfasser rät zu πραΰτης (»Sanftmut, Freundlichkeit, Milde«)[881], einer inneren Tugend, die in Eph 4,2 und Kol 3,12 neben ταπεινοφροσύνη[882] erscheint.[883]

Das eigentliche Interesse des Verfassers liegt in dem Hauptsatz: »Nehmt das eingepflanzte Wort an«. Der Ausdruck ἔμφυτος λόγος knüpft an das Syntagma λόγος ἀληθείας[884] und die Geburtsmetapher von V. 18 an: Das Wort der Wahrheit, durch das die Adressaten Christen geworden – metaphorisch: geboren – sind, also die Predigt[885], ist ihnen eingepflanzt. Die Pflanzenmetapher tritt zur Geburtsmetapher.[886] Damit wird der Gabe-Charakter der Predigt verstärkt.[887] Wieder wählt der Autor mit dem Adjektiv ἔμφυτος eine exquisite Vokabel[888], die weniger beschreibt oder

---

[874] S. zu Kap. 2.

[875] Hap. leg. in Jak.

[876] Ebenfalls hap. leg. in Jak. Sehr selten im NT.

[877] Vgl. noch Jak 5,20: dieselbe Formulierung. Zum antiken Begriff: G. Karamanolis / F. Zanella, Art. Seele, RAC 30, 2021, 107–177.

[878] Hap. leg. im NT, nicht in LXX. Zum Substantiv vgl. Spicq, NLNT II, 784 f.

[879] Hap. leg. in Jak. Vgl. 1Petr 2,1: Ἀποθέμενοι οὖν πᾶσαν κακίαν (Legt nun alle Bosheit ab).

[880] Für Jak typisches Syntagma. περισσεία, »Überfluss«, hap. leg. in Jak. NT: Röm 5,14; 2Kor 8,2, 10,15.

[881] Bauer / Aland, 1401. Vgl. Spicq, NLNT Supplément, 570–582. Paulinisch-deuteropaulinischer ethischer Sprachgebrauch. Noch Jak 3,13.

[882] Substantiv nicht in Jak, vgl. aber 1,9 (s. o.); 4,6.10.

[883] Die Entgegensetzung von Zorn (V. 20) und Milde (V. 21) begegnet auch bei Josephus, ant. Iud. XIX 334. Vgl. Burchard, Jak, 83.

[884] Dibelius, Jak, 145, dagegen lehnt auch hier einen Rückbezug auf V. 18 ab.

[885] Bauer / Aland, 520: »Wort des Evangeliums«.

[886] Dazu von Gemünden, Vegetationsmetaphorik.

[887] So Allison, Jak, 309: the ›implanted word‹ »implicitly appears to be a divine gift«.

[888] Hap. leg. im NT. LXX: SapSal 12,10 ἔμφυτος ἡ κακία αὐτῶν (ihre Bosheit ist eingepflanzt). Barn 1,2 (Die

C. Briefcorpus 195

definiert[889], sondern vielmehr die religiöse Bedeutung des Gesagten schmückend steigert. Dass bei dieser Wendung eine deutliche *sprachliche* Nähe zu stoischer Terminologie vorliegt, ist offensichtlich. Wieweit diese Nähe beabsichtigt ist, muss offenbleiben. Auf jeden Fall spricht Jak an dieser Stelle nicht philosophisch, sondern benutzt frühchristlichen Soziolekt[890]: Die Wendung »das Wort *annehmen*« gehört zum frühchristlichen Soziolekt und wird im 1. Thessalonicherbrief[891] und im lukanischen Doppelwerk[892] für die Predigt Jesu und der Apostel verwendet. Dass es sich hier um frühchristliche Verkündigung handelt und nicht um den stoischen Vernunft-Logos[893], wird aus der häufig gesetzten Wendung der »Rettung[894] der Seelen« ebenso deutlich wie aus V. 22. Die mögliche Nähe zu stoischer Diktion lässt sich noch einmal bei 2,12 diskutieren.

Jak 1,18.21 wird immer wieder mit 1Petr 1,22–2,2 verglichen. Damit stellt sich die Frage von Abhängigkeit oder Tradition.

Jak 1,18: βουληθεὶς ἀπεκύησεν ἡμᾶς λόγῳ ἀληθείας εἰς τὸ εἶναι ἡμᾶς ἀπαρχήν τινα τῶν αὐτοῦ κτισμάτων.
Willentlich hat er uns geboren durch das Wort der Wahrheit, damit wir gleichsam die Erstlingsgabe seiner Geschöpfe seien.
1,21: διὸ ἀποθέμενοι πᾶσαν ῥυπαρίαν καὶ περισσείαν κακίας ἐν πραΰτητι δέξασθε τὸν ἔμφυτον λόγον τὸν δυνάμενον σῶσαι τὰς ψυχὰς ὑμῶν.
Deshalb legt alle Unsauberkeit und den Überfluss der Bosheit in Sanftmut ab, nehmt das euch eingepflanzte Wort an, das eure Seelen retten kann.

Gnade der Geistesgabe ist eingepflanzt) und 9,9 (die eingepflanzte Gabe seiner [Jesu] Lehre). Verb: 1Kor 3,6.7.8 auf den Aufbau der korinthischen Gemeinde bezogen.

[889] Vgl. BURCHARD, Jak, 83: »Es ist kein Fachwort«. Anders die in den Kommentaren zu findenden Überlegungen zu der sprachlich parallelen Wendung λόγος σπερματικός und philosophischen, besonders stoischen sog. Parallelen: vgl. ALLISON, Jak, 312–315, besonders die Belege in Anm. 175–179; monographisch M. A. JACKSON-MCCABE, Logos and Law in the Letter of James: The Law of Nature, the Law of Moses, and the Law of Freedom, NT.S 100, Leiden 2001. Jackson-McCabe findet eine spezifische Soteriologie in dem Ausdruck: »The soteriology of the Letter of James … has been woven from strands of tradition that derive from Jewish, Christian *and* Greek philosophical discourse« (27), wobei J. an die Stoa denkt (s. u. zu 1,25 und 2,12).

[890] Dazu VON GEMÜNDEN, Vegetationsmetaphorik, 226 ff.270 f.

[891] 1Thess 1,6; 2,13 (Und dadurch danken auch wir Gott unablässig, dass ihr das Wort der Predigt von Gott, das von uns kam, nicht als Wort von Menschen, sondern – wie es auch in Wahrheit ist – als Wort Gottes aufgenommen habt, das auch in euch, den Glaubenden, wirkt).

[892] δέχεσθαι: Lk 8,13; Apg 7,38; 8,14 und 11,1 (λόγος τοῦ θεοῦ) und 17,11.

[893] JACKSON-MCCABE, Law. Vgl. KLOPPENBORG, James, 106: »Matt Jackson-McCabe has offered a reading that makes sense of Jas 1:21. The ›implanted word‹ reflects a philosophical notion of law, originally ›implanted‹ by God in humanity«. H. NAYMAN, A written Copy of the Law of Nature: An unthinkable Paradox?, in: Past Renewals, Interpretative Authority, Renewed Revelation and the Quest for Perfection in Jewish Antiquity, JSJ.S 53, Leiden 2010, 107–118, weist darauf hin, dass Philo das eingepflanzte Wort mit dem Gesetz des Mose gleichsetzt. – Zur Vegetationsmetaphorik in der Stoa vgl. VON GEMÜNDEN, Vegetationsmetaphorik, 351 ff.

[894] σῴζειν »retten« im NT sehr häufig, auch im Zusammenhang mit ψυχή. Jak 2,14; 4,12; 5,15 und 5,20 (die Seele retten).

196 Kommentar

1 Petr 1,22 f: Τὰς ψυχὰς ὑμῶν ἡγνικότες ἐν τῇ ὑπακοῇ τῆς ἀληθείας εἰς φιλαδελφίαν ἀνυπόκριτον ἐκ καθαρᾶς καρδίας ἀλλήλους ἀγαπήσατε ἐκτενῶς (23) ἀναγεγεννημένοι οὐκ ἐκ σπορᾶς φθαρτῆς ἀλλ᾽ ἀφθάρτου διὰ λόγου ζῶντος θεοῦ καὶ μένοντος. (22) Da ihr eure Seelen gereinigt habt im Gehorsam der Wahrheit zu aufrichtiger Bruderliebe, liebt einander eifrig aus reinem Herzen, (23) die ihr wiedergeboren seid nicht aus vergänglichem, sondern aus unvergänglichem Samen durch das lebendige und bleibende Wort Gottes. (2,1) Ἀποθέμενοι οὖν πᾶσαν κακίαν καὶ πάντα δόλον καὶ ὑποκρίσεις καὶ φθόνους καὶ πάσας καταλαλιὰς (2) ὡς ἀρτιγέννητα βρέφη τὸ λογικὸν ἄδολον γάλα ἐπιποθήσατε, ἵνα ἐν αὐτῷ αὐξηθῆτε εἰς σωτηρίαν. (2,1) Legt also alle Bosheit und allen Betrug und Heuchelei und Neid und alle Verleumdung ab (2) und verlangt wie neugeborene Kinder die geistige, unverfälschte Milch, damit ihr in ihr zunehmt zum Heil.

Beide Texte teilen wesentliche Elemente: die Geburtsmetapher, das »Wort« (der Wahrheit bzw. Gottes), die Wahrheit (Wort der Wahrheit bzw. Gehorsam der Wahrheit), das Schema von Ablegen und Annehmen (bzw. Verlangen nach), von Abkehr von Bosheit (κακία) und der Rettung (σωτηρία) (der Seelen). Die Unterschiede liegen vor allem in der Diktion und in der stilistischen Gestaltung der Metaphern. Dass hinter Jak 1,21 und 1 Petr 2,1 die gemeinsame Tradition eines »postkonversionalen Mahnwortes« aufscheine, wie M. Konradt formuliert, ist möglich, aber nicht zu belegen.[895] Der Jakobusbrief profiliert sich durch eine eigenwillige Metaphorik (Gott hat die Adressaten geboren) und Terminologie (»eingepflanztes Wort«, »Erstlingsgabe der Geschöpfe«). Gegenseitige Abhängigkeiten bzw. zeitliche Vor- oder Nachordnung lassen sich nicht wahrscheinlich machen. Deutlich ist die Rücknahme frühchristlichen Soziolekts in Jak. Lorenzo Scornaienchi weist darauf hin, dass in 1,23 und 1,25 »Wort« und »Gesetz« parallel verwendet werden, und schließt daraus, dass »es sich [bei dem λόγος] um das *Gesetz* handelt und nicht um das gepredigte Evangelium«.[896] Es ist aber typisch für Jak, derartige exkludierende Alternativen gerade mittels einer metaphorisch-vieldeutigen Diktion zu vermeiden.

2. Texteinheit: 1,22–25 Erstes Fallbeispiel: Hörer des Wortes
(22) **Seid**[897] **aber Täter des Wortes und nicht allein Hörer – (Menschen), die sich selbst betrügen**[898]. (23) **Wenn nämlich jemand (nur**[899]**) Hörer des Wortes ist und**

---

[895] M. Konradt, Christliche Existenz nach dem Jakobusbrief, StUNT 22, Göttingen 1998, 75. Dazu Metzner, Jak, 96 mit Anm. 73.

[896] Scornaienchi, Polemik im Jakobusbrief, 349.

[897] γίνομαι als Ersatz für »sein«: Bauer / Aland, 316; DBR, § 339,1 zum Part. Aor: zeitlich unbestimmt ingressiv, komplexiv oder effektiv (vgl. Burchard, Jak, 69).

[898] Wörtlich: »Sich selbst Betrügende«.

[899] »Nur« im Deutschen hinzugefügt.

nicht (auch[900]) Täter, gleicht er[901] einem Mann, der sein eigenes Gesicht[902] im Spiegel betrachtet – (24) er betrachtete nämlich sich selbst und ging fort und vergaß sogleich, wie er aussah[903]. (25) Wer aber in das vollkommene Gesetz – das der Freiheit – hineinschaute und in ihm[904] beharrte, indem er nicht ein Hörer der Vergesslichkeit, sondern ein Täter des Werkes wurde, der wird selig in seinem Tun sein.

Textkritik: V. 22 Statt ποιηται λογου (P74. 01. 02. 03. 04* und zahlreiche Minuskeln) lesen 04C2 und zahlreiche Minuskeln ποιηται νομου (wohl Angleichung an 4,11 und / oder Röm 2,13; in 4,11 keine abweichende Lesart). Λογου lesen P74. 01. 02. 03. 04*. 025. 044, zahlreiche Minuskeln. του λογου lesen 049. 69. νομου (vgl. 4,11; Röm 2,13) lesen 04C2, zahlreiche Minuskeln (wohl Beeinflussung durch 4,11). μονον ακροαται lesen P74. 01. 02. 04. 025. 044, zahlreiche Minuskeln. ακροαται μονον ist lectio difficilior. V. 23 οτι lesen 01. 03. 04. 025. 044, zahlreiche Minuskeln. οτι fehlt in P74V. 02, Minuskel 33 und weitere Minuskeln. οτι ist besser bezeugt.

Vers 22 führt die Ansprache an die Adressaten in der 2. Pers. Plur. fort. V. 23–25 dienen der Begründung. Dabei verwendet Jakobus einen als Kurzerzählung gestalteten Vergleich. Dies erste Fallbeispiel lenkt von der psychologischen Kultur des λόγος der V. 19–21 (wieder Stichwortanschluss) zum Aspekt des Handelns, der dem Verfasser vor allem wichtig ist. Er ermahnt die Adressaten, ποιηταὶ λόγου zu sein – eine Devise des ganzen Briefes.

V. 22 Der Verfasser kommt mit V. 22 zu einem Zentrum seiner ethischen Botschaft: dem Tun. Er fasst seinen imperativisch formulierten Rat in eine wuchtige Alternative: die suggestive binäre Opposition von »Hörer« und »Täter«, die er dreimal setzt (V. 22. 23. 25). Das Verhältnis von Hören und Tun (Umsetzung des Gehörten) wird öfter in den überwiegend mündlichen Lehrkulturen der Antike und so auch in den frühchristlichen Schriften thematisiert und unterschiedlich gewichtet. So wird Maria als »Hörerin des Wortes« in Lk 10,38–42 gelobt. Andererseits warnt das Doppelgleichnis Lk 6,46–49par vor dem bloßen Hören ohne Tun. ἀκροατής begegnet außer im Jak nur noch Röm 2,13 im NT: οὐ γὰρ οἱ ἀκροαταὶ νόμου δίκαιοι παρὰ [τῷ] θεῷ, ἀλλ' οἱ ποιηταὶ νόμου δικαιωθήσονται[905], dort ebenfalls in demselben Gegensatzpaar mit ποιηταί[906] und mit derselben Betonung des Tuns. Hier sind Paulus und Jakobus derselben Meinung. Der theologische *Kontext* ist bei Paulus aber ein anderer: das Gesetz und die Gerechtigkeit nach dem Gesetz, während Ja-

---

[900] »Auch« im Deutschen hinzugefügt.

[901] Im Griechischen: »dieser«.

[902] Wörtlich: »das Gesicht seiner Herkunft«. τῆς γενέσεως wird hier mit »sein eigenes« übersetzt.

[903] Griechisch: »war«.

[904] »In ihm« ist im Deutschen hinzugefügt. Es könnte auch »dabei« ergänzt werden.

[905] Vgl. auch Philo, congr. 70: »Hörer des Wortes«; Josephus, ant. Iud. 5,107.132: »Hörer der Gesetze«.

[906] Auch dies Substantiv nur in Röm 2,13 (vgl. 1Makk 2,67: ὑμᾶς πάντας τοὺς ποιητὰς τοῦ νόμου, euch alle, die ihr Täter des Gesetzes seid) und Jak 1,22. 23. 25 und 4,11 (vgl. auch das ntl. hap. leg. ποίησις 1,25). Dagegen in Apg 17,28: »Dichter«.

kobus vom Wort und vom Werk spricht (V. 25).[907] *Sprachlich* steht die paulinische Formulierung auf jeden Fall im Hintergrund des Jakobustextes. Jakobus überträgt aber *theologisch* die paulinische Aussage über das Gesetz aus dem Römerbrief auf die christliche Botschaft und ihre Anwendung im Leben der Adressaten. Das unterscheidet Jakobus auch von Sirach. Sirach dichtete im Rahmen seiner Pädagogik:

καὶ οὖς ἀκροατοῦ ἐπιθυμία σοφοῦ.

Das Ohr des Hörers ist die Begierde des Weisen (d. h. der Weise begehrt Gehör bei seinen Schülern) Sir 3,29[32].[908]

Bei Jakobus geht es nicht um das Hören, sondern um das Tun des Gehörten. Die bloßen Hörer betrügen[909] sich selbst, wie die nachgestellte Partizipialkonstruktion kritisch festhält – und verfehlen damit die Vollkommenheit, die Jakobus lehrt. Die Apposition zu »Hörer« verstärkt die negative Bedeutung des (bloßen) Hörens, das als παραλογίζεσθαι[910], täuschen, beschrieben wird.

V. 23–24 Die Verse begründen die Aufforderung von V. 22 mit einem Doppel-Beispiel, das mit dem Muster von falsch und richtig arbeitet: Ein bloßer Hörer des Wortes wird einem Täter des Wortes gegenübergestellt. Der Verfasser konstruiert einen kontrastiven Doppelvergleich, den zweiten expliziten Vergleich des Briefes (ἔοικεν).[911] Zunächst wird in V. 23.24 das *falsche* Verhalten dargestellt, indem Jakobus den bloßen Hörer des Wortes mit einem vergesslichen Mann (ἀνήρ[912]) vergleicht. V. 22.23 sind einander chiastisch zugeordnet: ποιηταὶ λόγου und ἀκροαταὶ in V. 22, ἀκροατὴς λόγου und ποιητής in V. 23. Der Vergleich erfolgt in Form einer ganz kurzen dreiteiligen Geschichte[913]: Ein Mann sieht[914] sein Bild im Spiegel[915], – er sieht es (*repetitio*), geht weg[916] und vergisst[917] es sogleich.[918] Es handelt sich um einen sprachlich sorgsam gestalteten[919], sachlich aber artifiziellen Vergleich, der wenig überzeugend wirkt:[920] Weshalb soll ein Mann sein Gesicht, das er im Spiegel betrachtet hat, bald wieder vergessen? Andererseits hat Dibelius überzeugend nach-

---

[907] Dazu siehe unten.

[908] FRANKEMÖLLE, Jak I, 326 f, zu weiteren Anklängen an Sirach. – Maria in Lk 10,39 verhält sich gemäß der Weisheit.

[909] παραλογίζομαι im NT nur noch in Kol 2,4. Vgl. das Substantiv παραλλαγή nur in Jak 1,17 (hap. leg. im NT).

[910] Hap. leg. in Jak. Im NT noch Kol 2,4.

[911] Erster Vergleich mit οὕτως 1,11 (Blume – der Reiche).

[912] Siehe zu 1,20.

[913] Vgl. Jak 1,14 f. In 1,23–25 aber Vergangenheitstempora.

[914] κατανοέω: betrachten, mehrfach im NT, in Jak nur in 1,23.24.

[915] Die Spiegelmetapher begegnet zweimal bei Paulus: ἔσοπτρον: 1Kor 13,12 (vgl. Jak 1,23) und verbal in 2Kor 3,18: κατοπτρίζομαι. Bei Paulus in theologisch und literarisch besonders qualifizierten Zusammenhängen. Jak nutzt die literarische Qualität der Metapher.

[916] ἀπέρχομαι: sehr häufig im NT, hap. leg. in Jak.

[917] ἐπιλανθάνομαι: selten im NT, hap. leg. in Jak. ἀπελήλυθεν καὶ εὐθέως ἐπελάθετο: Paronomasie.

[918] εὐθέως: sehr häufig in den erzählenden Schriften des NT, hap. leg. in Jak.

[919] Zu den rhetorischen Figuren vgl. besonders FRANKEMÖLLE, Jak I, 323 f.

[920] Anders 1,11: unmittelbar einleuchtend.

C. Briefcorpus 199

gewiesen, dass sachlich gesehen »der Vergleich ganz einfach ist und sich nur auf die Wertlosigkeit des Hörens ohne Tun bezieht«.[921] Der Spiegelvergleich hat keine weitere theologische Konnotation. Die Wendung πρόσωπον τῆς γενέσεως αὐτοῦ, eine typisch jakobeische Genitivverbindung, ist ebenfalls artifiziell. Am besten bleibt die Genitivverbindung unübersetzt oder wird mit »eigenes Gesicht« wiedergegeben.[922]

V. 25 V. 22–24 und V. 25 beziehen sich antithetisch aufeinander.[923] Der Spiegelvergleich erschließt sich im *zweiten* Teil des Vergleichsbeispiels. Es geht jetzt um den Mann, der sich *richtig* verhält. Die Satzkonstruktion von V. 25 beginnt mit dem vorangestellten, mit ὁ δὲ (antithetisch zu V. 23 f) eingeleiteten Relativsatz (ἐστιν fehlt wie oft bei Jakobus). Das betonte οὗτος des nachgestellten Hauptsatzes bezieht sich auf das ὁ δὲ des Relativsatzes zurück. Der Relativsatz verbindet zwei Partizipien: παρακύψας und παραμείνας (Anapher): Der Mann, der sich richtig verhält, *sieht* nicht – vielleicht eitel und selbstverliebt wie der Mann von V. 23[924] – in den *Spiegel*, sondern er *schaut* »in das vollkommene *Gesetz* der Freiheit«. Der Spiegelvergleich aus V. 22–24 fungiert also (lediglich) als Bildvorgabe für die richtige Schau, das παρακύπτειν (hineinschauen). Das im NT sehr seltene Verb ist hier übertragen gebraucht.[925] Ob wieder an einen Spiegel oder an ein Wasser gedacht ist, bleibt offen. Jedenfalls handelt es sich nicht um eine mystische Versenkung, sondern um die Art von Schau, die zum beständig geübten (παραμείνας[926]) *Tun* führt. Dieser Mann ist der »Täter des Wortes« von 1,22, wie der zweite erläuternde Teil des Relativsatzes deutlich macht: οὐκ ἀκροατὴς ἐπιλησμονῆς γενόμενος ἀλλὰ ποιητὴς ἔργου.[927] Jetzt spricht Jakobus vom »Täter der Tat« im Gegensatz zum »Hörer des Vergessens«.[928] Der Tataspekt wird ganz besonders akzentuiert: ποιητής[929], ἔργον[930], ποίησις.[931] Das tautologische Syntagma ποιητὴς ἔργου (semantische *variatio* im Syntagma) führt zu 1,4 zurück. ἔργον ist ein Vorzugswort bei Jakobus.[932] Der zweite Makarismus[933] von V. 25 nimmt V. 12 auf. Hieß es dort: Selig ist der Mann, der die Anfechtung

---

[921] DIBELIUS, Jak, 148. Ebenso METZNER, Jak, 98–100.

[922] γένεσις: Entstehung, Ursprung, Abkunft oder Dasein (BAUER / ALAND, 309). BAUER / ALAND übersetzt »sein natürliches Gesicht«, um den artifiziellen Stil nachzubilden.

[923] V. 22 und 25 sind außerdem chiastisch aufeinander bezogen

[924] Das wird nicht gesagt, lässt sich aber u. U. erschließen.

[925] BAUER / ALAND, 1251. παρακύπτειν hap. leg. in Jak, noch Lk 24,12 und Joh 20, 5.11 im eigentlichen Sinn, 1Petr 1,12 von der Schau der Engel.

[926] Παραμένειν 1Kor 16,6; Phil 1,25; Hebr 7,23; Jak 1,25 (hap. leg. in Jak).

[927] Das Partizip γενόμενος ist den beiden vorangehenden Partizipien modal untergeordnet: »indem er nicht Hörer, sondern Täter ist«.

[928] ἐπιλησμονή hap. leg. im NT. Seltenes Substantiv, aber Sir 11,27. Es handelt sich wieder um eine der artifiziellen Genitivwendungen des Jak. Sie hat hier eine ironische Konnotation.

[929] Jak 1,22. 23. 25; 4,11. Im NT nur noch Röm 2,13.

[930] Siehe oben zu 1,4: dort ἔργον τέλειον statt νόμος τέλειος.

[931] ποίησις hap. leg. im NT.

[932] Zwölfmal belegt, siehe zu Kap. 2.

[933] BURCHARD, Jak, 90, weist darauf hin, dass keine eigentliche Seligpreisung vorliege: »Das Futur ist echt und meint das künftige Leben«. Das gilt aber auch für die Mehrzahl der Seligpreisungen in Mt 5,1–10.

erduldet, so wird Jakobus jetzt konkret: Selig ist der Täter des Werkes in seiner Tat. Wieder liegt Septuagintastil vor, wie ihn alle frühchristlichen Autoren verwenden.[934]

Das Motiv von »Hören und Tun« findet sich in der synoptischen Tradition und bei Paulus in unterschiedlichen Zusammenhängen.[935] Hier wie öfter kommt Jakobus dadurch zu eigenständigen Aussagen, dass er synoptische Tradition und paulinische Aussagen verbindet. Auffallend ist die Nähe des Motivs zu bildhafter Rede und allegorischer Auslegung.

Röm 2,13: οὐ γὰρ οἱ **ἀκροαταὶ** νόμου δίκαιοι παρὰ [τῷ] θεῷ, ἀλλ᾽ οἱ **ποιηταὶ** νόμου δικαιωθήσονται.
Denn nicht werden die Hörer des Gesetzes gerecht vor Gott, sondern die Täter des Gesetzes werden gerechtfertigt werden.

Mt 7,24: Πᾶς οὖν ὅστις **ἀκούει** μου τοὺς λόγους τούτους καὶ **ποιεῖ** αὐτούς, ὁμοιωθήσεται ἀνδρὶ φρονίμῳ.
Jeder nun, der diese meine Worte hört und sie tut, kann einem klugen Mann verglichen werden. [Vergleich im Anschluss].

Lk 6,47: Πᾶς ὁ ἐρχόμενος πρός με καὶ **ἀκούων** μου τῶν λόγων καὶ **ποιῶν** αὐτούς, ὑποδείξω ὑμῖν τίνι ἐστὶν ὅμοιος.
Jeder, der zu mir kommt und meine Worte hört und sie tut – ich will euch zeigen, wem dieser gleicht.

Lk 8,15: τὸ δὲ ἐν τῇ καλῇ γῇ, οὗτοί εἰσιν οἵτινες ἐν καρδίᾳ καλῇ καὶ ἀγαθῇ **ἀκούσαντες** τὸν λόγον κατέχουσιν καὶ **καρποφοροῦσιν** ἐν ὑπομονῇ.
Das [Saatgut] in der guten Erde, das sind diejenigen, die in einem guten und aufrichtigen Herzen das Wort hören und daran festhalten und in Geduld Frucht bringen. [Im Zusammenhang einer allegorischen Auslegung].

Lk 8,21 μήτηρ μου καὶ ἀδελφοί μου οὗτοί εἰσιν οἱ τὸν λόγον τοῦ θεοῦ **ἀκούοντες** καὶ **ποιοῦντες**
Meine Mutter und meine Brüder sind diejenigen, die das Wort Gottes hören und tun. [Im Zusammenhang einer allegorischen Auslegung].

Lk 11,28: μακάριοι οἱ **ἀκούοντες** τὸν λόγον τοῦ θεοῦ καὶ **φυλάσσοντες**.
Selig sind, die das Wort Gottes hören und bewahren.

Jak 1,25: ὁ δὲ παρακύψας εἰς νόμον τέλειον τὸν τῆς ἐλευθερίας καὶ παραμείνας οὐκ **ἀκροατὴς** ἐπιλησμονῆς γενόμενος ἀλλὰ **ποιητὴς** ἔργου οὗτος μακάριος ἐν τῇ ποιήσει αὐτοῦ ἔσται.
Wer aber in das vollkommene Gesetz der Freiheit hineinschaute und in ihm beharrte, indem er nicht ein Hörer der Vergesslichkeit, sondern ein Täter des Werkes wurde, der wird selig in seinem Tun sein.

Das Motiv der notwendigen Kongruenz von Hören und Tun wird in der synoptischen Tradition im Zusammenhang von Wort Gottes (λόγος) oder Worten Jesu gesetzt und in Lk 11,28 und bei Jakobus in einen Makarismus gebracht, während Paulus es auf das Gesetz (νόμος) bezieht. Jakobus knüpft daran an, interpretiert

---

[934] S. o. zu 1,12.
[935] Eine komplexe Weiterbildung liegt in Joh 12,47 vor.

aber das Gesetz mit dem für den Stil des Jakobus typischen Syntagma νόμος τῆς ἐλευθερίας sehr eigenwillig und theologisch konträr zu Paulus. Jakobus qualifiziert das Gesetz qualitativ als vollkommen (adjektivisches Attribut) und sachlich als frei. Das Attribut τέλειος[936] nimmt das ethische Leitmotiv von 1,4 auf, das in 1,17 in theologischem Zusammenhang wiederholt wurde und in 3,2 nochmals ethisch verwendet wird. Die nachgestellte Bestimmung τὸν τῆς ἐλευθερίας trägt das theologisch gesetzte Motiv der Freiheit ein, das bei Jakobus nur hier begegnet, sich aber prominent bei Paulus (und nur bei Paulus[937]) im Zusammenhang mit der Gesetzesthematik findet. Das Syntagma »Gesetz der Freiheit« – stilistisch ein Paradoxon, wohl eine Neuschöpfung des Jakobus – weist terminologisch eindeutig auf paulinische Denk- und Sprachzusammenhänge, vor allem auf Gal 5,1.13 f[938]:

(1) Τῇ **ἐλευθερίᾳ** ἡμᾶς Χριστὸς ἠλευθέρωσεν … (13) Ὑμεῖς γὰρ ἐπ᾽ ἐλευθερίᾳ ἐκλήθητε, ἀδελφοί· μόνον μὴ τὴν ἐλευθερίαν εἰς ἀφορμὴν τῇ σαρκί, ἀλλὰ διὰ τῆς ἀγάπης δουλεύετε ἀλλήλοις. (14) ὁ γὰρ πᾶς **νόμος** ἐν ἑνὶ λόγῳ πεπλήρωται, ἐν τῷ· ἀγαπήσεις τὸν πλησίον σου ὡς σεαυτόν.

(1) Zur Freiheit hat euch Christus befreit … (13) Ihr nämlich seid zur Freiheit berufen, Brüder; nur [wählt] nicht die Freiheit zum Vorwand für das Fleisch, sondern durch die Liebe dient einander. (14) Denn das ganze Gesetz ist in dem einen Wort erfüllt, in dem ›Liebe deinen Nächsten wie dich selbst‹.

Während aber Paulus im Galaterbrief gegen eine nachträgliche Beschneidung Christus-bekennender nichtjüdischer Gemeindeglieder argumentiert und in diesem konkreten Zusammenhang die Freiheit *vom* Gesetz (der Tora Israels) für sog. Heidenchristen statuiert, gibt Jakobus hier dem paulinischen Zusammenhang eine ganz andere Wendung: Er lehrt die Freiheit *im* Gesetz. Die paulinische Gesetzesproblematik im Kontext der sog. Heidenmission ist für ihn nicht (mehr?) relevant[939], ihm geht es um die *Umsetzungspraxis* der ethisch verstandenen Tora. Was diese Tora, interpretiert als νόμος ἐλευθερίας, meint, wird in 2,8–11 expliziert und in 2,12 f abschließend auf das Tun der Adressaten appliziert.[940] In 1,25 ist aber bereits klar: Erst das kontinuierliche *Tun* des Gesetzes schafft jene Seligkeit (μακάριος), die schon in 1,12 angesprochen wurde. Jakobus formuliert gleichsam die zweite Stufe des paulinischen Arguments: Erstens sollt ihr das Gesetz als Gesetz der Freiheit

---

[936] Das Syntagma »das vollkommene Gesetz« sonst nicht im NT. Vor dem Jakobusbrief nicht bezeugt: vgl. METZNER, Jak, 101 mit Anm. 107. Ein spätes Echo bei J. W. VON GOETHES Gedicht: Natur und Kunst (»Und das Gesetz nur kann uns Freiheit geben«).

[937] Paulinischer Vorzugsbegriff (vgl. auch Verb und Adjektiv), dazu monographisch: S. VOLLENWEIDER, Freiheit als neue Schöpfung. Eleutheria bei Paulus und in seiner Umwelt, FRLANT 147, Göttingen 1989. Siebenmal bei Paulus, zweimal bei Jakobus (1,25, wiederholt in 2,12). Außerdem 1Petr 2,16 und 2Petr 2,19. Verb und Adjektiv öfter bei Paulus. Wichtig aber auch die Debatte in Joh 8,30–36 (die Abrahamskinder), die paulinische Motive aufnimmt. Mt 17,26 betrifft das politische Thema der Entrichtung der Tempelsteuer für Juden.

[938] Vgl. den präzisen Exkurs bei METZNER, Jak, 101 f. Metzner zählt die sechs in der Forschung vertretenen Interpretationen der Wendung auf. Siehe auch unten zu Kap. 2.

[939] Siehe dazu die Einleitung.

[940] Siehe dort.

verstehen, aber zweitens sollt ihr es auch *tun*. Auch hier verwendet Jakobus unterschiedliche frühchristliche Traditionszusammenhänge, um einen *eigenen* ethischen Beitrag zu formulieren. Rainer Metzner formuliert zutreffend:

> Am ehesten trifft die These zu, dass für Jakobus der schon von Paulus thematisierte Zusammenhang von Gesetz, Freiheit und Nächstenliebe ausschlaggebend ist (vgl. Gal 5,13 f; Röm 13,8–18; Jak 2,8–13).[941]

Allerdings sind auch die stoischen Aussagen über die Freiheit unter dem Gesetz[942] sachlich nahe an Jak 1. John Kloppenborg hat zurecht auf diese Nähe hingewiesen und zugleich in der Diskussion der Thesen von Jackson-McCabe deutlich gemacht, dass es hier nicht um »Abhängigkeiten« geht, sondern um ähnliche Überlegungen, die deutlich machen, dass bestimmte Paulus- und Jakobustexte bei stoischen Lesern durchaus auf Verständnis und Zustimmung stoßen konnten.

3. Texteinheit: 1,26–27 Zweites Fallbeispiel: der »Religiöse«, und Resümee

(26) Wenn jemand meint, religiös[943] zu sein, dabei[944] seine Zunge aber nicht zügelt, sondern sein Herz betrügt, dessen Gottesverehrung[945] ist leer. (27) Ein reiner und unbefleckter Gottesdienst[946] vor Gott dem Vater[947] ist [vielmehr[948]] dieser:[949] Waisen und Witwen in ihrer bedrängten Lage[950] zu besuchen, unbefleckt sich selbst zu halten von der Welt.

Textkritik: V. 27 01 und einige Minuskeln fügen nach θρησκεια noch γαρ ein. τω θεω lesen P74. 01Z. 02. 03. 04* 025. 044, Minuskel 33 und viele Minuskeln; 01T. 04C2. 5 und zahlreiche Minuskeln lassen τω aus. Die Hss zeigen hier eine auffällige Unsicherheit.

Bevor Jakobus das Thema des »Gesetzes der Freiheit« in Kap. 2 weiter ausführt, schaltet er eine kleine Texteinheit über θρησκεία, (Gottes-)Verehrung oder Religion, ein – ein im jüdisch-griechischen Lexikon insgesamt eher seltenes Substantiv[951],

---

[941] Metzner, Jak, 101f, besonders 101 Anm. 110. Nach Metzner ist der Genitiv ein »Genitiv des Zweckes und der Richtung«. Jak meint »wie Gal 5,13 f: Frei ist (nicht wer tun und lassen kann, was er will, oder die Wahl zur Entscheidung hat, sondern) wer das *Gesetz im Gebot der Nächstenliebe* befolgt. Freiheit bezieht sich also auf die Freiheit der Christen« (102).

[942] Epiktet, Diss. 4,1,158: »Das Gesetz erlaubt, frei zu sein«, und Philo, prob. 45: »Welche mit dem Gesetz leben, sind frei«.

[943] Eigene Übersetzung für θρησκός.

[944] Damit wird im Deutschen die logische Unterordnung der beiden Partizipien unter den Konditionalsatz »Wenn jemand meint« abgebildet.

[945] Eigene Übersetzung für θρησκεία.

[946] Eigene Übersetzung für θρησκεία.

[947] Wörtlich: »dem Gott und Vater«.

[948] Einfügung, um die gegensätzliche Struktur zu betonen.

[949] Zur Syntax vgl. Metzner, Jak, 105.

[950] Griechisch: »Bedrängnis«.

[951] Viermal in LXX, aber nicht positiv. SapSal 14,18.27 (beide Male im negativen Kontext: falsche Verehrung, vgl. Kol 2,18); 4Makk 5,7.13 (religiöses Brauchtum der Juden, aus heidnischer Sicht). Verb: SapSal 11,15; 14,16 (beide Male im negativen Kontext: falsche Verehrung).

das aber besonders von Josephus benutzt wird.[952] Jakobus thematisiert die θρησκεία nur hier.[953] Er wählt hier wie oft ein eher gehobenes Wort, nicht um eine Definition von θρησκεία[954] zu geben, sondern um eine sprachlich ausgefeilte Zwischenbilanz zum Thema von Kap. 1 zu ziehen. Sachlich geht es ihm um Erlangung von Vollkommenheit durch das Tun des Wortes. Wie kann das »Tun« aussehen? Jakobus spricht *drei* Aspekte an, zunächst die Sprachdisziplin. Damit bringt er zum ersten Mal in seinem Brief die γλῶσσα, die Sprache, ins ethische Spiel, die in Kapitel 3 zum Gegenstand einer eigenen Texteinheit werden wird. Zweitens verweist er auf klassische Beispiele barmherzigen Handelns, das Thema, das er in Kapp. 2 und 5 weiter verfolgt, drittens auf die ethische »Sorge um sich selbst«: ein Grundanliegen seiner Ethos-Lehre. Damit fungiert 1,26 f als Scharnier zwischen Kap. 1 und den folgenden Ausführungen.

V. 26 Der Vers zeigt den typischen Satzbau eines wertevergleichenden *exemplum*, hier wieder mit einem antithetisch konstruierten Negativbeispiel: Wenn für jemanden *x* gelten soll, aber nicht (positiv) *y*, sondern (negativ) *z*, dann hat *x* keinen Wert[955]: Der Mensch täuscht sich in seiner θρησκεία. Die Einleitungsformel »Wenn jemand meint …« findet sich häufiger in den Paulusbriefen und leitet stets eine Meinung ein, die Paulus als falsch korrigiert.[956] Positiv formuliert besagt V. 26: Gottesverehrung – in 1,25 als Vertiefung in das vollkommene Gesetz der Freiheit umschrieben[957] – ohne ethische Redekontrolle ist nichtig (μάταιος[958]). Damit führt der Verfasser das Thema der ethisch verantworteten Rede weiter, das er schon in 1,19 angesprochen hat und das in Kap. 3 ausführlich thematisiert wird. Die ethisch verantwortete Rede ist ihrerseits ein Teilaspekt jener Forderung, »Täter des Wortes sein«, die eine der wichtigsten theologischen Leitlinien im Jakobusbrief ist.

θρησκεία begegnet zweimal im Jakobusbrief, außerdem in Kol 2,18 vom Gottesdienst der Engel und in Apg 26,5 als Bezeichnung des Paulus für die jüdische Religion.[959] In Jak 1,26 trifft am ehesten »Gottesverehrung« zu.[960] Das Adjektiv θρησκός ist wohl hier zum ersten Mal bezeugt.[961] Durch dreimalige Nennung des Stammes θρησκ-, durch Anadiplose (V. 26 / 27), durch die ringförmige Verwendung des Be-

---

[952] ALLISON, Jak, 359 Anm. 84. A. zählt Sir 22,5 zu den LXX-Belegen (dort aber korrupte Lesart in Hs A).

[953] Jak 1,26.27.

[954] ROPES, Jak, 182: »This is not a definition of religion, but a statement (by an oxymoron) of what is better than external acts of worship«.

[955] Vgl. 1Kor 13,1–3. Öfter in den Weisheitsschriften.

[956] 1Kor 3,18, 8,2; 11,16; 14,37; Gal 6,3; Phil 3,4.

[957] BURCHARD, Jak, 92.

[958] Hap. leg. in Jak. Bedeutung: leer, nutzlos. μάται- steht für Nichtigkeit menschlicher Bestrebungen und ist ein beliebtes LXX-Motiv. Im NT selten: 1Kor 3,20 (Ps 93,11LXX); 15,17 (dort auch in V. 14 κενός bedeutungsgleich gebraucht); Tit 3,9; 1Petr 3,18.

[959] Apg 26,5: κατὰ τὴν ἀκριβεστάτην αἵρεσιν τῆς ἡμετέρας θρησκείας ἔζησα Φαρισαῖος (gemäß der strengsten Richtung unserer Religion Pharisäer); Kol 2,18: falsche Verehrung der Engel.

[960] Positiv im Sinne der Gottesverehrung, Religion: 1Clem 45,7; 62,1. Verb: 1Clem 45,7.

[961] SPIQC, NLNT I, 379 ff. θρησκός Jak 1,26 hap. leg. im NT, nicht in LXX.

204 Kommentar

griffs in V. 26 und durch die Hinzufügung des ungewöhnlichen Adjektivs in V. 26 erzielt Jakobus eine starke stilistische Wirkung. γλῶσσα wird hier ganz in der Linie des Sprachgebrauchs der Septuaginta als geläufige Metonymie für Rede gesetzt (3,5 ff). Mit dem ausgeführten Bild »die Zunge im Zaum halten« für »verantwortungsvoll sprechen« greift der Verfasser schon auf die Zaum-Metapher vor, die er in 3,2.3 verwendet.[962] Die Verbindung von Gottesverehrung und ethisch verantwortungsloser Rede wirkt an diesem Punkt des Jakobusbriefes noch eher künstlich. Das Thema der Sprachethik wird erst in Kap. 3 ausgeführt. Auch die partizipiale Wendung vom »Selbstbetrug des Herzens« (ἀπατῶν καρδίαν[963]) ist stilistisch bemüht.

V. 27 Jakobus bringt die ethische Botschaft des Verfassers nun positiv auf den Punkt und gibt eine schlüssige Definition richtigen Verhaltens »vor Gott«, der θρησκεία καθαρὰ καὶ ἀμίαντος.[964] Beide Adjektive sind hier nicht im kultischen, sondern im ethischen Zusammenhang gesetzt und stehen für Vollkommenheit. Auch das semantisch religiös konnotierte Verhalten wird von Jakobus ethisch eingesetzt. Wieder ist die stilistische Bemühung deutlich: Jakobus sucht nach einer Terminologie der Vollkommenheit und verwendet dabei kultische Vokabeln im ethischen Zusammenhang. Die Definition nimmt formal gesehen den vorherigen Vers antithetisch auf, geht aber inhaltlich weit über V. 26 hinaus. Ging es dort um einen bestimmten Mangel (1,4), nämlich das Fehlen verantworteter Rede, so gibt V. 27 eine positive Zusammenfassung des »vollkommenen (τέλειος) und untadeligen (ὁλόκληρος)« Wandels von 1,4. Trotz dieser Ausweitung arbeitet auch V. 27 nicht wirklich mit einer Definition, sondern mit exemplarischen ethischen bzw. nicht-ethischen Verhaltensformen, d. h. aspekthaft oder nach dem pars pro toto-Prinzip. Dabei ist V. 27 wie so oft im Jakobusbrief *zweipolig*. *Zunächst* wird das vollkommene Verhalten sozialethisch bestimmt und an dem Umgang mit Witwen und Waisen gemessen – eine nicht selbstverständliche ethische Thematik. Das aus Israel bekannte Thema der Witwen- und Waisenfürsorge[965] steht nicht im Zentrum neutestamentlicher Paränese. Zwar werden in den synoptischen Evangelien mehrfach Witwen erwähnt[966], Witwenfürsorge wird aber nur in Apg 6,1 und 1Tim

---

[962] χαλιναγωγεῖν im NT nur zweimal metaphorisch bei Jak: 1,16; 3,2. Vgl. χαλινοί Jak 3,3. Zügel der Pferde: Apk 14,20. Die Metapher stammt aus dem Bereich der Emotionenkontrolle: Burchard, Jak, 92.

[963] ἀπατᾶν hap. leg. in Jak. Eph 5,6 (Niemand betrüge euch mit leeren Worten); 1Tim 2,14 (Eva ließ sich verführen). Der Stamm ἀπατ- wird im Zusammenhang mit Sündenlisten gebraucht. Herz als Metonym für die Person öfter bei Jak: 1,26; 3,14; 4,8; 5,5.8. Vgl. D. Lincicum, Art. ἀπάτη, HTLS I, 877–888 (886: zahlreiche Belege bei Philo).

[964] Beide Adjektive hap. leg. in Jak. καθαρός in Mt 5,8 zusammen mit καρδία, in ethischen Zusammenhängen mehrfach in den Pastoralbriefen (mit καρδία auch in 1Petr 1,22), ἀμίαντος Hebr 13,4 (ἡ κοίτη ἀμίαντος) und 1Petr 1,4 (das unzerstörbare, unbefleckte und unvergängliche Erbe im Himmel).

[965] Vgl. Dtn 10,18 und öfter.

[966] Besonders bei Lk und in Mk 12,42par. Vgl. dazu M. Leineweber, Lukas und die Witwen. Eine Botschaft an die Gemeinden in der hellenistisch-römischen Gesellschaft, EHS.T 915, Frankfurt / M. 2011; E.-M. Becker, Was die »arme Witwe« lehrt. Sozial- und motivgeschichtliche Beobachtungen zu Mk 12,41–44par, NTS 65, 2019, 148–165.

5 thematisiert, Waisen werden nur noch in einer textkritischen Variante zu Mk 12,40 in der neutestamentlichen Paränese genannt.[967] »Witwen und Waisen« zusammen erscheinen im Neuen Testament nur in der textkritischen Variante von Mk 12 und hier in Jak 1. Öfter begegnen dann Waisen in den Apostolischen Vätern, auch zusammen mit Witwen.[968] Wie wichtig Jakobus das Thema ist, zeigt sich auch bei der Wahl des Verbs ἐπισκέπτεσθαι[969], das der gehobenen Septuagintasprache entstammt.

Die durchweg erhöhte Ausdrucksweise der Texteinheit zeigt sich dann im *zweiten* Aspekt: in der Wendung »sich selbst unbefleckt von der Welt erhalten«, in der die »Sorge um die eigene Person« ihren Ausdruck findet. ἄσπιλος[970], unbefleckt, ist wieder ein Adjektiv, das aus dem kultischen Zusammenhang in eine ethische Thematik überführt wird.[971] Die Wendung »unbefleckt von der Welt« ist ohne Parallele.

2. Zweiter Hauptteil: Belehrungen über das Ansehen der Person und über das Verhältnis von Glauben und Tun (Kap. 2)

Die Verse 2,1–13 stellen den ersten der beiden großen Teiltexte im 2. Hauptteil des Briefes dar (A). Der zweite Teil (B) ist der Belehrung über das Verhältnis von Glauben und Taten gewidmet. Thema von Teil A ist eine weitere *Gefahr* für den Glauben der Gemeinde: die προσωπολημψία, die für Jakobus sehr eng mit den Reichen bzw. der Bevorzugung der Reichen verbunden ist. In 2,1–7 werden beide Themen, Ansehen der Person und Reichtum bzw. Armut, zusammen behandelt. Der gesamte Text ist sorgfältig komponiert. Jakobus geht in vier Argumentationsschritten vor: 2,1–4; 2,5–7; 2,8–11; 2,12–13.

Das Thema der Parteilichkeit wird in V. 1 eingeführt und in seiner Relation zum Glauben beschrieben. Der Glaube wird doppelt bestimmt: erstens von seiner praktischen Ausübung her. Damit knüpft 2,1–13 direkt an 1,19–27, besonders an 1,27 an. Zweitens ist der Glaube theologisch-christologisch qualifiziert durch das lange Genitivobjekt »unseres Herrn Jesu Christi der Herrlichkeit«. Der Verfasser wendet sich an Christus-gläubige Gemeinden. Nachdem in 2,1 deutlich vor der Gefahr der Parteilichkeit gewarnt wird, entwirft der Verfasser in 2,2–4 ein exemplarisches Bild von sozialer Bevorzugung in einer Gemeindeversammlung. Hier kommen der Reiche und ein Armer als soziale *Typen* ins Spiel. Zunächst liegt das Interesse des

---

[967] Hss DWf[3], 28.565. ὀρφανός nur noch metaphorisch in Joh 14,18. Hss DWf[3], 28.565.

[968] Im Zusammenhang mit dem Wachsen der Gemeinden! ὀρφανός: Barn 20,2 (mit Witwen); 1Clem 8,4; IgnSmyr 6,2 (mit Witwen); Polyk 6,1; Herm vis II 4; Herm mand VIII; Herm sim I; V 3; IX 26 (mit Witwen). Offensichtlich werden Waisen erst allmählich in den Gemeinden als soziale Aufgabe wahrgenommen.

[969] ἐπισκέπτεσθαι verbindet die Aspekte von Aufsuchen und Helfen. Hap. leg. in Jak. Selten im NT. Vgl. J. ROHDE, Art. ἐπισκέπτομαι, EWNT 2, 1981, 83–85.

[970] Hap. leg. in Jak, im NT noch 1Tim 6,14; 1Petr 1,19; 2Petr 3,14.

[971] Weiteres bei METZNER, Jak, 105f mit Anm. 152.

Jakobus nicht bei dem Thema reich – arm, sondern bei dem Fehlverhalten der Gemeindeglieder gegenüber Reichen und Armen. Auf das *exemplum* folgt die dreiteilige auswertende *admonitio*. Zunächst klagt Jakobus in 2,5–7 dies ethische Fehlverhalten in scharfer Form an. Jetzt verlagert sich das Interesse auf die Existenzform der Armen und der Reichen: Jakobus qualifiziert die Armen theologisch und erklärt sie zu den Erben der Gottesherrschaft. Den Reichen macht er schwere Vorwürfe. Von V. 2 bis V. 7 steigert Jakobus seine Polemik gegen die Reichen. In einem nächsten Schritt erfolgt in V. 8–11 eine theologisch-ethische Vertiefung in Gestalt eines Hinweises auf das Gebot der Nächstenliebe. Die Argumentation lautet jetzt: Wenn durch soziale Bevorzugung das Gebot der Nächstenliebe missachtet wird, sind *alle* Gebote missachtet. V. 12.13 fügen schließlich die Endgerichtsperspektive hinzu und verschärfen dadurch das Verbot sozialer Bevorzugung noch einmal. Das ausführliche Beispiel, die teilweise aggressive Anrede (V. 4.6a) und die Gerichtsperspektive sind Ausdruck des hohen ethischen Engagements des Verfassers und weisen schon auf Kap. 4 und 5 voraus: Er sieht in Parteilichkeit und sozialer Differenzierung innerhalb der Gemeindeversammlungen eine deutliche Gefahr und spricht sie dementsprechend deutlich an.[972]

A. 2,1–13: Belehrung über das Ansehen der Person

1. Texteinheit: 2,1–4 Der Arme in der Gemeindeversammlung

(1) **Meine Brüder, übt**[973] **den Glauben an unsern Herrn der Herrlichkeit, Jesus Christus**[974]**, nicht in Ansehen der Person.**[975] (2) **Wenn nämlich in euren Versammlungsraum**[976] **ein Mann mit einem goldenen Ring in einem weißen Gewand einträte, aber auch ein Armer in schmutziger Kleidung einträte,** (3) **ihr aber auf den sähet, der das weiße Gewand trüge, und sagtet: »Du setz' dich hierhin auf den guten Platz«**[977]**, und zu dem Armen sagtet: »Du steh' oder setz' dich dort unten zu meinen Füßen«**[978]**,** (4) **würdet ihr (dann)**[979] **nicht miteinander im Streit liegen und würdet zugleich**[980] **zu schlecht denkenden Schiedsrichtern?**[981]

---

[972] Siehe eine detaillierte Gliederung des Textes bei ALLISON, Jak, 374 f.

[973] Wörtlich: »habt«. Dazu METZNER, Jak, 111: »Πίστιν ἔχειν meint hier also so viel wie »Glauben ausüben bzw. leben««.

[974] So als Hyperbaton übersetzt. Im Deutschen eleganter wäre die Auflösung: den Glauben an unsern Herrn Jesus Christus, (den Herrn) der Herrlichkeit. Weiteres s. Textkritik.

[975] BAUER / ALAND, 1429, übersetzt προσωπολημψία mit »Parteilichkeit«. »Ansehen der Person« bildet das griechische Substantiv direkter ab. Griechisch Plural lässt sich in der Übersetzung nicht gut abbilden: »Fälle von π.«. BAUER / ALAND übersetzt die ganze Phrase: »den Glauben haben und dabei parteiische Handlungen vornehmen«.

[976] Zu συναγωγή vgl. BAUER / ALAND, 1550 f.

[977] Wörtlich: »gut«.

[978] Wörtlich: »unter meine Fußbank«.

[979] »Dann« im Deutschen hinzugefügt.

[980] καί und καί: »zugleich«.

[981] Wörtlich: »Richter böser Gedanken«. Die Genitivkonstruktion wird analog zu dem Syntagma ὁ κριτὴς

C. Briefcorpus 207

Textkritik: Auffallend häufige Wortumstellungen in V. 3.5, die hier nicht dokumentiert werden. – V. 1 Das μ in προσωπολημψιαις fehlt in einer korrigierten Version von 03 und anderen Majuskeln, in Minuskeln und Byz. του κυριου ημων Ιησου Χριστου της δοξης lesen 01. 02. 03. 04, viele Minuskeln, Byz. und lat. Texttypen. της δοξης stellen voran: Minuskeln, koptische und syrische Manuskripte. Die Wendung fehlt in Minuskel 33.631 und Antiochus Monachus (7. Jh.). Bei beiden Varianten handelt es sich eindeutig um Glättungen des sperrigen Ausgangstextes. Die Lesart der großen Majuskeln ist die lectio difficilior. Die Diskussion um mögliche Interpolationen (ημων Ἰησου Χριστου oder της δοξης) lässt sich nicht auf der Basis der Textbezeugungen führen, sondern ist eine exegetische Entscheidung (s. d.). V. 3 επιβλεψητε δε lesen 03. 04, weitere Majuskeln, zahlreiche Minuskeln; και επιβλεψητε P74(V). 01. 02. 33 und zahlreiche andere Minuskeln. Die erste Lesart ist stilistisch anspruchsvoller, die 2. muss als Glättung gelten. Unklarer Text und unklare Syntax in V. 3: η καθου εκει 03, Minuskeln, εκει η καθου 02, 33 und andere M., εκει η καθου ωδε 01, zahlreiche Minuskeln (Verdeutlichung). η καθου εκει ist vorzuziehen, da der Anschluss zu συ στηθι eleganter ist. υπο το υποποδιον μου 01. 03T. 04, zahlreiche Minuskeln, Byz., επι το υποποδιον μου 03 Zusatzlesart, zahlreiche Minuskeln. επι το υποποδιον των ποδων μου Minuskel 33, υπο το υποποδιον των ποδων μου 02 f. L:V (Verbesserungen nach Jes 66,1 und Ps 109,1). επι ist eine sachliche Glättung von υπο.

Vers 1 eröffnet den Textabschnitt[982] mit einer kurzen Ermahnung im Imp. Plur. V. 2–4 stellen eine syntaktische Einheit dar. Eine Szene wird anschaulich gemalt und dient als negatives Exempel. Der einleitende Konditionalsatz (ἐὰν) verbindet fünf Verben: zunächst zweimal εἰσέλθη (Wiederholung und Antithese), bezogen auf die Beispielperson, dann drittens ἐπιβλέψητε, jetzt bezogen auf die imaginierten Adressaten, weiter zweimal εἴπητε (wieder Wiederholung und Antithese) – eingeschoben werden zwei kurze Anreden an den Reichen und an den Armen. Es folgt der Hauptsatz, gestaltet als doppelte Frage an die Adressaten und an ihr imaginiertes Verhalten und Reden.

V. 1 Die Texteinheit setzt mit der textgliedernden Anrede »meine Brüder« ein neues Thema[983]: die soziale Bevorzugung reicher Besucher bei den Versammlungen der Adressaten. Der Blick des Verfassers geht also von den *einzelnen* Gemeindemitgliedern – so die Adressaten in Kap. 1 – zur *Gemeinde*. Dabei muss grundsätzlich offenbleiben, ob im Folgenden eine bestimmte Gruppe oder ein Gruppennetzwerk im Blick ist. Literarisch sind die »zwölf Stämme in der Zerstreuung« angesprochen, vom Soziolekt her Christus-bekennende Gemeinden. Unter Umständen handelt es sich bei den Briefadressaten insgesamt um ein fiktives Korrespondenzgegenüber. Die Praxis der προσωπολημψία – ein sehr seltenes Nomen, das zuerst bei Paulus belegt ist[984], scheint den Verfasser umzutreiben. Das »Ansehen der Person« und

---

της ἀδικίας (Lk 18,6) attributiv aufgelöst (s. u. zum Vers).

[982] Dazu monographisch: I. A. K. Mongstad-Kvammen, Toward a Postcolonial Reading of the Epistle of James: James 2:1–13 in its Roman Imperial Context, Biblical Interpretation 119, Leiden / Boston 2013, Textexegese 101–204.

[983] Vgl. 1,2.9.16.19.–1,2.19 leiten ebenfalls neue Themen ein.

[984] Röm 2,11; Eph 6,9; Kol 3,25; Jak 2,1 (Paulinismus?); Verb nur Jak 2,9. Polyk 6,1 scheint ein Echo auf

die damit verbundene parteiliche Haltung in den Gemeinden sollen vermieden werden. Diese Haltung ist aus seiner Sicht eine ernste Gefahr des *gelebten Glaubens* seiner Adressaten, der seit 1,3 das Zentrum des paränetischen Interesses des Verfassers darstellt. Gewarnt wird vor προσωπολημψίαι[985] im internen, gemeindlich-sozialen Kontext: im Rahmen der Versammlung der Brüder. Das zugrunde liegende Verb προσωπολημπτέω (hap. leg. Jak 2,9), »to be a respecter of persons«,[986] oder: »das Aussehen in Augenschein nehmen / berücksichtigen«, ist auf der Grundlage der Septuaginta-Wendung πρόσωπον λαμβάνειν neu gebildet – ein Hebraismus bzw. Septuagintismus, dessen visuelle *und* moralische Aspekte verbindende Konnotation in der ursprünglichen verbalen Wendung am deutlichsten in Lev 19,15 hervortritt:[987]

> Οὐ ποιήσετε ἄδικον ἐν κρίσει· οὐ λήμψῃ πρόσωπον πτωχοῦ οὐδὲ θαυμάσεις πρόσωπον δυνάστου, ἐν δικαιοσύνῃ κρινεῖς τὸν πλησίον σου.
> Ihr sollt kein Unrecht tun beim Gericht. Nimm nicht in Augenschein das Angesicht des Armen und bestaune nicht das Angesicht des Mächtigen, in Gerechtigkeit beurteile (richte) deinen Nächsten.

Lev 19,15 kann sprachlich und thematisch als Prätext für Jak 2,1–4 angesehen werden. Dort bilden der Arme und der Mächtige ein Gegensatzpaar, in Jak 2 ein gesellschaftlich Einflussreicher bzw. Reicher und ein Armer. Hier wie dort folgt der grundsätzliche Verweis auf die Nächstenliebe (Lev 19,18 / Jak 2,8), weiterhin ist das Motiv des Richters in V. 4 aus Lev 19,15 vorgegeben. Dass es bei προσωπολημψίαι zuerst um den *Augenschein*, d. h. um die Einschätzung und Aufnahme eines unbekannten Menschen nach äußeren Zeichen von Reichtum und Rang geht, ist in Jak 2,1–3 ganz deutlich: ἐπιβλέψητε (V. 3). SapSal 6,7 kennt ebenfalls die Forderung, nicht nach dem Ansehen der Person, d. h. nicht nach dem sozialen Status einer Person zu urteilen:

> οὐ γὰρ ὑποστελεῖται πρόσωπον ὁ πάντων δεσπότης οὐδὲ ἐντραπήσεται μέγεθος, ὅτι μικρὸν καὶ μέγαν αὐτὸς ἐποίησεν ὁμοίως τε προνοεῖ περὶ πάντων.
> Der Gebieter über alles nämlich wird kein Ansehen der Person kennen, und er wird Größe nicht scheuen. Denn den Kleinen und den Großen hat er gemacht, und gleichermaßen sorgt er für alle.[988]

Das Motiv begegnet auch in 1Petr 1,17:

Jak 2,1 zu sein: Hier werden bei den Pflichten für die Presbyter u. a. aufgezählt: »nicht die Witwe, die Waise [Jak 1,27] oder den *Armen* vernachlässigen … sich enthalten von allem Zorn [Jak 1,19], dem *Ansehen der Person* …«. προσωπολήμπτης Apg 10,34 (von Gott gesagt, vgl. auch TestHiob 43,13, dort mit προσωπολημψία).

[985] Im Plural nur hier. Vgl. METZNER, Jak, III: vielleicht auf Armen und Reichen bezogen.

[986] LSJ, 1533.

[987] Sehr ausführlich dokumentiert bei ALLISON, Jak, 379–381. Allison weist darauf hin, dass der Ausdruck für die griechischsprachigen Adressaten kaum zu verstehen war. In jedem Fall handelt es sich einerseits um einen ungewöhnlichen und andererseits auf die Septuaginta und auf Paulus verweisenden Ausdruck. Vgl. auch KLOPPENBORG, The Author of James and His Lexical Profile, in: Who was ›James‹, 212.

[988] Übersetzung: Septuaginta Deutsch.

C. Briefcorpus 209

καὶ εἰ πατέρα ἐπικαλεῖσθε τὸν ἀπροσωπολήμπτως[989] κρίνοντα κατὰ τὸ ἑκάστου ἔργον …
und wenn ihr den als Vater anruft, der nach dem Tun eines jeden richtet ohne Ansehen
der Person.[990]

Der Glaube, der seit 1,3 das Grundthema der Ausführungen bildet, wird in 2,1
durch die unklare bzw. ungeschickt wirkende, grammatisch überfrachtete Genitivverbindung »der Glaube unseres Herrn Jesu Christi der Herrlichkeit« näher bestimmt.[991] Diese Wendung ist häufig als exegetische *crux* empfunden worden, ist in
den Handschriften aber gut bezeugt: Der Genitiv »(Jesu) Christi«[992] fehlt nirgends.
Seit den Arbeiten von Massebieau, Spitta, Halévy, Meyer u. a.[993] bis zu D. C. Allison und J. S. Kloppenborg wird trotzdem immer wieder vorgeschlagen, ἡμῶν Ἰησοῦ
Χριστοῦ als christliche Interpolation zu werten. Die Handschriftenlage gibt dies
Urteil ebenso wenig her wie die Syntax. Denn das Problem der überlangen Genitivkette liegt nicht so sehr in der christologischen Wendung, sondern in dem weiteren
Genitiv τῆς δόξης.[994] Christoph Burchard plädiert mit guten Gründen dafür, ein
Hyperbaton anzunehmen:

> Ein Genitivus qualitatis zu Ἰησοῦ Χριστοῦ (…) ist bei einem Namen kaum möglich,
> Apposition auch nicht, weil ἡ δόξα als Metonym für Christus frühchr. nicht belegt
> ist (…) Man muss wohl Hyperbaton (…) annehmen.[995]

Burchard bevorzugt eine Zuordnung des Hyperbatons zu τὴν πίστιν[996], betont aber
die Uneindeutigkeit des Hyperbatons.[997] Besser scheint eine Zuordnung von τῆς
δόξης als gen.qual. zu κυρίου zu passen: »Herr der Herrlichkeit« begegnet auch
1Kor 2,8 in christologischem Zusammenhang. δόξα ist hap. leg. im Jakobusbrief
und lässt sich am ehesten als eine Steigerung der Bedeutung Jesu Christi verstehen,
die ihn möglichst nahe an die für Gott in der Septuaginta und in der frühjüdischen
griechischsprachigen Literatur gebrauchte Wendung κύριος τῆς δόξης heranrückt.[998]

---

[989] Nicht in LXX. Hap. leg. im NT. LSJ, 230: Adverb hap. leg. in der Gräzität außer Suidas. Adjektiv noch
in TestHiob 4,8.

[990] TestHiob 4,8 macht deutlich, dass Gott selbst derjenige ist, der die Person nicht ansieht: »(Gott) sieht
die Person nicht an (ἀπροσωπόληπτος), er vergilt Gutes jedem, der auf ihn hört«.

[991] Zur Christologie des Jak siehe S. Luther, The Christ of James' Story, in: P. Dragutinović u. a. (Hg.),
Christ of the Sacred Stories, WUNT II / 453, Tübingen 2015, 191–200 (196 zu Jak 2,1: »The traditional predicate of God as ›Lord of glory‹ is transferred to Jesus and combined with the κύριος-formula«).

[992] Minuskel 2344 hat τοῦ Χριστοῦ.

[993] Zum Text ausführlich der Exkurs bei Allison, Jak, 382–384. Allison schließt sich der Linie Massebieaus
an. Siehe auch J. S. Kloppenborg, Judaeans or Judaean Christians in James? in: Z. A. Crook / P. A. Harland
(Hg.), Identity and Interaction in the Ancient Mediterranean: Jews, Christians and Others, FS. S. G. Wilson,
London 2007, 113–135.

[994] Vgl. die sorgfältige Analyse bei Ch. Burchard, Zu einigen christologischen Stellen des Jakobusbriefes,
in: C. Breytenbach / H. Paulsen (Hg.), Anfänge der Christologie, FS. F. Hahn, Göttingen 1991, 353–368.

[995] Burchard, Jak, 97.

[996] Vgl. die kritischen Bemerkungen bei Allison, Jak, 382 f.

[997] Ebd. Burchard, Jak, 14, listet die Hyperbata auf: 1,2. 5. 13; 2,1. 8. 14.16; 3,3. 8. 12; 5,10.17.

[998] Vgl. die Belege bei Allison, Jak, 381 Anm. 79. Auch H. Frankemölle, Jak II, 375; Luther, The
Christ of James' Story, 196.

Die Diktion in 2,1, »Herr der Herrlichkeit Jesus Christus«, lässt sich damit am besten in der Reihe stilistisch prätentiöser Genitivverbindungen anstelle von einfachen attributiven Adjektivverbindungen bei Jakobus verorten: Gesetz der Freiheit (1,25), Schiedsrichter böser Gedanken (2,5), Kosmos der Ungerechtigkeit (3,6), Rad der Entstehung (3,6), Sanftmut der Weisheit (3,13).

V. 2 V. 2–4 bilden ein zusammenhängendes Satzgefüge. In V. 2.3 wird in einem zweipoligen, antithetisch gebauten Bedingungssatz (ἐάν), der Protasis, ein *hypothetisches Szenario* nach dem kontrastiven Schema: »Angenommen, ein Reicher und ein Armer betreten eine Gemeindeversammlung und die Gemeinde behandelt beide Personen unterschiedlich nach ihrem Äußeren«, aufgebaut. V. 4 (Apodosis) bewertet dies Szenario kritisch, allerdings nicht in Form einer urteilenden Schlussaussage, sondern mit Hilfe einer doppelten rhetorischen Frage, die zugleich als Verurteilung des Gemeindeverhaltens fungiert. Das Exempel[999] von der unterschiedlichen Behandlung eines Reichen und eines Armen in einer Gemeindeversammlung veranschaulicht die Warnung vor der Gefahr der Parteilichkeit des gelebten Glaubens von 2,1 und bietet zugleich den Ausgangspunkt für eine grundsätzliche ethische Belehrung in V. 5–13. Dass der Verfasser des Briefes eine solche Bevorzugung eines Gemeindebesuchers nach seinem sichtbaren sozialen und wirtschaftlichen Status für *möglich* und realistisch hält, wenn er die Szene auch als hypothetisch entwirft (Eventualis), geht aus der Heftigkeit dieser Belehrung hervor.[1000] Wieweit die topische Szene eine reale Situation in den Gemeinden der Adressaten spiegelt, kann hier nicht entschieden werden.[1001]

V. 2 zeichnet den ersten Teil des ebenso knapp wie anschaulich und auf die visuelle Erfahrung hin entworfenen Szenarios, das wie oft bei Jakobus mit einer Antithese arbeitet: Zwei Personen kommen in eine Gemeindeversammlung. Beide wollen gleichermaßen an der Versammlung teilnehmen.[1002] Während der Eine von seinem Äußeren her – durch seinen Schmuck und seine Kleidung – als sozial und

---

[999] Vgl. DIBELIUS, Jak, 161–163: Exkurs: Die Beispiele im Jakobusbrief. Dibelius ist im Grundsatz zuzustimmen: Aus den Beispielen des Jak lässt sich nicht auf die Situation in seinen Gemeinden zurückschließen. Allerdings machen die Beispiele deutlich, an welchen Stellen der Verfasser, dem die Vollkommenheit der Gemeinden am Herzen liegt, besondere *Gefahren* sieht.

[1000] Vgl. die Auflistung der Exegeten, die von einer realen Situation ausgehen, und derjenigen, die wie Dibelius (161–163) nur mit einem hypothetischen Fall rechnen, bei METZNER, Jak, 113 Anm. 31. ALLISON, Jak, 384, bemerkt zutreffend: »The following situation, vividly depicted, is introduced as a hypothetical; but ... the circumstances, or something very close to them, were probably known to James and his readers«. Anders jetzt JÓNSSON, James, 260–274. Jónsson gibt eine Einführung in die topische Behandlung der Thematik von »Reicher« und »Armer« seit Aristoteles und bezieht sich besonders auf die Progymnasmataliteratur und die stoische und kynische Ethik. Damit weitet J. den kontextuellen Rahmen von Jak 2 aus: Neben LXX und den Schriften des antiken Judentums wird die allgemeine Relevanz des für Jakobus wichtigen Themas deutlich. Weiteres s. unten.

[1001] Vgl. unten zu 2,5–7.

[1002] Ob es sich um fremde oder zugezogene Christusbekenner oder um Neulinge handelt oder einfach um arme Gemeindeglieder, bleibt offen.

C. Briefcorpus

ökonomisch erfolgreich charakterisiert wird[1003], wird der Andere direkt von seiner ökonomischen Situation her als Armer (πτωχός) benannt, aber ebenfalls zusätzlich von seiner Kleidung her sozial kontrastiv zugeordnet.[1004] Der Erfolgreiche trägt einen goldenen Ring[1005] und weiße oder strahlende Kleidung. Auffallend ist die durchweg ausgesuchte und zum Teil prätentiöse sprachliche Formulierung: Neben dem einmaligen χρυσοδακτύλιος ist auch ἐσθῆτι λαμπρός wenigstens im Jakobusbrief hap. leg., und ἐσθής begegnet nur noch in 2,3. Das »weiße Gewand« begegnet mehrfach im lukanischen Werk.[1006] Mindestens bei dem χρυσοδακτύλιος ist eine ironische Note zu spüren.[1007] Der Verfasser will den *optischen* Eindruck wiedergeben, den ein wichtiger Mann beim Eintritt in eine Versammlung hervorruft. Antithetisch dazu ist der Arme ausschließlich durch seine schmutzigen (ῥυπαρός[1008]) Kleider, die man sich eher dunkel oder fleckig vorstellen muss, gekennzeichnet. Die kontrastive Charakteristik von »Reicher« und »Armer« begegnet auch in Lk 16,19 f:

> (19) Ἄνθρωπος δέ τις ἦν πλούσιος, καὶ ἐνεδιδύσκετο πορφύραν καὶ βύσσον εὐφραινόμενος καθ᾽ ἡμέραν λαμπρῶς. (20) πτωχὸς δέ τις ὀνόματι Λάζαρος ἐβέβλητο πρὸς τὸν πυλῶνα αὐτοῦ εἱλκωμένος.[1009]

> (19) Es war ein reicher Mann, und er kleidete sich in Purpur und Byssus und lebte Tag für Tag in Freude und Pracht. (20) Ein Armer aber mit Namen Lazarus lag vor seiner Tür, mit Geschwüren bedeckt.[1010]

Auch hier wird der Reiche, der anders als bei Jakobus gleich mit seinem ökonomischen Status vorgestellt wird, durch seine Kleidung charakterisiert[1011], während der

---

[1003] πλούσιος begegnet erst in V. 6.

[1004] Zur sozialen Bedeutung von Kleidung in der Antike vgl. die Beiträge in: A. J. Batten / K. Olson (Hg.), Dress in Mediterranean Antiquity: Greeks, Romans, Jews, Christians, London / New York 2021.

[1005] χρυσοδακτύλιος: Bauer / Aland, 1771. Hap. leg. in der griechischen Lit. Der Ring wird in der Literatur oft als besonderes Ehrenzeichen interpretiert (Cassius Dio, Römische Geschichte 48.45.7–9); vgl. M. Schmauder, Art. Ring, RAC 29, 2019, 123–130; ders. Art. Schmuck, RAC 29, 2019, 978–1006. Auch A. Weiss, Soziale Elite und Christentum. Studien zu ordo-Angehörigen unter den frühen Christen, Millennium-Studien 52, Berlin / Boston 2015, 153, denkt bei dem Ring an den *anulus aureus*, den zu tragen »ein exklusives Privileg der Angehörigen des zweiten Standes, des ordo equester, war«. Ob Jak sich darauf bezieht, muss offenbleiben.

[1006] Lk 23,11 (Königsgewand bei der Verspottung Jesu); Apg 1,10 und 10,30 dieselbe Wendung in Bezug auf Gottesboten.

[1007] Neologismus des Jakobus? Vgl. Metzner, Jak, 113 Anm. 23. Ironie: Popkes, Jak, 163.

[1008] Das Adjektiv, hap. leg. in Jak, steht im Gegensatz zu »leuchtend« und ist ebenfalls ungewöhnlich: nur noch Apk 22,11 (moralisch unrein). Das Substantiv im NT nur in Jak 1,21, dort ebenfalls für moralische Unreinheit.

[1009] TLG: die Suche nach πλούσιος, –α, –ον + πτωχός incl. Lemma und Nachbarschaft von 15 Wörtern ergibt 20 Ergebnisse in LXX: Ruth 3,10; Est 1,20; Spr 14,20 f; 19,22; 22,2.7; 28,6; Sir 10,22.30; 13,3. 19. 20.21.23; 25,2; 26,4; 30,14; 31,3; πλούσιος + πένης: 12 Ergebnisse in LXX: 2Kön 12,1.2; 1Esr 3,18; Ps 9,29; 48,3; Spr 14,20; 22,16; 23,4; 28,11; Sir 13,18.19.

[1010] Bauer / Aland, 507.

[1011] H. Bolkestein / A. Kalsbach, Art. Armut I, RAC I, 1950, 698–705; F. Hauck / W. Kasch, Art. πλοῦτος, ThWNT 6, 1959, 316–330; F. Hauck / E. Bammel, Art. πτωχός, ThWNT 6, 1959, 885–915; J.-U. Krause, Art. Klassen (Gesellschaftsschichten), RAC 20, 2004, 1169–1227; E. Baltrusch, Art. Luxus II (Luxuskritik), RAC 23, 2010, 711–738; M. Wacht, Art. Reichtum, RAC 28, 2018, 830–856 (Lit.).

Arme einerseits einen Namen hat, andererseits eher als nackend oder kaum bekleidet vorzustellen ist, da seine Geschwüre zu sehen sind. Die Typologie knüpft an das Alte Testament an: Der Reiche und der Arme sowie Reichtum und Armut werden vor allem in den Psalmen und bei Jesaja, aber auch in den Weisheitsschriften behandelt. Dabei werden beide Lebensformen als gegeben vorausgesetzt:

ἀγαθὰ καὶ κακά, ζωὴ καὶ θάνατος, πτωχεία καὶ πλοῦτος παρὰ κυρίου ἐστίν.
Gutes und Schlechtes, Leben und Tod, Armut und Reichtum sind vom Herrn (Sir 11,14).

In 2,1–4 zeichnet Jakobus das traditionelle Gegensatzpaar mit konventionellen Mitteln. Wichtig ist ihm zunächst das Thema der προσωπολημψία in den Gemeindeversammlungen. Jakobus spricht von »eurer συναγωγή«. Um welches Szenario geht es hier? Ist an den jüdischen Versammlungsort oder an die Gemeindeversammlungen der Christus-gläubigen Adressaten gedacht? Gegen Letzteres könnte sprechen, dass lexikalisch Jak 2,2 die einzige neutestamentliche Stelle wäre, an der Synagoge *nicht* für den jüdischen Versammlungsraum stände.[1012] Kommentatoren von Dibelius bis Metzner denken trotzdem an die Versammlung von Christusbekennern.[1013] Dafür lässt sich anführen, dass das Verb συνάγω von Paulus in 1Kor 5,4 für die Gemeindeversammlung der Christusbekenner gewählt wird. Das verwandte, sehr seltene Kompositum ἐπισυναγωγή wird Hebr 10,25 für Gemeindezusammenkünfte verwendet. συναγωγή kann auch einfach »Versammlung« heißen.[1014] Der Verfasser des Jakobusbriefes benutzt gern hapx legomena und Neologismen. Deshalb spricht nichts dagegen, hier die erste Bezeugung von συναγωγή als Christus-bekennender Versammlung zu finden: ein Neologismus in Bezug auf den religiösen Referenzrahmen. Allerdings ist auch deutlich, dass Jakobus einen Begriff wählt, der eher auf jüdische Versammlungsräume hindeutet. Damit wird die Linie von 1,1 fortgesetzt: eine jüdische oder zumindest mit dem Judentum der Zeit *kompatible* und ihm nahestehende Rahmung für das Selbstverständnis des Verfassers und der Adressaten zu entwerfen. In 5,14 benutzt der Verfasser dann den paulinischen Ausdruck ἐκκλησία – offensichtlich geht es um die gleiche Versammlung.[1015] Wieweit ein spezifisch ausgestaltetes Gebäude vorgestellt ist, geht aus dem Text nicht direkt hervor.

[1012] Zur Institution und Architektur der antiken jüdischen Synagoge vgl. L. I. Levine, Art. Synagogues, EDEJ 1260–1271; C. Claussen, Versammlung, Gemeinde, Synagoge. Das hellenistisch-jüdische Umfeld der frühchristlichen Gemeinden, StUNT 27, Göttingen 2002. – Die Christus-bekennenden Versammlungen und Gemeinden werden ἐκκλησία genannt (vgl. Jak 5,14). – Zum umfassenden Thema von antiken Vereinigungen vgl. R. Last / Ph.A. Harland, Group Survival in the Ancient Mediterranean: Rethinking Material Conditions in the Landscape of Jews and Christians, London 2020; R. S. Ascough (Hg.), Christ Groups and Associations. Foundational Essays, Waco TX 2022; B. W. Longenecker (Hg.), Greco-Roman Associations, Deities, and Early Christianity, Waco TX 2022.

[1013] Dibelius, Jak, 165 f; Metzner, Jak, 116 f.

[1014] LSJ, 1692. So auch Burchard, Jak, 98, mit Hinweis auf IgnPolyk 4,2; Herm mand XI 9. 13. 14; Justin, dial. 63,5. Vgl. auch Mk 1,23 (Versammlung) im Unterschied zu 1,21 (Raum).

[1015] S. u. zur Stelle. Bei Paulus seit 1Thess 1,1. Durchgängig in Apg für die Christus-bekennende Gemeinde. Vgl. auch Mt 18,17.

Gedacht ist auf jeden Fall an einen *Innenraum* mit Sitzgelegenheiten, in dem eine Versammlung oder gottesdienstliche Feier stattfindet. Die Eintretenden wollen beide gleichermaßen an der Versammlung teilnehmen.[1016] In dem Versammlungsraum gibt es Sitzplätze und Fußschemel.[1017] Die Gemeinde ist nach sozialem Status gestaffelt: Es gibt gute Plätze für die Honoratioren.

V. 3 Mit der Wendung zu den Adressaten, die die persönliche Relevanz des Bildes für die Adressaten steigert, wird der zweite Teil des Szenarios dargestellt: die Reaktion der Anwesenden bzw. Gemeindeglieder (»ihr«) auf die beiden Personen. Jakobus bedient sich des Stilmittels der Ethopoiie[1018], indem er im Rahmen der literarisch gestalteten Szene imaginierte Gemeindeglieder, die er mit den Adressaten identifiziert, sprechen lässt. Dabei ahmt er ihre Redeweise durchaus ironisch nach. Die Gemeindeglieder lassen sich vom optischen Eindruck der Hinzukommenden beeinflussen: ἐπιβλέψητε.[1019] Der wichtige Mann wird nochmals durch seine Kleidung charakterisiert. Die Gemeindeglieder reagieren auf das Erscheinungsbild der beiden Protagonisten mit unterschiedlicher sozialer Behandlung. Der Wichtige wird geehrt, indem ihm ein guter Sitzplatz angeboten wird (κάθου ὧδε καλῶς[1020]), der Arme wird mit »Desinteresse«, »Distanzierung« und »Degradierung« behandelt[1021], wie die lebhafte Beschreibung der Anweisung deutlich macht: »Du steh« – »oder setz dich dort unten an meinem Fußschemel hin« – also auf den Boden. Auch hier geht es nicht um Details des Szenarios – weshalb hat der imaginierte Sprecher einen Fußschemel?[1022] Es geht um soziale Differenzierung und Geringschätzung in der Gemeindeversammlung.

V. 4 In dem nachgestellten Hauptsatz, der als Frage formuliert ist, beurteilt der Verfasser, der gern mit rhetorischen Fragen arbeitet[1023], das imaginierte soziale Verhalten seiner Adressaten: διεκρίθητε ἐν ἑαυτοῖς, und bewertet es negativ: ἐγένεσθε

[1016] Ob es sich um fremde oder zugezogene Christusbekenner oder um Neulinge handelt oder einfach um arme Gemeindeglieder, bleibt offen. Vgl. 1Kor 14,23: Paulus rechnet mit Nicht-Mitgliedern, die eine Gemeindeversammlung besuchen. KLOPPENBORG, James, 93.96, plädiert für ein Synagogalgebäude (mit Berufung auf A. Batten): A. J. BATTEN, The Urbanization of Jesus Traditions in James, in: A. Batten / J. S. Kloppenborg (Hg.), James, 1&2 Peter and the Early Jesus Tradition, LNTS 478, London / New York 2014, 78–96.

[1017] J. S. Kloppenborg denkt an einen Versammlungsraum und vergleicht Nachrichten über Synagogengebäude (KLOPPENBORG, James, 96 f.).

[1018] Dazu in der Einleitung (s. o.).

[1019] In Jak nur hier. Im NT noch Lk1,48; 9,38 (Konnotation des »Sich Sorgens um«: LXX-Diktion).

[1020] »Setz dich hier gut hin«. Ein guter Sitzplatz ist stets Ausdruck eines guten sozialen Status, vgl. z. B. Mt 23,6. Weitere Einzelheiten werden hier genannt.

[1021] POPKES, Jak, 163.

[1022] ὑποπόδιον: seltenes Substantiv. LXX: Ps 98,5; 109,1; Jes 66,1; Klgl 2,1. Im NT meist als LXX-Zitat: Mt 5,35; Lk 20,43 (Ps 109,1LXX); Apg 2,35 (Ps 109,1LXX); 7,49 (Jes 66,1LXX); Hebr 1,13 (Ps 109,1LXX); 10,13. Jak 2,3 ist die einzige ntl. Bezeugung, die nicht-metaphorisch ist und sich auf den Fußschemel als Möbelstück bezieht. Entweder ist daran gedacht, dass der Arme sich neben den Fußschemel hinsetzen soll oder dass er einfach »unten« sitzt: METZNER, Jak, 118 Anm. 68, zu lokalem ὑπό.

[1023] 2,5.6.7.21.25; 4,1.4. Diese Fragen haben eine suggestive Intention. Sie evozieren ein »Nein« und sollen zugleich Betroffenheit bei den Adressaten hervorrufen.

κριταὶ διαλογισμῶν πονηρῶν. Was ist Inhalt der Kritik des Jakobus? διακρίνειν heißt »spalten«.[1024] διακρίνεσθαι kann »mit sich im Streite sein, Bedenken tragen, zweifeln« heißen.[1025] Dibelius übersetzt: »Habt ihr euch dann nicht untereinander geschieden?«[1026] Damit scheint er auf eine soziale Spaltung in den imaginierten Gemeinden abzuheben. Die Wendung »Schiedsrichter böser Gedanken« ist mit Dibelius attributiv aufzulösen, etwa als »böswillige / übelwollende Schiedsrichter«. Hier wie öfter im Jak ist der nachgestellte Genitiv, der ein adjektivisches Attribut ersetzt, Mittel eines prätentiösen Stils.[1027] Die »bösen[1028] Überlegungen[1029]« beziehen sich auf das Verhalten der Gemeindeglieder gegenüber dem Armen: die soziale Ungleichbehandlung der Eintretenden in der Gemeindeversammlung, die Bevorzugung des Reichen und die dadurch entstehende Spaltung der Gemeinde.[1030] Im Rückblick auf die exemplarische Szene der V. 2–4 muss betont werden, wie wirkungsvoll der Verfasser schreibt und wie ethisch selbstsprechend – auch weil aus der Erfahrung genommen – die Szene ist. Die starke Verknappung, bei der anders als in der Erzählung vom reichen Mann und dem armen Lazarus (Lk 16,19–31) alle erzählerischen Details fehlen[1031], hinterlässt einen nachhaltigen Eindruck, der geschickt in der anklagenden Frage in V. 4 aufgefangen wird.

An Jak 2,1–4 knüpfen sich vielfältige Überlegungen der Kommentatoren zu dem möglichen sozialen Stand des Reichen, zu seinem möglichen Status als Senator oder Patron, zu der Frage, ob beide Männer als Christen oder als zufällig eintretende Nichtchristen zu verstehen seien[1032], weshalb sie die Versammlung aufsuchen, ob es sich bei der συναγωγή um eine jüdische Synagoge handele, wie der Bau vorzustellen und ausgestattet sei, um welche Art von Sitzgelegenheiten es sich handele und ob der imaginierte Vorfall eher eine gottesdienstliche oder eher eine juristische Szene imaginiere. Diese Fragen sind für die Textaussage von nachgeordneter Bedeutung. Sie berücksichtigen nicht die *literarische* Qualität der Szene und ihre primär *moralische* Blickrichtung. Die allgemeinere Frage, wieweit hier *reale* Vorkommnisse aus den frühchristlichen Gemeinden geschildert werden, darf nicht übersehen,

---

[1024] LSJ, 399: »separate one from another«.

[1025] BAUER / ALAND, 370. Siehe Jak 1,6. Vgl. Jud 9.

[1026] DIBELIUS, Jak, 170.

[1027] Vgl. oben zu 2,1. Weiter DIBELIUS, Jak, 170: »Semitismus«, vgl. Lk 18,6. διεκρίθητε und κριταί: Wortspiel mit demselben Stamm.

[1028] πονηρός noch in 4,16.

[1029] διαλογισμός hap. leg. in Jak.

[1030] SCHLIESSERS Überlegungen, Zweifel, 283–286, zur Bedeutung von διακρίνειν in Jak 1,6 überschätzen die Kompliziertheit der Frage. Richtig ist aber Schliessers Hinweis darauf, dass Jak 2,4 im Zusammenhang von Einheit und Unparteilichkeit in der Gemeinde gelesen werden muss: »Die von Jakobus kritisierte Haltung steht nicht im Gegensatz zum Glauben, sondern vielmehr im Gegensatz zur Einfalt, konkret zur Unparteilichkeit« (286). Das ist zugleich das *eigene* Thema des Jak.

[1031] Vergleichbar: die topische Kontrastierung zwischen Reichem und Armem und die Betonung der prächtigen Kleidung des Reichen, der nicht die Kleidung, sondern die Geschwüre des Armen kontrastiert werden.

[1032] Ausführlich zu den Vorschlägen der Kommentatoren ALLISON, Jak, 389–399; METZNER, Jak, 113–118.

dass hier nicht einfach eine sozialgeschichtliche Quelle vorliegt. Einerseits ist das Beispiel gerade deswegen treffend, weil es reale Erfahrungen spiegelt. Andererseits werden keine Details mitgeteilt. All die von der Exegese gestellten Fragen werden *nicht* beantwortet. Das Beispiel ist eben deswegen so schlagend, weil es nicht um sozialgeschichtliche oder juristische Szenarien und deren Details geht, sondern um die mit schlichtesten topischen Erzählmitteln und literarischen Stereotypen erzielte *eine* ethische Mahnung: In der Gemeindeversammlung dürfen keine Unterschiede aus sozialen Gründen gemacht werden, denn das passt nicht zu dem Glauben an »unsern Herrn der Herrlichkeit, Jesus Christus« (2,1). Welchen nachhaltigen Eindruck der Text hinterließ, geht aus der Syrischen Didaskalia 12,20–25 hervor, die im direkten Anschluss an Jak 2 das vorbildliche Verhalten des Bischofs einfordert:

> Wenn aber ein armer Mann oder eine arme Frau kommt, entweder von deinen Gemeindemitgliedern oder aus einer anderen Gemeinde, und besonders, wenn sie in hohen Jahren stehen, und es ist kein Platz da für solche, so schaffe ihnen Platz von ganzem Herzen, o Bischof, selbst wenn du auf dem Boden sitzen müsstest, *daß du nicht seist wie einer, der die Person ansieht*, sondern daß bei Gott dein Dienst wohlgefällig sei.[1033]

2. Texteinheit: 2,5–7 Den Armen muss Ehre erwiesen werden

(5) Hört, meine geliebten Brüder: hat nicht Gott die Armen in Bezug auf[1034] die Welt auserwählt, die zugleich[1035] reich im Glauben sind und Erben der Königsherrschaft, die er denen verheißen hat, die ihn lieben, (6) während ihr dem Armen keine Ehre erwiesen habt?[1036] Tyrannisieren[1037] euch nicht die Reichen, und sind sie es nicht[1038], die euch vor die Gerichte ziehen? (7) Schmähen eben diese nicht den guten Namen, der über euch genannt ist?

Textkritik: V. 5 τω κοσμω πλουσιους: 01. 02 originale Lesart.03. 04 originale Lesart, Minuskel 33; του κοσμου πλουσιους 02C2 (korr).04C2 (korr.), viele Minuskeln; weitere Varianten: die Hss sind hier unsicher. Dat. der Beziehung (DBR, § 197) statt Genitiv ist lectio difficilior, die Genitivverbindung schafft eine Angleichung an κληρονομους της βασιλειας. εν πιστει würde als Einschub fungieren und das Paradoxon von »arm in Bezug auf die Welt (oder: im Urteil der Welt) – reich im Glauben« aufbrechen. V. 7 ουκ lesen 01. 03. 04, viele Minuskeln, Byz., και haben P74. 02. 33 und zahlreiche Minuskeln. Die Frage ist stilistisch vorzuziehen.

Jakobus führt die Thematik weiter aus und gibt ihr eine theologische Wende. Die weiterführende *admonitio* in drei Teilen (V. 5–7.8–11.12–13) wird ausführlich ein-

---

[1033] Die syrische Didaskalia, übersetzt und erklärt von H. Achelis und J. Flemming, Leipzig: Hinrich'sche Buchhandlung, 1904, 70. Syrischer Text: A. Vööbus, The Didascalia Apostolorum in Syriac I, CSCO 401; II, CSCO 407, Löwen 1979. Entstehungszeit des größtenteils verlorenen griechischen Originals: Mitte 3. Jh. in Syrien (B. Steimer, Art. Didaskalia, LACL ³2002, 196 f).

[1034] Die Übersetzung folgt der interpretierenden Glättung der Handschriften 322.323.

[1035] »Zugleich« wurde im Deutschen hinzugefügt. Der doppelte Akkusativ ist in seinen Relationen unklar.

[1036] Zur Übersetzung als Teil der Frage siehe den Kommentar.

[1037] Nach Bauer / Aland, 811.

[1038] Im Griechischen einfach: αὐτοί.

geleitet mit der nachdrücklichen, fast beschwörenden Eröffnungsformel: »Hört, meine geliebten Brüder«, die der Verfasser nur an dieser Stelle benutzt.[1039] Was sollen die Adressaten hören? Im ersten Teil (V. 5–7) folgt eine Anklagerede, die im Anschluss an die Szene von 2,1–4 auf drei rhetorischen Fragen (οὐχ, οὐχ, οὐκ) aufbaut: (1) Hat Gott nicht die Armen erwählt? (2) Sind es nicht die Reichen, die euch unterdrücken und vor die Gerichte ziehen? (3) Verlästern sie nicht »den guten Namen«? Die klimaktische Dynamik der Fragen ist offensichtlich. Die Anklage selbst wird im zweiten Teil der ersten rhetorischen Frage in V. 6a formuliert: »während *ihr* dem Armen Unehre getan habt«. Dieser Vorwurf bezieht die Gemeindeglieder in die Szene der V. 1–4 ein. Die fiktive Szene wird damit zur epistolaren und moralischen Realität. Das Verhalten der Gemeinde in V. 1–4 bildet den sachlichen Kern des ersten Teils der *admonitio* ab V. 5. Die weiteren rhetorischen Fragen dienen der argumentativen Unterstützung der Anklage, verschieben aber zugleich die Thematik hin zum Thema: die *Armen*. Die Vorstellung von der Erwählung der Armen spielt für mehrere Exegeten eine wichtige Rolle innerhalb der Interpretation des gesamten Briefes und erfordert einige Vorüberlegungen.

Bereits mit der ersten rhetorischen Frage: »Hat Gott nicht die Armen erwählt?«, die von einem imaginierten einzelnen armen und gleichsam zufällig in die Szene geratenden Versammlungsbesucher auf »die Armen« als soziale Gruppe in den Gemeinden überlenkt[1040], verleiht der Verfasser der Szene über προσωπολημψία eine

---

[1039] Eine ähnliche Eröffnungsform einer Rede findet sich in Apg 7,2 und 15,13. Zu den Aufrufen zum Hören METZNER, Jak, 120 Anm. 86.

[1040] Zum Thema: P. U. MAYNARD-REID, Poverty and Wealth in James, Maryknoll 1987; R. GARRISON, Redemptive Almsgiving in Early Christianity, JSNTS 77, Sheffield 1993; S. ELY WHEELER, Wealth as Peril and Obligation. The New Testament on Possessions, Grand Rapids 1995; S. K.-J. KIM, Stewardship and Almsgiving in Luke's Theology, JSNTS 155, Sheffield 1998; C. L. BLOMBERG, Neither Poverty nor Riches. A Biblical Theology of Material Possessions, NSBT 7, Leicester 1999; D. H. EDGAR, Has God not Chosen the Poor? The Social Setting of the Letter of James, JSNTS 206, Sheffield 2001; V. PRETACCA, Gott oder das Geld. Die Besitzethik des Lukas, TANZ 39, Tübingen / Basel 2003; F. S. KLOPPENBORG, Poverty and Piety in Matthew, James, and the Didache, in: H. de Sandt / J. K. Zangenberg (Hg.), Matthew, James and Didache. Three related Documents in Their Jewish and Christian Setting, SBLSymS 45, Atlanta 2008, 201–232; U. BERGES / R. HOPPE, Arm und Reich, NEB.T 10, Würzburg 2009; N. NEUMANN, Armut und Reichtum im Lukasevangelium und in der kynischen Philosophie, SBS 220, Stuttgart 2010; A. J. MALHERBE, Godliness, Self-Sufficiency, Greed, and the Enjoyment of Wealth I.II, NT 52, 2010, 378–405; NT 53, 2011, 73–96; R. DEINES, God or Mammon, The Danger of Wealth in the Jesus Tradition and in the Epistle of James, in: M. Konradt / E. Schläpfer (Hg.), Anthropologie und Ethik, 327–385; H. KRAMER, Lukas; JÓNSSON, James, 260–274; TH. R. BLANTON IV, Wealth, Poverty, Economy, in: St. P. Ahearne-Kroll (Hg.), Oxford Handbook of the Synoptic Gospels, Oxford 2023, 296–319 (Lit.). – Was BLANTON, Wealth 314, zum lukanischen Doppelwerk bemerkt, lässt sich unter Umständen auch auf die Armutsdarstellungen in Jak anwenden: »Greg Woolf (2006, 99 [= G. WOOLF, Writing Poverty in Rome, in: M. Atkins / R. Osborne (Hg.), Poverty in the Roman World, Cambridge 2006, 83–99]) notes that ›eloquent poets [like Martial], whose education and manners proclaim their status, play at paupers to amuse and tease their hosts and to extract from them a little of the wealth about which they have been made to feel uneasy.‹ Judging from the narratives in Luke-Acts, it appears that evangelists could deploy similar tactics to elicit donations among givers and recipients placed far lower on the economic scale«.

neue Dimension: In den Gemeinden *sind realiter* Arme, und das Verhalten, Arme zu beschämen oder zu verachten, richtet sich nicht nur gegen den Glauben an Jesus Christus, sondern gegen Gott selbst und gegen sein Erwählungshandeln. Jakobus stellt die These, Gott habe die Armen *erwählt*, in den Zusammenhang der βασιλεία-Theologie.[1041] Martin Dibelius hat hier die »Armentheologie« des Jakobusbriefes gefunden.[1042] Ihre Wurzeln verortet Dibelius in der Theologie des Alten Israel, sowohl in den Psalmen als auch in der Propheten- und Weisheitsliteratur.[1043] Hans Windisch und neuerdings wieder Dale C. Allison vermuten des Näheren einen ebionitischen Zusammenhang.[1044] Beides ist natürlich zu unterscheiden, und Beidem ist oft widersprochen worden, zuletzt mit unterschiedlichen Argumenten von John Kloppenborg und von Rainer Metzner. Kloppenborg gibt zu bedenken:

> The contrast of rich and poor was a standard rhetorical trope in Graeco-Roman moralizing literature.[1045]

Metzner betont zurecht, dass auch Reiche,

> wenn sie sich von Gott erniedrigen lassen, … Teilhaber der Basileia werden.[1046]

Die uneindeutige soziale Position der Adressaten und ihrer Gemeinden – Kloppenborg spricht von »urban, reasonably well educated groups of diaspora Judaeans«[1047] – verbietet, in V. 5 vorschnell eine eindeutige »Option für die Armen« im

---

[1041] βασιλεία hap. leg. in Jak. dazu ALLISON, Jak, 397f und KLOPPENBORG, James, 92–97. Weiteres bei ALLISON, Jak, Introduction, 56–62.

[1042] DIBELIUS, Jak, 170–172 und Einleitung, 58–66. Zur Verbindung von Armentheologie und Befreiungstheologie vgl. N. LOHFINK, Von der ›Anawim-Partei‹ zur ›Kirche der Armen‹. Die bibelwissenschaftliche Ahnentafel eines Hauptbegriffs der ›Theologie der Befreiung‹, Bibl 67, 1986, 153–176.

[1043] FRANKEMÖLLE, Jak I, 251–259; J. BREMER, Die Armentheologie als eine Grundlinie einer Theologie des Psalters, Hebrew Bible and Ancient Israel 5, 2016, 350–390.

[1044] H. WINDISCH / H. PREISKER, Die katholischen Briefe, HNT 15, Tübingen ³1951, 36; G. STRECKER, Art. Ebioniten, RAC 4, 1959, 487–500; J. FREY, Art. Ebionitenevangelium, WiBiLex, http://www.bibelwissenschaft.de/stichwort/47872/; ALLISON, Jak, 390. Allison denkt an »Christians within the synagogue«; allgemein zum ebionitischen Hintergrund: James,' 48–50. Dazu siehe oben die Einleitung.

[1045] KLOPPENBORG, Poverty and Piety, 228. Dazu auch M. TILLY, Besitzethik und Menschenbild bei Pseudo-Phokylides, in: M. Konradt / E. Schläpfer (Hg.), Anthropologie und Ethik, 309–325. E.N. NEILL, in: H.D. Betz (Hg.), Plutarch's Ethical Writings and Early Christian Literature, SCHNT 4, Leiden 1978, 289–362 (Kommentar zu Plutarch: Von der Liebe zum Reichtum).

[1046] METZNER, Jak, 120. Metzner wendet sich gegen Dibelius' »Armenfrömmigkeit« bei Jak (DIBELIUS, Jak, 46; vgl. auch »Armenliteratur«, 27; »Armenpathos«, 48.61; »Armenstolz«, 62; »patriarchalisch-pietistische Armenethik« und »pauperistische Reichtumsfeindschaft«, 66). Dibelius' Darstellung in seinem Exkurs »Arm und Reich« (58–66) gibt eine historische und traditionsgeschichtliche Skizze von der Armenfrömmigkeit Israels bis zum Hirten des Hermas. Damit zeichnet er den Rahmen, in dem Jak zu lesen sei. Es fehlt aber eine Unterscheidung zwischen Armentheologie, Armenfrömmigkeit und sozialgeschichtlichem Armenstatus. Differenziert urteilt BURCHARD, Jak, 102–103: »Man rechnet also wohl besser mit sozial verschieden gestellten Adressaten, die ihre Stellung auch verschieden auffaßten« (103).

[1047] KLOPPENBORG, Poverty and Piety, 231. Sicher ist das urbane Milieu der Adressaten: O. WISCHMEYER, Reconstructing the Social and Religious Milieu of James: Methods, Sources, and Possible Results, in: H. van de Sandt / J.K. Zangenberg (Hg.), Matthew, James and Didache, 33–41, 41.

Sinne einer Armen*soziologie* zu finden.[1048] Wohl aber liegt hier – hier muss man ausdrücklich Dibelius zustimmen – eine Art der Armen*theologie* vor.

Vor der Exegese sind vier *Unterscheidungen* zwischen den verschiedenen exegetischen Fragestellungen, die in der Literatur zu Jak 2,1–13 und besonders zu 2,5 zusammenlaufen, notwendig: *erstens* die allgemeine historische Unterscheidung zwischen der Realität wirtschaftlicher Armut (Mt 26,11) und einer korrespondierenden *sozial* basierten Parteinahme für die Armen im Alten Orient und in Israel einerseits und der *theologischen* Bedeutungsgebung des Status des Armen in der jüngeren Literatur Israels andererseits, *zweitens* zwischen theologischen Traditionen und eigener theologisch-ethischer Argumentation des Verfassers, *drittens* zwischen Rekonstruktion der realen sozialen Verhältnisse in den Adressatengemeinden und dem eigenen sozialen Status des Verfassers sowie *viertens* zwischen der literarischen Darstellung des Jakobus und weiterführenden theologiegeschichtlichen Zuordnungen, die den Text als Quelle für die Geschichte des Urchristentums im Rahmen der frühkaiserzeitlichen Sozialgeschichte lesen. In dieser komplexen Problemlage muss sich die *Versexegese* darauf konzentrieren, die *Argumentation* des Verfassers und seine literarischen Mittel freizulegen. Weiterführende Überlegungen zum Sozialstatus der Gemeinden und des Verfassers sowie zum sozialpolitischen Umfeld wurden auf der Basis des gesamten Briefes in der Einleitung angestellt.[1049] Die *admonitio* von V. 5–7 erschließt sich vornehmlich von der Rhetorik und der literarischen Dynamik des Arguments her, nicht von einer rekonstruierenden Sozialtheologie oder -theorie oder einer theologie- oder religionsgeschichtlichen Zuordnung.[1050] Das textpragmatische Gewicht liegt auf der Anklage in V. 6a, die sich aus der imaginierten Szene von V. 1–4 ableitet, das Anliegen des Verfassers von 2,1 aufnimmt und die Adressaten direkt attackiert. Um die Schwere der Anklage zu motivieren, konstruiert der Verfasser die drei genannten rhetorischen Fragen. Er beabsichtigt nicht, eine reale Beschreibung der sozialen Wirklichkeit in den Gemeinden zu geben, sondern will ein mögliches Fehlverhalten in Bezug auf die praktische Ausübung des Glaubens der Adressaten kritisieren.

V. 5[1051] Die pointierte Antithese Arm – Reich sprengt die strenge Form durch *variatio* auf: τῷ κόσμῳ (Dat. der Beziehung) und ἐν πίστει (lokale oder instrumentale Umstandsbestimmung).[1052] Mit der paradoxen Formulierung »reich im *Glauben*« bindet Jakobus seine Anklage an das Thema πίστις von 1,2–12 an. Die Armen werden doppelt theologisch charakterisiert: τοὺς πτωχοὺς τῷ κόσμῳ πλουσίους ἐν πίστει.

[1048] So auch Bammel, ThWNT 6: Die Gemeinde selbst identifiziert sich nicht mit den Armen. Der Verfasser »ist armenfreundlich, ohne daß aber von daher sein Denken bestimmt ist. Der Abschnitt [2,1–7] kann demnach nicht als ein Dokument christlichen Ebionitismus angesehen werden« (910).

[1049] S. o.

[1050] So auch Johnson, Jak, 227: »The force of James' example does not derive from its historical referentiality, but from its rhetorical function«.

[1051] Siehe zu allen Details des Verses die sehr sorgfältige Analyse bei Allison, Jak, 394–398.

[1052] Metzner, Jak, 121 Anm. 95.

Das Erwählungsargument ist das erste und wuchtigste der Dreierkette. Jakobus greift dabei auf religiöse Grundüberzeugungen Israels[1053] und der Jesustradition des Urchristentums[1054] zurück: *Gott hilft den Armen.* Diesen Grundsatz adaptiert, interpretiert und modifiziert Jakobus für sein Argument, indem er folgende *vier* Elemente hinzufügt: (1) Erwählung, (2) πτωχὸς τῷ κόσμῳ, (3) reich *ἐν πίστει*, (4) »Erben der βασιλεία, die er [Gott] denen verheißen hat, die ihn lieben«.

Ad (1): Dass die Armen in besonderer Weise von Gott *erwählt* seien, ist eine *ad-hoc*-Zuspitzung des Jakobus, die sich in dieser Weise weder im Alten Testament[1055] noch in den frühchristlichen Schriften findet. Jakobus scheint sich dabei an die theologische Vorstellung der Erwählung der Demütigen anzuschließen, die Johannes Bremer beschreibt:

> Die Erwählung von Demütigen durch JHWH (Ri 6,15; Jes 11,4; Jdt 9,11[13] u. ö.) hat schließlich zu der Überzeugung g4eführt, dass diese erstrebt werden kann und zum wahren Leben führt (Zeph 2,3; Spr 22,4 u. ö.).[1056]

Jak 2,5 liegt damit sachlich, strukturell und sprachlich besonders nahe bei 1Kor 1,26–29[1057], wo Paulus ebenfalls auf die alttestamentliche Vorstellung der Erwählung der Schwachen rekurriert:

> (26) Βλέπετε γὰρ τὴν κλῆσιν ὑμῶν, ἀδελφοί, ὅτι οὐ πολλοὶ σοφοὶ κατὰ σάρκα, οὐ πολλοὶ δυνατοί, οὐ πολλοὶ εὐγενεῖς·(27) ἀλλὰ τὰ μωρὰ τοῦ κόσμου ἐξελέξατο ὁ θεός, ἵνα καταισχύνῃ τοὺς σοφούς, καὶ τὰ ἀσθενῆ τοῦ κόσμου ἐξελέξατο ὁ θεός, ἵνα καταισχύνῃ τὰ ἰσχυρά, (28) καὶ τὰ ἀγενῆ τοῦ κόσμου καὶ τὰ ἐξουθενημένα ἐξελέξατο ὁ θεός, τὰ μὴ ὄντα, ἵνα τὰ ὄντα καταργήσῃ, (29) ὅπως μὴ καυχήσηται πᾶσα σὰρξ ἐνώπιον τοῦ θεοῦ.
>
> (26) Seht doch auf eure Berufung, Brüder: Nicht viele Weise nach dem Fleisch, nicht viele Mächtige, nicht viele Vornehme, (27) sondern was töricht ist vor der Welt, hat Gott erwählt, damit er die Weisen zuschanden mache; und was schwach ist vor der Welt, hat Gott erwählt, damit er zuschanden mache, was stark ist; (28) und was gering ist vor der Welt und was verachtet ist, hat Gott erwählt (ἐξελέξατο), was nichts ist, damit er zunichtemache, was etwas ist, (29) auf dass sich kein Fleisch vor Gott rühme,

---

[1053] Grundtexte zum Schutz des Armen und zur Parteinahme Gottes für den Armen: Ex 22,20–26; Dtn 15,7–11; Ps 113,5–9; 140,13 u. ö. Vgl. R. KESSLER, Art. Armut / Arme AT, WiBiLex, https://www.bibelwissenschaft.de/stichwort/13829/; BREMER, Die Armentheologie; DERS., Wo Gott sich auf die Armen einlässt. Der sozio-ökonomische Hintergrund der achämenidischen Provinz Yehud und seine Implikationen für die Armentheologie des Psalters, Göttingen 2016. Vgl. weiter DERS., Art. Demut (AT), WiBiLex https://www.bibelwissenschaft.de/stichwort/16317/.

[1054] Lk 6,20 fpar. Grundlegend: KRAMER, Lukas.

[1055] Vgl. SCHRENK / QUELL, Art. ἐκλέγομαι κτλ., ThWNT 4, 1942, 147–197, besonders 173–175 (Septuaginta). Hap. leg. in Jak.

[1056] BREMER, Art. Demut. Allerdings fehlt in den genannten Texten das Stichwort »Erwählung«.

[1057] SCHRENK, ThWNT 4, 180. J. Bremer findet in den nachexilischen Psalmen eine Tendenz zur Spiritualisierung der zunächst seit den altorientalischen Königreichen stets sozial und ökonomisch ausgerichteten Kategorie der »Armen«. So ist in dem späten Text Ps 149,4 die Kategorie der *anawim* deutlich spiritualisiert.

sowie bei dem lukanischen Magnificat (Lk 1,46–55), in dem Niedrige und Mächtige und Hungernde und Reiche kontrastiert werden. Statt des Motivs der Erwählung bei Paulus[1058] findet sich bei Lukas das entsprechende »Anschauen«:

(46) Μεγαλύνει ἡ ψυχή μου τὸν κύριον, (47) καὶ ἠγαλλίασεν τὸ πνεῦμά μου ἐπὶ τῷ θεῷ τῷ σωτῆρί μου, (48) ὅτι ἐπέβλεψεν ἐπὶ τὴν ταπείνωσιν τῆς δούλης αὐτοῦ … (52) καθεῖλεν δυνάστας ἀπὸ θρόνων καὶ ὕψωσεν ταπεινούς, (53) πεινῶντας ἐνέπλησεν ἀγαθῶν καὶ πλουτοῦντας ἐξαπέστειλεν κενούς.

(46) Meine Seele erhebe den Herren, (47) und mein Geist freue sich über Gott, meinen Heiland, (48) weil er auf die Niedrigkeit seiner Magd gesehen hat. … (52) Er hat die Mächtigen von den Thronen gestoßen und die Niedrigen erhöht, die Hungernden füllt er mit Gütern, und die Reichen lässt er leer ausgehen.

Während Paulus vor allem gegen die Weisheit argumentiert und die Armut nicht erwähnt, konzentriert sich Jakobus auf die Polemik gegen den sozialen Einfluss der Reichen.[1059] *Ad (2)*: Die Zusatzbestimmung τῷ κόσμῳ, in 1Kor 1,27 τοῦ κόσμου, bringt *sub contrario* die Perspektive Gottes zum Ausdruck.[1060] Der doppelte Akkusativ »die Armen in Bezug auf die Welt« und »die Reichen im Glauben« bilden ein sorgsam formuliertes antithetisches Paradoxon,[1061] stilistisch zwischen Dativ und präpositionaler Bestimmung variierend. *Ad (3)*: »Die Reichen *im Glauben*«[1062] sind als rhetorischer Gegenbegriff zu den »Armen in der Perspektive der Welt« konstruiert. Es geht nicht um Reiche im ökonomischen Sinne, sondern um die Adressaten, die den Glauben richtig leben. *Ad (4)*: Sie werden nun mit zwei Begriffen ausführlich charakterisiert, die traditionell sind und von Jakobus wegen dieses begrifflichen Gewichtes eingesetzt werden: zunächst als »Erben der Basileia«. Das metaphorische Syntagma ist fester Bestandteil des frühchristlichen Soziolekts, sowohl in den Synoptikern als auch in den Paulusbriefen.[1063] Hier spricht Jakobus denen, die richtig glauben, die *Gottesherrschaft* zu – bei Jakobus nur hier belegt. Hinzugefügt ist eine weitere formelhafte Bestimmung: »die er denen verheißen hat, die ihn lieben«. ἐπαγγελία ist ein Begriff, den Paulus in seiner Abraham-Bundestheologie besonders ausgearbeitet hat.[1064] Wie in Jak 1,12 dient die Wendung von der Verheißung auch hier nicht als spezielles theologisches Argument, sondern als rhetorische Überhöhung des »Reich-im-Glauben-Seins«. Dasselbe gilt für den letzten Zusatz: »denen,

---

[1058] Siehe die Lesarten in Jak 2,5.

[1059] Bei Paulus begegnet das Thema der Armut nur im Zusammenhang mit der Kollekte für die »Armen in Jerusalem«: Röm 15,26.

[1060] S. o. zur Textkritik: Dativ der Beziehung.

[1061] Vgl. die Paradoxa in 2Kor 6,10: »[wir], die Armen, die doch viele reich machen« und 8,9: »Unser Herr Jesus Christus … wurde arm um euretwillen, obwohl er reich war …« und Apk 2,9: »Ich kenne deine Bedrängnis und die Armut – aber du bist reich«.

[1062] Zur ἐν-Konstruktion vgl. Eph 2,4 (»reich an Erbarmen«).

[1063] Stets formelhaft: Mt 25,34; 1Kor 6,9 f; 15,50; Gal 5,21; (Eph 5,5 ex negativo). In Jak beide Begriffe hap. leg.

[1064] Siehe bes. im Galaterbrief. Weitere Belege im Hebräerbrief, bes. Kap. 9. Vgl. ἐπαγγέλλεσθαι Jak 1,12; 2,5.

die ihn lieben«, den Jakobus ebenfalls schon in 1,12 verwendet hat.[1065] Insgesamt zeigt er in 1,12 und 2,6 dieselbe Perspektive auf: »Der bewährte Glaube« von 1,3 wird zu Gott führen. Dafür werden topische Metaphern wie »den Kranz des Lebens erhalten« oder »Erben der Königsherrschaft sein« eingesetzt. Während 1,12 als Makarismus gestaltet ist, benutzt Jakobus in 2,5 die rhetorische Frage und entfernt sich damit stilistisch von der synoptischen Parallele in dem Makarismus von Lk 6,20par:

Lk 6,20: Μακάριοι οἱ πτωχοί, ὅτι [ὑμετέρα] ἐστὶν ἡ βασιλεία τοῦ θεοῦ.
Selig seid ihr Armen, denn euer ist das Reich Gottes.
Mt 5,3: Μακάριοι οἱ πτωχοὶ τῷ πνεύματι, ὅτι αὐτῶν ἐστιν ἡ βασιλεία τῶν οὐρανῶν.
Selig sind die Armen im Geist, denn ihrer ist das Reich der Himmel.
Jak 2,5: ὁ θεὸς ἐξελέξατο τοὺς πτωχοὺς τῷ κόσμῳ πλουσίους ἐν πίστει καὶ κληρονόμους τῆς βασιλείας.
Hat nicht Gott die Armen in Bezug auf die Welt auserwählt, die zugleich reich im Glauben sind und Erben der Königsherrschaft, die er denen verheißen hat, die ihn lieben?

Die Armen, die bei Lukas und in Q[1066] als *soziale* Gruppe angesprochen werden, erscheinen bei Mt und in Jak 2,5 als *religiös* definierte Gruppe. Dass der Verfasser hier auf ein ihm bekanntes Q-Logion anspielt, das er selbständig in ähnlicher Weise wie Mt interpretiert, ist wahrscheinlich.[1067]

V. 6 Mit der harten Opposition »ihr« im Gegenüber zu »Gott« in V. 5 wendet sich Jakobus in V. 6a mit seiner Anklage, die auf der Szene 2,1–4 beruht, direkt gegen die Adressaten: »Ihr habt dem Armen Unehre angetan«. Burchard schreibt zutreffend: »Arme zu ἀτιμάζειν[1068] ist herzlos und Sünde«.[1069] Allison macht die Textpragmatik deutlich: Die Adressaten sollen beschämt werden.[1070] Die Anklage ist in der Sache und in der Wortwahl äußerst kurz und schnörkellos. Jakobus wirft seinen Adressaten ein Verhalten in ihren Versammlungen vor, das sich am Ehre / Schande / Scham-Konzept ihrer Umwelt orientiert statt an Gottes Handeln.[1071] V. 6a lässt sich als unabhängiger Aussagesatz verstehen (so Nestle-Aland und ECM und die große

---

[1065] Siehe dort.

[1066] Vgl. auch EvThom 54.

[1067] Vgl. BURCHARD, Jak, 100: Hinter V. 5 kann »die in Lk 6,20 aufgenommen Seligpreisung liegen ... Jak wird aber mindestens für Welt opp. Glaube und den Relativsatz verantwortlich sein«. ALLISON, Jak, 397, weist darauf hin, dass Armut zuerst bei Lk und Mt mit der Basileia in Zusammenhang gebracht wird.

[1068] Selten im NT, hap. leg. in Jak. ἀτιμάζειν lässt sich im Deutschen eher mit dem passivischen »Unehre antun / Ehre verweigern« als dem aktivischen »entehren« wiedergeben. M. CARMINATI u. a., Art. ἀτιμάζω, HTLS I, 1262–1286 (das Substantiv ist paulinisches Vorzugswort, 1274).

[1069] Vgl. die atl., ntl. und altkirchlichen Belege bei BURCHARD, Jak, 101. Besonders LXX: Spr 14,21; 22,22; Sir 10,23 (mit ἀτιμάζειν). Vgl. auch 1Kor 11,22: καταισχύνετε τοὺς μὴ ἔχοντα (Beschämt ihr die, die nichts haben?).

[1070] ALLISON, Jak, 398.

[1071] Kurz und präzise JOHNSON, Jak, 225: »James gives a distinctive turn to the honor / shame axis of values characteristic of the Greco-Roman world«.

Mehrzahl der Kommentatoren). Besser ist es, die Anklage mit Christoph Burchard zur ersten rhetorischen Frage zu ziehen und zu übersetzen: »... während (δὲ) ihr den Armen verachtet?«[1072] Dadurch wird die Struktur der drei – unterschiedlich langen – rhetorischen Fragen deutlicher abgebildet.[1073]

Auf jeden Fall hat der Verfasser unter der Hand seiner Argumentation eine neue Richtung gegeben. Diese wesentliche Wendung wird in den Kommentaren nicht diskutiert. War das Szenario von 2,1–4 eine bloße (negativ gewertete) *Möglichkeit* und diente als *exemplum* für die Warnung: »Keine auf sozialer Differenzierung beruhende Parteilichkeit in Gemeindeversammlungen!«, scheint es jetzt so, als verhielten sich die Adressaten *tatsächlich* so, wie Jakobus es in 2,1–4 schildert. Das kann entsprechend der epistolographischen Situation *nicht* der Fall sein. Der Verfasser nutzt aber die Plausibilität der Szene zu einer verstärkten polemischen Attacke auf die Adressaten, die reale Vorkommnisse insinuiert, auf die er dann mit entsprechender rhetorischer Empörung reagieren kann. Die direkte Ansprache »Ihr aber« setzt die Adressaten in einen grundsätzlichen Gegensatz zum Handeln Gottes, und zwar nicht, weil sich die Adressaten tatsächlich sozial unverantwortlich verhalten hätten, sondern weil sie prophylaktisch durch die Wucht der Anklage beschämt werden sollen, um ihren Glauben desto besser zu schützen. Wenn diese rhetorische Qualität von V. 6a beachtet wird, verlieren die Überlegungen der Kommentatoren zu der Frage, wer denn die Reichen seien – Heiden, die Christen verfolgen, oder reiche Christen, die arme Christen schikanieren –, an Bedeutung.[1074] Was Jakobus mit den beiden nun folgenden kurzen rhetorischen Fragen tut, löst sich von dem Szenario von 2,1–4 ab. Er will den Adressaten die weiterreichenden Folgen ihres Tuns aufzeigen und kommt damit in einen *anderen Diskurs*, den von Arm und Reich, wie Jakobus ihn aus der Tradition Israels kennt und wie er allgemein in der hellenistisch-römischen Welt geführt wird. Die Reichen sind in diesem Diskurs nicht etwa *per se* böse[1075], aber mindestens latent *gefährlich*, da sie »meist zu den Herrschenden gehören«[1076], und von ihnen gilt – unabhängig von ihrer religiösen Zugehörigkeit: »Üben nicht die Reichen Gewalt gegen euch und schleppen euch vor die Gerichte?« An diesem Punkt taucht das Motiv der *Gewalt* als einer Spielart von *Unrecht* auf, dem besonders Sigurvin Jónsson nachgegangen ist.[1077]

Werden »die Reichen« – die Bezeichnung als πλούσιοι begegnet erst hier[1078] – in die Gemeinden integriert und u. U. noch besonders geehrt, wie Jakobus beobach-

---

[1072] Burchard, Jak, 101. B. übersetzt syntaktisch steif: »ihr dagegen«.

[1073] Eine eindeutige syntaktische Entscheidung lässt sich nicht herstellen.

[1074] Metzner, Jak, 124: vermutet werden a) reiche Juden, b) reiche Christen, c) reiche Heiden.

[1075] Darauf weisen Burchard, Jak, 101 (»Jak erklärt die Reichen nicht für verworfen«), und Metzner, Jak, 124, hin.

[1076] Burchard, Jak, 101.

[1077] Jónsson, James, 274–282.

[1078] Mongstad-Kvammen, Postcolonial Reading. »Die Reichen« ist »verbreitete, oft abschätzige Gruppenbezeichnung« (Burchard, Jak, 101, Beispiele).

C. Briefcorpus 223

tet, kann das auf die Gemeinden zurückschlagen. Es geht jetzt nicht mehr nur um προσωπολημψία, d. h. um soziale Bevorzugung, sondern um Macht und Gewaltausübung. Aus der Erfahrung Israels heraus weist Jakobus darauf hin, dass die Reichen Gewalt üben und Prozesse anstrengen. Die Propheten und die Weisheitsschriften warnen davor, den Armen, den Bedürftigen, den *personae miserae*, den Witwen und Waisen (Jak 1,27) Gewalt anzutun (καταδυναστεύειν[1079]). Ps 9,30LXX warnt vor dem Sünder und dem Gottlosen, »der zusammen mit den Reichen (9,29) im Hinterhalt liegt« und »den Armen wegreißt« (oder wegschleppt):

ἐνεδρεύει τοῦ ἁρπάσαι πτωχόν, ἁρπάσαι πτωχὸν ἐν τῷ ἑλκύσαι αὐτόν.
Er lauert, um die Armen zu fangen, er fängt den Armen, wenn er ihn in sein Netz zieht.

Das seltene Verb ἕλκω in Jak 2,6 kann auf Ps 9 anspielen.[1080] κριτήρια, Gerichte[1081], werden in den ntl. Schriften nur noch im 1Kor erwähnt. Die heftige Polemik, mit der Paulus in 1Kor 6,1–11 gegen Prozessführer in der Gemeinde in Korinth vorgeht, macht aber Zweierlei deutlich, einmal dass Prozessführen von Anfang an auch in den Christus-bekennenden Gemeinden geübt wurde,[1082] und zwar von Wohlhabenden, zum andern, dass verantwortungsvolle Gemeindeleiter dies Verhalten kritisierten. Die drastische Wendung ἕλκουσιν ὑμᾶς εἰς κριτήρια hält Burchard für »idiomatisch«.[1083] Die kontrastive Anrede mit ὑμεῖς δὲ[1084] steigert die Emotionalität der Rede. Jakobus versucht an dieser Stelle, rhetorisch besonderen Druck auf die Leserschaft aufzubauen, indem nicht mehr klar ist, wen er mit ὑμεῖς meint. Die Leserschaft soll sich fragen: »Sind wir das?«

V. 7 Es folgt die dritte rhetorisch-polemische Frage, die nun wieder in den theologischen Bereich führt: »Lästern sie nicht den guten Namen, der über euch ausgerufen ist?« Auch hier geht es nicht um eine Beschreibung realer Vorfälle in den Gemeinden[1085], sondern um *Gefahren*, die der Verfasser höchst eindrücklich mittels metaphorisch-topischer Sprache benennen will. Die Beziehung ist uneindeutig: Gehören die Reichen (αὐτοὶ) wie die ὑμεῖς von V. 6a doch bereits zu den Christengemeinden und ruinieren deren ethischen Ruf von innen gegenüber den Nicht-Christen (1Kor 6,1–11), oder handelt es sich um eine Christen-feindliche

---

[1079] Gewaltsam unterdrücken, nur hier in Jak, im NT noch Apg 10,38. LXX-Ausdruck: »den Armen und Bedürftigen unterdrücken« (Ez 18,12; 22,29), »Arme unterdrücken« (SapSal 2,10; Am 4,1; 8,4; Sach 7.10); »Witwen und Waisen unterdrücken« (Mal 3,5; Jer 7,6; 22,3; Ez 22,7).

[1080] ἕλκω: ziehen, schleppen, hap. leg. in Jak, selten im NT. Vgl. Ps 9,30LXX metaphorisch: Der Sünder reißt den Armen wie ein Löwe. Dazu Ps 9,35: Gott hilft der Waise (Jak 1,27).

[1081] κριτήριον: nur hier in Jak. Vgl. 1Kor 6,2.4. BAUER / ALAND, 92: »Gerichtshof«.

[1082] E.-M. BECKER/U. BABUSIAUX, Paulus, der »Sklave Christi Jesu« (Gal 1,10; Röm 1,1; Phil 1,1), im Lichte des römischen Rechts, NTS 69, 2023, 365–385.

[1083] BURCHARD, Jak, 101: Verweis auf P.Turin VI 11; Achilles Tatius (Ende 2. Jh. n. Chr.) VII 15,4; vgl. auch Apg 16,19.

[1084] Vgl. Apg 3,14.

[1085] So sehr häufig bei Paulus, besonders im 1Kor.

Gruppe, die Gemeindeglieder juristisch belangt und damit zugleich ethisch diskreditiert? Nun ist das Subjekt von V. 6b – »die Reichen« – auch das leitende Subjekt von V. 7. Der Verfasser bleibt also weiterhin in dem *polemischen Reichendiskurs Israels*, den er auf »seine« Adressaten bezieht. Es geht ihm nicht um die Abbildung konkreten sozialen Fehlverhaltens in den angeschriebenen Gemeinden, sondern um die Vermeidung von Missständen *a limine*. Welchen theologischen Vorwurf Jakobus »den Reichen« genau macht, bleibt offen. Er bedient sich wie öfter einer unklaren Wendung, die von den Kommentatoren entweder auf Gott – und damit auf die einfache Zugehörigkeit – oder aber auf Christus – und damit dann auf die Taufe – bezogen wird. »Den guten Namen lästern«, und zwar »den Namen, der über euch ausgerufen wurde«, bezieht sich in Dtn 28,10; Jer 14,9; Amos 9,11 f (Apg 15,17); 4Esr 4,25; 10,22 u. ö. auf den Gott Israels und kann auch in Jak 2 angenommen werden. Ein offener Bezug auf Christus und auf die Taufe findet sich jedenfalls nicht. Paulus dagegen beruft sich in 1Kor 6,11 im Zusammenhang mit seiner Prozesskritik auf den »Namen des Herrn Jesus Christus« und spielt mindestens mit ἀπελούσασθε auf die Taufe an. Eine vergleichbare Anspielung ist von Jak 2,1 her auch in V. 7 möglich.[1086] 1Tim 6,1 belegt andererseits, dass auch in den Christus-bekennenden Gemeinden vom »Namen Gottes« ohne Hinweis auf Christus gesprochen wurde. Jak 2,7 bleibt an diesem Punkt undeutlich und vermeidet jedenfalls eine Christus-bekennende oder Tauf-Sprache. Wie öfter geht es um die schöne Formulierung, nicht um die theologisch korrekte Zuordnung. Die Wendung »den Namen über jemandem nennen / ausrufen« bezeichnet auf jeden Fall ein Eigentumsverhältnis bzw. eine Zugehörigkeit.[1087] βλασφημεῖν gegen Gott (oder gegen Christus) ist ein schwerer Vorwurf[1088], der der Polemik des Verfassers geschuldet ist und die theologische Dimension des (möglichen) Fehlverhaltens »der Reichen« aufzeigen soll. Der »schöne Name« ist eine Allusion an Ps 53,8 und 134,3LXX (Gottes »guter / schöner Name«).

3. Texteinheit: 2,8–11 Nächstenliebe

(8) Wenn ihr jedoch[1089] das königliche Gesetz erfüllt gemäß der Schrift: ›Liebe deinen Nächsten wie dich selbst‹, handelt ihr gut, (9) wenn ihr aber parteilich seid, tut ihr Sünde und werdet vom Gesetz als Übertreter überführt. (10) Denn

---

[1086] Eine Bezugnahme von Jak 2,7 auf 1Kor 6 ist nicht ausgeschlossen. Die antithetische Verbindung von Prozessieren und dem »Namen« ist so ungewöhnlich, dass sie sich durchaus als Echo auf 1Kor 6 verstehen lässt.

[1087] Bauer / Aland, 596.

[1088] βλασφημεῖν hap. leg. in Jak: »Gottes Namen lästern«: Röm 2,24; 2Clem 13,2a; IgnTrall 8,2b (jeweils nach Jes 52,5); 1Tim 6,1; 1Petr 4,1 (Heiden); Apk 13,6; 16,9. In LXX: 4Kön 19,4. 6. 22; Jes 52,5; DanLXX 3,96. J. K. Aitken / R. Brucker, Art. βλασφημέω, HTLS I, 1638–1655.

[1089] μέντοι wird von Bauer, 1020, mit »wirklich« übersetzt. Weitere Bedeutungen: »freilich, allerdings, jedoch«. Im Zusammenhang mit Jak 2,1–7 sind beide Bedeutungsnuancen denkbar. Wichtig Burchard, Jak, 103: »Jedenfalls ist V. 8 eine captatio« (Werben um die Adressaten).

wer das ganze Gesetz hält, in einem Punkt[1090] aber sündigt, ist in Bezug auf alle Gebote schuldig geworden.[1091] (11) Der nämlich sagt: ›du sollst nicht ehebrechen‹, sagt auch: ›du sollst nicht töten‹; wenn du nun nicht die Ehe brichst, aber tötest, bist du ein Übertreter des Gesetzes geworden.

Textkritik: V. 8 νομον τελειτε βασιλικον: verschiedene Wortumstellungen und kleinere Abweichungen, zwei oder mehr sahidische Zeugen lesen νομον της ελευθεριας τελειτε (1,25; 2,12). κατα την γραφην: den gebräuchlicheren Plural κατα τας γραφας verwenden Minuskel 322.323 sowie sahidische und altkirchenslawische Zeugen, mehrere Papyri, Majuskeln und Minuskeln sowie lat. Zeugen lassen die Wendung aus. ως σεαυτον: 044 und andere Majuskeln, zahlreiche Minuskeln lesen εαυτον (zum Ersatz von σεαυτον durch εαυτον vgl. DBR, § 64,1). V. 9 προσωπολημπτειτε: das μ findet sich in P74V. 01. 02. 03*. 04, während 03C2, zwei weitere Majuskeln und viele Minuskeln das μ auslassen (vgl. zu Jak 2,1). V. 10 Das seltene Verb τηρηση bezeugen im Konjunktiv Aor. 01. 03. 04 und zwei Minuskeln (in der Form τηρησει 025 und zahlreiche Minuskeln). Zu τελεισει (Futur) glätten 044 und Minuskeln (vgl. V. 8), πληρωσει bevorzugen 02 und zahlreiche Minuskeln. Ähnliche Abweichungen bei πταιση. V. 11 Die Reihenfolge der Dekaloggebote und der Modus der Verben wechseln. μοιχευσης etc. nach μη haben 02. 03. 025 und zahlreiche Minuskeln (DBR, § 426, μη plus Konj.), μοιχευσεις etc. haben zahlreiche Minuskeln. Der Konj. Aor. ist besser bezeugt und lect. diff. (Ex 20 und Num 5 haben prohibitives Futur: DBR, § 361). Die Umstellung gilt auch für den ει- Satz. παραβατης: αποστατης haben P74. 02 (BAUER / ALAND, 197; 2Makk 5,8; Herm mehrfach, nicht im NT).

Mit V. 8 verlässt der Verfasser den allgemeinen Reiche-Arme-Diskurs und kehrt wieder zur direkten Kommunikation mit seinen brieflichen *Adressaten* zurück, indem er sich auf seinen Ausgangspunkt bezieht: das Szenario der möglichen – auch V. 8 ist hypothetisch[1092] – sozialen Bevorzugung in den Gemeindeversammlungen (προσωπολημπτεῖτε V. 9). Er nimmt eine weitere Vertiefung vor und entwickelt ein gedrängtes, aber präzises ethisches Argument aus der *Theologie des Gesetzes* heraus. Seine ethische Aussage ist klar: Handeln gemäß dem Gebot der Nächstenliebe ist gutes Handeln, Parteilichkeit ist Sünde. Die theologischen Koordinaten modifizieren und konkretisieren die Wendung von 1,25: »das vollkommene Gesetz der Freiheit«. In 2,8 spricht der Verfasser vom »königlichen Gesetz nach der Schrift«, um dann in 2,12 das »Gesetz der Freiheit« noch einmal aufzurufen. Jakobus meint die Tora, zusammengefasst in der Kombination des Gebotes der Nächstenliebe nach Lev 19,18 mit dem Dekalog. Für die leitende Thematik des bewährten Glaubens (1,3) bedeutet das Argument: Parteilichkeit ist Sünde und macht den Glauben unwirksam. Syntaktisch-stilistisch arbeitet der Verfasser mit einfachen Konditionalsätzen: Das Verhalten x (Konditionalsatz) hat ethisch die Konsequenz y (Aus-

---

[1090] »Punkt« ist im Deutschen ergänzt.

[1091] Wörtlich: »ist an allen schuldig geworden«.

[1092] Vgl. KONRADT, Christliche Existenz, 185. Das εἰ in V. 8. 9. 11 leitet jeweils einen Fall ein, der dann ethisch bewertet wird.

sagesatz). In die Konditionalkette eingeschoben sind zwei Relativsätze, die »Fälle« konstruieren: Wer x tut, von dem gilt y (V. 10 und 11).[1093]

V. 8 In dem antithetisch aufgebauten Satzgefüge der Verse 8 und 9 gibt der Verfasser eine klare ethische Richtschnur, indem er »gutes Handeln« von »Sünde tun« unterscheidet. Er beginnt mit dem positiven Handeln: der Anwendung der Nächstenliebe. καλῶς ποιεῖν im Sinne von »gut / richtig handeln« verwendet Jakobus auch in 2,19.[1094] Die Wendung »das Gesetz erfüllen« benutzt Paulus in Röm 2,27.[1095] Der Verfasser des Jakobusbriefes sucht hier nach einer stilistisch anspruchsvolleren Formulierung. Das hinzugefügte Adjektiv »königlich«[1096] ist mit Christoph Burchard am ehesten im Sinne von »majestätisch, erhaben« zu lesen.[1097] Gemeint ist hier speziell das Gebot der Nächstenliebe nach Lev 19,18. Der Zusatz »gemäß der Schrift« entspricht der (im Plural stehenden) Wendung in 1Kor 15,3 und gehört dem frühchristlichen Soziolekt an.[1098] Wichtig sind drei Punkte. *Erstens* zitiert Jakobus explizit Septuaginta und entnimmt damit die Grundnorm seiner ethischen Weisung dem »Gesetz« Israels. In Jak 2,8 liegt das erste von vier expliziten Septuagintazitaten vor.[1099] Durch die lobende Auszeichnung als »königliches Gesetz« erhält Lev 19,18 eine überragende Stellung im Gesamtgefüge des νόμος.[1100] Nur Jak 2,8 und Gal 5,14 sowie Röm 13,8–10 geben Lev 19,18 diese der Gesamtheit des νόμος übergeordnete Position.[1101] *Zweitens* unterscheidet der Verfasser zwischen νόμος und γραφή. Diese

---

[1093] ὁ γὰρ + Part. oft bei Paulus (vgl. Jak 1,6).

[1094] Vgl. auch 1Kor 7,37.38; Phil 4,14; 2Petr 1,19; 3Joh 6.

[1095] Im NT noch ähnlich Lk 2,39: ὡς ἐτέλεσαν πάντα τὰ κατὰ τὸν νόμον κυρίου (als sie alles vollendet hatten gemäß dem Gesetz des Herrn). Dort geht es um Gesetzesobservanz.

[1096] βασιλικός im Sinne des lobenden Adjektivs nur hier im NT. »Königlich« hap. leg. im NT. Joh 4,46 »ein Königlicher«; Apg 12,20 »Königsgebiet«.

[1097] BURCHARD, Jak, 104. Vgl. Burchards ausführliche Darstellung des antiken Sprachgebrauchs im Umkreis von königlichen Gesetzen seit PsPlaton. Burchard betont, dass es in Jak 2,8 nicht um einen religiösen, philosophischen (oder politischen) »Fachausdruck« geht (103). Noch ausführlicher dokumentiert ALLISON, Jak, 401–405. ALLISON, Jak, 405, schlägt vor, die verschiedenen Bedeutungszusammenhänge in der Wendung mitzuhören und auf eine eindeutige Bedeutungszuschreibung zu verzichten (mit Hinweis auf F. G. DOWNING, Ambiguity, Ancient Semantics, and Faith, NTS 56, 2010, 139–162). Beachtet man das Streben des Verfassers nach stilistischer *periphrasis* (Umschreibung: »königliches Gesetz« statt γραφή) und *variatio*, kann auf den Nachweis dieser zusätzlichen Bedeutungsdimensionen – die selbstverständlich in dem Adjektiv »königlich« mitschwingen, verzichtet werden.

[1098] Vgl. analoge Wendungen Röm 4,18; 2Kor 4,13; 2Tim 2,8. ALLISON, Jak, 406: »This secular formula … appears in the LXX with reference to religious instruction. James – with the singular instead of the plural accusative (cf. 1 Cor 15.3) – may supply the first and only Christian occurrence before Clement of Alexandria«.

[1099] Vgl. die Einleitung und WISCHMEYER, Scriptural Classicism?, 291–303. Die vier Zitate: Jak 2,8=Lev 19,18 (Nächstenliebe), Jak 2,11=Ex 20,3 f / Dtn 5:17 f (Dekalog), Jak 2,23=Gen 15,6 (Abraham), Jak 4,6=Spr 3,34LXX (Demut).

[1100] An dieser Stelle steht Jakobus in der theologischen Tradition des Paulus, vor allem von Röm 13,8–10 in der Zusammenstellung von Liebesgebot und Dekalog.

[1101] Jak 2,8 ist zu kurz, als dass man möglichen paulinischen Einfluss weiterverfolgen könnte. Dem Verfasser ist anders als Paulus nicht an einer Diskussion über die herausragende Bedeutung des Liebesgebotes gelegen, sondern daran, die Bedeutung dieses Gebotes für die Parteilichkeit zu zeigen. Aber Jak 2,8 ist neben Paulus die einzige neutestamentliche Schrift, die dem Liebesgebot diese Stellung zuschreibt. Die synoptischen

Unterscheidung zieht sich durch das gesamte Schreiben.[1102] *Drittens* befindet sich Jakobus mit seiner ethischen Weisung im *mainstream* frühchristlicher Regelung des internen Sozialverhaltens Christus-bekennender Gemeinden (»Wenn *ihr* ...«).[1103] Das Gebot der Nächstenliebe gehört zu den meistzitierten atl. Sätzen im NT:

Mt 5,43	Mt 19,19	Mt 22,39	Mk 12,31.33
Lk 20,27	Röm 12,19	Gal 5,14	Jak 2,8

V. 9 Der zweite Teil des Satzgefüges wiederholt die Struktur des ersten Teils mit Konditionalsatz und urteilendem Aussagesatz und fügt das sachliche negative antithetische Urteil hinzu: »Sünde tun« statt »Gutes machen« (*variatio* der Verben). Im Rückgriff auf 2,1 greift Jakobus noch einmal den negativen Fall der sozialen Parteilichkeit auf, die den Ausgangspunkt dieser *admonitio* darstellt, um nun aus der Sicht der Gesetzes*erfüllung* (2,8) zu urteilen: Parteilichkeit in Gemeindeversammlungen – προσωπολημπτέω ist ein *Neologismus* des Jakobus – ist Gesetzes*übertretung*.[1104] Damit wird Parteilichkeit als Sünde bezeichnet, genauer als ein Akt sündigen Handelns (ἐργάζεσθαι). ἁμαρτία hat der Verfasser schon in 1,15 thematisiert.[1105] Das Verb ἐλέγχειν, aufdecken, nachweisen, zurechtweisen, strafen[1106], als part. conj. eingesetzt, umfasst ethisch-pädagogische und juridische Aspekte. Im Hirten des Hermas deckt Rhode vor dem Herrn die Sünden des Hermas auf (ἐλέγξω).[1107] Jakobus argumentiert im Umfeld paulinischer Begrifflichkeit: sowohl in Bezug auf die Sünde[1108] als auch auf die Übertretung des Gesetzes, einerseits in Zitat und Allusion von Lev 19,15–18[1109], andererseits im Umfeld des paulinischen Gesetzesdiskurses, besonders in Röm 7. In Jak 2,9 hat das Gesetz dieselbe Funktion wie in Röm 7,7–13, ohne dass Jakobus hier die weiterführende Gesetzesdiskussion des Paulus

---

Evangelien verfolgen die Tradition des Doppelgebotes. Vgl. dazu O. WISCHMEYER, Love as Agape. The Early Christian Concept and Modern Discourse, Waco / Texas und Tübingen, 2021, 39–44.

[1102] γραφή 2,8.23; 4,5 (γράφειν begegnet anders als bei Paulus, den Synoptikern und Johannes nicht). νόμος 1,25; 2,8.9.10.11.12; 4,11 (viermal).

[1103] BURCHARD, Jak, 104 f, plädiert mit Hinweis auf 4,11 zurecht dafür, Jakobus habe das Gebot der Nächstenliebe »primär intern« verstanden (105).

[1104] Hap. leg. im NT. Vorbild: Lev 19,15: οὐ λήμψῃ πρόσωπον πτωχοῦ οὐδὲ θαυμάσεις πρόσωπον δυνάστου (Berücksichtige nicht das Gesicht des Armen und staune nicht über das Gesicht des Mächtigen). Das Verb begegnet nicht in LXX. Bei Jak liegt eine gleichsam »moderne« Zusammenfassung von Lev 19,15 vor.

[1105] Vgl. auch 4,17; 5,15.16.20.

[1106] BAUER / ALAND, 503. Hap. leg. in Jak. Nicht häufig im NT. Aufdecken von Taten, Fehlverhalten bzw. Sünden: Joh 3,20; 8,46; 16,8; 1Kor 14,24; Eph 5,11.13; 1Tim 5,20; Tit 1,9.13; 2,15; Jud 15.

[1107] Herm vis I 5. Der ermahnende Aspekt begegnet vor allem in den Pastoralbriefen.

[1108] 1,20: ὀργὴ γὰρ ἀνδρὸς δικαιοσύνην θεοῦ οὐ κατεργάζεται. Vgl. die verwandte Redewendung Röm 13,10; Gal 6,10.

[1109] ALLISON, Jak, 408–410. Die Gebote in Lev 19,15–18 verbinden die Motive von Gerichten (κρίσις), Parteilichkeit gegenüber dem Armen, ἐλέγχειν (tadeln), Sünde (ἁμαρτία), Nächstenliebe und Beachtung des Gesetzes (νόμος). Diese Motive liegen der Argumentation des Jakobus zugrunde, die aber anders als Lev 19 konkret auf die Sünde der Parteilichkeit fokussiert ist.

228 Kommentar

aufgreift. Röm 7 stand bereits hinter Jak 1,13–15. Es geht um die aufdeckende, überführende Rolle des Gesetzes, seine elenchtische Wirkung. In diesen Zusammenhang gehört auch das Motiv der Übertretung. παραβάτης/παράβασις[1110] wird von Paulus im Zusammenhang der Überschreitung des Gesetzes (νόμος) verwendet.[1111] Auch die folgenden Verse 10 und 11 stehen in diesem Kontext.

V. 10 Jakobus baut sein Argument, Parteilichkeit in den Gemeindeversammlungen sei Sünde und gegen das Gesetz gerichtet, durch ein weiteres Argument (begründendes γάρ) aus, das die Konsequenzen der Parteilichkeit benennt und V. 9 noch überbietet: Wer nur gegen *ein* Gebot verstößt, ist am *ganzen* Gesetz schuldig geworden. Dahinter steht folgende konkrete Pragmatik in Bezug auf die Adressaten: Es reicht nicht, wenn ihr im Allgemeinen die Gebote haltet, d. h. die Mehrzahl der Gebote befolgt. Euer Glaube wird nur dann vollkommen sein (1,2–4), wenn ihr *alle* Gebote haltet – so auch das Gebot der Nächstenliebe, das nach Lev 19,15 die Parteilichkeit ausschließt. Jakobus kleidet sein Argument in zwei pädagogisch anschauliche Beispielsätze. Der erste Satz formuliert einen antithetisch konstruierten Fall, der in ein Urteil mündet: »Denn wenn jemand x tut (positiv), zugleich aber andererseits y tut (negativ), ist er schuldig«. Die Basislogik ist eine gemeinantike, besonders bei den Stoikern formulierte Überzeugung von der Einheit der Tugend. Mit Seneca gilt daher im Umkehrschluss: *qui unum autem habet vitium, omnia habet*.[1112] Christoph Burchard weist aber zurecht darauf hin, dass Jak 2,10 hier nicht im engeren Sinne stoisch beeinflusst ist, sondern innerhalb des jüdischen Gesetzesdiskurses argumentiert, wie er sich auch bei Paulus und im Matthäusevangelium dokumentiert findet: »Jak steht also wohl in jüd. Tradition, zumal Schriftbeweis folgt«.[1113] Paulus argumentiert entsprechend in Gal 5,3 gegen Christus-bekennende galatische Gemeindeglieder, die sich beschneiden lassen wollen, ohne die Konsequenzen zu bedenken:

μαρτύρομαι δὲ πάλιν παντὶ ἀνθρώπῳ περιτεμνομένῳ ὅτι ὀφειλέτης ἐστὶν ὅλον τὸν νόμον ποιῆσαι.

Wer sich beschneiden lässt, nimmt die Verpflichtung auf sich, das ganze Gesetz zu tun.[1114]

[1110] παραβάτης hap. leg. in Jak (2,9.11). Vgl. Röm 2,25: Περιτομὴ μὲν γὰρ ὠφελεῖ ἐὰν νόμον πράσσῃς, ἐὰν δὲ παραβάτης νόμου ᾖς, ἡ περιτομή σου ἀκροβυστία γέγονεν (Die Beschneidung nämlich nützt, wenn du das Gesetz hältst, wenn du aber ein Übertreter des Gesetzes bist, hat sich deine Beschneidung in Unbeschnittenheit verwandelt).

[1111] Röm 2,23: ὃς ἐν νόμῳ καυχᾶσαι, διὰ τῆς παραβάσεως τοῦ νόμου τὸν θεὸν ἀτιμάζεις (Der du dich im Gesetz rühmst, schändest Gott durch die Übertretung des Gesetzes?); 4,15; Gal 3,19. Vgl. auch Röm 5,14; 1Tim 2,14; Hebr 2,2; 9,15.

[1112] Seneca, benef. V 15,1. Weiteres bei BURCHARD, Jak, 106. Vgl. besonders Diogenes Laertius VII 125: »Die Tugenden hängen nach ihnen alle wechselseitig zusammen, so daß, wer eine besitzt, alle besitzt« (Übersetzung: F. JÜRSS, Diogenes Laertius, Leben und Lehre der Philosophen, Stuttgart 2010, 341).

[1113] BURCHARD, Jak, 106. Weitere jüdische Texte bei ALLISON, Jak, 410–413.

[1114] Vgl. zur Sache auch Mt 5,19; 23,23. ὅλος ὁ νόμος auch Mt 22,37.40; Gal 5,3.

Das Argument heißt: Es gibt keine Auswahl von Gesetzesgeboten. Alle sind gleich wichtig und müssen gehalten werden. Das Gesetz ist eine Ganzheit. τηρεῖν τὸν νόμον Μωϋσέως[1115] begegnet auch in Apg 15,5 und mehrfach im 1Joh.[1116] Das im Neuen Testament sehr seltene Verb πταίειν[1117] bezeichnet »straucheln« als »fehlen, irren, sündigen«[1118]. ἐν ἑνί (Neutrum) betrifft das Einzelgebot. ἔνοχος c.gen., »schuldig sein, sich verfehlen an«, passt zur »Gerichtssprache«[1119] der Texteinheit und bereitet V. 13 vor.

V. 11 Zu dem harten Urteil von V. 10 fügt Jakobus eine letzte Begründung hinzu (γάρ). Die Satzstruktur führt die doppelte Kette von ὁ- und εἰ- Sätzen weiter, wechselt aber im εἰ- Satz in die 2.Pers.Sing. und steigert damit die Wirkung des Arguments und die Betroffenheit der Adressaten. Jakobus demonstriert nochmals die Einheit der Gesetzesgebote, diesmal unter Hinweis darauf, dass alle von ein und demselben Gott gegeben wurden (ὁ γὰρ εἰπών[1120]). Exemplarisch werden zwei der Dekaloggebote genannt. Hier liegt das zweite Septuagintazitat vor, und zwar als Kombination der beiden Gebote aus Ex 20,13.15 / Dtn 5,17.18 zu Ehebruch und Totschlag, die wie auch in anderen neutestamentlichen Texten exemplarisch für den Dekalog im Ganzen stehen.[1121] Die Reihenfolge bezieht sich auf Dtn 5: ehebrechen, töten. Für die Dekaloggebote gilt dasselbe wie für das Gebot der Nächstenliebe: Auch sie gehören zu den meistzitierten Sätzen aus der Septuaginta im Neuen Testament.[1122] Die Gebote gegen Ehebruch und Totschlag haben hier keine eigene Bedeutung und beziehen sich nicht auf mögliche Handlungen der Adressaten. Wichtig ist dagegen die Konfiguration von Gebot der Nächstenliebe und Dekaloggeboten. Der Verfasser assoziiert bei dem Gebot der Nächstenliebe den Dekalog und steht damit im Zusammenhang mit frühjüdischen Ansätzen und mit Mt 19,18 und Röm 13,9, d. h. sowohl paulinischer Tradition als auch synoptischer Jesustradition.[1123]

[1115] τηρεῖν in der Bedeutung von »befolgen« nur hier in Jak. Vgl. 1,27 »rein erhalten«.

[1116] 1Joh 2,3 (zweimal).5; 3,22.

[1117] Röm 11,11; Jak 2,10; 3,2 (zweimal), 2Petr 1,10. Vgl. Sir 37,12 (Zusammenhang mit Gesetz).

[1118] BAUER / ALAND, 1455.

[1119] BAUER / ALAND, 540.

[1120] Die Vorstellung, Gott selbst habe gesprochen und die Gebote gegeben, nehmen Ex 20,1 und Dtn 5,1–5 auf.

[1121] Deutliche Übereinstimmung besteht zwischen Jak 2,11 und Lk 18,20. Jak formuliert kürzer und konsequent exemplarisch.

[1122] Der Dekalog bzw. Sätze des Dekalogs werden in unterschiedlichem Umfang und in unterschiedlichen Zusammenhängen in den ntl. Texten zitiert. Mehrere Texte verbinden Dekalogsätze mit dem Gebot der Nächstenliebe: Jak 2,8–11; Mt 19,18; Röm 13,9. Im Einzelnen gibt es folgende Konstellationen: (a) *Dtn 5,16–20*: Mt 19,18f (zusammen mit dem Gebot der Nächstenliebe); Mk 10,19 (par zu Mt 19,18f, ohne Nächstenliebe); Lk 18,20 (par zu Mt 19,18f, ohne Nächstenliebe); (b) *Dtn 5,17*: Mt 5,21; (c) *Dtn 5,17f* Jak 2,11 (*in dieser Auswahl-Kombination nur hier, zusammen mit dem Gebot der Nächstenliebe*); (d) *Dtn 5,17–21*: Röm 13,9 (zusammen mit dem formalen Gebot »du sollst nicht begehren« und dem alles überbietenden und zusammenfassenden Gebot der Nächstenliebe); (e) *Dtn 5,18*: Mt 5,27.

[1123] Nachweise bei O. WISCHMEYER, Das Gebot der Nächstenliebe bei Paulus. Eine traditionsgeschichtli-

230 Kommentar

Das Resultat der Ausführungen ist in V. 11b formuliert: Die Übertretung eines Dekaloggebotes bedeutet (insgesamt) Gesetzesübertretung (Wiederholung von 2,9). Was das in der eschatologischen Perspektive bedeutet, wird in 2,12 f dargelegt.

4. Texteinheit: 2,12–13 Das Gesetz der Freiheit

(12) **So sollt ihr reden**[1124]**, und so sollt ihr handeln, wie (Menschen**[1125]**), die durch das Gesetz der Freiheit gerichtet werden wollen**[1126]**.** (13) **Das Gericht nämlich (ist) erbarmungslos über den, der nicht Erbarmen getan hat. Es triumphiert (aber) Erbarmen über das Gericht.**

Textkritisch: **V. 13** Einige Majuskeln, Minuskel 33 und viele Minuskeln lesen ανιλεως statt ανελεος. 04, Minuskel 33 und viele Minuskeln lesen den Akk. ελεον statt des Nominativs.

Mit dieser Texteinheit zieht Jakobus das Fazit seiner Mahnung zum Thema der Parteilichkeit in den Gemeindeversammlungen. Einerseits greift er mit der Wiederholung der Wendung »Gesetz der Freiheit« auf 1,25 zurück und knüpft wieder an die Thematik von Hören – Reden – Tun von Kap 1 an, zugleich leitet er mit der Doppelwendung von »Reden und Tun« zu seinen weiteren Ausführungen zu den ἔργα (2,14–26) und den λόγοι (3,1 ff) über.

V. 12 Damit nimmt Jakobus das Motiv der ποιηταὶ λόγου von 1,22 wieder auf und wiederholt zudem die Wendung vom »Gesetz der Freiheit« von 1,25. Als Abschluss der νόμος-Erörterung gibt er eine direkte ethische Anweisung an die Adressaten: Sprecht (1,19) und tut (3,18 »Frieden tun«, 4,17 »Gutes tun«) gemäß der Gerichtsnorm des »Gesetzes der Freiheit«. Das οὕτως lässt sich am besten auf die folgenden Imperative beziehen: »So sollt ihr sprechen und so sollt ihr tun«.[1127] Der eschatologische Horizont des Gerichtes[1128] wird im Folgesatz in V. 13 ganz deutlich: μέλλοντες enthält den futurischen Aspekt (»als solche, die [in Zukunft] durch das Gesetz der Freiheit gerichtet werden«[1129]). Wie öfter vermeidet Jakobus die explizite Begrifflichkeit wie »der Tag des Gerichtes« (so 2Petr 2,9 u. ö.) zugunsten seiner eigenen paradoxalen Formulierung des »Gesetzes der Freiheit«[1130], das den Maßstab des kommenden Gerichtes setzt. Nach 2,8 ist an das Gebot der Nächstenliebe gedacht, das Parteilichkeit ausschließt. Jakobus argumentiert hier von demselben Verständnis aus wie 1Petr 1,17:

---

che Untersuchung, in: DIES., Von Ben Sira zu Paulus, 137–162. Vgl. auch JEWETT, Romans, 809–815.

[1124] Die beiden Verben sind am besten als Imperative zu lesen: POPKES, Jak, 179 Anm. 200. Der Indikativ ergibt im paränetischen Zusammenhang keinen Sinn.

[1125] »Menschen« ist im Deutschen ergänzt.

[1126] Übersetzung von μέλλοντες.

[1127] BAUER / ALAND, 1209: »m. Bezug auf das Folgende: folgendermaßen«.

[1128] Gerichtslexik bei Jak: κρίνειν Jak 2,12; 4,11.12; 5,9; κρίσις 2,13; 5,12; κριτής 2,4; 4,11.12; 5,9; κρίμα 3,1. Eschatologisch konnotiert bei 2,12.13; 3,1; 4,12; 5,9.12.

[1129] METZNER, Jak, 134, weist auf die verschiedenen Übersetzungsmöglichkeiten hin (nach BAUER / ALAND, 1015 f). Hier liegt die einfache futurische Übersetzung am nächsten: BAUER / ALAND, 1015, 1cb.

[1130] Vgl. oben zu 1,25.

καὶ εἰ πατέρα ἐπικαλεῖσθε τὸν ἀπροσωπολήμπτως[1131] κρίνοντα κατὰ τὸ ἑκάστου ἔργον.
Und wenn ihr den als Vater anruft, der jeden ohne Ansehen der Person nach seinem Werk richtet.

V. 13 Die beiden asyndetischen Hauptsätze sind präzise formuliert und klingen sentenziös.[1132] Wie Burchard betont, sind sie aber nicht vor Jakobus belegt.[1133] Im Zentrum steht ἔλεος mit dem Wortspiel: ἔλεος – ἀνέλεος[1134], das im ersten Satz als Paradoxon eingesetzt wird: »Denn das Gericht ist erbarmungslos für den, der nicht Erbarmen getan hat[1135]« (Nominalsatz). Die Kommentatoren sprechen gern vom *ius talionis*.[1136] Die Paradoxie liegt darin, dass einerseits Erbarmen gefordert wird, um andererseits demjenigen verweigert zu werden, der selbst nicht »Erbarmen tut«. Im Endgericht – so die Logik – hat die Kette des Erbarmens ein Ende. Genau vor diesem Sachbestand will Jakobus warnen. Dieselbe sachliche Paradoxie liegt dem Gleichnis vom unbarmherzigen Gläubiger Mt 18,23–35 zugrunde, wenn der König sagt:

οὐκ ἔδει καὶ σὲ ἐλεῆσαι τὸν σύνδουλόν σου, ὡς κἀγὼ σὲ ἠλέησα;
Hättest du dich nicht auch erbarmen sollen über deinen Mitsklaven, wie ich mich über dich erbarmt habe? V. 33.[1137]

Das Adjektiv ἀνέλεος dürfte ein Neologismus des Jakobus sein.[1138] ἔλεος, 3,17 auch von der »Weisheit von oben« gesagt, ist hier das Erbarmen von Menschen gegenüber Menschen.[1139] Es geht weniger um Mitleid als vielmehr um die tätige barmherzige Hilfe (ποιεῖν) als Realisierung von Nächstenliebe wie im Gleichnis vom barmherzigen Samaritaner. Lk 10,37 ist eine geradezu schlagende Parallele. Auf die Frage, wer der Nächste des Mannes sei, der unter die Räuber gefallen war, lautet die Antwort:

ὁ δὲ εἶπεν· ὁ ποιήσας τὸ ἔλεος μετ᾽ αὐτοῦ. εἶπεν δὲ αὐτῷ ὁ Ἰησοῦς· πορεύου καὶ σὺ ποίει ὁμοίως.
Er aber sagte: der die Barmherzigkeit an ihm getan hat. Es sagte ihm aber Jesus: geh und tu du ebenso.[1140]

[1131] Hap. leg. im NT.

[1132] Dazu trägt die chiastische Struktur bei: Gericht – Mitleid, Mitleid – Gericht.

[1133] Burchard, Jak, 108.

[1134] Vgl. Jak 3,17.

[1135] »Erbarmen *tun*« ist ebenso in LXX wie in der allgemeinen Gräzität belegt.

[1136] Vgl. Allison, Jak, 420.

[1137] Zu der breiten frühjüdischen und frühchristlichen Überzeugung, das göttliche Gericht erfolge analog zum Handeln der Menschen, vgl. Burchard, Jak, 108.

[1138] Hap. leg. im NT. Insgesamt sehr selten, wohl zuerst bei Jak (vgl. Burchard, Jak, 108).

[1139] Bauer / Aland, 504. Vgl. R. Bultmann, Art. ἔλεος κτλ., ThWNT 2, 1935, 474–483.

[1140] Wischmeyer, Love, 34–37 (zu Lk 10) und 190–192 (zur Barmherzigkeit). Zur alttestamentlichen Barmherzigkeit vgl. M. Witte, Barmherzigkeit mit den Bedürftigen und Notleidenden und ihre anthropologischen Grundlagen, in: Konradt / Schläpfer (Hg.), Anthropologie und Ethik, 387–412.

232 Kommentar

Burchard bemerkt: Dass Barmherzigkeit »geboten ist ... hat lange jüd. Tradition; Jak übernimmt sie wohl schon als christliche«.[1141]

Der zweite Hauptsatz ist lapidar formuliert. Das sehr seltene κατακαυχᾶται κρίσεως[1142] (Alliteration), »triumphieren über«, wird mit ἔλεος verbunden. Burchard meint, Barmherzigkeit und Triumph passten nicht zusammen.[1143] Sieges- und Triumphmetaphorik findet sich aber auch bei Paulus (Röm 8,37 u. ö.). Es geht um den Sieg der Barmherzigkeit angesichts[1144] des (strengen) Gerichtes. Der Ausblick der gesamten dritten Texteinheit ist also auf das Endgericht bezogen, im Ergebnis aber nicht angstbezogen, sondern paränetisch-*positiv*.[1145] Hier ist die Logik von 5,20 vorweggenommen: Erbarmen und Rettung werden das letzte Wort haben. Diese Überzeugung ist der Motor der brieflichen Gemeindeparänese des Jakobus.

B. 2,14–26: Glaube ohne Taten ist tot

2,14–26 ist ein geschlossener Text[1146] und stellt den argumentativen Höhepunkt der beiden ersten Hauptteile und zugleich den Abschluss des zweiten Briefteils dar.[1147] Der Text bündelt mehrere neutestamentliche Themen: (1) Hauptthema ist der *richtige* Glaube.[1148] Jak 2,14–26 ist neben Röm 3 und 4, Gal 3 und Hebr 11 einer der zentralen *Glaubenstexte* des Neuen Testaments und eine wichtige eigene Stimme in dem frühchristlichen Diskurs um πίστις.[1149] (2) Die genannten Texte beziehen sich alle auf Abraham und seinen Glauben. Insoweit gehört Jak 2,14–26 auch zu den neutestamentlichen *Abrahamtexten* und muss in diesem Zusammenhang interpretiert werden.[1150] Das Thema des richtigen Glaubens zieht in dem genannten, von

---

[1141] BURCHARD, Jak, 108, mit zahlreichen Belegen, ebenso ALLISON, Jak, 423. Besonders nahe an Jak 2: Sib II 81.

[1142] κατακαυχᾶσθαι außer Jak 2,13; 3,14 noch Röm 11,18 (dort jeweils negativ konnotiert). LXX: Sach 10,12; Jer 27,11.38 (BAUER / ALAND, 835).

[1143] BURCHARD, Jak, 108 f.

[1144] So mit BURCHARD, Jak, 108: »κατά präpositional gemeint«.

[1145] Vgl. ALLISON, Jak, 424: Jakobus betont: »the *imitatio dei* is implicit: if mercy carries the day with God, it should carry the day with human beings«.

[1146] Darauf weist METZNER, Jak, 137, hin.

[1147] BURCHARD, Jak, 110, spricht von einem Exkurs. Er hält – mit Vorsicht – 1,12–25 für ein theologisches Hauptstück des Briefes. Ähnlich METZNER, Jak, 137 f.

[1148] Elfmal πίστις, zweimal πιστεύειν.

[1149] MORGAN, Roman Faith, 469 f. Morgan spricht vom »locus classicus« (468). Sie weist zurecht darauf hin, dass bei Jakobus der Glaube nicht nur äußere (»Taten«), sondern auch innere Aspekte hat; F. W. HORN, Glaube. Neues Testament, in: ders. (Hg.), Glaube, 33–63 (insgesamt umsichtige Darstellung und Lit.). Allerdings behandelt HORN, 50, Jak 2 lediglich im Zusammenhang mit Paulus (Stichwort: »Einspruch« gegen »Gerecht nicht durch Werke des Gesetzes, sondern durch Glauben an Jesus Christus«, 48). Diese Zuordnung ist unglücklich, denn sie verkennt (1.), dass Jak 1 und 2 grundsätzlich vom Glauben handeln und (2.), dass Jak 2,14–26 ein eigenständiger wichtiger ntl. Glaubenstext ist.

[1150] Röm 4; Gal 3. Beide Texte behandeln den Glauben Abrahams und thematisieren das Verhältnis von Glauben und Werken bei Abraham, und zwar unter dem leitenden Begriff der Gerechtigkeit, der in Jak 2 keine zentrale Rolle spielt, aber als Element aus Gen 15,6 in V. 21. 24. 25 begegnet. Dazu: O. WISCHMEYER, Glaube, der durch Liebe tätig wird (Galater 5,6). Überlegungen zu den Grundlagen paulinischer Theologie,

Paulus initiierten Glaubensdiskurs weiterhin das Thema der Taten bzw. Werke nach sich. (3) Jak 2,14–26 ist der neutestamentliche Spitzentext zum Thema ἔργα[1151], nicht aber der »Werke des *Gesetzes*«. Das Thema der ἔργα, seit Paulus als »(gute) Taten« im Verhältnis zu Gesetz, Rechtfertigung und Glaube thematisiert und problematisiert, findet in Jakobus seinen wichtigsten neutestamentlichen Bearbeiter. Jakobus löst die ἔργα anders als Paulus aus der νόμος-Thematik heraus und stellt sie als die konstitutiv-aktive Komponente der πίστις dar, darin aber nicht so fern von Paulus, wie es scheinen könnte: Röm 2,13. Die Vorstellung des Jakobus von ἔργα unterscheidet sich aber doch deutlich von der des Paulus. Jak 2,14–26 erschließt sich aus der Kombination der drei genannten Themen: Glaube, Abraham und Taten im Zusammenhang der genannten Diskurstexte.

Das Generalthema der beiden ersten Briefteile, *Gefahren des »bloßen Glaubens«* ohne praktische Verwirklichung[1152], konkret dargestellt als bloßes *Reden ohne Handeln* und speziell als Parteilichkeit in den Gemeinden, wird nun in einer eigenen *theologischen* Erörterung über *Glauben ohne Taten* zum Abschluss gebracht. Das Ziel des Verfassers, die Erziehung der Adressaten zur Vollkommenheit (1,4), wird noch einmal in 2,22 betont: Aus den Taten wird der Glaube *vollkommen*. Der Text ist dreigeteilt. *Erstens*: 2,14–17 führt den Beweis für die These »Glaube ohne Taten ist tot« anhand zweier praktischer Beispiele, die wieder wie 2,2 f aus dem Erfahrungsalltag der Gemeinden genommen sind und diesen Alltag kritisch beleuchten. *Zweitens*: In V. 18–19 wird ein Einwand entkräftet. Er lautet: Es mag doch Menschen geben, die »Glauben ohne Taten haben«, und auch solche, die »Glauben aus Taten« haben. Antwort: der Glaube ohne Taten ist der Glaube der Dämonen. *Drittens*: V. 20–25 beginnen und schließen mit der These des Verfassers: »Der Glaube ohne Taten ist tot« (*inclusio*). Zur Unterstützung beruft sich Jakobus auf das berühmte Glaubensexempel des Abraham und fügt als zweites Exempel Rahab an.

Dibelius hat zurecht den *stilistischen* Anspruch der »Abhandlung: von Glauben und Werken«[1153] akzentuiert:

> Wenn irgendwo, so muß bei dem zweiten mit V. 18 anhebenden Gedankengang die stilistische Betrachtung zunächst in den Vordergrund treten. Denn Jak gebraucht hier

---

in: B. Wißgott / A. Frank (Hg.), Christlicher Glaube in seinen Anfängen. Kulturelle Begegnungen und theologische Antworten. FS B. Heininger, Würzburg 2023, 101–130 (Lit.). In dem großen johanneischen Abrahamtext Joh 8,30–59 dagegen spielt die Glaubensthematik keine Rolle, sondern die kontroverse Argumentationsfigur »Abraham unser Vater«. Der umfangreiche Glaubenstext Hebr 11 stellt den Glauben Abrahams ins Zentrum der langen Reihe von Glaubenszeugen (11,8–22: Abraham und Sara, Isaak, Jakob). Das Thema Glaube – Werke spielt in Kap. 11 keine Rolle.

[1151] Zwölfmal in 2,15–26. συνεργεῖν einmal.

[1152] METZNER, Jak, 137, weist auf den Zusammenhang mit dem Thema von 1,19–27: »Hören und Tun« hin. Dies Thema wird jetzt theologisch vertieft.

[1153] DIBELIUS, Jak, 184.

234   Kommentar

die in der Diatribe übliche Form der fingierten Diskussion. Er selbst führt den Zwischenredner ein, er selbst gibt ihm Antwort.[1154]

Damit ist auch bereits etwas über den argumentativen Charakter und den theoretischen Anspruch dieses Textes ausgesagt. Allerdings weist Dibelius auch zurecht darauf hin, dass der Text stilistische – und wie sich in der Exegese zeigen wird – auch inhaltliche Unklarheiten und Schwächen hat. Dibelius stellt fest: »Es handelt sich ... nicht um eine dramatisch bewegte Szene, sondern um ein stilistisches Schema, das seine ursprüngliche dramatische Illusionskraft längst eingebüßt hat«.[1155]

1. Texteinheit: 2,14–17 Glaube ohne Taten ist tot (1)

(14) Was (wäre[1156]) der Nutzen, meine Brüder, wenn jemand sagte, er habe Glauben, Taten[1157] aber nicht hat? Kann ihn etwa der Glaube retten? (15) Wenn ein Bruder oder eine Schwester nackt wäre und die tägliche Nahrung nicht hätte, (16) jemand von euch aber zu ihnen sagte: »Geht hin in Frieden, wärmt und sättigt euch«, ihr ihnen aber (gleichzeitig[1158]) nicht die notwendigen Lebensbedürfnisse[1159] zur Verfügung stelltet, was würde das nützen[1160]? (17) So ist auch der Glaube, wenn er nicht Taten hat, tot in sich selbst.[1161]

Textkritik: V. 14 Statt des Konj. λεγη haben sehr viele Minuskeln den Ind. λεγει. Ähnlich bei εχη. V. 15 Einige Minuskeln verändern das seltene αδελφη zu αδελφοι. Mehrere Minuskeln setzen statt des Konj. υπαρχωσιν den Ind. υπαρχουσιν. 02. 33 und viele Minuskeln ergänzen zu λειπομενοι noch ωσιν.

V. 14 Der Verfasser eröffnet das Thema lebhaft mit einer latent rhetorischen *doppelten Frage*, die ein Gemeindeglied betrifft, das sich zum Thema Glaube und Taten äußert. Die Richtung der *Antwort*, die Jakobus bei den Lesern provozieren will, ist durch die in der griechischen Literatur öfter bezeugte Wendung τί τὸ ὄφελος[1162] bereits vorgegeben: Das *statement* des Gemeindegliedes ist nutzlos. Der Aspekt des Nutzens, soteriologisch verstanden (V. 14b), ist hier leitend. Jakobus wiederholt die Frage in V. 16 in derselben Absicht am Schluss der Doppelszene (Klammer und Achtergewicht). In die erste der beiden Fragen ist wieder die die literarische

---

[1154] DIBELIUS, Jak, 185. Philo, Flacc. 20 und Plutarch, mor. 791e zu der stummen Figur eines fingierten Gesprächspartners (κωφὸν προσωπεῖον).

[1155] DIBELIUS, Jak, 185.

[1156] »Wäre« ist im Deutschen ergänzt.

[1157] Mit BURCHARD, Jak, 111, und anderen Exegeten wird hier ἔργα als »Taten« übersetzt, um die anachronistische »Werke«-Diskussion zu vermeiden. Es geht Jakobus um das praktische Tun, die Umsetzung des Glaubens. So auch METZNER, Jak, 139: es geht nicht um die »Werke des Gesetzes« nach 4QMMT. Metzner stellt klar: »Die »Werke« bei Jak sind ... rein ethisch bestimmt ... Sie sind nicht funktional identisch mit den »Werken« des Gesetzes bei Paulus«.

[1158] »Gleichzeitig« ist im Deutschen ergänzt.

[1159] Übersetzung nach BAUER / ALAND, 598.

[1160] Wörtlich: »was (wäre) der Nutzen«.

[1161] Griechisch: »in Hinsicht auf sich selbst«.

[1162] Vgl. die Parallelen bei BURCHARD, Jak, 111. Besonders 1Kor 15,32.

C. Briefcorpus

Kommunikation weiterführende Anrede »meine Brüder« eingeschoben (1,2 u. ö.). V. 14–16 erinnern im syntaktischen Aufbau an 2,2–4: Eine hypothetische Situation wird narrativ entfaltet, um ein Urteil vorzubereiten.

Die *erste* Frage betrifft einen fingierten Zwischenredner: ein Gemeindeglied, das behauptet, πίστις zu haben, ohne aber Taten zu haben. Die einführende Wendung »Wenn jemand sagte (Konj. Präs.)«[1163] macht deutlich, dass es dabei um eine hypothetische Stellungnahme, um eine Konstruktion, nicht einfach um eine geläufige Parole aus einer Gemeinde geht. V. 14 ist also ein *erstes exemplum*, erfunden, um die Vorstellung des Jakobus von der richtigen πίστις zu illustrieren. Woran denkt der Verfasser bei der Konstellation von πίστις und Taten? Diese Antithese ist bereits bekannt. πίστις ist das Oberthema der beiden ersten Teile des brieflichen Schreibens (1,3). 1,6 hat deutlich gemacht, dass Glaube primär als festes Vertrauen auf Gott (1,5) in schwierigen Situationen (πειρασμοί) gemeint ist. Gegensatz ist nicht Unglaube oder falscher Glaube, sondern Zweifel (1,6). 2,1 hat den Aspekt des praktisch gelebten Glaubens in Solidarität mit den Armen und sozial Schwachen in den Gemeinden hinzugefügt. Die christologische Bestimmung von πίστις hat zusätzlich die Christus-bekennenden Gemeinden als Bezugsrahmen des Verfassers und der Adressaten des Briefes deutlich gemacht. Wenn Jakobus jetzt die Thematik von Glaube und Taten noch einmal aufgreift, sind die bisher gemachten Aussagen zu πίστις mitzuhören. Dasselbe gilt für ἔργα, die bereits in 1,4 und 1,25 angesprochen wurden. In 1,25 wurde derjenige, der in das vollkommene Gesetz der Freiheit hineinschaut und dabei beharrt, als ποιητὴς ἔργου bezeichnet.[1164] 2,14 benutzt den Plural und charakterisiert damit die eher abstrakte Kategorie des »Tuns« als Summe einzelner Taten. Wie diese Taten aussehen können, zeigen *ex negativo* V. 15.16. Jakobus denkt an praktische Hilfe und Unterstützung der Armen.

Die *zweite*, kurze Frage von V. 14: »Kann der Glaube den fingierten Zwischenredner retten?« weist auf die soteriologische Dimension der πίστις und damit auf die eschatologische Tiefenstruktur der ganzen Thematik hin. Es geht letzten Endes um das »Heil« des Zwischenredners. Damit ist dieselbe Dimension angesprochen wie schon in 1,12. 21. 25; 2,5.13 und später in 4,12 und 5,15.20.[1165] πίστις als Vertrauen erweist sich in den Taten. *Diese* πίστις kann »retten«. Dies Ergebnis ist dem Verfasser wichtig.

Dibelius weist auf die gewundene Formulierung von V. 14 hin. Der Verfasser spricht hier noch nicht von jemandem, der Glauben, nicht aber Taten hat, sondern von jemandem, der das von sich *sagt*: »Ein Mensch, dessen Glaube sich nicht in

---

[1163] Vgl. ähnliche Wendungen, mit denen ein entweder hypothetischer oder realer Interlokutor eingeführt wird: 1Kor 3,4; 15,12; 1Thess 5,3; Jak 4,13; 2Petr 3,4; 1Joh 2,4.6.9.

[1164] Vgl. auch das Verb 1,20; 2,9.

[1165] In 5,20 ist entsprechend zur Schlussstellung des Satzes die eschatologische Dimension von σῴζειν besonders deutlich: »vom Tode erretten«. σῴζειν bei Jak: 1,21; 2,14; 4,12; 5,15.20. Das Substantiv fehlt.

236 Kommentar

Taten ausdrückt, kann ihn nicht anders als durch Worte zeigen«.[1166] Die rhetorische Frage: »Kann ihn der Glaube retten?« schließt an die paulinische Vorstellung von der eschatologischen Rettung durch die πίστις an[1167], stellt aber klar, dass dieser Glaube nicht ohne Taten zu denken ist.[1168] Dabei spricht Jakobus nicht von den ἔργα νόμου[1169]: Dies paulinische Motiv findet sich hier nicht. Jakobus geht es nicht um die theologische Frage, ob der Mensch das Gesetz erfüllen und damit Gerechtigkeit vor Gott erlangen könne, sondern sehr einfach um soziales und caritatives Tun, das unabdingbar zum Glauben gehört. Ob der »Jemand« als Gegner zu bezeichnen sei, ist dem Text nicht zu entnehmen. Dibelius rechnet mit der »Möglichkeit«, »daß auch der Einwand V. 18 nur den Sophismus eines fingierten Gegners enthält, nicht aber einen ernsthaft zu beachtenden Gegengrund«.[1170] Burchard plädiert mit Rückblick auf Kap. 1,12–25 für einen Jemand, »der das dort Gesagte erst oder wieder nur halb beherzigt«.[1171]

V. 15–16 Der Verfasser verweist nun zur Klärung der Doppelfrage wie schon in 2,2–4 auf ein weiteres hypothetisches, wieder mit ἐάν eingeleitetes konstruiertes Beispiel aus dem Gemeindealltag. Dies *zweite*, längere und narrativ-szenisch ausgestaltete *exemplum* enthält in V. 16 noch einmal eine Redesituation, analog derjenigen des ersten *exemplum*. Die fingierte Szene dient der Illustration des ersten *exemplum* und ist darauf angelegt, dass Rede und Handlung eines Gemeindegliedes in skandalöser Weise auseinanderklaffen. Das Szenario ist zweiteilig: Zunächst wird eine Situation in der Gemeinde dargestellt, dann reagiert der fingierte Interlokutor auf diese Situation. Wieder wie schon in 2,3 arbeitet Jakobus mit Ethopoiie[1172], und wieder setzt er sie ironisch ein. Szene und Reaktion stehen in offenem Gegensatz zueinander.[1173] Der Erzählrahmen ist klar: Es geht um fingierte Personen aus den Gemeinden der Adressaten: »Jemand unter euch« (V. 16). Ausdrücklich werden hier Brüder und Schwestern[1174] genannt. Alle Beteiligten sind Gemeindeglieder. Der erste Teil der kleinen Erzählung in V. 15 ist durchaus realistisch: Arme gibt es immer in den Gemeinden (vgl. Mk 14,7; Mt 26,11). Die Armut wird durch Mangel an Kleidung und Nahrung konkretisiert. Das hyperbolische Motiv der Nacktheit

---

[1166] DIBELIUS, Jak, 187.

[1167] Röm 1,16; 10,9; 1Kor 1,21; Eph 2,8. Auch 1Petr 1,5.9.

[1168] Damit setzt Jakobus die Linie fort, die Paulus in Gal 5,6 aufzeigt: πίστις δι' ἀγάπης ἐνεργουμένη, allerdings verschiebt er den theologischen Kontext. Es geht nicht um Liebe statt Beschneidung als Gesetzeserfüllung, sondern um den Glauben, der sich in Taten erweist.

[1169] So der paulinische Werke-Diskurs, der Teil der Interpretation des Gesetzes ist. Für Jakobus ist das Gesetz das Gesetz der Freiheit: s. zu 1,25.

[1170] DIBELIUS, Jak, 186.

[1171] BURCHARD, Jak, 113.

[1172] Der Sprecher legt seine eigene Meinung einer anderen Person in den Mund.

[1173] MORGAN, Roman Faith, 471, weist auf die Liebe der griechischen Rhetorik zu binären Oppositionen hin: »a powerful heuristic device«. Das Gleiche gilt ebenso für die antike jüdische Literatur.

[1174] ἀδελφή hap. leg. in Jak, sehr selten im NT ausdrücklich als Gemeindeglieder genannt: Röm 16,1; 1Kor 7,15; 9,5. Vgl. auch Mk 3,35par (Jesuslogion) und 2Joh 13 (hier metaphorisch).

begegnet auch in dem christologisch zugespitzten Gleichnis in Mt 25,36.38.43 f zusammen mit Hunger und Durst. Jakobus formuliert stilistisch sorgfältig, aber doch mit nicht ungeläufigen Lexemen[1175]: ὑπάρχειν[1176] statt ἐισιν und λείπειν[1177] statt »nicht haben«. ἐφήμερος für »täglich« ist neutestamentliches hap. leg., begegnet aber zusammen mit τροφή im Sinne der für den jeweiligen Tag bestimmten Nahrung in der griechischen Literatur.[1178] Der Verfasser entwirft das herausfordernde, aber nicht unrealistische Bild von bettelarmen Menschen in der Gemeinde.[1179]

V. 16 spannt mittels zweier Konditionalsätze[1180] zwei einander entgegengesetzte mögliche Verhaltensformen zusammen: eine freundliche Ansprache und praktisches Fehlen von Hilfsbereitschaft. Dabei wechselt Jakobus im Satz das Subjekt: Die Ansprache wird von *einem* Gemeindeglied gehalten, das ethisch verheerende *Verhalten* schreibt Jakobus »euch« zu, d. h. den Adressaten bzw. den christlichen Gemeinden im Kollektiv. Durch diese Zuspitzung macht der Verfasser die Verantwortung der Gemeinden für den Glauben, der sich in Taten als lebendig erweist, deutlich.

Die kurze Ansprache des Interlokutors an die bettelarmen Gemeindeglieder erweist sich im Zusammenhang mit dem negativen Verhalten der Gemeindeglieder als Hohn auf die Situation. Wieder achtet Jakobus auf die Diktion: θερμαίνεσθαι[1181] καὶ χορτάζειν sind hap. leg. im Jakobusbrief, ἐπιτήδειος ist neutestamentliches hap. leg[1182], hier im Neutrum Pl. im Sinne von »täglicher Bedarf« gebraucht. Die Ansprache des Interlokutors ist zweiteilig und umfasst erstens einen geläufigen jüdischen Friedensgruß »zum Abschied«[1183], zweitens eine »wohlmeinend«[1184] klingende Verabschiedungsformel. Es könnte sich also um eine harmonische Abschiedsszene in einer Gemeinde handeln, wenn nicht der zweite Konditionalsatz wäre. Bezogen auf die Glaube-Taten-Thematik ist deutlich, dass der Interlokutor aus seiner πίστις heraus spricht, aber keine ἔργα hat. Dibelius weist auf die Typisierung in diesen Versen hin und betont zurecht, dass es nicht um reale Vorkommnisse in den Gemeinden geht.[1185] Der Verfasser konstruiert vielmehr einen äußerst unwahrscheinlichen Fall, der die Leser aufschrecken und für seine These: »Glaube ohne Taten ist tot« einnehmen soll.

[1175] Dibelius, Jak, 189.
[1176] Hap. leg. in Jak.
[1177] Noch Jak 1,4.5; Lk 18,22 und Tit 1,5; 3,13.
[1178] Bauer / Aland, 667.
[1179] Zur Definition von »bettelarm« vgl. Kramer, Lukas, 19–22.
[1180] Das ἐὰν von V. 14 und V. 15 wird nicht noch einmal wiederholt.
[1181] Noch Mk 14,54.67 und Joh 18,18.25.
[1182] Vgl. Dibelius, Jak, 189, zur Geläufigkeit des Wortes in der Gräzität (Stellenangaben).
[1183] Burchard, Jak, 116 (Beispiele).
[1184] Dibelius, Jak, 189.
[1185] Dibelius, Jak, 189.

238 Kommentar

V. 17 Hier wird in erneut sentenziöser Diktion das Urteil über die in V. 14–16 imaginierte Situation gefällt. Der Satz nimmt V. 14 auf (*inclusio*). Die Metapher, dass Glaube ohne Taten »tot« sei[1186], knüpft an die Diktion von Röm 6,11; 7,8; Hebr 6,1 an, die den Hintergrund von Jak 1,15 bildet. In 2,17 verwendet Jakobus die Metapher inhaltlich gegenteilig zu Hebr 6: Statt »toter Taten« spricht er vom »toten Glauben«.[1187] »Tot« bedeutet hier wie in Röm 7,8 »unwirksam«. Die These von V. 17: »Der Glaube, wenn er keine Taten hat, ist tot in sich selbst«, ist syntaktisch und inhaltlich aber auch nicht weit entfernt von 1Kor 13,2: »Wenn ich allen Glauben habe …, Liebe aber nicht habe, bin ich nichts«. Die Bedeutung der Nächstenliebe hat Jakobus in 2,8 formuliert: das königliche Gesetz. In 2,1–7 hat er ein Szenario entworfen, in dem die Liebe in der Gemeinde fehlt. In 2,17 zieht er ein vorläufiges Fazit und betont die Bedeutung des Tuns für den Glauben.

2. Texteinheit: 2,18–19 Ein Einwurf

(18aa) **Aber es könnte jemand sagen:** (ab) **»Du hast Glauben, und ich habe Taten«**[1188]; (ba) **zeige mir deinen Glauben ohne die Taten,** (bb) **und ich werde dir meinen Glauben aus meinen Taten zeigen.** (19) **Du glaubst, dass Gott Einer ist – gut tust du daran**[1189]**; auch die Dämonen glauben (das**[1190]**) und schaudern.**[1191]

Textkritik: V. 18 04 und mehrere Minuskeln fügen σου nach εργων hinzu. Zahlreiche Minuskeln (der ganze byzantinische Text) lesen εκ των εργων σου statt χωρις. P74. 02 und zahlreiche Minuskeln fügen σου nach την πιστιν ein. V. 19 εις εστιν ο θεος lesen P74. 01. 02 und einige Minuskeln. 04, Minuskeln 33V und andere lesen εις ο θεος εστιν. Zahlreiche Minuskeln lesen ο θεος εις εστιν, zahlreiche andere Minuskeln verkürzen zu θεος εις εστιν. Vor καλως fügen mehrere Minuskeln και ein.

V. 18 Im Folgenden unternimmt Jakobus einen weiteren Klärungsversuch. Dabei greift er noch einmal auf das Stilmittel der Ethopoiie[1192] zurück: Ein weiterer fiktiver Interlokutor kommt ins Spiel.[1193] Die erste texterschließende Frage ist: Wie weit reicht der Einwurf des Interlokutors? Das Ende des Einwandes ist stilistisch unklar, da die »du«-Anrede gleichermaßen die V. 18 und 19 regiert und sogar bis V.

[1186] νεκρός Jak 2,17 und 26 (zweimal). Der metaphorische Gebrauch findet sich bei Paulus: Röm 6,11; 7,8 (χωρὶς γὰρ νόμου ἁμαρτία νεκρά. Denn ohne Gesetz ist die Sünde tot). Auch Eph 2,1.5; Kol 2,13.

[1187] Über »Beziehungen« zwischen den Texten zu spekulieren, verbietet sich. Was sich sagen lässt: Hebr und Jak nehmen in ihrer jeweiligen theologischen Intention an dem durch Paulus geprägten Diskurs über das Verhältnis von Glauben und Taten teil.

[1188] Die Anführungsstriche sollen deutlich machen, dass nur der erste Satz dem Interlokutor zuzuschreiben ist.

[1189] »Daran« ist im Deutschen hinzugefügt.

[1190] »Das« ist im Deutschen hinzugefügt.

[1191] Die Interpunktion wird in der Exegese begründet.

[1192] Definition: s. o.

[1193] Zu der Wendung »Aber es könnte jemand sagen« vgl. BURCHARD, Jak, 117 (Mittel der Ethopoiie); ALLISON, Jak, 471 mit Anm. 254 (Diatribenstil). ALLISON, Jak, weist auch zurecht auf die sorgfältige Konstruktion von V. 18 hin (»artfully constructed«, 471).

C. Briefcorpus

23 reicht.[1194] Aus inhaltlichen Gründen beschränkt man mit Dibelius den Einwand des Interlokutors am besten auf den provokativen Satz V. 18a.b: »Du hast Glauben, und ich habe Taten«.[1195] Damit wird der Einwurf des ersten Interlokutors von V. 14 in modifizierter Form wieder aufgenommen (»ich habe Glauben«). Dabei *verschärft* Jakobus die Situation: Der zweite Interlokutor *trennt selbst* explizit Glauben und Taten, indem er *zwei* Personen sprechen lässt: ein »Ich« und ein »Du«. Das »Ich« ist nicht der Verfasser, der mit dem Interlokutor diskutiert. Vielmehr lässt der Verfasser den Interlokutor zwei Personen ihre Standpunkte formulieren. Dibelius kommentiert richtig:

> Jak behandelt den Zwischenredner, als wenn er gesagt hätte: ›Der eine hat Glauben, der andere Werke‹.[1196]

Darin liegt die gesteigerte Provokation für den Verfasser: Der Interlokutor dividiert definitiv zwei Begriffe auseinander, die für den Verfasser unlösbar zusammengehören, Glaube und Taten. Dabei ist zu bedenken, dass auch dieser Satz vom Verfasser stammt. Der Verfasser modelliert einen Standpunkt, den er selbst nicht teilt und als gefährlich markieren will: Wenn der Eine Glauben hat und der andere Taten, ist das doch in Ordnung. Für den Verfasser ist das Gegenteil der Fall. Der Satz ist – selbstverständlich – polemisch zugespitzt: Niemand würde in den Gemeinden so argumentieren. Hier wird *ex negativo* die in einen Pseudodialog umgesetzte Überzeugung des Verfassers ausgedrückt, dass Glaube ohne Taten »tot« ist. Es handelt sich um eine letztlich ungeschickte (weil unklare) diatribische Einkleidung einer Gefahr, die der Verfasser in den Gemeinden sieht: bloßer Glaube ohne praktische Konsequenzen – jener Position, die Jakobus bekämpft. Allison nennt im Zusammenhang seiner zwölf möglichen Auflösungen von V. 18 als eine mögliche Interpretation (vi) die folgende:

[1194] DIBELIUS, Jak, 190: »Nun versuche ich die Erklärung des problematischen V. 18 und damit einer der schwierigsten neutestamentlichen Stellen überhaupt.« Dibelius gibt eine äußerst detaillierte Darstellung der verschiedenen Interpunktions- und Interpretationsmöglichkeiten (190–195). BURCHARD, Jak, 117, spricht von den »strittigsten Sätzen des Briefs«. Er listet 7 Lösungstypen, jeweils mit Untertypen, auf (118–120). Sein eigener Lösungsvorschlag (120 f) ist unklar. Zur neueren Diskussion METZNER, Jak, 145 Anm. 75 (Lit.). Metzner schließt sich in einer ausführlichen Diskussion dem Dibelius-Vorschlag an (145–148), vgl. die Verseinteilung bei METZNER, 145, die in diesem Kommentar übernommen wird. ALLISON, Jak, 468–473, listet 12 verschiedene Erklärungsversuche auf und erklärt den Vers für nicht erklärbar. Weitere Lit: D. F. WATSON, James 2 in Light of Greco-Roman Schemes of Argumentation, NTS 39, 1993, 94–121; J. HEATH, The Righteous Gentile Interjects (James 2:18–19 and Romans 2:14–15), NT 55, 2013, 274–76; J.-N. ALETTI, James 2,14–26: The Arrangement and Its Meaning, Bibl 95, 2014, 88–101; A. MALINA, »I demoni credono e tremano« (Gc 2,19), ASEs 34, 2017, 457–68; K. M. WILSON, Reading James 2:18–20 with Anti-Donatist Eyes: Untangling Augustine's Exegetical Legacy, JBL 139, 2020, 385–407. – Die Schwierigkeit entsteht, wenn nicht beachtet wird, dass es sich nicht um eine *dialogische* Auseinandersetzung zwischen verschiedenen theologischen Positionen handelt, sondern um eine diatribisch-pädagogisch gestaltete Wiederholung der These: Glaube ohne Taten ist tot bzw. solchen Glauben gibt es nicht.

[1195] DIBELIUS, Jak, 191.

[1196] DIBELIUS, Jak, 192.

240 Kommentar

V. 18a represents an opponent, the speech is indirect and James is writing from his own perspective.

Diese Beschreibung ist richtig. Allerdings fährt Allison fort:

Thus ›you‹ is the opponent, ›I‹ the letter writer.[1197]

Er verlegt den Dialog also in V. 18ab und geht davon aus, dass der Verfasser in »Ich habe Taten« auf sich selbst verweist. Das ist gegen den Text gedacht, denn V. 18ab ist ja von »Aber es wird *jemand* sagen« abhängig.[1198] Genauer gesagt: es liegt in V. 18a kein argumentativer Dialog zwischen dem Ich (κἀγώ) des *Verfassers* und einem Du (σύ) vor, sondern zwei Positionen werden dargestellt. Burchard macht diese Interpretation Dibelius' noch plausibler, wenn er darauf hinweist, dass Zwischenredner in der Diatribe »nicht einen Dialog anfangen« sollen, sondern etwas »sagen oder fragen …, das in der Regel als Einwand gegen den Autor gemeint ist«[1199]. Das kann bedeuten: »Du und Ich sind unbestimmte Personen … Du und Ich bedeuten der eine, der andere.«[1200] Burchard selbst schließt sich allerdings dieser Interpretation nicht an. Er betont zwar, dass »das Du nicht Jak persönlich meint«, sondern »der lebhaften Exemplifizierung« dient[1201], bezieht aber das Ich inhaltlich auf den Interlokutor, der eine vorstellbare theologische Position vertritt. An diesem Punkt folgt der vorliegende Kommentar Burchard nicht.

Die Logik des Textes lässt sich zusammenfassend wie folgt explizieren: Der Verfasser konstruiert in V. 18a.b im Diatribenstil den Satz eines Interlokutors, der zwei Positionen vorstellt und damit dasjenige auseinandernimmt, das nach Jakobus nicht auseinandergenommen werden kann[1202]: »Du hast *Glauben*, und ich habe *Taten*«. In V. 18b.a nimmt der Verfasser argumentativ auf diesen Satz Bezug und sagt herausfordernd zu dem Interlokutor: »Zeige mir doch diesen Glauben *ohne* Taten«, wobei er innerlich hinzufügt: »Das kannst du nicht, denn den gibt es nicht!« Der Verfasser fährt fort: »Ich (dagegen) werde dir meinen Glauben *aus* den Taten zeigen« und fügt innerlich gleichsam trotzig hinzu: »Das kann ich, den gibt es nämlich, und diese Position ist richtig«. Dabei sind das »Du« wie das »Ich« beide fiktive Größen. Es geht weder um den Glauben noch um die Taten des *Verfassers*. Vielmehr geht es um eine in Diatribenform gestaltete Wiederholung des sachlichen Verdikts von V. 17: Es gibt keinen Glauben ohne Taten (vgl. V. 26). Argumentativ

---

[1197] ALLISON, Jak, 469–471 (zwölf Erklärungsmöglichkeiten), Zitat: 470.

[1198] Mit dieser Interpretation kommt Allison tatsächlich in eine Sackgasse. Er selbst verzichtet auf eine kohärente Erklärung des Argumentationsganges, da er den Text für korrupt oder unklar hält (471). Mit dem Vorschlag von Dibelius setzt er sich nicht auseinander.

[1199] BURCHARD, Jak, 117.

[1200] BURCHARD, Jak, 117.

[1201] BURCHARD, Jak, 121 (Hinweis auf DBR, § 281).

[1202] DIBELIUS, Jak, 192: »In V. 18a ist also – nach der Replik in v18b zu schließen – nicht die Verteilung von Glauben und Werke auf du und ich die Hauptsache, sondern die Teilung von Glauben und Werken überhaupt«.

steht χωρὶς gegen ἐκ: »ohne« ist die falsche, »aus« ist die richtige Verhältnisbestimmung von Glauben und Taten.

Wenn Dibelius hier von »eine(r) bloße(n) Konstruktion«, einer »sophistischen Trennung von Glauben und Werken« spricht[1203], hat er philologisch Recht. Allerdings geht es sachlich nicht nur um eine bloße Konstruktion. In 1Kor 12,9.10 liefert Paulus gleichsam die Vorlage für Jakobus[1204]: 9 ἑτέρῳ πίστις ἐν τῷ αὐτῷ πνεύματι 10 ἄλλῳ δὲ ἐνεργήματα δυνάμεων (dem Einen [gibt der Geist] Glauben[1205], dem anderen die Kraft zu Wundertaten). Hier nimmt Paulus die einzelnen Charismen auseinander, wenn auch, um gerade dadurch deutlich zu machen, dass sie *zusammengehören*. Wird in den Gemeinden dies *Caveat* überhört, kommt es zu genau jenem isolierten Verständnis einzelner Charismen, mit denen ihre Träger sich brüsten und die sie gegeneinander ausspielen, wie Jak in Kap. 2 skizziert. Dass ein solches Vorgehen schon von Paulus für möglich gehalten und bekämpft wurde, zeigt 1Kor 12,12–31. So kann »Glaube« tatsächlich gegen »Werke« – zum Beispiel ἐνεργήματα δυνάμεων – gestellt werden. Jakobus beobachtet in seinen Gemeinden entsprechendes Verhalten, assoziiert es mit einem zu kurz interpretierten paulinischen Glaubensbegriff und greift es seinerseits scharf an. Ob Jakobus hier polemisch oder affirmativ auf 1Kor 12 zurückgreift, lässt sich nicht sagen. Wichtiger ist: 1Kor 12,9 f ist der Text, der Jak 2,18 nicht nur argumentativ, sondern auch sachlich plausibel macht.

V. 19 Auch dieser Satz ist an den fiktiven Interlokutor gerichtet. Der Verfasser fügt seiner Attacke einen wichtigen Gedanken hinzu: Es gibt tatsächlich einen Glauben ohne Taten: Es ist der Glaube der Dämonen.[1206] Dieser Glaube ist zugleich in der Sache richtig und doch im Ergebnis falsch. Diese einfache Einsicht gewinnt der Verfasser aus einem weiteren fiktiven Beispiel, indem er dem erdachten Interlokutor nun die Position von V. 18a.b unterschiebt und unterstellt[1207], der Interlokutor berufe sich auf seinen Glauben in Gestalt des ersten Teils des Sch'ma Israel nach Dtn 6,4 f, das an verschiedenen Stellen in den neutestamentlichen Texten zitiert wird.

[1203] Dibelius, Jak, 193.

[1204] Vgl. Allison, Jak, 64.

[1205] Dabei spielt es keine Rolle, dass es sich in 1Kor 12 offensichtlich um Wunderglauben handelt.

[1206] Dämonen: häufig in den synoptischen Evangelien; 1Kor 10,20 f; 1Tim 4,1; Apk 9,20; 16,14; 18,2. Adjektiv δαιμονιώδης: Jak 3,15. Dazu: Wischmeyer, Zwischen Gut und Böse, 153–168.

[1207] Dibelius, Jak, weist auf S. 197 richtig darauf hin, »daß der Verf. im Bilde dieses Gegners nicht irgendeinen Zeitgenossen darstellen will. ... Der Verf. hat den Gegner nicht nach einem Modell gezeichnet; er ist nicht einmal als Typus gedacht«. Zugleich weist Dibelius darauf hin, wie sehr V. 19 dem antiken Judentum verpflichtet ist (ebenso Popkes, Burchard, Allison, Metzner u. a.).

242 Kommentar

Dtn 6,4: Ἄκουε, Ισραηλ· κύριος ὁ θεὸς ἡμῶν κύριος εἷς ἐστιν·(5) καὶ ἀγαπήσεις κύριον τὸν θεόν σου ἐξ ὅλης τῆς καρδίας σου καὶ ἐξ ὅλης τῆς ψυχῆς σου καὶ ἐξ ὅλης τῆς δυνάμεώς σου. Höre Israel, der Herr unser Gott ist einer. (5) Und du sollst den Herrn, deinen Gott, lieben aus deinem ganzem Herzen und aus deiner ganzen Seele und aus deiner ganzen Kraft.

Mk 12,29: ἄκουε, Ἰσραήλ, κύριος ὁ θεὸς ἡμῶν κύριος εἷς ἐστιν, (30) καὶ ἀγαπήσεις κύριον τὸν θεόν σου ἐξ ὅλης τῆς καρδίας σου καὶ ἐξ ὅλης τῆς ψυχῆς σου καὶ ἐξ ὅλης τῆς διανοίας σου καὶ ἐξ ὅλης τῆς ἰσχύος σου.

Mk 12,32: εἷς ἐστιν καὶ οὐκ ἔστιν ἄλλος πλὴν αὐτοῦ·(33) καὶ τὸ ἀγαπᾶν αὐτὸν ἐξ ὅλης τῆς καρδίας καὶ ἐξ ὅλης τῆς συνέσεως καὶ ἐξ ὅλης τῆς ἰσχύος καὶ τὸ ἀγαπᾶν τὸν πλησίον ὡς ἑαυτὸν περισσότερόν ἐστιν πάντων τῶν ὁλοκαυτωμάτων καὶ θυσιῶν.
Er ist einer, und es ist kein anderer außer ihm. (33) Und ihn zu lieben aus ganzem Herzen und aus ganzem Gemüt und aus aller Kraft und den Nächsten zu lieben wie sich selbst ist mehr als alle Brandopfer und (anderen) Opfer.

1Kor 8,4: οἴδαμεν ὅτι οὐδὲν εἴδωλον ἐν κόσμῳ καὶ ὅτι οὐδεὶς θεὸς εἰ μὴ εἷς.
Wir wissen, dass es keinen Götzen in der Welt gibt und dass kein Gott außer dem einen existiert.

Jak 2,19: εἷς ἐστιν ὁ θεός.

Jakobus zitiert Dtn nicht wörtlich, sondern gibt eine äußerste Kurzform, die seiner Ansicht nach auch diejenige der Dämonen ist: εἷς ἐστιν ὁ θεός.[1208] Das Sch'ma als solches ist nicht nur fester Bestandteil des zeitgenössischen Judentums[1209], sondern ein *rocher de bronze* der markinischen Jesustradition.[1210] Dtn 6,4 wird nur einmal im Neuen Testament wörtlich zitiert: in Mk 12,29[1211], und zwar mit höchster Zustimmung von Jesus und der nachträglichen geradezu emphatischen Bestätigung durch den Schriftgelehrten. In abgewandelter und gekürzter Form erscheint es als Wiederholung in Mk 12,33, sonst in 1Kor 8,4 und hier in Jak 2. 1Kor 8 und Jak 2 setzen Dtn 6,4 allerdings ganz anders ein als Mk 12. Während in der Jesustradition das Sch'ma im Zusammenhang der *Gebote* (ἐντολαί) thematisiert und eben als solches im Wortlaut zitiert wird, wird die Kurzform des Sch'ma in 1Kor 8 und Jak 2 als *Credo* behandelt: πιστεύεις ὅτι. Diese Formel interpretiert die πίστις in einer bestimmten Weise, nämlich als Wissensinhalt (1Kor 8,4 οἴδαμεν). Der Vertrauensaspekt tritt ganz zurück. Abraham dagegen verwirklicht den Vertrauensglauben (Jak 2,23 nach Gen 15,6: πιστεύειν c.Dat.).[1212] Mit einem *terminus* von Ingo Dalferth

---

[1208] Zu den zahlreichen Bezeugungen im antiken Judentum und der frühen christlichen Lit. vgl. die sehr sorgfältige Darstellung bei BURCHARD, Jak, 122f, und ALLISON, Jak, 474. Besonders eindrücklich ist Philo, virt. 216. Lit: W. POPKES / R. BRUCKER (Hg.), Ein Herr und ein Gott. Zum Kontext des Monotheismus im Neuen Testament, BThSt 68, Neukirchen-Vluyn 2004; S. MITCHELL / P. VAN NUFFELEN (Hg.), One God: Pagan Monotheism In The Roman Empire, Cambridge 2010.

[1209] DIBELIUS, Jak, 196.

[1210] Damit ist nichts darüber gesagt, wie weit Mk 12,28–34 auf den historischen Jesus zurückgeht.

[1211] Die Parallelen in Mt 22,34–40 und Lk 10,25–28 lassen Dtn 6,4 aus.

[1212] Vgl. A. WEISER / R. BULTMANN, Art. πιστεύω κτλ., ThWNT 6, 1959, 174–230, 210f: Differenzierung

handelt es sich bei dem Glauben der Dämonen an das Sch'ma um das doxastische »Fürwahrhalten«, den Glaubensinhalt der *fides quae*.[1213]

Damit wird dies doxastisch verstandene Credo in 1Kor 8 und Jak 2 zugleich implizit kritisiert: Das Sch'ma ist einerseits völlig unumstritten und wird explizit als Basistext einer Verständigung über die πίστις benutzt.[1214] Andererseits wird in beiden Texten deutlich, dass das bloße Zitieren und Behaupten des Sch'ma nicht ausreicht bzw. nicht nützt. Dem Credo fehlt die Handlungsdimension des Gebotes. Während Paulus in 1Kor 8 die bloße γνῶσις der »Starken« in der Gemeinde kritisiert (»Wir *wissen*, dass es keinen Gott gibt außer dem Einen«) und praktische Rücksichtnahme (ἀγάπη) gegenüber den »Schwachen« fordert (ἡ γνῶσις φυσιοῖ, ἡ δὲ ἀγάπη οἰκοδομεῖ 1Kor 8,1), fordert Jakobus generell ἔργα. Hinzu kommt der jeweilige kritische Kontext. Beide Autoren stellen das bloße Credo-Sch'ma in den Zusammenhang mit gegengöttlichen Größen. Paulus kritisiert eine γνῶσις, die die Furcht eines Teils der Gemeinde vor εἴδωλα mißachtet. Jakobus kritisiert eine πίστις ohne *caritas*[1215], die auch die Dämonen haben. Paulus wertet faktisch das bloße Sch'ma ab, wenn er sagt: Das Wissen der Starken nützt nichts, da es »aufbläst« (8,1). Jakobus ist hier noch schärfer mit seiner sarkastischen Bemerkung καλῶς ποιεῖς.[1216] Zudem lässt er die Dämonen das Sch'ma glauben, ohne dass es ihnen nützt, und stellt damit indirekt diejenigen, die diese Art von Credo-Glauben ohne Taten haben, auf eine Stufe mit den Dämonen. Zusammengefasst: 1Kor 8,1–6 ist mindestens *sachlich* der Prätext für Jak 2,19.[1217] Beide Texte zeigen, dass sich das Sch'ma nicht einfach als Credo eignet, sondern eine notwendige Handlungskomponente hat.

Das wird schneidend deutlich an der Reaktion der Dämonen: Statt Vertrauen zu haben, »schaudern« sie. φρίσσειν, hapax legomenon im NT, drückt Furcht und Schrecken aus.[1218] Für die Dämonen, die keine guten Taten tun können und so auch nicht den Sinn des Sch'mas erfüllen können, bedeutet das Sch'ma Schrecken. Jakobus ordnet damit die Menschen den Dämonen vor. Dieser theologisch-dämo-

---

von πιστεύειν εἰς oder c.gen.obj., πιστεύειν ἐν, πιστεύειν c.Dat.

[1213] I. Dalferth, Über Einheit und Vielfalt des christlichen Glaubens. Eine Problemskizze, in: W. Härle / R. Preul (Hg.), Glaube, MJTh4, Marburg 1992, 99–137, 108, differenziert zwischen doxastischem »Fürwahrhalten«, fiduzialem »Vertrauenschenken« und personalem »Sichverlassen«. Morgan, Roman Faith, 342, spricht von »propositional faith«.

[1214] 1Kor 8,4: »Wir wissen, dass …«; Jak 2,19: »Du tust gut daran«.

[1215] Jakobus verwendet nirgends γνῶσις, allerdings γινώσκειν 2,20.

[1216] Vgl. Mk 12,32 (καλῶς, διδάσκαλε, ἐπ' ἀληθείας εἶπες: gut, Meister, wahr redest du): gebräuchliche Zustimmung im Gespräch, hier aber anders als in Mk 12 oder in Jak 2,8 sarkastisch benutzt (vgl. Johnson, Jak, 241).

[1217] Zum Paulustext: E.-M. Becker, EIS THEOS und 1Kor 8. Zur frühchristlichen Entwicklung und Funktion des Monotheismus, in: W. Popkes / R. Brucker (Hg.), Ein Herr und ein Gott, 65–99. Zur Beziehung zwischen 1Kor und Jak vgl. Wischmeyer, Jak 3,13–18, 403–430; dort der Nachweis anhand von Jak 3,13–18, dass der Verfasser des Jak den 1Kor kannte. Jak 2,19 ergänzt die Argumentation zu Jak 3,13–18. – Zu den atl. Zitaten in Jak vgl. Wischmeyer, Scriptural Classicism.

[1218] Vgl. besonders Mayor, Jak, 94: das Verb bezeichnet »the physical signs of terror, especially of the hair standing on end«.

244 Kommentar

nologische Gedanke ist analogielos. Bei der ethischen Modellierung des Glaubens-
konzepts zeigt sich die theologische Originalität des Jakobus.

3. Texteinheit: 2,20–26 Glaube ohne Taten ist tot (2)

**(20) Willst du aber erkennen, o unvernünftiger Mensch, dass der Glaube ohne
die Taten nutzlos ist? (21) Abraham unser Vater – [1219]wurde er nicht aus Taten
gerechtgesprochen, als er seinen Sohn Isaak auf den Altar legte? (22) Du siehst,
dass der Glaube mit seinen Taten zusammengewirkt hat und sein[1220] Glaube aus
den Taten vollkommen geworden ist (23) und erfüllt ist die Schrift, die sagt: ›Es
glaubte aber Abraham Gott[1221], und es wurde ihm zur Gerechtigkeit angerechnet‹,
und »Freund Gottes« wurde er genannt. (24) Ihr seht, dass aus Taten der Mensch
gerecht wird und nicht aus Glauben allein. (25) Wurde aber nicht auch ebenso
Rahab, die Hure, aus Taten gerechtfertigt, als sie die Boten aufnahm und sie auf
einem anderen Weg herausließ? (26) Wie nämlich der Leib ohne Geist tot ist, so
ist auch der Glaube ohne Taten tot.**

Textkritik: V. **20** καινε statt des im Zusammenhang mit »Mensch« ungebräuchlichen κενε
lesen gegen den Sinn 01. 02 und einige Minuskeln. Das gebräuchliche νεκρα (V. 26) statt
des seltenen αργη wählen 01. 02. 04C2. 33 und sehr viele Minuskeln. αργη haben 03. 04*,
wenige Minuskeln (lectio difficilior). V. **23** Statt φιλος θεου lesen mehrere Minuskeln das
weniger konturierte δουλος θεου. V. **25** Der Ausdruck τους αγγελους (Botschafter) ist für
zahlreiche Abschreiber ein Problem. 04 und sehr viele Minuskeln schreiben nach Jos 2 und
6 (dort mehrfach das Verb) κατασκοπους (so auch Hebr 11,31), andere Hss. fügen »Israels«
oder »Jesu« zu αγγελοι oder κατασκοποι hinzu.

V. **20** Jakobus insistiert. Er ist nicht sicher, ob er den erdachten Interlokutor bereits
überzeugt hat. So setzt er noch einmal ein, um seine These von V. 17 zu bestätigen und die Diatribe auszuwerten. Dabei betreibt er erheblichen rhetorischen
Aufwand: Er eröffnet diesen letzten Argumentationsgang mit einer aggressiv formulierten Frage, um dann in V. 21–25 zwei *exempla* anzuführen. Die Frage richtet
sich an einen »unvernünftigen Menschen«, d. h. formal an den Interlokutor, kom-
munikationstechnisch aber letztlich an die Adressaten[1222], die Jakobus seit 2,14 im
Blick hat, nämlich an solche Gemeindeglieder, die ihren Glauben nicht durch ihr
persönliches soziales und caritatives Verhalten und Tun praktisch umsetzen.[1223]

Der Verfasser verschafft seiner These vom nutzlosen Glauben Nachdruck durch
die generelle Scheltanrede ὦ ἄνθρωπε κενέ. Die Anrede »o Mensch« gehört zum

---

[1219] Der griechische Satz ist nicht inkonzinn. Der Gedankenstrich soll die emphatische Betonung von
»Abraham« nachbilden.

[1220] Im Griechischen: »der«.

[1221] τῷ wird nicht übersetzt.

[1222] Vgl. Dibelius, Jak, 197. Dibelius weist darauf hin, dass Jakobus in V. 24 die Leser direkt anspricht
(»ihr«). Damit ist die Dialogform verlassen: »Sie war nur eine Episode«.

[1223] Zum folgenden Textabschnitt vgl. O. Wischmeyer, Polemik im Jakobusbrief, Formen, Gegenstände
und Fronten, in: dies. / L. Scornaienchi (Hg.), Polemik in der frühchristlichen Literatur. Texte und Kontexte,
BZNW 170, Berlin / Boston 2011, 357–379.

lehrhaften Diatribenstil[1224], ist aber auch ein Element der prophetischen Schelt-rede[1225] und begegnet bei Paulus in Röm 2,1.3 sowie in dem Diatribenabschnitt in Röm 9,20.[1226] κενός, ἀργός, νεκρός[1227]: Jakobus variiert mit diesen negativen Ad-jektiven die *eine* Aussage, die hinter der rhetorischen Frage von 2,14 steht, Glaube allein habe *keinen Nutzen* (2,14). κενός[1228] wird öfter von Paulus im Sinne von leer, hohl verwendet.[1229] 1Kor 15,14 bezieht er κενός auf einen Glauben, der sich nicht auf die Auferstehung Christi bezieht. ἀργός ist wie κενός hap. leg. im Jakobusbrief[1230] und changiert zwischen »faul, geschwätzig, leer«. Letzteres ist hier gemeint. Die Kommentare seit Windisch[1231] weisen auf das Wortspiel ἔργων – ἀργή (Paronoma-sie) hin.[1232] νεκρός bedeutet wie schon in V. 17 und wieder in V. 26 »wirkungslos«.

V. 21 Emphatisch setzt V. 21 mit dem Kronzeugen des Verfassers ein: mit der Wendung »Abraham unser Vater«.[1233] Wieder kleidet Jakobus seinen exemplari-schen Verweis in eine rhetorische Frage. Das bedeutet, dass er bei seinen Lesern nicht nur eine gewisse Kenntnis von Abraham voraussetzt, sondern auch davon ausgeht, dass sie sich als Abrahamskinder verstehen und seiner Argumentation mit Abraham folgen. Auch hier führt die Traditionslinie zu Paulus zurück. Die Eigenart von V. 21 liegt in der *Verbindung* folgender Elemente: (1) des Unser-Vater-Abra-ham-Motivs, (2) des erzählenden Verweises auf die Opferung Isaaks Gen 22[1234], (3) der Interpretation dieser Tat als ἔργα, die Abraham (4) *gerecht* machten. Jako-bus führt Abraham einerseits als Exempel ein wie Philo, benutzt ihn aber anderer-seits nicht wie Philo primär als Tugend- oder Frömmigkeitsbeispiel[1235], sondern als

---

[1224] Siehe oben zum Diatribenstil. ALLISON, Jak, 479, weist darauf hin, dass die spezifische Anrede »o leerer Mensch« ohne Analogie ist.

[1225] ALLISON, Jak, 480.

[1226] Weitere Beispiele bei BURCHARD, Jak, 126. In Röm 7,24 bezieht Paulus die Ansprache »o Mensch« in verwandelter Form auf sich selbst.

[1227] Zur Textkritik s. o. M. LATTKE, Art. κενός, EWNT II, 695, weist auch auf μωρός als verwandte Vokabel hin (vgl. ebenfalls Mt 5,22).

[1228] Hap. leg. in Jak.

[1229] BURCHARD, Jak, 126, schlägt »hirnlos« als Übersetzung vor und weist auf die Sachparallele Mt 5,22 (ῥακά, Dummkopf) hin. Im Jak noch in 4,5 κενός: »umsonst« (adverbial gebraucht). Zum hebräischen Hin-tergrund von κενός siehe ebd.

[1230] Selten im NT.

[1231] WINDISCH, Die katholischen Briefe, 18.

[1232] BURCHARD, Jak, 126, verweist auf SapSal 14,5: θέλεις δὲ μὴ ἀργὰ εἶναι τὰ τῆς σοφίας σου ἔργα (Du willst aber, dass die Werke deiner Weisheit nicht untätig sind).

[1233] Wichtige Quellen bei DIBELIUS, Jak, 197–200.206–214; K. BERGER, Art. Abraham II im Frühjuden-tum und Neuen Testament, TRE 1, 1977, 372–382; J.E. BOWLEY, Art. Abraham, EDEJ 2010, 294 f; ALLI-SON, Jak, 481–496. Vgl. auch: L. BORMANN (Hg.), Abraham's Family. A Network of Meaning in Judaism, Christianity, and Islam, WUNT 415, Tübingen 2018; ST. KRAUTER, Vater Abraham und *pater Aeneas*: Eine Auseinandersetzung mit einem neuen Interpretationsvorschlag zu Röm 4, in: J. Frey / J. Schröter / M. Wallraf (Hg.), Paulusmemoria und Paulusexegese, Tübingen 2023, 63–96.

[1234] Zur Aqeda (Bindung Isaaks) vgl. METZNER, Jak, 154.

[1235] So Elia in Kap. 5.

246 Kommentar

wichtiges Element seiner Argumentation wie Paulus. Dabei argumentiert er in der Sache *gegen* Paulus, was in V. 22–24 noch deutlicher wird.

Der Bezug auf Abraham garantiert im antiken Judentum und im entstehenden Christentum generell Zustimmung.[1236] Die Wendung »Vater Abraham« oder »Abraham unser / euer Vater« begegnet mehrfach in den Schriften des Neuen Testaments[1237]: meist positiv konnotiert.[1238] Wichtig ist der Vorwurf Jesu gegen »die Juden, die an ihn glaubten« (8,31) in Joh 8,39 f: Ihr tut nicht die »Taten Abrahams« – und deshalb seid ihr auch nicht »Abrahams Kinder«. Hier ist es explizit nicht die ethnische, sondern die *ethische* Genealogie, die jemanden zu »Abrahams Kind« macht.[1239] Paulus argumentiert ähnlich in den wichtigen Abrahamtexten Röm 4 und Gal 3.[1240] Auch Jakobus versteht Abraham mit großer Selbstverständlichkeit in ethischer Hinsicht als Stammvater der Adressaten[1241] und führt ihn als Vorbild des richtigen Glaubens, der sich in Taten erweist, an. Diese explizit exemplarische Rolle hat Abraham auch bei Philo. In De Abrahamo 167–199 beschreibt Philo ausführlich Isaaks Opferung unter dem Stichwort der gottgefälligen (θεοφιλής) Praxis. Während Abraham bei Philo Exempel der *Frömmigkeit*[1242] und »durch Belehrung erworbenen Tugend«[1243] ist, steht er in Hebr 11,8 wie bei Paulus für die πίστις. In Hebr 11,17 wird auch die Episode der Opferung Isaaks erwähnt. Insgesamt wird Abraham als Beispiel und ethisches Vorbild im Zusammenhang von Frömmigkeit, Glaube, Taten des Gehorsams,[1244] – diese vor allem auf Isaak bezogen – dargestellt,

---

[1236] Zum gewünschten Einverständnis und zu »Rezeption von Tradition« vgl. METZNER, Jak, 153.

[1237] Mt 3,9; Lk 13,16 (Tochter Abrahams); 16,24.30; 19,9; Joh 8,33.37 (σπέρμα Ἀβραάμ).39.53.56; Apg 7,2; 13,26 (»Söhne aus dem Geschlecht A.s«); Röm 4,1 (»Abraham unser Vorvater«).12; 9,7 (Same A.s); 11,1 (Same A.s); 2Kor 11,22; Gal 3,7 (Söhne A.s); 3,29 (Kinder A.s); Hebr 2,16. Vgl. auch 1Clem 31,2.

[1238] In Joh 8 wird die Wendung von »den Juden« als identitätsstiftende Selbstbezeichnung benutzt, ist in der Logik des Textes aber von Jesus polemisch gegen »die Juden« gerichtet.

[1239] O. WISCHMEYER, Abraham unser Vater. Biblische Gestalten in neutestamentlichen Texten, in: H. Lichtenberger / U. Mittmann-Richert (Hg.), Biblical Figures in Deuterocanonical and Cognate Literature, in: DCLY, Berlin / New York 2009, 567–585, 569 f.

[1240] O. WISCHMEYER, Wie kommt Abraham in den Galaterbrief? Überlegungen zu Gal 3,6–29, in: M. Bachmann / B. Kollmann (Hg.), Umstrittener Galaterbrief. Studien zur Situierung der Theologie des Paulus-Schreibens, BThSt 106, Neukirchen-Vluyn 2010, 119–163 (Lit. 119–121); DIES., Glaube, der durch Liebe tätig wird.

[1241] Ob er hier ethisch – und das heißt: transethnisch – oder ethnisch denkt, bleibt ungesagt. Keineswegs kann aus 2,21 auf ein jüdisches Lesepublikum geschlossen werden, wie ALLISON, Jak, 482, statuiert. Gegen jüdisches Lesepublikum schon DIBELIUS, Jak, 198, ebenso auch BURCHARD, Jak, 126 f: »Als ὁ πατὴρ ἡμῶν … ist er für Jak der erste, beste Christ und Stammvater der Adressaten«. Vgl. WISCHMEYER, Abraham unser Vater, 570, zu der paulinischen Wendung »Abraham, Vater aller Heiden« (Röm 4,17). Bereits Paulus hat die Bedeutung Abrahams für Nichtjuden erschlossen. So auch Barn 13,7: »Ich habe dich, A., zum Vater der Völker eingesetzt«.

[1242] Abr. 61: τῆς εὐσεβείας ἀποδείξεις.

[1243] Abr. 52.

[1244] In Gen 22,12 ist es die Gottesfurcht: νῦν γὰρ ἔγνων ὅτι φοβῇ τὸν θεὸν σὺ καὶ οὐκ ἐφείσω τοῦ υἱοῦ σου τοῦ ἀγαπητοῦ δι᾽ ἐμέ (Denn nun weiß ich, dass du Gott fürchtest und deinen geliebten Sohn nicht verschont hast um meinetwillen), die Abraham beweist.

ohne dass mit dem jeweiligen Interpretament eine spezifizierende Akzentuierung vorgenommen würde.

Diese Akzentuierung findet sich aber bei Paulus, der Abraham nicht als ethisches Exempel einführt, sondern zum Zeugen seiner Theologie macht, indem er in Gal 3 und Röm 4 jeweils eine komplizierte Schriftexegese zu Gen 16,5 vorlegt. Jak 2,20–26 befindet sich semantisch in der Nähe dieser Paulustexte. Allerdings fehlt bei Paulus der Hinweis auf die Isaakopferung. Paulus führt Abraham in Gal 3,6 und Röm 4,3.9 nicht im Zusammenhang mit Gen 22,2.9, sondern nur mit Gen 16,5 als Beispiel (καθώς Gal 3,6) für die Kraft des Glaubens an. Jakobus dagegen bezieht sich zunächst auf die Isaakerzählung in Gen 22 – auf Gen 22,9 weist der Terminus θυσιαστήριον hin[1245] – und zitiert erst im nächsten Satz Gen 16,5 im Sinne des entscheidenden Arguments für seine These zur Gerechtigkeit aus Taten. Er verbindet also verschiedene Abrahaminterpretationen für sein eigenes Argument. Mit dem Hinweis auf die ἔργα ist er nahe bei Philo, der ebenfalls Abrahams *Tat* als entscheidenden Faktor der Isaakopferung hervorhebt, ohne allerdings δικαιοσύνη ins Spiel zu bringen. Letzteres Thema führt zu Paulus. Darauf, dass in Jak 2,21 primär Paulus im Hintergrund steht, kann das Verb δικαιοῦν[1246] hinweisen.[1247] In V. 21–25 spitzt Jakobus seine eigentliche These: Glaube ohne Taten ist nutzlos (V. 20), dadurch zu, dass er in den paulinischen Gerechtigkeitsdiskurs eintritt, der bisher im Jakobusbrief keine Rolle gespielt hat[1248] und auch nur hier aufgerufen wird. Deutlich ist, dass Jakobus mit dem Thema der Rechtfertigung über sein eigentliches Ziel, den Glauben als *praktische* Größe zu erweisen, hinausgeht. Denn jetzt geht es nicht mehr »nur« um die praktische Verwirklichung des Glaubens, sondern um die Rechtfertigung des Glaubenden. Dies Thema wird bei Jakobus aber nicht selbständig erörtert. Wenn er in 2,21 von einer Rechtfertigung durch ἔργα spricht, bleibt er im Bereich der jüdischen Abrahaminterpretationen, ohne die theologischen Folgerungen des Paulus nachzuvollziehen.

Zudem basiert auch der paulinische Rechtfertigungsdiskurs, soweit er als Interpretation der Abrahamgestalt stattfindet, auf der frühjüdischen Abrahamtradition. Dass Abraham »aus Taten *gerechtfertigt* wurde«, betont auch 1Makk 2,51 f unter der Überschrift der ἔργα τῶν πατέρων (V. 51) mit einer rhetorischen Frage:

> (52) Αβρααμ οὐχὶ ἐν πειρασμῷ εὑρέθη πιστός, καὶ ἐλογίσθη αὐτῷ εἰς δικαιοσύνην;
>
> (52) Abraham, wurde er nicht in der Prüfung treu erfunden, und wurde es ihm zur Gerechtigkeit angerechnet?

[1245] Verb in Gen 22,9 ἐπιφέρω, in Jak 2,21 ἀναφέρω.

[1246] Dass dem Verfasser die Begrifflichkeit nicht unbekannt ist, zeigt Jak 1,20 (s. o.).

[1247] Apg 13,39 (Paulus in Antiochia in Pisidien): hier stellt das Theologumenon von der Gerechtigkeit aus Glauben den Höhepunkt der Predigt des Paulus dar. Sehr häufig in Röm 2–8, Gal 2 und 3. Bei Jak nur in Kap. 2: V. 21. 24. 25.

[1248] Der »Gerechte« begegnet erst in Kap. 5. »Gerechtigkeit« nur in 1,20.

Diese *Grundlage* interpretieren Paulus und Jakobus unterschiedlich. Während Paulus das Motiv der Treue Abrahams (πιστός) zur Grundbeziehung zu Gott (πίστις) weiterentwickelt und in antithetische Relation zum Gesetz und seiner Erfüllung (ἔργα νόμου) setzt, interpretiert Jakobus Abrahams Treue (πίστις) strikt von seinem Tun (ἔργα), dem Opfer seines Sohnes, her, ohne die Gesetzesthematik zu erwähnen. Indem Jakobus dabei nicht mehr die Treue bzw. den Glauben, sondern das *Gerechtfertigtwerden* betont an die ἔργα bindet, erhält sein Argument in der Sache eine antipaulinische Spitze, auch wenn Paulus – anders als in 2Petr 3,14–16 – nicht genannt wird.[1249] Ob diese in der Sache antipaulinische Front *intendiert* war, lässt sich dem Text nicht entnehmen.[1250] In V. 21 bemüht Jakobus Abraham als Zeugen für seine These zur πίστις.

Nun weist Allison darauf hin, dass δικαιοῦσθαι nicht ausschließlich auf Paulus weist, da in Mt 11,19 und 12,37 das Verb außerhalb des Rechtfertigungsdiskurses verwendet wird.[1251] Jakobus befindet sich zwar offensichtlich in der Nähe der paulinischen Texte, wie V. 23 zeigen wird. Dennoch sprechen die Matthäusbelege tatsächlich dafür, nicht zu einseitige Beziehungen zwischen den Paulustexten und Jak 2 zu konstruieren. Deutlich ist, dass der Verfasser durch die Abrahamthematik begrifflich in die Nähe des paulinischen Rechtfertigungsdiskurses gerät, ohne das paulinische Thema der δικαιοσύνη sachlich weiter zu verfolgen und ohne das die paulinische Argumentation tragende Element des Gesetzes (Syntagma der ἔργα νόμου) aufzugreifen. Er bedient sich vielmehr nur des Stichwortes ἔργα, das für seine eigene theologische These wichtig ist und das er aus der Tradition nimmt, aus der auch Paulus schöpft.[1252]

V. 22 Jakobus nimmt eine *erste* Auswertung des Abrahamexempels vor (βλέπεις[1253]), hier noch im Dialogstil der 2. Pers. Sing., während in V. 24 eine *zweite* Anwendung in der 2. Pers. Plur. (ὁρᾶτε) erfolgen wird. Wieder formuliert Jakobus sorgfältig, wie Burchard betont:

> zweimal Glaube als Subjekt, erst mit aktivischem, dann mit passivischem Prädikat. In verschiedenen Tempora, chiastisch gestellt.[1254]

Hinzu kommt die *figura etymologica* συνήργει τοῖς ἔργοις. Der Vers gibt weiterer Aufschluss über die eigentliche Absicht des Verfassers: Jakobus greift das Thema »Glaube« wieder auf und stellt die Rechtfertigung zugunsten von Synergie und Vollkommenheit zurück – Begriffen, die sein eigenes Anliegen präzise ausdrücken.

[1249] Zur Frage des »Antipaulinismus« s. die Einleitung.

[1250] Vgl. dazu die Einleitung.

[1251] Allison, Jak, 486.

[1252] Zur frühjüdischen Tradition vgl. vor allem Burchard, Jak, 125–128; zur »Rezeption von Tradition« vgl. Metzner, Jak, 153. ἔργον für das Isaakopfer: Josephus, ant. Iud. 1.233.

[1253] Vgl. 2Kor 7,8; Hebr 3,19.

[1254] Burchard, Jak, 128.

C. Briefcorpus 249

Die Auswertung erfolgt in zwei einander ergänzenden Aussagen: (1) Der Glaube (Abrahams) hat mit den Werken *zusammengewirkt*. (2) Durch die Werke ist der Glaube *vollkommen* geworden. Die beiden Verben συνεργεῖν[1255] und τελειοῦν hat Jakobus sorgfältig gewählt. συνεργεῖν, συνεργός werden im Neuen Testament außer hier bei Jak nur bei Paulus benutzt[1256], und zwar im Sinne von »helfen, gelingen, nützen«.[1257] Das Substantiv zielt auf die Zusammenarbeit (»Mitarbeiter«). συνεργεῖν nimmt also sachlich V. 14.20 wieder auf. τελειοῦν, »etwas vollkommen machen«[1258], knüpft an 1,4 (ἔργον τέλειον) und an die mehrfach Ermahnung des Verfassers, seine Adressaten sollten »vollkommen« sein, an.[1259]

V. 23 Dieser Vers enthält das gewichtigste Schriftzitat des Jakobusbriefes. Zugleich ist »der Schriftbeweis … die Spitze seiner Argumentation«, wie Metzner richtig formuliert.[1260] Gen 15,6 wird mit einer sog. Erfüllungsformel eingeleitet, die häufig bei den Synoptikern begegnet[1261], im Jakobusbrief aber nur hier verwendet wird. Jakobus verbindet Glauben und Gerechtigkeit Abrahams im Zitat von Gen 15,6, demselben Satz, den Paulus zweimal zitiert: in Röm 4,3.9 und Gal 3,6.[1262]

Gen 15,6: καὶ ἐπίστευσεν Ἀβραμ τῷ θεῷ, καὶ ἐλογίσθη αὐτῷ εἰς δικαιοσύνην.
Und es glaubte Abram Gott, und es wurde ihm zur Gerechtigkeit angerechnet.

1Makk 2,52: Ἀβρααμ οὐχὶ ἐν πειρασμῷ εὑρέθη πιστός, καὶ ἐλογίσθη αὐτῷ εἰς δικαιοσύνην;
Wurde Abraham nicht in der Versuchung als treu erfunden, und es wurde ihm zur Gerechtigkeit angerechnet?

Philo, mut. 177 f: ἐπίστευσε δὲ Ἀβραὰμ τῷ θεῷ, καὶ ἐλογίσθη αὐτῷ εἰς δικαιοσύνην.

Gal 3,6: Ἀβραὰμ *ἐπίστευσεν τῷ θεῷ, καὶ ἐλογίσθη αὐτῷ εἰς δικαιοσύνην.*

Röm 4,3: *ἐπίστευσεν δὲ Ἀβραὰμ τῷ θεῷ καὶ ἐλογίσθη αὐτῷ εἰς δικαιοσύνην.*

Röm 4,9: *ἐλογίσθη τῷ Ἀβραὰμ ἡ πίστις εἰς δικαιοσύνην.*

Jak 2,23: καὶ ἐπληρώθη ἡ γραφὴ ἡ λέγουσα· *ἐπίστευσεν δὲ Ἀβραὰμ τῷ θεῷ, καὶ ἐλογίσθη αὐτῷ εἰς δικαιοσύνην,* καὶ φίλος θεοῦ ἐκλήθη.

In 1Clem 10,6 wird ebenfalls Gen 15,5.6 ausführlich zitiert.[1263] Die genannten neutestamentlichen Zitate haben Gemeinsamkeiten in den Traditionen, auf die

---

[1255] Im Imperfekt: nur hier im Jakobusbrief, wohl auf die Tat Abrahams bezogen.

[1256] Das Substantiv noch 3Joh 8.

[1257] Bauer / Aland, 1570: »mitwirken, unterstützen, helfen«. Hap. leg. in Jak. Belege auch bei Burchard, Jak, 128 f – »Synergismus« im Sinne des Zusammenwirkens von göttlicher Gnade und menschlichem Tun ist hier nicht im Blick (vgl. Metzner, Jak, 155).

[1258] Bauer / Aland, 1615: »aus den Werken gewann der Glaube seine Vollkommenheit«, hap. leg. in Jak, vgl. Jak 2,8 τελεῖν. Adjektiv: Jak 1,4 (zweimal).17.25; 3,2.

[1259] Allison, Jak, verweist auf Philo, agr. 42; conf. 181 und praem. 49 für die Verbindung von τελειοῦν und ἐκ.

[1260] Metzner, Jak, 156.

[1261] Häufig bei Mt, mehrfach bei Joh und in Apg. In der Briefliteratur nur Jak 2,23.

[1262] Sonst nicht im NT zitiert.

[1263] Zitiert auch in 1Clem 31,2 und Barn 13,7 (beide Male im paulinischen Sinn interpretiert).

sie sich berufen und die sie im Rahmen ihrer Argumentation benutzen. (1) Sie zitieren explizit und nachdrücklich »die Schrift«, d.h. Gen 15,6. Damit bewegen sich sie sich im Zusammenhang der Schriftauslegung von Gen 15,6. Paulus fragt in Röm 4,3: »Was sagt die Schrift (γραφή)?« In Gal 3,6 wird zunächst Gen 15,6 zitiert und von Paulus interpretiert (»erkennt also, dass«), dann nennt Paulus in 3,8 »die Schrift« als Quelle seines theologischen Arguments. Jak 2,23 aber verleiht dem Schriftbezug besondere Bedeutung durch die Einleitungsformel eines sog. Erfüllungszitates. Die Anwendung der frühchristlichen Erfüllungszitat-Formel[1264] auf einen nicht-prophetischen Kontext ist ein exegetisches Problem. Allison zählt sechs verschiedene Lösungen auf.[1265] Am ehesten handelt es sich um die Übernahme der eindrucksvollen Einleitungsformel mit rhetorischer Absicht. Jakobus hat dabei den Verheißungs- Erfüllungszusammenhang außer Acht gelassen. Jakobus zitiert Gen 15,6 wörtlich.[1266] In V. 24 fährt er mit einer ähnlichen Interpretationsformel fort wie Paulus in Gal 3,6 (»Ihr seht, dass«).

(2) Das Genesiszitat wird jeweils theologisch oder ethisch interpretiert: theologisch im Galaterbrief im Zusammenhang der paulinischen Heidenmission und im Römerbrief im Rahmen einer umfassenden und thematisch komplexen Argumentation zur Glaubensgerechtigkeit Abrahams im Zusammenhang der paulinischen Christologie (Röm 3,21–26). Im Jakobusbrief geht es um eine ethische Frage: die praktische Umsetzung des Glaubens. Dabei ist durchaus eine theologische Komponente im Spiel: die richtige Interpretation von πίστις. Die ethische Komponente wird durch den zweiten Satz gestärkt: »Und Freund Gottes wurde er genannt«. Damit zeigt Jakobus, dass ihm mehr an der Gestalt Abrahams und seiner Vorbildfunktion als an dem Argument der Glaubensgerechtigkeit gelegen ist. Das Epitheton vom Gottesfreund begegnet sonst nicht im Neuen Testament[1267] und geht nicht auf Gen 15,6 zurück, die Vorstellung vom *Gottesfreund* ist aber sowohl im griechischen wie im jüdischen Kontext bekannt.[1268] Das antike Judentum verwendet diese Bezeichnung öfter als »Ehrenname(n)« für Abraham.[1269] Indem Jakobus sie hier hinzufügt, unterstreicht er die Bedeutung des Exempels. Das Verbum καλεῖν – im Brief nur hier – lässt sich mit »bezeichnen als« übersetzen und bestätigt den Ehrennamen.

[1264] Stellen bei ALLISON, Jak, 490.

[1265] Dazu ALLISON, Jak, 490 f. Allison weist auf das rabbinische Diktum hin: »There is no before or after in Scripture« (491).

[1266] Das einleitende καί fehlt.

[1267] Aber 1Clem 10,1 (Freund) und 17,2 (Freund Gottes).

[1268] Vgl. G. STÄHLIN, Art φίλος κτλ., ThWNT 9, 1973, 144–169, hier 165–167, zur »Freundschaft« zwischen Gott und Menschen bei Philo 156; K. TREU, Art. Gottesfreund, RAC 11, 1981, 1043–1060; weiter die Angaben bei JOHNSON, Jak, 244; METZNER, Jak, 157 Anm. 192 (Jub 19,9; ApkAbr B 4.10; 13.1.6; Philo, Abr. 273); BURCHARD, Jak, 129 f. Burchard meint, Jakobus habe den Nachsatz für einen Teil des Genesiszitats gehalten (19). Das kann für Irenäus, Haer IV 16,2 gelten. Vielleicht bezieht sich Irenäus aber auch auf Jak 2,23.

[1269] BURCHARD, Jak, 130.

C. Briefcorpus

V. 24 Jakobus wertet das Abrahamsbeispiel nun im Zusammenhang seiner Argumentation aus, indem er V. 21 verallgemeinernd aufgreift. Er schreibt weiter im Diatribenstil (Θέλεις δὲ γνῶναι, ὦ ἄνθρωπε, βλέπεις ὅτι, ὁρᾶτε ὅτι: *variatio*), wechselt aber das Subjekt und wendet sich seinen Adressaten zu (»ihr«). Der Satz ist zweigeteilt. Die *positive* Aussage lautet: »Der Mensch wird aus Taten gerechtfertigt.« Damit bleibt Jakobus im Anschluss an Gen 15,6 in der Diktion des Rechtfertigungsdiskurses. Was für Abraham gilt, gilt für alle Menschen.[1270] Die Aussage, die Jakobus hier zum zweiten Mal trifft, ist deutlich: Der Mensch wird ἐξ ἔργων gerechtfertigt. Das Präsens steht für die Allgemeingültigkeit der Aussage. Jakobus fügt eine *negative* Abgrenzung hinzu, um der These zusätzliches Gewicht zu verleihen: »nicht aus Glauben allein«. Hier scheint deutlicher als vorher paulinische Rechtfertigungstheologie als negative Folie durch. Statt um die ethische Frage nach der Vollendung des Glaubens im Tun – bisher im Zentrum des Jakobusbriefes und zugleich ein Gedanke, den auch Paulus kennt und bejaht[1271], geht es jetzt um das *eindeutig paulinische theologische Thema, wie* der Mensch *gerecht* werde. Die Zuspitzung des zweiten Teils der Antwort durch das Adverb μόνον[1272], das bei Paulus nicht in diesem Zusammenhang begegnet[1273], hat einen polemischen Effekt. Ob Jakobus hier Paulus in seiner komplizierten Rechtfertigungslehre angreifen will, muss aber offenbleiben, da Jakobus das Rechtfertigungsthema nicht eigens aufgreift. Deutlich ist dagegen zweierlei: *Erstens* argumentiert Jakobus gegen einen »Nur-Glauben«[1274] – jene Vorstellung, die ihn seit dem Anfang des Schreibens ängstigt. *Zweitens* zieht ihn das Genesiszitat in den paulinischen Rechtfertigungsdiskurs, der ihm bekannt zu sein scheint, aber nicht sein eigener ist. Ihm geht es ja nicht um die Rechtfertigung, sondern um die praktische Glaubensbewährung. Dementsprechend fehlt bei Jakobus das paulinische Syntagma »Werke des *Gesetzes*«. Die ἔργα sind bei Jakobus nicht auf die Erfüllung von Gesetzesvorschriften bezogen, sondern betreffen das soziale Ethos der Gemeindeglieder. Jak 2,24 ist damit sachlich weniger weit von Paulus entfernt, als der Wortlaut vermuten lässt. Auch Paulus ruft die Galater zu dem Glauben auf, der durch die Liebe tätig ist (πίστις δι᾽ ἀγάπης ἐνεργουμένη, Gal 5,6). Insgesamt muss gelten, dass Jak 2,24 und sein Kontext ohne einen polemischen Bezug auf Röm 3 bzw. Gal 2 nur schwer zu erklären sind. Jakobus sucht in diesem Text die polemische Auseinandersetzung und Abgrenzung, und als Gegenpart kommt nur Paulus in Frage.[1275]

[1270] Beispiele für allgemeine Aussagen über den Menschen bei METZNER, Jak, 158 Anm. 202.

[1271] S. o. zu 2,17.

[1272] Dazu METZNER, Jak, 159.

[1273] Ironischerweise hat Luther das »allein« in seiner Übersetzung von Röm 3,28 eingefügt und damit gewissermaßen auf Jakobus zurückgegriffen.

[1274] METZNER, Jak, 159.

[1275] Ausführliche Begründung und Auseinandersetzung mit der exegetischen Literatur bei WISCHMEYER, Polemik, 366–374.

Gen 15,6: καὶ **ἐπίστευσεν** Αβραμ τῷ θεῷ, καὶ **ἐλογίσθη** αὐτῷ εἰς **δικαιοσύνην.**

Röm 3,28: **λογιζόμεθα** γὰρ **δικαιοῦσθαι πίστει ἄνθρωπον** χωρὶς *ἔργων νόμου.*

Gal 2,16: εἰδότες [δὲ] ὅτι οὐ **δικαιοῦται ἄνθρωπος** *ἐξ ἔργων νόμου* ἐὰν μὴ **διὰ πίστεως** Ἰησοῦ Χριστοῦ.

Jak 2,24: ὁρᾶτε ὅτι *ἐξ ἔργων* **δικαιοῦται ἄνθρωπος** καὶ **οὐκ ἐκ πίστεως** μόνον.

V. 25 Bei dem zweiten Exempel, das Jakobus überraschend anführt, der Prostituierten Rahab[1276], scheint Jakobus auf eine frühjüdische oder frühchristliche Tradition zurückzugreifen, obgleich Rahab in der vorpaulinischen Literatur nicht mit Abraham in Zusammenhang gebracht wird.[1277] Anders als Abraham ist Rahab in der biblischen Tradition auch nicht mit πίστις/πιστεύειν verbunden. Sie steht vielmehr in Jos 2 und 6 für Schutz und Gastfreundschaft.[1278] So resümiert Allison zurecht:

> Why James follows the example of Abraham with that of Rahab is unknown.[1279]

Bei Paulus findet sich im Zusammenhang mit den Abrahamtexten kein Hinweis auf Rahab. Es ist also von einer bestimmten, von Paulus nicht rezipierten frühchristlichen Rahabtradition auszugehen, auf die sich außer im Jakobusbrief auch Hinweise in den Beispielreihen in Hebr 11 und 1Clem 12[1280], aber auch in der Genealogie in Mt 1,5[1281] finden.

Auffallend ist die syntaktisch-stilistisch parallele Struktur der beiden Beispiele in V. 21 und 25: Einführung des Vorbilds in einer rhetorischen Frage, Rechtfertigung aus Taten in einer rhetorischen Frage, Bezeichnung der Tat (Opfer des Sohnes,

---

[1276] H. WINDISCH, Zur Rahabgeschichte, ZNW 37, 1917/18, 188–198. Ῥαάβ Hebr 11,31; Jak 2,25; Ῥαχάβ Mt 1,5. Vgl. 1Clem 12,1–3.

[1277] Erhalten sind nur frühchristliche Rahab-Traditionen. Die Mehrheit der Exegeten rechnet aber mit einer frühjüdischen Vorgeschichte.

[1278] DIBELIUS, Jak, 204 f, weist besonders auf das verbindende Motiv der Gastfreundschaft in 1Clem 10 hin, wo Abraham, Lot und Rahab durch die Tugend der Gastfreundschaft verbunden sind, Abraham und Rahab zusätzlich durch den Glauben. ALLISON, Jak, 500 f, ausführlich dazu: Rahab begegnet im Tanak nur in Jos 2 und 6, nicht in Apokryphen und Pseudepigraphen (besonders wichtig 500 Anm. 438: Rahab fehlt in Glaubenslisten), in Qumran und bei Philo. Josephus, ant. Iud. 5.8. Vgl. auch ALLISON, Jak, 501 Anm. 445. Allison betont, dass in der älteren Tradition nirgendwo Abraham und Rahab zusammen genannt werden. Erst in 1Clem 12,1 wird Rahab wegen ihrer Gastfreundschaft und ihres *Glaubens* gerühmt. In Hebr 11 fungiert Rahab unter den *Glaubenszeugen*, ihre Gastfreundschaft wird zusätzlich hervorgehoben. In beiden Texten steht Rahab nahe neben Abraham. – Zu den rabbinischen Rahabtraditionen siehe STRACK-BILLERBECK I, 20–23 (Kommentar zu Mt 1,5: Rahab im Stammbaum Jesu). – Vgl. allgemein den ausführlichen Art. Rahab von S. BIEBERSTEIN, WiBiLex, https://www.bibelwissenschaft.de/de/wibilex/das-bibellexikon/lexikon/sachwort/anzeigen/details/rahab-person/ch/eaa36c114c2683d3357040eed6aa5885/#h11 (Lit.!). JÓNSSON, James, 249 f, weist auf R. W. WALL, The Intertextuality of Scripture: The Example of Rahab (James 2:25), in: P. W. Flint (Hg.), The Bible at Qumran: Text, Shape, and Interpretation, Grand Rapids 2001, 217–226, 226, hin: Wall schlägt eine Verbindung von Jak 2,25 und Hebr 13,2 zu Gen 18 (Abraham) vor.

[1279] ALLISON, Jak, 501.

[1280] 1Clem 9–12: Rahab erhält neben Abraham den längsten Text. Sie wurde »wegen Glauben und Gastfreundschaft gerettet« (12,1).

[1281] Dazu STRACK-BILLERBECK I, 23.

Aufnahme der Boten). Anders als in V. 23 fehlt bei Rahab ein explizites Zitat. Rahab (Ῥαάβ) wird wie in Jos 6,17.25 als πόρνη eingeführt. Ihre »Tat«, die Aufnahme der Kundschafter, wird aber frei nach Jos 2 erzählt. Allison weist darauf hin, dass ὑποδέχεσθαι, ἄγγελος, ἐκβάλλειν einerseits nicht aus LXX stammen und andererseits im Jakobusbrief nur hier verwendet werden. Der Verfasser bemüht sich um eine eigene geschickte Zusammenfassung von Jos 2. Ebenso betont Allison, dass das Urteil οὐκ ἐξ ἔργων ἐδικαιώθη nicht aus dem Josuatext stammt, sondern Jak 2,21 wiederholt.[1282] Auffallend ist, dass Jakobus das Rahab-Beispiel wählt: Er scheint vorauszusetzen, dass es bekannt und plausibel ist.

V. 26 Noch überraschender als das Rahabbeispiel ist der Schlusssatz der Ausführung von 2,14–26 zu Glauben und Taten, der ein letztes Fazit zieht. ὥσπερ γὰρ: auch das zweite Beispiel dient der Evidenz der Begründung von 2,17. Jakobus wiederholt hier nicht nur in Variation den Satz aus 2,17, sondern fügt dies Urteil über den Glauben in einen Vergleich aus dem Bereich paulinischer Anthropologie ein. Noch einmal stößt man also auf paulinische Diktion, ohne dass damit eine positive Anleihe bei paulinischer Theologie gemacht würde.[1283] Vielmehr ist hier wie öfter der Jakobusbrief ein Zeuge dafür, dass paulinische Diktion in verschiedenen frühchristlichen theologischen Milieus Verwendung fand. σῶμα begegnet mehrfach bei Jakobus: 2,16 (»lebensnotwendiger Bedarf«) und 3,2.3.6 (Leib im Sinne von Körper) ohne spezifische anthropologische Bestimmung. Das gilt auch für 2,26: Die Dichotomie von σῶμα und πνεῦμα (vgl. 4,5) ist topisch.[1284] Sie wird hier nicht in einem anthropologischen Diskurs verwendet, sondern dient der Abrundung der Abhandlung über Glaube und Taten durch ein Beispiel sich ergänzender Begriffe, die nur im Zusammenspiel ein sinnvolles Ganzes darstellen. Zu erwarten wäre: Glaube und Taten verhalten sich zueinander wie Leib und Geist. Diese Analogie liegt aber nicht im Interesse des Verfassers. Metzner weist richtig auf folgende Inkonzinnität hin: »Der Vergleich überrascht insofern, als nicht Leib … und Taten … einerseits sowie Geist … und Glaube … andererseits gegenübergestellt werden, sondern Leib und Glaube auf der einen sowie Geist und Taten auf der anderen Seite.«[1285] Richtig schließt Metzner daraus, dass es Jakobus (nur) »um ein Zusammenwirken von Glaube und Taten analog zum Zusammenwirken von Leib und Geist« gehe.[1286]

Im Rückblick auf Jak 2,14–26 ist festzuhalten, dass das Glaubensverständnis des Jakobus sachlich unscharf bleibt. Einerseits will er mit den Ausführungen der beiden ersten Kapitel den Glauben seiner Adressaten stärken (1,3), indem er auf die Bewährung (δοκίμιον 1,3) des Glaubens in Geduld dringt, die zur Vollkommenheit

---

[1282] ALLISON, Jak, 505.

[1283] Zu σῶμα als paulinischem anthropologischem Begriff vgl. L. SCORNAIENCHI, Sarx und Soma bei Paulus. Der Mensch zwischen Destruktivität und Konstruktivität, NTOA / StUNT 67, Göttingen 2008.

[1284] Vgl. BURCHARD, Jak, 132 f, und ALLISON, Jak, 508 Anm. 493.

[1285] METZNER, Jak, 162.

[1286] Ebd.

führt. Er bezeichnet die Geduld als ἔργον und beschreibt sie als praktische Vollendung des Glaubens. Andererseits legt er schon in 1,22 f.25 den Akzent einseitig auf das Tun. Indem er dann in 2,14 ff den Fall eines Gemeindegliedes, das sagt, Glauben zu haben, ohne Taten vorzuweisen, konstruiert, reißt er Glauben und Tun so auseinander, dass die folgende Argumentation theologisch undeutlich bleibt und der Glaube selbst gegenüber dem Tun ganz an Bedeutung verliert. Das zeigt sich auch in den beiden Exempeln. In seiner Interpretation der *Akedah* tritt Abrahams Glaube zurück, bei Rahab spielt der Glaube gar keine Rolle. Dazu führt das Genesiszitat in den Zusammenhang der paulinischen Rechtfertigungstheologie, die aber nicht eigenes Thema des Jakobus ist. Am Ende versucht Jakobus mit Hilfe einer Formulierung aus der paulinischen Anthropologie sein eigentliches Votum: »Glaube benötigt Taten« plausibel zu machen. Es bleibt festzuhalten, dass Jakobus theologisch nicht am paulinischen Glaubens-Gerechtigkeits-Diskurs interessiert ist, sondern an der Stärkung des *tätigen Glaubens*, den er in seinen Gemeinden gefährdet sieht.

3. Dritter Hauptteil: Warnungen vor Gefahren (Kap. 3)

Auf die Diatribe in Kapitel 2 folgt in Kapitel 3 erneut Paränese.[1287] Jakobus teilt die Thematik in zwei Teile: die Warnung vor den Gefahren der Zunge (A) und die Warnung vor der irdischen Weisheit (B). 3,1 bringt einen völligen Neueinsatz und formuliert das neue Thema: die *Gefahren des Lehrers*. Zugleich ist der zweite Hauptteil eng mit den beiden ersten Hauptteilen und ihrer Thematik, den *Gefahren eines Glaubens ohne Taten*, verzahnt: Wieder (3,2) geht es um Vollkommenheit (1,4). Und schon im ersten Hauptteil ging es mehrfach um das Schwerpunktthema des 3. Kapitels, das Wort bzw. die Rede (λόγος). Die Motive der Vorsicht beim Sprechen und der Zähmung der Zunge, die in 3,1–12 im Mittelpunkt stehen, wurden bereits in 1,19.26 angesprochen, ebenso das Thema des Gerichts in 2,12.13 (doppelt). Das Thema der Weisheit, die vertieft in 3,13–18 behandelt wird, wurde in 1,5 präludiert. *Neu* dagegen ist das Motiv des Streits und der Feindschaft (ζῆλος, ἐριθεία), das in 4,1–6 weiter ausgeführt wird. Kapitel 3 basiert also auf Kapitel 1 und 2 und führt gleichzeitig die Thematik in Richtung auf die Kapitel 4 und 5 weiter.[1288] Der Verfasser warnt vor Verfehlungen oder Sünden (πταίω) der *Rede*. Aber auch diese Warnung hat schon ein Vorspiel in 2,10. Insgesamt stellt Kapitel 3 einen eigenen thematischen Zusammenhang dar. 3,1–12 ist auf »die Zunge« fokussiert[1289], V. 13–18 enthalten eine ethisch-weisheitliche Vertiefung.

[1287] METZNER, Jak, 167 f. Vgl. aber einschränkend das unten zum literarischen Anspruch der Texteinheit Gesagte.

[1288] Anders gewichtet DIBELIUS, Jak, 222.

[1289] Vgl. JOHNSON, Jak, 254: »3:1–12 stands as an intelligible discourse in its own«.

In Kapitel 3 ruft Jakobus massiv dazu auf, die Rede als das Hauptinstrument der Lehre zu kontrollieren. Diesem Aufruf zur *Kontrolle der Rede* verleiht er eingangs in zwei impliziten Vergleichen Farbe, die die pars pro toto-Verengung des Themas der Rede auf »die Zunge« von V. 5 an vorbereiten: Pferde werden durch Trensen kontrolliert, Schiffe durch Steuerruder. Die Zunge wird analog zu Trense und Steuer verstanden: Sie kann und soll, obgleich ein kleines Glied, doch den Menschen kontrollieren. Jakobus spricht weder die Analogie zwischen Lehrer, Pferd und Schiff, noch zwischen Zunge, Trense und Steuerruder aus, sondern setzt voraus, dass sie von seinen Adressaten vollzogen wird. Allerdings hinken beide Vergleiche oder müssen jedenfalls nicht als analoges *exemplum*, sondern als Gegenbeispiel zur Zunge verstanden werden: Während Trense und Steuerruder gerade von den Menschen kontrolliert und erfolgreich als Steuerungsinstrumente eingesetzt werden, ist Jakobus davon überzeugt, dass die Zunge sich *nicht* vom Menschen kontrollieren lässt (V. 8). Daher *verzichtet* er auch auf konkrete Anweisungen zur Kontrolle, etwa im Sinne einer konstruktiven Humanisierung der Rede (*speech ethics*).[1290] Eigentliche *speech ethics* liegt hier nicht vor. Stattdessen fügt er einen dritten, nun expliziten Vergleich hinzu: Die Zunge ist mit derselben Gewalt destruktiv tätig wie ein kleines Feuer, das einen ganzen Wald in Flammen setzt. In V. 5–8 beschreibt Jakobus mit rhetorischer Verve diese dämonische destruktive Macht der Zunge.[1291] Erst in V. 9 findet er zu einer ausgewogenen Beurteilung der Zunge zurück. V. 10 enthält eine kurze auswertende Mahnung (»Das soll nicht so sein«), die in V. 11.12 noch durch das doppelte Bildwort von der Quelle und dem Feigenbaum unterstützt wird.

Der zweite Teil des Kapitels, V. 13–18, nimmt dann das Thema friedlicher Rede in veränderter Form wieder auf bzw. treibt es weiter voran und ändert zugleich die Thematik, indem eine friedenstiftende »*Weisheit* von oben« einer bösen, streitsüchtigen »Weisheit von unten« gegenübergestellt wird. Die Thematik einer weisheitlich geleiteten *Rede* tritt dabei ganz in den Hintergrund. Allerdings schreibt der Verfasser selbst im Duktus der weisheitlichen Lehrrede.[1292] Das *Ziel* der Belehrung wird am Ende des 2. Hauptteils klar definiert: »Frieden *tun*«, nicht friedlich sprechen oder lehren. Damit wird das theologische Grundanliegen des Briefes, das ethische *Handeln*, konkretisiert.

Das Kapitel ist weder primär argumentativ wie 2,14–26 aufgebaut noch konsequent paränetisch ausgerichtet wie 1,2–2,13. Vorherrschend ist rhetorisch-metaphorische Rede über »die Zunge«. Die literarische Anstrengung des Verfassers überwiegt die Sachaussage deutlich. Die Binnengliederung des 1. Teils ist klar: V. 1.2 formulieren die Mahnung aufgrund der von Jakobus gesehenen Gefahr, die Lehrer betreffen kann. V. 3.4 bereiten mit zwei Beispielen die Ausführungen über »die

---

[1290] Luther, Sprachethik im Neuen Testament, 145–170 und 337–343.

[1291] Vgl. Allison, Jak, 517: »3.1–12 is more lament than help, because James offers no counsel on how to tame the tongue … His chief goal is to warn, not instruct«.

[1292] Luther, Sprachethik, 157.

Zunge« (V. 5–9) vor, die das Zentrum des 2. Hauptteils bilden. V. 10–12 unterstützen diese Ausführung. Dabei weist V. 12 schon auf die zweite Texteinheit voraus.[1293]

Bilderrede und rhetorische Instrumentierung prägen insgesamt den ersten Teil des Kapitels. Das Thema der »Zunge« und der Gefahren der Zunge trifft so sehr einen Nerv des Verfassers, dass er das angestrebte Ziel der friedlichen Lehre, die einen Lehrer vollkommen macht, über seinem rhetorischen Kabinettstück zur Zunge in V. 5–8 aus dem Blick verliert. Der thematische Text über die Zunge ist literarisch auffallend sorgfältig gestaltet und gewinnt eine gewisse Eigendynamik, die der Verfasser in den V. 9–12 wieder einfangen muss. Die Verse 5–9 lassen sich mit Susanne Luther als Ekphrasis, als bildhafte Beschreibung der Rede unter dem Bild der Zunge, klassifizieren.[1294]

Beide Textteile sind nicht nur jeweils in sich homogen, sondern auch eng aufeinander bezogen, der Einschnitt ist formal kaum zu verifizieren. Deutlich ist aber die thematische Verschiebung von der Warnung vor der Gefahr der Rede zur Darstellung der konstruktiven Weisheit auf der Negativfolie der irdischen Weisheit in V. 13–18. Jakobus wirbt für die »Weisheit von Oben«, die er rein ethisch definiert. V. 18 bringt einen klaren Abschluss des Kapitels.[1295]

Der übergreifende Zusammenhang der Themen der »Zunge« und der »Weisheit«, die sich im richtigen Tun erweist, ist in der alttestamentlichen Weisheitsliteratur vorgegeben. Die Psalmisten und die Weisheitslehrer, deren Schullehre in den Sammlungen des Sprüchebuches und im Buch Jesus Sirach niedergelegt ist, verstanden die Rede als eine Quelle ethischer Gefahren und betrachteten sie daher als wesentlichen Gegenstand ihrer Erziehung. Dieser positive pädagogische Aspekt fehlt aber bei Jakobus. In den Psalmen wird die Metapher der »Zunge« sowohl mit dem Lobpreis Gottes assoziiert[1296] als auch mit τὸ κακόν und ἀδικία.[1297]

[1293] Zu anderen Einteilungen des Textes vgl. METZNER, Jak, 168 f.

[1294] LUTHER, Sprachethik, 157 (Lit.). Ekphrasis begegnet im Brief nur hier: Das Thema der »Zunge« hat für den Verfasser eine besondere Bedeutung und wird in besonderer Weise literarisch herausgehoben. Zu dem beliebten antiken Thema vgl. vor allem Plutarch, de garrulitate (Plutarque: Œuvres morales. Band 7 Teil 1, hrsg. Jean Dumortier, Jean Defradas, 1975). Dort begegnen neben der Metapher der Zunge auch die Metaphern von Schiff (10), Feuer (10) und Zügel (7.19). Zu Zügen von E. in Jak 4,17 s.u.

[1295] Zum Aufbau des Kapitels besonders BURCHARD, Jakobus, 134 f (»V. 1–11 … setzen neu ein, sind aber schwer auf die Reihe zu bringen«). DIBELIUS, Jak, 223, urteilt ähnlich: »Wir merken …, wie die Gedanken sich stoßen oder auch sich kreuzen«. Dibelius schließt daraus auf »Schulgut«.

[1296] Ps 15,9LXX; 50,16LXX u. ö.

[1297] So Ps 33,14LXX παῦσον τὴν γλῶσσάν σου ἀπὸ κακοῦ (Halte deine Zunge vom Bösen zurück); Ps 51,4–6LXX 4 ἀδικίαν ἐλογίσατο ἡ γλῶσσά σου· ὡσεὶ ξυρὸν ἠκονημένον ἐποίησας δόλον. 5 ἠγάπησας κακίαν ὑπὲρ ἀγαθωσύνην, ἀδικίαν ὑπὲρ τὸ λαλῆσαι δικαιοσύνην. διάψαλμα. 6 ἠγάπησας πάντα τὰ ῥήματα καταποντισμοῦ, γλῶσσαν δολίαν (Deine Zunge ersann Ungerechtigkeit. Wie ein geschärftes Schermesser begingst du Betrug. Du liebtest Bosheit mehr als Rechtschaffenheit, Ungerechtigkeit mehr als Gerechtigkeit zu reden … Du liebtest alle ertränkenden Worte, eine betrügerische Zunge).

A. 3,1–12: Warnung vor der Macht der Zunge

(1) Lasst[1298] nicht (so / zu) viele (von euch) Lehrer sein[1299], meine Brüder, und bedenkt[1300], dass wir ein strengeres[1301] Urteil empfangen werden. (2) In Vielem[1302] verfehlen wir uns nämlich alle. Wenn sich jemand in der Rede[1303] nicht verfehlt, ist[1304] er[1305] ein vollkommener Mann, der[1306] im Stande ist, auch den ganzen Körper zu zügeln. (3) Wenn wir aber die Zügel in die Mäuler der Pferde legen, damit sie uns gehorchen, lenken[1307] wir auch ihren ganzen Körper. (4) Siehe, auch die Schiffe, die so groß sind und von rauhen Winden getrieben werden, werden mit einem sehr kleinen Steuerruder gelenkt, wohin die Absicht[1308] des Steuernden will – (5) so ist auch die Zunge ein kleines Glied und vermisst sich doch[1309] großer Dinge[1310]. Siehe welch kleines Feuer welch großen Wald[1311] anzündet. (6) Auch die Zunge ist[1312] ein Feuer: die Welt der Ungerechtigkeit, die Zunge, präsentiert sich[1313] in unseren Gliedern, indem sie den ganzen Körper beschmutzt[1314] und das Rad des Werdens in Brand setzt und selbst[1315] von der Gehenna in Brand gesetzt ist[1316]. (7) Jede Spezies von Landtieren nämlich und Vögeln, Schlangen und Seetieren wird gebändigt und ist gebändigt worden von der menschlichen Spezies[1317], (8) die Zunge aber kann kein Mensch bändigen, das unruhige Übel, voll todbringenden Giftes. (9) Mit ihr loben wir den Herrn und Vater, und mit ihr

---

[1298] Ob hier »seid« oder »werdet« zu übersetzen ist, muss offenbleiben. Beides ist möglich (BAUER / ALAND, 316–321). DIBELIUS plädiert mit gutem Grund für »sein«: Jak, 223.

[1299] Übersetzung nach DIBELIUS, Jak, 223. Wörtlich: »Seid nicht viele Lehrer« oder »Nicht viele von euch sollen Lehrer sein«. Zur Trennung der Negativpartikel vom Verb vgl. DBR, § 433 Anm. 1. Vgl. Jak 1,7; 2,1. Hier ist die Verneinung aber eher auf πολλοί zu beziehen. πολλοί gehört der Stellung nach zum Prädikativum »Lehrer«. BURCHARD, Jak, 135, hält die Frage der Beziehungen nicht für entscheidend.

[1300] Partizip.

[1301] Wörtlich: »größeres«.

[1302] Auch möglich: »oftmals«. Vgl. BAUER / ALAND, 380: »Der Akk. wird als Adv. gebraucht«. BAUER / ALAND schlägt »sich vielfach verfehlen« vor.

[1303] λόγος hier »Rede«, sonst »Wort« (1,18. 21. 22.23).

[1304] »Ist« fehlt: Nominalsatz.

[1305] Griechisch: »dieser«.

[1306] Das Partizip ist im Relativsatz aufgelöst.

[1307] BURCHARD, Jak, 140, will statt »in eine andere Richtung lenken« (so BAUER / ALAND, 1034) genauer übersetzen: »hinführen«. S.133 übersetzt Burchard den Text: »bewegen wir auch ihren ganzen Körper (hin zum Ziel)!« Der Unterschied ist unerheblich.

[1308] Übersetzung nach BAUER / ALAND, 1178. LSJ, 1253: »impulse to do a thing«.

[1309] »Doch« ist im Deutschen ergänzt.

[1310] Übersetzung nach BAUER / ALAND, 250.

[1311] Nach BAUER / ALAND, 700.

[1312] »Ist« ist im Deutschen hinzugefügt.

[1313] Medium von καθιστάναι: sich darstellen als, eingesetzt sein, wirken. LSJ, 855: »to set oneself down, settle, stand in his presence« (vgl. Jak 4,4). METZNER, Jak, 181, schlägt vor: »sich platzieren«.

[1314] Das Partizip ist modal aufgelöst.

[1315] »Selbst« ist im Deutschen hinzugefügt.

[1316] γέεννα wird mit »Gehenna« übersetzt, um den Charakter des Fremdwortes abzubilden.

[1317] Nach LSJ, 1965.

258 Kommentar

verfluchen wir die Menschen, die (doch[1318]) nach dem Bilde Gottes gemacht sind. (10) Aus ein und demselben Mund gehen Lob und Fluch hervor. Nicht soll, meine Brüder, dies so geschehen. (11) Lässt etwa[1319] die Quelle aus derselben Öffnung süßes und bitteres (Wasser)[1320] quellen? (12) Kann etwa[1321], meine Brüder, ein Feigenbaum Oliven produzieren[1322] oder ein Weinstock Feigen? Auch kann nicht eine Salz(quelle)[1323] Süßwasser produzieren.[1324]

Textkritik: V. 1 Majuskeln L (9. Jh.) und Minuskel 630 (12./13. Jh.) – beide Zeugen für den Koinetext – haben im handschriftlichen Befund statt πολλοι διδασκαλοι: πολυ δ., (beide Hss mit *einem* λ und mit Akzenten bei πολύ und διδάσκαλοι, d. h. in zwei eigenständigen Wörtern zu denken), wie man auf den im Internet bereitgestellten Abbildungen der Hss ersehen kann. Für den Hinweis danke ich Herrn Dr. Klaus Wachtel im Institut für Neutestamentliche Textforschung Münster. Ob es sich um eine orthographische Variante zur Textlesart handelt oder um einen Neologismus (πολυδιδασκαλοι, »Viellehrer«, nicht in der Gräzität), kann kaum entschieden werden. Die mehrfach vorgeschlagene Itazismusthese (DBR, § 115 Anm. 2: οι und υ austauschbar) sowie die »Buchstabenverwechslungen«, die DIBELIUS, Jak, 223, diagnostizieren will, basieren auf TISCHENDORF, der in der Editio octava critica maior (1869–1872) für L fälschlich die Lesart πολλυ angibt. Die ECM entschied sich dafür, eine eigenständige Variante anzunehmen. Zu älteren Emendationen vgl. kritisch DIBELIUS, Jak, 223. ληψεσθε statt λη(μ)ψομεθα lesen mehrere Minuskeln; die Lesart ληψεσθε, die die 2.Ps.Pl. des Vordersatzes aufnimmt, ist am ehesten als Angleichung an V. 1a zu werten. Die Lesarten mit 1.Ps.Pl. sind sehr viel besser bezeugt. V. 2 οι und mehrere Minuskeln lesen δυναμενος statt δυνατος. V. 3 Mit ει δε leiten 03C2, weitere Majuskeln und viele Minuskeln, darunter 33, den Satz ein. ιδε (öfter im Joh; Gal 5,2) lesen 056 und sehr viele Minuskeln wohl unter dem Einfluss von V. 4.5. P54. 02 und mehrere Minuskeln lesen το στομα statt des besser bezeugten Plurals τα στοματα. προς το lesen zahlreiche Minuskeln, εις το haben 01. 03. 04. 044 und einige Minuskeln (bessere Bezeugung). V. 5 μεγαλαυχει (sich brüsten) lesen P20. 01. 04C2. 044 und sehr viele Minuskeln. Besser bezeugt ist μεγαλα αυχει (P74. 02. 03. 04*. 025 und einige Minuskeln). V. 6 025 und zahlreiche Minuskeln schieben ουτως bzw. ουτως και (020. 056 und einige Minuskeln) zwischen αδικιας und η γλωσσα ein. [1325] οι und einige Minuskeln haben γενεσεως ημων. V. 7 Mehrere Minuskeln zeigen abweichende Lesarten bei den komplexen Wendungen θηριων τε και πετεινων, ερπεων τε και εναλιων einerseits und dem doppelten Verb δαμαζεται και δεδαμασται. V. 8 Dasselbe gilt für das Hyperbaton ουδεις δαμασαι δυναται ανθρωπων. Beides sind Zeichen für die Schwierigkeiten, die Kopisten mit dem literarisch manierierten Stil hatten. Statt ακαταστατον κακον (01. 02. 03) lesen 04 und sehr viele Minuskeln ακατασχετον, unbändig (öfter bei Philo; MPol 12,2). V. 9 Statt κυριον (P20. 01. 02. 03. 04. 33) lesen sehr viele Minuskeln θεον. Dadurch wird das Akk.objekt

---

[1318] »Doch« ist im Deutschen hinzugefügt.

[1319] μήτι »Fragepartikel in Fragen, die e. verneinende Antwort verlangen« (BAUER / ALAND, 1053).

[1320] »Wasser« ist im Deutschen hinzugefügt.

[1321] μή: »Fragepartikel, wenn eine verneinende Antwort erwartet wird« (BAUER / ALAND, 1047, vgl. DBR, § 427,2.4.)

[1322] ποιῆσαι lässt sich am besten mit »produzieren« übersetzen.

[1323] Übersetzung mit BURCHARD, Jak, 152.

[1324] Zu V. 12 vgl. DBR, § 445,1 (DBR urteilt: »ganz verdorben«).

[1325] Zur Syntax vgl. den Kommentar zur Stelle.

verdeutlicht. Statt γεγονοτας (01.02.03.04, viele Minuskeln) haben 02.33 und weitere Minuskeln γεγενημενους. V. 11 Zahlreiche kleine Abweichungen bei der Wendung το γλυκυ και το πικρον. V. 12 Zahlreiche Varianten im Nachsatz: ουτε αλυκον γλυκυ ποιησαι υδωρ lesen 02. 03. 04. 044 und wenige Minuskeln. ουδε lesen 01. 33 und wenige Minuskeln. Zahlreiche Minuskeln fügen eine erläuternde Ergänzung ein: ουδεμια πηγὴ αλυκον και γλυκυ ποιησαι υδωρ.

V. 1 Jakobus eröffnet den neuen Textabschnitt mit einer imperativisch formulierten Ermahnung an seine Adressaten, die er im Sinne der epistolaren Kommunikation wieder als »meine Brüder« anspricht.[1326] Die Ermahnung wird mit einer partizipial formulierten Begründung abgerundet. Die Adressaten werden davor gewarnt, »in der Mehrzahl«[1327] διδάσκαλοι zu sein oder zu werden[1328], ohne dass weitere Details gegeben werden. Das Thema *Lehrer* oder Lehre / lehren begegnet hier unvermittelt und taucht im Brief sonst nicht auf.[1329] Dibelius erklärt einleuchtend,

> daß Jak nicht an gelegentliches Auftreten der Christen als Lehrer denkt, sondern an einen gewissen Andrang zum Beruf des διδάσκαλος.[1330]

Es geht um eine Gemeindefunktion, die schon in den paulinischen Gemeinden bezeugt ist (1Kor 12,28 f[1331]) und auch in den nachpaulinischen Briefen positiv gesehen wird.[1332] Jakobus scheint sich selbst als Lehrer zu verstehen, wenn das »wir« der Begründung in V. 1b wörtlich genommen werden darf.[1333] Seiner Wahrnehmung nach streben zu viele Gemeindeglieder ebenfalls nach dieser Funktion. Das weist auf eine sozial und intellektuell dynamische Entwicklung der Gemeinden, mit denen er kommuniziert, hin. Neben den πρεσβύτεροι (5,14) sind die διδάσκαλοι die einzigen Funktionsträger in den Gemeinden, die der Jakobusbrief erwähnt.[1334] Anders als gegenüber den Ältesten lässt Jakobus eine gewisse Vorsicht gegenüber den Lehrern walten, ohne aber explizit negativ zu werden. In einigen späten und nach-neutestamentlichen Schriften finden sich analoge, sehr offen kritische Überlegungen zu

---

[1326] 1,2; 2,1.14; 3,1.10.12; 5,10.12.19.

[1327] DBR, § 45,1.

[1328] πολλοὶ ist am besten auf »Lehrer« (Prädikatsnominativ) zu beziehen: »zahlreich Lehrer werden« (gleich πάντες, Bauer / Aland, 1380).

[1329] διδάσκαλος ist hap. leg. in Jak. Weder διδαχή noch διδάσκειν begegnet in Jak.

[1330] Dibelius, Jak, 224.

[1331] Vgl. auch Eph 4,11; 1Tim 2,7 (auf Paulus bezogen: »Lehrer der Völker«); 2Tim 1,11 (ebenfalls auf Paulus bezogen). Wichtig ist Hebr 5,12: »Und ihr, die ihr der Zeit nach schon Lehrer sein solltet, braucht wieder jemand, der euch die Anfangsgrundlagen der Lehre von Gott (oder: der Worte Gottes) beibringt«. Der Verfasser scheint anzunehmen, dass alle Gemeindeglieder Lehrer (im Sinne von Belehrten) werden können. Vgl. zum Thema: W. Horbury, Pedagogues and Primary Teachers, from Paul to Mishnah, in: G. J. Brooke / R. Smithuis (Hg.), Jewish Education from Antiquity to the Middle Ages: Studies in Honour of Philip S. Alexander, Leiden 2017, 95–127; A. Falcetta, Early Christian Teachers: The ›Didaskaloi‹ from Their Origins to the Middle of the Second Century, WUNT II / 516, Tübingen 2020.

[1332] Außerdem wird in den synoptischen Texten die Lehrerrolle Jesu sehr betont.

[1333] Allison, Jak, 521: »This is our author's only real autobiographical statement«. 1.Pers.Plur. in 1,18; 2,2; 3,3.6.11.21; 5,17 ist generisch.

[1334] ἀπόστολος fehlt, vielleicht von δοῦλος in 1,1 ersetzt (siehe 2Petr 1,1). δοῦλος drückt aber keine eigentliche Funktion aus.

260 Kommentar

den Lehrern und ihren Lehren, die aber in eine andere Richtung zielen als Jakobus.[1335] So wenden sich 1Tim 1,3 und 6,1–5 gegen das ἑτεροδιδασκαλεῖν. Die Pastoralbriefe diagnostizieren ζητήσεις καὶ λογομαχίας[1336] in den Gemeinden, krankes Denken und Abkehr von der Wahrheit. Auch der Vorwurf von Bereicherung – wohl durch Unterricht – steht im Raum (1Tim 6,5). Im Hirten des Hermas sim IX 22,1f findet sich eine scharfe polemische Passage gegen christliche Lehrer:

> Vom fünften Berg … kommen solche Gläubigen: Sie haben Glauben [vgl. Jak 2,14!], sind aber unbelehrbar, anmaßend und selbstgefällig, wollen alles wissen und wissen doch gar nichts. … Sie rühmen sich selbst als Weise und spielen sich selbst als Lehrer auf – die Toren! (ὡς σύνεσιν ἔχοντας καὶ θέλουσιν ἐθελοδιδάσκαλοι εἶναι ἄφρονες ὄντες).[1337]

1Tim 6 und Herm sim IX 22 illustrieren die Furcht des Jakobus vor zu vielen Lehrern / Lehre gut. Jak 3 setzt aber einen eigenen Akzent. Es gibt auf der einen Seite die notwendige Gemeindefunktion der Lehrer, auf der anderen Seite die Erfahrung von »Schulgezänk« (διαπαρατριβαί 1Tim 6,5). Vor dieser Gefahr scheint Jakobus zu warnen, ohne allerdings sachliche Beispiele zu geben, wie sie im 1Tim und den anderen Pastoralbriefen unter dem Stichwort διδασκαλία vorliegen.[1338] An welche Lehren Jakobus denkt, bleibt – offensichtlich nicht zufällig – ungesagt. Anders als die Pastoralbriefe und der Hirte des Hermas hat Jakobus *erstens* nicht an der theologischen[1339], sondern an der ethischen Seite der Lehre Interesse, wie der Fortgang seiner Ermahnung in V. 2 sogleich zeigt.[1340] Es geht um Verfehlung und Vollkommenheit, d. h. um Haltungen, nicht um theologische Inhalte und Positionen, besonders nicht um die Abwehr von »Falschlehren«. Debatten wie die um die Christologie im 1Joh oder um das Gesetzesverständnis im 1Tim werden im Jakobusbrief nicht geführt und scheinen auch nicht im Hintergrund von Kap. 3 auf. *Zweitens* ist der Verfasser mehr an der rhetorischen Darstellung der Gefahren der Zunge interessiert als an falschen Lehrinhalten. Ethische Kritik an den »Lehrern« und ihren Lehren üben die Pastoralbriefe, die Johannesbriefe, Jak und der Hirt des Hermas gleichermaßen, aber Jakobus betont die ethische Thematik besonders stark. Über die Lehrer, ihren Status und ihre Lehrinhalte erfährt man nichts. *Drittens* möchte

---

[1335] 2Tim 4,3 (kritisch auf zukünftige Lehrer bezogen). Kritisch gegenüber »mancherlei fremden Lehren« ist Hebr 13,9. »Irrlehren«: Apk 2,14.15.24 (Lehre Balaams und der Nikolaiten). Schon Röm 2,21: kritischer Hinweis auf jüdische Lehrer. In LXX begegnet der Begriff des Lehrers nur in 2Makk 1,10 (Aristoboulos, Lehrer des Königs Ptolemaios), διδαχή nur Ps 59,1. Häufig dagegen διδάσκειν (Deuteronomium, Psalmen, Weisheitsliteratur u. a.). Vgl. den Exkurs »Die Lehrer«, bei METZNER, Jak, 170–171. BURCHARD, Jak, 135, weist auf entsprechende Warnungen kaiserzeitlicher Philosophen hin.

[1336] 1Tim 6,4.

[1337] Hier wie öfter ist eine Bezugnahme des Hirten auf Jak nicht auszuschließen (vgl. die Einleitung zum Thema Intertextualität).

[1338] Ca. 15 Bezeugungen, nicht in Katholischen Briefen.

[1339] Stichworte: »gesunde, gute, fromme« Lehre in Bezug auf die Gesetzesauslegung (1Tim 1,7: νομοδιδάσκαλοι).

[1340] Klar ALLISON, Jak, 520: »The subject is not heresy but ethics«.

C. Briefcorpus   261

Jakobus die Gemeindeglieder davon abhalten, Lehrer zu werden, wie die Begründung deutlich macht.

Es ist nur diese im Partizipialsatz folgende *Begründung,* die auf einen besonderen Status der Lehrer hinweist. Die Perspektive ist latent eschatologisch: κρίμα λαμβάνειν[1341], futurisch ausgerichtet. Die Gerichtsthematik begleitet den Jakobusbrief durchgehend[1342], meist ohne offen eschatologisch zu sein. Manifest eschatologisch ist nur die Texteinheit 5,7–11. Hier wird die Ankündigung des Richters (V. 9) mit der Verheißung verbunden: »Die Ankunft des Herrn ist nahe herbeigekommen«. In 3,1 wird dieser Aspekt – wenn überhaupt – nur durch das Futur angedeutet. Wichtig ist die besondere Gefährdung der Lehrer, der die Androhung des verschärften Urteilsspruches folgt. Eine entsprechende Gefahr sagt Jesus in Mk 12,40[1343] den Schriftgelehrten voraus: Wegen ihrer Scheinfrömmigkeit (nicht wegen ihrer Lehrtätigkeit) werden sie περισσότερον κρίμα empfangen (λαμβάνειν im Fut.). κρίμα ist der Richterspruch oder das richterliche Urteil. Ob Jakobus an Gott oder an Christus als Richter denkt, bleibt unausgesprochen.[1344] Richtig ist Metzners Hinweis darauf, Jakobus beziehe

> seine Gerichtsaussagen fast ausschließlich auf die christlichen Adressaten (2,12 f; 4,11 f; 5,9.12; anders 5,1–6) … Er meint nicht das allgemeine Weltgericht mit Urteil über Leben und Tod aller Menschen …, sondern die Beurteilung des Lebenswerkes der Christen.[1345]

Dass Lehrer in einer besonderen Verantwortung stehen, ist nicht nur jüdisch-weisheitliche Überzeugung, sondern darüber hinaus auch antikes Gemeingut.[1346] Jakobus weist mit εἰδότες darauf hin.[1347]

V. 2 Jakobus fährt in der 1.Pers.Plur. fort, wobei aber unklar bleibt, ob er weiterhin von den Lehrern und damit auch von sich selbst spricht oder ob er jetzt ein generelles »wir« gewählt hat. Dibelius verneint den Bezug auf die Lehrer und damit auch auf den Verfasser. Er versteht den ganzen Vers als »Übergangsvers« und spricht von einem »Gemeinplatz«.[1348] Aber V. 2 gilt als Begründung von V. 1, und zumindest V. 2a führt V. 1 weiter, während V. 2b ein neues, wenn auch eng verwandtes Thema anschlägt. Metzner hält daher zurecht die »wir alle« für die frühchristli-

---

[1341] κρίμα ist hap. leg. in Jak. κρίμα λαμβάνειν noch Mk 14,40par und Röm 13,2.

[1342] κρίμα 3,1; κρίνειν 2,12; 4,11.12; 5,9; κρίσις 2,13 (zweimal); 5,12; κριτής 2,4; 4,11.12; 5,9; κριτήριον 2,6; διακρίνειν 1,6 (zweimal); 2,4.

[1343] Vgl. Lk 20,47; Mt 23,14 nach *f* 33 und anderen späteren Hss. Vgl. auch Röm 13,2 (»sie ziehen sich selbst das Urteil zu«). Ob hier Jesustradition vorliegt (JOHNSON, Jak, 255 f), muss offenbleiben.

[1344] Vgl. zur Eschatologie die Einleitung.

[1345] METZNER, Jak, 172.

[1346] Vgl. die jüdischen Belege bei DIBELIUS, Jak, 224 Anm. 3. Weiteres bei BURCHARD, Jak, 136.

[1347] Vgl. 4,4. εἰδότες ὅτι oft bei Paulus für »traditional teaching«, ALLISON, Jak, 521.

[1348] DIBELIUS, Jak, 225 Anm. 1 (dort Belege für den »Gemeinplatz«, ausführlicher BURCHARD, Jak, 136).

262 Kommentar

chen Lehrer.[1349] Auf jeden Fall weitet der Verfasser die Argumentation bzw. die Reichweite seiner Warnung aus, indem er ἅπαντες als Subjekt setzt und sich selbst und die anderen »Lehrer« beschuldigt, häufig (Akk. πολλὰ »vielfach«) zu »straucheln« – eine Metapher aus der Wegmetaphorik.[1350] Jakobus formuliert sorgfältig mit π-Alliteration und dem seltenen πταίω.[1351] Die generalisierende Diktion erlaubt keine genauere Interpretation. Allerdings weist Burchard zurecht darauf hin, dass es sich in der Perspektive auf Kapitel 4 nicht nur um Verfehlungen beim Reden handeln wird[1352], sondern auch um

> einen allgemeinen Satz, nicht als anthropologische These[1353], sondern als Beschreibung eines gegebenen Mißstands.[1354]

V. 2b führt das Motiv des »Strauchelns« weiter und kehrt kurz zum Diatribenstil des »Jemand« (τις) zurück. ἐν λόγῳ πταίειν hält Jakobus für besonders gefährlich und offensichtlich für die Hauptgefahr des Lehrers, auch wenn er dies nicht explizit sagt. λόγος ist mit 1,18.21 ein zentraler Begriff im Brief, ohne dass sich ein klares semantisches Profil zeichnen ließe: Das »Wort der Wahrheit« und das »eingepflanzte Wort« sind theologisch aufgeladene Wortschöpfungen des Jakobus, die den λόγος als Gabe Gottes interpretieren und der menschlichen Willkür entziehen wollen. In 1,22.23 hat Jakobus auf den zweiten Aspekt des λόγος hingewiesen: Das Wort muss in Tun umgesetzt werden. In Kap. 3 fügt er den dritten Aspekt hinzu: Das menschliche Wort ist gefährlich und entzieht sich der ethischen Kontrolle. Dieser Aspekt wird in 3,1–4,12 ausgeführt. Das Stichwort τέλειος ἀνήρ in V. 2c nimmt das Grundthema des Jakobus von 1,4 wieder auf und bereitet mit dem metaphorisch gesetzten Verb χαλιναγωγεῖν aus dem Bereich des Reitens, das Jakobus schon in 1,26 verwendet hat (die Zunge im Zaum halten), die folgenden Bilder vor: (1) Pferd und Zügel, (2) Schiff und Steuerruder (beide Bilder konstruktiv)[1355], (3) Zunge und

---

[1349] Auch METZNER, Jak, 172, votiert mit guten Gründen für den Bezug auf die Lehrer.

[1350] Noch Jak 2,10. BURCHARD, Jak, 136 f weist auf zahlreiche Parallelaussagen über die Verfehlungen der Menschen aus der griechischen und jüdischen Literatur hin (u. a. auch Röm 3,12).

[1351] Schon in 2,10.

[1352] Vgl. dazu die Parallelen in Pred 5,1; Sir 15,16 (»Wer sündigt nicht mit seiner Zunge?«); Av 1,17.

[1353] So in Röm 3.

[1354] BURCHARD, Jak, 137.

[1355] Allgemein zum Thema: vgl. Einleitung (Lit.). Zum Text vgl. den Exkurs bei BURCHARD, Jak, 138 f: Zum Hintergrund der Pferd / Wagen- und Schiffsmetaphorik in Jakobus 3,3 f (mit Spezialliteratur). Wichtig sind die Anwendungsgebiete dieser Metaphern. Burchard nennt u. a. »Beherrschung des eigenen Selbst, der Triebe, Bewegungen, Zunge und Worte, des Lebens« (138). Beispiele: Aristipp bei Stobaeus III 17,17. Burchard resümiert: »Daß gerade Philo Pferd / Wagen und Schiff gern verbindet, deutet nicht auf die Quelle, aber vielleicht den Quellbereich; Jak imitiert wohl niemanden« (139). Dass Pferd und Schiff zusammen genannt werden, ist eher trivial, da es sich um die effektivsten Verkehrsmittel handelt. Allerdings begegnet ἵππος im NT nur in Jak 3,3 (die Belege in Apk sind Teil der visionären Kriegsszenarien). Burchard weist zurecht darauf hin, dass Pferde »Prestigebesitz« waren (139) und nicht in der Landwirtschaft eingesetzt wurden. Auch wenn nicht gesagt wird, dass der Verfasser selbst Pferde- oder Schiffsbesitzer war, stammt der Doppelvergleich jedenfalls nicht aus dem gesellschaftlichen Niveau der Unterschichten.

C. Briefcorpus   263

Leib (ambivalent), (4) Feuer und Wald (destruktiv). In V. 2c wird damit die Weiche für die Bildersprache der V. 3–12 gestellt.

Bildhafte Vergleiche gehören zur paränetischen Sprache des Jakobus und begegnen schon in 1,6.10 f.15.23 f: Meereswelle, Blume, Spiegelbild, gezähmte Zunge. Kap. 2 bietet im Kontext von »Glaube und Taten« größere fingierte Szenarien aus dem Gemeindeleben, die ebenfalls paränetischen Zwecken dienen.[1356] 3,2b–12 ist die längste bildhafte Passage des Briefes. Jakobus setzt sein literarisches Können ein, um die Bedeutung des Redens – positiv wie vor allem negativ – unmissverständlich deutlich zu machen. Dabei geht es wieder um den Zusammenhang von kontrollierter Rede und Vollkommenheit. Die argumentative Pointe der Metapher vom »Zügeln des ganzen Körpers« lässt sich leicht erfassen. Sie arbeitet auf der Basis des paradoxen Erfahrungssatzes: »Kleines bezwingt Großes«. Ihre Evidenz liegt darin, dass die Kontrolle der Rede die schwierigste ethische Leistung ist und gleichzeitig die Rede das leitende ethische Kontrollorgan des Menschen darstellt. Das heißt: Kontrollierte Rede bewirkt ethisches Verhalten der ganzen Person. Wer seine Rede kontrolliert, ist »ein vollkommener Mann« und entspricht dem ethischen Ideal des Verfassers. In der folgenden Darstellung der Macht der »Zunge« geht diese spezielle ethische Perspektive aber verloren. Erst im zweiten Teil des Kapitels kehrt Jakobus zum Thema des »guten Wandels« zurück (3,13).

Schon mit der Wendung vom »vollkommenen Mann, der den ganzen Körper beherrscht«, formuliert Jakobus einen überschüssigen Gedanken: Die Fokussierung auf das *Reden*, in V. 2a angelegt, erfolgt erst wieder in V. 5. Das Ideal des vollkommenen Mannes[1357] knüpft an 1,4 an: an die Eingangsermahnung an die Adressaten, vollkommen zu sein, und an 2,22, den Glauben, der aus den Taten vollkommen wird. Vom vollkommenen Menschen spricht SapSal 9,6 im Modus der Möglichkeit, Sir 44,17 gibt Noah (als Einzigem) das Prädikat des »vollkommenen Gerechten«. Den »Vollkommenen« kennt Paulus: In 1Kor 14,20 fordert er die Korinther auf, »vollkommen im Verstehen« zu sein.[1358] Jakobus scheint hier allgemein an Selbstzucht zu denken, ohne dass von Askese die Rede wäre. Vom Körper spricht er selten, und zwar in unspezifischer Weise ohne anthropologische Vertiefung.[1359]

V. 3 Das metaphorisch gesetzte Verb »zügeln bzw. zäumen« wird nun zu einem ersten vollständigen Bild ausgeweitet, das die Bedeutung der Rede für den gesamten Menschen erläutert. Das *Pferdebild* ist das erste von vier Bildern aus dem Bereich des täglichen Lebens, die die These des Verfassers veranschaulichen: Das Kleine regiert und kontrolliert das Große. Dabei verschiebt sich aber die Perspektive zwischen den einzelnen Bildern. Zuerst geht es um die Lenkung des Pferdes durch

---

[1356] Zu weiteren bildhaften Passagen s. u.

[1357] ἀνήρ ist hier wie sonst bei Jakobus Äquivalent für das generalisierend verstandene »Mensch« (1,8.12.20.23; 2,2).

[1358] Vgl. auch 1Kor 2,6; Phil 3,15. Dazu WISCHMEYER, Liebe als Agape, 201–204.

[1359] 2,16.26; 3,2.3.6.

den Zaum bzw. die Trense (χαλινοί[1360]). Der Vergleich mit der Rede ist implizit, aber sehr leicht herzustellen, denn das Trensenbild bezieht sich ebenfalls auf die Zunge: Die Trense wirkt über die Zunge auf das Pferd. Jakobus schreibt weiter im »Wir«-Modus, nun mit der Absicht, auf eine allgemeine Wahrheit zu verweisen: Pferde, die als schwer regierbare Tiere gelten[1361], werden durch die Trense geleitet.[1362] πείθειν[1363] und μετάγειν[1364] sind sorgfältig gewählte Verben.

V. 4 Das zweite Bild ist das *Bild von Schiffen auf dem stürmischen Meer.* Jakobus schließt das Bild mit der Demonstrativpartikel ἰδού[1365] an[1366], die ein LXX-Vorzugswort als Übersetzung von hebr. *hinnē* ist und sehr häufig in den synoptischen Sprüchen und in der Offenbarung, dort im prophetisch-apokalyptischen Sprachgestus begegnet.[1367] Das Schiffsbild[1368] ist genauso bekannt wie das Pferdebild und spricht ebenso unmittelbar für sich selbst. Burchard weist eigens darauf hin, dass nicht das Pferd mit dem Schiff verglichen wird. Vergleichspunkt zwischen V. 3 und 4 ist vielmehr das »Geführtwerden« (Wiederholung: μετάγομεν – μετάγεται). Das »auch« gilt dem Grundsatz: »Das Kleine steuert das Große«.[1369] Das Vokabular entspricht dem Gegenstand und ist durchweg sorgfältig gewählt: Rauhe (σκληρός[1370]) Winde treiben (ἐλαύνειν[1371]) die großen (τηλικαῦτα ὄντα[1372]) Schiffe.[1373] Diese lassen sich aber mit einem ganz kleinen (ἐλάχιστος[1374]) Steuerruder (πηδάλιον[1375]) lenken, wohin die Absicht (ὁρμή[1376]) des Steuernden führt (εὐθύν).[1377]

[1360] Hap. leg. in Jak. Im NT nur noch Apk 14,20 (die Zäume der Pferde).

[1361] Vgl. z. B. Philo, opif. 86. »Und selbst das mutigste Tier, das Pferd, wird leicht am Zügel geführt (χαλιναγωγηθείς), damit es nicht im Springen durchgeht«; migr. 62: »Du siehst ein Pferd, d. h. die freche, sich aufbäumende Leidenschaft, wie sie die Zügel abwirft«.

[1362] Zur Trense vgl. BURCHARD, Jak, 139, mit zahlreichen Belegen.

[1363] Hap. leg. in Jak.

[1364] Hap. leg. im NT (nur Jak 3,3.4). BAUER / ALAND, 1034: »in eine andere Richtung lenken«. Vgl. Philosophensprüche S. 486,18: Pferde werden in eine Richtung gelenkt. S. o. zur Übersetzung.

[1365] Auch 3,5. Auffallend häufig in Kap. 5: 5,4.7. 9. 11.

[1366] Erstarrter Imperativ Aorist (BURCHARD, Jak, 140), Funktion nach BAUER / ALAND, 754: »Aufforderung zu genauerer Überlegung u. Betrachtung«. Aber es geht auch um Auflockerung der Vergleichskette und um Erzeugung von Aufmerksamkeit. Die Partikel weist deutlich auf LXX-Sprache hin.

[1367] Mt und Lk, selten bei Mk.

[1368] πλοῖον hap. leg. in Jak. Oft bei den Synoptikern und in Apg. Jak 3,4 und Apk 8,9; 18,19.

[1369] BURCHARD, Jak, 141.

[1370] Hap. leg. in Jak. LSJ, 1612: vom Wind gebraucht bei Pollux 1.110 und Aelianus, nat. 9.57.

[1371] Hap. leg. in Jak. Vgl. 2Petr 2,17 ebenfalls im Bild. In der Gräzität gern im Zusammenhang mit Schiffen verwendet: LSJ, 529.

[1372] Hap. leg. in Jak. Im NT noch in 2Kor 1,10; Hebr 2,3; Apk 16,18.

[1373] BURCHARD, Jak, 140.

[1374] Hap. leg. in Jak.

[1375] Hap. leg. in Jak. Im NT noch Apg 27,40 (dort Plural, vgl. LSJ, 1400: griechische Schiffe hatten zwei Steuerruder) im NT.

[1376] Hap. leg. in Jak. Im NT noch Apg 14,5.

[1377] Hap. leg. in Jak. Im NT noch Joh 1,23.

V. 5 Mit οὕτως beginnt die Übertragung der Bilder von Zaum und Steuer auf das Bild der Zunge. Die V. 5.6 und 8 bilden einen eigenen Metaphernzusammenhang, der die Thematik der V. 2–4 aufnimmt und verändert. Jakobus leitet zu seinem eigentlichen Thema, der Zunge[1378], metaphorisch für Rede gebraucht, über. Das Thema γλῶσσα als menschliche Rede begegnet im NT ausschließlich im Jak. Es handelt sich um eine gängige antike Metapher, die sich in ethischen Zusammenhängen bei Autoren wie Menander und Jesus Sirach findet. Menander stellt fest:

ἡ γλῶσσα πολλῶν ἐστιν αἰτία κακῶν.
Die Zunge ist Ursache vielfachen Übels.[1379]

Jakobus fokussiert auf die Perspektive ethischer Gefahr: Rede ist nicht zu kontrollieren und schafft Streit und Gewalt, wie schon Jesus Sirach gewarnt hat. Jakobus konkretisiert mit diesem Motiv seine Warnung von 3,1 f: Verfehlung im Wort. Die V. 5.6.8 können auf der Grundlage von Sir 28 gelesen werden, während V. 7 die Metapher der Zähmung von V. 2–4 aufgreift. Dass bereits in V. 5 die zunächst scheinbar nur als weiteres Beispiel für Zähmung gewählte Feuermetapher auf gewalttätigen Streit zwischen Menschen zielt, macht ein Blick auf Sir 28,8–26 deutlich[1380]:

(8) Halte dich fern von *Streit* (μάχης), und du wirst *Sünden* verringern;
    ein wütender Mensch nämlich wird Streit entfachen
    (ἄνθρωπος γὰρ θυμώδης ἐκκαύσει μάχην);
(9) ein sündiger Mann aber wird Freunde in Unruhe versetzen,
    und zwischen diejenigen, die in Frieden leben, wird er Zwietracht bringen.
(10) Je nach dem *Holz* (ὕλη) des *Feuers* (τοῦ πυρὸς), so wird es entflammen,
    und je nach der Hartnäckigkeit des Streits, so wird er sich auswachsen.
    Je nach der Kraft des Menschen, so wird sein Zorn sein,
    und je nach dem Reichtum, so wird seine Wut sich steigern.
(11) Hitziger Hader entfacht Feuer (ἔρις κατασπευδομένη ἐκκαίει πῦρ),
    und hitziger Streit vergießt Blut.
(12) Wenn du in die Funken bläst, wird es (die Glut) entfachen,
    und wenn du hineinspuckst, wird sie verlöschen;
    und beides wird aus deinem *Mund* hervorgehen
    (καὶ ἀμφότερα ἐκ τοῦ στόματός σου ἐκπορεύεται).[1381] ...
(17) Der Schlag einer Geißel macht Striemen,
    der Schlag einer *Zunge* (πληγὴ δὲ γλώσσης) aber zerbricht Gebeine.
(18) Viele sind gefallen durch die Schneide eines Schwertes,
    jedoch nicht (so viele) wie die, die durch eine *Zunge* gefallen sind. ...
(21) Ein übler *Tod* (θάνατος πονηρὸς) (ist) der von ihr (bewirkte) Tod[1382]
    Und vorteilhafter als sie ist der *Hades* (ὁ ᾅδης).

1378 Jak 1,26; 3,5.6 (zweimal).8.
1379 Menander, Sententia graeca *965 (467 P.), Text: C. Pernigotti, Menandri Sententiae, Florenz 2008.
1380 Dazu Frankemölle, Jak II, 499–521. Dass Sir 28 als Prätext zu Jak 3 zu lesen ist, lässt sich angesichts der Motivkombination nicht bezweifeln.
1381 Zu diesem Bild s. zu Jak 3,10. Übersetzung nach Septuaginta Deutsch.
1382 D. h. der durch sie verursachte Tod.

266 Kommentar

(22) Nicht soll sie herrschen über Fromme,
   (damit diese) in ihrer *Flamme* (φλογὶ) nicht verbrannt werden.[1383]

Jakobus bindet auf der Basis von Sir 28 das Thema der *Zunge*, das er in V. 5 gleichsam spielerisch einführt, an das große Thema des gefährlichen Streits, verstanden als die grundlegende Gefahr, in der sich die διδάσκαλοι befinden. Der Sirachtext zeichnet vor, wie Jakobus von 3,1 an zielgerichtet das Thema des *Streites*, der aus unkontrollierter Rede der Lehrer entsteht, unter Rückgriff auf die Metaphern und theologischen Verurteilungen Sirachs entfaltet: Zunge, Feuer, Hölle, Tod, Ungerechtigkeit bzw. Sünde. Auch das Motiv der höllischen (3,6) und dämonischen (3,15) Qualität dieses Streites übernimmt Jakobus aus Sirach. Dabei sind die syntaktischen und stilistischen Veränderungen gegenüber Sirach deutlich: thematische Fokussierung (»die Zunge«), Verknappung, Verzicht auf Wiederholungsstrukturen, Verselbständigung der Metaphern und Bilder. Der Text befindet sich formal auf dem Weg von der thematischen Sprucheinheit zur Ekphrasis. Die Stichworte sind von Sir 28 vorgegeben.

In V. 5 werden die Bilder von Zaum und Ruder mit οὕτως explizit gemacht und in ihrer ethischen Bedeutung für die menschliche Rede, die »Zunge«, ausgewertet. V. 5a ist präzise antithetisch formuliert. Noch einmal wird mit dem Gegensatz »klein-groß« gespielt. Die *dritte Metapher, die Zunge, die den Leib regiert*, scheint auf einer Linie mit den beiden vorangehenden Bildern zu liegen. Allerdings fehlt das Äquivalent zu dem »ganzen Leib« des Pferdes und dem »großen Schiff«. Stattdessen fokussiert Jakobus auf das kleine Glied (μέλος[1384]), das sich »großer Dinge« vermisst oder rühmt. Mit dem nicht mehr eindeutig positiven αὐχεῖν[1385] verlässt der Verfasser das Muster der beiden ersten Bilder. Die *vierte Metapher*, das *Feuer*, πῦρ[1386], wieder mit ἰδού eingeleitet, bezieht sich auf die destruktive Kraft der Zunge. In der Logik von ›klein – groß‹ knüpft Jakobus zwar wieder an die beiden vorigen Bilder an (ἡλίκον-ἡλίκην). Dazu verwendet er ein Wortspiel, indem er die doppelte Bedeutung von ἡλίκος: wie groß / wie klein, ausnutzt. In der Sache verlässt er aber die argumentative Linie der V. 1–5a, denn bei dem Bild vom waldverzehrenden Feuer[1387] fehlt das Thema der Steuerung. Anders als Zaum und Ruder ist das Feuer zwar klein, aber weder dient es der Zähmung, noch kann es gezähmt werden. Es steuert nicht, es vernichtet. Das Bild vom Waldbrand ist im Gegensatz zu den Bildern von den Pferden und Schiffen in höchstem Grade destruktiv aufgeladen.

[1383] Zum Sirachtext und zum Vergleich mit Jak 3 vgl: WISCHMEYER, The Book of Ben Sira, 285–300.

[1384] μέλος Jak 3,5.6; 4,1. »Glieder« sind ein wichtiges Thema in Röm; 1Kor.

[1385] αὐχέω hap. leg. im NT. LSJ, 285: »to boast«. »Sich vermessen« trifft den bereits ins Negative spielenden Ton des Vergleichs besser.

[1386] Feuer begegnet im NT in unterschiedlichen materialen und übertragenen Zusammenhängen, häufig im eschatologischen Kontext. Es besteht eine Verbindung zur Hölle und zum ewigen Feuer. Vgl. unten zu Jak 5,3. Vgl. F. LANG, Art. πῦρ κτλ., ThWNT 6, 1959, 927–953.

[1387] ὕλη hap. leg. im NT. ἡλίκος hap. leg. in Jak, im NT noch in Kol 2,1. ἀνάπτειν: hap. leg. in Jak, im NT noch Lk 12,49.

C. Briefcorpus

V. 6 Jakobus vollzieht nun die Gleichsetzung von Zunge und Feuer. Der apodiktische Nominalsatz deckt den destruktiven Charakter der *Rede* im doppelten Bild (Rede=Zunge, Zunge=Feuer) auf, das im Verlauf des Verses bis zum Äußersten, nämlich bis zur Hölle, ausgedehnt wird. »Feuer«, Zweitmetapher und Prädikativ zur Erstmetapher »Zunge«, macht explizit, dass die Zunge jetzt nicht Metapher für die Rede allgemein, sondern nur für die *destruktive* Rede ist. V. 6 bringt eine sich verselbständigende Bilderhäufung auf kleinstem Raum. Stilistische Pointe ist die Metapher τροχὸς τῆς γενέσεως, verbunden mit der Assonanz von γενέσεως und γεέννης. Der Fortschritt von V. 5 zu V. 6 liegt darin, dass deutlich wird, welch Ziel die Satzfolge von V. 2 an verfolgt: Die Kritik an der »Verfehlung im Wort« wird nun durch einen Tadel »der Zunge« anschaulich gemacht. Zugleich bietet die Zweitmetapher »Feuer« das negative Potential, das in diesem Satz weiter ausgeführt wird.

Der Vers wird mit dem stilistisch unglücklichen dritten καὶ eingeleitet (V. 4.5.6), das hier aber dem Vergleich dient und als »auch« übersetzt werden muss. Die Syntax ist wenig stringent und war immer umstritten.[1388] Die Häufung von Nominalwendungen wirkt künstlich. Am ehesten bietet sich folgende Zuordnung der meist nominalen Satzglieder an: vorangestellter Nominalsatz (»Die Zunge Feuer«), asyndetisch gefolgt von dem Hauptsatz (»Die Zunge präsentiert sich[1389] in unsern Gliedern«) mit dem vorangestellten Prädikativum (»die Welt des Unrechts«). Das Subjekt des Hauptsatzes (Zunge) zieht drei erweiterte Partizipien nach sich. Während der Nominalsatz ἡ γλῶσσα πῦρ an die Bilder des vorangehenden Verses anknüpft und sie moralisch auswertet, entfernt sich der Verfasser im Verlauf des Satzes von den anschaulichen Bildern und bevorzugt ethisches Vokabular: ἀδικία, oder ein Bild, das ethisch gewertet ist: beschmutzen (σπιλοῦν), oder das Vokabular des Bösen: γέεννα. Auf die metaphorische Gleichsetzung von Zunge und Feuer folgt das zweite metaphorische – vorangestellte – Prädikativ[1390]: Die Zunge ist κόσμος τῆς ἀδικίας.[1391] Wie schon in 1,27 und dann wieder in 4,4 ist κόσμος durch das attributive Genitivobjekt negativ konnotiert.[1392] Wenn Jakobus die Zunge als »eine Welt des Unrechts«[1393] bezeichnet, benutzt er eine verallgemeinernde Wendung, die auch in 1Hen 48,7 begegnet.[1394] Die seltene Wendung »die Zunge präsentiert sich in unseren Gliedern« enthält eine implizite Kritik: Statt zu dienen oder zu steuern,

---

[1388] Vgl. Burchard, Jak, 143, und Metzner, Jak, 179 f.

[1389] καθίσταται ist einziges Vollverb im Satzgefüge.

[1390] So mit Burchard, Jak, 144.

[1391] Zu diesem Syntagma vgl. Lk 18,6: ὁ κριτὴς τῆς ἀδικίας.

[1392] Anders 2,5.

[1393] ἀδικία hap. leg. in Jak. Paulinisches Vorzugswort: vgl. Röm 6,13: μηδὲ παριστάνετε τὰ μέλη ὑμῶν ὅπλα ἀδικίας τῇ ἁμαρτίᾳ (Bietet nicht eure Glieder als Waffen der Ungerechtigkeit für eure Sünden dar).

[1394] Vgl. weitere Sachparallelen bei Burchard, Jak, 143.

268 Kommentar

»präsentiert sich« (καθίστημι) die Zunge.[1395] Die »Glieder« stehen als Synekdoche für »Körper«, zugleich wird das Gliederbild von V. 5 weiterverwendet.[1396]

Die drei *Partizipien* sind mit besonderem semantisch-stilistischen Anspruch gesetzt: σπιλοῦσα, φλογίζουσα, φλογιζομένη (*repetitio*). (1) σπιλοῦν[1397] begegnet im Neuen Testament ebenfalls bildlich noch in Jud 23 (beflecktes Gewand). (2+3) φλογίζειν ist neutestamentliches hap. leg. Die Ergänzungen der Partizipien sind klimaktisch angeordnet: der eigene Leib, Kosmos, Hölle. Jakobus bietet in diesem Satz alles auf, was sich an Feuer und Destruktion anschließen lässt, und weitet die Perspektive der Ungerechtigkeit, die durch die Zunge geübt wird, über den Weltbrand bis zur Hölle aus. Für die Partizipialkonstruktionen benutzt Jakobus weiter bildhafte Sprache mit generalisierendem Anspruch[1398] und ethischer Konnotation. Die *beiden ersten* Partizipien beschreiben die aktiv zerstörende Wirkung der Zunge auf den Menschen und das Leben. Zunächst geht es um das Verhältnis der Zunge als eines Gliedes zum ganzen Leib, den sie beschmutzt.[1399] Es folgt die ungewöhnliche bildhafte Wendung vom »Rad des Werdens«, das durch die Zunge in Brand gesetzt wird.[1400] τροχὸς τῆς γενέσεως knüpft an die frühere Wendung von πρόσωπον τῆς γενέσεως an (1,23).[1401] τροχός, das Rad, ist hier am besten vom Verb τρέχω, laufen, her zu übersetzen. Es geht um den Lebenslauf, eine bildliche Umschreibung[1402] des in seiner zeitlichen Erstreckung gedachten »ganzen Lebens« analog zum »ganzen Körper«.[1403] Die »Zunge« kann das ganze Leben, den gesamten Lebenslauf vernichten. Die *dritte* Partizipialkonstruktion, nun im Passiv, φλογίζουσα, beleuchtet den Ursprung der Destruktionskraft der Zunge in der Hölle. Das Bild evoziert die Vorstellung eines Höllenbrandes, der die Zunge entflammt, die ihrerseits Welt und Menschen verbrennt. Das Motiv der Totenwelt findet sich bereits bei Sir 28,21. Das γέεννα-Motiv[1404] ist verwandt, stammt aber nicht aus LXX, sondern findet

---

[1395] Die Bedeutung des Verbs καθίστημι geht in die Richtung von »sich breit machen« und weiter: »usurpieren«, »herrschen«.

[1396] Vgl. auch 4,1.

[1397] Hap. leg. in Jak.

[1398] »Der ganze Körper«: 3,2.3.6.

[1399] σῶμα: »Körper« mit defizitärem Status wie 2,16.26.

[1400] φλογίζειν hap. leg. im NT.

[1401] τροχός hap. leg. in der frühchristlichen Literatur. γένεσις: außer in Jak 1,23; 3,6 auch Mt 1,1.18; Lk 1,14.

[1402] Ähnlich im paulinischen Sprachgebrauch: Röm 9,1; 1Kor 9,24.26; Gal 2,2.16; 5,7; Phil 2,16; 2Thess 3,1; Hebr 12,1.

[1403] LSJ, 1829, führt als parallele Metapher ὁ τῆς εἱμαρμένης τε καὶ γενέσεως τροχός aus Simplikios, CAG 377.14 (6. Jh. n. Chr.) an. Die sprachliche Übereinstimmung bedeutet nicht eine kosmologische Konnotation in Jak 3. BURCHARD, Jak, 144–146, dokumentiert die antike Geschichte der Radmetapher und weist besonders auf Ps-Phok 27 hin: ὁ βίος τροχός.

[1404] Gräzisierung von gê(')hinnom (»Hinnomtal«). Hap. leg. in Jak. BAUER / ALAND, 306: »Talschlucht südl. v. Jerusalem. Dort sollte nach späterem jüd. Volksglauben dereinst das Gericht stattfinden« (Justin, apol. 19,8). Wichtige Parallelen im NT, besonders bei Mt: Mt 5,22 (Gehenna *des Feuers*).29 (und nicht *dein ganzer Leib* in die Gehenna geworfen werde).30 (und nicht dein ganzer Leib in die Gehenna komme); Mt 10,28;

sich vereinzelt in griechischen Schriften des antiken Judentums.[1405] Jakobus ist hier der endzeitlichen Motivwelt von Mt 7 und 23 besonders nahe, allerdings ohne die bei Matthäus gegebene eschatologische Perspektive zu verwenden. Die Gehenna ist ein feuriger Ort, von dem die Zunge, als zerstörendes Feuer verbildlicht, ihre Zerstörungskraft empfängt. Die Gehenna ist also ein Ursprungsort des Bösen[1406] und damit in ethischer, nicht in zeitlicher Perspektive vorgestellt.[1407] Die doppelte Partizipialwendung φλογίζουσα τὸν τροχὸν τῆς γενέσεως καὶ φλογιζομένη ὑπὸ τῆς γεέννης ist vor allem des *stilistischen* Effektes willen gewählt. Im Gegensatz zu den δαιμόνια, die Jakobus in 2,19 erwähnt, und zum Hades[1408] ist die »Gehenna« nicht Bestandteil der allgemeinen Gräzität, sondern ein Spezialbegriff aus der frühjüdisch-frühchristlichen religiösen Sprache und verleiht der bildlichen Szene besonderen Nachdruck.

V. 7–8 Die Verse 7 und 8 nehmen das Motiv des Zähmens noch einmal auf, jetzt aber nicht auf den Gegensatz zwischen klein und groß bezogen, sondern auf den paradoxen Gegensatz zwischen allen Geschöpfen, die der Mensch zähmen kann, einerseits und der Zunge – seinem eigenen Glied, das niemand zähmen kann, andererseits. Die Verse sind antithetisch (δέ) zugeordnet: V. 7 formuliert positiv, V. 8 negativ. Der Verfasser arbeitet durchweg mit Wiederholung und Wiederaufnahme von Verben[1409] (δαμάζειν) und Substantiven (φύσις), um einen dichten Stil zu erzeugen. V. 7 wiederholt in veränderter semantischer und logischer Form die Verse 3–5a. Statt um »zähmen« geht es jetzt um das stärkere δαμάζειν[1410], »bändigen«, in V. 7 im eigentlichen Sinne gesetzt, in V. 8 wieder metaphorisch auf die Zunge bezogen. δαμάζειν wird als Stichwort in V. 7.8 dreimal in unterschiedlichen Verbformen eingesetzt. Die Bilder von V. 7 knüpfen steigernd an V. 3 an: Mittels des Zaumes beherrschen die Menschen die Pferde. Mehr noch: die Menschen beherrschen alle Arten von Tieren. Die Akzentverschiebung von »zügeln«, »steuern« zu »bändigen« bereitet schon auf die destruktive Gewalt der Zunge von V. 8 vor. V. 8 bringt die höchste Steigerung: Die Zunge ist stärker als die Menschen –, die doch alle Tiere zähmen können. Es handelt sich um eine rhetorische Pointe. Die Zunge ist stärker als die Tiere und widersteht jedem Domestizierungsversuch – eine logische Unmöglichkeit, die, nähme der Verfasser sie sachlich ernst, jede Paränese sinnlos machte und den Menschen selbst zum Sklaven seiner Zunge machte.

18,9 (Gehenna des Feuers); Mk 9,43 (in die Gehenna, in das Feuer, das nie erlischt).45.47; 23,15.33 (Nattern, Gezücht von *Giftschlangen*, wie wollt ihr vor dem Gericht der Gehenna fliehen?); Lk 12,5.

[1405] 4Esr 7,36; Sib IV 186.

[1406] In Analogie zum Ursprungsort der Sünde im Menschen selbst in 1,13–15. Die Vorstellungen sind nicht kohärent.

[1407] Anders METZNER, Jak, 182 f, der φλογιζομένη futurisch lesen möchte und an die zukünftige Bestrafung mit dem Höllenfeuer denkt. Doch diese eschatologische Perspektive liegt in Jak nicht vor.

[1408] Hades begegnet zehnmal im NT, nicht in Jak.

[1409] Beispiele für die Wiederholung des Verbs in einer Vergangenheitsform: BURCHARD, Jak, 146.

[1410] In LXX nur Dan 2,20; im NT nur Mk 5,4 und Jak 3,7 f.

270   Kommentar

Die Wendung »φύσις der Tiere«[1411] meint hier »Spezies«. Wieder geht es wie in V. 6 generalisierend um »alle« Tiere. Die Aufzählung der Arten erfolgt paarweise (τε καὶ): Landtiere (θηρία[1412]) und Tiere der Luft (πετεινά[1413]), Kriechtiere (ἑρπετόν[1414]) und Seetiere (ἐναλία).[1415] φύσις ἀνθρώπινη[1416] steht parallel zu »φύσις der Tiere«. Texte wie Gen 1,26.28; 9,2[1417] stehen im Hintergrund, werden aber nicht zitiert, sondern variiert.[1418] Auf die höchste Steigerung folgt die heftigste Schmähung; V. 8b wiederholt die Schmähung der Zunge von V. 6, nun mit zwei nachgestellten negativen Bestimmungen.[1419] Die erste Bestimmung benutzt mit der phonetisch raffinierten Wendung ἀκατάστατον κακόν[1420] schon aus V. 6 bekanntes ethisches Vokabular. Die zweite Bestimmung, ebenfalls sorgfältig formuliert, ist wieder bildhaft: »voll[1421] todbringenden Giftes«. ἰός, Gift[1422], ist wie in Röm 3,13 (Ps 139,4LXX, dort explizit Schlangengift) als Schlangengift zu denken und schließt an V. 7 an. Das Unheilsensemble von Feuer, Hölle, Gift und Tod (V. 5–8) kommt hier an sein Ende.

V. 9–10a Mit diesen Versen nähert sich der Verfasser seinem Thema, den Gefahren der Rede Christus-gläubiger Lehrer, wieder an und findet damit auch zu neuer ethischer Differenzierung. Erst in V. 9 wird nämlich deutlich, dass seit V. 5 die »Zunge« im Sinne der Metonymie für »qualifizierte Rede« verwendet wird, ob spezifisch als Rede des Lehrers oder allgemein als menschliche Fähigkeit, bleibt offen, Ersteres ist aber aus dem Kontext von 3,1 wahrscheinlich. Diese Rede kann aber nicht *in toto* todbringend sein, wie die Passage über die Zunge insinuiert, sondern zeigt die übliche antithetische Struktur antiker jüdischer Ethik, wie sie sich in

---

[1411] φύσις hap. leg. in Jak. LSJ, 1965: »creature, frequent in collective sense«. Belege bei BURCHARD, Jak, 146. Siehe Philo, spec.leg. IV 116, Sib V 157.

[1412] δαμάζειν hap. leg. in Jak. Selten im NT (nur in Apk häufig im metaphorischen Zusammenhang).

[1413] Hap. leg. in Jak. Mehrfach in den synoptischen Evangelien.

[1414] Hap. leg. in Jak. Apg 10,12; 11,6; Röm 1,23 (ähnliche Aufzählung wie in Jak 3: πετεινῶν καὶ τετραπόδων καὶ ἑρπετῶν).

[1415] ἐνάλιος (»im Meer befindlich«: BAUER / ALAND, 527) hap. leg. im NT. ἐ. begegnet aber in der griechischen Literatur (poetisches Wort). Nicht aus Gen: nicht in LXX (aber Philo, decal. 54). Die drei anderen Bezeichnungen sind für die Tierwelt nicht ungewöhnlich, aber hap. leg. in Jak.

[1416] ἀνθρώπινος hap. leg. in Jak. BURCHARD, Jak, 147: »Geläufiger Ausdruck für die menschliche Natur« (Belege von Platon bis Philo, opif. 114 und ebr. 166, und Josephus, keine anderen frühchristlichen Belege).

[1417] Weitere LXX-Stellen bei BURCHARD, Jak, 146.

[1418] Gen 1,26: καὶ ἀρχέτωσαν τῶν ἰχθύων τῆς θαλάσσης καὶ τῶν πετεινῶν τοῦ οὐρανοῦ καὶ τῶν κτηνῶν καὶ πάσης τῆς γῆς καὶ πάντων τῶν ἑρπετῶν τῶν ἑρπόντων ἐπὶ τῆς γῆς (Und sie sollen herrschen über die Fische im Meer und über die Vögel unter dem Himmel und über das Vieh und über die ganze Erde und über alles Gewürm, das auf Erden kriecht). Zwei von vier Substantiven stimmen überein: stilistische *variatio*.

[1419] BURCHARD, Jak, 147, schwankt zwischen »Prädikative(n) eines Nominalsatzes« und »lockere(n) Appositionen«. Letzteres scheint plausibler.

[1420] ἀκατάστατος: unbeständig, im NT nur hier und in Jak 1,8 (Jes 54,11LXX). τὸ κακόν: sehr häufig in Röm, vgl. Jak 1,13.

[1421] μεστός mehrfach im NT mit Gen: Röm 1,29 (Lasterkatalog). Vgl. Jak 3,17 (Tugendkatalog, vgl. Röm 15,14).

[1422] In Jak 5,3 »Rost« (s. d.). θανατηφόρος, todbringend: hap. leg. im NT, mehrfach in LXX.

C. Briefcorpus

der Septuaginta, in den Testamenten der zwölf Patriarchen, in der Jesustradition, bei Paulus und in anderen frühchristlichen Traditionen findet: gut *und* böse, hier in V. 9.10a als Loben und Fluchen auf das Thema der Rede appliziert. Mit dieser *antithetischen* Struktur steht Jakobus in der Tradition von Texten wie den folgenden:

θάνατος καὶ ζωὴ ἐν χειρὶ γλώσσης, οἱ δὲ κρατοῦντες αὐτῆς ἔδονται τοὺς καρποὺς αὐτῆς.
Tod und Leben liegen in der Hand der Zunge, die sie meistern, werden ihre Früchte essen (Spr 18,21).

δόξα καὶ ἀτιμία ἐν λαλιᾷ, καὶ γλῶσσα ἀνθρώπου πτῶσις αὐτῷ.
Ruhm und Unehre liegen zugleich in der Rede, und die Zunge des Menschen ist sein Verderben (Sir 5,13).

ἐὰν φυσήσῃς εἰς σπινθῆρα, ἐκκαήσεται, καὶ ἐὰν πτύσῃς ἐπ᾽ αὐτόν, σβεσθήσεται· καὶ ἀμφότερα ἐκ τοῦ στόματός σου ἐκπορεύεται.
Wenn du in die Funken bläst, wird es (die Glut) entfachen, und wenn du hineinspuckst, wird sie verlöschen; und beides wird aus deinem Mund hervorgehen (Sir 28,12[1423]).

ἡ ἀγαθὴ *διάνοια* οὐκ ἔχει δύο γλώσσας, εὐλογίας καὶ κατάρας.
Der gute Sinn hat nicht zwei Zungen, Segen und Fluch (TestBen 6,5[1424]).

V. 9 formuliert das Verhalten der Zunge in zwei durch »und« verbundenen, parallel gebauten Aussagesätzen, die von der antithetischen Struktur und der Anapher ἐν αὐτῇ bestimmt sind: εὐλογεῖν[1425] steht gegen καταρᾶσθαι.[1426] Die beiden Akkusativobjekte sind durch Appositionen erweitert. Die zweite Apposition bezieht sich auf die erste zurück (»Herr und Vater« – »Ebenbild Gottes«) und beschreibt das Handeln der Zunge als paradoxal gegen Gott gerichtet. Jakobus verwendet wieder das epistolare »Wir« von 3,1 f und appliziert damit die Aussagen über die »Zunge« auf die Adressaten: V. 10b (»meine Brüder«). V. 10a wiederholt und strafft V. 9 in substantivierter Form der traditionellen Antithese[1427] von εὐλογία (Segen)[1428] und κατάρα (Fluch)[1429]. Der Septuagintabezug ist offensichtlich. Segen und Fluch stehen über dem Gesetz seit Dtn 11,26–32 (vgl. 30,15.20):

(26) Ἰδοὺ ἐγὼ δίδωμι ἐνώπιον ὑμῶν σήμερον εὐλογίαν καὶ κατάραν, (27) τὴν εὐλογίαν, ἐὰν ἀκούσητε τὰς ἐντολὰς κυρίου τοῦ θεοῦ ὑμῶν, ἃς ἐγὼ ἐντέλλομαι ὑμῖν σήμερον, (28) καὶ τὰς κατάρας, ἐὰν μὴ ἀκούσητε τὰς ἐντολὰς κυρίου τοῦ θεοῦ ὑμῶν.
(26) Siehe, ich lege euch heute vor Segen und Fluch: (27) den Segen, wenn ihr gehorcht den Geboten des Herrn, eures Gottes, die ich euch heute gebiete; (28) den Fluch aber, wenn ihr nicht gehorchen werdet den Geboten des Herrn, eures Gottes.

1423 Hier mit der Metapher des Feuers verbunden.

1424 Nächste Parallele zum Jakobustext.

1425 Hap. leg. in Jak. Überaus häufig in LXX und griechischsprachiger jüdischer Lit., besonders in Genesis, Deuteronomium, Psalmen und Sirach. Häufig im NT.

1426 Hap. leg. in Jak. Mt 25,41; Mk 11,21; Lk 6,28; Röm 12,14 (fluchen und segnen).

1427 Vgl. Lk 6,28; Röm 12,14; Mt 25,31–46 (das Endzeitgleichnis ist nach der Struktur von »Gesegnete« und »Verfluchte« aufgebaut).

1428 Hap. leg. in Jak. Sehr häufig in LXX. Häufiger bei Paulus.

1429 Hap. leg. in Jak. κατάρα öfter in LXX. Wichtig besonders: Dtn 11,26–28; 30,1.19; Jos 9,2LXX (jeweils »Segen und Fluch« im Zusammenhang mit dem Gesetz); Gal 3,10.13 f (Fluch und Segen); Hebr 6,7.8 (Segen und Fluch); 2Petr 2,14 (Kinder des Fluches). Vgl. auch Mt 25,34.41 (partizipial: Gesegnete und Verfluchte).

272 Kommentar

Jakobus stellt die Zunge, also die Rede des Lehrers, in den Kontext des Gesetzes und versteht die Rede der frühchristlichen Lehrer von ihrer Tatdimension her. Damit ist bereits die Weiche für den zweiten Teil des Kapitels gestellt, in dem es um die Taten des Weisen geht. In V. 9 nimmt Jakobus eine Aufteilung vor: Die *Sprache des Lobens*[1430] hat »den Herrn und Vater« zum Gegenstand, die *Sprache des Fluches*[1431] die Menschen. Dass mit κύριος hier Gott selbst gemeint ist, macht das zweite Akkusativobjekt klar: πατήρ (vgl. 1,17.27[1432]). Die Vorstellung vom Gotteslob – sei es durch das Volk Israel oder den Einzelnen – ist besonders für die Psalmen zentral. Ob Jakobus hier an öffentliches oder privates Gotteslob denkt, bleibt unwesentlich. Die Zusammenstellung κύριος καὶ πατήρ ist analogielos, aber ebenso nahe an Sir 23,1.4 wie an Mt 11,25.[1433] Wie so oft sucht Jakobus nach einer neuen, eigenen Wendung.

Woran denkt der Verfasser bei der »Verfluchung des Menschen«? Liegt hier eine rein topische Formulierung vor, oder bestehen auch aktuelle Bezüge? Die Exegeten machen verschiedene Vorschläge. Dibelius denkt an Flüche, wie sie im Alten Testament erwähnt werden[1434], und meint, bei Jakobus »Kritik an jüdischen« Sitten finden zu können, da Fluchen nicht zum »Ethos urchristlicher Gemeinden« gehört habe.[1435] Dibelius verweist u. a. auf Röm 12,14 und Lk 6,28. Aber gerade diese Mahnungen belegen ja, dass auch in den frühchristlichen Gemeinden das Übel des Fluchens bestand. Burchard argumentiert ähnlich wie Dibelius: »Ausformulierten Menschenfluch neben Gotteslob kann man sich bei den Adressaten schwer vorstellen«.[1436] Schon ein Blick auf 3,1.2 und 3,14 zeigt aber, dass dies Argument nicht stichhaltig ist. Jakobus diagnostiziert bei seinen Adressaten und gerade bei den Lehrern »viele Verfehlungen«. Burchard erwägt dann, ob Jakobus hier an »besondere Verwerfungen unter den Adressaten« denke, ob er sich »allgemein gegen Fluchen« wende oder, ob sich Jakobus hier »indirekt gegen Paulus« richte (Gal 1,8 f; 1Kor5; 16,22; 1Tim 1,20 analog zu 1Kor 5).[1437] In die Nähe dieser letzten Vermutung kommt Metzner, wenn er in Aufnahme von J. P. L. Wolmarans schreibt: »Das Fluchen kann sich im vorliegenden Zusammenhang nur auf christliche Mitmenschen beziehen, die in Opposition zu den nach Ämtern strebenden Lehrern stehen, also

---

[1430] Zur Eulogie vgl. H. Beyer, Art. εὐλογέω κτλ., ThWNT 2, 1935, 751–763.

[1431] Zum Fluch allgemein vgl: M. Hölscher / M. Lau / S. Luther (Hg.), Antike Fluchtafeln und das Neue Testament: Materialität – Ritualpraxis – Texte, WUNT 474, Tübingen 2021.

[1432] Hier dieselbe Konstruktion mit καί. Im NT vergleichbare Aussagen zum Gotteslob: Lk 1,64.68; 24,53 (Schluss des Lk).

[1433] ἐξομολογοῦμαί σοι, πάτερ, κύριε τοῦ οὐρανοῦ καὶ τῆς γῆς (Ich preise dich, Vater, Herr des Himmels und der Erde). Burchard, Jak, 148, mit verwandten Doppelprädikationen. Vgl. auch 1Clem 62,2.

[1434] Dibelius, Jak, 245 f mit Anm. 5.

[1435] Dibelius, Jak, 245.

[1436] Burchard, Jak, 149.

[1437] Burchard, Jak, 149. Weitere Belegstellen nach Burchard: Apg 13,10 f; 23,3.

konkret auf konkurrierende Lehrer und / oder deren Anhänger«.[1438] Eben dies Phänomen können wir bei Paulus studieren. Paulus ist selbst frühchristlicher Lehrer und arbeitet mehrfach mit dem Mittel des Fluches, wie Burchard dokumentiert.[1439] Metzners klare Stellungnahme gewinnt an historischer Plausibilisierung, wenn sie auf Paulus bezogen wird. Jak 3,9 lässt sich zwar nicht als offene Polemik gegen Paulus lesen, wohl aber gegen das Ethos des Paulus, dem Fluch bzw. Anathema nicht fremd ist. Allerdings ist Jakobus selbst nicht weit von diesem kämpferischen Ethos entfernt, wenn er die Zunge als Höllenbrand bezeichnet. Dibelius' Erklärung wirkt demgegenüber eher harmlos.[1440]

Das Objekt des Fluches, der Mensch[1441], wird durch eine weitere nachgestellte Partizipialbestimmung theologisch qualifiziert, die den Gegensatz zwischen Loben und Fluchen zuspitzt: »die Menschen, die nach dem Ebenbilde Gottes gemacht sind«. Die Wendung καθ' ὁμοίωσιν θεοῦ nimmt Gen 1,26 auf (ποιήσωμεν ἄνθρωπον κατ' εἰκόνα ἡμετέραν καὶ καθ' ὁμοίωσιν) und schließt zugleich an V. 7 an: die Anspielung auf die Tiere in Gen 1,24f: Gen 1 steht hinter Jak 3,7–9. Mit dieser schöpfungs-anthropologischen Vorstellung ergänzt Jakobus seine metaphorische Aussage von 1,18. Dort sind die Christus-bekennenden Adressaten die »Erstlingsfrucht« von Gottes Geschöpfen.

Die bildliche Wendung »Beides geht aus dem Munde hervor« findet sich ebenso in Sir 28,12.[1442] Sir 28 ist auch Bildgeber für die folgenden Verse, die das Bild der doppelten Rede, die aus dem Mund hervorgeht, durch das Bild von der Quelle weiter veranschaulichen.

V. 10b Der Verfasser setzt neu ein mit einer epistolaren Anrede: »meine Brüder« und zieht gleichzeitig eine ganz kurze negative Bilanz, die er dann in V. 11 und 12 mit zwei Bildworten veranschaulicht. Die elegante Wendung χρή[1443] mit Akk.c.Inf. lässt sich als Verbot übersetzen: »Das darf nicht so geschehen.«

V. 11 V. 10b ist nicht das letzte Wort des Verfassers zum Thema des »Wortes«. Jakobus fährt mit zwei rhetorischen Fragen[1444] fort, um danach den gesamten Text über die »Zunge« mit einer lehrhaften Sentenz zu schließen. Noch einmal zeigt der Verfasser sein literarisches Können, indem er zwei selbständige Bildworte, die das Bild von V. 10a *kontrastiv* illustrieren, ineinander fügt: *erstens* in Anknüpfung an V.

[1438] METZNER, Jak, 189; J. L. P. WOLMARANS, The Tongue Guiding the Body: The Anthropological Presuppositions of James 3:1–12, Neotest. 26, 1992, 523–530.

[1439] Vgl. dazu J. S. KLOPPENBORG, Cursing in the Corinthian Christ Assembly, in: Hölscher / Lau / Luther (Hg.), Antike Fluchtafeln, 409–424.

[1440] Dibelius und andere zitieren auch Midrasch BerR 24. Hier liegt eine schlagende Sachparallele vor.

[1441] Es geht nicht um die Menschheit, sondern um bestimmte Menschen.

[1442] καὶ ἀμφότερα ἐκ τοῦ στόματός σου ἐκπορεύεται. Jak 3,10 variiert zu ἐξέρχεται.

[1443] In der frühchristlichen Literatur nur hier, vgl. DBR, § 358,2: χρή enthält »eine Aufforderung«.

[1444] μήτι: im NT mehrfach als Einleitung einer rhetorischen Frage, vgl. besonders Mt 7,16 (Sammelt man auch von Dornen Trauben oder von Disteln Feigen?). BURCHARD, Jak, 153, verneint eine besondere Nähe zu Mt 7 und weist auf unterschiedliche Sachparallelen hin, besonders auf Epiktet II 20,18.

10 das Bild von der Quelle, aus der *nicht* gleichzeitig süßes und salziges Wasser fließen kann, gestützt *zweitens* durch ein weiteres übliches Bild zum Thema ›Einheit‹, den Feigenbaum, der nur *eine* Sorte von Früchten, nämlich Feigen, tragen kann. Die argumentative Logik beider Bildworte besagt, auf das Thema der Rede bezogen: Ein Mensch kann – d. h. *soll – nicht* gleichzeitig loben und fluchen. Dies Urteil ist auf die paränetische Intention der V. 9.10 bezogen. Was fehlt, ist eine logische Verbindung zur Schmähung der Zunge in den V. 5–8. Konsequent gedacht würde sein logischer Schluss in V. 12 die vorangehenden Ausführungen *ad absurdum* führen bzw. einfach überflüssig machen: Wenn aus dem Mund nur Lob hervorgehen kann, ist die Vorstellung von der Zunge, die nicht (zum Guten) gezähmt werden kann, überflüssig. Hier wird noch einmal im Rückblick deutlich, dass der Verfasser in 3,1–12 nicht ein kohärentes logisches Argument zum Thema der Rede der christlichen Lehrer aufbaut, sondern unter Zuhilfenahme von Elementen alttestamentlich-frühjüdischer Sprachethik eine vehemente Warnung, deren Ernst er durch einen elaborierten Stil Nachdruck verschafft, an die frühchristlichen Lehrer formuliert. Die Passage über die böse Zunge erweist sich als literarisches *superadditum*. Letztlich setzt der Verfasser ja gerade nicht auf die *Bosheit* der Zunge, sondern auf ihre *Beherrschung*.

Das kontrastive Bild von der *Quelle*[1445], aus der nur Süßwasser fließt, ist durch das Bild aus Sir 28,12 (s. o.) evoziert und vorbereitet: Aus dem Mund geht »Beides« hervor. Auf diesem Bild hat der Verfasser schon in den V. 9.10 aufgebaut. Jetzt kehrt er mit den Bildern von der Quelle und dem Feigenbaum zu seiner eigentlichen Intention zurück: Christliche Lehrer *können* die Rede nicht destruktiv nutzen. Hinter beiden Bildern steht das leitende Ideal der Einheit, das der Verfasser seit dem 1. Kapitel entwirft: kein Zweifel, keine doppelte ψυχή, Einheit von Wort bzw. Glaube und Tat. Bei dem Quellbild, das als implizite Metapher für die menschliche Rede gesetzt ist, handelt es sich um ein geläufiges und plausibles Bild aus der Natur[1446], das der Verfasser wieder semantisch und stilistisch schmückt. βρύειν, quellen lassen[1447], ist nicht nur hap. leg. im NT, sondern insgesamt ein eher seltenes Verb.[1448] ὀπή, »Loch, Spalt, Höhlung« ist hier »die Öffnung, aus der eine Quelle fließt«.[1449] Das Paar τὸ γλυκὺ καὶ τὸ πικρόν[1450] – »Wasser« fehlt – sind »geläufige Attribute von Wasser«[1451]. Das Motiv des »Bitteren« bereitet schon die ethische Anwendung in V. 14 vor.

[1445] πηγή hap. leg. in Jak, selten im NT, metaphorisch auch 2Petr 2,17 über die falschen Propheten: sie sind πηγαὶ ἄνυδροι.

[1446] Vgl. Burchard, Jak, 150: Philo det 40; migr. 71. Von Gemünden, Vegetationsmetaphorik, 268f, zu der Frage der Herleitung des Bildes von Mt 7,16 (v. G. plädiert zurecht gegen synoptische Abhängigkeit).

[1447] Bauer / Aland, 295.

[1448] Burchard, Jak, 150. LSJ, 332: »Poet. and later prose«.

[1449] Bauer / Aland, 1164. Hap. leg. in Jak. Im NT noch Hebr 11,38 (»Höhle«).

[1450] γλυκύς noch Apk 10,9f (süß und bitter). πικρός nur Jak 3,11.14 im NT (Adverb Mt 26,75par).

[1451] Burchard, Jak, 150, mit Beispielen.

V. 12 Die Wiederholung der epistolaren Anrede aus V. 10 verstärkt die Eindringlichkeit der Applikation. Die beiden weiteren Bilder – Feigenbaum und Weinstock – sind syntaktisch und stilistisch analog zum ersten Bild gestaltet[1452] und wieder aus dem Bereich der Vegetationsmetaphorik genommen. Die συκῆ, der Feigenbaum, begegnet in der synoptischen Tradition im *exemplum*[1453], ebenso der ἄμπελος, der Weinstock.[1454] Der Gedanke entstammt der Erfahrungsweisheit, wie sie sich in Mt 7,16par

> ἀπὸ τῶν καρπῶν αὐτῶν ἐπιγνώσεσθε αὐτούς. μήτι συλλέγουσιν ἀπὸ ἀκανθῶν σταφυλὰς ἢ ἀπὸ τριβόλων σῦκα.
> An ihren Früchten werdet ihr sie erkennen. Erntet man von Dornen Trauben oder von Disteln Feigen?

ebenso findet wie bei Plutarch, mor. 472 f.[1455] Im Zusammenhang der V. 9–12 heißt das: Der Mensch, das Ebenbild Gottes, kann nicht dem Menschen fluchen. Die rhetorische Frage weist darauf hin, dass dies nicht sein soll (V. 10b οὐ χρή), aber sein kann. Der kurze Schlusssatz bestätigt dies mit einer inversiven Formulierung[1456]: »Nicht [kann] S / salziges süßes Wasser machen«. Die Kürze des Satzes erlaubt unterschiedliche sprachliche Auflösungen. Entweder fügt man nach »salziges« noch »Wasser« ein, was eine Plattitüde wäre, oder man liest ἁλυκόν[1457] als Substantiv, oder man fügt »Quelle« hinzu. Die ältere Exegese ist von einer Textverderbnis ausgegangen oder hat diese wenigstens nicht ausgeschlossen.[1458] Die Textkritik bietet keine Grundlage dafür. Metzner hat Recht, wenn er den Kurztext für »verständlich« hält[1459] und ἁλυκόν als »Salziges« bzw. »Salzquelle« übersetzt.[1460] Jakobus schließt hier wie öfter mit einer lakonisch formulierten Gnome. Dabei spielt er mit der Assonanz von ἁλυκόν und γλυκύ[1461] und dem Gegensatz von salzig und süß (*variatio* zu πικρόν). Der Schlussgedanke ist dann nicht eine bloße Wiederholung von V. 9–11, sondern verengt die Perspektive von dem Einheitsgedanken (V. 11) und dem

---

[1452] Anapher, zweimal rhetorische Frage. Zum Vers vgl. S. LUTHER, Von Feigenbäumen und Oliven. Die Rezeption, Transformation und Kreation sprachethischer Traditionen im Jakobusbrief, ASEs 34, 2017, 381–401. L. bietet eine ausführliche Dokumentation zum traditionsgeschichtlichen Feld von Jak 3,10–12 (389–398). Ergebnis S. 398: »Die zentrale Bedeutung des Motivs der Sprachethik im Jakobusbrief verweist auf eine Verortung primär im jüdisch-weisheitlichen Kontext; zugleich zeigt sich das Schreiben jedoch im positiven Sinne offen für Motive aus unterschiedlichen Traditionsbereichen. Dadurch ermöglicht der Jakobusbrief m. E. eine Einbindung des frühchristlichen Diskurses in den gemeinantiken Diskurs zur Sprachethik.«

[1453] Mt 21,19–21par; 24,32par. Hap. leg. in Jak.

[1454] Mt 26,29par; Joh 15,1–5 (Bildwort); Apk 14,18 f. Hap. leg. in Jak.

[1455] »Nun aber verlangen wir zwar nicht, dass der Weinstock Feigen trägt oder der Ölbaum Trauben …«. BURCHARD, Jak, 153, weitere Beispiele. Eine einseitige Ableitung von Mt 7 verbietet sich daher.

[1456] Chiasmus von V. 11.12.

[1457] Hap. leg. im NT.

[1458] BAUER / ALAND, 1206, nach DBR, § 445,1. Vgl. die komplizierten Überlegungen bei DIBELIUS, Jak, 248 f (mit älterer Lit.).

[1459] METZNER, Jak, 193.

[1460] METZNER, Jak, 194.

[1461] Hap. leg. in Jak. Im NT noch Apk 10,9 f.

276 Kommentar

Argument mit der Artenfolge (V. 12a) zu dem Ausschlussargument 12b. Dies letzte Bild von der salzigen Quelle, die kein süßes Wasser führt, unterstreicht abschließend den wichtigen Gedanken von V. 9: Ein Mensch, Ebenbild Gottes, kann einen Menschen nicht verfluchen.

Im Rückblick wird deutlich, wie sehr 3,1–12 an Vorstellungen und Traditionen der Septuaginta gebunden ist. Das eigene Anliegen des Verfassers, nämlich Vorsicht bei der Rede Christus-gläubiger διδάσκαλοι zu empfehlen, tritt dabei teilweise zugunsten literarischer Übung in den Hintergrund. Dabei vermeidet der Verfasser jedes Zitat, sondern umspielt Texte wie Sir 5 und 28 oder Gen 1. Als Kontrastbeispiel kann 1Petr 3,10–12 dienen. Hier wird Ps 33,13–17LXX mit leichten Abwandlungen zitiert.[1462] Jak 3,8 dagegen nimmt die Verbindung von Zunge und κακόν in einer selbständigen, literarisch stilisierten Wendung auf, ohne an Ps 33 anzuschließen. In 3,1–12 demonstriert der Verfasser seine literarischen Ambitionen, nicht seine Treue zum Schrifttext. Andererseits bleibt er sowohl den alttestamentlichen Themen (Gefahren der Zunge, gutes und böses Sprechen) verbunden als auch dem Motiv- und Begriffsnetz von Sir 28 und der jüdisch-frühchristlichen Semantik (Gehenna). Seine Innovation bezieht sich auf Sprache und Stil.

B. 3,13–18: Warnung vor der irdischen Weisheit

Die zweite Texteinheit beginnt mit einer direkten Frage an die Adressaten, mit der die briefliche Kommunikation ein weiteres Mal aktualisiert wird.[1463] Viermal setzt der Verfasser σοφ- in dieser kurzen Texteinheit. Das Stichwort von der Weisheit hatte Jakobus schon in 1,5 gegeben: Als ersten und wichtigsten möglichen Mangel, der die Brüder an der Vollkommenheit hindere, nannte er dort die Weisheit. Das bedeutet im Umkehrschluss: Weisheit ist die wichtigste oder eine der wichtigsten Erscheinungsformen ethischer Vollkommenheit. Mit seiner Frage kommt Jakobus nun vertieft auf das Thema der Weisheit zurück, um sie an die Taten zu binden – eine Verbindung, die sich schon in der ersten Texteinheit andeutete.[1464] Der kurze, homogene und sorgfältig gestaltete Text ist nach 1Kor 1 und 2 der zweite bedeutende Weisheitstext des NT.

(13) **Wer ist**[1465] **weise und verständig unter euch? Der zeige aus seinem guten Wandel seine Taten in weiser Sanftmut.**[1466] **(14) Wenn ihr aber bittere Rivalität**[1467]

[1462] Einleitendes γάρ.

[1463] Vgl. Burchard, Jak, 154, zu entsprechenden Fragen in Sir 6,34; 1Kor 1,20; 1Clem 54,1 u. ö. 1Clem 54,1–4 zu Spaltungen in der Gemeinde, s. u.

[1464] Zu dem Abschnitt vgl. O. Wischmeyer, Jak 3,13–18 vor dem Hintergrund von 1Kor 1,17–2,16. Frühchristliche Weisheitstheologie und der Jakobusbrief, ASEs 34, 2017, 403–430.

[1465] »Ist« hinzugefügt.

[1466] Griechisch: »Sanftmut der Weisheit«.

[1467] ζῆλος hier: Neid, Rivalität, destruktiver Wettstreit (LSJ, 755: »rivalry«).

und Selbstsucht[1468] in eurem Herzen habt, triumphiert[1469] nicht und lügt nicht gegen die Wahrheit.[1470] (15) Nicht ist das die Weisheit, die von oben herabkommt, sondern die irdische, physische[1471], dämonische. (16)Wo nämlich Eifersucht und Streit sind[1472], da ist[1473] Aufruhr und jede Art von[1474] schlechter Sache[1475]. (17) Die Weisheit von oben aber ist erstens rein, dann friedfertig, gütig, gehorsam, voll von Erbarmen und guten Früchten, unparteiisch[1476], ohne Heuchelei. (18) Die Frucht der Gerechtigkeit aber wird gesät in Frieden von denen, die Frieden tun.

Textkritik: V. 13 Mehrere Minuskeln lesen ει τις, so dass nicht eine rhetorische Frage, sondern ein Nebensatz zu δειξάτω vorläge. V. 14 κατακαυχασθε: P74V. P100. 01. 02. 03. 04, weitere Majuskeln und sehr viele Minuskeln. Zu καυχασθε verkürzen 02, weitere Majuskeln und zahlreiche Minuskeln.

V. 13 σοφός und ἐπιστήμων sind hap. leg. im Jakobusbrief, ἐπιστήμων begegnet nur hier im NT.[1477] Die Zusammenstellung betont die Bedeutung des Weiseseins und zeigt das Interesse des Verfassers an einer anspruchsvollen Ausdrucksweise. Statt einer Antwort auf die Ausgangsfrage formuliert der Verfasser in V. 13b eine Aufforderung an die Adressaten, die er jetzt im Singular anspricht, d. h. auf die einzelne ethisch verantwortliche Person hin: δειξάτω.[1478] Was soll die Einzelperson zeigen? Die Antwort ist sehr einfach: τὰ ἔργα αὐτοῦ. Damit wiederholt Jakobus den praktischen Ertrag von 2,14–26, ohne nochmals auf das Thema des Glaubens zurückzukommen. Im Duktus von Kapitel 3 geht es jetzt um »den guten Wandel«. ἀναστροφή ist hap. leg. bei Jakobus, begegnet aber auch Gal 1,13 und häufiger in den späteren Briefen des NT, besonders im 1Petr.[1479] καλός im Sinne von »sittlich gut«[1480] wird oft im NT gesetzt, vor allem in den Briefen. 1Petr 2,12 spricht in der Paraklese (2,11 ff) ebenfalls vom guten Wandel und den Taten, ohne aber den Zusammenhang zur Weisheit herzustellen:[1481]

[1468] ἐριθεία hier: »Selfish or factious ambition« (LSJ, 688, zur Stelle).

[1469] Vgl. 2,13, dort keine abweichende Lesart.

[1470] Kein Fragesatz, »sondern wie in 1,7 ein Verbot« (METZNER, Jak, 200, mit Verweis auf DBR, § 427,4).

[1471] ψυχικός ist hier mit »physisch« übersetzt, weil so am besten die materiell-irdische Qualität des Adjektivs wiedergegeben werden kann.

[1472] »Sind« ist im Deutschen hinzugefügt.

[1473] »Ist« ist im Deutschen hinzugefügt.

[1474] »Art von« ist im Deutschen hinzugefügt.

[1475] Deutsch besser: »alles Schlechte« (BAUER / ALAND, 1397).

[1476] Nach BAUER / ALAND, 31.

[1477] ἐπιστήμη fehlt im NT ganz, ἐπίστασθαι mehrfach im NT, auch in Jak 4,14. BURCHARD, Jak, 154, verweist auf Barn 6,10 (ebenfalls σοφὸς καὶ ἐπιστήμων) und vermutet »Biblizismus« (Belege).

[1478] Imp. Aor. von δείκνυμι. Vgl. 1,2 ἡγήσασθε. δεικνύναι hier wie in 2,18 im Sinne belehrenden Zeigens oder Nachweisens verstanden: Mt 16,21; Joh 5,20; 10,32 (καλὰ ἔργα); Apg 10,28; 1Kor 12,31.

[1479] Ebenso das Verb.

[1480] BAUER / ALAND, 812.

[1481] Das Thema fehlt ganz im 1Petr.

278   Kommentar

τὴν ἀναστροφὴν ὑμῶν ἐν τοῖς ἔθνεσιν ἔχοντες καλήν ἵνα ἐν ᾧ καταλαλοῦσιν ὑμῶν ὡς κακοποιῶν ἐκ τῶν καλῶν ἔργων ἐποπτεύοντες δοξάσωσιν τὸν θεὸν *ἐν ἡμέρᾳ ἐπισκοπῆς*.
Führt euren Wandel unter den Heiden als guten, damit die, die euch als Übeltäter verleumden, gerade darin eure guten Taten sehen und Gott preisen am Tag der Heimsuchung.

1Clem 38,2 bindet dagegen Weisheit und gute Taten zusammen:

Der Weise zeige (ἐπιδεικνύσθω) seine Weisheit nicht in Worten, sondern in guten Taten (ἐν ἔργοῖς ἀγαθοῖς).

Der Zusammenhang von guten Taten und Weisheit wird von Jakobus in das Syntagma »in der Sanftmut der Weisheit« gefasst. σοφία agiert mit πραΰτης, jener Sanftmut, die Jakobus schon in 1,21 beschworen hatte – ebenfalls im Kontext von Sprachethik, von Vermeidung des Zornes und dem Ethos des Tuns. Die logische Zuordnung des Syntagmas zum Verb oder zu der Wendung »aus seinem guten Wandel«[1482] muss offenbleiben. Es kommt Jakobus nicht auf genaue Abhängigkeitsverhältnisse an, sondern auf die Herstellung eines ethischen Beziehungsgeflechts. Entscheidend sind die Taten. Durch die Bestimmung »in der Sanftmut der Weisheit« wird die σοφία als friedenstiftende Größe bestimmt (Vorbereitung von V. 18) und ausschließlich dem Feld der Ethik zugeordnet.

V. 14 Der vorangestellte Bedingungssatz fungiert als Test: Was erfüllt das Herz[1483] der Adressaten, die jetzt wieder im Plural angesprochen werden? Die Adressaten, die sich aus der Sicht des Jakobus offensichtlich für weise halten, sollen bei sich selbst nach Streit und Zwietracht suchen. Finden sie diese Laster, dann fehlt ihnen die gute Weisheit, die sanftmütig ist. ζῆλος[1484] und ἐριθεία[1485] sind typische Aspekte von Lasterkatalogen, wie Paulus sie verwendet. Sie beschreiben das egoistisch-destruktive Moment in der sachlichen und rhetorischen Dynamik der σοφία, also das Gegenteil von πραΰτης. ζῆλος erhält hier das Attribut πικρός, das auf 3,11, das bittere Quellwasser, rückverweist und die implizite ethische Komponente dieses Bildes nochmals aufgreift und explizit macht. Paulus hat in Röm 3,14 im Zitat von Ps 9,28LXX dieselbe ethisch-negative Konnotation hergestellt:
ὧν τὸ στόμα ἀρᾶς καὶ πικρίας γέμει.
Ihr Mund ist voll von Fluch, von Bitterkeit und von Betrug.

Der Nachsatz, wieder imperativisch als Mahnung und implizite Warnung formuliert, beleuchtet das Ergebnis einer Weisheit ohne Sanftmut: Es ist Selbstruhm und

---

[1482] BURCHARD, Jak, 154f, erwägt auch die Zuordnung zu »seine Taten«.
[1483] Sitz des Ethos: siehe 1,26 (allgemeiner jüdischer und frühchristlicher Sprachgebrauch). Auch 4,8; 5,5.8.
[1484] ζῆλος noch in Jak 3,16, Verb in 4,2. Öfter bei Paulus: Röm 13,13; 1Kor 3,3; 2Kor 12,20.
[1485] ἐριθεία noch in Jak 3,16. Mehrfach bei Paulus: Röm 2,8; 2Kor 12,20; Phil 1,17; 2,3. Das sachlich eng verwandte ἔρις in Röm 1,29; 13,13; 1Kor 1,11; 3,3; 2Kor 12,20; Gal 5,20; Phil 1,15; IgnPhld 8,2. BAUER / ALAND, 626, zu ἐριθεία und ἔρις: beide Laster stehen in 2Kor 12,20 und Gal 5,20 nebeneinander. ἐριθεία scheint anders als ἔρις, Streit, eher die Selbstsucht zu bezeichnen. BURCHARD, Jak, 158, zu ἐριθεία: B. übersetzt »Eigennutz«, lässt aber auch »Streitsucht« (»in falscher Ableitung von ἔρις«) sowie »Geltungsdrang« zu.

C. Briefcorpus 279

Lüge. Das sehr seltene κατακαυχᾶσθαι begegnet außer in Jak 2,13 und 3,14 noch Röm 11,18 im Sinne eines unbegründeten Selbstruhmes.[1486] ψεύδεσθαι ist hap. leg. im Jakobusbrief, hier mit κατά c.gen. gebraucht (Alliteration). Das Thema der Wahrheit hat Jakobus schon in 1,18 prominent gesetzt: Die Adressaten sind durch »das Wort der Wahrheit« geboren. Daher ist ihnen die Welt der Lüge verschlossen. Was will der Verfasser mit dieser Mahnung sagen? Er scheint implizit auf eine Situation anzuspielen, wie Paulus sie in 1Kor 1–4 ausführlich schildert: Dort geht es um Streit zwischen verschiedenen Gemeindegruppen, die »Weisheit« für sich in Anspruch nehmen. ζῆλος und ἔρις herrschen nach der Wahrnehmung des Paulus in der korinthischen Gemeinde (1Kor 1,11; 3,3). Während Paulus aber Parteiungen und Auseinandersetzungen um das theologische Sachthema des Evangeliums (1Kor 1,17) in Korinth diagnostiziert, konzentriert Jakobus seine implizite Kritik gänzlich auf den Mangel an ethischen Verhaltensweisen bei seinen Adressaten. Bevor er diese Kritik in Kap. 4 expliziert, schließt er den zweiten Hauptteil über den Lehrer mit einer Belehrung über die richtige Weisheit ab.

V. 15 In den Versen 15 bis 17 stellt Jakobus die richtige und die falsche Weisheit einander gegenüber. Die Verse sind ein kleines Lehrstück über die himmlische[1487] Weisheit, die auf der Folie der irdischen Weisheit in einer Reihe von Adjektiven und Substantiven, d. h. von ihren Verhaltensformen her, entfaltet wird. Im Hintergrund stehen die Tugend- und Lasterkataloge der frühjüdischen und frühchristlichen Literatur.[1488] Strukturbildend ist die Opposition von ἄνωθεν und ἐπίγειος. Paulus verwendet eine analoge Struktur in Gal 4,25.26 (gegenwärtiges und himmlisches Jerusalem)[1489] und Phil 3,14 (ἄνω κλῆσις: »himmlische Berufung«).[1490] Eine direkte Strukturparallele zu Jak 3 stellt Kol 3,1 f dar:

τὰ ἄνω φρονεῖτε, μὴ τὰ ἐπὶ τῆς γῆς.

Das, was oben ist, denkt, nicht das auf der Erde.

Die Opposition von »himmlisch – irdisch« verbindet die spatiale Dimension mit der Dimension der Herkunft. Sie wird bei Jakobus anders als im paulinischen Zusammenhang ethisch instrumentiert. ἄνωθεν[1491] bedeutet hier wie in 1,17: Die Weisheit kommt aus der Sphäre Gottes und ist eine Gabe. Wie in 1,16–18 benutzt Jakobus eine bewusst metaphorisch-verschlüsselnde religiöse Sprache, wie sie in Joh

---

[1486] Zu Jak 2,13 s. zur Stelle.

[1487] Mit »von oben« umschrieben.

[1488] Ähnliche Reihen bei BURCHARD, Jak, 161. Burchard weist darauf hin, dass Gal 5,22 »formal und inhaltlich anders« als Jak 3,17 ist: Substantive (Tugenden), abhängig von πνεῦμα, nicht von der Weisheit. Trotzdem zeigen beide Reihen eine nahe semantische und inhaltliche Verwandtschaft: καρπός, εἰρήνη, ἀγαθωσύνη.

[1489] Die Opposition ist hier temporal: τῇ νῦν Ἰερουσαλήμ.

[1490] Keine direkte Opposition, vgl. aber 3,13: »was hinten ist« und »was vorne ist«. Zu Phil 3,14 vgl. A. STANDHARTINGER, Der Philipperbrief, HNT 11/I, Tübingen 2021, 242 f. Standhartinger weist für Phil 3 auf Philo, plant. 23, hin: Denn es ist angemessen, dass das Göttliche die von ihm Begeisterten nach oben (ἄνω) ruft.

[1491] Jak 1,17; 3,15.17. Auch Joh 3,31; 19,11.

3,3. 7. 31; 8,23 Verwendung findet. Statt des plastischeren Verbs καταβαίνειν (1,17) setzt Jakobus hier das blassere κατέρχεσθαι.[1492] Hier wie in 1,16–18; 1,25; 2,12 verzichtet der Verfasser auf explizit und eindeutig theologische Terminologie – Gott, Christus, Geist –, sondern *umschreibt* die göttliche Herkunft der Weisheit. Wenn Jakobus hier auch weniger um gehobene religiöse Sprache bemüht ist, wie sie in Kap. 1 vorliegt, so formuliert er doch weiterhin stilistisch sorgfältig.[1493] In den folgenden Versen werden antithetisch Laster und Tugenden der irdischen und der himmlischen Weisheit zugeordnet. Die antithetische Struktur verdeckt Inkonzinnitäten und Varianzen im Detail. Der »Weisheit von oben her«, deren göttliche bzw. himmlische Herkunft und Qualität nicht genannt, sondern umschrieben werden, steht nicht eine ebenfalls spatial bezeichnete »untere« Weisheit gegenüber, sondern diese Weisheit wird dreifach explizit charakterisiert als ἐπίγειος, ψυχική, δαιμονιώδης. Diese Charakteristik kommt einer Schmähung gleich. Demgegenüber wird die Weisheit von oben mit sieben bzw. acht Eigenschaften im Sinne des literarischen Lobes charakterisiert. Auch die jeweiligen Resümees in V. 16 und 18 variieren in Satzbau und Aussage. V. 16 führt drei Laster an und schließt mit einer generalisierenden Wendung. V. 18 fügt stattdessen einen weiterführenden Gedanken hinzu.

ἐπίγειος, irdisch, begegnet wie ἄνωθεν in Joh 3,12, sonst mehrfach bei Paulus.[1494] ψυχικός, hap. leg. im Jakobusbrief, wird viermal bei Paulus verwendet[1495], und zwar stets im Gegensatz zu πνευματικός, im Sinne von menschlich, irdisch, stofflich, diesseitig, physisch[1496]:

ψυχικὸς δὲ ἄνθρωπος οὐ δέχεται τὰ τοῦ πνεύματος τοῦ θεοῦ.

Der physische Mensch nimmt das, was vom Geist Gottes ist, nicht an (1Kor 2,14).

ἐπίγειος und ψυχικός sind fast bedeutungsgleich. δαιμονιώδης, hap. leg. im Neuen Testament[1497], setzt einen anderen grellen Akzent: Die irdische Weisheit ist ge-

---

[1492] Hap. leg. in Jak, lukanisches Vorzugsverb.

[1493] Alliteration, Syntagma, Klimax, Homoioteleuton, variatio: doppelte Verben und Substantive. Form: Ekphrasis.

[1494] 1Kor 15,40; 2Kor 5,1; Phil 2,20; 3,19; IgnPolyk 2,1.

[1495] 1Kor 2,14; 15,44 (zweimal).46; Jud 19 (ebenfalls im Gegensatz zu πνεῦμα).

[1496] »Bez. für das Diesseitige« (BAUER / ALAND, 1783). BURCHARD, Jak, 159f, stellt die Vorstufen des tendenziell negativen Gebrauchs von ψυχή, ψυχικός in SapSal und bei Philo dar, allerdings fehlt das Adjektiv. Daher kommt B. zu dem Schluss: »Vorläufig spricht offenbar nichts dagegen, daß es erst im griechisch sprechenden Urchristentum von der Seele, der Gottes Geist fehlt, bzw. dem geistlosen Menschen gebraucht wurde.«

[1497] Am besten mit »dämonenartig« übersetzt. Weitere Differenzierungen (s. BURCHARD, Jak, 160) bleiben spekulativ. Sehr selten in der Gräzität. Späte Bezeugungen bei LSJ, 365. Herm mand IX 11 greift Motive aus Jak auf. Wichtig ist der Beitrag von J. M. DALE, Demonic Faith and Demonic Wisdom in James: A Response to Kenneth M. Wilson, JBL 121, 2022, 177–195: »Of particular importance is a passage about two types of wisdom (3:13–18); one type, labeled demonic, provides an interpretive parallel for the statement in 2:19 that ›the demons believe.‹ I seek to advance the conversation about the unity of the epistle by demonstrating how the themes of faith and wisdom resonate throughout chapters 1–3. In the Jacobean perspective, there are genuine forms of faith and wisdom that are gifts from above as well as deficient forms of each that are connected with the demonic realm. In this light, it makes sense to read the statement about the demons believing as part of the author's argument rather than an objection from the interlocutor« (Text des *abstract*).

gengöttlich und destruktiv. Im Hintergrund steht die Charakteristik des Glaubens der Dämonen von 2,19: Ihr theologisch korrektes Wissen ist nutzlos, da sie nicht ethisch handeln können. Die »Weisheit von oben« ist dagegen ethisch ausgerichtet. Während die beiden ersten Adjektive aus dem Umkreis paulinischer theologischer Diktion stammen, fügt Jakobus mit dem dritten Adjektiv eine eigene (negative) religiöse Bestimmung hinzu. In der Kritik an der irdischen Weisheit schließt er sich an die Darstellung des Paulus in 1Kor 1,15–2,16 an, bezieht sich aber nicht auf das göttliche πνεῦμα[1498], das Einsichten in Gottes Heilsplan vermittelt, sondern ausschließlich auf ethische Verhaltensformen.

V. 16 Diese werden zunächst *ex negativo* benannt: Der Verfasser knüpft an V. 14 an und nennt noch einmal ζῆλος und ἐριθεία. Sie führen zu[1499] ἀκαταστασία und πᾶν φαῦλον πρᾶγμα. ἀκαταστασία, nur hier bei Jakobus, begegnet öfter bei Paulus und changiert zwischen Unordnung und Aufruhr.[1500] »Jede schlechte Handlung« ist in so allgemein ethischer Sprache formuliert[1501], dass das Profil der irdischen Weisheit durch diese Bezeichnung nichts gewinnt. V. 16 bleibt sehr allgemein und dient eher als Negativfolie denn als eigene Bestimmung der irdischen Weisheit.

V. 17 Erst jetzt kommt Jakobus zur positiven Weisheit. Die Weisheit »von oben her« wird in acht Aspekten oder Wirkungsweisen beschrieben: Hier liegt das Interesse des Verfassers. Er benutzt – anders als Paulus in 1Kor 13,4 bis 7 – keine Verben, sondern Adjektive. Durch die Aufzählung πρῶτον[1502], ἔπειτα[1503] wird die erste Eigenschaft besonders hervorgehoben: ἁγνός, rein, »gottgemäß«[1504], ist ein religiöses Qualitätsprädikat. Die Weisheit wird damit noch einmal als der religiösen Sphäre zugehörig bezeichnet. εἰρηνικός, hap. leg. in Jak, ist dann das sachlich wichtigste Adjektiv[1505]: Weisheit, wie Jakobus sie darstellt, ist friedlich und schafft Frieden. ἐπιεικής, ebenfalls hap. leg. in Jak, changiert zwischen »nachgiebig«, »billig denkend« und »mild, gütig«[1506] und begegnet einige Male in den neutestamentlichen Briefen.[1507] εὐπειθής, »gehorsam, folgsam«, ist ntl. hap. leg.[1508] Weiterhin ist die

---

[1498] Der theologische πνεῦμα-Begriff fehlt gänzlich bei Jakobus. 2,26; 4,5 (unbekanntes Zitat) bedeutet πνεῦμα Lebensgeist, Inneres des Menschen.

[1499] ὅπου und ἐκεῖ begründen kein logisches, sondern ein locker spatiales Verhältnis. Vgl. Mt 6,21par; 24,28; Mk 6,20; Lk 17,37; Joh 12,26; Apk 12,6.14.

[1500] 1Kor 14,33; 2Kor 6,5; 12,20. Auch Lk 21,9 (dort politisch). 1Clem 3,2 (Lasterkatalog, bezogen auf die korinthische Gemeinde); 14,1 allgemein von Streit (Thema des ganzen Kap. 14); 43,6 (zu Israel).

[1501] φαῦλον πρᾶγμα: (beide Wörter hap. leg. in Jak), häufig im Hirten des Hermas.

[1502] πρῶτον μὲν hap. leg. in Jak.

[1503] ἔπειτα noch 4,14. Öfter bei Paulus.

[1504] Hap. leg. in Jak. BAUER / ALAND, 21. Öfter in den ntl. Briefen: 2Kor 7,11; 11,2; Phil 4,8 (eine Reihe ethischer Adjektive); 1Tim 5,22; Tit 2,5; 1Petr 3,2 (mit ἀναστροφή); 1Joh 3,3.

[1505] Im NT nur noch Hebr 12,11. Vgl. 1Clem 14,5. εἰρήνη dagegen im NT häufig, besonders in den Briefen. S. zu Jak 3,18.

[1506] BAUER / ALAND, 593. ἐπιείκεια: »Nachsicht, Milde«, BAUER / ALAND, 592 (Apg 24,4; 2Kor 10,1).

[1507] Phil 4,5; 1Tim 3,3: δεῖ οὖν τὸν ἐπίσκοπον … εἶναι … ἐπιεικῆ ἄμαχον (Ein Bischof soll gütig sein, nicht streitsüchtig); Tit 3,2; 1Petr 2,18 (gute und milde Herren).

[1508] BAUER / ALAND, 655, vgl. SPICQ, NLNT I, 323 f.

»obere« Weisheit μεστὴ ἐλέους καὶ καρπῶν ἀγαθῶν. ἔλεος hat Jakobus schon in dem Wortspiel in 2,13 an theologisch prominenter Stelle gesetzt. Betont er dort den Gegensatz zwischen gerechtem Strafgericht und Erbarmen, verstärkt ἔλεος hier den Aspekt der Milde, mit der die obere Weisheit agiert. μεστὴ[1509] ἐλέους καὶ καρπῶν ἀγαθῶν[1510] korrespondiert antithetisch mit φαῦλον πρᾶγμα[1511]: Gute »Früchte« stehen gegen schlechte »Sachen«. καρπός wird häufig im Neuen Testament als Metapher für ethisches Handeln gewählt.[1512] Gal 5,22 eröffnet Paulus den Katalog der Geistesgaben mit der Wendung: ὁ δὲ καρπὸς τοῦ πνεύματος. Die Verbindung καρπὸς ἀγαθός findet sich in den neutestamentlichen Schriften nur hier. Die Spruchquelle Q überliefert zwei Logien, in denen zweimal καρπὸς καλός begegnet – vielleicht wegen der Alliteration, die Jakobus hier gerade nicht wählt, vielleicht auch, weil durch καλός die Fruchtmetapher gestärkt wird.[1513] In diesen Logien ist das Bild vom guten Baum, der gute Früchte trägt, und vom bösen Baum, der böse Früchte trägt, ausgeführt. Bei Jakobus dagegen fehlt das ausgeführte Bild. Es findet sich lediglich die Früchtemetapher im Kontext eines Tugendkatalogs. Jakobus schließt in V. 18 mit »säen« an das Bild an und rundet das Argument von der oberen Weisheit ab.

Den stilistisch betonten Abschluss der Dreier-Reihe bilden die beiden positiv konnotierten Adjektive ἀδιάκριτος und ἀνυπόκριτος, verbunden durch Alliteration und Alpha privativum. ἀδιάκριτος ist ntl. hap. leg. und lässt sich mit »unparteiisch« oder »unerschütterlich« wiedergeben[1514], ἀνυπόκριτος, ungeheuchelt, echt, ist hap. leg. im Jakobusbrief und begegnet einige Male in ethischem Zusammenhang in der ntl. Briefliteratur.[1515] Stilistisch und inhaltlich vergleichbar ist Röm 1,31, wo Paulus viermal asyndetisch das Alpha privativum setzt, um die »Völker« als ἀσυνέτους ἀσυνθέτους ἀστόργους ἀνελεήμονας zu bezeichnen.

[1509] Hier übertragene Bedeutung c.gen. (schon in 3,8, dort eigentliche Bedeutung: »voller Gift«). μεστός c.gen. im Zusammenhang mit Tugenden bzw. Lastern auch: Mt 23,28; Röm 1,29; 15,14; 2Petr 2,14.

[1510] Vgl. Mt 3,10par; 7,17ffpar; 12,33par.

[1511] Zu dieser Wendung vgl. Joh 3,20; 5,29; Röm 9,11; 2Kor 5,10 (jeweils mit dem Verb πράσσω).

[1512] Vgl. Phil 1,11; Eph 5,9 u.ö.

[1513] Q 3,9; 6,43=Mt 3,10par: πᾶν οὖν δένδρον μὴ ποιοῦν καρπὸν καλὸν ἐκκόπτεται καὶ εἰς πῦρ βάλλεται (Jeder Baum nun, der nicht gute Frucht trägt, wird abgehauen und ins Feuer geworfen); Mt 7,17–19par: πᾶν δένδρον ἀγαθὸν καρποὺς καλοὺς ποιεῖ (Jeder gute Baum trägt gute Früchte); 12,33par: Ἢ ποιήσατε τὸ δένδρον καλὸν καὶ τὸν καρπὸν αὐτοῦ καλόν, ἢ ποιήσατε τὸ δένδρον σαπρὸν καὶ τὸν καρπὸν αὐτοῦ σαπρόν· ἐκ γὰρ τοῦ καρποῦ τὸ δένδρον γινώσκεται (Nehmt an, ein Baum ist gut, und so ist auch seine Frucht gut, oder nehmt an, der Baum ist faul, und so ist auch seine Frucht faul – denn an seiner Frucht wird der Baum erkannt.) »δένδρον καλόν« mag auch auf Gen 3,6 anspielen.

[1514] BAUER / ALAND, 31. Vgl. IgnEph 3,2; IgnMagn 15; IgnTrall 1,1. Adverb: IgnRöm inscr.; Phld inscr. »Unparteiisch« passt zu Jak 2,1–7. »Nicht zweifelnd« würde zu διακρίνειν Jak 1,6; 2,4 (zweifeln, Bedenken tragen) passen. Der Text erlaubt keine genaue Festlegung.

[1515] Röm 12,9 (mit ἀγάπη); 2Kor 6,6 (ebenso); 1Tim 1,5 (ebenso); 2Tim 1,5 ὑπόμνησιν λαβὼν τῆς ἐν σοὶ ἀνυποκρίτου πίστεως (Denn ich erinnere mich an deinen aufrichtigen Glauben); 1Petr 1,22 (mit εἰς φιλαδελφίαν ἀνυπόκριτον). Adverb: 2Clem 12,3.

Welches Profil dieser kurzen Ekphrasis der Weisheit von oben, die formal nicht weit von 1Kor 13,4–7 entfernt ist[1516], ergibt sich bis hierhin? Die Weisheit ist auf den Frieden ausgerichtet: nachgiebig, milde, folgsam, unparteiisch. Sie agiert ausschließlich ethisch und wird an ihren Taten erkannt. Noetische und rhetorische Aspekte fehlen dagegen ganz. Das wird abschließend in V. 18 deutlich. Hier wird der Friede eigens betont.

V. 18 Noch einmal wird die ethische Metapher καρπός aufgegriffen, nun nicht mehr wie in V. 17 in Verbindung mit σοφία, sondern mit dem bereits zweimal genannten ethischen Grundwert δικαιοσύνη.[1517] Dibelius denkt hier an einen frühchristlichen Spruch.[1518] Deutlich ist die traditionelle Sprache, mit der das Thema der Weisheit zum Abschluss gebracht und zugleich mit dem Thema Frieden der Übergang zur nächsten Texteinheit vorbereitet wird. Jakobus verbindet den Grundwert der Gerechtigkeit mit einem zweiten, schon in V. 17 als Eigenschaft der Weisheit von oben genannten Wert: εἰρήνη, dem Frieden. Durch die Saat-Fruchtmetapher stellt der Verfasser eine lockere Verknüpfung zwischen beiden Werten her. Das Bild ist schief und künstlich: »Die Frucht der Gerechtigkeit wird gesät«. Das ist vom Ende her gedacht: Nicht der Same, sondern bereits die Frucht[1519] wird gesät.[1520] Der Verfasser denkt an die Taten der Gerechtigkeit.[1521] σπείρειν ist hap. leg. bei Jakobus. Aber weder das Syntagma »Frucht der Gerechtigkeit«[1522], d. h. gute Taten, noch das Bild des Säens der Frucht, d. h. der Beginn des gerechten Tuns, sind ungewöhnlich. Vielmehr benutzt Jakobus wie zuvor gängige Bilder aus dem ethischen Repertoire. »Säen« wird in verschiedenen Zusammenhängen metaphorisch verwendet, so in Gal 6,7.8 Paulus spricht von der Liebe als Frucht des Geistes (Gal 5,22) und attestiert den Philippern, sie seien erfüllt von der »Frucht der Gerechtigkeit« (Phil 1,11). Dasselbe lesen wir im Epheser- und im Hebräerbrief:

ὁ γὰρ καρπὸς τοῦ φωτὸς ἐν πάσῃ ἀγαθωσύνῃ καὶ δικαιοσύνῃ καὶ ἀληθείᾳ.

Denn die Frucht des Lichtes liegt in aller Güte und Gerechtigkeit und Wahrheit (Eph 5,9).

Jede Züchtigung aber scheint im Augenblick nicht Freude, sondern Schmerz zu sein, später aber [bringt sie] denen, die dadurch geübt sind, als friedenstiftende Frucht (καρπὸν εἰρηνικὸν) die Gabe der Gerechtigkeit (ἀποδίδωσιν δικαιοσύνης) (Hebr 12,11).

[1516] Unterschied s. o.: 1Kor 13 formuliert verbal, Jak 3 adjektivisch.

[1517] Jak 1,20 (δικαιοσύνη θεοῦ: die Gerechtigkeit, die vor Gott gilt); 2,23 (Zitat Gen 15,6).

[1518] DIBELIUS, Jak, 258. Zurecht skeptisch METZNER, Jak, 209, mit Hinweis auf ALLISON, Jak, 584 f.

[1519] καρπός in Jak 3,17.18; 5,7.18.

[1520] Das spricht gegen Dibelius' These.

[1521] BURCHARD, Jak, 163. B. weist für καρπός auf die Bedeutung »der künftige Ertrag« hin (Belege aus der Gräzität).

[1522] Parallelen bei BURCHARD, Jak, 163.

Gerechtigkeit und Friede – in Septuaginta bei den Propheten prominent verbunden[1523] – hängen zusammen. In Spr 10 sind Sprüche zu Weisheit und Gerechtigkeit zusammengestellt. Der Weise und Gerechte ist auch ein Friedensstifter:

ὁ δὲ ἐλέγχων μετὰ παρρησίας εἰρηνοποιεῖ.
Wer mit Freimut zurechtweist, stiftet Frieden (Spr 10,10).

In dieselbe Richtung zielt Jak 3,18. Das Element des Friedenstiftens oder Frieden-Tuns findet sich ebenso in den Seligpreisungen (Mt 5,9[1524] μακάριοι οἱ εἰρηνοποιοί). In den Deuteropaulinen wird Christus als Friedenstifter bezeichnet: Kol 1,20 (εἰρηνοποιήσας) und Eph 2,15 (ποιῶν εἰρήνην). In Jak 3,18 sind es die Friedenstifter, denen in besonderer Weise Gerechtigkeit und Friede zukommen. Wie die verschiedenen Werte sich zueinander verhalten, ob als Ursache und Wirkung oder als Anfang und Ergebnis, bleibt ungesagt. Es geht nicht um logische und funktionale Abhängigkeiten[1525], sondern um ein möglichst dichtes Bild von Gerechtigkeit und tatkräftigem Frieden als der Wirkungsweise der Weisheit von oben. Stilistisch arbeitet der Verfasser mit der Wiederaufnahme von Stichworten (Frucht, Friede) und einer Art von tautologischer Inklusion im zweiten Satzteil: Gerechtigkeit wird in *Frieden* gesät von denen, die *Frieden* tun. »Friede« steht am Schluss. Was »in Frieden säen« eigentlich bedeutet, bleibt ungesagt. Der Dativ τοῖς ποιοῦσιν ist mit Allison und Metzner als *Dativus auctoris* zu lesen[1526]: Die Friedenstäter bzw. Friedensstifter sind es, die Gerechtigkeit tun. Der Friede, den Jakobus beschwört, ist auf die Gemeinde bezogen. Die Lehrer sollen in ihrer Redetätigkeit zum Frieden und zu guten Taten ermuntern, statt Zwietracht und Streit zu säen. Damit ist das ethische Thema für 4,1–12 gesetzt.

4. Vierter Hauptteil: Mahn- und Gerichtsreden gegen verschiedene Gruppierungen (Kap. 4,1–5,6)

Der vierte Hauptteil führt formal und inhaltlich Teil 3 direkt weiter. Drei Abschnitte lassen sich in diesem Hauptteil unterscheiden. (A) In 4,1–12 wendet sich Jakobus gegen streitsüchtige und hochmütige Gemeindeglieder, ohne allerdings ihr soziales Profil deutlicher zu zeichnen. (B) 4,13–17 und (C) 5,1–6 zeigen demgegenüber jeweils ein klares soziales und wirtschaftliches Gruppenprofil: Es handelt sich um Schelt- und Gerichtsreden gegen Kaufleute und gegen Reiche. Wieweit diese Gruppen innerhalb der Adressatenschaft und ihren Gemeinden zu verorten sind, ist aber

---

[1523] E. Dinkler / E. Dinkler-von Schubert, Art. Friede, RAC 8, 1972, 434–505.

[1524] Gerechtigkeit ebenfalls in Mt 5,6, weiter Erbarmen 5,7 und Sanftmut 5,5. Metzner, Jak, 211 Anm. 289, erwägt eine Nähe zwischen den Seligpreisungen und Jak 3,18. Weder eine direkte Abhängigkeit noch eine Allusion lassen sich wahrscheinlich machen. Deutlich ist das verwandte *Ethos*.

[1525] Anders Burchard, Jak, 164, der verschiedene logische Zuordnungen diskutiert.

[1526] Metzner, Jak, 211, mit Hinweis auf Allison, Jak, 586. Der von Burchard, Jak, 164, wohl bevorzugte *Dativus commodi* (Gerechtigkeit wird gesät für die, die Frieden tun) ergibt keinen Sinn.

ebenfalls unklar und exegetisch umstritten. Deutlich ist, dass 4,1–10 antithetisch an 3,13–18 anschließt: Das Stichwort *Friede* evoziert das Gegenteil, *Kriege* und *Kämpfe*. Damit wird das Thema *Streit* aus Kapitel 3 sprachlich radikalisiert.

Ein Blick auf die briefliche Kommunikation zeigt eine gewisse Unsicherheit bei Jakobus. Formal sind nach 3,1 weiterhin »meine Brüder« die Adressaten. Jakobus spricht sie in Kap. 4 zunächst einfach mit »ihr« an (V. 1). Erst in 4,11 kehrt er zu der freundlichen Anrede »Brüder« zurück. In 4,4.8 verwendet er für die brieflichen Adressaten stattdessen hochpolemische Schimpfworte. Jakobus steigert sich in eine so scharfe Anklage mit viel allgemeiner Gerichtstopik gegen die »Ehebrecherinnen« und »Gottesfeinde« (V. 1–6) und »Sünder« und »Zweiseeler« (V. 7–10) hinein, dass der Bezug auf reale Gemeindesituationen mindestens fraglich wird. Die Rhetorik der Gerichtsrede scheint sich zu verselbständigen.[1527] In V. 11.12 ändert der Verfasser den Ton und geht zu einer sprachlich moderaten Form über. Nun *ermahnt* er die *Brüder*, einander nicht zu verleumden oder zu verurteilen. An diesem Punkt scheint er wieder die realen Gemeinden und ihre Zwistigkeiten im Blick zu haben. Allerdings schließt dieser Abschnitt mit dem Hinweis auf die Gerichtsthematik und mit einer polemisch klingenden rhetorischen Frage.

4,13 bringt einen formalen Neueinsatz. In den Abschnitten V. 13–17 und 5,1–6 verlässt Jakobus das Thema des Streites, bleibt aber bei dem Ton des scharfen moralischen Vorwurfs. Seine Vorwürfe gelten nun anderen Themen. Beide Texte sind formal und thematisch deutlicher profiliert als 4,1–6 und 4,7–12. Sie werden mit dem klassischen ἄγε νῦν eingeleitet und sind anders als in 4,1–12 direkt an bestimmte Gruppen adressiert: an (reiche) Kaufleute und an »die Reichen« generell. Diese stereotyp gezeichneten Gruppen können aber nicht einfach der brieflichen Adressatenschaft zugerechnet werden. Sie geben auch nicht spiegelbildlich Auskunft über die Zusammensetzung der Gemeinden. Eher will der Verfasser hier Gefahren aufzeigen, die den wachsenden Gemeinden drohen. Wieder zeigt sich eine gewisse Verselbständigung der topischen Polemik. Die Vorwürfe folgen einer Klimax. Gegenüber der letzten Gruppe steigert sich die Polemik bis zum Mordvorwurf (so aber schon 4,2). Zugleich baut der Verfasser die eschatologische Kulisse der »letzten Tage« auf, auf die er schon in 4,12 angespielt hat und an die er bei seinen Schlussermahnungen ab 5,7 anknüpft. Die dreigliedrige Scheltrede gegen die unfriedlichen Gemeindeglieder, gegen Kaufleute und gegen »die Reichen« bricht mit dem letzten Vorwurf in 5,6 unvermittelt ab, ohne dass konkrete ethische Folgerungen wie in 4,7–10 gezogen werden. Stattdessen verfolgt Jakobus im Folgenden das Thema der Endzeit thematisch explizit weiter. Aus Kap. 4 kann keineswegs spiegelbildlich auf die soziale Zusammensetzung der Adressatenschaft des Jak geschlossen werden: Die Gemeinden, an die sich der Verfasser brieflich wendet, sind weder von Streit noch von Gier und Begierden zerfressen, noch handelt es sich um reiche Kaufleute oder

---

[1527] Vgl. dieselbe Tendenz bei der Texteinheit über »die Zunge«.

286 Kommentar

überhaupt um Reiche, die den Armen Gewalt bis zum Tode antun. Dass Jak hier mit Stereotypen arbeitet, geht besonders aus dem Abschnitt über die Kaufleute hervor.[1528] Andererseits macht gerade Kap. 4 wie schon Kap. 2 deutlich, dass Jak an wohlhabende Gemeindeglieder gerichtet ist, in deren Reihen sowohl Reiche als auch speziell Kaufleute Platz haben. Weitere sozialgeschichtliche Einzelheiten der Adressatengemeinden lassen sich dem Text nicht entnehmen.

A. 4,1–12: Gegen Sünder

Die thematisch-strukturelle *Zuordnung* von 4,1–12 ist nicht eindeutig. Dibelius betont die Verbindung zu Kapitel 3 und rechnet 3,13–4,12 zur 6. Spruchgruppe: »Wider Streitsucht«.[1529] Metzner und Allison verstehen diesen Abschnitt dagegen als eigene Größe[1530]. Burchard wählt eine formale Einteilung: die Form der Schelt-rede. Daher trennt er anders als Dibelius zwischen 3,11 und 3,12 und lässt bereits mit der rhetorischen Frage von 3,12 den 2. Hauptteil beginnen: »Schelte der Un-vollkommenen« (3,12–5,6)[1531]. Johnson teilt wie Dibelius zwischen 3,12 und 3,13. Er liest 3,13–4,10 als Einheit unter der Überschrift: »Call to Conversion«.[1532] Alle Vorschläge haben Anhaltspunkte im Text. 4,1 knüpft thematisch sehr eng an 3,18 an, allerdings stellt 3,18 eine Schlussgnome dar, und mit der Frage in 4,1 liegt formal ein Neueinsatz vor. Die Anbindung von 4,1–12 an die folgenden Teiltexte 4,13–17 und 5,1–6, die in diesem Kommentar vorgeschlagen wird, ist vor allem von der *Redeform* her begründet: Es handelt sich dreimal um eine Buß- oder Gerichtspre-digt bzw. Scheltrede[1533], zuerst adressiert an die »Ehebrecherinnen« und »Sünder« bzw. »Zweiseeler«. Die erste Rede wendet sich nicht an bestimmte Gruppierungen, sondern an alle »Brüder«. Die Wortwahl, besonders die mehrfache Anrede der Ad-ressaten als Ehebrecher, Sünder und »Zweiseeler« und die Bezeichnung als »Feinde Gottes« sowie die Aufforderung in V. 8–10 weisen textpragmatisch auf die Bußpre-digten des Täufers und Jesu. Der Schlüsselbegriff dieser Bußpredigten, μετάνοια[1534], begegnet allerdings nicht bei Jakobus.

Die *erste* Gerichtsrede 4,1–12 ist länger und weniger formal durchstrukturiert als die *zweite* in 4,13–17 und die *dritte* in 5,1–6. Eine gewisse formale Zäsur besteht innerhalb der ersten Rede zwischen V. 6 und 7. Dibelius bemerkt richtig: Von der Bußpredigt in V. 1–6

[1528] S. u. den Kommentar.

[1529] DIBELIUS, Jak, 191.

[1530] METZNER, Jak, Teil VIII: »Kriege und Kämpfe sind Feindschaft mit Gott« (212). ALLISON, Jak, 588: »Friendship with the World versus Friendship with God«.

[1531] BURCHARD, Jak, 152.

[1532] JOHNSON, Jak, 267.

[1533] BURCHARD, Jak, findet diese Form schon in 3,12. Aber erst in 4,1–6 begegnen die scheltenden Anreden (V. 4).

[1534] Mt 3,8: ποιήσατε οὖν καρπὸν ἄξιον τῆς μετανοίας (Tut nun rechtschaffene Frucht der Umkehr).

heben sich … die imperativischen Mahnungen 47 ff. deutlich ab … Wir stehen offenbar vor einer Reihe formgleicher, aber inhaltlich verschiedener Mahnungen, wie wir sie in der Paränese nicht selten finden; vgl. Röm 12,9–13. Der Autor hat sie übernommen und vielleicht variiert.[1535]

Jakobus hat hier deutlich traditionelle Materialien übernommen und überarbeitet. Die *zweite* und *dritte* Rede ist jeweils kürzer, präziser und auf eine bestimmte soziale Gruppe zugeschnitten: erstens auf die Kaufleute, zweitens auf die Reichen. Die dritte Gerichtsrede endet abrupt mit dem Vorwurf gegen die Reichen, »den Gerechten« getötet zu haben.

Der Stil ist teils diatribisch-belehrend, teils anklagend und insgesamt äußerst lebhaft. Die Anrede erfolgt in häufigem Wechsel zwischen »ihr« und einzelnen Gruppierungen, auch spitzt der Verfasser seinen Angriff durch den Wechsel von »Brüder« zu »du« zu (V. 11.12). Fragen, Aufforderungen, Anklagen und Zitate wechseln einander ab. Eine klare Zuordnung der einzelnen Texteinheiten zu bestimmten literarischen Kleinformen aus der prophetischen Tradition Israels wie Scheltrede[1536], Gerichtsrede[1537] oder Bußpredigt[1538] muss unterbleiben. Jakobus verbindet verschiedene Motive und Formen und schafft neue Kleinformen.

1. Texteinheit: 4,1–6 Mahnrede gegen »Ehebrecher« und Weltfreunde
(1) Woher (kommen)[1539] die Kämpfe und woher die Streitigkeiten bei euch? Nicht daher: aus den[1540] Lüsten, die in euren Gliedern streiten? (2) Ihr begehrt und erlangt[1541] [es] doch nicht[1542], ihr tötet[1543] und eifert und könnt doch[1544] nichts[1545] erreichen, ihr kämpft und streitet, (und)[1546] ihr habt doch[1547] nichts[1548], weil ihr nicht bittet, (3) ihr bittet und empfangt doch[1549] (nichts)[1550], weil ihr in böser

---

[1535] Dibelius, Jak, 250.

[1536] Vgl. oben.

[1537] Vgl. dazu M. Reiser, Die Gerichtspredigt Jesu. Eine Untersuchung zur eschatologischen Verkündigung Jesu und ihrem frühjüdischen Hintergrund, NTA NF 23, Münster 1990. Das Schema der prophetischen Gerichtsrede mit Anklage und Gerichtsankündigung findet sich in Röm 1 und 2, nicht aber bei Jakobus. Jakobus verwendet eschatologische Gerichtsmotive, ohne aber ein Gerichtsszenario herzustellen. Die Motive von Geduld und Leiden überwiegen.

[1538] Windisch, Die Katholischen Briefe, 26. Es fehlt aber das Motiv der Buße und Umkehr.

[1539] »Kommen« ist im Deutschen hinzugefügt.

[1540] Griechisch: »euren«.

[1541] Griechisch: »habt«.

[1542] »Doch« ist im Deutschen hinzugefügt.

[1543] Siehe Textkritik.

[1544] »Doch« ist im Deutschen hinzugefügt.

[1545] Im Griechischen nur οὐ.

[1546] Zu »und« siehe Textkritik.

[1547] »Doch« ist im Deutschen hinzugefügt.

[1548] Im Griechischen nur οὐ.

[1549] »Doch« ist im Deutschen hinzugefügt.

[1550] Im Griechischen nur οὐ.

288 Kommentar

Absicht[1551] bittet, um es für eure Begierden[1552] auszugeben. (4) Ehebrecherinnen, wisst ihr nicht, dass die Freundschaft mit der Welt Feindschaft gegenüber Gott[1553] ist? Wer nun Freund der Welt sein will, agiert[1554] als Feind Gottes. (5) Oder meint ihr, dass umsonst die Schrift sagt: ›Nach Neid strebt der Geist, den er in uns hat wohnen lassen.[1555] (6) Er gibt aber größere Gnade‹? Deshalb heißt es: ›Gott widersteht den Hochmütigen, den Demütigen aber gibt er Gnade‹.

Textkritik: V. 2 Die Textbezeugung spricht ausschließlich für φονευετε (METZNER, Jak, 217 f). Seit Erasmus wird öfter φθονειτε konjiziert (Minuskel 918Z, 16. Jh.).[1556] Diese Lesart wäre zwar sowohl vom Sinn als auch von 1Petr 2,1 und anderen Belegen her sinnvoll, aber eine Verschreibung ist nicht plausibel zu machen. Außerdem werden in Röm 1,29; Gal 5,21 gerade φονος und φθονος zusammen aufgezählt. Jakobus selbst verbindet dreimal Ehebruch und Tötung: 2,11 (zweimal) und 4,2.4 (siehe Mk 10,19par und Röm 13,9 im Zitat von Ex 20,13 f). Die Zuordnung der Verben ist nicht klar. και ουκ εχετε in V. 2 lesen 01. 025. 044 und sehr viele Minuskeln. ουκ εχετε lesen P100. 02(*Vf). 03. 33 und andere Minuskeln: bessere Bezeugung, daher in ECM. Ich bevorzuge mit DIBELIUS[1557] die Lesart mit και, da sie der Struktur der Passage gerecht wird und Jakobus stets auf Strukturierung Wert legt. V. 4 μοιχοι και μοιχαλιδες lesen Majuskel 01C2. 025. 044 und zahlreiche Minuskeln (glättend gegenüber der besonders schimpflichen femininen Form: ein Beleg dafür, dass die antiken christlichen Autoren durchaus zwischen männlicher und weiblicher Anrede unterscheiden konnten und die maskuline Anrede nicht automatisch die weibliche Hörerschaft mit anspricht). ος εαν … κοσμου: diese schwerfällige Wendung existiert in den Handschriften in sieben Varianten, ohne dass sich eine Sinnänderung ergäbe (ein Beispiel für die die Schreiber oft irritierende gewollte Schwerfälligkeit und Überladenheit des Ausdrucks). V. 5 Statt φθονον lesen Minuskel 181. 1243 und 2492 φονον (siehe zu V. 1). Statt κατωκισεν, »er hat angesiedelt« (P74. 01.03. 044.049, mehrere Minuskeln) lesen 025. 33 und viele Minuskeln κατωκησεν, »er hat gewohnt«. εν υμιν statt εν ημιν lesen zahlreiche Minuskeln. Text: P74. 01. 02. 03. 025. 044. 33 und sehr viele Minuskeln. V. 6 ECM setzt erst nach χαριν das Fragezeichen, d. h. ECM versteht V. 6a als Teil des ersten Zitats. ο θεος lesen P74V. 01. 02. 03. 33 und viele Minuskeln. ο κυριος (so Spr 3,34) lesen 056 und mehrere Minuskeln. Die Vereindeutigung des Zitates lässt sich eher Jakobus als einem Kopisten zuschreiben.

Die Verse 1–6 stellen die erste Texteinheit dar. Auf eine doppelte rhetorische Frage in V. 1, die eine Anklage eröffnet, folgt in V. 2 und 3 eine rücksichtslose und rhetorisch überzogene Schilderung der Situation der Angesprochenen (ἐν ὑμῖν), die in V. 4 in der schimpflichen Anrede »Ehebrecherinnen« gipfelt, wieder mit einer rhetorischen Frage verbunden und in V. 4b durch eine theologische Aussage kommentiert.

[1551] Griechisch: »böse«.

[1552] δαπανάω: »ausgeben, aufwenden«, BAUER / ALAND, 341.

[1553] τοῦ bleibt unübersetzt.

[1554] S. o. zu 3,6. καθιστάναι »machen, bewirken«, BAUER / ALAND, 792.

[1555] φθόνος; vgl. dazu SPICQ, NLNT II, 919–921. SapSal 2,24; 6,23; 1Makk 8,16; 3Makk 6,17 negativ. Jak ist auf der Linie von Weish.

[1556] WINDISCH, Die Katholischen Briefe, 27, und DIBELIUS, Jak, 261 f, sprechen von »Konjektur«.

[1557] DIBELIUS, Jak, 261.

C. Briefcorpus 289

Eine weitere rhetorische Frage, verbunden mit einem ersten Schriftzitat, folgt in V.
5.6a, ein zweites Schriftzitat in V. 6b dient als sentenziöser Abschluss der Verse 1–6.

V. 1 Jakobus setzt formal übergangslos mit zwei Fragen ein, die beide rhetorischer
Natur sind. Der Ton ist aggressiv-anklagend. Der Verfasser gibt die Antwort auf die
erste Frage in Form einer zweiten Frage, die durch das vorangestellte οὐκ ἐντεῦθεν
noch gesteigert wird und zugleich deutlich macht, dass die Adressaten die erste
Frage selbst beantworten können. Dadurch wird der vorwurfsvolle Ton verschärft.
Sachlich werden zwei Themen aufgegriffen: die »Begierde« aus 1,14 f und das Thema
von 3,14.16, das jetzt zugespitzt wird. Statt »Rivalität und Selbstsucht« wirft Jakobus
nun den Adressaten »Kämpfe und Streitigkeiten« vor und schafft ein sprachliches
Szenario von Kriegsterminologie, das in übertragener Weise ethisch-polemisch eingesetzt wird. πόλεμοι, eigentlich »Krieg« oder »Schlacht«, wird hier übertragen für
»Streitigkeiten« (Plur.) gebraucht.[1558] μάχαι, eigentlich »Kämpfe«, steht für heftige Streitigkeiten und begegnet in V. 2 nochmals in verbaler Form.[1559] Die Lüste
(ἡδοναί[1560]) »ziehen zu Felde« in den Gliedern (στρατεύομαι[1561]). Die μέλη[1562] hatte
Jakobus schon in 3,5.6 im Blick: die Zunge, das kleine Glied, das große Dinge
anrichtet und den ganzen Leib befleckt. Hier in 4,1 stehen »die Glieder« *pars pro
toto* für das σῶμα (2,16.26), das »Kampfplatz der Lüste« ist. Eine sehr ähnliche Metaphorik verwendet Paulus in Röm 6,13:

μηδὲ παριστάνετε τὰ μέλη ὑμῶν ὅπλα ἀδικίας τῇ ἁμαρτίᾳ.
Setzt eure Glieder nicht als Waffen der Ungerechtigkeit und der Sünde ein.

V. 2–3 Das eindrückliche Bild der Glieder als Kampfplatz der Lüste setzt das Thema
für 4,1–6. Das leitende Thema dieser Verse ist aber nicht das σῶμα selbst – das gar
nicht genannt, sondern durch das *pars-pro-toto*-Bild von den Gliedern vertreten
wird –, sondern die *Begierde*: ἡδονή (V. 1.3) und ἐπιθυμεῖν (V. 2) sowie ἐπιποθεῖν
(V. 5). Damit ist Begierde auch der Schlüsselbegriff für den schwierigen Vers 5.
ἐπιθυμία hat Jakobus bereits in 1,14.15 als Ursache von Sünde und Tod genannt.
An diesem Punkt befindet er sich im Zusammenhang der paulinischen und nachpaulinischen Briefliteratur, in der ἐπιθυμία[1563] stets negativ verwendet wird, häufig
im Zusammenhang mit σάρξ.[1564] Jakobus kann diese Verbindung hier als bekannt
voraussetzen. Um welche Begierden es geht, bleibt ungesagt.[1565] Als anthropologi-

---

[1558] Hap. leg. in Jak. BAUER / ALAND, 1374 (im NT nur hier übertragen gebraucht).

[1559] Hap. leg. in Jak. BAUER / ALAND, 1006: in der frühchristlichen Lit. nur im Plural und nur übertragen
(2Kor 7,5; 2Tim 2,23; Tit 3,9). Verb ebenfalls hap. leg. in Jak, im NT noch dreimal.

[1560] Hap. leg. in Jak, vgl. Tit 3,3; 2Petr 2,13. Vgl. G. STÄHLIN, Art. ἡδονή, ThWNT 2, 1935, 911–928.

[1561] Hap. leg. in Jak, vgl. 1Petr 2,11 (zusammen mit ἐπιθυμίαι). Vgl. O. BAUERNFEIND, Art. στρατεύομαι
κτλ., ThWNT 7, 1964, 701–713. B. betont den Aspekt des Aufmarschierens. Weitere Präzisionen verbieten
sich angesichts der wenigen Belege (gegen METZNER, Jak, 216).

[1562] Im NT ein typisch paulinischer Vorzugsbegriff (Röm 6;12; 1Kor 12).

[1563] Vgl. F. BÜCHSEL, Art. θυμός κτλ., ThWNT 3, 1938, 167–173.

[1564] Z. B. Gal 5,16.

[1565] Vgl. z. B. die Konkretionen, die 4Makk 1,25–27 aufzählt: »Prahlerei, Ehrgeiz, Geldgier, Streitsucht und

scher Hintergrundtext bietet sich nochmals Röm 7,14–25[1566] an: die Konstellation von Leib und Gliedern und dem Kampf zwischen »innerem Menschen« und »der Sünde in den Gliedern«. Jakobus übernimmt aber nicht die anthropologische Perspektive des Paulus. σῶμα fehlt in Jak 4, auch sonst spielt der Begriff bei Jakobus keine Rolle. σῶμα bezeichnet einfach den physischen Körper.[1567] Auch πνεῦμα wird in V. 5 nicht im paulinischen Sinn gebraucht, sondern ebenso wie σῶμα rein physisch als Lebenskraft verstanden. Die paulinische Rechtfertigungsperspektive, die im Hintergrund von Römer 7 steht, fehlt hier gänzlich. Jakobus reduziert den paulinischen Diskurs rigoros auf die ethische Sünde (V. 8) der Zwistigkeiten, als deren Ursache er die Begierden ausmacht, ohne dies weiter zu konkretisieren. Stattdessen führt Jakobus in V. 2.3 das Bild des *Kampfes* mit rhetorischen Mitteln weiter aus. Da er das Bild nicht verlässt, bleibt die Anwendung auf reale Gemeindesituationen unklar. Es geht hier nicht um Anwendung auf σχίσματα wie beispielsweise in 1Kor 1–4, sondern um den Verweis auf einen allgemein-antiken Ethikdiskurs, in dem Streit auf Begierden oder Lüste zurückgeführt wird.[1568]

Der Einsatz der stilistischen Mittel ist erheblich. Jakobus veranschaulicht den Prozess des Streites in einer Kette asyndetisch gereihter verbaler Aussagen – zwei dieser Aussagen paarweise angeordnet – über die Adressaten in der 2.Pers.Pl.[1569] Sechs Verben des Strebens: ἐπιθυμεῖτε, φονεύετε καὶ ζηλοῦτε, μάχεσθε καὶ πολεμεῖτε, αἰτεῖτε stehen vier verbale Wendungen des Nicht-Gewinnens gegenüber: οὐκ ἔχετε, οὐ δύνασθε ἐπιτυχεῖν, οὐκ ἔχετε (mit Erweiterung), οὐ λαμβάνετε. Die Aussagen sind einander in vier antithetisch strukturierten Paaren in der Weise zugeordnet, dass auf das vordere Glied »Ihr tut x« stets folgt: (aber) »Ihr erzielt nicht das Resultat y«. Jakobus nimmt Erweiterungen, Variationen und Wiederaufnahmen innerhalb diese Schemas vor: Zweimal verdoppelt er das Verb, zweimal fügt er ähnlich formulierte Begründungen hinzu, am Ende von V. 3 folgt noch eine finale Bestimmung. Die Vergeblichkeit der Bestrebungen wird durch viermal gesetztes »nicht(s)« ausgedrückt. Folgende Verhaltens- bzw. Ergehensformen stehen einander gegenüber:

Begehren	nicht erlangen
Töten und eifern	nicht erreichen können (erweitertes Verb)
Kämpfen und streiten	nicht haben (plus Begründung)
Bitten	nicht empfangen (plus Begründung und Angabe der Absicht).[1570]

Missgunst« sowie »Allesfresserei, Schlemmerei und Allein-Essen«. Vgl. METZNER, Jak, 215 Anm. 26.

[1566] Mit DIBELIUS, Jak, 259.

[1567] 2,16.26; 3,2.3.6.

[1568] Vgl. die ausführliche Dokumentation bei DIBELIUS, Jak, 258–260.

[1569] Hag 1,6 könnte als Vorbild gedient haben: ἐσπείρατε πολλὰ καὶ εἰσηνέγκατε ὀλίγα, ἐφάγετε καὶ οὐκ εἰς πλησμονήν, ἐπίετε καὶ οὐκ εἰς μέθην, περιεβάλεσθε καὶ οὐκ ἐθερμάνθητε ἐν αὐτοῖς (Ihr sät viel und bringt wenig ein; ihr esst und werdet doch nicht satt; ihr trinkt und bleibt doch durstig; ihr kleidet euch und könnt euch doch nicht erwärmen).

[1570] Vgl. die Darstellung bei DIBELIUS, Jak, 261.

Die Verben ἐπιθυμεῖν, ἐπιποθεῖν, φονεύειν, ζηλοῦν, ἐπιτυγχάνειν, μάχεσθαι, πολεμεῖν, αἰτεῖν, λαμβάνειν, δαπανεῖν gehören unterschiedlichen Bildkreisen an. Den *ersten* Kreis bilden die Begierde als Grundlage von Streit und ihre Erscheinungsformen. Dabei bemüht sich Jakobus um gewählte Sprache und benutzt Verben, die sonst weder von ihm noch anderswo in den frühchristlichen Schriften häufiger verwendet werden. ἐπιθυμεῖν[1571] ohne Akkusativobjekt wird von Paulus in Röm 7,7 und 13,9 (!) als Quintessenz der zehn Gebote gesetzt. Dazu passt das Verb φονεύειν[1572], das Jakobus bereits in 2,11 im Zusammenhang mit Ex 20,13 f genannt hat. ζηλοῦν[1573]: Jakobus hat schon in 3,14 auf den Zusammenhang von Streit und »bitterem« Neid, Rivalität, destruktivem Wettstreit (εἰ δὲ ζῆλον πικρὸν ἔχετε καὶ ἐριθείαν) hingewiesen. μάχεσθαι[1574] und πολεμεῖν[1575] sind verbale Variationen zu V. 1.

Der *zweite* Bildkreis umfasst Verben des Bittens und Empfangens: αἰτεῖν[1576], ἐπιτυγχάνειν[1577], λαμβάνειν[1578] und δαπανεῖν.[1579] Die Relation von »bitten und empfangen« wird mit gebräuchlichen Verben bezeichnet. Es handelt sich um ein bekanntes frühchristliches Thema, das bereits in 1,5–7 von Jakobus angesprochen wurde.[1580] αἰτεῖσθαι ist dabei entscheidend[1581]: Jakobus wirft den gedachten Adressaten zunächst vor, nicht zu bitten und daher nicht zu empfangen. Da diese Konstellation aber 1,5 nicht entsprechen würde, präzisiert er: Sie bitten *falsch*, nämlich mit der Absicht, das Erbetene zu vergeuden. Das entspricht der Einschränkung in 1,6 f: Dort empfängt der Zweifler nichts trotz seiner Bitte. Beide Male wendet sich Jakobus gegen einen formalen Automatismus von Bitte und Empfang. Die beiden Verben ἐπιτυγχάνειν und δαπανεῖν sind ähnlich selten wie die Verben des ersten Bildkreises und belegen den sprachlichen Anspruch, mit dem Jakobus formuliert. Die gesamte Verbalreihe spiegelt vor allem das rhetorische Können des Verfassers. Interpretierende Konkretionen verbieten sich. Allison bezieht den Text auf die Reichen[1582], während Windisch und Burchard an die Unterschichten denken.[1583] Metzner bezieht die Adressatenschelte auf »rivalisierende Lehrer«.[1584] Die

---

[1571] Hap. leg. in Jak, aber 1,14 f Substantiv.

[1572] Jak 2,11 (zweimal); 4,2; 5,6.

[1573] Hap. leg. in Jak, aber 3,14.16 Substantiv.

[1574] Hap. leg. in Jak, selten im NT.

[1575] Hap. leg. in Jak, im NT noch sechsmal in Apk.

[1576] Häufig im NT. Vgl. Jak 1,5.6.

[1577] Hap. leg. in Jak, selten im NT (öfter τυγχάνειν).

[1578] Eines der häufigsten Verben im NT. Vgl. Jak 1,7.12; 3,1; 5,7.10.

[1579] Hap. leg. in Jak, selten im NT. Die neutrale Bedeutung »ausgeben, aufwenden« (BAUER / ALAND, 341) wird hier durch die Zweckbestimmung »um es in euren Begierden auszugeben« zum Negativen hin verändert (etwa: verschwenden).

[1580] Siehe dort zur synoptischen Tradition (Mt 7,7–11par). Die Relation bitten – empfangen ist auch in der johanneischen Tradition bekannt: Joh 16,23 f und 1Joh 3,22 u. ö.

[1581] Dreimal in der Verbalreihe.

[1582] ALLISON, Jak, 607.

[1583] BURCHARD, Jak, 169.

[1584] METZNER, Jak, 220. Damit beachtet er zwar den Kontext, bleibt aber hinter seinen eigenen Überlegun-

Bußpredigt in 4,1–12 ist aber gerade dadurch gekennzeichnet, dass sie im Gegensatz zu 4,13–17 und 5,1–6 keine konkreten Adressaten und keine konkreten Verfehlungen im Blick hat. Es geht vielmehr um die klassische Anklage gegen die Begierde (ἐπιθυμία) und ihre Erscheinungsformen: Zwietracht, Sünde (ἁμαρτία, siehe 4,8) und Tod (θάνατος, siehe 4,2), wie Jakobus in 1,14 f dargestellt hat. Jakobus verzichtet auf die fundamentalanthropologische Grundlegung, die Paulus in Röm 7 gegeben hat. Für Jakobus sind ἐπιθυμία und ἡδοναί einfach grundlegende Sünden, die sündige Verhaltensformen nach sich ziehen.

V. 4 So liegt der Fluchtpunkt der Verbalkette auch in dem ganz allgemeinen Vorwurf in V. 4, in dem den »Ehebrecherinnen« Freundschaft mit dem κόσμος vorgeworfen wird, da diese gleichzeitig Gottesfeindschaft ist. Erst in diesem Satz werden die Adressaten direkt angesprochen, und zwar mit einer aggressiven Frage, die eine beleidigende Metapher aus dem Soziolekt der Jesusüberlieferung enthält, die ihrerseits die aggressive Metaphorik der Propheten Israels aufgreift. In der brieflichen Kommunikation des Paulus, die seinen real existierenden Gemeinden gilt, hat diese Form der aggressiven moralischen Verurteilung keinen Platz.[1585] V. 4 macht deutlich, dass es sich anders als in den Paulusbriefen im Jakobusbrief um *literarische* Polemik handelt, die mit stereotypen Vorwürfen arbeitet. Reale Gemeinden sind nicht im Blick. μοιχαλίς, in der Septuaginta zweimal im eigentlichen, viermal im metaphorischen Sinn verwendet[1586], begegnet in der synoptischen Tradition dreimal im metaphorischen Sinn in der allgemeinen Wendung »das böse und ehebrecherische Geschlecht« (Mk 8,38 und Mt 12,39; 16,4: das Zeichen des Jona). Jak 4,4 steht in dieser Tradition, deren bildliche Dimension sich aus der »Vorstellung vom Ehebund Gottes mit Israel, der durch Untreue der Glaubenden … gebrochen wird«, herleitet.[1587] Rainer Metzner kommentiert: »Die Anklage ist prophetisch«. Er weist auf den Dekalogbezug von 4,2.4 hin (töten, ehebrechen), der die Schwere der Anklage unterstreicht. Mit dem Bild der »Ehebrecherin« transformiert Jakobus allerdings das Laster des Ehebruchs[1588] ins Metaphorische und verwendet einen Vorwurf, den Jesus in seiner Scheltrede gegenüber seiner Generation, die Johannes den Täufer ablehnte, benutzt.[1589]

Die schimpfliche Anrede »Ehebrecherinnen« zieht ein erstes Fazit aus der Kette der Angriffe in V. 1–3. Wie in V. 1 wird die Anklage zunächst in V. 4a in Form einer rhetorischen Frage formuliert, deren Aussage dann in V. 4b in einem Ur-

---

gen von S. 215 zur Allgemeinheit antiker Charakterisierung von Begierde(n) und Lüsten zurück.

[1585] Vgl. aber die aggressive moralische Polemik in Röm 1,18–32: sie gilt »Heiden«.

[1586] Spr 18,22LXX und 24,55 (30,20)LXX im wörtlichen Sinn: Ehebrecherin. Übertragen: Ez 16,38; 23,45LXX; Hos 3,1; Mal 3,5. Im NT im eigentlichen Sinn: Röm 7,3 und 2Petr 2,14. Die Handschriften 01C2 und andere Handschriften missverstehen den Text im wörtlichen Sinn und »verbessern« »Ehebrecherinnen« in »Ehebrecher und Ehebrecherinnen« – ein unerwarteter »Modernismus«! (s. Textkritik).

[1587] METZNER, Jak, 221. Ebenso ALLISON, Jak, 607. Allison weist besonders auf Hos 3,1 hin.

[1588] Jak 2,11 im Zusammenhang der Dekaloggebote (vgl. Mk 10,19par und Röm 13,9).

[1589] Vgl. LUZ, Mt I / 2, 276 f zu Mt 12,38–42 mit Hinweis auf Mt 11,16 (LUZ, 187 f).

C. Briefcorpus

teilsatz (wer x tut, ist y) wiederholt wird. Der Urteilssatz wiederholt variierend die Leitbegriffe der Frage: Freundschaft, Feindschaft. V. 4a ist abstrakt und formuliert einen religiösen Grundsatz, der auf dem antithetischen Denken beruht, wie es sich im antiken Judentum und im entstehenden Christentum gleichermaßen findet. V. 4b konkretisiert dieselbe Anklage, indem sie auf Personen bezogen wird (»wer«, »wenn jemand«, φίλος[1590], ἐχθρός[1591]). Die Anklage hat zwei Seiten, die ein bekanntes antithetisches Paar bilden: Freundschaft (φιλία) und Feindschaft (ἔχθρα), Welt (κόσμος)[1592] und Gott.[1593] »Freundschaft[1594] mit der Welt« ist eine singuläre Wendung im Neuen Testament[1595], während »Feindschaft gegen Gott« – wieder ein Begriff aus der Sprache von Kampf und Streit – auch in Röm 8,7 begegnet.[1596] κόσμος ist hier genauso negativ verwendet wie in 1,27.[1597] Die Opposition »Welt – Gott«[1598] ist Ausdruck des Pessimismus des Autors.[1599] Zu der sprachlich sorgfältig gearbeiteten Formulierung von V. 4a bemerkt Allison:

> James' nicely balanced, memorable aphorism is evidently his invention.[1600]

V. 5–6a Es folgt eine weitere vorwurfsvolle rhetorische Frage, an die sich zwei Schriftzitate anschließen, die die Warnung vor Streit und seinen Ursachen nachdrücklich unterstützen und das Thema, das den Verfasser so stark beschäftigt, zum Abschluss bringen. Vers 5b (bzw. Verse 5b.6a) gilt in der Geschichte der Exegese als einer der schwierigsten nicht nur im Jakobusbrief (wie 2,18; 3,6), sondern im Neuen Testament.[1601] Dies Urteil scheint aber überzogen: In den Text ist zu viel an Problematik gelegt worden.[1602] Zunächst einmal ist die vieldiskutierte textliche Überlieferung nicht der Grund für die Schwierigkeiten. Konjekturen sind überflüssig. Burchard schreibt zurecht zur Frage der Textkritik: »Der Text steht wohl fest«.[1603] Schwierigkeiten liegen einerseits in dem unbekannten Schriftzitat, andererseits in

---

[1590] Vgl. Abraham als Freund Gottes 2,23.

[1591] Hap. leg. in Jak.

[1592] φιλία τοῦ κόσμου: Gen. obj. (ebenso ἔχθρα τοῦ θεοῦ).

[1593] BURCHARD, Jak, 170: Belege zur oppositionellen Verwendung.

[1594] φιλία hap. leg. im NT.

[1595] Siehe aber 1Joh 2,15–17: Liebe zum κόσμος mit dem Verb ἀγαπᾶν bezeichnet. Vgl. auch 2Tim 4,10.

[1596] Hap. leg. in Jak. In Röm 8 mit εἰς statt mit Gen. ἔχθρα noch Gal 5,20 im Zusammenhang eines Lasterkatalogs. In Eph 2,14.16 in übertragenem Zusammenhang.

[1597] 2,5: neutral; 3,6: negativ in einem Bild.

[1598] ALLISON, Jak, 588, stellt die Texteinheit 4,1–12 unter die Überschrift: »Friendship with the world versus friendship with God«.

[1599] ALLISON, Jak, 609. Allison verweist auf die jüdische apokalyptischen Literatur.

[1600] ALLISON, Jak, 608.

[1601] ALLISON, Jak, 611: »This is one of the most challenging lines in early Christian literature. It is of uncertain sense and uncertain source«.

[1602] Hier wie auch in 2,18 und 3,6 kann exegetischer Ballast (im Sinne des immer wieder Zitierens bekannter Positionen) abgeworfen werden.

[1603] BURCHARD, Jak, 171.

der grammatischen und semantischen Interpretation von 5b.[1604] Außerdem ist das Ende des ersten Zitats unklar. Nach der Interpunktion der ECM reicht das Zitat bis V. 6a, so dass auch V. 6a als Frage zu lesen ist. Dem schließt sich dieser Kommentar an.[1605] V. 5b.6a werden hier als Einheit behandelt.

Die Interpretationen gehen weit auseinander.[1606] Statt die Fragen und unterschiedlichen Antworten noch einmal im Detail aufzulisten, ist es sinnvoller, zunächst den Gesamtzusammenhang von 4,1–12 zu skizzieren, der die interpretatorischen Rahmenbedingungen setzt.[1607] Außerdem muss die manieristische Ausdrucksweise berücksichtigt werden, die Jakobus hier wie schon oft sucht – oder aus einer unbekannten Schrift übernommen hat – und die von den Exegeten häufig inhaltlich überinterpretiert wurde. Auffallend sind die drei hapax legomena in V. 5b (φθόνος, ἐπιποθεῖν, κατοικίζειν). Hinzu kommt viertens χάρις in V. 6a.[1608] Die ältere Exegese vermutet in V. 5b einen unreinen Hexameter.[1609] Diese Eigenarten können entweder auf Jakobus zurückgehen oder aber Bestandteil des unbekannten Zitats sein.

Zunächst sind folgende *Koordinaten* des Gesamtzusammenhanges deutlich: Jakobus tadelt heftig die *Streitigkeiten* »zwischen euch« (V. 1), die aus den »Lüsten, die in den Gliedern streiten«, stammen und die er als ständiges *Begehren* qualifiziert. Für Jakobus führt ständiges Begehren und Verlangen – aus seiner Sicht kurz als die »Liebe zum κόσμος« bezeichnet – zu innerer Unrast, ständigem Streben nach Lust und damit zu Streit. Jakobus versucht, das Phänomen des unersättlichen Haben-Wollens als Ursache ständigen Streites zu beschreiben. Dabei bleibt er sehr unscharf. Sein Interesse ist nicht die anthropologische oder psychologische Analyse, sondern der *Tadel*, der dem falschen Haben-Wollen gilt. Dies Wollen erhält nichts. Den Gegenwert bildet die *Gabe* Gottes, hier in V. 6 als χάρις ausgedrückt, bereits in 1,17 als δόσις und δώρημα thematisiert. Die Gabe Gottes empfangen die Demütigen, nicht die Streitenden, die nur haben wollen. Schon in Kapitel 1,9.10 hat

---

[1604] METZNER, Jak, 223–227, gibt eine klare Definition der Probleme von V. 5b: Wo beginnt das Schriftzitat? Wo endet es? Was bedeuten φθόνος und πνεῦμα, und worauf sind die Substantive zu beziehen? Welche Subjekte sind für ἐπιποθεῖ und κατῴκισεν anzunehmen? Schließlich: welche Schriftstelle zitiert Jakobus?

[1605] Die Kommentare von Mayor, Windisch, Johnson, Burchard und Metzner ignorieren das Fragezeichen in V. 6. ALLISON, Jak, hält sich in seiner Übersetzung an das Fragezeichen (588), ist aber bei der Versexegese eher unentschieden (622). Er weist aber darauf hin, dass das Thema »Gnade« gut zu »Eldad und Modad« passt.

[1606] Vollständige Übersicht über die Interpretationsvorschläge bei ALLISON, Jak, 610–622. Für die Interpretation des Verses sei insgesamt auf die umfangreiche Dokumentation bei Allison hingewiesen. Allison verzeichnet drei Vorschläge für »der Geist, der in euch / uns wohnt«, sowie 19 verschiedene Interpretationen des Sinnes von V. 5b im Ganzen! Zur Frage der Herleitung des Schriftzitates bietet Allison 12 unterschiedliche Lösungen. Seine eigene Option unterstützt er dann mit 15 Argumenten!

[1607] Anders BURCHARD, Jak, 171: »Der Kontext hilft leider nicht entscheidend.«

[1608] Im Jakobusbrief nur hier zweimal im Zitat.

[1609] WINDISCH, Die Katholischen Briefe, 27. Windisch folgert: »Ist das nicht zufällig, dann ist die γραφή ein jüdisch-hellenistisches Lehrgedicht gewesen«.

C. Briefcorpus 295

Jakobus den *Demütigen* als Vorbild für die Brüder bezeichnet und die *Begierde* als Quelle der Sünde definiert (V. 14.15). Die Demütigen empfangen die Gnade bzw. Gabe. Sie müssen nicht dafür kämpfen.

In diesen Interpretationsrahmen des *Vorwurfs* sollen 4,5.6a eingezeichnet werden. V. 5 wird mit der vierten rhetorischen Frage dieses Kapitels eröffnet. Dabei spielt der Verfasser im Modus des Vorwurfs auf das Wissen der Adressaten an, das sie vernachlässigen, und knüpft mit »oder« an das »Wisst ihr nicht?« von V. 4 an: »Oder meint ihr etwa, dass die Schrift umsonst sagt …?« κενός, »leer, nutzlos« ist ein paulinisches Vorzugswort[1610], während das Adverb κενῶς [1611] sonst nicht in den neutestamentlichen Schriften begegnet. Bereits in Jak 2,20 wird das Adjektiv in der tadelnden Anrede »du leerer Mensch« gesetzt. Die Wendung »die Schrift sagt« ist ebenfalls eine paulinische Vorzugswendung. Jakobus hat sie schon in 2,23 benutzt.[1612] Auf die Einleitungsformel folgt jeweils das Schriftzitat.[1613] Das Zitat beginnt in V. 5b und reicht bis V. 6a:

πρὸς φθόνον ἐπιποθεῖ τὸ πνεῦμα ὃ κατῴκισεν ἐν ἡμῖν, μείζονα δὲ δίδωσιν χάριν.
Nach Neid strebt der Geist, den er in uns hat wohnen lassen. Er gibt aber größere Gnade.[1614]

Das Zitat muss im Zusammenhang der Rhetorik des *Vorwurfs* interpretiert werden. »Die Schrift sagt *tadelnd*«, ist zu ergänzen. Die Voranstellung des Adverbs verstärkt den *Vorwurf*, den Jakobus den Adressaten macht. Dieselbe Figur des Hyperbatons gilt für die präpositionale Wendung πρὸς φθόνον. Das Zitat selbst findet sich – wie auch andere neutestamentliche »Zitate unbekannter Herkunft«[1615] – nicht in der uns überlieferten Literatur. Zwei Fragen sind zu klären: erstens die Frage nach der Bedeutung des Satzes, zweitens die Frage nach seiner Herleitung.

(1) Zur *Bedeutung*: im Zusammenhang der Rahmenthematik von Streit und Begierden ist der zweigliedrige Satz als negatives ethisches Statement zu verstehen, dem der Hinweis auf Gottes gute Gabe folgt. Beide Sätze sind durch das steigernde

---

[1610] 1Kor 15,10.14.58 und öfter.

[1611] BAUER / ALAND, 871: »hohl, leer, grundlos, umsonst«.

[1612] Mit Zitat von Gen 15,16. Häufiger in Röm; Gal 4,30; 1Tim 5,18. Mit εἶπεν ἡ γραφή in Joh 7,38 (vgl. 7,42; 19,37).

[1613] Die zahlreichen Spekulationen über den Beginn des Zitats sind überflüssig, siehe BURCHARD, Jak, 172, sowie METZNER, Jak, 224.

[1614] In der Rekonstruktion des Zusammenhanges und damit auch in der Übersetzung und der inhaltlichen Interpretation von V. 5b stimmen Burchard und Metzner im Gegensatz zu DIBELIUS, Jak, 264–268, überein: »Zum Neid hin strebt der Geist, den er in uns hat wohnen lassen«, d. h. die Menschen sind neidisch. Anders als Allison und als in diesem Kommentar vorgeschlagen beziehen beide Exegeten aber V. 6a nicht in das Zitat ein.

[1615] METZNER, Jak, 226 mit Anm. 128. Metzner nennt: Mt 2,23; Joh 7,38; 1Kor 2,9; 9,10; 2Kor 4,6 (? nicht klar als Schriftzitat eingeleitet); Eph 5,14 (? nicht klar als Schriftzitat eingeleitet); 1Tim 5,18; 1Clem 46,2; 2Clem 11,2.

μείζονα[1616] und die Partikel δέ verbunden.[1617] Der längere, stilistisch anspruchsvolle *Vordersatz* tadelt das neidische Streben des menschlichen Geistes. Das πνεῦμα ist der innere Geist oder die innere Disposition des Menschen. Jakobus selbst hat keine pneumatologische oder anthropologische πνεῦμα-Konzeption.[1618] Dementsprechend wählt er auch ein Zitat, in dem πνεῦμα nicht den Geist Gottes, sondern den Lebensgeist oder das Streben des Menschen bezeichnet, der »in uns«, d. h. in den Menschen »wohnt«. Dieser Lebensgeist, das innere Streben des Menschen, ist auf φθόνος, Neid, gerichtet.[1619] φθόνος gehört in das Vokabular der Lasterkataloge und ist eindeutig negativ konnotiert.[1620] In V. 2.3 wurden bereits ἐπιθυμεῖν und ζηλοῦν angesprochen. Damit drückt der erste Satz des Zitates genau das aus, was Jakobus seit 4,1 kritisiert: den Geist der streitenden und begehrenden *competition*, der am Ende zu Krieg, Mord und Zerstörung führt. πρὸς φθόνον wird von BAUER / ALAND als adverbiale Wendung attributiv mit »eifersüchtig« übersetzt.[1621] Das ist sprachlich möglich, aber nicht nötig. Bei dieser Auflösung würde die Zielangabe, das Streben, das im Verb ἐπιποθεῖ[1622] begegnet und durch πρός verstärkt wird, wegfallen. Das Verb κατῴκισεν[1623], (er hat eine Wohnung angewiesen) hat Gott zum Subjekt (V. 4: »Feind *Gottes*«, V. 6b im Zitat Gott als nachgestelltes Subjekt für V. 5b.6a). Die Quintessenz des Zitates ist: Gott hat den Menschen den Lebensgeist gegeben, aber sie nutzen ihn gegen Gott (V. 4). Ihr Geist strebt in die falsche Richtung: hin zu Neid und damit zu jenem Streit, den Jakobus bekämpft. Ganz einfach gesagt: Die Menschen sind neidgetrieben. Der einfache kurze *Nachsatz* eröffnet demgegenüber (δέ) Hoffnung[1624]: Gott »aber gibt größere Gnade«.[1625] Das Zitat ist also nach der traditionellen Antithetik: »Gottes Gabe im Gegensatz zum menschlichen Verhalten« strukturiert.

[1616] Vgl. in Jak 3,1.

[1617] Daher ist eine Trennung zwischen V. 5b und 6a unwahrscheinlich. V. 5b / 6a lassen sich grammatisch und inhaltlich eher als Einheit verstehen, d. h. als Zitat, das der Verfasser als anklagende Frage einsetzt.

[1618] πνεῦμα in Jak nur 2,26 als »Lebensprinzip« im Gegensatz zum unbelebten Körper. Hier ähnlich gebraucht. Es geht nicht um den Geist Gottes oder das πνεῦμα ἅγιον, das Gott den Menschen gibt. Sehr klar BURCHARD, Jak, 174: πνεῦμα ist hier »etwas Anerschaffenes …, [bezeichnet] aber kaum den bösen Trieb … prophetische Inspiration … oder einen Dämon«. Das ist gegen die Interpretation von Dibelius gerichtet.

[1619] Hap. leg. in Jak.

[1620] Materialien bei BURCHARD, Jak, 173, und SPICQ, NLNT II, 919–921. Kein Septuaginta-Vorzugswort. LXX: SapSal 2,24; 6,23; 1Makk 8,16; 3Makk 6,7. – Exegetische Vorschläge, φθόνος im Sinne von ζῆλος, »Eifer Gottes« zu übersetzen und *positiv* zu konnotieren, sind unbegründet. In 4,2 ist ζηλοῦν negativ konnotiert.

[1621] BAUER / ALAND, 1423.

[1622] ἐπιποθεῖν hap. leg. in Jak. Paulinisches Vorzugswort.

[1623] Hap. leg. im NT. Vgl. Herm mand III 1: »damit der Geist, den Gott in diesem Fleischesleib hat wohnen lassen (κατοικίζειν), bei allen Menschen als wahrhaftig erwiesen werde« (Übers: LINDEMANN / PAULSEN, Die Apostolischen Väter, 379). DIBELIUS, Jak, 266–268, nimmt das Hermas-Zitat als Ausgangspunkt seiner Erklärung.

[1624] BURCHARD, Jak, 174: »Es gibt aber noch Hoffnung«.

[1625] METZNER, Jak, 227 f, zieht V. 6a nicht zum Zitat und sucht nach einer anderen Interpretation. Er liest μείζονα als Objekt und χάριν als Ergänzung: »Größeres aber gibt er, nämlich Gnade«. Das lässt sich nicht plausibel machen.

(2) Zur *Herleitung* des Zitats: zunächst ist noch einmal festzuhalten, dass es sich, wenn man die Einleitungsformeln betrachtet, in V. 5b.6a und V. 6b deutlich um *zwei* unterschiedliche Zitate handelt.[1626] Während die hapax legomena und der mögliche Hexameter[1627] für V. 5b in die Richtung einer eigenen Formulierung des Jakobus weisen könnten, mit der er auf einen – uns unbekannten – Text *anspielt*, macht die Einführungsformel ein *Zitat*, d. h. eine wörtliche Wiedergabe, doch wahrscheinlich. In 4,5.6 verbindet Jakobus also zwei Zitate, deren erstes einer unbekannten Quelle entstammt, während das zweite aus dem Sprüchebuch öfter in den Schriften des frühen Christentums erscheint. Zitate aus uns nicht überlieferten Schriften finden sich mehrfach im Neuen Testament.[1628] Jakobus mag das Zitat wegen seiner prätentiösen Formulierung, die seinem eigenen Stil entgegen kommt, und wegen seiner antithetischen Struktur gewählt haben. Ein Referenztext findet sich nicht. Nun ist es für die Texterklärung auch nicht nötig, die komplizierte Suche nach einem verlorenen Referenztext zu dokumentieren und fortzusetzen.[1629] Der Sinn von V. 5b.6a lässt sich nicht aus einem verloren gegangenen Werk erschließen, über das wir nichts wissen. Allerdings hätte die Suche durchaus für die Rekonstruktion der *Bibliothek* des Jakobus Bedeutung.[1630] Daher wird sie hier in aller Kürze dargestellt.

Es ist sinnvoll, die Dokumentation der Rekonstruktionsversuche auf Spitta und Allison zu konzentrieren. Friedrich Spitta[1631] hat an die im Hirten des Hermas erwähnte Schrift »Eldad und Modad«[1632] gedacht und als Hintergrund für Jak 4,5 und für beide Zitate in V. 5.6 Num 11,25–29 namhaft gemacht: Eldad und Modad wird ihr Geistbesitz geneidet, sie aber bleiben demütig. Spitta verweist auf die Ausgestaltung der Episode aus Numeri in der späteren jüdischen Literatur, der das Buch »Eldad und Modad« entstammt, das im Hirten des Hermas zitiert wird.[1633] Die Basis findet er in Num 11,29:

[1626] Beide Male mit λέγει eingeleitet. Vgl. auch weitere Argumente für ein Zitat bei Burchard, Jak, 172: hapax legomena (nicht stichhaltig, da Jakobus selbst hapax legomena liebt), möglicherweise Hexameter (nicht stichhaltig: siehe 1,17), ὅτι fehlt am Anfang vor πρός. Anders Johnson, Jak, 280–282. Johnson versteht V. 5a allgemein: »Meint ihr, dass die Schrift nutzlos spricht / nichts bedeutet?« V. 5b nimmt er dementsprechend nicht als Zitat, sondern als weitere rhetorische Frage: »Ist dies der Weg, auf den das Trachten des menschlichen Geistes gerichtet sein soll, der Neid?« (282).

[1627] Windisch, Die Katholischen Briefe, 27: πρὸς φθόνον ἐπιποθεῖ τὸ πνεῦμ᾽ κατῴκισ᾽ ἐν ἡμῖν.

[1628] Mt 2,23; Joh 7,38; 1Kor 2,9; 9,10; 2Kor 4,6; Eph 5,14; 1Tim 5,18; 1Clem 23,3 f; 2Clem 1,2–4.

[1629] Burchard, Jak, 173, verzichtet auf Vorschläge. Metzner, Jak, 226 f, bleibt vage und schließt auch eine Eigenformulierung des Verfassers nicht aus.

[1630] Vgl. Wischmeyer, Scriptual Classicism, 292–303.

[1631] F. Spitta, Zur Geschichte und Literatur des Urchristentums. 2. Band, Der Brief des Jakobus, 1–239; Studien zum Hirten des Hermas, 241–437. 120–123 entwickelt Spitta seine Interpretation. Vgl. auch R. J. Bauckham, The Spirit of God in Us Loathes Envy. James 4:5, in: G. N. Stanton / B. W. Longenecker / S. C. Barton (Hg.), The Holy Spirit and Christian Origins. Essays in Honor of James D. G. Dunn, Grand Rapids 2004, 270–281.

[1632] In Herm vis II 3.4 erwähnt.

[1633] Vgl. zu der Schrift Eldad und Modad auch Allison, Jak, 617 Anm. 171, weiter D. C. Allison, Eldad and Modad, JSPE 21, 2011, 99–131. Allison, Jak, 617, bezieht sich auf Spitta und Bauckham: »This writer

Μὴ ζηλοῖς σύ μοι; καὶ τίς δῴη πάντα τὸν λαὸν κυρίου προφήτας, ὅταν δῷ κύριος τὸ πνεῦμα αὐτοῦ ἐπ᾽ αὐτούς.

Eiferst [bist du neidisch] du um meinetwillen? Wollte Gott, dass alle im Volk des Herrn Propheten wären und der Herr seinen Geist über sie kommen ließe!

Hier sind die Merkmale von Vorwurf, Geist und Neid auf den Geistbesitz mit der Demut der beiden Protagonisten verbunden. Dale Allison folgt Spitta[1634] und sucht, ihn zu präzisieren: Das Jakobus-Zitat müsse im Buch »Eldad und Modad« Teil der Antwort des Moses an Josua gewesen sein, der gegen die Prophezeiungsgabe von Eldad und Modad protestierte. Allison weist darauf hin, dass auch das zweite Zitat aus V. 6 mit dem Motiv der Demut in diesen Zusammenhang passt. Außerdem verweist Allison nochmals auf die Nähe zum Hirten des Hermas[1635], der wiederum der einzige Zeuge für das Buch »Eldad und Modad« ist. Drei Einwände können gegen diese These erhoben werden: (1) Nach Allison ist πνεῦμα als Gottes Geist zu verstehen, während die in diesem Kommentar vorgelegte Exegese deutlich auf den »Lebensgeist« der Menschen verweist. Vom Geist Gottes ist im Jakobusbrief nirgends die Rede. Sollte der Verfasser ein Zitat benutzt haben, das gerade dies ihm fremde Thema behandelt? Es ist nicht auszuschließen, aber sehr unwahrscheinlich, dass Jakobus πνεῦμα in diesem Sinne verstanden hat. (2) Es geht im Kontext um den Streit im Sinne von Uneinigkeit christlicher Lehrer, der durch Begierde und falsches Streben ausgelöst wird, nicht um Streit im Sinne des *contest* von Geistesgaben wie in 1Kor 12–14, der Hochmut und »Rühmen« erzeugt. Der 1.Korintherbrief ist thematisch deutlich näher an Num 11 als Jak 4,5. (3) Der zweite Teil des Zitats lässt sich in dem von Allison vorgeschlagenen Rahmen nur teilweise plausibel machen: Worauf soll sich »in uns« bezogen haben? Es wäre (gegen Allison) allerdings möglich, dass das Zitat nur den ersten Teil von V. 5b umfasst und der 2. Teil die Applikation des Verfassers auf die Adressaten (»in uns«) ist.[1636] Der Verfasser hätte dann den ganzen Satz in Anlehnung an einen Hexameter gestaltet. Unklar bliebe bei dieser Interpretation die Stellung von V. 6a. Fazit: der Verweis auf das literarische Milieu des Hirten des Hermas und seiner Referenztexte – und damit des Buches Eldad und Modad – als Quelle des unbekannten Zitats und als Teil der virtuellen Bibliothek des Jakobus ist verlockend, konnte aber von Allison

---

shares the view of Spitta and Bauckham«. Allgemein: A.-M. DENIS, Introduction à la littérature religieuse judéo-hellénistique, 2 Bd., Turnhout 2000, 482–485; SIEGERT, Einleitung, 296.

1634 Spittas Übersetzung von V. 5b unterscheidet sich von Allison und wird hier nicht erörtert.

1635 Vgl. die hilfreiche Dokumentation bei METZNER, Jak, 18–20. Das mögliche Zitat aus 4,5 fehlt dort. Grundlegend bleibt das Urteil von DIBELIUS, Jak, 49 f: »In Wahrheit handelt es sich wohl darum, daß beide Schriften über einen verhältnismäßig großen gemeinsamen paränetischen Besitz verfügen, den Hermas meist in verarbeitetem Zustand …, Jak in Spruchform wiedergibt« (50).

1636 ALLISON, Jak, 620 f, schließt von Herm mand III 1 und sim V 6 als den einzigen christlichen Belegen, in denen κατοικίζειν, πνεῦμα und ἐν vor Justin zusammen begegnen und von dem Einfluss von »Eldad und Modad« auf den Hirten des Hermas auf ein Eldad und Modad-Zitat, das auf Traditionen im Zusammenhang mit Num 11,26–29 beruht und von Jakobus benutzt wird.

C. Briefcorpus

nicht wahrscheinlich gemacht werden und wird im vorliegenden Kommentar nicht übernommen.

V. 6b Der Referenztext des zweiten Zitats ist klar: Spr 3,34.

Spr 3,34: κύριος ὑπερηφάνοις ἀντιτάσσεται, ταπεινοῖς δὲ δίδωσιν χάριν.
Der Herr widersteht den Hochmütigen, den Demütigen aber gibt er Gnade.
Lk 1,51 f: Ἐποίησεν κράτος ἐν βραχίονι αὐτοῦ, διεσκόρπισεν ὑπερηφάνους διανοίᾳ καρδίας αὐτῶν·(52) καθεῖλεν δυνάστας ἀπὸ θρόνων καὶ ὕψωσεν ταπεινούς.
(51) Er übt Gewalt mit seinem Arm, er zerstreut, die hochmütig sind in ihres Herzens Sinn. (52) Er stößt die Herrscher vom Thron und erhebt die Demütigen.
Jak 4,6: ὁ θεὸς ὑπερηφάνοις ἀντιτάσσεται, ταπεινοῖς δὲ δίδωσιν χάριν.
1Petr 5,5: κύριος ὑπερηφάνοις ἀντιτάσσεται, ταπεινοῖς δὲ δίδωσιν χάριν.

Spr 3,34 wird in Lk 1 alludiert, in Jak 4,10 und 1Petr 5,6 wörtlich zitiert. Die Einleitung in das Zitat: »Darum[1637] heißt es« findet sich mehrfach im Neuen Testament.[1638] Jakobus zitiert wörtlich, ersetzt aber κύριος durch das eindeutige θεός.[1639] Das Proverbienzitat »gehört zum frühchristlichen Zitatenschatz«[1640] und führt den Gedanken des ersten Zitats fort: Die wirkliche Gabe, nämlich die Gnade, wird von Gott den Demütigen gegeben. Daneben steht die antithetische Behauptung: Den Hochmütigen widersteht er. Das Zitat passt in den allgemeinen Zusammenhang von Streit, Begierde, falscher Bitte und neidischem Streben, dem die demütige Haltung gegenübersteht, die Gnade, χάρις, empfängt. χάρις ist ein paulinisches Vorzugswort. Jakobus benutzt es nur hier in der Einführung des Zitats und – wiederholend – im Zitat selbst. Das Thema der Gabe hat er in Kapitel 1 verbal (1,5) und substantivisch (1,17) prominent angesprochen, auf Bitte und Gebet bezogen. In 4,6 begegnet das Verb δίδωμι ebenso wie χάρις zweimal: in beiden Zitaten. Damit fällt von dem zweiten Zitat noch einmal Licht auf den Umfang des ersten Zitats. Die Doppelung von V. 6a und 6b wäre stilistisch äußerst ungeschickt, wenn V. 6a vom Verfasser stammte und eine Art Ankündigung des folgenden Zitats wäre.[1641] Außerdem ist μείζονα schwer zu verstehen, denn es fehlt ein Vergleichsbegriff.[1642] Beachtet man das Fragezeichen der ECM, entfällt die ungeschickte Einleitung, stattdessen setzt das erste Zitat das Stichwort für das zweite und macht das zweite Zitat plausibel. Das ist die einleuchtendste exegetische Lösung.

[1637] διό noch 1,21.
[1638] Eph 4,8; 5,14; Hebr 3,7; 10,5; Apg 13,35.
[1639] Vgl. 1Petr 5,5; 1Clem 30,2; IgnEph 5,3 (überall ebenfalls θεός).
[1640] BURCHARD, Jak, 175.
[1641] So aber BURCHARD, Jak, 174: »V. 6a greift auf den Wortlaut des Zitats voraus, auch wenn χάρις, (im Brief nur hier) gern Objekt zu διδόναι ist.«
[1642] In 1Kor 12,31 verwendet Paulus den Ausdruck »größere Charismen«, bezogen auf ἀγάπη. In Herm sim V 2.10 findet sich dieselbe Konstruktion. Die Arbeiter beten für den Herrn des Weinbergs, »dass er größere Gnade bei dem Herrn [sc. Gott] fände«. Auch hier fehlt der Vergleich.

300 Kommentar

2. Texteinheit: 4,7–10 Mahnrede gegen Sünder und Zweiseeler

(7) **Ordnet euch nun Gott unter**[1643], **widersteht aber dem Teufel, dann**[1644] **wird er von euch fliehen, (8) naht euch Gott, dann wird er sich euch nahen. Reinigt die Hände, Sünder, und heiligt die Herzen, Zweifler. (9) Jammert und klagt und weint. Euer Lachen verkehre sich in Trauer und eure Freude in Niedergeschlagenheit. (10) Demütigt euch vor dem Herrn, so**[1645] **wird er euch erhöhen.**

Textkritik: V. 9 μετατραπητω, »umkehren«, Passiv »sich verkehren« lesen P100.03.025 und Minuskeln, μεταστραφητω, »sich verkehren«, lesen 01. 02. 044. 33 und zahlreiche Minuskeln. Die äußere Bezeugung spricht für μεταστραφητω. μετατραπητω ist hap. leg. im NT, lectio difficilior und wohl ursprünglich: Jakobus liebt hap. leg. Beide Verben sind in LXX bezeugt, μεταστρεφειν öfter, μετατρεπειν nur in 4Makk, μεταστρεφειν auch Gal 1,17 und Apg 2,20.

Die Verse 7–10 stellen die zweite Texteinheit im Zusammenhang von Teil 4 dar. Der Verfasser schreibt im Stil der *Bußpredigt*. Stil und Motive sind traditionell. Der Text ist stilistisch sorgfältig gearbeitet. Jakobus eröffnet mit dem applikativen οὖν[1646] und setzt die denkbar strengste und grundlegendste Antithese: Gott und Teufel. Die Adressaten stehen dazwischen. Der Verfasser sieht seine Aufgabe darin, der Leserschaft in dieser Situation sehr konkrete Anweisungen zu geben. Die Verse enthalten eine zweite Reihe von Verben, jetzt ermahnenden Inhaltes im Gegensatz zu den beschreibenden Verben in V. 2–3. Auffallend ist der parataktische Stil mit sieben καί (LXX-Stil). Jakobus setzt insgesamt neun Imperative in der 2.Pers.Pl.[1647], die zum Teil Untergruppen bilden: Ordnet euch unter, widersteht (ein Zweierpaar), nähert euch (erweitert durch korrespondierenden Nachsatz), reinigt euch, heiligt euch (ein Dreierpaar), jammert, klagt, weint (zweites Dreierpaar), demütigt euch (erweitert durch korrespondierenden Nachsatz wie schon beim 3. Imperativ). Die *repetitio* der Imperative dient der Intensivierung der Ermahnung. Hinzu kommt die zweimalige aggressive Anrede als »Sünder« und »Zweiseeler«. Zusätzlich setzt Jakobus syntaktische *variatio* ein. Die Imperative werden teilweise ergänzt: Wenn ihr *x* tut, wird reziprok *y* eintreten (V. 7b.c reziprok, V. 10 antithetisch). V. 9b fällt mit dem Imperativ der 3.Pers.Sing. formal aus dieser Verbkette heraus. Das inhaltliche Profil der Verben ist sehr allgemein gehalten: Es handelt sich nicht um konkrete Verhaltensangaben, sondern um religiös konnotierte Topoi gängiger Sünden- bzw. Bußpredigt. Auffallend viele der Verben sind hapax legomena im Jakobusbrief. Das Ziel der Ermahnung liegt in V. 10: Es geht um Unterordnung und Demut (vgl. Jak 1,9f) im Gegensatz zu den »Übermütigen« aus dem Zitat Spr 3,34. Der Abschnitt ist nach der Matrix des Proverbienzitates vorwiegend antithetisch in Oppositionspaaren strukturiert: Gott und Teufel, Lachen und Weinen, Demütigung und Er-

---

[1643] τῷ ist nicht übersetzt.

[1644] Wörtlich: »und«.

[1645] Im Griechischen »und«.

[1646] Jak 4,7.17; 5,7.16.

[1647] BURCHARD, Jak, 175: »Zehn Imperative prasseln«. Er zählt den Imperativ von V. 9 mit.

höhung. Die sorgfältige stilistische Gestaltung ist auf größtmögliche Wirkung hin angelegt.

V. 7.8a eröffnet die Texteinheit mit der allgemeinen Aufforderung: »Gehorcht nun Gott«. ὑποτάσσω ist ein paulinisches Vorzugswort, auch häufiger in Hebr und 1Petr gebraucht, im Jakobusbrief nur hier. Die weiteren Aufforderungen in V. 7b.8a folgen demselben Bauplan: Tut *x*, dann folgt *y*. V. 7 setzt den Ton mit der Antithese von Gott und Teufel. Auch ἀντίστημι[1648] sowie διάβολος und φεύγειν begegnen im Jakobusbrief nur hier. Der Satz gehört einer Tradition an, die sich auch in 1Petr 5,8f findet:

> (8) ὁ ἀντίδικος ὑμῶν διάβολος ὡς λέων ὠρυόμενος περιπατεῖ ζητῶν τινα καταπιεῖν (9) ᾧ ἀντίστητε.
>
> (8) Euer Widersacher, der Teufel, geht umher wie ein brüllender Löwe und sucht, wen er verschlinge. (9) Dem widersteht.

Die Wendung »der Teufel flieht« ist so oder ähnlich auch in TestIss 7,7[1649]; TestDan 5,1[1650]; TestNaph 8,4; TestBen 5,2[1651]; Herm mand XII 4,6f; XII 5,2 bezeugt. Der erste Teil von V. 8 gehört zu V. 7 und stammt aus demselben traditionellen Umfeld. τῷ θεῷ wird wieder aufgenommen, ἐγγίζειν wird wiederholt. Die Satzstruktur wiederholt V. 7b. Die Wiederholungen dienen der Intensivierung der Ermahnung. ἐγγίζειν, »sich nähern«[1652], »ursprünglich kultisch gemeint«, ist hier wie in TestDan 6,1f »Metapher für die ganzheitliche Hinwendung zu Gott und zu seinem Willen«.[1653] ἐγγίζειν ist das erste von drei ursprünglich kultisch orientierten Verben, die hier bildlich im Zusammenhang einer Bußpredigt eingesetzt werden.

V. 8b.c Jakobus fährt mit zwei parallel gebauten imperativischen Kurzsätzen fort (synthetischer Parallelismus: Herzen und Hände, reinigen und heiligen). Die Anrede ist jeweils nachgestellt. Die metaphorischen Wendungen καθαρίσατε[1654] χεῖρας[1655] und ἁγνίσατε[1656] καρδίας[1657] führen das Motiv des ἐγγίζειν weiter: Wieder benutzt Jakobus kultisch-rituelle Metaphorik Israels zur Annäherung an Gott[1658], wobei die zweite Aufforderung das kultische Vokabular ethisiert. Diese Wendungen be-

---

[1648] BURCHARD, Jak, 175, weist auf die Beziehung zwischen ἀντίστητε und ἀντιτάσσεται im Zitat hin. Das Zitat scheint für V. 7 als Stichwortgeber gedient zu haben, wie das erste Zitat Stichwortgeber des zweiten Zitats war.

[1649] »Der Geist Belials«.

[1650] »Der Geist Belials«.

[1651] »Die unreinen Tiere«.

[1652] 5,8 zeitlich gemeint.

[1653] BURCHARD, Jak, 176 (Belege). Burchard verweist auch auf das Zitat aus Eldad und Modad in Herm vis II 3,4.

[1654] Hap. leg. in Jak.

[1655] Hap. leg. in Jak. Vgl. 2Kor 7,1; Eph 5,26; Tit 2,14; mehrfach in Hebr. BURCHARD, Jak, 176, weist darauf hin, dass χείρ »metonymisch für Handeln« steht.

[1656] Hap. leg. in Jak.

[1657] Siehe 1Petr 1,22: »Seelen« statt »Herzen«. Vgl. 1Clem 29,1.

[1658] Nachweise bei BURCHARD, Jak, 176.

302 Kommentar

gegnen im Neuen Testament nur hier. Während der Vorwurf »Sünder« auf den Soziolekt vor allem der synoptischen Evangelien weist, ist δίψυχος, »Zweiseeler«, ein Ausdruck des eigenen Jakobus-Vokabulars.[1659] Wenn der Verfasser, der seit V. 7 im Ton des ernsten, verpflichtenden Mahnwortes zu den Adressaten spricht, diese als »Sünder« qualifiziert, wird deutlich, dass es seit 4,1 nicht um ein bestimmtes Auditorium bzw. um eine reale briefliche Kommunikation mit einer oder mehreren bestimmten Gemeinden geht, sondern um eine literarische Bußpredigt, die Topoi aus der prophetischen Bußpredigt verwendet.

V. 9 Dieser Ton wird in V. 9 verstärkt fortgeführt. ταλαιπωρήσατε καὶ πενθήσατε καὶ κλαύσατε: die drei Imperative von V. 9a bringen die hochemotionale Komponente des dreigliedrigen Weherufs gegen die Reichen von Lk 6,24 f in die Bußpredigt ein:

> (24) Πλὴν οὐαὶ ὑμῖν τοῖς πλουσίοις, ὅτι ἀπέχετε τὴν παράκλησιν ὑμῶν. (25) οὐαὶ ὑμῖν, οἱ ἐμπεπλησμένοι νῦν, ὅτι πεινάσετε. οὐαί, οἱ γελῶντες νῦν, ὅτι πενθήσετε καὶ κλαύσετε.

> (24) Wehe euch Reichen, denn ihr habt schon euren Trost gehabt. (25) Wehe euch, die ihr jetzt satt seid, denn ihr werdet hungern. Wehe euch, die ihr jetzt lacht, denn ihr werdet weinen und klagen.[1660]

Burchard kommentiert:

> Trauerbezeugungen gegenüber Gott gehören traditionell zur Buße.[1661]

Jakobus verbindet den traditionellen Doppelausdruck »Klagen und weinen«[1662] mit dem vorangestellten hap. leg. ταλαιπωρεῖν, »unglücklich sein, wehklagen«.[1663] V. 9b ist zweigliedrig und parallel gebaut: Lachen und Freude – Weinen und Trauer. Jakobus nimmt das Motiv von Klage und Trauer mit dem Substantiv πένθος verstärkt auf.[1664] Zu den drei Imperativen von 9a fügt Jakobus einen weiteren hinzu, der das Bußmotiv von »Umkehr« aufgreift: μετατρέπειν, sich verkehren.[1665] Von dem Imperativ hängt das doppelte antithetische Begriffspaar »Lachen«[1666] und »Klage« und »Freude« und »Niedergeschlagenheit« (κατήφεια[1667]) ab.

V. 10 Es folgt ein weiterer Imperativsatz, der die ethische Summe aus 4,1–9 zieht. Damit knüpft Jakobus an das Zitat aus V. 6 an. ›Sich demütigen‹ im Sinne von »Niedrig-Gesinnung«[1668] ist ein wichtiges ethisches Motiv im Jakobusbrief seit 1,9

[1659] Siehe oben zu 1,8. Vgl. Herm mand IX 7.

[1660] Vgl. unten zu 5,1–6.

[1661] BURCHARD, Jak, 177. Die motivische Nähe zu Lk 6,24 f ist deutlich: Doppelausdruck »Weinen und Klagen« (vgl. auch Apk 18,11.15.19) und Gegenbegriff »Lachen«.

[1662] Außer Lk 6: 2Sam 19,2; Apk 18,11.15.19.

[1663] Vgl. das Substantiv in 5,1. ταλαιπ- zweimal bei Paulus. Vgl. SPICQ, NLNT II, 875.

[1664] Hap. leg. in Jak. Vgl. Apk 18,7.8; 21,4 (endzeitliche Gerichtssemantik).

[1665] Hap. leg. im NT.

[1666] Hap. leg. im NT (Verb Lk 6,21.25).

[1667] Hap. leg. im NT.

[1668] BECKER, Demut, VII Anm. 1.

C. Briefcorpus

(Adjektiv).10 (Substantiv).[1669] Die Opposition von ›Sich selbst erniedrigen‹ und ›Erhöht werden‹ in 4,10 geht auf LXX zurück[1670] und begegnet in verschiedenen thematischen, literarischen Zusammenhängen in der synoptischen Tradition, bei Paulus sowie im 1Petr.

2Kor 11,7	Phil 2,8 f	Lk 14,11	Lk 18,14	Mt 23,12
Paulus' Verhalten in Korinth	Jesu Tod und Erhöhung	Sitzordnung beim Gastmahl	Pharisäer und Zöllner	Nicht Lehrer, sondern Diener
Jak 4,10	1Petr 5,6	Mt 11,23	Lk 1,52	
Allgemeine Bußpredigt gegen Streit unter den Adressaten 4,6=Spr 3,34	Allgemeine Aufforderung zur Unterordnung in der Gemeinde 5,5=Spr 3,34	Gerichtsrede gegen Kapernaum	Magnifikat: Erhöhung der Niedrigen	

Der Topos wird in dem Paralleltext 1Petr 5,6[1671] thematisch im Zusammenhang der Gemeindeparänese verwendet und dient als Abschluss eines parakletischen (5,1) Abschnittes, der an die Ältesten gerichtet ist. Jakobus setzt den Topos im Zusammenhang seiner literarischen Bußpredigt ein. Paulus verwendet den Topos christologisch und autobiographisch. Die synoptischen Texte sind statuszentriert: Lk 14 ist thematisch nahe bei Jak 2,1–7, Lk 18 wendet den Topos kritisch auf die Formen der Frömmigkeit an, Mt 23 auf die Art der Leitung in der Gemeinschaft der Jünger. In Jak 4 geht es nicht um den Status, sondern um die Gesinnung.[1672]

3. Texteinheit: 4,11–12 Mahnrede gegen das Richten

(11) Verleumdet einander nicht, Brüder, wer seinen Bruder verleumdet oder seinen Bruder richtet, verleumdet das Gesetz und richtet (oder: verurteilt) das Gesetz, wenn du aber das Gesetz richtest, bist[1673] du nicht Täter des Gesetzes, sondern Richter. (12) Einer ist der Gesetzgeber und Richter, der retten und verderben kann; du aber – wer bist du, der den Nächsten richtet?

Textkritik: V. 12 Mehrere Minuskeln lesen ετερον statt πλησιον. 018 und einige Minuskeln haben den erklärenden Zusatz: οτι ουκ εν ανθρωπω αλλα εν θεω τα διαβηματα ανθρωπου κατευθυνεται.

[1669] BECKER, Demut, 188–195.

[1670] Vgl. Sir 2,17: »Und vor ihm [dem Herrn] demütigen sie ihre Seelen«. Weitere Belege bei BURCHARD, Jak, 177.

[1671] 1Petr und Jak scheinen auf eine gemeinsame Tradition zurückzugehen (Zitat von Spr 3,34 und Verbindung mit dem Motiv des Teufels).

[1672] So auch BECKER, Demut, 196.

[1673] Im Deutschen ergänzt.

304 Kommentar

Die Anrede »Brüder«, die für die Verse 11 und 12 gilt, signalisiert einen Neuansatz, der durch das kommunikationsintensive »Du« in V. 11c unterstützt wird: Der Verfasser verlässt den literarischen Gestus der Bußpredigt und kehrt zur brieflichen Kommunikation zurück. Der kleine Textabschnitt V. 11.12 hat im Gesamtduktus des Briefes erhebliches Gewicht, denn hier verknüpft Jakobus seine Bußpredigt mit seinem theologischen Hauptthema: Gesetz, Nächstenliebe und Tun des Gesetzes. Damit kommt er noch einmal auf die Thematik von 2,8–26 zurück und wendet seine Ethik des Tuns auf das innergemeindliche Fehlverhalten der Verleumdung an.

V. 11 Der Vers stellt ein kurzes selbständiges ethisches Lehrstück mit einer deutlichen dreigliedrigen Binnengliederung dar. (1) In V. 11a formuliert Jakobus eine knappe ethische Forderung in der 2. Pers. Plur. (2) Die Formulierung in V. 11b: »der verleumdet oder be(ver)urteilt das Gesetz« wiederholt den Vordersatz und formt die Forderung in einen allgemeinen zweigliedrigen Rechtssatz um. (3) V. 11c zieht daraus eine applikative Schlussfolgerung in der 2. Pers. Sing. Auch V. 12 weist eine dreiteilige Binnengliederung auf: (1) Gott wird mit zwei *Funktionen* umschrieben. (2) Eine weitere Umschreibung bezieht sich auf seine *Wirkung* auf die Menschen. (3) Der Satz schließt mit einer anklagenden rhetorischen Frage in der 2. Pers. Sing. ab und greift thematisch V. 11b auf (Ringkomposition).

Ethisch geht es in V. 11 um zwei Formen des Fehlverhaltens, zunächst um Verleumdung, üble Nachrede: καταλαλεῖν[1674], ein topisches soziales Fehlverhalten unter Brüdern, d. h. in den Gemeinden, das Paulus in den Lasterkatalogen von Röm 1,30 (κατάλαλος) und 2Kor 12,10 (καταλαλία) nennt.[1675] Wie in Jak 1,9 und 2,15 wird hier eine Bruder-Ethik etabliert, deren Soziolekt und ethische Regeln sich ebenso bei Paulus wie im 1Joh finden. Diese Texte weisen darauf hin, dass auch die Adressaten des Jakobus Mitglieder Christus-bekennender Gemeinden sind. Jakobus verpflichtet sie auf eine Ethik, die sich an der Nächstenliebe orientiert, wie V. 12 zeigt. Jakobus spitzt die Verurteilung des Topos der Verleumdung dann ethisch zu, indem er im Sinne der Steigerung (Klimax) die »Verleumdung« mit dem wichtigeren Thema der »Verurteilung« verbindet: καταλαλῶν ἢ κρίνων (Alliteration), die er als eigentliche Gefahr des Verleumdens ausmacht.

Damit stellt er die Verleumdung in einen theologisch-ethisch qualifizierten Zusammenhang. Das schwerwiegende ethische Fehlverhalten, den Bruder »zu richten«, d. h. sein Verhalten zu beurteilen und zu verurteilen, wird in den frühchristlichen Texten verschiedentlich kritisch thematisiert: in dem Logion Q 6,37 ebenso wie mehrfach und ausführlich in den paulinischen Briefen. Die Tabelle zeigt, an welchem *breiten frühchristlichen Diskurs* Jakobus hier teilnimmt:

[1674] Hap. leg. in Jak (4,11 zweimal).

[1675] Vgl. 1Petr 2,1; 3,16 (keine Zusammenstellung mit κρίνειν. Schon in LXX und auch bei den Apostolischen Vätern).

Lk 6,37	Mt 7,1f	Röm 2,1–3	Röm 14,4.10–13.23	1Kor 5,12f
Und **richtet** (κρίνειν) nicht, und auch **ihr** werdet nicht gerichtet werden. Und verurteilt (καταδικάζειν) nicht, und auch ihr werdet nicht verurteilt werden.	[1]**Richtet** nicht, damit **ihr** nicht gerichtet werdet. [2]Denn nach welchem Urteil ihr richtet, werdet ihr gerichtet werden, und mit welchem Maß ihr messt, wird euch gemessen werden.	[1]Deshalb bist **du** unentschuldbar, **o Mensch**, wer auch immer du bist, der du **richtest**. Denn worin du den anderen richtest, verurteilst du dich selbst (κατακρίνειν), der du, der du richtest, dasselbe tust. [2]Wir wissen aber, dass das Urteil Gottes der Wahrheit entsprechend ergeht über die, die solches tun. [3]Denkst du aber das, o Mensch, der du die richtest, die solches tun, und dasselbe tust, dass du dem Urteil Gottes entkommen wirst?	[4]Wer bist **du**, der du einen fremden Knecht **richtest**? [10]**Du** aber – was richtest du deinen **Bruder**? Oder auch du – was verachtest du deinen Bruder? Wir werden alle vor den Richterstuhl Gottes gestellt werden. [13]Darum wollen **wir** uns nun nicht mehr gegenseitig richten. [23]Wer aber zweifelt und dennoch isst, der ist gerichtet.	[12]Denn was gehen mich die draußen an, dass ich sie **richten** sollte? Richtet **ihr** nicht **die, die drinnen sind**? [13]Die die draußen sind, wird Gott richten.

Weiterhin können auch 1Kor 6,1–11 und Kol 2,16 in diesen Zusammenhang gestellt werden. 1Kor 6 ist eine kleine Abhandlung über das κρίνειν der Christus-bekennenden Gemeinden. Die Texte beziehen sich bei gleicher Thematik auf unterschiedliche Grundlagen: Basis sind das Talionsrecht, das Gottesgericht und die Bruderthematik der Gemeinden. Situation und Adressaten der Sprüche sind unterschiedlich. Während Q 6,37 nicht situativ gerahmt ist, setzt Mt 7,1–5 den Rahmen der Bruderliebe. Wieweit in Mt 7 konkrete Gemeindeprobleme angesprochen werden, muss offenbleiben.[1676] Ganz deutlich ist dagegen die Applikation auf die Gemeinde bei Paulus. Paulus thematisiert das κρίνειν in den Gemeinden in unterschiedlichen Zusammenhängen. Die grundsätzliche Behandlung des Themas in Röm 2,1–3 im Zu-

---

[1676] U. Luz, Mt I/1, 489. Luz fragt: »Ist Jak 4,11f ein Nachhall unseres Jesuswortes?«.

306 Kommentar

sammenhang des Gesetzes ist für Jak 4 von besonderem Interesse. Die Pointe von Röm 2 liegt – wie in Mt 7,1–5 in metaphorischer Weise ausgedrückt[1677] – darin, dass niemand *berechtigt* ist, den Anderen zu kritisieren, da jeder Mensch sich selbst dauernd verfehlt und *das Gesetz nicht halten kann*. Die Pointe in Jak 4 ist aber eine andere. Ohne es zu explizieren, greift Jakobus hier *erstens* auf 2,8 zurück: Das Gesetz erfüllt sich in der Nächstenliebe[1678] – nicht in der Verleumdung und Verurteilung des Nächsten. Das Gesetz fordert also zum eigenen *Tun* der Nächstenliebe auf, nicht zum Richten über den Anderen. Dabei reflektiert Jakobus nicht wie Paulus auf die Möglichkeit oder Unmöglichkeit, das Gesetz zu erfüllen, sondern weist ganz einfach darauf hin, dass die Adressaten das Gesetz *tun* sollen, statt sich die kritische Funktion des Richters anhand des Gesetzes anzumaßen. Diese Funktion gehört allein Gott, wie V. 12 klarstellt. Jakobus greift implizit *zweitens* auf 2,12 f zurück: die Adressaten sollen nicht »richten«, sondern werden selbst gerichtet werden, und zwar nach dem Maßstab ihres barmherzigen Handelns (ποιεῖ ἔλεος). Jakobus spitzt das Argument rhetorisch noch weiter in Richtung auf das Gesetz zu: Verleumdung oder Verurteilung des Bruders ist Verleumdung oder Verurteilung des Gesetzes statt Gesetzesbefolgung. Die Konsequenz ist die Verkehrung der Gewichte: Statt »Täter des Gesetzes« zu sein und Nächstenliebe und Erbarmen zu üben, macht sich der Verleumder zum Richter des Gesetzes und nimmt damit Gottes Stellung ein. In Jak 4,11 liegt eine selbständige ethische Interpretation des Talionsrechtes, wie es in Q 6,37 formuliert ist, vor, bezogen auf die Gemeinden wie bei Paulus (»Brüder«). Jakobus gibt hier einen eigenen Beitrag zur frühchristlichen Gesetzesthematik: Das Gesetz ist darauf angelegt, »getan« zu werden, nicht als Maßstab zu dienen. Die Adressaten sollen »Täter des Gesetzes« sein, nicht Ausleger und Diskutanten. Hier sind noch einmal die Lehrer von 3,1 im Blick: Es liegt eine Ringkomposition vor. Die Tätigkeit der Lehrer vollzieht sich vor dem Forum eines »strengeren Gerichtes« (κρίμα), das Gott, nicht den Lehrern vorbehalten bleibt.

V. 12 Jakobus formuliert eine abschließende theologische Aussage von grundsätzlicher Bedeutung für den Textabschnitt 4,1–12. Die theologische Aussage ist analog zu 2,19 im Duktus des Sch'ma (Dtn 6,4 κύριος ὁ θεὸς ἡμῶν κύριος εἷς ἐστιν) formuliert und erhält dadurch besonderen Nachdruck: Gott (allein) ist Gesetzgeber und Richter. Ausschließlich *Gott* ist das *Richten* nach dem Gesetz, das er gegeben hat, vorbehalten, während die *»Brüder«* auf das *Tun* des Gesetzes verwiesen sind. Jakobus führt hier zwei Gottesprädikate zusammen, die sonst in den neutestamentlichen Schriften nicht verbunden werden und unterschiedliche Wurzeln haben. Beide Funktionen begegnen nur selten in substantivischer Formulierung im Neuen Testament. νομοθέτης ist sogar hap. leg. im Neuen Testament. Die Vorstellung von

---

[1677] Insofern ist mindestens Röm 2 ein sachlicher Nachhall von Mt 7.

[1678] 4,12 spielt auf diesen Zusammenhang an: Du sollst den Nächsten (πλησίον) nicht verurteilen, sondern lieben.

Gott als *Gesetzgeber* klingt nur in Röm 9,4 an.[1679] Die *Richterfunktion* (κριτής) Gottes ist in Jak 4 und in Hebr 12,23 allein auf Gott bezogen.[1680] In 2Tim 4,1 (verbal).8 und Apg 10,42 wird dieser Titel dagegen Christus zugesprochen. In verbaler Formulierung ist die alttestamentlich-frühjüdische Vorstellung von Gott als Richter[1681] Paulus präsent, so prominent in Röm 2,16; 3,4; 1Kor 5,13. Apg 17,31 verbindet beide Aspekte: Gott setzt Christus als Richter ein. Beide Prädikate verbinden die heilsgeschichtliche Perspektive vom Gesetz Gottes mit der apokalyptischen Perspektive von seinem endzeitlichen Gericht.[1682]

Hier fällt noch einmal Licht auf das Thema des νόμος, das für Jakobus eine wichtige Rolle spielt: 1,25 (νόμος τέλειος ὁ τῆς ἐλευθερίας); 2,12 (ν. ἐλευθερίας, verbunden mit κρίνεσθαι); 2,8 (ν. βασιλικός).9.10; 4,11 (dreimal). Den Begriff »Gesetz« setzt er voraus. Während die Erwähnungen in 1,25; 2,8 und 2,12 eher umschreibenden Charakter haben und dem Lob des Gesetzes dienen, begrifflich aber unscharf bleiben, ist 4,12 deutlicher. Ist »der Eine« der Gesetzgeber, dann ist das Gesetz gemeint, das Mose von Gott empfangen hat.[1683] Jakobus befindet sich hier im Umkreis des antiken jüdischen Sprachgebrauchs. Philo schreibt in sacr. 131[1684]:

> Unter den besten göttlichen Kräften nämlich wird eine einzige (μία οὖσα), die allen anderen gleichwertig ist: die gesetzgebende (Kraft) (νομοθετική) – denn Gesetzgeber (νομοθέτης) und Gesetzesquelle (πηγὴ νόμων) ist er selbst, von dem alle Einzelgesetzgeber abhängig sind – zwiefach geteilt: teils (dient sie) zur Belohnung der Gerechten, teils zur Bestrafung der Sünder.

Theologisch ist damit das Entscheidende gesagt. Jakobus hat ein originelles theologisches Argument generiert, das seine Ethik des *Tuns* begründet: Das Gesetz ist den Menschen von Gott dazu gegeben, dass es umgesetzt, d.h. getan wird, nicht dazu, dass Menschen sich die Rolle Gottes anmaßen und selbst zu Richtern machen. Damit verzichtet Jakobus mindestens theoretisch auf das für die Rechtskultur Israels ebenso wie für die hellenistisch-römische Rechtsordnung zentrale Amt des Richters und konzentriert die Bedeutung des Gesetzes darauf, Antrieb für das Tun des einzelnen Christus-gläubigen Gemeindegliedes zu sein.[1685]

[1679] νομοθετεῖται Hebr 7,11; 8,6 geht in eine andere Richtung.

[1680] Vgl. auch Apg 7,7 (Gen 15,13 f). F. HERNTRICH / F. BÜCHSEL, Art. κρίνω κτλ., ThWNT 3, 920–955; W. SCHENK, Art. κριτής, EWNT 2, 795–797.

[1681] Hebr 10,30 zitiert Dtn 32,36; vgl. Hebr 13,4. Im Joh wird die Gerichtsthematik kritisch interpretiert.

[1682] Vgl. 5,9 endzeitliches κρίνεσθαι.

[1683] Ob an den Dekalog (Jak 2,8–11) oder die gesamte Tora zu denken sei, bleibt aber offen.

[1684] Die Wortfamilie νομοθέτ- findet sich häufig bei Philo. Vgl. Weiteres bei TH. KLEINKNECHT / W. GUTBROD, Art. νόμος κτλ., ThWNT 4, 1016–1084, S. 1082 f zu νομοθέτης (Gutbrod).

[1685] Auch Paulus distanziert sich von der Funktion des Richters und verweist die Gemeinde auf das Ethos der Tugenden: 1Kor 6,1–11, billigt allerdings doch den Gemeindegliedern die Funktion zu, Rechtsstreitigkeiten in den Gemeinden zu schlichten. Zur internen Gerichtsbarkeit vgl. ZELLER, Der erste Brief an die Korinther, 212. Seine Position bleibt insgesamt vage und ist aus einer deutlich eschatologischen Perspektive

Das zweite Glied des Satzes (2) fügt traditionelle Aussagen zu Gott hinzu: Er ist wirkmächtig (δυνάμενος)[1686] und kann retten und verderben.[1687] Die Opposition »Retten und verderben« ist geläufig. Das dritte Glied des Satzes (3) nimmt in einer scharf formulierten rhetorischen Frage die Pointe des theologischen Argumentes auf: »Du – wer bist du (Mensch), dass du den Nächsten verurteilst?« Positiv gewendet: das steht allein Gott zu. Die vorangestellte Anrede an die Adressaten in der 2.Pers.Sing. betont nochmals die Dringlichkeit des ethischen Appells, den Nächsten nicht zu richten, sondern zu lieben.[1688] Dieselbe Frage begegnet schon in Röm 14,4: σὺ τίς εἶ ὁ κρίνων ἀλλότριον οἰκέτην; (Du – wer bist du, dass du einen fremden Knecht richtest?) Paulus bezieht die Frage auf den innergemeindlichen Streit zwischen »Starken« und »Schwachen«:

> Μηκέτι οὖν ἀλλήλους κρίνωμεν· ἀλλὰ τοῦτο κρίνατε μᾶλλον, τὸ μὴ τιθέναι πρόσκομμα τῷ ἀδελφῷ ἢ σκάνδαλον.
>
> Darum lasst uns nicht mehr gegenseitig richten, sondern achtet vielmehr darauf, nicht einen Anstoß oder ein Ärgernis dem Bruder zu geben (Röm 14,13).

Ob eine entsprechende oder ähnliche Konstellation in den Gemeinden, an die sich Jakobus brieflich wendet, bestand, wissen wir nicht.

B. 4,13–17: Gegen Kaufleute

(13) Wohlan nun ihr, die ihr sagt: »Heute oder morgen werden wir in die und die Stadt reisen und uns dort ein Jahr betätigen und Handel treiben und Gewinn machen« – (14) die ihr doch[1689] nicht den nächsten Tag[1690] kennt, wie euer Leben sein wird[1691]; Rauch nämlich seid ihr, der eine kleine Zeit sichtbar wird und dann verschwindet[1692], – (15) statt dass ihr sagt: »Wenn der Herr will, werden wir leben und dies oder jenes tun«. (16) Nun aber rühmt ihr euch in euren Prahlereien; jedes derartige Rühmen ist schlecht. (17) Wer[1693] nun weiß, was Gutes tun ist, es aber[1694] nicht tut, der sündigt[1695].

Textkritik: V. 13 und V. 15 liest ein größerer Teil der Hss jeweils das Futur der Verben (πορευσομεθα usw.), während ein kleinerer Teil den Aorist hat. Das Futur ist besser über-

---

geschrieben. Dazu allgemein G. Thür / P. E. Pieler, Art. Gerichtsbarkeit, RAC 10, 1978, 360–492; S. Schima, Art. Prozessrecht, RAC 28, 2017, 744–771.

[1686] Hap. leg. in Jak. Gott als der mächtige: Mt 3,9; Mk 2,7; Apg 20,32; Phil 3,21 (von Christus); Eph 3,20.

[1687] Mk 3,4par; 8,35par; Lk 19,10; 1Kor 1,18 u. ö.

[1688] Jak 2,8.

[1689] »Doch« im Deutschen hinzugefügt.

[1690] Wörtlich: »das morgen«.

[1691] »Sein wird« ist im Deutschen hinzugefügt. Übersetzung mit Burchard, Jak, 180.

[1692] Das Partizip ist nebengeordnet übersetzt. Das Wortspiel φαινομένη und ἀφανιζομένη lässt sich im Deutschen nicht nachbilden.

[1693] Wörtlich: »für den aber«.

[1694] »Aber« ist im Deutschen hinzugefügt.

[1695] Wörtlich: »für den ist es Sünde«.

liefert und passt zur Aussage. **V. 16** lesen 43 und 330 ασθενειας ὑμων καὶ αλαζονειας – ein Anklang an die paulinischen Peristasenkataloge?

Der Abschnitt ist bis V. 16 in der 2. Person Plural verfasst und als direkte Anrede an eine bestimmte Gruppe gestaltet, während V. 17 ein allgemeines ethisches Fazit zieht. Jakobus spricht Kaufleute an, die Handel außerhalb ihrer eigenen Stadt treiben – ob zu Lande oder mit Handelsschiffen, bleibt ungesagt. Der Textabschnitt ist sprachlich[1696], formal und argumentativ sehr sorgfältig gestaltet. Den Begriff »Kaufmann«, ἔμπορος, verwendet Jakobus nicht.[1697] Stattdessen benutzt er eine *Umschreibung* mit Hilfe von *sermocinatio* bzw. Ethopopoiie: Die Kaufleute werden charakterisiert, indem ihnen bestimmte Sätze in den Mund gelegt werden.[1698] Dabei stellt der Verfasser in den Versen 13–15 zwei Reden gegenüber (ἀντί), in denen er seine eigene Position gegenüber derjenigen der Kaufleute akzentuieren kann: eine erste vom Verfasser fingierte negativ konnotierte prahlerisch-großspurige Rede der Kaufleute (V. 13) und eine zweite positiv konnotierte, in der er sein eigenes Votum formuliert und den Kaufleuten als gutes Beispiel vorhält (V. 15). V. 14 stellt eine eingeschobene Reflexion (Parenthese) dar, die V. 15 vorbereitet. Die V. 16–17 sind noch einmal antithetisch konstruiert: V. 16 beschreibt das Verhalten der Kaufleute im Gegensatz zu V. 15 und bewertet dies Verhalten negativ. V. 17 schließt mit einer auswertenden ethischen Gnome.[1699] Die belehrende Rede ist im Modus des ethischen Vorwurfs verfasst: Die Kaufleute machen sich des Übermutes schuldig und werden sündig. Der Verfasser verwendet das bekannte anthropologische Motiv der Vergänglichkeit. V. 15 ist als sog. *conditio Iacobea* zum geflügelten Wort geworden. Die literarische Zuwendung zu den Adressaten (Apostrophe und 2. Person Plural), die fingiere Rede, die knappe Formulierung und die gnomische Zuspitzung verleihen dem Text besondere Intensität.

V. 13 Jakobus setzt mit der Apostrophe ἄγε νῦν rhetorisch versiert ein[1700], – ein Neuanfang, der Aufmerksamkeit bei den Adressaten erzeugt. Was folgt, ist nicht eine Bußpredigt an das Volk und an einzelne Gruppierungen (Zöllner, Soldaten) wie in Lk 3,7–14 oder ein apokalyptisches Szenario mit Wehklagen der Kaufleute und Seeleute wie in Apk 18[1701], sondern ein moralischer Appell bzw. ein Warnruf an

---

[1696] Hapax legomena!

[1697] ἔμπορος im NT: Mt 13,45 und Apk 18 mehrfach, das Verb in Jak 4,13 (in 2Petr 2,3 metaphorisch gebraucht). Ausführliche Belege zum Thema Handel bei Burchard, Jak, 184 f. Allgemein zum Handel vgl. H. J. Drexhage, Art. Handel I.II, RAC 13, 1986, 519–547; J. Renger, u. a., Art. Handel, DNP 5, 1998, 106–127; Blanton IV, Wealth, Poverty, Economy.

[1698] Zu Prosopopoiie siehe A. Bendlin, Art. Personifikation I und II, DNP 9, 2001, 639–643: »Der frühneuzeitliche Begriff der *personificatio* gibt das hell. rhetor. Konzept der προσωποποιία … wieder, welche die Darstellung fiktiver Personen, konkreter Sachen oder abstrakter Begriffe als Redende und Handelnde bezeichnet« (639).

[1699] G. Thür, Art. Gnome, DNP 4, 1998, 1108–1116.

[1700] Im NT nur Jak 4,13: 5,1. Bauer / Aland, 14: Interjektion mit folgendem Anakoluth.

[1701] Im NT in Mt 13,45: ein Kaufmann, der besonders wertvolle Perlen sucht; Apk 18,3: Reichtum der Kaufleute; 18,11–17a Klagelied der Kaufleute; vgl. 18,17b–19 Klagelied der Seeleute über den Fall »Babylons«.

310 Kommentar

eine Berufsgruppe, die Jakobus für ethisch gefährdet hält. Es ist die zweite Bezugnahme auf eine Gruppe nach den Lehrern in 3,1. Während der Verfasser sich selbst
den *Lehrern* zurechnet, spricht er jetzt eine fremde Berufs- oder Standesgruppe an.
Ohne moralische Einseitigkeit schildert er das Selbstbewusstsein und die Selbstherr-
lichkeit der großen *Kaufleute*, die Überland- und Überseehandel betreiben.[1702] Mit
den Kaufleuten wendet sich Jakobus an diejenige Gruppe des städtischen Lebens,
deren Vertreter den Handel im Imperium Romanum tragen und organisieren. Dabei kann er sich auf klassische Texte Israels stützen. Kaufleute werden schon in Jes
23,8 und Ez 27,1–36 als wichtigste Vertreter der großen Handelsstädte Tyrus und
Sidon und ihres mittelmeerumspannenden Handels gesehen und in ihrer Überheblichkeit dargestellt. In Jes 23,8 heißt es von den Kaufleuten von Tyrus: οἱ ἔμποροι
αὐτῆς ἔνδοξοι, ἄρχοντες τῆς γῆς (»Ihre Kaufleute sind hoch angesehen, Große der
Erde«). In dem Klagelied über Sor in Ez 27 wird Tyros (»Sor«) als ἐμπόριον τῶν
λαῶν bezeichnet. Der Prophet schildert das Selbstverständnis und den Dünkel der
Kaufmannsstadt Tyrus im Spiegel einer ironischen Gottesrede:

> Dies sagt der Herr zu Sor: Du hast gesagt: »Ich habe mir meine Schönheit angelegt«
> (27,2).

Was folgt, ist eine umfangreiche und detaillierte Beschreibung des mittelmeeri-
schen und vorderorientalischen Handels zu Wasser und zu Lande mit Luxusgütern.
Wie stark die Kontinuität in der Wahrnehmung der Großkaufleute durch die religiösen Schriftsteller Israels und des antiken Judentums ist, macht ein Blick auf Philo
und auf Apk 18 deutlich. Philo erwähnt öfter Kaufleute und Reeder. Aus seiner
alexandrinischen Perspektive in der frühen Kaiserzeit lassen sich die Kaufleute folgendermaßen charakterisieren:

> Man spricht auch darüber, wie ungeziemend es ist, daß zwar Groß- (ἔμποροι) und
> Kleinkaufleute schmutzigen Gewinstes willen die Meere durchsegeln und um die gan-
> ze bewohnte Erde im Kreise herumfahren, indem sie weder Hitze noch Kälte, weder
> Ungestüm noch Ungunst der Winde, weder Jugend noch Alter, nicht Krankheit, nicht
> Verkehr mit Freunden, nicht die unaussprechliche Freude bei Weib und Kind und den
> anderen Hausangehörigen, weder den Genuß des Vaterlandes und staatlicher Gesit-
> tung, noch die Nutzung von Geld und Gut und sonstigem Überfluß noch irgendetwas
> anderes, was und wie es auch sein mag, ob groß oder klein, als Hindernis erachten.[1703]

Die Ankündigung des Falls »Babylons« in Apk 18,3 schließt einerseits an die prophetischen Texte Israels an[1704]:

[1702] Den Status dieser Kaufleute genauer bestimmen zu wollen (so Burchard, Jak, 184), verbietet sich.
Allgemein zum Thema vgl. Renger u. a., DNP 5, 117–121 und Drexhage, RAC 13.
[1703] Migr. 217.
[1704] Apk 18,7: Ethopoiie wie in Ez 27,2.

C. Briefcorpus 311

καὶ οἱ ἔμποροι τῆς γῆς ἐκ τῆς δυνάμεως τοῦ στρήνους αὐτῆς ἐπλούτησαν.
(Und die Kaufleute der Erde sind reich geworden aus der Fülle ihres [Babylons] Luxus),

andererseits werden in 18,11–13 die Luxusgüter des zeitgenössischen römischen kaiserzeitlichen Großhandels genannt, der die Kaufleute und Reeder bzw. Schiffseigner reich gemacht hat (18,15). Die Waren unterscheiden sich nicht wesentlich von den Handelsprodukten, die in Ez 27 aufgezählt wurden:

… γόμον χρυσοῦ καὶ ἀργύρου καὶ λίθου τιμίου καὶ μαργαριτῶν καὶ βυσσίνου καὶ πορφύρας καὶ σιρικοῦ καὶ κοκκίνου …

… Gold und Silber und Edelsteine und Perlen und feines Leinen und Purpur und Seide und Scharlach … (Apk 18,12 f).

Philo tadelt den Erwerbseifer der Kaufleute und ihrer aufwendigen Handelsreisen (»schmutzigen Gewinstes willen«) und sähe diesen Aufwand lieber auf den Erwerb der Weisheit angewendet.[1705] Die Johannesoffenbarung verurteilt die »Wucht« oder »Macht« ihres üppigen Luxus (18,3). Jakobus' Pointe ist eine andere. Er tadelt den *Planungswahnsinn* des Überland- und Überseehandels, dessen Ursprung er in der übergroßen Selbstsicherheit und Überheblichkeit der Kaufleute findet. Ausdruck dieser Selbstsicherheit ist die fingierte Rede der Kaufleute in V. 13: Sie sprechen von einer einjährigen Geschäftsreise[1706], die ihnen Gewinn bringen soll (κερδαίνω[1707]). Die Formulierung des Zeitpunktes »heute oder morgen«[1708] bringt die Nonchalance der Kaufleute zum Ausdruck, die davon ausgehen, die Zeitwahl sei in ihr Belieben gestellt. Dasselbe gilt für die Wahl der Stadt: »diese oder jene« wollen sie aufsuchen.[1709]

V. 14 Jakobus schließt an die fingierte Rede der Kaufleute eine zweigliedrige Reflexion an. Die unerbittliche anthropologische Diagnose, die dem Selbstbewusstsein und Verhalten der Kaufleute entgegengesetzt ist, lautet *erstens* konkret: Man kann nicht für den morgigen Tag – und darüber hinaus – planen. Die Zeit gehört nicht den Kaufleuten. *Zweitens* allgemein: die eigene Existenz ist kurz und flüchtig. Syntaktisch knüpft V. 14 an »ihr, die ihr sagt« von V. 13 an. In V. 14a benutzt Jakobus die direkte Anrede in der 2. Pers. Pl. und hält den Kaufleuten eine tadelnde Rede des Inhalts, sie wüssten[1710] nicht, »was morgen ist«. Die explikative Fortsetzung: ποία ἡ ζωὴ ὑμῶν (»wie euer Leben aussehen wird«), kann als direkter[1711] oder als indirekter

---

[1705] Vgl. die bekannte differenzierende Kritik Ciceros am Handel aus der Sicht des Standesdenkens des Grundbesitzers und Philosophen: off. 1,151. Für Cicero ist der Großhandel ethisch unbedenklich, während der kleine Kaufmann schmutzige Geschäfte macht.

[1706] ἐμπορεύεσθαι: Handel treiben, hap. leg. in Jak. Im NT noch 2Petr 2,3 (übertragen).

[1707] Hap. leg. in Jak. Vgl. Platon, leg. 952e, und Xenophon, mem. 2,9,4.

[1708] σήμερον hap. leg. in Jak, αὔριον noch in V. 14.

[1709] πόλις hap. leg. in Jak (in allen ntl. Briefen sehr selten). BAUER / ALAND, 1121 f: εἰς τήνδε τὴν πόλιν, »in die und die Stadt« (mit Belegen). Weitere Belege bei BURCHARD, Jak, 183 f.

[1710] ἐπίσταμαι hap. leg. in Jak, sehr selten im NT außer mehrfach in Apg.

[1711] So die Lutherübersetzung: »Was ist euer Leben?«

312 Kommentar

Fragesatz aufgelöst werden[1712] und spitzt die Aussage auf das persönliche Leben der Angesprochenen zu. Das Wissen um die Unverfügbarkeit des »Morgen« ist antikes Allgemeingut.[1713] In V. 14b behält Jakobus die direkte Ansprache bei und sagt den Kaufleuten die Flüchtigkeit ihrer Existenz mittels der Metapher von ἀτμίς (Rauch oder Dampf[1714]) auf den Kopf zu: »Rauch seid ihr nämlich«. *Tertium comparationis* der Metapher ist die Flüchtigkeit, verbunden mit der sehr kurzen Zeitdauer: πρὸς ὀλίγον.[1715] Auch hier formuliert Jakobus stilistisch sorgfältig: Er benutzt die Paronomasie von φαινομένη und ἀφανιζομένη[1716]: »aufscheinen und verschwinden«.[1717]

V. 15 Im Gegensatz zur Position der Kaufleute formuliert Jakobus nun den Satz, der als *conditio Iacobaea* (c.I.) bekannt geworden ist und sich als geflügelte Wendung von seinem Kontext emanzipiert hat.[1718] V. 15 erfordert eine eigene grammatische Analyse, denn der Umfang der c.I. ist nicht eindeutig, und auch die syntaktische Verknüpfung des Verses muss diskutiert werden. Eingeleitet wird die c.I. mit der Genitivwendung des substantivierten Infinitivs ἀντὶ τοῦ λέγειν (»anstatt des Sagens«)[1719], die sich am besten auf V. 13 »Nun zu euch, die ihr sagt« zurückbeziehen lässt und antithetisch mit »anstatt dass ihr sagt« an die Rede der Kaufleute anknüpft.[1720] Die c.I. selbst wurde in der Vulgataübersetzung als zweigliedrig verstanden. Die Vulgata beschränkt die c.I. nicht (nur) auf den kurzen einleitenden Konditionalsatz (Eventualis, ἐὰν mit Konjunktiv): »Wenn der Herr will«[1721], sondern weitet die Bedingung aus, indem sie καὶ ζήσομεν zum Konditionalsatz zieht:

si dominus voluerit et vixerimus[1722], faciemus hoc aut illud.

Wenn der Herr will und wir leben, werden wir dies und jenes tun.

Damit unterschlägt die Vulgata aber das zweite καί.[1723] Der griechische Text legt es nahe, den Hauptsatz – etwas ungewöhnlich – bereits mit dem ersten καί be-

---

[1712] ποίος als indirektes Fragepronomen: BAUER/ALAND, 1372 (so meine Übersetzung). BAUER/ALAND hält auch direkten Fragesatz für möglich.

[1713] Vgl. die Belege bei BURCHARD, Jak, 185 f.

[1714] BAUER/ALAND, 241, vgl. die parallelen Beispiele mit den Flüchtigkeits-Metaphern »Wolke«, »Strom«, »Traum«, »Schatten« bei BURCHARD, Jak, 186. Im NT nur noch in Apg 2,19 im Zitat aus Jo 3,3.

[1715] ὀλίγος hap. leg. in Jak. Die präpositionale Wendung »für eine kurze Zeit« ist öfter belegt, aber nicht in der frühchristlichen Literatur: BAUER/ALAND, 1143.

[1716] φαίνομαι: sichtbar werden, BAUER/ALAND, 1698. Hap. leg. in Jak. ἀφανίζω: verschwinden, BAUER/ALAND, 249: »unsichtbar machen«, sehr selten im NT, hap. leg. in Jak.

[1717] Ps.-Aristoteles, mund. 399a im Zusammenhang des Auf- und Untergangs der Gestirne.

[1718] Vgl. BACKHAUS, Conditio Jacobaea.

[1719] ἀντί mit Gen. »anstatt«: DBR, § 403. ἀντί hap. leg. in Jak.

[1720] Mit ALLISON, Jak, 659; METZNER, Jak, 249. DIBELIUS, Jak, 278, weist darauf hin, »wie locker in diesem Satzgefüge die Konstruktion ist«.

[1721] BURCHARD, Jak, 187; METZNER, Jak, 249 (weitere Lit.).

[1722] Ähnlich wie Vulgata übersetzt K. BEYER, Semitische Syntax im Neuen Testament I, Göttingen 1962, 69: »Wenn der Herr will, dass wir noch am Leben sind (καὶ ζήσομεν), werden wir …«. Das zweite καί versteht er als *waw apodoseos* (»und«, das den Hauptsatz eröffnet).

[1723] Die Vulgata scheint sich an dem doppelten καί gestört zu haben.

ginnen zu lassen.[1724] Wird V. 14 so gelesen, sind die beiden Prädikate ζήσομεν und ποιήσομεν durch doppeltes καί (»sowohl als auch«) verbunden, das das doppelte καί von V. 13 spiegelt.[1725] Damit wird die Bedingung eingliedrig und bezieht sich ausschließlich auf den Willen des Kyrios, und zugleich wird der Faktor des Noch-am-Leben-Seins der Kaufleute betont und damit das Thema von V. 14 aufgenommen. Wenn die c.I. also lapidar lautet: »Wenn der Herr will«, verliert sie an gnomischem und literarischem Eigengewicht, da sie zu kurz ist. Diese Überkürze hatte die Vulgata vermieden. Die c.I. in dieser Kurzform ist eine bloße Formel ohne eigenes sachliches Profil. »Wenn der Herr will« findet sich in der antiken griechischen und jüdischen Literatur gleichermaßen.[1726] James H. Ropes kommentiert den Befund etwas einseitig folgendermaßen:

> It just appears that James is here recommending to Christians a Hellenistic pious formula of strictly heathen origin. His own piety finds in it a true expression of Christian submission to divine providence.[1727]

Besonders nahe kommt die c.I. dem Text von Sir 39,6:
ἐὰν κύριος ὁ μέγας θελήσῃ, πνεύματι συνέσεως ἐμπλησθήσεται.
Wenn der Herr, der große, es will, wird er mit dem Geist der Erkenntnis erfüllt.[1728]

1Kor 4,19 ist mit Jak 4,15 identisch: ἐὰν ὁ κύριος θελήσῃ, dort und an anderen Stellen bei Paulus auf seine eigenen Reisepläne bezogen. Luke T. Johnson weist besonders darauf hin, dass sich der Verweis auf Gottes Willen häufig im Neuen Testament findet[1729]: Apg 18,21; 21,14; Röm 1,10; 12,2; 15,32; 1Kor 1,1; 4,19; 16,7; Hebr 6,3; 10,36; 1Petr 3,17 und in den Evangelien (auffallend: Mt 26,42 und Mt 6,10).[1730] Kyrios dürfte hier wie öfter im Jakobusbrief für Gott stehen (1,7; 3,9; 4,10; 5,11).[1731]

V. 16 Die Analyse des Verhaltens der Kaufleute schließt sich antithetisch an V. 15 an: Sie verhalten sich *nicht* gemäß der c.I., sondern »rühmen sich in ihrem Übermut«, d. h. sie beharren auf ihrem Standpunkt von V. 13. νῦν δὲ (vgl. ἄγε νῦν in V. 13) bezieht sich auf den »wahren Sachverhalt«[1732], der der (unrealistischen) Position der Kaufleute entgegengestellt wird. Der Vers ist zweigeteilt. Im ersten Hauptsatz formuliert Jakobus seine Diagnose als Vorwurf – weiter in direkter An-

---

[1724] DBR, § 442 Anm. 14.

[1725] DIBELIUS, Jak, 278 f.

[1726] Dokumentation in den Kommentaren (DIBELIUS, Jak, 278 Anm. 3; BURCHARD, Jak, 187).

[1727] ROPES, Jak, 280. ROPES bezieht sich besonders auf Minucius Felix, Octavius 18.11, der in Zweifel zieht, ob die gebräuchliche Formel des »Volkes«: *si deus dederit*, schon christlich (*Christiani confitentis oratio*) sei oder nur allgemeine religiöse Formel (*vulgi naturalis sermo*). Vgl. auch METZNER, Jak, 250, zu der römischen Formel *deo volente* (unter der Voraussetzung, dass Gott will).

[1728] Zur frühjüdischen Weisheitsliteratur vgl. FRANKEMÖLLE, Jak II, 639–641.

[1729] In unterschiedlichsten Wendungen. 1Kor 4,19 fehlt merkwürdigerweise bei JOHNSON.

[1730] JOHNSON, Jak, 296 f.

[1731] Vgl. Sir 39,6.

[1732] BAUER / ALAND, 1104. BURCHARD, Jak, 187: »aber wie die Dinge jetzt liegen«.

314 Kommentar

rede in der 2. Person Plural. Der Vorwurf lautet auf Prahlereien (ἀλαζονείαι), ein Vorwurf, der in mehreren ntl. Lasterkatalogen begegnet.[1733] Die Wendung: »Ihr rühmt (καυχᾶσθε) euch in euren Prahlereien« verdoppelt den Vorwurf stilistisch (Tautologie) und macht ihn dadurch nachhaltiger. Der zweite Hauptsatz formuliert ein allgemein gültiges ethisches Urteil in Bezug auf das Prahlen bzw. Sich-Rühmen (καύχησις). Ruhm / sich rühmen ist ein klassisches paulinisches Motiv. Die Wurzel begegnet im NT nur (sehr häufig) bei Paulus und einige Male im Jakobusbrief.[1734] Anders als Paulus bezieht sich Jakobus aber nur auf die moralisch negative Seite des Ruhm-Motivs: »Jeder derartige Ruhm ist schlecht«.[1735]

V. 17 Die Rede an die Kaufleute schließt mit einer Gnome, die die moralische Verurteilung von V. 16 in eine theologische Verurteilung überführt, indem sie das Verhalten – Jakobus bezeichnet es als ποιεῖν, Tun – der Kaufleute als Sünde qualifiziert. Dabei ist die sachliche Beziehung zu V. 13–16 undeutlich. V. 17 ist trotz des resümierenden οὖν nicht aus dem vorausgehenden Text entwickelt[1736], sondern stellt eine allgemeine ethisch-theologische Maxime (bezogen auf αὐτῷ: »jeden, der das tut«) dar, die im Textzusammenhang das Verhalten der Kaufleute in den großen Zusammenhang von Sünde (ἁμαρτία) einordnet. Jakobus überführt damit die spezielle Thematik des Verhaltens der Kaufleute am Ende der Texteinheit in den großen Zusammenhang der religiösen Ethik. Dass das paulinische Vorzugswort[1737] auch im Jakobusbrief eine gewisse Rolle spielt, zeigte bereits Jak 1,15.[1738] Die Gnome betont die Notwendigkeit, die Kenntnis[1739] des Guten in das *Tun* des Guten umzuwandeln. Das Unterlassen dieser Um- oder Anwendung ist Sünde. Dadurch verbindet Jakobus die spezielle Thematik mit einem zentralen Motiv des Briefes (2,12: reden und tun; 2,13: Mitleid tun; 3,18: Frieden tun): Gutes Handeln als solches ist Gegenstand der ethischen Mahnung des Briefes (2,8).[1740] V. 17 erfüllt dieselbe Funktion wie 2,26 und 3,18: Eine längere Argumentation, die einem speziellen Thema gilt, wird mit einer allgemeinen ethischen Gnome abgeschlossen.[1741] Ähnlich

---

[1733] Das Substantiv ἀλαζονεία hap. leg. in Jak, im NT nur noch 1Joh 2,16 (»d. Prahlen mit d. Vermögen«: BAUER / ALAND, 67). ἀλάζων, der Prahler: Röm 1,30; 2Tim 3,2 (in Lasterkatalogen).

[1734] Verb: Jak 1,9; 4,16; καύχησις Jak 4,16: hap. leg. in Jak. Vgl. 1Clem 21,5: ἐγκαυχάομαι ἐν ἀλαζονείᾳ τοῦ λόγου ([die Menschen, die] sich in Prahlerei ihrer Rede rühmen).

[1735] πονηρός noch in 2,4. Sehr häufig in den synoptischen Evangelien. BAUER / ALAND, 1385: »im sittl. Sinn schlecht, böse«.

[1736] Anders BURCHARD, Jak, 188.

[1737] Sehr häufig im Hebr, häufiger auch im Joh und im 1Joh.

[1738] 1,15 (Nähe zu Röm 7: vgl. zu Jak 1,15); 2,9 (konkrete Verfehlung der Bevorzugung bestimmter Personen); 4,17; 5,15.16.20.

[1739] BURCHARD, Jak, 188, möchte εἰδότι nicht als »der etwas weiß«, sondern als »der sich versteht auf« übersetzen: »Die Rede ist von dem, der ›also‹ Gutes zu tun … vermag und nicht tut«. Aber das passt nicht besser zu den ruhmsüchtigen Reden der Kaufleute. Ein näherer Zusammenhang zwischen V. 17 und dem vorangehenden Text stellt sich auch bei dieser Interpretation von εἰδότι nicht her.

[1740] Dort in der abgeschwächten Wendung: καλῶς ποιεῖτε (»ihr handelt richtig«).

[1741] Die folgende Texteinheit 5,1–6 enthält keinen allgemeinen Schlusssatz.

wie bei der c.I. benutzt Jakobus eine allgemein bekannte und anerkannte Einsicht: Wer wissentlich gegen die Wahrheit oder gegen die Erkenntnis handelt, wird zugrunde gehen.[1742]

C. 5,1–6: Gegen Reiche

(1) **Wohlan ihr Reichen, weint und heult**[1743] **über das Elend**[1744]**, das auf euch kommen wird.** (2) **Euer Reichtum ist verfault, und eure Gewänder sind mottenzerfressen,** (3) **euer Gold und Silber verrostet, und ihr Rost wird gegen euch zeugen**[1745] **und euer Fleisch**[1746] **verzehren wie Feuer. Ihr habt Schätze gesammelt in der Endzeit**[1747]**!** (4) **Siehe der Lohn der Arbeiter, die eure Ländereien gemäht haben, den ihr ihnen vorenthalten habt**[1748]**, schreit, und die Rufe der Erntearbeiter haben Eingang gefunden in die Ohren des Herrn Zebaoth.** (5) **Ihr habt geschwelgt auf der Erde und geschlemmt, ihr habt eure Herzen ernährt am Schlachttag,** (6) **verurteilt, getötet habt ihr den Gerechten, und**[1749] **nicht hat er euch Widerstand geleistet.**

Textkritik: V. 5 εν ημερα lesen 01*. 03. 33. 43 (lectio difficilior), εν ημεραις liest 02, ως εν ημερα lesen 01C2. 044 und sehr viele Minuskeln (Abschwächung).

Wieder wendet sich der Verfasser an eine sozial klar definierte Gruppe, diesmal an die Reichen, und spricht ihre Mitglieder wieder direkt in der 2.Pers.Plur. an. Formal schließt die Texteinheit an die vorangehende Einheit an: Sie wird mit derselben Formel eröffnet. Zugleich greift der Verfasser auch auf Motive aus der ersten Bußpredigt gegen die Sünder und Zweiseeler zurück. Angegriffen werden jetzt nicht Kaufleute, sondern reiche *Grundbesitzer*. Die Form ist eine *Anklagerede* mit endzeitlichen Motiven. Der Ton ist besonders heftig. Jakobus spielt auf Prophetenworte an und verweist auf »die letzten Tage« und bereitet damit schon die nächste Texteinheit (5,7–11) vor. Der Text stellt wie schon die Rede an die Kaufleute eine sorgfältig komponierte kurze Einheit dar und endet – anders als die Rede gegen die Kaufleute – nicht mit einer ethischen Gnome, sondern gipfelt abrupt in dem unerwarteten Vorwurf des Mordes an dem Gerechten.

V. 1 Jakobus setzt mit der Wiederholung der Apostrophe ἄγε νῦν ein. Die Angesprochenen werden – wieder anders als die Kaufleute – aber nicht durch ihre Reden charakterisiert, sondern direkt als Reiche bezeichnet. Eine entsprechende Anrede findet sich in Lk 6,24:

[1742] Belege bei BURCHARD, Jak, 188.
[1743] Das Partizip ist parataktisch aufgelöst.
[1744] Im Griechischen Plural.
[1745] Wörtlich: »euch zum Zeugnis sein«.
[1746] Im Griechischen Plural.
[1747] Wörtlich: »in den letzten Tagen«.
[1748] Die Partizipien sind relativisch aufgelöst.
[1749] »Und« ist im Deutschen hinzugefügt.

Πλὴν οὐαὶ ὑμῖν τοῖς πλουσίοις, ὅτι ἀπέχετε τὴν παράκλησιν ὑμῶν.
Wehe euch Reichen, denn ihr habt euren Trost schon gehabt.

Der Zusammenhang mit dem Motiv des Weinens und Klagens, der Lukas und Jakobus verbindet, wurde schon zu Jak 4,9 dargestellt. Jakobus nimmt die Anklage des Abschnittes, der gegen die »Sünder« gerichtet ist, verstärkt wieder auf.

»Der Reiche« begegnet im Neuen Testament *thematisch* in zwei Schriften: im Lukasevangelium und im Jakobusbrief (1,10.11; 2,6.7; 5,1).[1750] Hatte Jakobus die Reichen schon in Kapitel 1 (die Reichen werden dahinwelken und vergehen) und 2 (die Reichen führen Prozesse gegen die Gemeindeglieder) negativ geschildert, hält er ihnen jetzt eine Anklagerede, die in den Mordvorwurf mündet. In 2,6 hatte Jakobus den Reichen vorgeworfen, gewaltsam gegen »euch« vorzugehen und Prozesse gegen »euch«, d. h. die Adressaten, zu führen[1751], die damit in der Logik der Epistel – nicht zu verwechseln mit der sozialen Realität in frühchristlichen Gemeinden – auf die Seite der Armen, nicht der »Reichen«, gehören. Einen entsprechenden, aber viel schärfer formulierten Vorwurf stellt Jakobus an das Ende seiner Anklagerede in 5,1–6.

Jakobus beginnt mit einer Aufforderung zur Trauer, gebunden an die Ansage zukünftigen Elends. Die Sprache ist nahe bei den Unheilsankündigungen der Propheten. ταλαιπωρία, Elend, wird in Septuaginta häufiger verwendet[1752], begegnet im Neuen Testament nur noch in Röm 3,16 im Zitat aus Jes 59,7. ἐπέρχεσθαι wird auch in Lk 21,26 im Zusammenhang der Furcht der Menschen in den Endzeitereignissen gesetzt.[1753] Die dreigliedrige Aufforderung von 4,9: ταλαιπωρήσατε καὶ πενθήσατε καὶ κλαύσατε, wird in 5,1 variiert zu: κλαύσατε ὀλολύζοντες ἐπὶ ταῖς ταλαιπωρίαις ὑμῶν ταῖς ἐπερχομέναις. ὀλολύζειν ist hap. leg. im Neuen Testament, begegnet aber öfter in Septuaginta in den Unheilsankündigungen der Propheten.[1754]

V. 2–3 Jakobus stellt in vier Aussagesätzen – je zwei Hauptsätze sind durch »und« verbunden, der vierte Hauptsatz hat zwei erweiterte Prädikate – den Reichen die Nichtigkeit ihres Besitzes vor. Dabei knüpft er variierend an Kapitel 2 an: Wieder werden Reichtum und Armut durch die äußeren Zeichen von Edelmetall und Kleidung definiert. Am Schluss von V. 3 wird in einem sentenziösen kurzen Aussagesatz der Grund für die Aufforderung zur Trauer in V. 1 genannt, gleichsam der entscheidende Anklagepunkt: Es ist das Anhäufen von Schätzen (ἐθησαυρίσατε) »in den letzten Tagen«. Diese Anklage wird in einer Anrede in der 2. Pers. Plur. den Adressaten gleichsam auf den Kopf zugesagt. Zuvor wird in V. 2 die Nichtigkeit des θησαυρίζειν[1755] in zwei geläufigen exemplarischen Bildern aus dem Bereich organischen und anorganischen Zerfalls entfaltet. *Erstens* ist der Reichtum der Rei-

---

[1750] Zum Themenkomplex Reichtum und Armut vgl. oben zu Jak 2,5.
[1751] Schima, Art. Prozessrecht, RAC 28, 434–459 zum Thema des Prozessführens (vgl. 2,6).
[1752] ταλαιπωρία hap. leg. in Jak. Öfter in LXX. Verb: Jak 4,9 (hap. leg. im NT), Adjektiv: Röm 7,2; Apk 3,17.
[1753] Eph 2,7: die kommenden Zeiten.
[1754] Jes 13,6; 15,3 (mit »Weinen«); Jer 31,31; Am 8,3; Sach 11,2.
[1755] Hap. leg. in Jak. Vgl. Mt 6,19 f und Lk 12,21.

C. Briefcorpus 317

chen verfault (Perf. 2 σέσηπεν von σήπειν[1756]), *zweitens* sind die Kleider von Motten zerfressen (Adj. σητόβρωτος[1757]). V. 2 ist im »prophetischen Perfekt« gehalten und knüpft schon grammatisch an prophetische Rede an.[1758]

In V. 3 wechselt Jakobus zum Futur als Zeichen endzeitlicher Rede. Zu den zwei genannten Zerfallsbildern fügt er ein *drittes* hinzu: Gold und Silber sind verrostet (Perf. Pass. κατίωται von κατιοῦσθαι[1759]). In V. 2 wird der Reichtum abstrakt als πλοῦτος[1760] bezeichnet, in V. 3 dann mit der Metonymie »Gold und Silber«[1761] umschrieben. Die beiden Verben σήπειν[1762] und κατιοῦσθαι[1763] sowie das Adjektiv σητόβρωτος[1764] in V. 2 sind hapax legomena im Neuen Testament. Für das Kleidungsmotiv gilt die gewählte Wortwahl nicht: Statt des feinen ἐσθής von 2,2 setzt Jakobus hier für »Kleidung« das geläufige τὰ ἱμάτια.[1765]

Das Motiv des Rostes[1766] von V. 3a wird in V. 3b weitergeführt. Es entsteht eine *dreigliedrige* Klimax, die das Motiv der Korrosion besonders anschaulich macht. (1) Die Aussage: »euer Gold und Silber sind verrostet bzw. korrodiert«[1767], verweist auf die Erfahrung von Gefährdung und Vergänglichkeit des Reichtums hin, die auch in Mt 6,19par ausgesprochen wird:

Μὴ θησαυρίζετε ὑμῖν θησαυροὺς ἐπὶ τῆς γῆς, ὅπου σὴς καὶ βρῶσις ἀφανίζει.

Sammelt euch nicht Schätze auf der Erde, wo Motte und Rost sie zerfressen.

Das Bild vom Rost in V. 3a wird in zwei Bildworten radikalisiert, in denen sich der Rost gleichsam verselbständigt und personifiziert. (2) Zunächst wird dieser Rost gegen die Reichen als »Belastungszeuge«[1768] auftreten (Personifikation): εἰς μαρτύριον ὑμῖν ἔσται. Die Wendung ist ein deutlicher »Septuagentismus«.[1769] Jakobus benutzt das Gerichtsszenario. Es folgt (3) ein weiteres krudes Bild: »Der Rost wird das Fleisch der Reichen fressen bzw. zersetzen«. In diesem Bild gelingt Jakobus der bildliche Übersprung vom *Material* des *Schatzes*, dem Metall, zur *materiellen* Seite der *Reichen*, ihren Körpern (Plural!), und damit die persönliche Zuspitzung

---

[1756] Grundbedeutung: »make rotten or putrid« (LSJ, 1594). Hap. leg. im NT.

[1757] Hap. leg. im NT.

[1758] Zum sog. prophetischen Perfekt (Jes 60,1LXX) vgl. DBR, § 344,1 und Metzner, Jak, 258 mit Anm. 127.

[1759] Hap. leg. im NT.

[1760] Hap. leg. in Jak. Vgl. Apk 18,17 zum Reichtum der Kaufleute: μιᾷ ὥρᾳ ἠρημώθη ὁ τοσοῦτος πλοῦτος (Denn in einer Stunde ist ein solcher Reichtum verwüstet).

[1761] Im Neuen Testament öfter zusammen: Apg 3,6 (χρυσίον); 1Petr 1,18 (χρυσίον); Mt 10,9.

[1762] Vgl. Hi 16,8; 19,20; 33,21; 40,12; Sir 14,19.

[1763] Auch hap. leg. LXX: Sir 12,11 (korrodierter Metallspiegel).

[1764] Auch hap. leg. LXX: Hi 13,28 mit ἱμάτιον.

[1765] Sehr häufig in LXX, hap. leg. in Jak; häufig im NT.

[1766] ἰός im NT »Gift«: Röm 3,13 (Zitat von Ps 139,4); »Gift« Jak 3,8; »Rost« 5,3.

[1767] Vgl. dazu die ausführliche Dokumentation bei Burchard, Jak, 191. B. übersetzt »von Zersetzung befallen«, 181.

[1768] Burchard, Jak, 191.

[1769] Burchard, Jak, 191 (LXX-Belege). Hap. leg. in Jak., im NT öfter: Mt 8,4; 10,18; 24,14; Mk 6,11; Hebr 3,5.

318 Kommentar

seiner Anklagerede. Die neue Doppel-Metonymie, »Fleisch«[1770] statt »Körper« und »fressen«[1771] statt »töten« kann in Richtung auf das Todesurteil interpretiert werden. Damit bliebe Jakobus bei dem Gerichtsszenario.[1772] Unter Umständen hat sich das Bild von der Rost-Korrosion aber auch verselbständigt. Dafür spricht der Zusatz ὡς πῦρ. »Feuer« wird im Jakobusbrief als negativ konnotierte Metapher schon in 3,5.6 eingesetzt und steht für Zerstörung und Vernichtung im endzeitlichen Kontext.[1773] Dasselbe Bild findet sich in Apk 17,16 für das Ende der Hure Babylon. Für die Hörner und das Tier gilt:

τὰς σάρκας αὐτῆς φάγονται καὶ αὐτὴν κατακαύσουσιν ἐν πυρί.
Sie werden ihr Fleisch essen und sie mit Feuer verbrennen.[1774]

Der Grund der Anklage: »Ihr habt Schätze gesammelt[1775] in den letzten Tagen[1776]« bezieht sich auf den *Zeitpunkt*. Der gleiche Vorwurf begegnet auch in der synoptischen Tradition. Die Reichen verhalten sich nicht zeitgemäß, d. h. endzeitgemäß. Auch hier wird das endzeitliche Gerichtsszenario vorausgesetzt: In der Endzeit wird irdischer Reichtum nichts nützen (Mt 6,20; Lk 12,21)[1777] – im Gegenteil: Er wird vernichtet werden. Mt 6,19 und Lk 12,33 zeigen verwandte Traditionen der endzeitlich motivierten Reichtumskritik:

[1770] Hap. leg. in Jak.

[1771] φάγομαι Fut. von ἐσθίειν (DBR, § 74,2), hap. leg. in Jak.

[1772] So Burchard, Jak, 191 f: »Der Belastungszeuge vollstreckt auch das Todesurteil«. Zum Gerichtsszenario als Rahmen für 5,3 vgl. auch Apk 19,35 (dort eschatologisch gewendet).

[1773] Jak 3,6: die Zunge ist »von der Hölle entzündet«.

[1774] Das Bild von Fressen auch Apk 19,35 (dort in der apokalyptischen Vision von Kap. 19,11–21 nicht-bildhaft von den Vögeln, die das Fleisch der Könige fressen). Weitere Belege zum »fressenden Feuer« bei Burchard, Jak, 192. φάγειν ist hap. leg. in Jak.

[1775] θησαυρίζειν ist hap. leg. in Jak. Das Verb »kann ohne Objekt stehen« (Burchard, Jak, 192: dort Belege).

[1776] ἐν ἐσχάταις ἡμέραις: die Wendung ist in LXX nur wörtlich bei Jes 2,2 belegt, abgewandelt Spr 31,26 und Dan 11,20. Sie gehört zum frühchristlichen eschatologischen Soziolekt: Joh 3,19; 11,24; 12,48 (stets Singular: »der jüngste Tag«); Apg 2,17; 2Tim 3,1; 2Petr 3,3 (stets Plural: »die Endzeit«).

[1777] Burchard, Jak, 192, kommentiert: »Der Satz ist dann keine Gerichtsansage, sondern unterstreicht, daß die Reichen Toren sind«. Aber der Satz ist bei aller Knappheit eben der entscheidende Anklagepunkt.

Mt 6,19	Lk 12,33[1778]
Μὴ **θησαυρίζετε** ὑμῖν θησαυροὺς ἐπὶ τῆς γῆς, ὅπου **σὴς** καὶ **βρῶσις** ἀφανίζει καὶ ὅπου κλέπται διορύσσουσιν καὶ κλέπτουσιν.	Πωλήσατε τὰ ὑπάρχοντα ὑμῶν καὶ δότε ἐλεημοσύνην· ποιήσατε ἑαυτοῖς βαλλάντια μὴ παλαιούμενα, **θησαυρὸν** ἀνέκλειπτον ἐν τοῖς οὐρανοῖς, ὅπου κλέπτης οὐκ ἐγγίζει οὐδὲ **σὴς** διαφθείρει.
Sammelt euch nicht Schätze auf der Erde wo Motte und Holzwurm sie zerstört und wo Diebe einbrechen und stehlen.	Verkauft euren Besitz und gebt Almosen. Schafft euch Geldbeutel, die nicht veralten, einen Schatz, der nicht abnimmt, in den Himmel, wohin kein Dieb kommt und keine Motte Zerstörung anrichtet.

V. 4 Wo sind die »Reichen« dieser Gerichtsrede sozial verortet? Es handelt sich um reiche Landbesitzer (χώρα) wie in Lk 12,16.[1779] Den Reichen stehen die Arbeiter[1780] gegenüber, genauer als Schnitter, d. h. als Erntearbeiter bezeichnet. Jakobus verschärft das Gerichtsszenario, indem er die soziale Situation literarisch mit den Mitteln biblischer Metaphernsprache überhöht und radikalisiert. Die Opfer rufen den Herrn Zebaoth an. Grund ist ein neuer Vorwurf, der in eine andere Richtung als V. 3 zielt. Es geht jetzt nicht um das unzeitgemäße Verhalten der Reichen, sondern darum, dass ihr Reichtum auf ungerechter Lohnbemessung bzw. Lohnverweigerung beruht. V. 4 verbindet durch »und« zwei Hauptsätze, die unterschiedliche Subjekte haben (synthetischer Parallelismus).

Der *Vordersatz* enthält ein kühnes Bild und ist analog zu V. 3 konzipiert. Das Subjekt ist hier der personifizierte vorenthaltene Lohn der Erntearbeiter, der schreit – ob nach dem Lohn oder nach Gerechtigkeit oder einfach als Ausdruck der Verzweiflung, bleibt ungesagt. Das Bild enthält eine paradoxe Komponente: Der *nicht vorhandene* Lohn *schreit*. κράζειν steht für lautes Rufen bzw. Schreien.[1781] Die deutsche bildliche Wendung: »Diese Sache schreit zum Himmel« geht auf Gen 4,10; 18,20[1782] und Jak 5,4 zurück. ὁ μισθὸς τῶν ἐργατῶν begegnet als Wendung im Jakobusbrief nur hier. Jakobus denkt bei den Arbeitern des Näheren an Schnitter: ἀμᾶν, ein hap. leg. im Neuen Testament, bezieht sich auf das Abmähen von Feldern.

[1778] Vgl. auch Lk 12,21 οὕτως ὁ θησαυρίζων ἑαυτῷ καὶ μὴ εἰς θεὸν πλουτῶν (So ist der, der Schätze für sich selbst sammelt und nicht reich bei Gott ist).

[1779] ἀνθρώπου τινὸς πλουσίου εὐφόρησεν ἡ χώρα (Das Feld eines reichen Menschen hatte gut getragen). χώρα ist hap. leg. in Jak und begegnet in der Bedeutung »Felder / Landbesitz«. Felder als Metonymie für Landbesitz und als Grundlage des Reichtums nur noch in Lk 12 im NT.

[1780] ἐργάτης: einige Male im Literalsinn bei den Synoptikern, hap. leg. in Jak.

[1781] Hap. leg. in Jak, häufig im NT. Vgl. Beda, Expositio, 176, der auf Hiob 31,38–40 (Vulgata) verweist (Metaphorik des Schreiens).

[1782] Gen 4,10: φωνὴ αἵματος τοῦ ἀδελφοῦ σου βοᾷ πρός με ἐκ τῆς γῆς (Die Stimme des Blutes deines Bruders ruft zu mir aus der Erde). 18,21: καταβὰς οὖν ὄψομαι εἰ κατὰ τὴν κραυγὴν αὐτῶν τὴν ἐρχομένην πρός με συντελοῦνται (Ich werde also hinabsteigen und sehen, ob sie es entsprechend dem Geschrei treiben, das zu mir dringt). Beide Male reagiert Gott auf das laute Rufen von der Erde.

320 Kommentar

Die Reichen – so der Vorwurf – berauben die Erntearbeiter ihres Lohnes. Das im NT seltene ἀποστερεῖν wird hier wie in 1Kor 6,8 metaphorisch eingesetzt.[1783] Damit bezieht sich Jakobus auf Dtn 24,14 f und Sir 31,25–27:

Dtn 24,14: Οὐκ ἀπαδικήσεις[1784] μισθὸν πένητος καὶ ἐνδεοῦς ἐκ τῶν ἀδελφῶν σου ἢ ἐκ τῶν προσηλύτων τῶν ἐν ταῖς πόλεσίν σου. (15) αὐθημερὸν ἀποδώσεις τὸν μισθὸν αὐτοῦ, οὐκ ἐπιδύσεται ὁ ἥλιος ἐπ᾽ αὐτῷ, ὅτι πένης ἐστὶν καὶ ἐν αὐτῷ ἔχει τὴν ἐλπίδα· καὶ οὐ καταβοήσεται κατὰ σοῦ πρὸς κύριον, καὶ ἔσται ἐν σοὶ ἁμαρτία.

(14) Dem Tagelöhner, der bedürftig und arm ist, sollst du seinen Lohn nicht vorenthalten, er sei von deinen Brüdern oder den Fremdlingen, die in deinem Land und in deinen Städten sind, (15) sondern du sollst ihm seinen Lohn am selben Tage geben, dass die Sonne nicht darüber untergehe – denn er ist bedürftig und verlangt danach –, damit er nicht wider dich den Herrn anrufe und es dir zur Sünde werde.

Sir 34, 21 f.LXX: ἄρτος ἐπιδεομένων ζωὴ πτωχῶν, ὁ ἀποστερῶν αὐτὴν ἄνθρωπος αἱμάτων. 22 φονεύων τὸν πλησίον ὁ ἀφαιρούμενος ἐμβίωσιν, καὶ ἐκχέων αἷμα ὁ ἀποστερῶν μισθὸν μισθίου.

21 Brot der Bedürftigen (ist) Leben der Armen; derjenige der es raubt, (ist) ein Mensch des Blutvergießens. 22 Den Nächsten tötet, wer (ihm) den Lebensunterhalt wegnimmt; und Blut vergießt, wer den Lohn des Tagelöhners raubt.[1785]

Hinter dem Bild steht sowohl die gemeinantike Überzeugung aus Lk 10,7 / Mt 10,10:

ἄξιος γὰρ ὁ ἐργάτης τοῦ μισθοῦ αὐτοῦ bzw. ἄξιος γὰρ ὁ ἐργάτης τῆς τροφῆς αὐτοῦ.[1786]
Denn der Arbeiter ist seines Lohnes / seines Unterhaltes wert,

als auch die im antiken Judentum breit bezeugte Verpflichtung, den Tageslohn am Abend rechtzeitig zu bezahlen (Mt 20,1–16).

[1783] Hap. leg. in Jak. Ähnlich 1Kor 6,7 (»berauben«: metaphorisch für »finanziell und juristisch übervorteilen«).8 (Aber ihr tut Unrecht und ›beraubt‹ – und das bei Brüdern). Mk 10,19 fügt in die Reihe von Geboten aus der zweiten Tafel des Dekalogs ein: μὴ ἀποστερήσῃς (fehlt in B*KW𝑓¹³ u. a. Hss.), vgl. dazu A. YARBO COLLINS, Mark. A Commentary (Hermeneia), Minneapolis 2007, 478. COLLINS verweist auf Lev 5,20–26LXX; Mal 3,5LXX und Sir 4,1LXX. Zum Thema Reiche – Lohnarbeiter vgl. JÓNSSON, James, 258–282; M. PEACHIN, Attacken und Erniedrigung als alltägliche Elemente der kaiserzeitlichen Regierungspraxis, in: R. Haensch / J. Heinrichs (Hg.), Herrschen und Verwalten. Der Alltag der Administration des römischen Reiches in der Kaiserzeit, KHAb 46, Köln / Weimar / Wien 2007, 117–125; MORALES, Rich and Poor in James; H. RHEE, Loving the Poor, Saving the Rich: Wealth, Poverty, and Early Christian Formation, Grand Rapids 2012; DERS. (Hg.), Wealth and Poverty in Early Christianity, Ad Fontes, Minneapolis 2017, xvii-xxii und 1–21.

[1784] Codex A: ἀποστερήσῃς.

[1785] Vgl. auch Sir 4,1 τὴν ζωὴν τοῦ πτωχοῦ μὴ ἀποστερήσῃς (Das Leben des Armen sollst du nicht berauben) und Mal 3,5: καὶ προσάξω πρὸς ὑμᾶς ἐν κρίσει καὶ ἔσομαι μάρτυς ταχὺς … καὶ ἐπὶ τοὺς ἀποστεροῦντας μισθὸν μισθωτοῦ (Und ich will zu euch kommen zum Gericht und will ein schneller Zeuge sein … gegen die, die den Lohn des Lohnarbeiters rauben).

[1786] Das Thema wird in einer Gleichniserzählung erörtert in Mt 20,1–16 (μισθός).

Der *Nachsatz*[1787] nimmt das Bild auf und führt es in veränderter Form weiter. Jetzt sind es die Schnitter (Part. Aorist von θερίζειν[1788]) selbst, die rufen.[1789] Diese Rufe dringen zu Gott. Jakobus befindet sich hier nicht nur semantisch und metaphorisch in der Bilderwelt der Septuaginta. Die Wendung »εἰς τὰ ὦτα κυρίου σαβαώθ eingehen«[1790] spielt auf Jes 5,9 an. Dort heißt es im Kontext eines prophetischen Werufs über die Reichen, die dem Nächsten etwas wegnehmen:

(8) Οὐαὶ οἱ συνάπτοντες οἰκίαν πρὸς οἰκίαν καὶ ἀγρὸν πρὸς ἀγρὸν ἐγγίζοντες, ἵνα τοῦ πλησίον ἀφέλωνταί τι· μὴ οἰκήσετε μόνοι ἐπὶ τῆς γῆς; (9) ἠκούσθη γὰρ εἰς τὰ ὦτα κυρίου σαβαωθ ταῦτα.

(8) Wehe (über) sie, die Haus an Haus reihen und Acker an Acker fügen, damit sie dem Nächsten etwas wegnehmen. Wollt ihr etwa allein auf dem Land leben? (9) Denn dies ist dem Herrn Zebaoth zu Ohren gekommen.

Der Titel κύριος σαβαώθ begegnet im Neuen Testament nur noch in Röm 9,29 im Zitat von Jes 1,9LXX.[1791] σαβαώθ ist in LXX[1792] fast ausschließlich bei Jesaja bezeugt, der den Titel sehr häufig verwendet. Jakobus setzt hier also einen der wenigen *expliziten* semantischen Verweise auf seine jüdische literarisch-religiöse Tradition, die Septuaginta[1793], sowie auf die hebräische Sprache. Damit erschließt sich auch die ganze Texteinheit als von alttestamentlichem, speziell prophetischem Stil geformt. In V. 5 und 6 wird dieser Hintergrund noch deutlicher.

V. 5 Die Anklage geht weiter: Jakobus inkriminiert jetzt in einem dritten Anklagepunkt das üppige Leben der Reichen. Wieder verwendet er zwei Hauptsätze, diesmal asyndetisch gereiht. Der erste Hauptsatz hat zwei Prädikate, die fast bedeutungsgleich sind (Hendiadyoin). τρυφᾶν: »ein üppiges Leben führen, schwelgen« ist hap. leg. im NT.[1794] Einen ähnlichen Vorwurf macht der 2. Petrusbrief den »falschen Propheten« (2,1) in 2,13:

[1787] BURCHARD, Jakobus, 193, weist auf die Bedeutung des Perfekts hin: Gott hat die Schnitter bereits gehört.

[1788] θερίζειν hap. leg. in Jak. Vgl. Mt 6,26par; 25,24.26par; Joh 4,36 (Beziehung von Arbeit des Schnitters und Lohn, metaphorisch verwendet); Gal 6,7 (Beziehung von Saat und Ernte).

[1789] βοή: hap. leg. im NT, »feierliches lautes Rufen«. Vgl. Gen 4,10 (Verb); Ex 2,23 (Substantiv). Öfter in LXX, so in Ex 2,23: ἀνέβη ἡ βοὴ αὐτῶν πρὸς τὸν θεὸν ἀπὸ τῶν ἔργων (Ihr Schreien wegen der Arbeiten stieg auf zu Gott). Lk 18,7 (verbal) feierliches Rufen der Gerechten zu Gott: ὁ δὲ θεὸς οὐ μὴ ποιήσῃ τὴν ἐκδίκησιν τῶν ἐκλεκτῶν αὐτοῦ τῶν βοώντων αὐτῷ ἡμέρας καὶ νυκτός (Sollte Gott nicht auch Recht schaffen seinen Auserwählten, die zu ihm rufen Tag und Nacht?). – Das Motiv vom Rufen des Blutes Abels aus Gen 4,10 wird in Hebr 12,24 aufgenommen: »das Blut der Besprengung, das besser spricht als das Abels«.

[1790] »Ohr« hap. leg. in Jak. »Eingehen« noch Jak 2,2 (nicht metaphorisch).

[1791] Vgl. auch 1Clem 34,6 (Jes 6,3).

[1792] Hebr. ṣəvā'ôt wird in LXX als σαβαωθ und (häufiger) als παντοκράτωρ (2Kor 6,18 im Zitat und mehrfach in Apk) übersetzt.

[1793] Vgl. WISCHMEYER, Social and Religious Milieu, 33–41.

[1794] BAUER / ALAND, 1652. In LXX selten, dagegen ist τρυφή häufig bezeugt (Bedeutung überwiegend positiv wie Gen 3,23). Lk 7,25: kritisch. Vgl. auch Herm sim VI 64,4 negativ.

322 Kommentar

ἀδικούμενοι μισθὸν ἀδικίας, ἡδονὴν ἡγούμενοι τὴν ἐν ἡμέρᾳ τρυφήν. …
den Lohn der Ungerechtigkeit davontragend, halten sie es für eine Lust, bei Tage ein
üppiges Leben zu führen.

Der Parallelbegriff σπαταλᾶν, »schwelgen, üppig leben« ist hap. leg. bei Jakobus.[1795]
Im 1Tim wird er auf den falschen Lebenswandel christlicher Witwen bezogen.[1796]
Jakobus benutzt hier seltene Verben in eindeutig negativer moralischer Konnotati-
on, die sich auch vereinzelt in den moralischen Anlagereden der Pastoralbriefe und
Katholischen Briefe finden. ἐπὶ τῆς γῆς ist eine gebräuchliche Wendung in LXX und
im NT.[1797]

Der zweite Hauptsatz: ἐθρέψατε τὰς καρδίας ὑμῶν ἐν ἡμέρᾳ σφαγῆς, wechselt wieder in die metaphorische Rede. Herz[1798] steht als Metonymie für Person. τρέφειν (im
Aorist wie die vorangehenden Verben), füttern, aufziehen, ernähren, unterhalten,
ist hap. leg. bei Jakobus.[1799] σφαγή ist »das Schlachten, die Schlachtung«.[1800] Das
Substantiv, hap. leg. bei Jakobus, begegnet im NT außer in Jak 5,5 in Apg 8,32 (Jes
53,7 »das Lamm, das zur Schlachtbank geführt wird«) und Röm 8,36 (Ps 43,23LXX
»wir werden geachtet wie Schlachtschafe«), also im Zusammenhang von LXX-Zitaten, die sich auf den Opfertod beziehen. Auch in Jak 5,5 kann ein Anklang an LXX
vorliegen. ἡμέρα σφαγῆς findet sich als Wendung nur in Jer 12,3: ἅγνισον αὐτοὺς εἰς
ἡμέραν σφαγῆς αὐτῶν (Weihe sie für den Tag ihrer Schlachtung). Der Prophet setzt
die Wendung metaphorisch und bezieht sich auf die Männer von Anathoth (11,21),
deren Vernichtung der Prophet von Gott erbittet.

Im Zusammenhang von V. 5 ist das Bild vom Schlachttag in den Kommentaren
unterschiedlich interpretiert worden. (1) Liest man die drei Verben von V. 5: τρυφᾶν,
σπαταλᾶν und τρέφειν in einer Reihe, betrifft der Vorwurf das schwelgerische Leben der Reichen. Der »Schlachttag« ist in diesem Zusammenhang als Tag eines
Opferfestes mit Opferschmaus oder auch nur als Schlachttag auf dem Landbesitz
der Reichen zu verstehen, der ihnen den Anlass zu einem üppigen Festmahl bietet.
Dafür plädiert zuletzt Rainer Metzner.[1801] Es liegt dann weder eine Gerichts- noch
eine *theologische* Opfervorstellung zugrunde, sondern Kritik am üppigen Leben der

---

[1795] BAUER / ALAND, 1519.

[1796] Vgl. im NT nur noch 1Tim 5,6: eine Witwe, »die schwelgerisch lebt, ist lebendig tot«; Barn 10,3. Verb
in LXX nur Sir 21,15 (negativ) und Ez 16,49 (negativ), Substantiv nur Sir 27,13 (negativ).

[1797] Vgl. noch Jak 5,17.

[1798] Jak 1,26; 3,14; 4,8; 5,5.8.

[1799] Mehrfach im NT, Substantiv Jak 2,15: (auch mehrfach in LXX). Die Übersetzungen wählen gern die
Übersetzung »mästen« mit einer speziell negativen Konnotation, die aber bei LSJ, 1814, nicht vorgeschlagen
wird.

[1800] BAUER / ALAND, 1587. σφάζειν im NT 1Joh 3,12 (Kain tötete seinen Bruder) und mehrfach in Apk
6,9–11 und 18,24 für den Tod der Gerechten: καὶ ἐν αὐτῇ αἷμα προφητῶν καὶ ἁγίων εὑρέθη καὶ πάντων τῶν
ἐσφαγμένων ἐπὶ τῆς γῆς (Das Blut der Propheten und der Heiligen ist in ihr gefunden worden und das Blut
aller derer, die auf Erden umgebracht worden sind).

[1801] So POPKES, Jak, 310, und METZNER, Jak, 268 f. Beide lesen die Wendung »am Schlachttag« generisch
(»jedes Mal beim Schlachtfest«, METZNER, 269), dagegen ALLISON, Jak, 683.

Reichen analog zu 2Petr 2,13.[1802] (2) Dale Allison entscheidet sich dagegen unter Hinweis auf den deutlichen Gerichtskontext und auf 1Hen für die Variante des »eschatological reading«.[1803] Jakobus würde nach dieser Interpretation den Reichen das Endgericht ankündigen. Dagegen spricht der Aorist der drei Verben, die alle dieselbe Zeitstufe der nahen Vergangenheit, die in die Gegenwart reicht, anzeigen und nicht auf das zukünftige Gericht bezogen werden können.[1804] Das gilt besonders, wenn man den Hinweis von Burchard ernstnimmt, dass die beiden Zeitbestimmungen »in den letzten Tagen« und »am Schlachttag« zueinander in Beziehung stehen.[1805] Jak 5,7–11 macht aber deutlich, dass das »Kommen des Herrn« und »Richters« zwar nahe ist, aber eben noch aussteht.[1806] (3) Auch Dibelius hält fest, dass »die Worte … aus dem Bewußtsein der Endzeit heraus geredet« sind.[1807] Bei der Deutung des »Tages« ist er vorsichtiger: »In diesem Pathos des Armenpietismus könnte auch ein Unglückstag ἡμέρα σφαγῆς heißen, bei dem es nur den Armen schlecht erging oder gar an dem die Armen von den Reichen zu leiden hatten«.[1808] Diese Deutung bleibt aber unbestimmt. (4) Frankemölle bezieht den Schlachttag dagegen auf »den Tag der Ermordung des Gerechten, da Schlachten und Morden zum gleichen semantischen Feld gehören«.[1809] Diese Deutung wird dem Tempus der Verben gerecht und berücksichtigt zugleich den eschatologisch gefärbten Ton der Metaphern und den Gerichtsrahmen. Diese Deutung ist zu bevorzugen: das dritte Verb von V. 5 weist also auf V. 6 voraus.[1810]

V. 6 Jetzt formuliert Jakobus die letzte und schwerste Anklage (Klimax): κατεδικάσατε, ἐφονεύσατε. Die Anklage, in auffallender Kürze vorgetragen (*brevitas*), besteht aus zwei asyndetisch gesetzten Verben und einem gemeinsamen Akkusativobjekt im Singular. Es handelt sich bei den Verben nicht um ein weiteres Hendiadyoin[1811], sondern um zwei Aspekte eines ungerechten bzw. willkürlichen Gerichtsverfahrens: Verurteilung[1812] und Tötung[1813] des Gerechten. Damit ist ein

---

[1802] Vgl. die ähnliche Verwendung von ἐν ἡμέρᾳ (»am Tage«, »am helllichten Tage«).

[1803] ALLISON, Jak, 684. A. verweist auf 1Hen 16,1 (die Tage »des Umbringens, Verderbens [σφαγή] und des Todes der Riesen«) und 98,3 (die Reichen werden verderben in »in Schande, in Verderben [σφαγή] und großer Armut«), übersetzt von S. UHLIG, Das äthiopische Henochbuch, JSHRZ V 6, Gütersloh 1984.

[1804] So sehr klar FRANKEMÖLLE, Jak II, 657 f.

[1805] BURCHARD, Jak, 194, votiert für die eschatologische Deutung.

[1806] Vgl. dazu die Kommentierung von 5,7–11.

[1807] DIBELIUS, Jak, 285.

[1808] Ebd. mit Hinweis auf 1Hen 100,7.

[1809] FRANKEMÖLLE, Jak II, 658.

[1810] Im Deutschen wäre ein Doppelpunkt zwischen V. 5 und 6 zu setzen.

[1811] So METZNER, Jak, 269, der »töten« uneigentlich versteht.

[1812] καταδικάζειν (Aorist). Hap. leg. in Jak. LXX: selten, viermal in SapSal, in 2,20 im Zusammenhang mit der Tötung des Gerechten: θανάτῳ ἀσχήμονι καταδικάσωμεν αὐτόν (Zu einem schändlichen Tod wollen wir ihn verurteilen). Im NT: Mt 12,7.37; Lk 6,37: μὴ καταδικάζετε, καὶ οὐ μὴ καταδικασθῆτε (Richtet nicht, und ihr werdet auch nicht gerichtet werden). Substantiv: Apg 25,15.

[1813] φονεύειν (Aorist). Im NT öfter im Zusammenhang mit Ex 20,13 / Dtn 5,17 (so auch Jak 2,11). Mt 23,31.35; Jak 4,2 und 5,6: Vorwurf der willkürlichen Tötung. Substantivisch Apg 7,52 in der Stephanusrede:

anderer Personenkreis im Blick: nicht mehr die *sozialgeschichtlich* definierte Gruppe der betrogenen Lohnarbeiter auf den Feldern der Reichen, sondern eine *theologisch* qualifizierte Personengruppe, hier im Singular als »der Gerechte« bezeichnet. Es ist nicht auszuschließen, dass Jakobus die Lohnarbeiter als »Gerechte« qualifiziert, eher ist aber wahrscheinlich, dass er seine Gerichtsrede gegen die Reichen mit einem dritten, eigenen Anklagepunkt schließt: (1) Anhäufung von Reichtum »in den letzten Tagen«, (2) Vorenthalten des Lohnes der Erntearbeiter, (3) gewaltsames Gerichtsverfahren und Tötung »des Gerechten«. Ebenfalls asyndetisch wird das *Verhalten* des Gerechten mit einem einzigen Verb beschrieben: ἀντιτάσσεσθαι (keinen) Widerstand leisten, d. h. passiv bleiben.[1814]

Die Exegese hat die Frage gestellt, wer »der Gerechte« sei.[1815] (1) Die große Mehrheit der Exegeten versteht τὸν δίκαιον »generell«[1816] oder »generisch«[1817] vor dem Hintergrund der alttestamentlichen Figur des Gerechten, der verfolgt wird.[1818] Besonders wichtig für Jak 5 sind SapSal 1–5 mit der Gegenüberstellung der Gerechten und der Ungerechten und SapSal 10. Hier wird die Urgeschichte von Adam bis zu Joseph als die Geschichte der immer neuen Errettung »des Gerechten« dargestellt, wobei ohne Namensnennung *e contrario* auf Kain (»der Ungerechte«[1819]), dann auf Noah, Abraham, Lot, Jakob und Joseph angespielt wird. Jedes Mal wird nur von »dem Gerechten« gesprochen. In 10,20 wird dann im Zusammenhang des Zuges durch das Rote Meer das »heilige Volk« als »die Gerechten« bezeichnet:

διὰ τοῦτο δίκαιοι ἐσκύλευσαν ἀσεβεῖς.

So kam es, dass Gerechte Gottlosen die Waffen abzogen.[1820]

τίνα τῶν προφητῶν οὐκ ἐδίωξαν οἱ πατέρες ὑμῶν; καὶ ἀπέκτειναν τοὺς προκαταγγείλαντας περὶ τῆς ἐλεύσεως τοῦ δικαίου, οὗ νῦν ὑμεῖς προδόται καὶ φονεῖς ἐγένεσθε (Welchen der Propheten haben eure Väter nicht verfolgt? Und sie haben getötet, die die zuvor verkündigten das Kommen des Gerechten, dessen Verräter und Mörder ihr nun geworden seid). »Der Gerechte« bezieht sich hier auf Jesus.

[1814] ἀντιτάσσεσθαι (Präsens). Selten in LXX und NT, kein ausgeprägtes Profil. Vgl. Jak 4,6 und 1Petr 5,5 (jeweils Zitat von Spr 3,34: κύριος ὑπερηφάνοις ἀντιτάσσεται, ταπεινοῖς δὲ δίδωσιν χάριν. Gott widersteht dem Hoffährtigen, den Demütigen aber gibt er Gnade); Apg 18,6; Röm 13,2.

[1815] Die zweite Erwähnung des Gerechten in Jak 5,16 muss aus dem dortigen Kontext interpretiert werden. – Zu den verschiedenen Deutungsmöglichkeiten sehr ausführlich ALLISON, Jak, 685–687 (sieben Optionen).

[1816] DIBELIUS, Jak, 285.

[1817] BURCHARD, Jak, 194. So schon MAYOR, Jak, 149.

[1818] ὁ δίκαιος sehr breit bezeugt in LXX. Der *verfolgte* Gerechte: Jes 3,10LXX καταδυναστεύσωμεν πένητα δίκαιον (Lasst uns den Gerechten fesseln, denn er ist uns lästig); Spr 1,11fLXX: 11 Ελθὲ μεθ᾽ ἡμῶν, κοινώνησον αἵματος, κρύψωμεν δὲ εἰς γῆν ἄνδρα δίκαιον ἀδίκως, 12 καταπίωμεν δὲ αὐτὸν ὥσπερ ᾅδης ζῶντα καὶ ἄρωμεν αὐτοῦ τὴν μνήμην ἐκ γῆς; (Komm mit uns, mache gemeinsame Sache am Blut und lasst uns den gerechten Mann in der Erde verbergen – ungerechterweise, und lasst uns ihn verschlingen wie der Hades – lebendig, und lasst uns seine Erinnerung von der Erde wegnehmen …); 11,31; SapSal 2,10–20: 10 καταδυναστεύσωμεν πένητα δίκαιον (Lasst uns den Gerechten unterdrücken).

[1819] Abel fehlt: vgl. aber Mt 23,35; Hebr 11,4; 12,24.

[1820] NIEBUHR (Hg.), Sapientia Salomonis, 73.

Die Bezeichnung einzelner Personen mit dem Ehrentitel »Gerechter« im Neuen Testament ist in diesem Zusammenhang zu sehen.[1821] (2) So wird Jesus selbst im Neuen Testament mehrfach als »der Gerechte« bezeichnet: Mt 27,19[1822]; Lk 23,47; Apg 3,14; 7,52; 22,14; 1Petr 3,18; 1Joh 2,1 (Jesus Christus).[1823] Beda hat mit Hinweis auf die Stephanusrede in Apg 7,52 den »Gerechten« in Jak 5,5 mit Jesus identifiziert.[1824] (3) Für den Herrenbruder Jakobus ist der Titel »Gerechter« nicht im Neuen Testament, sondern zuerst in Logion 12 des Thomasevangeliums bezeugt.[1825] Exegeten, die den Jakobusbrief als pseudonymes Schreiben lesen, finden hier Ethopoiie und interpretieren den »Gerechten« als Hinweis auf den Herrenbruder.[1826] Dem Jakobusbrief ist nun keine explizite Verbindung zu Jesus oder zu dem Herrenbruder Jakobus zu entnehmen, aber die *theologische Figur* des »Gerechten« deckt alle Genannten: die Gerechten des Alten Bundes, Jesus und Jakobus wie andere frühchristliche Zeugen ebenso wie die armen Mitglieder der Christus-bekennenden Gemeinden.

Wer ist in V. 6 gemeint, und worauf zielt Jakobus in der Texteinheit 5,1–6? Eine Gesamtinterpretation muss verschiedene Faktoren berücksichtigen: die aggressive Polemik gegen »die Reichen« einerseits, die Metaphorik, die verschiedene Bezugsebenen eröffnet und die Intention der Rede zwischen Topik und konkreter Situation bewusst offenhält[1827], andererseits. Hinzu kommen der doppelte Gerichtskontext – sowohl in Bezug auf die Gewalt, die die Reichen durch Prozesse gegen die Armen ausüben, als auch auf die eschatologische Gerichtskulisse, die in der Semantik durchscheint –, die prophetische Sprache und der prophetisch-erregte Redegestus, der in der Mordanklage gipfelt. Zusammengefasst: Jakobus setzt zum Schluss seiner dreiteiligen Warn- und Gerichtsrede gegen »Zweiseeler« (4,1–4,12), Kaufleute (4,13–17) und Reiche (5,1–6) gezielt die Mittel prophetischer topischer Buß- und Gerichtsrhetorik ein, wie sie sich auch in der Bußpredigt Johannes des Täufers (Lk 3,7–9) oder in der Stephanusrede findet (Apg 7,49–53). Entscheidend ist hier jeweils nicht der realistische Bezug auf soziale und ökonomische Verhältnisse, sondern der *Effekt* der Gerichtsrhetorik. Die Zuhörer sollen emotional tief

---

[1821] Mt 1,19 (Joseph); 23,35 (Abel); Mk 6,20 (Johannes d. T.); Lk 1,6 (Zacharias und Elisabeth); 2,25 (Simeon); 23,50 (Joseph von A.); Apg 10,22 (Kornelius); Hebr 11,4 (Abel).

[1822] Variante in 27,24.

[1823] Siehe auch Justin, dial. 136,2.

[1824] BEDA, Expositio, 179. Ausführliche Liste der Belege bei ALLISON, Jak, 685 Anm. 309.

[1825] PLISCH, Thomasevangelium, 63–65. Zur Bezeugung bei Hegesipp vgl. Eusebius, HE. II 23.4 (Hegesipp. Übersetzt und eingeleitet von F. SCHLERITT, Göttingen 2016, 19–36). Dazu DEINES, Jakobus, 49–51. Vgl. auch Hieronymus, vir. ill. II 13 (Zitat aus dem Hebräerevangelium).

[1826] Zuletzt JÓNSSON (s. u.).

[1827] So richtig ALLISON, Jak, 687, zu den unterschiedlichen Deutungen des »Gerechten«: »Commentators should be open to the possibility of a double entendre or even an open-ended expression. One can imagine a Christian and a non-Jew hearing two different things in 5.6 or a Christian mulling several possibilities. A veiled allusion to James' fate remains an enticing possibility … Prophetic invective lends itself to hyperbole and is otherwise hardly objective, and accusing one's enemies of murder was a common topos.«

getroffen werden. Intendiert ist, dass sie fragen: »Was sollen wir tun«? (Lk 3,10) Möglich ist aber auch, dass sie den Redner töten (Apg 7,54–58). Jakobus setzt auf die erste Reaktion. So erklärt sich der Übergang zu 5,7: Er ist sich sicher, dass seine Gerichtsrede gewirkt hat, so dass er jetzt wieder zu der freundlichen Anrede ἀδελφοί übergehen kann.

In der exegetischen Literatur wird die Frage nach der möglichen Rekonstruktion der sozialen *Realität* hinter Jak 5 seit Martin Dibelius breit diskutiert. Wendet sich 5,1–6 an Mitchristen, oder handelt es sich um eine Rede »nach außen«? Die Exegeten vertreten unterschiedliche Positionen, die sich vor allem aus der mangelnden Deutlichkeit sozialgeschichtlicher Profilierung im Jakobusbrief ergeben.[1828] Wichtige Interpretationsvorschläge stammen von Dibelius, Metzner und zuletzt von Sigurvin L. Jónsson. (1) Dibelius dachte an »reiche Christenfeinde«:

> Seine christlichen Leser redet Jak hier ebenso wenig an wie der Verf. des Henoch-Buches in den Weherufen Hen 946 ff. sein jüdisches Publikum. Die Drohung gegen die Reichen ist aber auch eine Warnung für die Christen: es besteht die Gefahr, daß mit dem Eintritt vermögender Leute in die Christengemeinden auch die Gesinnung der »Reichen« Einzug hält; darum laßt es euch gesagt sein, daß diese ganze Welt der Reichen dem Untergang verfallen ist.[1829]

(2) Rainer Metzner[1830] weist darauf hin, dass in Jak 5,1–6 »eine Bußmahnung wie in 4,1–10 fehlt«.[1831] Die Rede gegen die Kaufleute sei noch als Rede an *Christen* zu verstehen, in 4,17 sei mit ἁμαρτία »das Fehlverhalten von Christen gemeint«. Die Gerichtsrede gegen die Reichen wende sich dagegen an *Nichtchristen*. Metzner geht also trotz der gleichen Einführungswendung Ἄγε νῦν von verschiedenen Gruppen in 4,13–17 und 5,1–6 aus – ein Vorschlag, der angesichts der auffallend gleichen Eingangsformulierung wenig plausibel ist. 5,1–6 liest Metzner mit René Krüger nicht als Appell, sondern als »öffentliche Proklamation«[1832]: »Jakobus leiht den Opfern eine Stimme«.[1833] (3) Sigurvin Jónsson interpretiert die Aussagen des Jakobusbriefs zu Reichtum, Armut und Gewalt *insgesamt* als Reflex realer Verhältnisse *in den Gemeinden*:

> The working hypothesis is that the author of James addresses the rich as a part of his community and that the language of violence reflects a historical reality of in-group

---

[1828] Vgl. den ausgewogenen Exkurs »Zur sozialen Lage der Adressaten des Jakobusbriefs« bei BURCHARD, Jak, 102 f.

[1829] DIBELIUS, Jak, 286.

[1830] METZNER, Jak, 271–274 (»Exkurs: Die Adressaten von 4,13–5,6« mit ausführlicher Dokumentation der Positionen).

[1831] METZNER, Jak, 272.

[1832] R. KRÜGER, Arm und Reich im Jakobusbrief von Lateinamerika aus gelesen. Die Herausforderung eines prophetischen Christentums, Diss. Universität Amsterdam 2003 (=Der Jakobusbrief als prophetische Kritik der Reichen, Münster 2005), 259.

[1833] METZNER, Jak, 274.

conflict.[1834] … While the author does not explicate the social standing of the rich within the community, he does address them repeatedly and his rhetoric makes little sense if he does not expect them to be among his intended audience.[1835]

Sein Fazit lautet daher:

In addressing this in-group violence and socio-economic disparity, the author presents an authoritative paraenetic letter written mainly in an imperative mood.[1836]

Auf die Interpretation zugespitzt heißt das: Jakobus

addresses a community where socio-economic disparity and communal strife, has led to a variety of in-group violence ranging from economic subjugation (Jas 2.1–6; 5.4–6) to fighting (Jas 3.13–18; 4.1–6) and murder (Jas 4.2; 5.6). In exegetical literature, there has been a clear tendency to interpret this as rhetoric and not as reality, yet the prevalence of this discussion in the letter calls for a reevaluation of this interpretation. When exegetes propose hypotheses regarding the location of authorship or intended audience of the letter of James, such proposals must fit with the topics and ethical constraints that are urgent in the text. In this regard, it seems evident that there is a wealthy elite present among James' intended readers along with violated destitute poor, which has led our author to urgently address this socio-economic disparity in theological terms.[1837]

Im Rückblick auf die genannten Interpretationsvorschläge und auf die Texte, 1,9–11; 2,1–7 und 5,1–6, ergibt sich ein differenziertes Bild, das mit keiner der genannten Positionen übereinstimmt. Zwei Faktoren müssen bedacht werden: (1) das Texttableau, (2) die unterschiedlichen Redeformen der Teiltexte. Als Schlüssel dient der *literarische* Anspruch des Jakobusbriefes, den Jónsson zwar ins Zentrum seiner Gesamtinterpretation des Briefes stellt, nicht aber für 5,1–6 gelten lässt. Hier gibt er dem Wortsinn den Vorzug vor einer stärkeren Berücksichtigung der metaphorischen Sprache.

(Ad 1) Das *Texttableau* enthält sehr unterschiedliche Nuancen. Jakobus thematisiert schon im ersten Teil seines Briefes Reiche und Arme gleichzeitig. In 1,9 spricht er nur die Armen explizit als Gemeindeglieder an: ὁ ἀδελφὸς ὁ ταπεινὸς. Ob sich ὁ δὲ πλούσιος ebenso auf die Gemeinde bezieht, bleibt undeutlich. In 2,5 fragt Jakobus rhetorisch die »Brüder«: οὐχ ὁ θεὸς ἐξελέξατο τοὺς πτωχοὺς τῷ κόσμῳ πλουσίους ἐν πίστει? Wieder sind die Armen unbestritten als Gemeindemitglieder vorgestellt. In V. 6a fährt Jakobus dann in Bezug auf sein Beispiel von 2,1–4 aber erstaunlicherweise fort: ὑμεῖς δὲ ἠτιμάσατε τὸν πτωχόν. Einerseits spricht er hier deutlich seine Adressaten an (ὑμεῖς), andererseits greift er sie explizit scharf an: ὑμεῖς. Jakobus scheint hier die bzw. »den Armen« im Sinne der Armentheologie von Martin

---

[1834] JÓNSSON, James among the Classicists, 258. Kap. 6: Wealth and Community in the Letter of James, 258–282, bietet eine umfassende aktuelle Einführung in die Literatur und die Positionen zum Thema.

[1835] JÓNSSON, James among the Classicists, 278.

[1836] JÓNSSON, James among the Classicists, 280.

[1837] JÓNSSON, James among the Classicists, 282.

328 Kommentar

Dibelius[1838] außerhalb der Gemeinden bzw. der Adressatenschaft zu positionieren. Allerdings fährt er sogleich fort, »die Reichen« anzugreifen, καταδυναστεύουσιν ὑμῶν. Jetzt sind »die Reichen« wieder außerhalb der Gemeinden, die als »ihr« bezeichnet werden, zu denken. V. 7 macht das ganz deutlich: »Die Reichen« lästern (βλασφημοῦσιν) den Christus-Namen, der über den Gemeindegliedern ausgerufen worden ist. Sind also die Gemeindeglieder arm? Und sind die »Reichen« Christenfeinde? Das bleibt offen. Für 4,13–5,6 gilt: Jakobus macht gar nicht deutlich, dass die genannten Gruppen zu den Gemeindegliedern gehören. Hier geht es nicht um »Brüder« wie in 1,9, sondern um mit Stereotypen gekennzeichnete Gruppen, die *quer* zu der Gruppe der einleitenden Adressatenschaft der »zwölf Stämme in der Diaspora« (1,1) bzw. den »Brüdern« (1,2) stehen: Es sind Kaufleute und Reiche, die Jakobus mit typischen Vorwürfen beschreibt. Welche Rolle diese Gruppen in den Gemeinden spielen, denen Jakobus sein literarisches Schreiben widmet, lässt sich dem Jakobusbrief *nicht* entnehmen. Deutlich ist einerseits, dass Jakobus »die Reichen« als Gefahr der Gemeinden betrachtet und den Sog kennt, den ihr sozialer und monetärer Status auf Gemeinschaften ausübt (2,1–4). Dem setzt er die Achtung vor dem Armen und die soziale Gleichheit in den Gemeinden entgegen. Andererseits geht er in seinem Beispiel in Kap. 2 davon aus, dass »Reiche« und Angesehene in die Gemeinden kommen, dort gut aufgenommen werden und die Armen deklassieren können, ohne dass die Adressaten (»ihr«), die anscheinend weder »reich« noch »arm« sind, dies bemerken.

(Ad 2) Entscheidend sind die jeweiligen *Redeformen* der unterschiedlichen Texteinheiten und Briefteile. Kap. 1 und 2 sind paränetische Texte, die eindeutig an die »Brüder« gerichtet, d. h. auf die imaginierten Gemeindeglieder bezogen sind. Die Gestalt des »Reichen« taucht hier als typische Kontrastfolie auf: Die Brüder sollen in Anfechtungen geduldig sein (Kap. 1) und frei vom Ansehen der Person (Kap. 2). Die Reichen müssen vorsichtig sein: demütig (1,10) und auf soziale und juristische Gewalt verzichten (2,6). Kapitel 4 und 5 gehören dagegen zu den Gerichtsreden gegen bestimmte Gruppen: »Zweiseeler«, Kaufleute und Reiche. Hier herrscht nicht die Logik der *Gemeindeparänese*, die erst in 5,7 mit ἀδελφοί wieder aufgenommen wird, sondern die *Gerichts-Anklage*. Der Verfasser verfolgt eine bestimmte literarisch-emotionale Intention. Er beabsichtigt nicht, die briefliche Leserschaft zu stärken und zu ermahnen (Kap. 1), zu belehren (Kap. 1,19 ff; 2 und 3) und zu trösten (5,7–11), sondern mit rhetorischen Mitteln anzuklagen und in Schrecken zu versetzen. Dabei folgt er dem Prinzip der Steigerung. In Kap. 4 ist noch Raum für Umkehr (4,7–10). Die Adressaten werden nach heftigen Anklagen wieder als ἀδελφοί angesprochen und auf diesen Bruderstatus verpflichtet. Bei den beiden konzisen Gerichtsanklagen in 4,13–17 und 5,1–6 fehlt dagegen jede positive Perspektive. Jakobus liefert zwei ebenso kurze wie brillante Gerichtsreden, in denen

---

[1838] Dibelius, Jak, 58–66.

der Verfasser auf Topoi aus den prophetischen und weisheitlichen Schriften der Septuaginta Bezug nimmt. Der Eindruck, hier hätte sich sein literarischer Ehrgeiz thematisch verselbständigt, legt sich nahe. Anders lässt sich die übergangslose Wiederaufnahme der brüderlichen Tröstung (5,7) nicht erklären.

Zusammengefasst: Jakobus denkt, schreibt und formuliert auf der Grundlage der traditionellen prophetischen und weisheitlichen Kritik Israels an »den Mächtigen« und »Reichen«, die seine eigene Weltsicht strukturiert und ihm auch als literarische Inspirationsquelle dient. Er verwendet die Septuaginta-Stereotypen von »Arm« und »Reich«, »Gerechter« und »Sünder« usw. zur Aufdeckung und Erklärung zeitgenössischer Fehlentwicklungen. Er bedient sich vor allem in 4,13–17 und 5,1–6 der scharfen Gerichtspolemik der Septuaginta-Tradition und ihrer semantischen und rhetorischen Mittel, um die Leserschaft vor gefährlichen Entwicklungen in den Gemeinden zu warnen. Dabei liegt ihm nicht an realistischer Darstellung gemeindlicher Vorgänge, sondern an der Erzeugung von Angst und Schrecken, um die befürchteten Fehlentwicklungen zu verhindern. Wieweit in den Gemeinden, an die sich der Verfasser schriftlich wendet, die Gefahr der Dominanz reicher und sozial dominierender Personen *real* war, lässt sich nicht beantworten, zumal die intendierte Leserschaft des fingierten Diasporabriefes ja nicht aus *einer* Gemeinde stammt und nicht als homogen vorgestellt werden kann. Sicher ist allerdings, dass Jakobus die Gefahren von Reichtum und hohem Sozialstatus für die Gemeindestruktur wahrnahm und dass Szenen wie die in 2,1–4 entworfenen eine gewisse Plausibilität hatten. Das Mittel, mit dem der Verfasser diese Gefahren bekämpft, ist die *literarische Gerichtsrhetorik*. Jakobus kämpft als *theologischer Schriftsteller* gegen die sozialen Fehlentwicklungen, die er in den Gemeinden diagnostiziert.

5. Schlussteil (Kap. 5,7–20)

Die Gliederung ist klar: 5,7–11.12.13–18.19–20. Die einzelnen Texteinheiten sind formal und thematisch deutlich voneinander abgesetzt. Die erste Texteinheit 5,7–11 ist der Mahnung zur μακροθυμία in Bezug auf die Parusie gewidmet. V. 12 stellt einen kurzen Einschub zum Thema »Warnung vor dem Schwören« dar. In V. 13–18 gibt der Verfasser Ratschläge für das Gebet bei Krankheit. Die Epistel schließt in V. 19.20 mit einem Hinweis auf die Bekehrung von Sündern und einem Septuagintazitat.

Nach der fulminanten Anklage in 5,6: »Verurteilt, getötet habt ihr den Gerechten«, ändert der Verfasser in 5,7 abrupt den Ton. Er kehrt zu der epistolaren Anrede »Brüder«, mit der er sein Schreiben eröffnet hatte und die seit 3,12 ausgesetzt war, zurück und setzt diese Anrede dreimal ein. Damit stellt er in 5,7 ff in Anknüpfung an die beiden ersten Kapitel den *Rahmen* des Schreibens her. Die Kommunikationssituation ist wieder die der freundlichen Ermahnung und Belehrung wie in

330 Kommentar

Kap. 1 und 2. Der Verfasser findet nicht nur zu dem Ton, sondern auch zu der Thematik dieser Kapitel zurück: Ab 5,7 richten sich die Ermahnungen wie in Kapitel 1 und 2 wieder an die Mitglieder der Christus-bekennenden Gemeinden.

Die Verse 5,7–19 fungieren als Schluss des Briefes. Eingeleitet wird der Schlusstext mit der paränetischen Texteinheit 5,7–11, die thematisch explizit an Kapitel 1 anknüpft (Ringkomposition): an die Geduld (1,12; 5,11). Die Geduld wird jetzt in eine apokalyptische Perspektive gerückt und mit einem Bild verbunden, das vorzugsweise von Paulus verwendet wird: der Parusie des Herrn (V. 7). Beide Themenbereiche, Paränese und Eschatologie, finden sich mehrfach im letzten Teil der Paulusbriefe. Mit dem theologischen Satz in V. 11 ist bereits der sachliche Schluss erreicht. Allerdings wendet sich der Verfasser im Folgenden noch zwei Themen aus dem Frömmigkeitsverhalten und dem Gemeindeleben zu: dem Schwur bzw. der aufrichtigen Rede und dem Gebet. Ein Schlussgruß fehlt. Stattdessen formuliert Jakobus in der Schlussgnome 5,19 f noch einmal ein theologisches Urteil in einer gewissen Analogie zu 5,11.

Der Text ist wieder stilistisch sehr sorgfältig gestaltet: Der Wortschatz ist gewählt, sprachliche Bilder, Vergleiche und *exempla* beleben die Paränese. Im Zentrum stehen die Leittugenden des geduldigen Wartens, der Geduld und der Barmherzigkeit für die Gegenwart, die nach vorn offen gedacht ist. Große Bilder aus der Tradition Israels werden aufgerufen: der endzeitliche Richter und die Propheten, namentlich Hiob. Vers 7 hat eine bedeutende Rezeption in Brahms' Deutschem Requiem (II 2) gefunden. Der Brief schließt pointiert mit einer theologischen Gnome aus Spr 10,12.

1. Texteinheit: 5,7–11 Mahnung zur Geduld

(7) Seid nun geduldig, Brüder, bis zur Parusie[1839] des Herrn. Siehe, der Landmann wartet geduldig[1840] auf die kostbare Frucht der Erde, bis er die frühe und die späte (Frucht) empfängt. (8) Seid auch ihr geduldig, stärkt eure Herzen, denn die Parusie des Herrn ist nahe herbei gekommen. (9) Seufzt nicht gegeneinander, Brüder, damit ihr nicht gerichtet werdet; siehe, der Richter steht bereits[1841] vor der Tür[1842]. (10) Als Beispiel des Leidens und der Geduld nehmt, Brüder, die Propheten, die im Namen des Herrn gesprochen haben. (11) Siehe, wir preisen selig, die geduldig waren; von der Geduld Hiobs habt ihr gehört, und ihr kennt das Ende, das der Herr bereitet hat[1843], denn überaus[1844] mitleidig und barmherzig ist der Herr.

[1839] Das griechische Fremdwort soll deutlich machen, dass es sich bei »Ankunft des Herrn« um terminologische Sprache handelt (vgl. »adventus domini« im Lateinischen zur Bezeichnung der Ankunft des Kaisers).

[1840] Das Partizip ist adverbial aufgelöst, ἐπ᾽ αὐτῷ bleibt unübersetzt.

[1841] »Bereits« wurde im Deutschen hinzugefügt, um das Perfekt abzubilden.

[1842] Griechisch Plural.

[1843] Wörtlich: »das Ende des Herrn«.

[1844] Damit wird πολύ abgebildet.

C. Briefcorpus

Textkritik: **V. 7** Minuskel 1735 liest κυριου, 1729 hat χριστου, 1440 erweitert zu του κυριου ημων Ιησου Χριστου, 2674 hat του σωητρος. προιμον και οψιμον haben 01. 02. 03* und eine Reihe von Minuskeln, πρωιμον και οψιμον ohne Erweiterung lesen P74. 03. 048 und wenige Minuskeln. Einige Majuskeln fügen das erklärende Objekt ein: υετον προιμον και οψιμον (so 02. 33 und sehr viele Minuskeln sowie Byz.). 01C2 ergänzt καρπον, 01* fügt den Artikel hinzu. **V. 9** P20. 23. 54. 74. 04 und einige Majuskeln sowie 33 und mehrere Minuskeln haben die finale Ergänzung »damit ihr nicht gerichtet werdet« nicht. **V. 10** Die Wortstellung in V. 10a ist unübersichtlich und hat bei den Abschreibern zu Varianten geführt. Die Hss. bieten 25 verschiedene Lesarten. ECM wählt die am besten bezeugte Lesart von 03C2 und einer Anzahl von Minuskeln. Interessant: 01* und 01C ersetzen das seltene κακοπαθεια durch καλοκαγαθια. **V. 11** Das schwierige τελος wird von mehreren Minuskeln durch ελεος ersetzt. Auch ειδετε (01. 03* und sehr viele Minuskeln) wird als schwierig empfunden und durch ιδετε (02. 03C2 und sehr viele Minuskeln) ersetzt.

V. 7 Der Vers beginnt mit dem ersten von fünf Imperativen (Plur.), die diese ermahnende Texteinheit prägen. Zu dem οὖν bemerkt Burchard richtig:

> Die Konjunktion … folgert hier wohl nichts, … sondern zeigt die Reprise des Hauptthemas an.[1845]

Die Anrede »Brüder« bzw. »meine Brüder« hat der Verfasser schon in 1,2; 2,1.14; 3,1.10.12; 4,11 benutzt. Er setzt sie nun noch einmal verstärkt im Schlussteil des Briefes: 5,7.9.10.12.19. Μακροθυμήσατε: die kurze und klare Mahnung zur Geduld knüpft nicht weiterführend oder kontrastierend an 5,1–6 an[1846], sondern eröffnet thematisch die Schlussparänese. Der Stamm μακροθυμ- begegnet nur in Kapitel 5, hier aber gehäuft: verbal in 5,7 (zweimal) und 8, substantivisch in V. 10. Damit ist 5,7–11 der wichtigste neutestamentliche Text zu μακροθυμεῖν/μακροθυμία. Es handelt sich also um eine Mahnung zur Geduld, die in diesem Text eine besondere Qualität erhält.

Das Verb steht im Imp. Aor.[1847] am Anfang der prägnanten Mahnung, die wieder auf die brieflichen Kommunikationsbedingungen zurückgreift, wie sie der Verfasser in 1,2 gesetzt hatte. Μακροθυμεῖν/μακροθυμία changiert zwischen der Haltung oder Tugend des »Langmuts« einerseits und einem geduldig-hoffnungsvollen Verhalten gegenüber der Zukunft, der »Geduld«[1848], andererseits.[1849] Das Verb wird selten im

---

[1845] Burchard, Jak, 198, weist darauf hin, dass »die atl. und frühjüd. Texte, die von Präsenz oder Ankunft Gottes zu verschiedenen Zeiten und Zwecken reden … ihn dabei nicht einfach Herr« nennen. »Deshalb meint Jak hier wohl den Herrn Christus«.

[1846] Zu den verschiedenen Anstrengungen, einen Bezug zur vorangehenden Texteinheit zu finden, vgl. die Kritik bei Metzner, Jak, 275f mit Anm. 2 und 3 (Lit.).

[1847] Vgl. DBR, § 337,2.

[1848] Zu ὑπομονή in Jak siehe zu 5,11.

[1849] Bauer / Aland, 990. Vgl. M. Spanneut, Art. Geduld, RAC 9, 1976, 243–294. Spanneut zeigt, dass in dem Begriff »Geduld« zwei Aspekte verbunden sind: μακροθυμία und χρηστότης (ebenfalls ein vorzugsweise bei Paulus gebrauchter ethischer Terminus, der wie μακροθυμία auch als Beschreibung des Wesens Gottes Verwendung findet).

332   Kommentar

Neuen Testament gebraucht.[1850] Das Substantiv begegnet häufiger in der neutestamentlichen Briefliteratur[1851], vor allem in paränetischen Zusammenhängen bei Paulus. μακροθυμία »ist keine griechische Tugend«, wie M. Spanneut gezeigt hat.[1852] In LXX ist μακροθυμία eine der Eigenschaften Gottes. Gott übt Langmut und Erbarmen gegenüber den Menschen.[1853] Damit gilt auch:

> Wenn die Verfasser der biblischen Bücher einem Menschen Langmut zuschreiben, sehen sie darin eine herrscherliche Tugend.[1854]

Im Jakobusbrief tritt aber eine eigene Bedeutungsnuance hinzu. Der Geduld wird eine Zeitbestimmung hinzugefügt, und damit bestimmt der *Gegenstand* des Verbs hier seine Bedeutung, die παρουσία des Herrn. Es handelt sich also nicht einfach um ethische, sondern um eschatologische Sprache wie in Lk 18,7 und 2Petr 3,9.15.

Die παρουσία ist ein paulinischer Vorzugsbegriff und findet sich besonders in der Thessalonicherkorrespondenz.[1855] κύριος ist in Jak 5,7 wie mehrfach im Jakobusbrief unterbestimmt.[1856] Die Ergänzung Ἰησοῦ Χριστοῦ fehlt anders als in 1,2 und 2,1.[1857] Im paulinischen Zusammenhang ist die Parusie allerdings stets mit Christus verbunden.[1858] Von daher ist es zunächst wahrscheinlich, dass es auch in Jak 5,7 um geduldiges Warten auf die Wiederkunft des Herrn Jesus Christus geht.[1859] Auf-

---

[1850] In theo-logischem Zusammenhang Mt 18,26 (Erbarmen und Schuldenerlass), in theologisch-eschatologischem Sinn in Lk 18,7 und 2Petr 3,9. Ethisch: 1Kor 13,4 und 1Thess 5,14. – Der Wortstamm wird kaum in der griechischen Literatur verwendet und begegnet auch eher selten in LXX, das Verb mehrfach bei Sirach, das Adjektiv öfter als Gottesprädikat zusammen mit »Erbarmen« (Ex 34,6; Num 14,18; Neh 9,17; Ps 85,15LXX; 102,8LXX; Jo 2,13), so auch Jak 5,11.

[1851] Vor allem bei Paulus und in den deutero- und tritopaulinischen Briefen: Röm 2,4; 9,22; 2Kor 6,6 (Geistesgabe); Gal 5,22 (Geistesfrucht); Eph 4,2; Kol 1,11; 3,12; 1Tim 1,16; 2Tim 3,10; 4,2; Hebr 6,16. Auch 1Petr 3,20 und 2Petr 3,15 (deutlich eschatologisch).

[1852] Spanneut, RAC 9, 254.

[1853] Das Adjektiv wird ca. 15mal in LXX verwendet. Belege aus LXX und NT bei Spanneut, RAC 9, 254. Burchard, Jak, 198, weist besonders auf TestHiob 26,4f hin.

[1854] Spanneut, RAC 9, 254.

[1855] 1Kor 15,23; 1Thess 2,19; 3,13; 4,15; 5,23; 2Thess 2,1.8 (9); 2Petr 1,16; 3,4.12 (»Ankunft des Tages Gottes«); 1Joh 2,28. Außerdem ist die Vorstellung von der »Ankunft des Menschensohnes« auch ein Motiv in der matthäischen Endzeitrede Kap. 24: 24,3 (»deine Ankunft«).27.37 und 39 (»Ankunft des Menschensohnes«). Synoptische Parallelen fehlen. Zur Vorstellung bei Paulus vgl. B. Heininger, Die Parusie des Kyrios, in: F. W. Horn (Hg.), Paulus Handbuch, Tübingen 2013, 299–305, 301. Vgl. dazu auch A. J. Malherbe, The Letters to the Thessalonians, AYB, New Haven / London 2000, 271f. Malherbe weist auf 1Kor 16,22 hin: Die Formel *Maranatha* deutet auf den Sitz der Vorstellung in den aramäisch sprechenden vorpaulinischen Gemeinden (weitere Lit.). Bereits Adolf Deissmann hatte auf das hellenistische Motiv von der Ankunft des Herrschers hingewiesen (A. Deissmann, Licht vom Osten, Tübingen ⁴1923, 214–220).

[1856] 1,7; 4,10.15; 5,7.8.10.11.14.15.

[1857] Weitere Bestimmungen, beide Mal auf Gott bezogen: 3,9: εὐλογοῦμεν τὸν κύριον καὶ πατέρα, 5,4: τὰ ὦτα κυρίου σαβαὼθ (Zitat). Die Hss sehen hier kein Problem. Nur jeweils eine Hs ergänzt »Christi«, »unseres Herrn Jesu Christi«, »des Heilands«.

[1858] Jak 5,7 ist die einzige neutestamentliche Erwähnung des Motivs der »Parusie des Herrn«, bei der der Bezug zu Jesus nicht expliziert wird.

[1859] Vgl. Burchard, Jak, 198.

fallend bleibt aber, dass Jakobus hier Jesus Christus nicht nennt und in 5,10.11[1860] offensichtlich mit »Herr« wieder Gott selbst meint. Das kann auf eine theozentrische Tendenz bei Jakobus hinweisen, könnte aber auch eine implizite »Erhöhung« Christi bedeuten. Allerdings bliebe auch diese eschatologisch gefärbte Christologie im Jakobusbrief implizit und würde nicht ausgesprochen. Ob es sich um eine lebendige Naherwartung wie in 1Thess handelt oder ob diese Naherwartung verblasst ist wie in 2Petr (2Petr 3,1–13) und der Verfasser zur Belebung der ursprünglichen Naherwartung aufrufen muss, geht aus dem Jakobusbrief ebenfalls nicht hervor. Jedenfalls macht 5,8 deutlich, dass der Verfasser an der Naherwartung festhält und diese nicht in Frage stellt. Der Fortgang des Textes zeigt aber, dass es Jakobus hier vor allem um *einen bestimmten* Aspekt der Naherwartung geht: den des *Richters*. Diese Funktion ist bei Jak eindeutig mit Gott selbst verbunden. Daher legt sich für die gesamte Texteinheit eine theo-logische Interpretation nahe: Die paulinische Parusie-*Christologie* wird gleichsam zurückgenommen und auf eine Parusie-Richter-*Theologie* reduziert.

Zunächst vertieft Jak den zeitlichen Aspekt des geduldigen Wartens durch eine Analogie aus dem Bereich der Landwirtschaft[1861], eingeleitet durch die Demonstrativpartikel ἰδού, »seht«. Diese begegnet sechsmal im Jakobusbrief, viermal davon in 5,7–20, dreimal in der Texteinheit 5,7–11.[1862] Jakobus setzt sie hier »zur Belebung der Rede«[1863] und leitet so einen stilistisch sorgfältig gestalteten Hinweis auf die exemplarische Geduld des Bauern ein: Der Bauer wartet (variatio: ἐκδέχεται[1864] statt μακροθυμεῖν). γεωργός begegnet selten im Neuen Testament, und zwar stets in figurativer Rede im Zusammenhang mit Weinanbau.[1865] Hier in Jak 5,7 ist aber wohl eher der Kornbauer im Blick. Auf jeden Fall denkt Jakobus an Bodenfrüchte. ὁ γεωργός: »Der Artikel ist ... generisch«.[1866] γῆ als »Acker« begegnet öfter in den synoptischen Evangelien, im Jakobusbrief dreimal in Kapitel 5. Den Gegenstand des Wartens hat Jakobus stilistisch besonders sorgfältig formuliert: τὸν τίμιον[1867] καρπὸν τῆς γῆς. Dies pretiöse Syntagma verrät Septuagintaeinflüsse (καρπὸς[1868] τῆς γῆς Gen 4,3; 43,11 u. ö.)[1869], ist als ganzes aber ohne antike Parallele.[1870] Hier wird durch das

---

[1860] Dazu s. u. Mindestens in V. 11 ist Gott selbst gemeint.

[1861] Dazu VON GEMÜNDEN, Vegetationsmetaphorik, 296f.

[1862] 3,4.5; 5,4.7.9.11.

[1863] BAUER / ALAND, 753.

[1864] Selten im NT, hap. leg. in Jak. Hebr 10,13 apokalyptisch konnotiert, Hebr 11,10 auf Abraham bezogen: Aspekt seiner Glaubenstugend.

[1865] Im Gleichnis von den Weinbergpächtern (Mk 12,1–12par); Joh 15,1 (Weinstockrede) und 2Tim 2,6.

[1866] BURCHARD, Jak, 199.

[1867] τίμιος, wertvoll, geehrt: hap. leg. in Jakobus, selten im NT, öfter in Apk als Adjektiv bei Edelsteinen.

[1868] καρπός noch 3,17 (übertragen) und 5,18.

[1869] Aufgeschlüsselt bei BURCHARD, Jak, 199. Allerdings ist der Hinweis auf Spr 8,19 wenig aussagekräftig: βέλτιον ἐμὲ καρπίζεσθαι ὑπὲρ χρυσίον καὶ λίθον τίμιον (Besser ist es, mich [die Weisheit] zu ernten als Gold und Edelsteine).

[1870] Laut TLG.

334 Kommentar

Attribut τίμιος die Bedeutung des geduldigen Wartens gestärkt: Der Gegenstand der Erwartung ist besonders wertvoll. Daher ist das Warten selbst ebenfalls notwendig und wertvoll. Denselben Effekt hat die Wiederholung von μακροθυμεῖν im angefügten Partizipialsatz[1871], dessen Subjekt der Landmann ist: μακροθυμῶν ἐπ᾽[1872] αὐτῷ, ἕως λάβῃ πρόϊμον καὶ ὄψιμον. αὐτῷ lässt sich am besten auf »die Frucht der Erde«, d. h. die Ernte beziehen.

Der angehängte Temporalsatz zeichnet sich durch besondere Kürze aus: Das Subjekt ist ebenso unklar oder unterbestimmt wie das Akkusativobjekt πρόϊμον καὶ ὄψιμον. Einige Handschriften ergänzen hier »Regen«, so dass es um Früh- und Spätregen geht. In diesem Fall ist die Frucht im Boden, die den Regen empfängt (λαμβάνειν), Subjekt. Andere Handschriften ergänzen die »Frucht«[1873], wodurch der Bauer zum Subjekt der Partizipialkonstruktion wird: Er wartet geduldig darauf, die Früh- und Späternte zu empfangen. Beide Ergänzungen sind sprachlich möglich und sachlich sinnvoll. Die Lutherübersetzung bevorzugt den »Frühregen und Spätregen«.[1874] Zudem ist 5,17.18 explizit dem Thema des Regens gewidmet, das aber in V. 7 fehlt. In Dtn 11,14; Jer 5,24; Jo 2,23; Sach 10,2 und Hos 6,4(3) ist vom »Frühregen« die Rede, während in Hos 9,10; Jer 24,2 das substantivierte Adjektiv mit frühem Erntegut verbunden wird.[1875] Burchard bemerkt daher salomonisch:

> Lexikalisch steht es zwischen Regen und Frucht unentschieden.[1876]

Hält man sich an die *lectio difficilior* (ohne explizites Objekt), bezieht die Wendung sich auf jeden Fall auf die Erntefrucht, und es ist hier die Frühfrucht und Spätfrucht, d. h. die frühe und die späte Ernte gemeint.[1877] Der Bauer wartet also geduldig auf die Frühjahrs- und die Herbsternte, nicht auf den Früh- und Spätregen. Die LXX-Nähe des Syntagmas ist auf jeden Fall deutlich.[1878]

V. 8 Der zweite Imperativ wiederholt den Anfang von V. 7 (Anapher) und enthält mit dem καὶ ὑμεῖς die applikative Übertragung von V. 7b. Dabei arbeitet Jakobus mit einer doppelten steigernden Wiederholung: μακροθυμήσατε, στηρίξατε. στηρίζειν ist hap. bei Jak. Das Verb begegnet bei Paulus und in nachpaulinischen Briefen stets in

---

[1871] Beispiele solcher Partizipialkonstruktionen bei BURCHARD, Jak, 199, besonders 2Makk 6,14: μακροθυμῶν ὁ δεσπότης μέχρι τοῦ καταντήσαντας αὐτοὺς πρὸς ἐκπλήρωσιν ἁμαρτιῶν κολάσαι (Während nämlich der hochherzige Herr auch bei anderen Völkern mit der Züchtigung wartet, bis sie selbst zur Erfüllung ihrer Verfehlungen gelangen).

[1872] Μακροθυμεῖν mit ἐπί Sir 18,11; Mt 18,26.

[1873] Ausführlich BURCHARD, Jak, 199 f. Kürzer METZNER, Jak, 280.

[1874] Die Vulgata folgt dem griechischen Text: ecce agricola expectat pretiosum fructum terrae / patienter ferens donec accipiat temporivum et serotinum.

[1875] Belege aus der griechischen Lit. bei LSJ, 1543.

[1876] BURCHARD, Jak, 199. VON GEMÜNDEN, Vegetationsmetaphorik, 297, scheint die Regen-Variante zu bevorzugen.

[1877] Siehe die Handschriften 01C2 und 01*. BURCHARD, Jak, 199, weist auf Parallelen aus LXX und griechischen Schriftstellern hin.

[1878] LXX schreibt πρόϊμος oder πρωϊνός (nicht in den Jak.hss.).

C. Briefcorpus   335

paränetischem Zusammenhang.[1879] Dieser dritte Imperativ στηρίξατε ist mit dem
Akk.objekt »eure Herzen« verbunden. Den Appell an das Herz hat Jakobus schon
in 4,8 benutzt.[1880] Die Wendung »das Herz stärken« (im Sing.) begegnet öfter in
LXX[1881], in 1Thess 3,13[1882] auch im Plural, dort in demselben eschatologischen Zusammenhang, bezogen auf die Parusie Christi:

> (12) ὑμᾶς δὲ ὁ κύριος πλεονάσαι καὶ περισσεύσαι τῇ ἀγάπῃ εἰς ἀλλήλους καὶ εἰς πάντας
> καθάπερ καὶ ἡμεῖς εἰς ὑμᾶς, (13) εἰς τὸ στηρίξαι ὑμῶν τὰς καρδίας ἀμέμπτους ἐν ἁγιωσύνῃ
> ἔμπροσθεν τοῦ θεοῦ καὶ πατρὸς ἡμῶν ἐν τῇ παρουσίᾳ τοῦ κυρίου ἡμῶν Ἰησοῦ μετὰ πάντων
> τῶν ἁγίων αὐτοῦ.

> (12) Euch aber lasse der Herr wachsen und zunehmen an Liebe untereinander und
> allen gegenüber, wie auch wir sie zu euch haben, (13) dass eure Herzen gestärkt werden
> und untadelig sind in Heiligung vor Gott, unserem Vater, bei der Ankunft unseres
> Herrn Jesus mit allen seinen Heiligen.

Den Motivzusammenhang von geduldigem Warten und der Parusie des Herrn von
5,7 greift Jakobus hier noch einmal auf, jetzt präzisiert durch eine Zeitangabe: Die
Parusie ist nahe. Das Verb ἐγγίζειν[1883] in zeitlicher Bedeutung wird in der synoptischen Tradition pointiert im Zusammenhang der eschatologischen Botschaft Jesu
verwendet, vor allem in der Ansage der Gottesherrschaft:

> πεπλήρωται ὁ καιρὸς καὶ ἤγγικεν ἡ βασιλεία τοῦ θεοῦ.
> Erfüllt ist der Zeitpunkt, und genaht hat sich die Königsherrschaft Gottes (Mk 1,15par).

Lk 21,8 belegt, dass falsche Messiasse verkünden konnten: ὁ καιρὸς ἤγγικεν. Demgegenüber lässt Lukas Jesus in 21,28 formulieren:

> ἀρχομένων δὲ τούτων γίνεσθαι ἀνακύψατε καὶ ἐπάρατε τὰς κεφαλὰς ὑμῶν, διότι ἐγγίζει ἡ
> ἀπολύτρωσις ὑμῶν.
> Wenn das zu geschehen anfängt, seht auf und erhebt eure Häupter, weil eure Erlösung
> nahe ist.

Für die Parusie Christi wird das Verb sonst nicht gebraucht, vergleichbar ist aber
Phil 4,5: ὁ κύριος ἐγγύς. 1Petr 4,7 formuliert knapp:

> Πάντων δὲ τὸ τέλος ἤγγικεν.
> Es ist aber nahe gekommen das Ende aller Dinge

und ruft zum Gebet auf. Jakobus bringt in 5,7–9 geduldiges Warten der *Gemeinde*
auf der einen Seite und das baldige Kommen des *Herrn* auf der anderen Seite zusammen. 2Petr 3 verschiebt dies Gleichgewicht und legt den Akzent auf die Geduld
(μακροθυμία) des *Herrn*, der seine Parusie (2Petr 1,16; 3,4.12) noch hinausschiebt,
um den Menschen die Möglichkeit zur Untadeligkeit zu geben:

[1879] Röm 1,11; [16,25]; 1Thess 3,2.13; 2Thess 2,17; 3,3; 1Petr 5,10; 2Petr 1,12.

[1880] καρδία 1,26; 3,14; 4,8; 5,5.8.

[1881] Ri 19,5.8; Ps 103,15LXX u. ö.

[1882] Vgl. ähnlich 2Thess 1,17.

[1883] Noch in Jak 4,8. Hier wird das Verb nicht temporal, sondern übertragen spatial (»sich nähern«) verwendet.

336 Kommentar

2Petr 3,9: οὐ βραδύνει κύριος τῆς ἐπαγγελίας, ὥς τινες βραδύτητα ἡγοῦνται, ἀλλὰ μακροθυμεῖ εἰς ὑμᾶς.
Der Herr verzögert nicht die Verheißung, wie es einige für eine Verzögerung halten; sondern er hat Geduld mit euch ...
2Petr 3,15: τὴν τοῦ κυρίου ἡμῶν μακροθυμίαν σωτηρίαν ἡγεῖσθε.
Und erachtet die Geduld unseres Herrn für eure Rettung.

Der Blick auf 2Petr 3 macht es wahrscheinlich, dass Jakobus (noch) nicht gegen das Verblassen der Naherwartung kämpfen musste wie der Verfasser des 2. Petrusbriefes.

V. 9 Jakobus formuliert in V. 9 einen weisheitlichen Mahnspruch, der formal und inhaltlich nahe bei Mt 7,1 liegt. Dabei bezieht sich der vierte Imperativ: μὴ στενάζετε, ἀδελφοί, κατ᾽ ἀλλήλων konkret auf das Miteinander der Adressaten, d. h. der angeschriebenen Gemeindeglieder. Das im Neuen Testament seltene Verb στενάζειν[1884], seufzen, wird hier am besten mit »murren gegen« im Sinne von »Klage führen gegen« übersetzt und trägt in dieser Bedeutungsnuance einen negativen Akzent.[1885] BAUER / ALAND bietet als Übersetzung von κατά c.gen. an:

> nach Wörtern u. Ausdrücken, die ein feindseliges Reden, bes. auch eine Anklage bezeichnen.[1886]

Damit verwendet Jakobus στενάζειν hier als Synonym zu κρίνειν. Metzner weist nachdrücklich auf die formale und sachliche Parallele zu 4,11 hin[1887]: ὁ καταλαλῶν ἀδελφοῦ ἢ κρίνων τὸν ἀδελφὸν αὐτοῦ καταλαλεῖ νόμου καὶ κρίνει νόμον. Auch dort geht es bereits um Verträglichkeitsparänese unter »Brüdern« und um den Hinweis auf den Richter, allerdings im Zusammenhang der Gesetzesthematik. κρίνειν setzt Jakobus sechs Mal, vor allem in 4,11.12, im Sinne von »moralisch verurteilen«. Das Verbot, den Nächsten (Jak 4,12) oder den Bruder (Jak 4,11) anzuklagen oder moralisch zu verurteilen, gehört zu den Standardforderungen der antiken jüdischen und der frühchristlichen Paränese. Zahlreiche Mahnungen aus den Paulusbriefen, so vor allem Röm 2,1 und 14,13, fordern den Verzicht auf die Verurteilung der Brüder, d. h. der Gemeindeglieder.

Die finale Wendung ἵνα μὴ κριθῆτε, dient hier als Warnung im eschatologischen Horizont des kommenden Richters. Die direkte spiegelbildliche Kongruenz der Verhaltensform gemäß der goldenen Regel, wie sie sich in Mt 7,1.2 (Lk 6,37) als weisheitlicher Mahnspruch findet, hat Jakobus hier vermieden, indem er στενάζειν statt κρίνειν setzt (*variatio*). Ob hier allerdings eine *intendierte aemulatio* eines Je-

---

[1884] Aber häufig z. B. in der griechischen Literatur.
[1885] LSJ, 1638: »to moan« (Klage führen gegen). Ein negativer Akzent findet sich auch in Hebr 13,17: »seufzen« konträr zu »Freude«. Vgl. ähnlicher Duktus der Paränese in 1Kor 10,10: »murrt nicht« mit Hinblick auf das Todesschicksal der Murrenden.
[1886] BAUER / ALAND, 824. Beispiele: Apk 2,4.14.20; Joh 18,19; Röm 8,33; Lk 23,14; Jak 3,14 und 5,9 u. a.
[1887] METZNER, Jak, 283.

C. Briefcorpus

suslogions in der Fassung von Mt 7,1 vorliegt[1888] oder ob Jakobus selbständig im Kontext der weisheitlich-ethischen Tradition des »Nicht-Richtens« und der goldenen Regel formuliert, kann nicht entschieden werden. Dale Allison weist zurecht darauf hin, dass die Finalkonstruktion ἵνα μὴ κριθῆτε nicht außerhalb griechischer christlicher Texte begegnet. Allison urteilt daher, es sei »indeed close to certain«, dass Jakobus hier Kenntnis von Mt 7,1.2 zeige:

> It occurs only in the saying of Jesus, James, and quotations of those texts.[1889]

Allerdings verweist Jakobus eben nicht auf »den Herrn« wie Polykarp in Polyk 2,3. Jakobus benutzt nicht die Autorität des Herrenwortes, sondern formuliert *selbst*. Zudem legt er den Akzent stärker auf die *eschatologische* Paränese.[1890]

Mt 7,1: Μὴ κρίνετε, **ἵνα μὴ** κριθῆτε. (2) ἐν ᾧ γὰρ κρίματι κρίνετε κριθήσεσθε.
(1) Richtet nicht, damit ihr nicht gerichtet werdet. (2) Denn nach welchem Recht ihr richtet, werdet ihr gerichtet werden.
Lk 6,37: Καὶ μὴ κρίνετε, καὶ οὐ μὴ κριθῆτε· καὶ μὴ καταδικάζετε, καὶ οὐ μὴ καταδικασθῆτε.
Und richtet nicht, und ihr werdet nicht gerichtet, und verdammt nicht, und ihr werdet nicht verdammt werden.
Jak 5,9 μὴ στενάζετε, ἀδελφοί, κατ᾽ ἀλλήλων, **ἵνα μὴ** κριθῆτε.

Autorisiert wird seine μακροθυμία-Mahnung in 5,9 also nicht durch ein Herrenwort, sondern durch den nun *eschatologisch* zugespitzten Verweis auf den Richter: ἰδοὺ ὁ κριτὴς πρὸ τῶν θυρῶν ἕστηκεν.[1891] Der Satz wiederholt und überbietet V. 8b in *abgewandelter* und *bildhafter* Form. Mit einem weiteren Aufruf der Demonstrativpartikel ἰδού wird die Ankündigung der Nähe des Kyrios von V. 8 intensiviert. Jakobus benutzt weitere Mittel der Intensivierung: Der Kyrios wird der κριτής, und das Motiv des Nahens wird durch das Bild »(bereits) vor der Tür stehen« (Verb im Perfekt!) verstärkt. Das Motiv des »Vor der Tür Stehens bzw. Naheseins« gehört in den frühchristlichen eschatologischen Bildschatz und variiert hier V. 8b. In Apk 3,20 findet sich dasselbe Motiv. Der Herr – hier eindeutig Christus – steht vor der Tür: Ἰδοὺ ἕστηκα ἐπὶ τὴν θύραν.[1892] Auf die Endereignisse bezogen findet sich dieselbe Wendung in Mt 24,33:
ὅταν ἴδητε πάντα ταῦτα, γινώσκετε ὅτι ἐγγύς ἐστιν ἐπὶ θύραις.
Wenn ihr all das seht, wisst, dass [es] nahe vor der Tür ist.[1893]

[1888] Dazu Luz, Mt I/1, 487–494.

[1889] Allison, Jak, 706. Viel vorsichtiger Burchard, Jak, 200 (mit Verweis auf S. 17): »V. 9a ist vielleicht mit Mt 7,1 par verwandt«.

[1890] Luz, Mt I/1, 490 f, sieht allerdings auch in Mt 7,1 die eschatologische Komponente.

[1891] »Tür« hap. leg. in Jak. Plural: »Der Pl. kann, was bei Klassikern häufig ist, von einer Tür gebr. werden« (Bauer/Aland, 743).

[1892] Ebenfalls das Verb im Perfekt und Einleitung mit ἰδού. »Tür« im Singular, ἐπί statt πρό.

[1893] »Tür« im Plural, ἐπί statt πρό, ἐγγύς ἐστιν statt ἕστηκα.

338 Kommentar

Auch der übergeordnete Themenkomplex von Richter, Gericht (κρίμα[1894]), richten (κρίνειν[1895]), Urteil (κρίσις[1896]) in theologischer oder speziell eschatologischer Bedeutung ist im Jakobusbrief durchgehend präsent. Demgegenüber wird der Begriff des κριτής als Gottesepitheton im Neuen Testament nur viermal gesetzt, immerhin zweimal davon bei Jakobus.[1897] Dass Gott allein der Richter sei, hat Jakobus bereits in 4,12 statuiert. Dort ist der Richterbegriff an den Begriff des Gesetzgebers gebunden. Hier in 5,9 geht es um das Endgericht. Das Verhalten der »Brüder« gegeneinander wird in den Horizont der Parusie und des Gerichts gestellt.

V. 10 Jakobus lässt jetzt die eschatologische Zuspitzung seiner Geduldsparänese hinter sich und setzt – wieder – einen ethischen Akzent: μακροθυμία wird jetzt als geduldiges Ertragen und Leiden konkretisiert, in den Zusammenhang der ὑπομονή gestellt und durch den Hinweis auf die *Propheten* verdeutlicht, auf die dreimal verwiesen wird (5,10.11.17 f). Jakobus hat bisher fünfmal in unterschiedlichen Formulierungen auf die »Schrift« hingewiesen, in 4,5.6 ausdrücklich in ethischem Kontext.[1898] Jetzt fügt er den allgemeinen Verweis nicht auf den Wortlaut der Schrift, sondern auf das Vorbild der Propheten hinzu. Wieder bildet also die Septuaginta den religiös-kulturell-ethischen Hintergrund für Jakobus und sein Lesepublikum. Jakobus kehrt hier ein letztes Mal zu der Geduldsparänese von 1,2–4 zurück, die den Anfang der Epistel prägt, jetzt vertieft durch die Einbeziehung der Propheten. Der fünfte Imperativ: »nehmt die Propheten als Beispiel« ist wieder mit der eindringlichen Anrede »Brüder« eingeleitet.

Der Vers ist stilistisch besonders sorgfältig gestaltet. Zunächst fallen zwei hapax legomena auf, ὑπόδειγμα und κακοπάθεια. ὑπόδειγμα ist hap. leg. in Jak und begegnet selten im Neuen Testament.[1899] Jakobus befindet sich hier in der Nähe des Septuaginta-Sprachgebrauchs: Sir 44,16 bezeichnet Henoch als beispielhaftes Vorbild der μετάνοια.[1900] Jakobus setzt bei seiner Leserschaft die Kenntnis der Prophetenerzählungen – hier im besonderen Hiob und Elia – voraus. Er erläutert, in welcher Beziehung die Propheten als Beispiel genommen werden sollen: Es geht um ihre μακροθυμία – das Oberthema der Texteinheit –, die nun als κακοπαθία/

[1894] Jak 3,1.

[1895] Jak 2,12; 4,11.12; 5,9.

[1896] Jak 2,13.

[1897] Apg 10,42 (auf Christus bezogen); 2Tim 4,8 (auf Christus bezogen); Hebr 12,23 (auf Gott bezogen); Jak 4,12 (auf Gott bezogen); 5,9.

[1898] 2,8. 11. 23; 4,5.6 (siehe dort).

[1899] Joh 13,15; Hebr 4,11; 8,5; 9,23; Jak 5,10; 2Petr 2,6. Paulus verwendet für »Beispiel« entweder τύπος oder die personalisierte Form μιμηταί. ὑπογραμμός 1Petr 2,21, öfter in 1Clem (5,7 Paulus als ὑπογραμμὸς ὑπομονῆς).

[1900] Ενωχ εὐηρέστησεν κυρίῳ καὶ μετετέθη ὑπόδειγμα μετανοίας ταῖς γενεαῖς (Henoch gefiel dem Herrn und wurde verwandelt, ein Beispiel an Umkehr für Generationen). ὑπόδειγμα aber auch in LXX sehr selten: Ez 42,15; 2Makk 6,28.31 und 4Makk 17,23. ὑπόδειγμα mit λαμβάνειν nicht in LXX. Klassische Texte bevorzugen παράδειγμα (nicht im NT, mehrfach in LXX).

κακοπάθεια bestimmt wird.[1901] Das neutestamentliche hap. leg. κακοπάθεια[1902], das auch das in der Gräzität eher selten begegnet, weist wieder auf die Septuaginta. In 2Makk 2,26 f wird das Substantiv für »Beschwerlichkeit, schwere Arbeit«, in 4Makk 9,8 für »schlimmes Leiden« gesetzt. Letzteres scheint im Hinblick auf Hiob in Jak 5 angemessen.[1903] Die Verbindung beider Substantive ist nur in Jak 5,10 belegt, aber in 4Makk 9,8 begegnet die verwandte Verbindung von κακοπάθεια und ὑπομονή.[1904] 4Makk 18,10–19 darf damit als allgemeiner Hintergrund der ethisch-exemplarischen Interpretation der Propheten bei Jakobus gelten: Der Vater der sieben Brüder »lehrte [sie] das Gesetz und die Propheten« (18,10) und las unter anderem aus Daniel, Jesaja und Ezechiel vor.[1905] Die Wendung »jemanden zum Vorbild nehmen«, ὑπόδειγμα λαμβάνειν, ist noch bei Eupolemos belegt.[1906]

Neben der Wortwahl ist auch die Wortstellung im Satz auffallend: ὑπόδειγμα, das als Ergänzung zum Akkusativobjekt »die Propheten« fungiert, ist *vor* das Verb λάβετε gestellt (Hyperbaton) und durch das eingeschobene doppelte Genitivobjekt τῆς κακοπαθείας καὶ τῆς μακροθυμίας (Gen. der Sache zu ὑπόδειγμα) von seinem Bezugswort »die Propheten« getrennt. Die Textkritik hat gezeigt, dass diese Wortstellung bei den Abschreibern für Verwirrung sorgte. Die Ergänzung: οἳ ἐλάλησαν ἐν τῷ ὀνόματι κυρίου[1907] ist ein traditionelles Epitheton der Propheten und findet sich ebenso in Dan 9,6.[1908] Sie fügt keinen inhaltlichen ethischen Aspekt hinzu. Die Propheten sind nicht nur die Vorbilder der Ausdauer, der Geduld und des Ertragens von Leid, sondern auch die religiösen Autoritäten Israels – obgleich Jakobus kein Prophetenwort zitiert. »Herr« meint wieder Gott selbst.

V. 11 Eine nähere inhaltliche Bestimmung der Haltung der Propheten erfolgt in V. 11, der die Texteinheit zur μακροθυμία abschließt. Noch einmal geht es um die Geduld, zunächst verbal um ὑπομένειν (so 1,12), dann substantivisch um die ὑπομονή aus 1,3.4. Um das Thema der Geduld ein letztes Mal zu akzentuieren, greift Jakobus nicht nur zum sechsten Mal zu der Demonstrativpartikel ἰδού[1909], sondern verweist auf Vorbilder aus der Schrift, um mit einer grundsätzlichen theo-

---

[1901] Die Hss haben mehrheitlich κακοπάθεια, einige haben κακοπαθία (vgl. dazu BAUER / ALAND, 806).

[1902] Zum Verb s. u. zu V. 13.

[1903] BAUER / ALAND, 806, bevorzugt »Ausdauer«.

[1904] ἡμεῖς μὲν γὰρ διὰ τῆσδε τῆς κακοπαθείας καὶ ὑπομονῆς τὰ τῆς ἀρετῆς ἆθλα ἕξομεν (Denn wir werden wegen dieses schlimmen Leidens und der Geduld den Siegespreis der Tugend erhalten).

[1905] Vgl. auch VitProph. Die Viten der Schriftpropheten, zusätzlich Nathan, Achia von Silo, Joad, Azarja, Elia, Elisa, Sacharja ben Jojada. XXI: Elia-Vita. Hiob ist nicht vertreten.

[1906] »Wobei er den von Mose im Zelt des Zeugnisses aufgestellten [Leuchter] zum Vorbild nahm«: Eusebius, Pr. EV. IX 43,7 (Übersetzung bei N. WALTER, Fragmente jüdisch-hellenistischer Historiker, JSHRZ I 2, Gütersloh 1976, 104; Text bei C. R. HOLLADAY, Fragments from Hellenistic Jewish Authors I: Historians, Chico 1983, 126).

[1907] »Herr« meint wieder Gott selbst.

[1908] καὶ οὐκ ἠκούσαμεν τῶν παίδων σου τῶν προφητῶν, ἃ ἐλάλησαν ἐπὶ τῷ ὀνόματί σου (Und wir haben nicht auf deine Knechte, die Propheten, gehört, was sie in deinem Namen sprachen).

[1909] Jak 3,4.5; 5,4.7.9.11. Richtig BURCHARD, Jak, 202: ἰδού führt »etwas Bekanntes ein«.

340 Kommentar

logischen Aussage über Wesen und Verhalten Gottes zu schließen. μακαρίζομεν τοὺς ὑπομείναντας fungiert als Echo von 1,12. Dort hatte Jakobus statuiert: Μακάριος ἀνὴρ ὃς ὑπομένει πειρασμόν. In 5,11 wiederholt Jakobus dies Urteil im Plural. Damit bezieht er seine Leserschaft in die Formulierung ein. Zugleich löst er den Makarismus in einen reinen Aussagesatz auf und ändert das Objekt. μακαρίζειν ist hap. leg. bei Jakobus und begegnet im Neuen Testament nur noch in Lk 1,48. In LXX wird μακαρίζειν häufiger verwendet. Nahe an Jak 5,11 ist 4Makk 18,13: In der Reihe der bedrängten Propheten bzw. Gerechten[1910] wird Daniel selig gepriesen.[1911] Die Kommentatoren fragen, wer die Geduldigen hier bei Jakobus sind.[1912] Grundsätzlich gilt der Makarismus von 1,12 für alle Geduldigen in den Christus-gläubigen Gemeinden. In 5,11 geht es aber um das Vorbild der *Propheten*.

Das macht der folgende Aussagesatz mit zwei Prädikaten (ἀκούειν/ἰδεῖν[1913]) deutlich. Jakobus fokussiert nun sein ὑπόδειγμα der Geduld (Stichwortanschluss ὑπομένειν/ὑπομονή) auf *Hiob*: τὴν ὑπομονὴν Ἰὼβ ἠκούσατε. Hiob wird in den neutestamentlichen Schriften nur hier erwähnt.[1914] Dabei setzt der Verfasser voraus, dass die Adressaten Hiob und seine Lebensgeschichte aus der Septuaginta kennen. Mit der anknüpfenden Wendung »ihr habt gehört«[1915] benutzt Jakobus die Einleitung in eine erzählende Homilie ethischer Abzweckung. Er beschränkt sich allein auf die ὑπομονή des Hiob, ohne die Hioberzählung weiter heranzuziehen.[1916] Den Hintergrund des Paradigmas finden wir in der antiken jüdischen Schrift »Das Testament Hiobs«, die schon für Jak 1 und 2 wichtig war.[1917] Es geht wieder nicht um die Frage, ob Jakobus diese Schrift gekannt habe oder gar auf sie anspiele, sondern um den Hinweis auf die ethische *Bedeutung*, die die Hiobgestalt und die Hioberzählung im antiken Judentum und im frühen Christentum erhielten.[1918]

Jakobus fügt für seine Leser einen Kommentar an, der die ὑπομονή Hiobs verdeutlichen soll: καὶ τὸ τέλος κυρίου εἴδετε, ὅτι πολύσπλαγχνός ἐστιν ὁ κύριος καὶ οἰκτίρμων. Das zweite Verb: »ihr habt gesehen« nimmt die Wendung »ihr habt gehört« auf und

---

[1910] 18,15: Πολλαὶ αἱ θλίψεις τῶν δικαίων (Zahlreich sind die Trübsale der Gerechten).

[1911] [Der Vater der sieben Jünglinge] rühmte auch den Daniel in der Löwengrube, den er seligpries (ἐδόξαζεν δὲ καὶ τὸν ἐν λάκκῳ λεόντων Δανιηλ, ὃν ἐμακάριζεν). Vgl. auch 4Makk 7,22.

[1912] Die Erörterung bei BURCHARD, Jak, 202, ist sehr umständlich.

[1913] Vgl. die entsprechende pädagogisch-kommunikative Wendung mit βλέπειν in 2,22.

[1914] 1Clem 17,3 und 2Clem 6,8 nennen Hiob als Gerechten. Zu Hiob in der Alten Kirche vgl. den umfangreichen Beitrag von E. DASSMANN, Art. Hiob, RAC 15, 1991, 366–442.

[1915] So schon Jak 2,5.

[1916] Im Buch Hiob in LXX fehlt ὑπομονή. Für die Kirchenväter seit Clemens von Alexandria ist Hiob ein Vorbild der Geduld (vgl. SPANNEUT, RAC 9, besonders 270 f).

[1917] S. oben zu 1,4 und 12 sowie 2,1. B. SCHALLER ordnet die Schrift in den Zeitraum 1. Jh. v.Chr. bis 2. Jh. n. Chr. ein: Das Testament Hiobs, JSHRZ III 3, Gütersloh 1979, 311. Vgl. A. YOSHIKO REED, Art. Job, Testament of, EDEJ, 814–816 (Datierung: zwischen 150 v. Chr. und 116–117 n. Chr.).

[1918] BURCHARD, Jak, 202, spricht von »einem haggadischen Hiobbild«. Vgl. DASSMANN, RAC 15, 374: »das Test. Job als bedeutendes Zeugnis der jüd. Haggadah«.

C. Briefcorpus 341

steigert und konkretisiert diese.[1919] Das Syntagma τὸ τέλος κυρίου ist uneindeutig und verunklärt die Aussage des Jakobus. Da der anschließende Kausalsatz einige Klärung anbietet, lässt sich τὸ τέλος κυρίου am besten von der Gottesprädikation her aufschlüsseln. Jakobus beschreibt Gott als mitleidig[1920] und barmherzig[1921] und unterstreicht damit die Bedeutung der Geduld Hiobs (ὑπομονή) im Zusammenhang des μακροθυμία-Abschnitts. Er variiert Ex 34,6 f:

(6) Κύριος ὁ θεὸς οἰκτίρμων καὶ ἐλεήμων, μακρόθυμος καὶ πολυέλεος καὶ ἀληθινὸς (7) καὶ δικαιοσύνην διατηρῶν καὶ ποιῶν ἔλεος εἰς χιλιάδας.

(6) (Gott) der Herr ist mitleidig und barmherzig, großmütig und voller Erbarmen und wahrhaftig (7) und übt Gerechtigkeit und tut Barmherzigkeit.

Das in LXX wichtige Gottesprädikat οἰκτίρμων[1922] behält Jakobus bei, statt πολυέλεος setzt er das ausgefallene πολύσπλαγχνος. Anders als σπλάγχνος ist οἰκτίρμων in LXX ein wichtiges Gottesprädikat: (Ex 34,6). Die Verbindung findet sich dann zweimal in der paulinischen Literatur: Phil 2,1 (als Hendiadyoin: εἴ τις σπλάγχνα καὶ οἰκτιρμοί) in christologisch-ethischem Zusammenhang und Kol 3,12 in ethischem Zusammenhang:

ἐνδύσασθε οὖν, ὡς ἐκλεκτοὶ τοῦ θεοῦ ἅγιοι καὶ ἠγαπημένοι, σπλάγχνα οἰκτιρμοῦ χρηστότητα ταπεινοφροσύνην πραΰτητα μακροθυμίαν.

So zieht nun an, als die auserwählten Gottes, als die Heiligen und Geliebten, herzliches Erbarmen, Freundlichkeit, Demut, Sanftmut, Geduld.

Jakobus findet sich hier also in einem festen Kontext alttestamentlicher und frühjüdischer Theo-logie, die auch bei Paulus vorausgesetzt ist.[1923] Paulus wie Jakobus verwenden die theo-logische Prädikation im ethischen Zusammenhang.

Von dieser Perspektive lässt sich die Wendung τὸ τέλος κυρίου εἴδετε zuordnen.[1924] Zwei Übersetzungs- und Verstehensmöglichkeiten bietet die Wendung. Erstens lässt sich »Herr« auf Christus beziehen, es würde sich um einen Gen.subj. handeln. Mit τέλος[1925] wäre der Tod Jesu gemeint.[1926] Die enge Verbindung zwischen dem Schicksal Hiobs und Jesu ist aber nicht einsichtig. Jakobus würde die Leserschaft auf ihre Kenntnis der Passionsgeschichte ansprechen und zugleich auf das barmherzige Handeln Gottes verweisen. Κύριος wäre im ersten Fall Jesus, im zweiten Fall

---

[1919] Vgl. 1Joh 1,1.

[1920] πολύσπλαγχνος fehlt in LXX, ist hap. leg. im NT, begegnet in Herm mand IV 3,5 u.ö. σπλάγχνον bei Paulus: 2Kor 6,12; 7,15; Phil 1,8; 2,1; Kol 3,12; Phlm 7.12.20. Auch Lk 1,78 Gottesprädikat (διὰ σπλάγχνα ἐλέους θεοῦ ἡμῶν). Das Verb begegnet mehrfach bei den Synoptikern für Jesus (z.B. Lk 7,13).

[1921] οἰκτίρμων im NT: Lk 6,36 und Jak 5,11 (hap. leg. in Jak). οἰκτιρμός im NT: Röm 12,1; 2Kor 1,3; Phil 2,1; Kol 3,12; Hebr 10,28.

[1922] Häufiger in den Psalmen, stets in Verbindung mit ἐλεήμων.

[1923] Paulus interpretiert sie christologisch.

[1924] Vgl. die grammatische Darstellung bei BURCHARD, Jak, 203.

[1925] Hap. leg. in Jak.

[1926] Die Wendung wäre dann vergleichbar mit Mt 2,15: ἕως τῆς τελευτῆς Ἡρῴδου (bis zum Tod des Herodes).

342 Kommentar

Gott selbst. Dieser Bedeutungswechsel ist äußerst unwahrscheinlich.[1927] Zweitens kann der Genitiv als Gen.auct. gelesen werden: Gott hat ein (gutes) Ende für Hiob herbeigeführt (Hi 42,10–16LXX): Das Syntagma lässt sich dann auflösen als »das Ende, das der Herr herbeigeführt hat«. Ob Jakobus hier speziell auf 42,12:

ὁ δὲ κύριος εὐλόγησεν τὰ ἔσχατα Ιωβ ἢ τὰ ἔμπροσθεν.
Der Herr segnete die letzte Lebenszeit Hiobs mehr als die frühere,

oder auf 42,17 anspielt und damit eine eschatologische Tendenz impliziert, lässt sich nicht sagen. Hier wie oft bleibt Jakobus äußerst kurz, gradlinig und einfach. Seine Paränese gilt der Geduld, für die er die Propheten ins Feld führt. Hiob ist ein Beispiel für diese Geduld. Gott ist barmherzig und führt eine Existenz in Geduld und Leiden wie die Hiobs zu einem guten Ende.

2. Texteinheit: 5,12 Warnung vor dem Schwören

(12) **Vor allem aber, meine Brüder, schwört nicht, weder beim Himmel noch bei der Erde noch mit[1928] irgendeinem anderen Eid. Es sei aber euer »Ja« ja und euer »Nein« nein, damit ihr nicht dem Gericht verfallt[1929].**

Textkritik: **V. 12** Der ινα-Satz enthält ein Problem: ινα μη υπο κρισιν πεσητε lesen 01. 02. 03. 33V (bessere Bezeugung) und einige Minuskeln, ινα μη εις υποκρισιν πεσητε lesen 025. 044 und viele Minuskeln.

V. 12 Wieder werden die Brüder – hier ist die Beziehung noch durch »meine« verstärkt – im Sinne epistolarer paränetischer Kommunikation persönlich angesprochen. Πρὸ πάντων δέ stellt einerseits den direkten Zusammenhang zum Vorangehenden her, obgleich das Thema von V. 12 nicht zum Themenkreis »Geduld« gehört, und impliziert andererseits eine finale Steigerung. Der Wortlaut der Hervorhebungsformel ist in der griechischen Literatur gängig.[1930] Inhaltlich geht es um eine weitere Mahnung, die hier geradezu beschwörenden Charakter hat: Die Leserschaft soll auf keinen Fall und in keiner Weise *schwören*. Das Thema »Schwören« ist Jakobus so wichtig, dass er ihm in V. 12 eine eigene kleine Texteinheit gegen Ende des Briefes widmet. Im Vergleich mit anderen Texten zum Thema fällt die Kürze und Prägnanz des Jakobustextes auf. Die Bedeutung des Schwurverbotes ist trotz der Unverbundenheit zum vorangehenden Thema der Geduld im Zusammenhang des Briefes plausibel: Der begründende Finalsatz »damit ihr nicht dem Gericht verfallt« stellt V. 12 in den eschatologischen Gerichtszusammenhang der V. 7–11. Außerdem ist das Schwurverbot Teil der Sprachethik des Briefes: Gerade der feierli-

---

[1927] So auch DIBELIUS, Jak, 294.
[1928] Griechisch: Akkusativ.
[1929] Wörtlich: damit ihr nicht unter das Gericht fallt.
[1930] Beispiele BURCHARD, Jak, 207; ALLISON, Jak, 730. NT: Kol 1,17; 1Petr 4,8. Allgemein: F. O. FRANCIS, Form and Function of the Opening and Closing Paragraphs of James and I John, ZNW 61, 1970, 110–126.

C. Briefcorpus   343

che Sprechakt (John Searle / J. L. Austin) des Schwurs muss sprachethisch beurteilt werden.[1931]

Der Eid bzw. Schwur[1932] (hebr. *šbʿ*) spielt im Alten Testament wie im gesamten Alten Orient eine wichtige Rolle sowohl im juristischen Zusammenhang wie im Alltagsleben.[1933] Ähnliches gilt für die griechisch-römische Welt.[1934] Die Geltung und korrespondierend der Schutz des Eides sind von besonderer Wichtigkeit. Lev 19,12 enthält an prominenter Stelle das Verbot des Falschschwurs oder Meineides: καὶ οὐκ ὀμεῖσθε τῷ ὀνόματί μου ἐπ᾽ ἀδίκῳ καὶ οὐ βεβηλώσετε τὸ ὄνομα τοῦ θεοῦ ὑμῶν. Ihr sollt nicht unrecht schwören bei meinem Namen und den Namen eures Gottes nicht entheiligen.[1935]

Gefahren beim Viel-Schwören sieht besonders Jesus Sirach. Im Zusammenhang seiner Sprachethik warnt er ausführlich vor dem Vielschwörer (ἀνὴρ πολύορκος)[1936]: 23,9 ὅρκῳ μὴ ἐθίσῃς τὸ στόμα σου καὶ ὀνομασίᾳ τοῦ ἁγίου μὴ συνεθισθῇς· (10) ὥσπερ γὰρ οἰκέτης ἐξεταζόμενος ἐνδελεχῶς ἀπὸ μώλωπος οὐκ ἐλαττωθήσεται, οὕτως καὶ ὁ ὀμνύων καὶ ὀνομάζων διὰ παντὸς ἀπὸ ἁμαρτίας οὐ μὴ καθαρισθῇ. (11) ἀνὴρ πολύορκος πλησθήσεται ἀνομίας.

(9) Gewöhne deinen Mund nicht ans Schwören, und gewöhne dir das Aussprechen des heiligen (Namens) nicht an; (10) denn wie ein Sklave, der fortwährend verhört wird, an (blutigen) Striemen nicht Mangel haben wird, so wird auch der, der schwört und dauernd den Namen (Gottes) ausspricht, von Sünde nicht gereinigt werden. (11) Ein Mann, der viel schwört, wird voll von Gesetzlosigkeit sein.

Im Neuen Testament erscheint das Thema *Schwur* im Hebräerbrief, zweimal im Matthäusevangelium und bei Jakobus. Die Bedeutung dieses Verbotes zeigt sich darin, dass Jesus dies Verbot in der vierten Antithese in Mt 5,33 aufgreift und seine eigene Position zum Schwur neben seine neue Deutung der *Dekalogverbote* von Töten und Ehebruch stellt: auch hier eine hervorgehobene Positionierung des Themas.

In Hebr 6,13–20 verweist der Verfasser auf die Abrahamsverheißung Gottes, die Gott mit einem ›Schwur bei sich selbst‹ unterstützte[1937], um die Hoffnung der Ge-

---

[1931] Dazu besonders die sehr umsichtige und gründliche Darstellung des Themas »Schwören« und »Eid« bei LUTHER, Sprachethik, 247–280 (Vergleich zwischen Mt 5 und Jak 5); zum Sprechakt: 278.

[1932] *Schwur* ist die allgemeinere Version einer feierlichen Beteuerung der Wahrheit einer Aussage (genaue Definition von »Schwur« bei S. ESDERS, Art. Schwur, RAC 30, 2021, 29–79, Sp. 30; Lit.!). *Eid* bezieht sich vor allem auf die Beteuerung der Wahrheit einer Aussage vor juristischen und öffentlichen Institutionen.

[1933] A. FLURY, Art. Eid / Schwur (AT), WiBiLex (https://www.bibelwissenschaft.de/stichwort/16992/); J. SCHNEIDER, Art. ὀμνύω, ThWNT 5, 1954, 177–185. Vgl. für Jak 5,12 auch die Belege aus der nichtjüdischen und jüdischen (besonders Philo) Antike bei BURCHARD, Jak, 207.

[1934] ESDERS, Art. Schwur, verweist besonders auf die Eidkritik in der griechischen Philosophie: Sp. 35.

[1935] Gegen Meineid auch Ps-Phok 16 und 1Tim 1,10.

[1936] Hap. leg. in der Gräzität. FRANKEMÖLLE, Jak II, 697–704, stellt ausführlich Sirachs Position zum Schwören dar und positioniert sie im Zusammenhang von Sirachs Sprachethik, die ihrerseits eine große Rolle für Jak 3 spielt. Frankemölle konstatiert aber zurecht: »So sehr diese Vorstellungen auch motivgeschichtlich auf Jakobus eingewirkt haben, im strengen Sinn formale und inhaltliche Parallelen sind diese Stellen nicht« (700). Es geht hier weder um Parallelen noch um Allusionen oder gar Zitate, sondern um ein traditionelles ethisches *Thema* von großer Bedeutung im jüdischen Kontext.

[1937] Die »zwei πράγματα« in Hebr 6,18 beziehen sich auf die Verheißung und den (zusätzlichen) Schwur, der

344 Kommentar

meinde zu stärken und ihnen Geduld zu empfehlen (6,9–12). Der Verfasser fügt in diesem Zusammenhang eine Beschreibung (V. 16a) und eine Definition (V. 16b) des Schwurs hinzu:

ἄνθρωποι γὰρ κατὰ τοῦ μείζονος ὀμνύουσιν, καὶ πάσης αὐτοῖς ἀντιλογίας πέρας εἰς βεβαίωσιν ὁ ὅρκος.

Menschen nämlich schwören bei dem Höheren, und der Eid dient ihnen als Bestätigung gegenüber jedem Einwand.

Auf eben diese Sitte, bei »etwas Größerem« zu schwören, bezieht sich kritisch Jesu dritter Weheruf gegen die »Schriftgelehrten und Pharisäer« in Mt 23,16–22. Dieser Text wirft ein grelles und polemisches Licht auf die Realität des Schwörens im Zusammenhang der Polemik Jesu: Die hier geübte Kritik an heuchlerischer Schwurpraxis, nämlich den Schwur bei der höchsten und daher gültigen Instanz absichtlich zu vermeiden, um damit den Konsequenzen des Schwures zu entgehen, ist kaum zu überbieten.[1938]

Bei Jakobus geht es aber weder um die Kritik des Vielschwörens oder der Vermeidung von Konsequenzen noch primär um ein Schwurverbot, sondern *positiv* um eine Vorschrift zu einfacher und wahrer Rede.[1939] Damit steht das Gebot in Jak 5,13 in derselben Linie wie die Kritik am »Zweiseeler« in 1,8; 4,8.[1940] Die nächste Parallele zu 5,13 findet sich Mt 5,33–37.[1941] Außerdem heranzuziehen ist 2Hen 49,1 f.[1942] Ein Vergleich der beiden neutestamentlichen Mahnsprüche weist auf eine gemeinsame Grundlage.

---

der Verheißung noch mehr Sicherheit gibt.

[1938] Luz, Mt I/3, 325–329. Esders' Urteil, Art. Schwur, RAC 30, Sp. 46: »Die eidkritische Position Jesu steht in der Tradition religiös begründeter Ablehnung des E.(des) in der griechischen Philosophie … u. konnte auch an zahlreiche eidkritische Stimmen im hellenistischen Judentum anschließen …, ist also keineswegs als Fundamentalkritik an ›jüdischer Vielschwörerei‹ zu verstehen«, enthält gleich mehrere Ungenauigkeiten. Dass die Jesuslogien in Mt 5 und 23 sich aus der griechischen philosophischen Tradition herleiten, ist angesichts der Beispiele in beiden Texten eher abwegig. Es geht um spezifisch *jüdische* Eidvermeidungspraktiken, die aus *jüdischen* theologischen Erwägungen abgelehnt werden. Vgl. bereits die prophetische Kritik bei Hos 4,15 (μὴ ὀμνύετε ζῶντα κύριον). Fundamentalkritk an der Praxis jüdischer *Vielschwörerei* übt Jesus Sirach eben gerade auch mit dem singulären Neologismus πολύορκος (Übersetzung des Enkels!). Eben dasselbe kritisiert Jesus in Mt 23. Vgl. auch die innerjüdische Schwurkritik in den Qumranschriften und bei Philo (Esders, Art. Schwur, 48 f). Richtig ist dagegen E.s Hinweis auf die Verbindung von Schwurthematik und Torakritik in Mt 5, die in Jak 5 fehlt.

[1939] So in der Tendenz auch bei Diogenes Laertius von Pythagoras überliefert: Diogenes Laertius VIII 22 (Auch soll man nicht bei den Göttern schwören, vielmehr sich bemühen, selbst glaubwürdig zu erscheinen); vgl. auch Jamblichos, v.P. 28,115,10. Pythagoras ist sehr nahe bei dem Schwurverbot, legt den Akzent aber stärker auf die wahrhaftige Rede.

[1940] Vgl. Luther, Sprachethik, 279.

[1941] Zum Text Luz, Mt I/1, 369–382; zum hellenistischen und jüdischen Kontext von Eidkritik ebd. 373 f. Zum Vergleich Jak 5 und Mt 5 vgl. Luther, Sprachethik, 276 f.

[1942] Zu 2Hen 49,1 f vgl. Luther, Sprachethik, 264 f. Ausführlicher Kommentar zum Schwur in der Henochtradition bei Ch. Böttrich, Das slavische Henochbuch, JSHRZ V 7, Gütersloh 1995, 968–970. Böttrich erörtert die Möglichkeit, die Passage »doch siehe … ja ja« als christlichen Einschub zu interpretieren. Er bevorzugt die Erklärung, die Einschaltung sei »ursprünglich« (969). Deutlich ist: Das Thema in 2Hen

C. Briefcorpus 345

Jak 5,12: μὴ ὀμνύετε μήτε τὸν οὐρανὸν μήτε τὴν γῆν μήτε ἄλλον τινὰ ὅρκον, ἤτω δὲ ὑμῶν τὸ ναὶ ναὶ καὶ τὸ οὒ οὔ, ἵνα μὴ ὑπὸ κρίσιν πέσητε.

Mt 5,34: ἐγὼ δὲ λέγω ὑμῖν μὴ ὀμόσαι ὅλως· μήτε ἐν τῷ οὐρανῷ, ὅτι θρόνος ἐστὶν τοῦ θεοῦ, (35) μήτε ἐν τῇ γῇ, ὅτι ὑποπόδιόν ἐστιν τῶν ποδῶν αὐτοῦ, μήτε εἰς Ἱεροσόλυμα, ὅτι πόλις ἐστὶν τοῦ μεγάλου βασιλέως, (36) μήτε ἐν τῇ κεφαλῇ σου ὀμόσῃς, ὅτι οὐ δύνασαι μίαν τρίχα λευκὴν ποιῆσαι ἢ μέλαιναν. (37) ἔστω δὲ ὁ λόγος ὑμῶν ναὶ ναί, οὒ οὔ, τὸ δὲ περισσὸν τούτων ἐκ τοῦ πονηροῦ ἐστιν.

(34) Ich aber sage euch, dass ihr überhaupt nicht schwören sollt, weder bei dem Himmel, denn er ist Gottes Thron; (35) noch bei der Erde, denn sie ist der Schemel seiner Füße; noch bei Jerusalem, denn sie ist die Stadt des großen Königs, (36) noch sollst du bei deinem Haupt schwören; denn du vermagst nicht ein einziges Haar weiß oder schwarz zu machen. (37) Eure Rede aber sei: Ja, ja; nein, nein. Was darüber ist, ist vom Bösen.

2Hen 49,1: »Denn ich schwöre euch, meine Kinder – doch siehe, ich schwöre weder mit einem einzigen Schwur, noch beim Himmel, noch bei der Erde, noch bei einem anderen Geschöpf, das der Herr geschaffen hat. Denn der Herr hat gesprochen: ›Bei mir sind weder Schwur noch Unrecht, sondern Wahrheit.‹ So, wenn unter Menschen keine Wahrheit ist, so sollen sie schwören mit dem Wort: Ja, ja; wenn aber so: Nein, nein. (2) Und ich schwöre euch: Ja, ja« usw.

Jak 5,12 gliedert sich nach der Anrede in ein *Verbot* mit einer dreigliedrigen Konkretisierung und in ein zweigliedriges *Gebot* mit einem angehängten Finalsatz. Eine explizite antithetische Zuordnung von Verbot und Gebot fehlt. Das Verbot bezieht sich auf jede Art des Schwörens. Auch Mt 5,34–37 enthält keine antithetische Zuordnung von Verbot und Gebot.[1943] Die Sprucheinheit erweitert das *Verbot* in zweifacher Hinsicht: erstens von zwei konkreten Gliedern auf vier, zweitens durch vier ὅτι-Sätze, die jeweils auf die Beziehung des Schwurgegenstandes bzw. Schwurgaranten zu Gott verweisen. Gemeinsam sind die beiden ersten Glieder: Himmel und Erde[1944], während Matthäus anstelle des allgemeinen »irgendein anderer Schwur(-gegenstand)« Jerusalem und das eigene Haupt zufügt – »geläufige Beteuerungsformeln«[1945], die der Vermeidung des Gottesnamens dienen.[1946] Die Doppelstruktur des *Gebots* ist in beiden Mahnsprüchen gleich: zuerst die Empfehlung, dann die Begründung mit dem Hinweis auf die negativen Folgen des Schwörens. Die Empfehlung setzt allerdings jeweils einen eigenen Akzent. Jak 5,12 ist an der Wahrhaftigkeit und Glaubwürdigkeit jeder Form von *Rede* interessiert: τὸ ναὶ

---

49 ist der Henochschwur. Der Einschub dient der ethischen Korrektur des Schwurs. Statt eines klassischen Schwures verwendet Henoch das »Ja ja«. Das deutet m. E. auf Kenntnis von Mt 5,37 hin. In 2Hen 49,1 ersetzt das verdoppelte Ja bzw. Nein den Schwur bzw. fungiert als Schwur.

[1943] Die antithetische Stoßrichtung gehört in die Rahmung V. 33.34a. – Zum Vergleich zwischen Jak 5 und Mt 5 vgl. die klaren Schemata bei DIBELIUS, Jak, 297, und ALLISON, Jak, 728.

[1944] Diese drücken per se eine Totalität aus und bedürfen keiner Ergänzung.

[1945] LUZ, Mt I/1, 377. Luz verweist auf BILLERBECK I, 334, und WETTSTEIN I, 305 f.

[1946] LUZ, Mt I/1, 371 Anm. 8, erklärt die ὀμόσαι ἐν-Fassung bei Matthäus als »Septuagintismus«. Jak 5,12 dagegen mit LSJ, 1223, klassisch: ὀμνύειν c. Akk.

(mit Artikel) soll eben »Ja« und nichts anderes bedeuten. Hier geht es direkt um Sprachethik.[1947] Burchard fasst zusammen: »ehrliches Ja und Nein«.[1948] Metzner präzisiert:

Jakobus bietet also keine Schwurersatzformel »Ja, Ja« oder »Nein, Nein« an.[1949]

Mt 5,37 ist dagegen auf die Vermeidung des religiös konnotierten Schwurs fokussiert. Mt betont die Einfachheit und Nachdrücklichkeit eines *Schwurersatzes* durch Verdoppelung des »Ja« oder »Nein«: ναὶ ναί, οὒ οὔ (»ja, ja« = »wirklich ja«, »tatsächlich«), der auf jede Beziehung zur göttlichen Sphäre verzichtet und aus sich selbst heraus gültig ist. Auch die Folgen werden unterschiedlich benannt: Jakobus verweist auf das *Gericht* und damit auf den eschatologischen Rahmen von 5,9.[1950] Mt 5,37 dagegen urteilt im Kontext der neuen *Gesetzes*-Hermeneutik der Antithesen.

Jak 5,12 im Vergleich mit Mt 5,37 stellt erneut die Frage nach möglicher *Jesusüberlieferung* bzw. nach der Anspielung auf diese Tradition. Ulrich Luz nimmt für das Schwurverbot in Mt 5,34 jesuanische Herkunft an:

Da das kategorische Schwurverbot im Judentum singulär ist, stammt es wohl von Jesus.[1951]

Welche Bedeutung hat dies Urteil, das mehrheitlich von den Exegeten geteilt wird, für Jak 5,13? Im Zusammenhang der Texteinheit in Jak 5 dürfen *vier* Faktoren als offensichtlich und unbestritten gelten: *Erstens* zitiert Jakobus anders als Mt 5 nicht explizit ein Jesuslogion. Das bedeutet auch, dass er sich nicht explizit auf Jesu Autorität stützt.[1952] Ebenso wenig verwendet Jakobus *zweitens* die antithetische Rahmenlogik von Mt 5,33–37 und damit die Abgrenzung von der Tora in 5,33[1953]. Das heißt auch: Jak 5,12 befindet sich nicht im Zusammenhang der Diskussion um die Toraauslegung. *Drittens* akzentuiert Jak 5,12 das Logion über das Schwurver-

---

[1947] So auch Luther, Sprachethik, 279: Jakobus ist »auf die Wahrhaftigkeit des Menschen und die Glaubwürdigkeit seiner Rede ausgerichtet«.

[1948] Burchard, Jak, 208. Dibelius, Jak, 296: »Es handelt sich um eine sittliche Mahnung« mit dem Inhalt: »Euer Ja sei wahr und euer Nein sei wahr«. Dasselbe formuliert Paulus in 2Kor 1,17 f: ἵνα ᾖ παρ' ἐμοὶ τὸ ναὶ ναὶ καὶ τὸ οὒ οὔ (Damit bei mir das Ja ja und das Nein nein sei). Allison, Jak, 732, ordnet den Paulussatz fälschlich Mt 5,37 zu.

[1949] Metzner, Jak, 294.

[1950] κρίσις schon Jak 2,13. »Dem Gericht verfallen«: seltene Formulierung. Burchard, Jak, 208, weist auf Sir 29,19 hin: ἁμαρτωλὸς ἐμπεσὼν εἰς ἐγγύην καὶ διώκων ἐργολαβίας ἐμπεσεῖται εἰς κρίσεις (Ein Sünder stolpert in eine Bürgschaft hinein, und wer Gewinnstreben nachjagt, wird in Prozesse hineinstolpern).

[1951] Luz, Mt I/1, 372. Es ist hinzuzufügen: Als generelles Verbot ist es auch im paganen Bereich ohne Parallele.

[1952] Darauf verweist besonders Burchard, Jak, 207, und schließt: Jakobus »muß sie nicht als Ausspruch oder Meinung Jesu gekannt haben«. Dieser Schluss ist aber im frühchristlichen Kontext eher unwahrscheinlich (so Allison).

[1953] Für Mt 5,33 weist Luz, Mt I/1, 372, einen allgemeinen frühjüdischen Hintergrund nach. Direkte Anspielung auf Ex 20,7 (Missbrauch des Gottesnamens), Ex 20,16 (falsches Zeugnis) oder Lev 19,12 (Verbot des Meineids) verneint Luz.

C. Briefcorpus 347

bot allgemein ethisch und rückt es damit sachlich in die Nähe zeitgenössischer Schwurkritik hellenistisch-römischer Herkunft. Trotzdem darf *viertens* auch gelten: Die Liste der formalen und sachlichen Übereinstimmungen zwischen Mt 5 und Jak 5 ist überdeutlich. Dass hier von Tradition zu sprechen ist, zeigt der andere Zusammenhang in 2Hen 49, in den die Schwurtradition eingefügt ist. Es wird bei einer vergleichenden Analyse also weniger um das »Dass« als um das zeitliche und *traditionsgeschichtliche »Wie«* der gegenseitigen Beziehung gehen.

Wie beurteilen die Kommentare die Traditionszusammenhänge? Wichtige Beiträge haben vor allem Dibelius, Allison und Metzner geleistet. Dibelius weist darauf hin, dass »eine der Jak-Form ähnliche Gestalt des Spruches … noch von einer Anzahl altchristlicher Texte zitiert« wird und schließt:

> Das Wort scheint also in doppelter Gestalt umgelaufen zu sein.[1954]

Er hält die Jakobusfassung für die einfachere und ältere.[1955] Ob es sich ursprünglich um einen Spruch Jesu handelte, lässt Dibelius offen.[1956] In der Einleitung bezeichnet er den Spruch allerdings als »Einzelfall«, der neben anderem »für die Bekanntschaft des Jak mit der Überlieferung von Jesus« spricht.[1957]

Allison plädiert gegen Burchard für die Abhängigkeit des Jakobustextes von Mt 5.[1958] In seiner ausführlichen und unübertroffen genauen und vorsichtig abwägenden Einführung präsentiert er die Liste der Logien, die nach seinem Urteil Jakobus bekannt waren und von ihm benutzt wurden.[1959] Dazu gehört die Tradition in Jak 5,12, die für Allison besonders wichtig ist. Mt 5,33–37 ist nach Allison *erstens* das einzige Jesuslogion bei Jakobus, das nur bei Matthäus überliefert ist, *zweitens* aber auch das einzige, das wörtlich wiedergegeben wird:

> Just as James can rewrite the LXX in his own words …, so he can rewrite sayings of Jesus. Indeed, with the exception of 5.12 = Mt 5.33–37, emulating logia without reproducing them is characteristic of him.[1960]

Nach Abwägung aller Möglichkeiten tendiert Allison dazu, eine besondere Nähe zwischen Matthäus und Jakobus anzunehmen:

> The hypothesis that James knew Matthew is a real possibility. It neatly accounts at a stroke for most of the Jesus tradition in our epistle. But it remains just that, a hypothe-

---

[1954] DIBELIUS, Jak, 297 (Belege von Justin und Clemens Alexandrinus, jeweils ohne Hinweis auf Jak 5,12).

[1955] DIBELIUS, Jak, 298.

[1956] DIBELIUS, Jak, 299.

[1957] DIBELIUS, Jak, 46.

[1958] ALLISON, Jak, 729.

[1959] ALLISON, Jak, 56–62.

[1960] ALLISON, Jak, 57. Allison bezieht sich auf R. BAUCKHAM, Brother, 74–111, und auf KLOPPENBORG, Reception, und: Emulation.

348 Kommentar

sis. We have only hints, nothing approaching proof. Moreover, even if James did use Matthew, the latter may not have been his only source for the Jesus tradition.[1961]

Allison dokumentiert auch mögliche Gründe dafür, dass Jakobus Jesus nicht als Urheber des Schwurverbotes nennt, obgleich er sich auf die Jesustradition bezieht. Der wichtigste Grund könnte sein: Zu der Adressatenschaft des Jakobusbriefes gehören auch Juden und Judenchristen. Allison zieht damit Jak 5,12 als Beleg für seine Zuordnung des Briefes zum Ebionitenmilieu heran.

> Our text does not appeal to Jesus as an authority because Jesus was not an authority for all of the envisaged audience.[1962]

Metzner unterscheidet drei Lösungsmöglichkeiten: (1) Jak 5,12 steht am Anfang der Überlieferung. Ob der Spruch als Jesuslogion bekannt war, bleibt offen (Dibelius). (2) Jakobus verwendet Mt 5,33–37 und »gestaltet das Mt-Wort zu einem kurzen Mahnwort um«.[1963] (3) Mt 5 hängt von Jak 5 ab, was aber zeitlich und sachlich unwahrscheinlich ist. Metzner votiert für die zweite Lösung und erläutert mögliche Gründe »für die briefliche Kurzfassung«.[1964] Er vermutet, dass der Jakobusbrief die zu enge Beziehung zu Jerusalem vermeiden möchte, um die generelle Tendenz des Wortes zu steigern. Zugleich sieht er in dieser Tendenz ein wichtiges Argument gegen die These der Verfasserschaft durch den Herrenbruder.[1965] Zusammenfassend ist deutlich, dass Jakobus innerhalb eines breiten ethischen Diskurses zum Thema »Schwur« eine eigene Position vertritt, die Mt 5,33–37 modifiziert. Ob Jakobus das Jesuslogion kannte und weshalb er das Schwurverbot nicht als Herrenwort zitiert, muss offenbleiben.[1966]

3. Texteinheit: 5,13–18 Mahnung zum Gebet

(13) Es leidet jemand unter euch, – er bete; es ist jemand froh, – er singe Psalmen; (14) es ist jemand unter euch krank, – er rufe die Ältesten der Ekklesia herbei, und sie sollen über ihm beten und ihn mit Öl salben[1967] im Namen des Herrn. (15) Und das Gebet des Glaubens wird den Kranken retten, und aufrichten wird ihn der Herr; und wenn er Sünden begangen hat[1968], wird ihm vergeben werden. (16) Bekennt nun einander eure[1969] Sünden und betet füreinander, dass ihr geheilt werdet. Viel vermag das wirksame[1970] Gebet des Gerechten. (17) Elias war ein

---

[1961] ALLISON, Jak, 62. Zur Bedeutung von Mt für die Ebionitenthese Allisons s. Einleitung.
[1962] ALLISON, Jak, 59. Der vorliegende Kommentar teilt diese Meinung nicht.
[1963] METZNER, Jak, 295.
[1964] METZNER, Jak, 295.
[1965] METZNER, Jak, 296: »Jak 5,12 passt nicht zum überlieferten Jakobusbild«.
[1966] Allison beruft sich auf ein Gesetz der Paränese: »since *paraenesis* ... is not argument, but exhortation, sources are not usually cited« (ALLISON, Jak, 59). Dazu kritisch die Einleitung.
[1967] Das Partizip ist parataktisch aufgelöst.
[1968] Das Partizip ist konditional aufgelöst.
[1969] Griechisch: »die«.
[1970] Griechisch: partizipial.

Mensch, der denselben Leiden ausgesetzt war[1971] wie wir, und er betete ein Gebet, es solle nicht regnen, und es regnete nicht auf der Erde drei Jahre und sechs Monate. (18) Und er betete noch einmal, und der Himmel gab Regen, und die Erde brachte ihre Frucht hervor.

Textkritik: V. 13 Statt ευθυμει lesen 044 und die Minuskeln 614. 945. 2412 und L884 αθυμει (glättend: lectio facilior, schlecht bezeugt). V. 14 Minuskel 88 erweitert zu εν τω ονοματι του κυριου Ιησου, Minuskel 6 liest εν τω ονοματι Ιησου Χριστου.

Mit κακοπαθεῖ nimmt Jakobus das Stichwort aus 5,10 auf und knüpft damit an die Thematik von 5,7–11 an. So erweist sich auch im Nachhinein das Schwurverbot von V. 12 als eine Art von thematischem Einschub. Allerdings arbeitet Jakobus in der gesamten Schlusspassage 5,7–20 mit einer verschränkten Stichwortkette[1972]: Leiden (5,10→13), Gericht (5,9→12), Krankheit (5,13→15.16), Sünden (5,15.16→20), Rettung (5,11→20), Gebet (5,13→15. 16. 17.18). Das Endgewicht liegt auf dem Thema des *Gebets*[1973] in der Verknüpfung mit Krankheit. So wie 5,7–11 ein Text über die *Geduld* ist, ist 5,13–18 einer der wichtigen neutestamentlichen Texte über das *Gebet*. Dabei benutzt Jakobus προσεύχεσθαι/προσευχή[1974] und εὔχεσθαι/εὐχή[1975] sowie δέησις.[1976] Das Gebet hat Jakobus schon im Zusammenhang der Geduldsparänese in Kapitel 1 thematisiert.[1977] Im Matthäusevangelium sind das Schwurverbot in den Antithesen in Kapitel 5 und die Gebetsbelehrung in Kapitel 6 im Rahmen der Frömmigkeitsparänese einander zugeordnet: Schwören und Gebet gehören zu den zentralen Themen der Bergpredigt. Das Gebet ist fester Bestandteil des persönlichen und gemeinschaftlichen Frömmigkeitslebens der frühjüdischen und frühchristlichen Gemeinden wie auch der vielfältigen griechisch-römischen Religionspraxis.[1978] Jakobus spricht also in der Schlusspassage seines Schreibens wichtige

---

[1971] Griechisch: ὁμοιοπαθής.

[1972] ALLISON, Jak, 746 (Tabelle).

[1973] 5,13.14.15.16a.16b.17 (figura etymologica).18. Zum Gebet im Jak: S. KAISER, Krankenheilung. Untersuchungen zu Form, Sprache, traditionsgeschichtlichem Hintergrund und Aussage zu Jak 5,13–18, WMANT 112, Neukirchen-Vluyn 2006, 236–274.

[1974] V. 13. 14. 17.18 (verbal), V. 17 (substantivisch).

[1975] V. 15.16.

[1976] V. 16c.

[1977] 1,5–8; 4,3.

[1978] Exemplarisch: Apg 4,23–31. Detaillierte Einblicke vermittelt 1Kor 14,13–19 (individuelles Gebet und Gebet in der gottesdienstlichen Versammlung). In Mt 6,7–15 / Lk 11,2–4 und 7,7–11 sind Jesustraditionen zum Thema Gebet gesammelt. Zum allgemeinen antiken Umfeld vgl. E. VON SEVERUS, Art. Gebet I, RAC 8, 1972, 1134–1258. Vertieft: H. LÖHR, Studien zum frühchristlichen und frühjüdischen Gebet: Untersuchungen zu 1Clem 59 bis 61 in seinem literarischen, historischen und theologischen Kontext, WUNT 16, Tübingen 2003; R. HAYWARD / B. EMBRY (Hg.), Studies in Jewish Prayer, JSSt.S 17, Oxford 2005; K.-H. OSTMEYER, Kommunikation mit Gott und Christus: Sprache und Theologie des Gebets im Neuen Testament, WUNT 19, Tübingen 2006; W. URBANZ, Gebet im Sirachbuch. Zur Terminologie von Klage und Lob in der griechischen Texttradition, HBS 60, Freiburg 2009. Siehe die kommentierte Textsammlung von K.-H. OSTMEYER, Jüdische Gebete aus der Umwelt des Neuen Testaments. Ein Studienbuch, BTSt37, Leuven 2019 (umfangreiches Literaturverzeichnis 429–460).

350 Kommentar

konkrete Themen frühchristlicher Paränese und des frühchristlichen Gemeindelebens an. Formal geht die allgemein gehaltene ethische Paränese von 5,7–11 und 12 jetzt in praktische Gemeindeparänese über, wie wir sie von Paulus kennen.

Diese letzte Texteinheit des Briefes ist noch einmal konzeptionell[1979] und sprachlich sorgfältig gestaltet. Untereinheiten sind die Verse 13 und 14, 15, 16a.b sowie viertens V. 16c–18. Die Verse 13 und 14, die die *erste* Untereinheit bilden, sind nach demselben Muster aufgebaut: Sie enthalten *drei Imperative* (die beiden ersten Imperative stehen im Sing. Präs.), die Anweisungen zu drei jeweils vorweg im Aussagesatz formulierten Situationen geben. Es bilden sich folgende Fall-Paare: bei Leiden – beten, bei Wohlbefinden – Psalmen singen, bei Krankheit – die Ältesten rufen. Dieser dritte Imperativ (Sing. Aor. Med.) trägt das Achtergewicht der Imperativkette und wird durch einen mit καί angeschlossenen *vierten Imperativ* (Subjektwechsel zu den Ältesten: Plur. Aorist), der zum ersten Imperativ zurückführt, ergänzt und konkretisiert[1980]: Die Ältesten sollen für den Kranken *beten*. Hier liegt der thematische Akzent des Satzverbandes der V. 13.14. Eine letzte Erweiterung wird in dem *Partizip* (Plur. Aor.) ἀλείψαντες vorgenommen: Dem Gebet sollen die Ältesten eine Krankensalbung hinzufügen. Die *zweite* Untereinheit (V. 15) nimmt das Ergebnis des Gebets der Ältesten vorweg. Die *dritte* Einheit (V. 16) fügt einen doppelten Ratschlag (erneuter Subjektwechsel zu den Gemeindegliedern): zwei Imperative Plur. Präs. und eine finale Ergänzung, hinzu. Die *vierte* Einheit in V. 16–18 wird aus einer Gnome (V. 16a) mit einem erläuternden Beispiel aus der Geschichte Israels (V. 16b–18) gebildet.

V. 13–14a[1981] Der Neueinsatz in V. 13 ist auffallend, eine asyndetisch gereihte Dreierkette von Situationsangaben, die in kurzen verbalen Aussagesätzen skizziert werden, mit anschließenden imperativisch formulierten Ratschlägen: Man bete, lobsinge, rufe die Ältesten. So wird der Text zum Thema »Gebet« rhetorisch besonders wirkungsvoll eingeleitet.[1982] Mit dem eher seltenen Verb κακοπαθεῖν[1983] nimmt Jakobus das Motiv der leidenden Propheten aus 5,10 wieder auf, verschiebt die Bedeutung aber bereits in Richtung Krankheit, wie V. 14a zeigt. Thema ist jetzt nicht mehr der allgemeine Zusammenhang von Geduld und Leiden bzw. das Ertragen der Zeit vor der Parusie, sondern das praktische Problem von Schwäche als *Krankheit* in den Gemeinden, dem mit dem *Gebet* begegnet wird. Damit wendet sich

---

[1979] ALLISON, 749.

[1980] Lange Apodosis in V. 14.

[1981] Zum Text: A. WYPADLO, Viel vermag das inständige Gebet eines Gerechten (Jak 5,16). Die Weisung zum Gebet im Jakobusbrief, FzB 110, Würzburg 2006; O. WISCHMEYER, The Prayer of Faith – the Prayer of the Righteous (Jas 5,13–18): Where the »Ways« Intersect, in: N. Calduch-Benages / M. W. Duggan / D. Marx (Hg.), On Wings of Prayer: Sources of Jewish Worship. Essays in Honor of Professor Stefan C. Reif on the Occasion of his Seventy-Fifth Birthday, DCLS 44, Berlin / Boston 2019, 151–168 (Lit.).

[1982] »Lebhafter Stil«: BURCHARD, Jak, 208 (Beispiele von Demosthenes u. a.).

[1983] Hap. leg. in Jak. Vgl. 2Tim 2,9 und 4,5 (Leiden des Apostels und des Timotheus). Gräzität: öfter für Krankheit (Belege bei LSJ, 862). Detailliert: KAISER, Krankenheilung, 26–29.

C. Briefcorpus 351

Jakobus einer weiteren möglichen realen Gemeindesituation zu, wie er sie schon in 2,1 ff gezeichnet hatte. Ging es dort um den Umgang mit sozial Niedrigen in den Gemeindeversammlungen, entwirft Jakobus jetzt die realistische Situation eines Krankheitsfalles (τις ἐν ὑμῖν). *Krankheit*[1984] ist ein zentrales Phänomen in den Evangelien: Überall trifft Jesus auf Kranke und wirkt als Heiler.[1985] Auch Paulus und seine Begleiter werden mit Krankheit konfrontiert (Apg 19,11 f) und vollbringen Heilungstaten. Im Jakobusbrief geht es nicht um Krankheit als solche, sondern um Kranke in den *Gemeinden*. Auch dies Thema wird bereits von Paulus angesprochen. In 1Kor 11,29–32 stellt Paulus den Zusammenhang zwischen Sünde, Krankheit, auch tödlicher Krankheit, und Gericht bei Gemeindegliedern her. 1Clem 59,4 und Polyk 6,1[1986] greifen das Thema von Gebet und Krankheit weniger vertieft auf[1987]: Für Polykarp sind Krankenbesuche schon eine selbstverständliche Aufgabe der Presbyter. Der 1.Clemensbrief ordnet Gebet und Krankheit einander zu.[1988]

Was ist im Krankheitsfall zu tun? Zunächst gilt der Ratschlag des Jakobus dem Betroffenen selbst: προσευχέσθω/προσεύχεσθαι/προσευχή werden im Neuen Testament sehr häufig für das Gebet bzw. das Beten gesetzt. Jakobus verwendet das Substantiv in 5,17, das Verb in 5,13.14.16.17.18. In V. 15.16 setzt er die eher seltene Kurzfassung εὔχεσθαι/εὐχή. Der einfache Aufruf zum Gebet begegnet topisch in der paulinischen Paränese, dort allerdings vor allem im Gebet des Apostels und der Gemeinden füreinander.[1989] Das Gebet im Krankheitsfall wird in Sir 38,9 empfohlen. Sirach stellt auch den Zusammenhang zwischen Krankheit und Sünde her, ohne ihn weiter auszuführen:

Τέκνον, ἐν ἀρρωστήματί σου μὴ παράβλεπε, ἀλλ᾽ εὖξαι κυρίῳ, καὶ αὐτὸς ἰάσεταί σε.
Kind, in deiner Krankheit sei nicht unachtsam, sondern bete zum Herrn, und er selbst wird dich heilen.[1990]

Im Neuen Testament ist es Paulus, der in 2Kor 12 auf ein persönliches Gebet im Zusammenhang mit Krankheit zu sprechen kommt.[1991] Er habe »dreimal den Herrn angerufen«, der Satansengel, der ihn »schlug«, möge von ihm weiche. Paulus benutzt religiöse Metaphorik bei der Beschreibung seiner Krankheit – am ehesten handelte es sich um Migräne. Im Zusammenhang mit Jak 5,13–16 ist wichtig, dass

---

[1984] Einführend G. B. FERNGREN, Art. Krankheit, RAC 21, 2006, 966–1006, dort 973 f zum neutestamentlichen Vokabular für »Krankheit«; EaC 5, 2014 / 3 (Themenheft: Frühchristliche Heilungen und antike Medizin, Hg. J. SCHRÖTER, Beiträge von R. VON BENDEMANN, A. WEISSENRIEDER, PH. VAN DER EIJK, V. NUTTON). Monographisch zu Jak 5: KAISER, Krankenheilung.

[1985] FERNGREN, RAC 21, 985–989.

[1986] Polyk 6,1: »Aber auch die Presbyter (sollen) barmherzig (sein), … nach allen Kranken sehen …«.

[1987] Im Schlussgebet 1Clem 59,4: »Die unter uns in Bedrängnis sind, rette, die Gestrauchelten richte auf, den Betenden zeige dich, die Kranken heile …«.

[1988] Vgl. LÖHR, Studien zum frühchristlichen und frühjüdischen Gebet.

[1989] 1Thess 5,17.25; 2Thess 3,1; 1Tim 2,8; Hebr 13,8. Vgl. auch Mt 5,44.

[1990] Zum Text vgl. P. W. SKEHAN / A. A. DI LELLA, The Wisdom of Ben Sira, AncB 39, New York 1987, 442 f.

[1991] Zum Zusammenhang von Satan und Krankheit vgl. FERNGREN, RAC 21, 989.

352 Kommentar

der Herr – bei Paulus ist Christus gemeint – Paulus gerade *nicht* heilt, sondern ihm mitteilt:

ἀρκεῖ σοι ἡ χάρις μου, ἡ γὰρ δύναμις ἐν ἀσθενείᾳ τελεῖται.

Meine Gnade reicht dir, denn die Kraft vollendet sich in Schwäche (2Kor 12,9).

Jakobus fährt rhetorisch wirkungsvoll mit einer Antithese fort: Im Falle des Wohlbefindens soll man lobsingen! Wieder wählt Jakobus seine Worte sorgfältig: εὐθυμεῖν ist hap. leg. im Jakobusbrief, εὔθυμ- begegnet vier Mal in der Apostelgeschichte.[1992] Auch ψάλλειν ist hap. leg. im Brief und begegnet nur noch dreimal in der paulinischen Briefliteratur.[1993] Es kann sich hier um ein individuelles Lob Gottes außerhalb einer gottesdienstlichen Versammlung handeln. Nach diesem rhetorisch wirkungsvollen kontrastiven Einschub kommt Jakobus auf die erste Situation zurück: auf den Krankheitsfall. Das geläufige ἀσθενεῖν[1994] variiert nun das seltene κακοπαθεῖν. Jakobus verlagert jetzt den Akzent vom Gebet des Betroffenen auf das Gebet *für* den Betroffenen durch die Ältesten. Zum Gebet des Einzelnen tritt damit das Gebet als religiöse Handlung der Presbyter. Über die Art der Krankheit sagt Jakobus nichts, allerdings weist κάμνειν, krank sein bzw. schwerkrank sein[1995] in V. 15, eher auf eine schwere Krankheit. Der Kranke liegt zu Bett.[1996] Er kann nicht in die Gemeindeversammlung kommen, sondern ruft die Ältesten zu sich.

Mit dem Syntagma »die Ältesten der Ekklesia« wird zum zweiten Mal im Jakobusbrief auf die reale organisatorisch-institutionelle Verfasstheit der Leserschaft Bezug genommen. Sprach Jakobus in 2,2 von der συναγωγὴ ὑμῶν und meinte damit den *Raum*, in dem sich die Leserschaft versammelt, wählt er jetzt ἐκκλησία[1997], um die *Organisation* zu bezeichnen, der die Adressaten – in der literarischen Fiktion die Diasporajudenschaft – jeweils am Ort angehören. Auffallend ist die Selbstverständlichkeit, mit der Jakobus die Zugehörigkeit seiner Leserschaft zur ἐκκλησία voraussetzt. Was schon in 2,2 auffiel, das Fehlen einer näheren landsmannschaftlichen (Apg 6,9), örtlichen (Apg 9,2), polemischen (Apk 2,9; 3,9) oder allgemein ethnisch-religiösen Zuordnung[1998], gilt auch für den Gebrauch von ἐκκλησία. Wieder fehlt eine lokale[1999], ethnische oder religiöse Einbindung.[2000] Dennoch handelt es

---

[1992] In LXX nur εὔθυμος 2Makk 11,26.

[1993] Röm 15,9; 1Kor 14,15; Eph 5,19. Sehr häufig in LXX: Psalmen. Daher im NT die Bedeutung: »lobsingend preisen, lobsingen«: BAUER / ALAND, 1777. Allgemein »mostly of the string of musical instruments« (LSJ, 2018).

[1994] Doppelbedeutung: krank sein (Mt 10,8; Mk 6,56; Lk 4,40; 2Tim 4,20), schwach sein (so häufiger bei Paulus). KAISER, Krankenheilung, 29–41.

[1995] BAUER / ALAND, 816. KAISER, Krankenheilung, 41–48.

[1996] Vgl. Mk 1,30.

[1997] Hap. leg. in Jak. Paulinisches Vorzugswort.

[1998] »Synagoge der Juden / Judäer« sehr oft in den Evangelien und in Apg. Keine Belege in der paulinischen Literatur.

[1999] Röm 16,1; 1Kor 1,2; 2Kor 2,1; Gal 1,2; Kol 4,16; 1Thess 1,1; 2,14; 2Thess 1,1. Oft in Apk.

[2000] »Ekklesia Gottes« häufig bei Paulus. Gal 1,22: ταῖς ἐκκλησίαις τῆς Ἰουδαίας ταῖς ἐν Χριστῷ (die Gemeinden Judäas, die in Christus sind). Eph 2,21 u. ö.

C. Briefcorpus 353

sich nicht um eine bloße Versammlung, ein *gathering*, sondern das Syntagma deutet auf eine Organisation bzw. auf einen *terminus technicus*.[2001] Jakobus setzt als gegeben voraus, dass die Leser jeweils einer ἐκκλησία angehören, d. h. einer ortsgebundenen Vereinigung von Christus-bekennenden Männern und Frauen, die ein Ältestengremium haben. ἐκκλησία als Bezeichnung Christus-gläubiger Ortsgemeinden stammt aus der vorpaulinischen Gemeinde und ist durch Paulus zum festen Bestandteil ekklesiologischer Terminologie des Christentums geworden.[2002] Jakobus benutzt hier den frühchristlichen Soziolekt.[2003] Die ἐκκλησία hat *Älteste*, d. h. sie ist eine Vereinigung oder ein binnendifferenzierter Sozialkörper mit einer Leitungsstruktur. Diese wird im Vergleich mit den Paulusbriefen und vor allem mit den Pastoralbriefen im Jakobusbrief allerdings so gut wie gar nicht thematisiert. Während in 1Tim 5,17–22 die Ältesten als Gemeindevorsteher charakterisiert werden und von der Gemeinde unterhalten werden sollen, ist in Jak 5 der bloße Hinweis auf die Ältesten das einzige Zeichen der organisatorischen Binnendifferenzierung. Jakobus ist in seiner Paränese nicht an der Ämterfrage der ἐκκλησία interessiert, sondern an sozialem und statusbezogenem Ausgleich (Kap. 2). Deutlich ist auch der Unterschied zu den anderen Katholischen Briefen: Der Verfasser des Jakobusbriefes verwendet den Titel Ältester nicht für sich selbst.[2004] Das heißt auch, dass er keinen Leitungsanspruch für eine oder mehrere Gemeinden formuliert. Er bezeichnet sich lediglich indirekt als Lehrer (3,1f). Die πρεσβύτεροι[2005] haben bei Jakobus ein ähnlich flaches Profil wie der Begriff ἐκκλησία. Jakobus setzt ihr Vorhandensein und ihre Funktionen voraus, ohne diese als solche zu thematisieren. Über den Aufbau der Gemeinden, an die Jakobus schreibt, und über mögliche Leitungsfunktionen geht aus 5,14 ebenso wenig Näheres hervor wie über Anzahl und leitende Stellung der Ältesten: Das Interesse des Autors gilt den einzelnen *Gemeindegliedern*, d. h. den Adressaten, und der speziellen *Aufgabe* der Ältesten für kranke Gemeindeglieder. »Älteste« sind eine allgemeine »Funktionsbezeichnung« und ebenso aus »griechisch-römischen Verei-

---

[2001] »Summon to an assembly«: LSJ, 509.

[2002] R. Last, The Pauline Church and the Corinthian Ekklēsia. Greco-Roman Associations in Comparative Context, MSSNTS 164, Cambridge 2015; M. Öhler, Geschichte des Urchristentums, Göttingen 2018, 147.256–259. Öhler fasst zusammen: »Die christliche Selbstbezeichnung als *ekklēsia* verweist auf die Septuaginta als Hintergrund und stammt aus vorpaulinischer Zeit … Im Kontext der griechisch-römischen Welt sind mit diesem Begriff allerdings sowohl politische wie auch vereinsbezogene Konnotationen verbunden« (256). Zugleich weist er auf den Unterschied zu griechisch-römischen Vereinen hin: »Allerdings begegnet *ekklēsia* sonst nicht als Titel einer Vereinigung, sondern nur als Bezeichnung konkreter Versammlungen … So findet sich auch hierin eine Besonderheit frühchristlicher Gemeinschaften im Rahmen des antiken Vereinswesens« (257). Vgl. auch Kaiser, Krankenheilung, 100–136.

[2003] So auch in Mt 18,17: ἐκκλησία als Gemeindeversammlung.

[2004] 1Petr 5,1 Πρεσβυτέρους τοὺς ἐν ὑμῖν παρακαλῶ ὁ συμπρεσβύτερος καὶ μάρτυς τῶν τοῦ Χριστοῦ παθημάτων (Eure Presbyter ermahne ich, der Mitpresbyter und Zeuge der Leiden Christi); 2Joh 1 und 3Joh 1: Presbyter.

[2005] Hap. leg. in Jak. J. G. Mueller, Art. Presbyter, RAC 28, 2017, 86–112; Öhler, Geschichte des Urchristentums, 320f. Zu unterscheiden von πρεσβύτερος sind πρεσβύτης und πρεσβῦτις, die Gruppe alter Männer und alter Frauen in der Gemeinde (Tit 2,1–3). Zum Text: Kaiser, Krankenheilung, 100–136.

354 Kommentar

nigungen« bezeugt[2006] wie im antiken Judentum.[2007] Während Paulus nicht von Presbytern spricht, geht der Verfasser der Apostelgeschichte (Apg 11,27–30) davon aus, dass »Presbyter Teil der Jerusalemer Gemeindeordnung waren«.[2008] Für die Datierung des Jakobusbriefes ist der Hinweis von Markus Öhler wichtig:

> In den Quellen begegnet das Amt des Presbyters erst in Texten vom Ende des 1. und Anfang des 2. Jh. n. Chr.[2009]

Die Ältesten sollen von dem kranken Gemeindeglied gerufen werden. προσκαλεῖσθαι, herbeirufen, ist hap. leg. bei Jakobus.[2010] Jakobus setzt hier eine auffällige Alliteration.[2011]

V. 14b Dieser Imperativ bezieht sich auf die Ältesten: Ihr Gebet über dem Kranken und die Salbung sind gefordert. »Beten über jemandem« ist »weder im NT noch in der LXX belegt«.[2012] Allison betont zurecht:

> The meaning is not ›pray for‹ but ›pray over‹.[2013]

Gegen Burchard[2014] ist hier durchaus eine lokale Komponente vorstellbar, so dass sich die Presbyter über das Bett des Kranken beugen.[2015] Das bedeutet persönliche Anwesenheit und intensive Zuwendung. Entscheidender als die Gebetshaltung der Ältesten ist aber die Salbung. Die Krankensalbung mit Öl[2016] wird zwar nur zweimal im Neuen Testament erwähnt (Mk 6,13 und Jak 5,14), kann aber wohl als »geläufiger Gemeindebrauch« angesehen werden.[2017] Über seine Entstehung lässt sich auf der Basis von Jak 5,14 nichts sagen. Das Markusevangelium führt den frühchristlichen Brauch auf Jesus und die Zwölf zurück.[2018] Mk 6 ist eine Ursprungserzählung. Der kurze Jakobustext, dem jede religiöse oder praktische Begründung

---

[2006] ÖHLER, Geschichte des Urchristentums, 35.

[2007] Die Frage der Bezeugung ist hier nicht einfach: MUELLER, Art. Presbyter, 94: »In der ntl. Zeit gibt es keine einheitliche Bezeichnung für Synagogenvorsteher«.

[2008] ÖHLER, Geschichte des Urchristentums, 320 (320 f allg. zu Presbytern im frühen Christentum). Vgl. MUELLER, Art. Presbyter, 97. Nach Apg 14,23 setzen Paulus und Barnabas überall in den gegründeten Gemeinden Presbyter ein.

[2009] ÖHLER, Geschichte des Urchristentums, 320: Apg, 1Petr, Jak, 2.3.Joh, 1Tim, Tit, 1Clem, Ign, Polyk, Herm (fehlt in Did).

[2010] Öfter in den synoptischen Evangelien und in der Apg.

[2011] ALLISON, Jak, 755: πρεσβύτεροι, προσκαλεῖσθαι, προσεύξασθαι.

[2012] KAISER, Krankenheilung, 237. Nicht bei LSJ, bei BAUER / ALAND, 1430, vgl. 584 f zu ἐπί als Antwort »auf die Frage wo?« bzw. »auf etwas«.

[2013] Allison, Jak, 758.

[2014] BURCHARD, Jak, 209.

[2015] So auch KAISER, Krankenheilung, 238.

[2016] KAISER, Krankenheilung, 138–199; B. KRANEMANN, Art. Krankenöl, RAC 21, 2006, 915–965, 921 f zu Jak 5,14.

[2017] KRANEMANN, RAC 21, 920, zu Mk 6,13. Ebd. 921 zu Jak 5: »Diese Form der Ölsalbung wird hier weniger angewiesen … denn als üblicher Brauch vorausgesetzt«.

[2018] Zur Salbung mit Öl im AT: KAISER, Krankenheilung, 158–167. Fazit: Kaiser findet ein Grundmuster: »Dieses Grundmuster bildet sowohl bei Rechtsakt, Weihe und Ehrung als auch bei den mit der Salbung ver-

und Detailvorschrift fehlt, kann nur als Beleg für die selbstverständliche Praxis der Krankensalbung in den Gemeinden, an die der Brief im Blick hat, gelten.[2019] Benedikt Kranemann weist zurecht darauf hin, dass im Jakobusbrief »die Salbung … im Zusammenhang eines Gebets [steht], dem hier das größere Gewicht zukommt«.[2020] Die religionsgeschichtliche Problematik des Salbungsvorganges wird detailliert von Sigurd Kaiser erörtert.[2021] Jak 5,14 trägt aber keine Erkenntnisse zu Kaisers Fragen bei. Die Aufforderung an die Ältesten bringt drei Aspekte zusammen: die caritative Funktion der Ältesten als leitender Vertreter der Gemeinde, ihr Gebet am Krankenbett und die Salbung mit Öl. Der parallele Markustext reduziert diese Aspekte:

> (Die Zwölf) ἤλειφον ἐλαίῳ πολλοὺς ἀρρώστους.
> Sie salbten mit Öl viele Kranke.

ἀλείφειν begegnet Mt 6,17; Mk 16,1 und Lk 7,38par.[2022] In diesen Texten geht es um verschiedene Aspekte der Körperpflege.[2023] ἔλαιον dürfte das übliche Olivenöl sein, während μύρον »das teure, parfümierte Salböl oder speziell die Myrrensalbe« ist.[2024] Die Krankensalbung dagegen steht im Zusammenhang mit dem Gebet um Genesung. Der Ritus erfolgt ἐν τῷ ὀνόματι τοῦ κυρίου. Kranemann interpretiert in Bezug auf den Namen:

> wohl unter Anrufung des Namens Jesu Christi als Kyrios … Sie [die Anrufung] wird nicht natürlich-medizinisch verstanden, sondern besitzt übernatürliche Kraft.[2025]

Er spricht auch von der Salbung als von einem »Handeln ›im Namen Jesu‹«.[2026] Burchard lehnt diese Deutung strikt ab.[2027] Metzner weist darauf hin, dass in 5,10 – dort dieselbe Formulierung – und 5,15 mit κύριος Gott selbst gemeint ist.[2028] Der

---

bundenen Assoziationen von Freude und Segen die im profanen Kontext der Einreibung mit Öl geschätzte, stärkende und gelegentlich schützende Wirkung des Öls« (166 f).

[2019] BURCHARD, Jak, 210, formuliert pointiert: »Die Herkunft des Ritus ist unbekannt«. Zu den ersten Belegen einer christlichen Ölsalbung in den ersten Jahrhunderten« vgl. KAISER, Krankenheilung, 192 f. Did 10,8 im koptischen Text hat »eine Formel über das Salböl, deren Zuordnung zum ursprünglichen Did-Text unsicher ist« (LINDEMANN / PAULSEN, Die Apostolischen Väter, 1).

[2020] KRANEMANN, RAC 21, 921.

[2021] KAISER, Krankenheilung, 137 f.

[2022] Hap. leg. in Jak. Zum Verb KAISER, Krankenheilung, 138–141: »Die Wahl von ἀλείφω für den Krankheitsfall in Jak 5,14 entspricht damit dem Septuaginta-Sprachgebrauch, der außerhalb des kultisch-sakralen Bereichs ἀλείφω für die Salbung bevorzugt« (141).

[2023] Zu den verschiedenen anderen Aspekten der Salbung im Alten Testament und im antiken Judentum ausführlich KAISER, Krankenheilung, 150–173. Kaiser, 173, kommt nach Sichtung der Texte des AT, der atl. Pseudepigraphen, der Qumrantexte und der Texte des rabbinischen Judentums zu dem Urteil: »Damit bleibt das Postulat einer Salbung mit apotropäischer Wirkung – insbesondere zum Zweck der Krankenheilung – für das Judentum des 1. Jh. unbestätigt.«

[2024] KAISER, Krankenheilung, 141. ἔλαιον ist hap. leg. in Jak und begegnet einige Male in den Evangelien sowie Hebr 1,9 (Ps 44,8LXX), Jak 5,14 und Apk 6,6; 18,13.

[2025] KRANEMANN, RAC 21, 921.

[2026] Ebd.

[2027] BURCHARD, Jak, 210.

[2028] METZNER, Jak, 300 f erörtert die verschiedenen exegetischen Möglichkeiten der Wendung ἐν τῷ

Blick auf 2,7 könnte auf Jesus weisen.[2029] Der Text gibt keine Entscheidung her. Was deutlich wird, ist: Jakobus *vermeidet* anders als alle anderen katholischen Briefe den Namen Jesu fast vollständig[2030], ohne dass hier ein eindeutiger Grund genannt werden könnte. Möglich sind: Vermeidung eines »christlichen« Profils, Scheu vor dem »Namen«, schriftstellerische Attitüde. Alles mag zusammenspielen.[2031] Jedenfalls ist nicht auszuschließen, dass der Verfasser oder die Adressaten an Jesus dachten. Die Wendung ist ein weiteres Beispiel für das flache religionsgeschichtliche Profil des Textes.

V. 15 In drei jeweils mit καί verbundenen einfachen Hauptsätzen nimmt Jakobus den dreifachen Erfolg des Gebetes der Ältesten vorweg: Der Kranke wird gerettet werden, der Herr wird ihn aufrichten, mögliche Sünden werden ihm vergeben werden. Die beiden ersten Sätze sind einander chiastisch zugeordnet.[2032] Der dritte Aussagesatz ist erweitert: Ihm ist ein ebenfalls mit καί eingeleiteter Konditionalsatz vorangestellt. Die drei καί-Verknüpfungen lassen die verschiedenen Aspekte der Wirkung des Gebetes wie einen einzigen Vorgang, der mit einer gewissen Selbstverständlichkeit stattfindet, erscheinen. Die Wirkungen werden *eintreten*. Zweifel, wie Jakobus sie in 1,5–8 angesprochen hatte, tauchen hier nicht auf. Grund für diesen Optimismus ist das Syntagma ἡ εὐχὴ τῆς πίστεως. Damit greift Jakobus auf 1,3–8 zurück: auf das Gebet des Glaubens (αἰτείτω δὲ ἐν πίστει μηδὲν διακρινόμενος 1,6). In Kapitel 1 hat Jakobus dargelegt, Gott gebe allen einfach, die ihn bitten (vgl. Mt 7,7). Die Bitte soll im Glauben erfolgen, der Bittende soll nicht zweifeln. Ein Zweifler werde nichts empfangen (1,5–7). Diese Konstellation von Gebet und Glaube wird hier durch die Sündenvergebung erweitert und auf die Krankheit von Gemeindegliedern angewendet.

Mit dem Thema des *Gebetsglaubens* kehrt Jakobus wie schon bei dem Thema *Geduld* (5,7–11) noch einmal zum Anfang des Briefes zurück (*inclusio*). εὐχή als Gebet ist in der Septuaginta belegt[2033], aber hap. leg. im Neuen Testament.[2034] Die Wendung »Gebet des Glaubens«, eine für Jak typische Genitivverbindung, in der das Attribut als Genitivobjekt gesetzt wird, ist analogielos, wie Allison betont.[2035] Die Kraft des Glaubensgebets bewirkt die Rettung des Kranken. Die Verben, die die Rettung aussagen, sind merkwürdig doppeldeutig. Sie lassen sich sowohl rein technisch als auch theologisch lesen. σῴζειν bezieht sich sonst im Brief[2036] auf das eschatologische Geschick des Menschen, hier wohl auf die Genesung[2037] des Kran-

---

ὀνόματι τοῦ κυρίου.

[2029] Siehe oben zu der Wendung τὸ καλὸν ὄνομα τὸ ἐπικληθὲν ἐφ' ὑμᾶς (2,7).

[2030] Ausnahmen: 1,1; 2,1.

[2031] Siehe auch die Einleitung zur »Christologie«.

[2032] Satzglieder: Subjekt – Prädikat, Prädikat – Subjekt.

[2033] Bedeutung: Gebet, Gelübde, Darbringung.

[2034] Apg 18,18 und 21,23 ist εὐχή »Gelübde«.

[2035] ALLISON, Jak, 764.

[2036] Jak 1,21; 2,14; 4,12; 5,14.20.

[2037] So BURCHARD, Jak, 210, mit Beispielen aus Diodorus Siculus I 82,3 und Philo, decal. 12.

C. Briefcorpus 357

ken. V. 20 wird das Motiv der endgültigen Rettung des Menschen noch einmal abschließend aufnehmen. κάμνειν kann physische oder übertragene Bedeutung haben.[2038] ἐγερεῖ αὐτὸν ὁ κύριος: ἐγείρειν, hap. leg. bei Jakobus, wird in den neutestamentlichen Schriften mehrheitlich für die religiöse Vorstellung der Auferstehung gebraucht, heißt aber ebenso auch »aufstehen, sich aufrichten, sich erheben, auftreten«. In Mk 1,31 richtet Jesus die Schwiegermutter des Petrus von ihrem Bett auf. Hier wird das Verb metaphorisch für »gesundmachen, heilen« (V. 16) eingesetzt.[2039] Auch κύριος bleibt wieder unterbestimmt. Erst das dritte Verb ist eindeutig theologisch konnotiert: ἀφιέναι[2040] ist mit ἁμαρτίαι[2041] verbunden und bedeutet daher »vergeben«. ἁμαρτίας ποιεῖν begegnet öfter im Neuen Testament.[2042] Der Ausdruck κἂν ἁμαρτίας ᾖ πεποιηκώς ist *conjugatio periphrastica* nach dem Konjunktiv ᾖ[2043], der die bloße *Möglichkeit* sündigen Tuns des Kranken beschreibt. Jakobus setzt also nicht voraus, dass der Kranke gesündigt *hat*, sondern weist darauf hin, dass *im Fall* sündigen Handelns mit dem Glaubensgebet und der Salbung auch die Sünden vergeben werden. Jakobus verbindet hier Krankheit, Glaubensgebet und Sünde bzw. Sündenvergebung *ohne* Kausalzusammenhang. Die Sünden werden nicht näher charakterisiert. Die Aussagen bleiben auch hier in verschiedener Hinsicht theologisch unbestimmt. Mit dem bloßen καί wird jeder innere Zusammenhang zwischen Krankheit und Sünde wie bei Paulus in 1Kor 11,27–32 vermieden. Der Sündenbegriff selbst ist von Jakobus in 1,15 im Zusammenhang mit dem Begriff der Versuchung definiert worden, und Jakobus hat ihre tödlichen Folgen im Sinne paulinischer Theologie aufgedeckt.[2044] Wer aber hier die Sünden vergibt, bleibt wieder ungesagt: ἀφεθήσεται hat kein Subjekt. Die Vergebung liegt in der Zukunft.

V. 16a.b Zwei mit »und« verbundene Imperativsätze ziehen den Schluss aus den Zusagen von V. 14f. Jakobus kehrt zum Imperativ der 2. Pers. Pl. zurück und formuliert einen praktischen Doppelrat für die Adressaten. Das οὖν macht deutlich: Jakobus nimmt den Ton seiner gewohnten allgemeinen Paränese wieder auf. Auch unabhängig von einem ernsten Krankheitsfall und der Intervention der Ältesten gilt der Ratschlag zu Sündenbekenntnis und Gebet. Dieser Ratschlag erstaunt. Denn hier werden scheinbar die Akzente verschoben: Jakobus empfiehlt jetzt *gegenseitiges* Sündenbekenntnis, Gebet *füreinander* – er setzt nun ὑπέρ[2045] statt ἐπί – und verheißt Heilung ohne Älteste und ohne Salbung. Liegt ein neuer Gedanke bzw. ein neuer Ratschlag vor, oder handelt es sich nur um eine verkürzte *ad hominem*-Zusammenfassung des zuvor Gesagten? Letzteres ist wahrscheinlicher. Die

---

[2038] κάμνειν hap. leg. in Jak. NT noch Hebr 12,3 für das Ermatten der Seelen. BAUER / ALAND, 794.

[2039] Vgl. Joh 5,8: »aufstehen«.

[2040] Hap. leg. in Jak.

[2041] Feste Verbindung im NT.

[2042] Joh 8,34; 2Kor 11,7; 1Petr 2,22; 1Joh 3,4.8.9.

[2043] DBR, § 352: Umschreibung für das Perfekt durch Part. Perf. + ᾖ ist beim Konjunktiv notwendig.

[2044] S. o. zu 1,15.

[2045] Vgl. Herm sim 5,2,10 (dort aber eher »bitten«).

Verbindung von Gebet und Sünden*bekenntnis* – bisher ging es nur um mögliche Sünden, nicht um ein Sündenbekenntnis – ist im antiken Judentum geläufig (Dan 9,20LXX; JosAs 11,11 und 12,3). Ausführlich schildert Sir 38 den Zusammenhang in einem besonderen Ratschlag für Kranke:

> (9) Τέκνον, ἐν ἀρρωστήματί σου μὴ παράβλεπε, ἀλλ᾽ εὖξαι κυρίῳ, καὶ αὐτὸς ἰάσεταί σε
>
> (10) ἀπόστησον πλημμέλειαν καὶ εὔθυνον χεῖρας καὶ ἀπὸ πάσης ἁμαρτίας καθάρισον καρδίαν
>
> (11) δὸς εὐωδίαν καὶ μνημόσυνον σεμιδάλεως καὶ λίπανον προσφορὰν ὡς μὴ ὑπάρχων.
>
> (9) Kind, in deiner Krankheit sei nicht unachtsam, sondern bete zum Herrn, und er selbst wird dich heilen.
>
> (10) Halte fern Vergehen und lenke gerade die Hände, und von aller Sünde reinige (dein) Herz.
>
> (11) Gib süßen Duft und ein Gedächtnisopfer aus feinstem Weizenmehl und mache die Opfergabe fett, als seiest du nicht da [als müsstest du sterben].

Im Neuen Testament begegnet der Ausdruck ἁμαρτίας ἐξομολογεῖν allerdings nur noch in Mk 1,5 / Mt 6,3 im Zusammenhang der Johannestaufe.[2046] 1Joh 1,9 hat ὁμολογεῖν. Die Didache spricht von παραπτώματα:

> In der Gemeindeversammlung sollst du deine Übertretungen (παραπτώματα) bekennen (ἐξομολογήσῃ), und du sollst nicht hintreten zu deinem Gebet (ἐπὶ προσευχήν) mit schlechtem Gewissen (Did 4,14).

Das Thema Krankheit fehlt im 1Joh und in der Didache. Jak 5,16b bezieht sich aber noch einmal auf den Krankheitsfall, wenn der logische Zusammenhang zwischen V. 15 und 16a.b auch lose ist. ὅπως ἰαθῆτε[2047]: ὅπως nach einem Verb des Bittens wird mit »dass« übersetzt.[2048] Es geht also um den Inhalt des Gebets füreinander. ἰᾶσθαι[2049], geheilt werden, in der Passivform wird öfter im Neuen Testament gebraucht. Hier steht es in Variation von ἐγείρειν (V. 15). Jakobus formuliert hier dieselbe Zuversicht zu Gottes Handeln am Kranken wie Sirach.

V. 16c Diese Zuversicht beruht auf der *Kraft* des Gebets. Jakobus verschiebt jetzt die theologischen Koordinaten: Er spricht nicht mehr vom *Glaubens*gebet, sondern vom Gebet des *Gerechten*[2050], δέησις δικαίου (Alliteration). Damit wird sachlich auch auf Abraham in Kapitel 2 angespielt, ohne dass das Thema Glaube-Taten-Ge-

---

[2046] ἐξομολογεῖν heißt »bekennen« oder »anerkennen, preisen« (BAUER / ALAND, 560f), hap. leg. in Jak. 1Joh 1,9 über die Bedeutung des Sündenbekenntnisses: ἐὰν ὁμολογῶμεν τὰς ἁμαρτίας ἡμῶν, πιστός ἐστιν καὶ δίκαιος, ἵνα ἀφῇ ἡμῖν τὰς ἁμαρτίας καὶ καθαρίσῃ ἡμᾶς ἀπὸ πάσης ἀδικίας (Wenn wir unsere Sünden bekennen, ist er treu und gerecht, dass er uns die Sünden erlässt und uns von aller Ungerechtigkeit reinige). Der christologische Bezug fehlt bei Jakobus.

[2047] Aor. Konj.

[2048] DBR, § 392,1.

[2049] Hap. leg. in Jak.

[2050] Zum Text insgesamt: WYPLADO, Weisung zum Gebet; WISCHMEYER, The Prayer of Faith – the Prayer of the Righteous. Zum »Gerechten« im Jak vgl. oben zu 5,6. Im Rückblick wird deutlich, dass Jakobus in 5,6 auch Gestalten wie die Propheten und Elia im Blick hat.

rechtigkeit hier nochmals erörtert würde. Burchard weist zurecht darauf hin, dass es sich bei δέησις um ein Bittgebet handelt.[2051] Die Frage, ob der Verfasser hier auch an den Herrenbruder Jakobus denkt, wird von einigen Exegeten positiv beantwortet.[2052] Hegesipp berichtet, der Herrenbruder habe anhaltend im Tempel für das Volk Vergebung erbeten.[2053] Nach Hegesipp

> rief [bei der Steinigung des Jakobus] einer der Priester … und sagte: »Haltet ein! Was tut ihr? Der Gerechte betet für euch«.[2054]

Jakobus ist nach dieser Tradition als Gerechter und als Beter modelliert, Jak 5,16c kann in dieser Tradition stehen.[2055] Metzner argumentiert aber von Jak 5,16c her plausibel in eine andere Richtung: Der Gerechte (im Griechischen ohne Artikel) ist kein bestimmter, sondern irgendein Gerechter oder jeder Gerechte.[2056] V. 16c spielt noch nicht auf eine bestimmte Person an – diese exemplarische Konkretisierung erfolgt erst in V. 17 –, sondern ist als allgemeine Sentenz formuliert. Dibelius hat das klassisch formuliert:

> Dieses Wort [der Gerechte] ist ohne jede Belastung mit dogmatischen Fragestellungen einfach im jüdisch-traditionellen Sinne als Bezeichnung des Frommen zu nehmen.[2057]

Der asyndetische Anschluss von V. 16c an die V. 13–16b dient der rhetorischen Akzentuierung der Sentenz. Erfahrungswissen wird zu einer Regel kondensiert. Die Tautologie von »leisten« und »wirksam werden« verstärkt ihrerseits die Sentenz. ἰσχύειν[2058] ist hier am besten mit »vermögen, können, leisten« wiederzugeben.[2059] ἐνεργεῖν[2060] im Medium bedeutet »wirksam werden«.[2061] Das Partizip ἐνεργουμένη kann sich attributiv auf δέησις beziehen. So übersetzt Bauer / Aland mit »e. wirksames Gebet«.[2062] Das Partizip lässt sich aber ebenso als Verkürzung eines Konditionalsatzes verstehen: »wenn es nachhaltig bzw. wirkungsvoll ist« (part. coniunct.). Eindeutiger wäre eine Formulierung wie πολὺ ἰσχύει δέησις ἐνεργουμένη διὰ

[2051] Burchard, Jak, 212. Hap. leg. in Jak.

[2052] Vgl. Metzner, Jak, 307 Anm. 331.

[2053] Eusebius, HE. II 23,6.16.17.

[2054] Hegesipp, 24.

[2055] In allgemeiner theologischer und frömmigkeitsgeschichtlicher Hinsicht umfasst die Sentenz in V. 16c auch Jakobus den Herrenbruder, aber der Verfasser des Briefes bezieht sich nicht explizit oder implizit auf »Jakobus den Gerechten«. Zu dieser Tradition vgl. N. Förster, »Elia war ein Mensch uns gleichartig« (Jak 5,17): Jakobus, Elia und das Gebet des Gerechten in der Perspektive des Jakobusbriefes, in: Who was ›James‹?, 15–27.

[2056] Metzner, Jak, 307.

[2057] Dibelius, Jak, 305.

[2058] Hap. leg. in Jak.

[2059] Bauer / Aland, 778.

[2060] Hap. leg. in Jak.

[2061] DBR, § 316 Anm. 1: »sich als wirksam erweisen«.

[2062] Bauer / Aland, 535.

360   Kommentar

δικαιοσύνης (vgl. Gal 5,6: οὔτε περιτομή τι ἰσχύει οὔτε ἀκροβυστία ἀλλὰ πίστις δι’ ἀγάπης ἐνεργουμένη. Weder Beschneidung bewirkt etwas noch Unbeschnittenheit, sondern Glaube, der in der Liebe wirksam wird). In Jak 5,16c ist aber die Wendung »Gebet des Gerechten« vorrangig und soll nicht auseinandergerissen werden. Die Wendung vom Erfolg des Gebetes des Gerechten entspricht der Überzeugung Israels: Ps 33,16LXX (1Petr 3,16):

> ὀφθαλμοὶ κυρίου ἐπὶ δικαίους, καὶ ὦτα αὐτοῦ εἰς δέησιν αὐτῶν.

Die Augen des Herrn [sind] auf den Gerechten und seine Ohren auf ihr Gebet [gerichtet]

oder – noch näher – Spr 15,29:

> μακρὰν ἀπέχει ὁ θεὸς ἀπὸ ἀσεβῶν, εὐχαῖς δὲ δικαίων ἐπακούει.

Gott hält sich weit entfernt von Gottlosen, Gebete von Gerechten aber erhört er.

V. 17–18 Die allgemeine Sentenz von V. 16c weist zugleich auf *Elia* voraus, der in den folgenden Versen als *exemplum* für das »Gebet des Gerechten« herangezogen wird. Die Verse 17 und 18 bilden eine thematische und stilistische Einheit. Sie sind Elia gewidmet.[2063] Ohne eine Vergleichspartikel oder eine andere Einführung greift Jakobus noch einmal auf einen Protagonisten Israels zurück. In 2,20–26, hatte er auf *Abraham* und *Rahab* verwiesen: Sie wurden beispielhaft durch Taten *gerecht*. In 5,10 f verwies er auf die *Propheten* und *Hiob* als Beispiel der *Geduld*. Ebenso verweist er jetzt noch einmal in 5,16c–18 auf Elia als Beispiel des *Gebetserfolges*. V. 17 setzt sich aus drei kurzen Aussagesätzen zusammen, deren zweiter und dritter mit »und« eingeleitet wird. In V. 17a charakterisiert Jakobus seinen Protagonisten, in 17b und 17c erzählt er kurz von dem Gebet Elias und seinem Erfolg. Das doppelte καί in der Einleitung der Aussagesätze ist erzählender Septuagintastil. In V. 18 wiederholt und steigert Jakobus diesen narrativen Stil noch, indem er wieder drei kurze, jetzt alle drei jeweils durch καί eingeleitete Aussagesätze aneinanderreiht und so den zweiten Teil des sog. Regenwunders erzählt.

Joachim Jeremias leitet seinen Eliaartikel im Theologischen Wörterbuch folgendermaßen ein:

> Keine biblische Persönlichkeit hat das religiöse Denken des nachbiblischen Judentums so stark beschäftigt wie diejenige des Propheten Elias.[2064]

Auch in den Schriften des Neuen Testaments spielt Elia eine erhebliche Rolle.[2065] Jeremias nennt zwei Gründe für die besondere Stellung des Elia: »seine geheimnis-

---

[2063] J. Jeremias, Art. Ἠλ(ε)ίας, ThWNT 2, 1935, 930–943; K. Wessel, Art. Elias, RAC 4, 1959, 1141–1163; vgl. M. Kamell Kovalishyn, The Prayer of Elijah in James 5. An Example of Intertextuality, JBL 137, 2018, 1027–1045; Förster, Elia, in: Who was ›James‹?

[2064] Jeremias, Art. Ἠλ(ε)ίας, 930 f.

[2065] Hap. leg. in Jak. Im NT noch in Mt, Mk, Lk, Joh, Röm 11,2. M. Öhler, Elia im Neuen Testament. Untersuchungen zur Bedeutung des alttestamentlichen Propheten im frühen Christentum, BZNW 88, Berlin / New York 1997, 257–260 zu Jak 5.

C. Briefcorpus 361

volle Entrückung« und »die Weissagung von der Wiederkehr«.[2066] Vor diesem Hintergrund wird die eigene Eliainterpretation des Jakobusbriefes, die beide genannten Motive gerade nicht aufgreift, umso deutlicher. Anders als wichtige Eliatexte des antiken Judentums wie Sir 48,1–11[2067] und die Elia-Vita (VitProph 21) bezieht sich Jakobus ausschließlich auf die Regenepisode in 3Kön 17 fLXX.[2068] Die Eliagestalt ist damit aus dem umfangreichen alttestamentlichen Erzählzusammenhang um Ahab und Isebel und den Kampf um die wahre Gottesverehrung herausgenommen. Aus der Elia-Erzählung wählt Jakobus lediglich den Erzählstrang 17,1 und 18,1.41–45 aus und konzentriert sich auf Elias zweimaliges erfolgreiches Gebet in Bezug auf Regen. Allerdings folgt er auch hier nicht dem Septuagintatext, in dem keine Rede vom Gebet Elias ist. In 3Kön 17 f ist Gott jeweils der allein Handelnde, sowohl in 17,1 und 18,1 als auch in 18,42–45, wo zwar von der komplizierten Stellung Elias berichtet wird, ohne dass aber von einem Gebet oder einer Gebetshaltung gesprochen wird.[2069] Elia ist jeweils lediglich der Kommunikator. Jakobus hat hier Teil an einer jüdischen Eliatradition, die ebenfalls in der Elia-Vita der VitProph 21,4 ihren Niederschlag gefunden hat. Allerdings erwähnt die Vita auch andere Episoden aus 3Kön 17 fLXX. Das Regengebet wird hier als erstes *Wunder* Elias bezeichnet:

> Die Wunder (σημεῖα) aber, die er tat, sind folgende:
> Elias betete (εὔχεσθαι) und es regnete drei Jahre nicht.
> Und er betete wiederum nach drei Jahren,
> Und es gab viel Regen.[2070]

Damit ist die Elia-Vita wie Jak 5,17 f Zeuge der jüdischen Tradition des Regengebetes, wie überhaupt das Gebet Elias eine zentrale Rolle in der Vita spielt. Aber die Vita beschränkt sich nicht auf diese eine Episode und hebt letzten Endes auf die eschatologische Richterfunktion Elias ab.[2071]

Jakobus fokussiert sein Eliabild weiter, indem er auch den für Elia so wichtigen Prophetentitel (3Kön 17,1LXX) übergeht und ihn stattdessen als Gerechten bezeichnet.[2072] Damit wird Elia zu einem *exemplum* für den Erfolg des »Gebetes

---

[2066] JEREMIAS, Art. Ἠλ(ε)ίας, 932.

[2067] Zu Sir 48 vgl. FRANKEMÖLLE, Jak II, 732 f.

[2068] Vgl. ALLISON, Jak, 777, stellt Gemeinsamkeiten zwischen 3Kön 17 f und Jak 5 her und resümiert: »That James knew the LXX version of the tale, not just Jewish lore about it, seems likely given the common vocabulary.« Das ist richtig, erklärt aber nicht die rigorose Auswahl und die besonderen Erzählzüge des Jakobus.

[2069] JEREMIAS, Art. Ἠλ(ε)ίας, 963 Anm. 53, ist vorsichtig gegenüber der Interpretation als Gebetsgestus. Weiteres bei ÖHLER, Elia, 258 Anm. 26.

[2070] A. M. SCHWEMER, Studien zu den frühjüdischen Prophetenlegenden. Vitae Prophetarum Band II. Die Viten der kleinen Propheten und der Propheten aus den Geschichtsbüchern, Tübingen 1996, 224–260. Text und Übersetzung: 224. Beachtenswert ist der parataktische Erzählstil mit »und«. Vgl. weiter zu Elias Regengebet 4Esr 7,109: »Elia [betete] für jene, die Regen erhielten«, J. SCHREINER, Das 4. Buch Esra, JSHRZ V 4, Gütersloh 1981, 357.

[2071] A. M. SCHWEMER, Vitae Prophetarum, JSHRZ I 7, Gütersloh 1997, 645, mit Verweis auf SCHWEMER, Studien II, 245 f.

[2072] METZNER, Jak, 309, weist zurecht darauf hin, dass für das antike Judentum und das frühe Christentum

362   Kommentar

des Gerechten« aus V. 16c. Für die Plausibilität seiner Gemeindeparänese – die Gemeindeglieder sollen füreinander beten (V. 16b) – geht Jakobus einen weiteren Schritt. Die Gestalt Elias wird ein ethisches Vorbild für die Adressaten, denn nach Jakobus war Elia nicht nur ein Gerechter, sondern gleichzeitig auch ein ἄνθρωπος ὁμοιοπαθής, »ein Mensch wie wir«. ὁμοιοπαθής, gleichgeartet, ist ein bemerkenswerter Begriff, hap. leg. im Jakobusbrief[2073], und wird in der philosophischen Literatur[2074] allgemein anthropologisch für die Gleichheit der Menschen und ihrer Natur benutzt, steht aber auch für gleiche Emotionen bzw. Seelenlagen.[2075] Mit dieser erstaunlichen Interpretation des alttestamentlichen Propheten, die nicht nur einen gewissen Gegensatz zum Epitheton des »Gerechten« enthält, sondern sich auch deutlich von der Interpretation Elias im eschatologischen Kontext des antiken Judentums und des frühen Christentums entfernt[2076], gelingt Jakobus eine rein ethisch-frömmigkeitsgetragene Interpretation: Elia ist gleichsam ein vorbildliches Gemeindemitglied.[2077]

Die V. 17f sind nicht nur in der Nachahmung des narrativen Septuagintastils sorgfältig gestaltet. Jakobus legt Wert auf sprachliche Intensität. Elias Gebet wird in Jak 5,17b durch die *figura etymologica* προσευχῇ προσηύξατο betont.[2078] Der Gegenstand seines Gebetes wird mit einem substantivierten Infinitiv Aor. im Genitiv beschrieben: τοῦ μὴ βρέξαι. βρέχειν, regnen, begegnet sehr selten im Neuen Testament, wird hier aber in 17c wiederholt[2079], so dass auch dieser Vorgang intensiviert wird.[2080] Die Wendung βρέχειν ἐπὶ τῆς γῆς[2081] erinnert an Gen 2,5: οὐ γὰρ ἔβρεξεν ὁ θεὸς ἐπὶ τὴν γῆν. Die Zeitangabe ἐνιαυτοὺς τρεῖς καὶ μῆνας ἕξ findet sich ebenso in dem Eliatext in Lk 4,25:

»Elia ... selbstverständlich zu den gerechten Propheten« gehörte (vgl. Mt 13,17 u. ö.).

[2073] Vgl. im NT noch Apg 14,15 (»sterbliche Menschen«). Vgl. SapSal 7,3 und 4Makk 12,13 (auch dort jeweils auf die Gleichheit aller Menschen bezogen); Philo, conf. 7.

[2074] LSJ, 1224.

[2075] ALLISON, Jak, 775, weist darauf hin, dass Plutarch und Justin den Begriff gern verwendeten.

[2076] Vgl. aber 1Makk 2,58: »Elia wurde in den Himmel erhoben, weil er großen Eifer für das Gesetz bewies«.

[2077] So auch FÖRSTER, Elia, 24, der allerdings noch eine gegen eine Überhöhung von »Jakobus dem Gerechten« gerichtete Spitze in der ›egalitären‹ Eliagestalt vermutet (25).

[2078] ALLISON, Jak, 776: »The result is emphasis«. ALLISON weist ebendort (mit Anm. 236 und 237) auf den Semitismus der Wendung hin. Der Dativ des Substantivs προσευχή (»Er betete *mit* einem Gebet«) statt eines Akkusativs (»Er betete ein Gebet«) begegnet nicht im klassischen Griechisch: »dative nouns with cognate verbs match the similar Hebrew construct state«.

[2079] Βρέχει (unpersönlich): »es regnet« (BAUER / ALAND, 294).

[2080] Mt 5,45; Lk 7,38.44; 17,29 (met.); Apk 11,6 (Hinweis auf Elia). Eher selten in LXX (Gen 2,5 u. ö.), nicht im Zusammenhang mit Elia.

[2081] Vgl. 3Kön 17,7 οὐκ ἐγένετο ὑετὸς ἐπὶ τῆς γῆς (Denn es fiel kein Regen auf das Land); 18,42 καὶ Ηλιου ἀνέβη ἐπὶ τὸν Κάρμηλον καὶ ἔκυψεν ἐπὶ τὴν γῆν καὶ ἔθηκεν τὸ πρόσωπον ἑαυτοῦ ἀνὰ μέσον τῶν γονάτων ἑαυτοῦ (Und Elia ging auf den Karmel hinauf und beugte sich zur Erde nieder und legte sein Angesicht zwischen seine Knie).

C. Briefcorpus   363

πολλαὶ χῆραι ἦσαν ἐν ταῖς ἡμέραις Ἠλίου ἐν τῷ Ἰσραήλ, ὅτε ἐκλείσθη ὁ οὐρανὸς ἐπὶ ἔτη τρία καὶ μῆνας ἕξ.
Es waren viele Witwen in Israel zur Zeit Elias, als der Himmel verschlossen war drei Jahre und sechs Monate.

Apk 11,2 spricht von der kommenden Zerstörung der heiligen Stadt »zweiundvierzig Monate lang«, d. h. dreieinhalb Jahre. Apk 11,3 weissagt, dass zwei Zeugen auftreten werden, die »prophezeien werden tausendzweihundertundsechzig Tage«, d. h. dreieinhalb Jahre. 11,6 macht deutlich, dass der Apokalyptiker Johannes auf Elia anspielt:

οὗτοι ἔχουσιν τὴν ἐξουσίαν κλεῖσαι τὸν οὐρανόν, ἵνα μὴ ὑετὸς βρέχῃ τὰς ἡμέρας τῆς προφητείας αὐτῶν.
Diese haben Macht, den Himmel zu verschießen, damit es nicht regne in den Tagen ihrer Weissagung.

Diese Parallelen können auf eine gemeinsame Quelle deuten. Allison bevorzugt eine apokalyptische Deutung:

The number, three and a half, was symbolically charged because it is half of seven, and in Dan 7.25 and 12.7 it is the length of the apocalyptic period of distress. This explains Rev 11. It may also account for the tradition common to James and Lk 4.25.[2082]

Burchard betont aber zurecht, dass mögliche Quellen für das Eliabild des Jakobus nicht rekonstruierbar sind.[2083] Die Bedeutung der Zeitangabe bleibt offen.[2084] Jeremias scheint das Richtige zu treffen, wenn er zu Jak 5,17 schreibt:

»drei Jahre und sechs Monate« heißt also einfach: »gut drei Jahre«, »eine geraume Zeit«.

Denn, anders als Allison akzentuieren möchte, ist Jak 5,13–18 kein apokalyptisch grundierter Text.

In V. 18 setzt Jakobus noch ein letztes Mal in dem Abschnitt 5,13–18 das Verb προσεύχεσθαι, wenn er von dem zweiten[2085] erfolgreichen Gebet Elias erzählt: καὶ πάλιν προσηύξατο, καὶ ὁ οὐρανὸς[2086] ὑετὸν ἔδωκεν καὶ ἡ γῆ[2087] ἐβλάστησεν τὸν καρπὸν αὐτῆς. Damit schließt Jakobus den Kreis zu V. 13. Das Begriffspaar »Himmel und Erde« strukturiert die parallel gebauten Aussagesätze: »Regen geben« und »Frucht wachsen lassen« korrespondieren einander. In LXX findet sich öfter die Wendung: »Gott gibt Regen« (Lev 26,4 u. ö.), bei Jakobus ist hier poetisch οὐρανός das Subjekt.[2088] Allison weist auch hier auf den Semitismus hin.[2089] ὑετός, Regen, begegnet

---

[2082] ALLISON, Jak, 778.
[2083] BURCHARD, Jak, 214.
[2084] METZNER, Jak, 310, stellt verschiedene Deutungen zusammen.
[2085] πάλιν, wiederum hap. leg. bei Jak.
[2086] Noch Jak 5,12.
[2087] Jak 5,5. 7. 12.17.
[2088] οὐρανός und ὑετός: beide Elemente der Wendung sind hapax legomena in Jak.
[2089] ALLISON, Jak, 779: »δίδωμι+ὑετόν is a Semitism«.

364 Kommentar

sehr selten im Neuen Testament.[2090] Jakobus bezieht sich auf 3Kön 18,45 zurück: καὶ ἐγένετο ὑετὸς μέγας (Und es ereignete sich ein großer Regen), verändert aber den Ton hin in Richtung auf ein Schöpfungsszenario, nicht unähnlich Jak 5,7. ἡ γῆ ἐβλάστησεν erinnert an Gen 1,11: βλαστησάτω ἡ γῆ βοτάνην χόρτου (Die Erde lasse eine Weide von Grünpflanzen wachsen). βλαστάνειν, »wachsen lassen, hervorbringen«[2091] begegnet viermal im Neuen Testament.[2092] Die Wendung »Früchte der Erde«, die sich schon in Jak 5,7 findet, knüpft ebenfalls an Gen 4,2; 43,11 an. Stilistisch schließt Jakobus sich wieder eng an die Septuaginta an. V. 18 ist im Ton einer biblischen Idylle gehalten, inhaltlich weit entfernt von der eschatologischen Eliagestalt des antiken Judentums und des frühen Christentums.

4. Texteinheit: 5,19–20 Schlussbelehrung zur Umkehr

(19) Meine Brüder, wenn jemand unter euch in die Irre ginge, fort[2093] von der Wahrheit, und ihn jemand zur Umkehr bewegte, (20) dann soll er wissen, dass der, der den Sünder von seinem falschen Weg bekehrt[2094], seine Seele vom Tod retten und eine Menge von Sünden bedecken wird.

Textkritik: V. 19 απο της αληθειας lesen die Majuskeln 02. 03. 025 und viele Minuskeln, zu απο της οδου της αληθειας erweitern 01. 33 und viele Minuskeln. V. 20 Statt γινωσκετω (lectio difficilior) lesen 03 und wenige Minuskeln Plural: γινωσκετε. Mehrere Minuskeln schließen mit αμην. Erweiterte Doxa-Formel + αμην in Minuskel 999.

V. 19–20 Die Gebetsthematik ist mit V. 18 abgeschlossen.[2095] Jakobus setzt ein letztes Mal neu mit der Anrede ein: meine Brüder.[2096] Damit kommt er zu dem brüderlich-amikablen Kommunikationston von 1,2 zurück. Die Schlusspassage wird aus *einem* Satzgefüge gebildet: vorangestellter doppelter, durch »und« verbundener Konditionalsatz im Aor. Konj., Imperativsatz mit anschließendem doppelten, durch »und« verbundenen Objektsatz im Futur. Burchards Urteil zu V. 20: »V. 20 erklärt sich als gewollter volltönender Abschluss«[2097] lässt sich auf die ganze Schlusspassage ausweiten. Jakobus formuliert hier noch einmal mit sprachlich-stilistischer Sorgfalt und schließt mit einer Anspielung auf ein Septuaginta-Diktum. Thema dieses kurzen Schlussabschnitts ist das »Jemanden von etwas abwendig machen[2098], zur Abkehr von etwas oder zur Umkehr zu etwas bewegen«. Damit ist die *Belehrung über die Bedeutung der Umkehr* das Schlusswort des Verfassers. Es geht

---

[2090] Apg 14,17; 28,2; Hebr 6,7; Apk 11,6 (im Zusammenhang mit Elia).

[2091] BAUER / ALAND, 284. Hap. leg. in Jak.

[2092] Mt 13,26; Mk 4,27; Hebr 9,4 und Jak 5,18. LXX: eher selten, mehrfach metaphorisch (z. B. Jes 45,8).

[2093] »Fort« ist im Deutschen hinzugefügt.

[2094] Das Partizip ist relativisch aufgelöst.

[2095] F. MUSSNER, Jak, 230, weist aber darauf hin, dass Jak 5,13–18 und 19 f unter demselben Oberthema stehen: »geistliche Hilfe des Christen«.

[2096] Jak 1,2. 16. 19; 2,1. 5. 14; 3,1. 10. 12; 4,11; 5,7. 9. 10. 12. 19. Dreimal setzt Jakobus den Zusatz »geliebt« (1,16.19; 2,5). Viermal fehlt »meine«: 4,11; 5,7. 9. 10.

[2097] BURCHARD, Jak, 216.

[2098] So BAUER / ALAND, 609.

C. Briefcorpus

dabei nicht um Ermahnung, sondern um brüderliche Belehrung (γινωσκέτω). Das Verb ἐπιστρέφειν wird im Jakobusbrief nur zweimal hier in V. 19.20 in auffallender Position am Briefende gesetzt, beide Male transitiv. Im Neuen Testament begegnet das Verb häufig. Überwiegend wird es im Zusammenhang mit ἐπί oder πρός + τὸν κύριον/ τὸν θεόν u. ä. verwendet.[2099] Ohne Objekt findet es sich in Mt 13,15 im Zitat aus Jes 6,10 im Sinne von »sich bekehren«. In Jak 5,19 übersetzt man am besten: »zur Umkehr bewegen«[2100], d. h. zu einer existentiellen Wende verhelfen, da wie in Mt 13 eine Ergänzung mit ἐπί im Sinne des »wozu bzw. woraufhin« fehlt. In V. 19 geht es darum, dass jemand aus dem Adressatenkreis (τις) ein verirrtes Gemeindeglied (τις ἐν ὑμῖν) zur Umkehr bewegt. Rahmen ist also der Adressatenkreis bzw. die dahinterstehende Gemeinde. Im Zentrum des Konditionalsatzes von V. 19 stehen zwei Personen, zuerst ein Gemeindeglied, das »von der Wahrheit abirrt«, dann jemand aus dem Adressatenkreis, der das Gemeindeglied »umkehrt« bzw. zur Umkehr bewegt, ἐπιστρέψῃ. Derselbe Fall wird noch dreimal in den neutestamentlichen Schriften angesprochen. Lev 19,17 gibt das ethische Muster vor: Die wechselseitige Verantwortung für die Israeliten aufgrund der Nächstenliebe ist das Fundament der Zugehörigkeit zum Volk Israel:

οὐ μισήσεις τὸν ἀδελφόν σου τῇ διανοίᾳ σου, ἐλεγμῷ ἐλέγξεις τὸν πλησίον σου καὶ οὐ λήμψῃ δι᾽ αὐτὸν ἁμαρτίαν.

Du sollst in deinem Geist deinen Bruder nicht hassen, mit Tadel sollst du deinen Nächsten tadeln, und [so] wirst du dir seinetwegen keine Sünde zuziehen.

Lev 19,17LXX benutzt das Substantiv ἀδελφόν und legt damit die Grundlage für die spätere Bezeichnung *correctio fraterna*.[2101] Mussner formuliert zurecht:

Jak bewegt sich … sprachlich und sachlich vollkommen in überlieferten Auffassungen und Anweisungen.[2102]

Dabei spielt Lev 19,17 eine entscheidende Rolle.[2103] Das zeigt ein Blick auf ausgewählte alt- und neutestamentliche Texte:

[2099] Lk 1,16; Apg 9,35 u. ö.

[2100] Vgl. G. BERTRAM, Art. ἐπιστρέφω, ThWNT 2, 1935, 722–729.

[2101] J. ERNST, Art. Brüderliche Zurechtweisung. I. Biblisch, ³LThK 2, 1994, 715f; A. SCHENK-ZIEGLER, Correctio fraterna im Neuen Testament. Die »brüderliche Zurechtweisung« in biblischen, frühjüdischen und hellenistischen Schriften, FzB 84, Würzburg 1997; L. T. JOHNSON, Brother of Jesus and Friend of God: Studies in the Letter of James, Grand Rapids, MI, 2004, 131 f.

[2102] MUSSNER, Jak, 231. Mussner weist auch auf Ez 34,4: τὸ πλανώμενον οὐκ ἐπεστρέψατε (Das Verirrte habt ihr nicht zurückgeführt); Sir 28,2 f; 1QS X,26–XI,1; CD XIII,9 f hin. Vgl. weiter zu V. 20.

[2103] ALLISON, Jak, 784f, liest V. 19.20 von Ez 34 und von TestAbr Langfassung 10,14 her: [Gott spricht] »Siehe, Abraham sündigt nicht, aber er erbarmt sich nicht der Sünder. Ich habe die Welt geschaffen, aber ich will keinen von ihnen [den Menschen] vernichten. Ich schiebe den Tod des Sünders auf, bis daß er sich bekehre und lebe« (E. JANSSEN, Testament Abrahams, JSHRZ III / 2, Gütersloh 1975, 227); D. C. ALLISON, Job in the Testament of Abarahm, JSPE 12, 2001, 1131–147.

366 Kommentar

οὐ μισήσεις τὸν **ἀδελφόν** σου τῇ διανοίᾳ σου, **ἐλεγμῷ ἐλέγξεις** τὸν πλησίον σου καὶ **οὐ λήμψῃ** δι᾽ αὐτὸν **ἁμαρτίαν.**
Du sollst in deinem Geist deinen Bruder nicht hassen; mit Tadel sollst du deinen Nächsten tadeln, und so wirst du dir seinetwegen keine Sünde zuziehen (Lev 19,17).

Ἀδελφοί, ἐὰν καὶ **προλημφθῇ** ἄνθρωπος ἔν τινι **παραπτώματι,** ὑμεῖς οἱ πνευματικοὶ **καταρτίζετε** τὸν τοιοῦτον ἐν πνεύματι πραΰτητος.
Brüder, wenn ein Mensch sich zu einer Verfehlung hinreißen lässt, so sollt ihr, die ihr geistlich seid, ihn wieder im Geist der Sanftmut zurechtbringen (Gal 6,1).

Ἐὰν δὲ **ἁμαρτήσῃ** [εἰς σὲ] ὁ **ἀδελφός** σου, ὕπαγε **ἔλεγξον** αὐτὸν μεταξὺ σοῦ καὶ αὐτοῦ μόνου. ἐάν σου ἀκούσῃ, **ἐκέρδησας** τὸν **ἀδελφόν** σου.
Wenn dein Bruder an dir sündigt, geh, weise ihn zurecht zwischen dir und ihm allein (Mt 18,15).

Ἐάν τις ἴδῃ τὸν **ἀδελφὸν** αὐτοῦ **ἁμαρτάνοντα ἁμαρτίαν** μὴ πρὸς **θάνατον, αἰτήσει** καὶ δώσει αὐτῷ ζωήν, τοῖς ἁμαρτάνουσιν μὴ πρὸς **θάνατον.** ἔστιν ἁμαρτία πρὸς θάνατον.
Wenn jemand seinen Bruder ein Sünde begehen sieht, die nicht zum Tod führt, möge er bitten, und [Gott] wird ihm Leben geben – jenen die nicht zum Tod sündigen. Es gibt [aber] eine Sünde zum Tod (1Joh 5,16).

Ἀδελφοί μου, **ἐάν τις** ἐν ὑμῖν **πλανηθῇ** ἀπὸ τῆς ἀληθείας καὶ **ἐπιστρέψῃ** τις αὐτόν, γινωσκέτω ὅτι ὁ ἐπιστρέψας **ἁμαρτωλὸν ἐκ πλάνης ὁδοῦ αὐτοῦ** σώσει ψυχὴν αὐτοῦ ἐκ **θανάτου** καὶ καλύψει πλῆθος **ἁμαρτιῶν.**
Meine Brüder, wenn jemand unter euch in die Irre gehen würde, fort von der Wahrheit, und ihn jemand zur Umkehr bewegte, dann soll er wissen, dass der, der den Sünder von seinem falschen Weg bekehrt, seine Seele vom Tod retten und eine Menge von Sünden bedecken wird (Jak 5,19 f).

Zugleich zeigt sich im Vergleich auch die charakteristische Behandlung des Motivs bei Jakobus. Unterschiedlich sind Vokabular, inhaltliche Rahmung und Aussage der Texte. Lev 19 gibt das Thema des Zusammenhanges von Sünde und korrigierendem Tadel unter »Brüdern« vor. Allerdings spricht Lev nicht von einem Sünder, sondern von der Vermeidung der Sünde durch die *correctio fraterna.* Lev 19 schützt denjenigen, der den Bruder korrigiert. Sünde begegnet auch bei Matthäus und Jakobus, hier aber im Zusammenhang mit demjenigen, der sich verfehlt. Paulus spricht dagegen von παράπτωμα, einem Fehltritt oder Vergehen. Er unterscheidet genauer zwischen dem Menschen, der den Fehltritt begeht, und den geistbegabten Gemeindegliedern, die diesen Menschen zurechtbringen (καταρτίζειν). Matthäus geht es um das *procedere* des Tadels in Rahmen der Gemeinde. Die brüderliche Hilfe kommt an ihre Grenze. Dasselbe gilt für 1Joh. Hier wird die Unterscheidung von »Sünden, die den Tod bringen« (»Sünden zum Tod«), und Sünden, die vergeben werden können, eingeführt. Die *fraterna correctio* besteht außerdem bei Johannes im Gebet für den Sünder, nicht in der persönlichen Zurechtweisung. Damit *verbindet* 1Joh 5 die beiden Motive des Gebets für eine andere Person und der *fraterna correctio,* die in Jak 5 aufeinander folgen. Jakobus selbst formuliert *grundsätzlich* und zugleich wie so häufig umschreibend: πλανηθῇ ἀπὸ τῆς ἀληθείας. πλανάω – hap. leg.

im Jakobusbrief – begegnet häufiger im Neuen Testament im Sinne von »irren«.[2104] In Jak 1,16 setzt Jakobus das Verb im Passiv für »abirren von«[2105]: »Lasst euch nicht täuschen, irrt euch nicht«. Dieser Appell μὴ πλανᾶσθε steht im Zusammenhang mit einem falschen Verständnis von dem Ursprung der Sünde. Das »Abirren von der Wahrheit« in 5,19 nimmt zudem 1,18 auf: Die Adressaten sind »geboren durch das Wort der Wahrheit«. 5,19 greift also abschließend auf wichtige Motive aus 1,16–18 zurück und passt das Leviticusmotiv dem eigenen ethischen Entwurf an.

V. 20 beginnt mit dem Imperativ γινωσκέτω[2106]: Jakobus spricht hier noch ein letztes Mal als Lehrer. Der Imperativ gibt dem Inhalt der anschließenden Lehre mehr Gewicht. Was ist der Inhalt dieser Belehrung? Zunächst wiederholt Jakobus variierend V. 19b, das Motiv des Zur-Umkehr-Bewegens: ὅτι ὁ ἐπιστρέψας ἁμαρτωλὸν ἐκ πλάνης ὁδοῦ αὐτοῦ. Jakobus benutzt eine Septuagintawendung. Das Syntagma »die Verirrung der Wege« findet sich in SapSal 12,24, dort noch durch die *figura etymologica* verstärkt:

καὶ γὰρ τῶν πλάνης ὁδῶν μακρότερον ἐπλανήθησαν.
Auf ihren Irrwegen waren sie nämlich zu weit in die Irre gegangen.

In Jak 5,19 f wird zunächst das Verb πλανάω[2107] gesetzt, dann in der variierenden Wiederholung das Substantiv πλάνη.[2108] Von den Sündern hat Jakobus schon in seiner Anklagerede in 4,8 gesprochen. Das Thema der Sünde ist eines der wenigen Themen, die Jakobus in seinem Schreiben theologisch vertieft anspricht: 1,13–15.[2109] Die Schlussbelehrung in 5,19 f als ganze bezieht sich also in besonderer Weise auf Inhalte aus 1,13–18 zurück.

Abschließend wird dann das doppelte Ergebnis dieser Bemühung des »Jemanden zur Umkehr Leitens« dargestellt. Der Sünder wird gerettet, und viele Sünden werden »bedeckt«: σώσει ψυχὴν αὐτοῦ ἐκ θανάτου καὶ καλύψει πλῆθος ἁμαρτιῶν. Auch die Wendung von der Rettung der Seele(n) – ein durch die Septuaginta transportierter Semitismus[2110] – hat Jakobus schon verwendet: δέξασθε τὸν ἔμφυτον λόγον τὸν δυνάμενον σῶσαι τὰς ψυχὰς ὑμῶν (1,21). »Seele« bedeutet auch hier »Leben«. In 5,20 wird ἐκ θανάτου hinzugefügt. Bereits in 1,15 hatte Jakobus den *Tod* auf die Sünde zurückgeführt: ἡ δὲ ἁμαρτία ἀποτελεσθεῖσα ἀποκύει θάνατον. Die Konstellation von Sünde und Tod findet sich prägnant bei Ez 18,20:

[2104] Sehr häufig im Alten Testament, öfter im Zusammenhang mit Sünde bzw. Sünder einerseits und der Weg-Metapher andererseits (z. B. Spr 21,16).

[2105] BAUER / ALAND, 1338.

[2106] Γινώσκειν Jak 1,3; 2,20; 5,20.

[2107] Hap. leg. in Jak.

[2108] Hap. leg. in Jak.

[2109] Weitere Erwähnungen: 2,9; 4,17; 5,15.16. Es ist deutlich, dass Jakobus bei seinen Adressaten Sünde(n) diagnostiziert und den Sündern zur Umkehr verhelfen will. ἁμαρτωλός Jak 4,8 und 5,20.

[2110] ALLISON, Jak, 786.

368 Kommentar

ἡ δὲ ψυχὴ ἡ ἁμαρτάνουσα ἀποθανεῖται.
Die Seele aber, die sündigt, wird sterben.[2111]

Allison betont besonders die enge Beziehung von Jak 5,20 zu Ez 34 und dessen Umfeld und kommt zu folgender Interpretation:

> We have already seen that Ezek 34 supplies part of the background to James' conclusion. So too does Ezekiel's famous refrain, according to which God does not wish the death of sinners but rather waits so that they might ›turn and live‹. Rabbinic and patristic authorities often cite this byword, which also plays an important role in the long recension of the Testament of Abraham and the extant fragments of the Apocryphon of Ezekiel. James seems to echo it and associated motifs.[2112]

Allison sieht damit *insgesamt* nicht Lev 19,17 und die Tradition der *fraterna correctio*, sondern Ez 34 und die Vorstellung, Gott wolle die Umkehr des Sünders, als Hintergrund von Jak 5,19 f. Hier liegt aber keine Alternative vor, sondern Jakobus *verbindet* gerade die beiden theologischen Motive, indem er das Ezechiel-Motiv von der Umkehr des Sünders zum Leben mit dem Motiv der brüderlichen Verantwortung in der Gemeinde, das auf Lev 19 zurückgeht, verknüpft. Wie Mussner feststellt, hat Jakobus in seinem Schlusssatz ganz und gar traditionelle Motive kombiniert. Dabei ist er nicht allein, denn die frühchristlichen Schriftsteller haben diese und andere Motive wie das »Bedecken der Sünden« ihrerseits produktiv verarbeitet, wie die obige Tabelle zeigt.

Ob Jakobus hier am Ende des Briefes eine Perspektive eröffnet, die über den Tod hinausführt, muss offenbleiben.[2113] Aber entgegen den heftigen Angriffen der Kapitel 3, 4 und 5 schließt der Brief mit einem vorsichtig positiven Ausblick (Konjunktiv), wenn auch »Sünden« das letzte Wort ist. Umkehr ist aber möglich. Die metaphorische Wendung καλύψει πλῆθος[2114] ἁμαρτιῶν ist 1Petr 4,8 verwandt. Dort ist das Motiv des Bedeckens auf die ἀγάπη bezogen: ἀγάπη καλύπτει πλῆθος ἁμαρτιῶν (Liebe bedeckt die Menge der Sünden). Das Bild von der einhüllenden Liebe findet sich in Spr 10,12: ist dort aber auf das Vermeiden von Hass und Streit bezogen.

Spr 10,12LXX: μῖσος ἐγείρει νεῖκος, πάντας δὲ τοὺς μὴ φιλονεικοῦντας καλύπτει φιλία.
Hass weckt Streit, alle aber, die nicht streitsüchtig sind, hüllt Freundschaft ein.
1Petr 4,8: πρὸ πάντων τὴν εἰς ἑαυτοὺς ἀγάπην ἐκτενῆ ἔχοντες, ὅτι *ἀγάπη καλύπτει πλῆθος ἁμαρτιῶν*.
Vor allen Dingen habt untereinander beharrliche Liebe; denn Liebe deckt der Sünden Menge zu.

[2111] Siehe die Tabelle bei ALLISON, Jak, 785, mit Anm. 304 und 306.

[2112] ALLISON, Jak, 784 f.

[2113] Vgl. insgesamt den Exkurs »Zukunftshoffnungen im Jakobusbrief« bei BURCHARD, Jak, 203 f (5,20 wird nicht erwähnt). ALLISON, Jak, 786, mit Anm. 309 kommentiert: »salvation will be won at the end«. Im Zusammenhang von Kap. 5 ist dies Urteil plausibel. Aber Jakobus führt anders als die paulinische und nachpaulinische Eschatologie das Thema nicht aus.

[2114] καλύπτειν und πλῆθος sind hapax legomena in Jak.

D. Subscriptio

Jak 5,20: γινωσκέτω ὅτι ὁ ἐπιστρέψας ἁμαρτωλὸν ἐκ πλάνης ὁδοῦ αὐτοῦ σώσει ψυχὴν αὐτοῦ ἐκ θανάτου καὶ *καλύψει πλῆθος ἁμαρτιῶν.*

Jakobus benutzt also auch am Briefende eine sprachliche Wendung, die aus der Septuaginta vertraut ist, und passt sie seinem Thema an. »Die Menge der Sünden« in den Gemeinden treibt den Verfasser des Jakobusbriefes um. Er selbst will mit seinem Rundschreiben zur Vollkommenheit der Gemeindeglieder beitragen (1,4) und vor der Sünde warnen (1,13–15). Seine Adressaten belehrt er abschließend über die Bedeutung des gegenseitigen Gebets und des Sündenbekenntnisses (5,13–18) und der *fraterna correctio* in den Gemeinden als wesentlicher Instrumente zum Kampf gegen die Sünde.

D. Subscriptio

Minuskel 5.33 und zahlreiche Minuskeln (Byz) haben keine *subscriptio*. 03 hat ιακωβου, 01. 044 und wenige Minuskeln haben επιστολη ιακωβου, 02 und einige Minuskeln haben ιακωβου επιστολη. Jeweils einzelne Minuskeln haben längere Schlussformeln (τέλος …) und benutzen Varianten der Formulierung καθολικη επιστολη ιακωβου. Jakobus wird in einzelnen Minuskeln mit »heilig« und »Apostel« benannt. Minuskel 1739 und 2544 fügen hinzu: αδελφοθεου.